Warsaw

Kiev

Cracow

Gran
Buda-Pest

Black Sea

Belgrade

Danube River

Viddin
Nicopolis
Trnovo
Varna

Sinope

Trebizond

Amastris

PONTUS

Ragusa

Pompeiopolis

Amasia
Sebasteia (Sivas)

Constantinople

Brusa
Ancyra

Halys River

Aegean Sea

NEGROPONTE

Corinth

Mistra
Modon
Coron

Ionian Sea

RHODES

CYPRUS

CRETE

Sea

Mediterranean Sea

RUTGERS BYZANTINE SERIES

PETER CHARANIS
GENERAL EDITOR

Frontispiece: *Manuel as Emperor*. Illuminated Miniature, Bibliothèque Nationale, Paris, *Cod. suppl. gr. 309*, f. VI (photo courtesy Bibliothèque Nationale, Paris; see Appendix XXIV, A, I, 4).

JOHN W. BARKER

MANUEL II PALAEOLOGUS
(1391–1425):
A Study in
Late Byzantine Statesmanship

RUTGERS UNIVERSITY PRESS
New Brunswick *New Jersey*

The first printing of this work has been produced with the help of a grant-in-aid from the Ford Foundation in support of publication in the field of the humanities.

To My Parents
As the Barest Acknowledgment
of Unpayable Debts
I Dedicate This Book

Foreword

On May 11 in 330 A.D., Constantine the Great dedicated the ancient Greek colony of Byzantium on the Bosphorus as Constantinople, the splendid new capital of the recently Christianized Roman Empire. If that dedication may be taken to mark the beginning of what modern historians call the Byzantine Empire—distinguished from the earlier Roman Empire by the abandonment of Rome as the capital and by such cultural developments as the triumph of Christianity—then that Empire lasted for over eleven hundred years.

In the course of this long existence, the Byzantine Empire faced and survived a number of crises. That it achieved a longevity unique in European history was due to many factors, one of the most important being the emergence at critical moments of brilliant and capable leadership. But if such men as Heraclius, Leo III, Alexius I Comnenus, and Michael VIII Palaeologus succeeded in checking the forces which threatened to destroy the Byzantine Empire, they did so not only through sheer ability but also because the resources necessary for survival were there.

The Empire finally succumbed on May 29, 1453, not for lack of capable leadership but as the result of a multiplicity of conditions which, by the end of the fourteenth century, could not be changed. The man was there, but the Empire no longer had the potential to save itself. Manuel II Palaeologus, as readers of this study by John W. Barker will learn, was one of the most gifted statesmen Byzantium ever produced, but it was his fate to rule the State at a time when the forces which threatened its existence could not be checked. Intelligent, energetic, and a man of character, he tried hard to turn back the tide, but failed in the end—failed because the tide was irreversible. Nevertheless, he emerges as a fascinating personage, a consummate statesman, and a brilliant man of letters. His career, moreover, is inextricably intertwined with developments of major significance in the history of Europe: the consolidation of the Ottoman position in the Balkan peninsula, and the consequent subjugation of its Christian peoples.

The author's task was by no means easy; sources of information on Manuel are sparse, widely scattered, and difficult to interpret and evaluate. Professor Barker, however, has been highly successful in surmounting these difficulties; he has produced a volume which, in addition to being scholarly, is also very readable. His book is likely to remain the standard study on the subject for many years to come.

Professor Barker's manuscript was completed and accepted for publication some time ago; in the interim, the author has added whatever new information has come to his attention, so that the book as it now appears may be considered abreast with the most recent published research. We are happy indeed that the book has finally seen the light, and happier still that we have been able to include it in the Rutgers Byzantine Series.

Peter Charanis
General Editor
Rutgers Byzantine Series

Preface

The purpose of this book is to trace the development of a fascinating Emperor as a statesman and, to a lesser extent, as a man of letters. The book is not intended to give a detailed account of Byzantine history during the seventy-five years of his life. Nor is it intended to be an all-embracing and "definitive" study of this man as an individual. It is designed rather to provide a basis for fuller evaluation of Manuel II by synthesizing the already extensive scholarly work on details or aspects of his life, by sampling in translation his surviving literary work, and by pointing ahead to work yet to be done on these subjects.

Since the background, aims, and methods of this study are set forth more fully in the Introduction following, this space may be confined to a few vital acknowledgments.

The major portions of this book, and its basic premises, appeared as a thesis submitted to Rutgers University in the spring of 1961 in partial fulfillment of doctoral degree requirements. The five original chapters of the dissertation were revised, and the two additional chapters (VI and VII) were written, during the following year. For the academic years 1959–1962 I was privileged to be a resident Fellow at Dumbarton Oaks, Harvard University's center for Byzantine studies. While delays have postponed publication, I have attempted to bring the scholarly apparatus up to date as thoroughly as possible. My first expressions of gratitude go therefore to the two institutions which enabled me to pursue this work: Rutgers University, which sustained me generously through my years of graduate study; and the Dumbarton Oaks Trustees for Harvard University, without whose generosity and matchless facilities my subsequent research would have been, at the very least, far more difficult, and its results perhaps different.

Within these two institutions there were many individuals who were bountiful in their help. Primacy in this category belongs to my master and sponsor, Peter Charanis, Voorhees Professor of History at Rutgers University, who guided and supported me through crucial training with a degree of staunchness far exceeding the customary teacher-student relationship. Whatever merit may be found in my work may perhaps serve to justify his exertions on my behalf. To another of the faculty members then at Rutgers, Professor Clayton M. Hall of the Classics Department, I am indebted for much useful advice in the early stages of my work in the thorny arbors of Palaeologan literary texts.

Among the faculty and staff members of Dumbarton Oaks, with whom I enjoyed enriching contacts both professional and personal, there are many to whom I owe particular gratitude. One of these is the late Dr. George Soulis, then librarian of Dumbarton Oaks, whose suggestions and encouragement were of constant significance. His untimely death in the summer of 1967 has prevented his seeing in completed form this book he helped so much, adding for me a further poignance to the personal grief I feel at the tragic loss of this brilliant scholar and fine man. To Professor Romilly J. H. Jenkins I owe the warmest thanks for invaluable advice on the demanding problems of translating the original texts which appear throughout this book. In my present ignorance of Slavonic languages I was given generous and indispensable assistance with Russian by Dr. Cyril Mango, at that time director of the institution's publications, and with Russian and particularly Serbian by Mrs. Jelisaveta S. Allen of the library staff. Among other members of this staff, I must also single out Mr. Isham Perkins, the indefatigable interlibrary-loan expert, for his endless and devoted labor in securing hard-to-find titles. Though limitations of space hinder a full enumeration of the names, I must also note the valuable exchanges of information, assistance, and ideas that I enjoyed with those who were my contemporaries as Fellows at Dumbarton Oaks during the years of my residence there.

There were also several individuals beyond the confines of these two institutions who were of great help to me. Chief among these is the Reverend Father Raymond-Joseph Loenertz, O.P., of the Istituto Storico Domenicano in Rome. This learned and kind scholar has been unselfishly and endlessly generous in his wise advice, encouragement, and even contributions of material, during the course of a long and fruitful correspondence between us. His imprint upon my work may be seen throughout the book. I wish also to acknowledge my thanks to Dr. Enrica Follieri of the Istituto di Studi Bizantini e Neoellenici in Rome, for her important contributions to this correspondence as well. I am also greatly indebted to Father Loenertz' student, the Reverend George T. Dennis, S.J. Our nearly simultaneous work on the same Emperor, mutually discovered in midstream, has proved happily complementary rather than competitive. He very kindly sent me a copy of his published dissertation on Manuel in Thessalonica at precisely the right moment for me, and he also was generous enough to provide me with a transcription of the short chronicle texts published by M. Gedeon in the rare periodical Ἐκκλησιαστικὴ ἀλήθεια, which would otherwise have been unavailable to me. I am also indebted to Professor Oliver Strunk, the eminent musicologist, formerly of Princeton University, for an illuminating exchange of ideas on the question of the liturgical acclamations in honor of Manuel II and his Empress.

Finally, there were a number of individuals who were of great assistance to me in assembling the illustrative material for this book. For the sake of convenience and pertinence, I have expressed my thanks to most of them at the conclusion of Appendix XXIV. Nevertheless, I will take this opportunity to offer my gratitude to Professor Randall D. Sale, and especially Mr. David A. Woodward, of the Cartographic Laboratory of the Department of Geography at the University of Wisconsin, for their generous contribution of the three maps to be found in this book.

JOHN W. BARKER

University of Wisconsin
Madison, Wisconsin
October, 1967

Contents

List of Illustrations

FIGURES

FIGURES

MAPS

Chronological Outline
of the Life and Reign
# of Manuel II Palaeologus

1350   Manuel Palaeologus born (June 27), the second son of John V Palaeologus and Helena Cantacuzena, amid the struggle between John V and John VI Cantacuzenus for the throne.

1354   Capture of Gallipoli by the Osmanli Turks (March); the position of Cantacuzenus deteriorates; aided by Francesco Gattilusio, John V enters Constantinople and forces Cantacuzenus to abdicate (November); Gattilusio rewarded with marriage to John V's sister Maria and the lordship of Lesbos.

1355   The heir to the throne, Manuel's brother Andronicus (IV, b. 1348) is betrothed to the Princess Maria-Kyratza of Bulgaria (August); awed by the mounting Turkish menace, John V appeals to Pope Innocent VI for aid, offering (bull, December 15) Manuel as a hostage; the death of Stefan Dušan (December 20), ending the great age of Serbia.

1357   John V renews his pleas for aid and offer of Manuel as hostage to the Pope (bull, November 7), but these are ignored.

1360   The Turks capture Didymoteichos.

1362   The Turks capture Adrianople; accession of Murad I as Osmanli Emir (Sultan).

1363   Turkish capture of Philippopolis; mission of the Patriarch

Kallistos I of Constantinople to Serbia to win an alliance; his death during the mission.

1364   Restoration of Philotheos as Patriarch of Constantinople (October 8), marking a resurgence of Cantacuzenian influence at court; Byzantine war with Bulgaria.

1366   Leaving Andronicus as regent, John travels to Buda to seek aid from Hungary, committing himself further to Church union and personal conversion; leaving Manuel and another son Michael as hostages, John sets out for home, but is blocked in Viddin by the King of Bulgaria; Count Amadeo VI (the "Green Count") of Savoy mounts a private crusade to aid the Empire; seizing Gallipoli from the Turks (August), Amadeo threatens Bulgaria, winning passage for John V and territorial concessions to the Empire.

1367   Union negotiations pressed by the Papal legate accompanying Amadeo, Cantacuzenus (now the monk Ioasaph) as Byzantine spokesman; John V commits himself to a personal visit to Rome.

1369   Establishing Manuel as Despot in Thessalonica and leaving Andronicus as regent in the capital again, John V sails to Italy; in Rome, John adopts Latin Catholicism personally (October) and promises to work toward Church union.

1370   Departing from Rome (March), John travels to Venice to complete negotiations with the Republic; in view of his indebtedness to Venice, he is honorably detained until terms are reached; Andronicus, appealed to, provides no help, but Manuel comes to his father's aid.

1371   After further negotiations, John V agrees to the cession of Tenedos to Venice; departing, John leaves Manuel in Venice as a temporary hostage; with the neutrality, if not the cooperation, of Andronicus, the Turks defeat the Serbians under Vukašin and Uglješa at Černomen on the River Marica (September 26), beginning the destruction of Serbia; John V returns to Constantinople (October 28), and Manuel, to Thessalonica; John purges nobles (?supporters of Andronicus) in the capital (December 5); John issues a bull on behalf of Manuel and begins to favor him over Andronicus; Manuel makes some brief progress in seizing Macedonian territory amid the breakdown of Serbian authority; Manuel writes his Letter ε'.

1373 Abandoning hope of Western aid by this time, John V begins a policy of cooperation with the Turks, becoming their vassal; outbreak of a joint revolt by Andronicus and Murad's son Saudji (spring); defeat and surrender of Andronicus (May 25–30); Manuel is crowned as co-Emperor and heir (September 25); Saudji is defeated, captured (September 29), and blinded by Murad; John V is ordered by him to do likewise to Andronicus and the latter's son, but carries out this command only in part; Andronicus and his son John (VII) are imprisoned in the Tower of Anemas.

1374 Disillusionment in the West over Byzantine accommodation with the Turks; Imperial friction with Venice.

1376 Andronicus and his family escape to Galata; winning Genoese support and Turkish approval, Andronicus besieges Constantinople (July) and enters it (August 12); blockaded in the fortress of the Golden Gate, John V and his sons Manuel and Theodore finally capitulate and are imprisoned in the Tower of Anemas; death of the Patriarch Philotheos (October); Andronicus goes (October 3?) to the Turks to arrange the surrender of Gallipoli in return for their support of his coup; death of Maria Palaeologina (October); about this time(?) Demetrius Cydones, Manuel's old tutor, produces his *Oratio de non reddenda Callipoli* and refuses to serve Andronicus; Andronicus' cession of Tenedos to his Genoese supporters (August 23) is not honored on the island, and, instead, Carlo Zeno wins it for Venice after all; the beginning of the Chioggia War against Venice.

1377 Andronicus IV is involved in the Chioggia War, fighting on the side of Venice; a Venetian squadron raids Constantinople (July); failure of a Genoese-Imperial expedition against Tenedos; coronation of Andronicus as Emperor (October 18) by his new Patriarch Makarios;

Andronicus' position deteriorates amid unpopularity and limited support at home.

1379   Escape of John V and his sons from the Tower of Anemas (June?); winning Turkish support, they enter Constantinople (July 1) and re-establish John V's government; some Genoese resist, but Andronicus and his family escape to Galata, taking old Cantacuzenus, the Empress Helena, and her sisters as hostages; Galata is besieged by Manuel; the Patriarch Makarios is deposed and replaced by Neilos.

1381   Fighting before Galata is ended by a truce and then a new settlement among the Imperial family (May), by which Andronicus is recognized as heir, to the exclusion of Manuel, and is given an appanage on the Marmora coast with Selymbria as capital; released with his daughters, Cantacuzenus finally departs to the Morea to join his son, the Despot Matthew.

1382   Formal ending of the Chioggia War by the Treaty of Turin (August 23), sponsored by Amadeo of Savoy, providing for the neutralization of Tenedos; final peace between the Empire and Genoa (November 2); departure of Theodore to the Morea (autumn); disaffected, Manuel leaves secretly for Thessalonica (autumn–winter?).

1383   Manuel begins an independent stand against the Turks in Macedonia, recovering Serres and winning several victories over them; death of John Cantacuzenus (June 15) and then of Matthew Cantacuzenus, both in the Morea; a Turkish counteroffensive is launched against Manuel under Khairaddin Pasha, taking Serres (September 19) and beginning the siege of Thessalonica (autumn); Manuel composes his *Discourse of Counsel to the Thessalonians When They Were Besieged,* later writing his Letter ιαʹ to accompany a copy of it sent to Cydones; he also writes his Letters γʹ and ιʹ, and those in between.

1384   Theodore emerges unchallenged as Despot of the Morea; Theodore and Manuel cooperate militarily and make various alliances with neighbors; failure of their joint plea to Venice for help (April 18); death of Francesco I Gattilusio of Lesbos, succeeded by his son Francesco II (August).

1385   New hostilities between Andronicus IV and John V; Andronicus is defeated (spring) and dies in Selymbria (June 25), his son John (VII) succeeding to his appanage and pretensions; Manuel's independent negotiations with Pope Urban VI for possible Church union to win Western aid; Manuel writes his Letter η' and (about this time) Letter ς'; failure of mediation attempts between Manuel and the Turks, who at this time take Sofia.

1386   The Turks capture Niš.

1387   His position in Thessalonica precarious, Manuel is forced to leave it (April 6), and it is surrendered to the Turks (April 9); Manuel escapes to Lesbos, where he writes his *Discourse in Letter Form to Cabasilas;* unwelcome in Constantinople, Manuel moves to desolate Tenedos and is approached by envoys of Murad; he is invited to Brusa and is received affably by Murad; sent back to Constantinople (autumn), he is sentenced to exile on Lemnos by John V.

1388   Death of the Patriarch Neilos (February); Serbian victory over the Turks at Bileće (August 27).

1389   Antonios made Patriarch of Constantinople (January 12); great Turkish victory over the Serbians at Kossovo (June 15), beginning the end of their independence; during the battle Murad is assassinated and is succeeded by his son Bayazid I.

1390   In Genoa, John VII, with his mother, conspires with the Genoese; winning Turkish support as well, he besieges Constantinople (March); returning from exile (then or earlier), Manuel arrives (March 31); a plot in the capital on John VII's behalf is defeated (April 2); John VII wins entry to the city (April 13/14) and takes the throne, while John V and Manuel continue to resist from the Golden Gate fortress; John VII signs the latest treaty renewal with Venice (June 3); the Patriarch Antonios is deposed, and Makarios is restored (July 30); Maria-Kyratza returns home by way of Venice (summer); Manuel makes efforts to win outside aid; with help from the Hospitalers of

Rhodes, he drives John VII out of Constantinople (September 17), together with John's (then or later?) father-in-law Francesco II of Lesbos; the Empire's vassalage to the Turks now tighter than ever, Manuel campaigns (together with John VII) in Bayazid's army, assisting in the Turkish reduction of Philadelphia.

1391   Compelled by Bayazid to destroy fortifications in Constantinople on threats of harm to Manuel, John V dies (February 16); Manuel escapes to Constantinople and secures the throne; Bayazid acquiesces, but exacts further concessions; after the death of Makarios, Antonios is restored to the Patriarchal throne (March); leaving his mother, Helena Cantacuzena, as regent, Manuel departs from Constantinople (June 8) to rejoin Bayazid's army as a vassal, campaigning in northeastern and central Asia Minor; he writes his Letters ιδ′, ιε′, ις′, ιζ′, ιη′, ιθ′, κ′, and κα′, and perhaps also κβ′, and his *Dialogue Which Was Held with a Certain Persian, the Worthy Mouterizes, in Angkyra of Galatia*.

1392   Returning to Constantinople (early January), Manuel finally takes a wife, Helena Dragaš, daughter of the Serbian prince Konstantin Dejanović; she arrives in Constantinople (February 7/8) and is married to Manuel (February 10), both being then crowned formally (February 11); plans for further vassalage service by Manuel with Bayazid, which were not carried out(?); birth of Manuel's first son, the future John VIII (December 17/18).

1393   Protests of the Patriarch of Constantinople against non-recognition of Manuel as Emperor by the Muscovite Church and Prince; Bayazid captures Trnovo and subjects Bulgaria; successful Hungarian raid on Nicopolis Minor; plan for a reconciliation, with reciprocal adoptions, between Manuel and John VII, with the support of the Genoese of Galata; John changes his mind and reveals the plan to Bayazid; seeking to use similar complaints against other Christian vassals, Bayazid gathers the Balkan princes by trickery for a meeting at Serres (winter); his brief scheme to have at least Manuel and his brother assassinated is abandoned; he dismisses Manuel, but retains Theodore in an effort to extort cessions in the Morea from him.

1394 When Bayazid moves on Greece, Theodore escapes and is able to forestall his unwilling cessions; in the wake of the Serres gathering, Manuel decides to abandon accommodation with the Turks, rejecting Bayazid's latest summons; the Turkish siege of Constantinople begins (spring); (?)Thessalonica is retaken by the Turks (?April); provisions made with Venice for Manuel's flight from Constantinople if necessary, and aid sent; the first Turkish assaults are held back; Manuel writes his Letter κθ′ about this time; at this time, or early in the following year, Bayazid sends Evrenos-Bey to ravage the Peloponnesus.

1395 Indecisive Battle of Rovine between Bayazid and Mircea of Wallachia (May 17), but the beginning of Wallachian subjection; death of Marko Kraljević and Konstantin Dejanović in the battle; Manuel and Helena establish a pious foundation in Constantinople in her father's honor (October); in spite of Turkish ravages, the victory of Theodore I's forces over the Navarrese of Achaia (June 4); new Turkish assaults on Constantinople, led by John VII (September), in whose name the city is claimed; first organization of a Christian coalition against the Turks under Sigismund of Hungary.

1396 Manuel's ambassador to Buda, Manuel Philanthropenos, concludes an alliance between the Empire and Sigismund (February); Venice agrees to cooperate; the Crusade of Nicopolis organized; its initial progress through Bulgaria (summer); its siege of Nicopolis on the Danube and its crushing defeat by Bayazid there (September 25); Sigismund and others escape the capture and slaughter of prisoners and stop at Constantinople on their way home; Sigismund plans a new expedition in the following year; Manuel writes his *Ethical Dialogue, or Concerning Marriage,* and his Letter ξδ′; Theodore I sells Corinth to the Hospitalers; death of Manuel's mother, Helena Cantacuzena (November), as the nun Hypomene.

1397   Bayazid renews active assaults on Constantinople (winter) and on Galata; Venice sends some aid; with this and other help the Turks are beaten off; hardship mounts in the city; Manuel sends appeals to various rulers; likewise the Patriarch, who writes (January) to Jagiello of Poland-Lithuania, holding out prospects of Church union after aid is given and also to the Muscovite Church and Principality; failure of Sigismund's plans for a new expedition; death of Patriarch Antonios (May); his successor, Kallistos II, dies after a few months and is followed in his See by Matthaios; amid a slight relaxation of the Turkish blockade Manuel makes new appeals to the West, sending Nicholas Notaras and then Theodore Palaeologus Cantacuzenus as his ambassadors to France and England; John VII attempts vainly to sell his rights to the Imperial title to the King of France (July–August); a Turkish force under Timurtash and Iakoub Pasha ravages the Peloponnesus.

1398   Charles VI of France promises to aid the Emperor; Pope Boniface IX issues an appeal (April) for Western help to Byzantium.

1399   Boniface assists Manuel's son-in-law, Hilario Doria, in fund raising in the West, producing some contributions (Siena; England); Charles VI of France mounts a small expedition under Marshal Boucicaut, a veteran of the Crusade of Nicopolis, which sets sail (June 26) and is cordially welcomed at Constantinople, to which it brings some relief; Manuel and Boucicaut lead it in minor raids in surrounding areas, but can accomplish substantially little; Boucicaut recommends a personal appeal by Manuel in the West; John VII is brought from Selymbria to Constantinople (December 4) and a reconciliation with Manuel is effected; leaving John as regent, with some French troops under Chateaumorand, Manuel sails with Boucicaut (December 10), taking his family; the Patriarch Matthaios writes to the Metropolitan of Kiev to explain the new arrangement and to beg aid.

1400   John VII holds Constantinople, despite Bayazid's threats and mounting hardship in the city; final arrangements for

Manuel's journey are completed in the Morea, where Manuel leaves his wife and children, sailing for Venice (spring); there, Manuel is received with honor, and Boucicaut proceeds ahead of him to France; Manuel crosses Italy, through Padua, Vicenza, and Pavia, and is grandly received by Gian Galeazzo Visconti in Milan, where Manuel Chrysoloras is then visiting; Pope Boniface IX issues a new bull on Manuel's behalf (May 27), but Manuel probably does not meet him yet; from Milan Manuel proceeds to France, and is received at Charenton, outside Paris, by the King and a vast throng (June 3), being thereafter ceremoniously entertained; Manuel writes his Letter λζ´; aid and a new expedition under Boucicaut are promised; Manuel enters into contact, through his ambassador Alexios Vranas, with King Martin I of Aragon, King Henry III of Castile, King Charles of Navarre (summer and thereafter), and other kings, to ask their participation in the new expedition; through Peter de Holt of the Hospitalers Manuel negotiates (summer and thereafter) a visit to England; Charles VI suffers a fit of insanity (August–September); Manuel goes to Calais with Holt (October) and eventually crosses to England; he is received with great honor at Canterbury (December 13) and London (December 21) by Henry IV, who promises his aid; Timur (Tamerlane) begins his campaigns in Asia Minor and beyond, capturing Sivas (Sebasteia: August) and Aleppo; Theodore I, needing their aid against the Turks, cedes more of the Morea, including Mistra, to the Hospitalers, but riots and popular resistance hamper the scheme; apparently about this time Manuel's third son, Adronicus, is born while Helena is in the Morea.

1401   In London, Manuel writes his Letter λη´; he receives belated English financial contributions made good by Henry IV (letter of thanks, February 3); Manuel returns to France (mid-February); reaching Paris (late February), he joins King Charles VI in ceremonies at Saint-Denys; amid mounting hardships, hopes of relief, and negotiations with the Turks, the Patriarch Matthaios defends himself against rumors of secret dealings with Bayazid; Timur continues his campaign, taking Baghdad and attacking Egypt; Christian attempts begin to contact him and make an alliance; further contacts (summer) through Vranas with Spanish monarchs and with the anti-Pope Benedict XIII, and with other rulers; Manuel's optimism continues, and he writes his Letters λθ', μ', and μα'; Demetrius Palaeologus fails to win help in Italy; Martin I of Aragon puts off his contribution; beginnings of disillusionment as expedition plans founder; appointment of Boucicaut instead as Governor of Genoa (autumn), now a French dependency.

1402   Manuel informs John VII of at least Henry IV's failure to give help; John VII writes (June 1) on his own to the English King, begging aid; Manuel writes (then, or earlier?) his Letter μβ', passing time also by writing his description of a tapestry in the Louvre, and a long refutation of Latin doctrines; continuing contacts and appeals to win help prove vain; Benedict XIII issues a bull on Manuel's behalf (June 26); Manuel lingers hopelessly in France, while the situation in Constantinople deteriorates; in spite of hopes for help from Timur, John VII takes steps to arrange the surrender of the city to Bayazid; before this is carried out, Bayazid and Timur clash in the Battle of Ancyra (July 28), in which the Turkish army is shattered and Bayazid is taken prisoner; lack of consistent Christian policy, and some help given the Turks; John fails to live up to promises to Timur; Chateaumorand sent (August) to France to report (September); Manuel prepares to return and leaves Paris (November 21?); as Bayazid's sons secure parts of Turkish territory, Suleyman establishes himself in Rumelia (Europe) and presses for an accommodation with the Christians; John VII stalls for time, but joins a league of Aegean Christian powers; Timur takes Smyrna from the Hospitalers, storming and sacking it (December).

1403   Manuel arrives in Genoa (January 22) and attempts negotiations for anti-Turkish action with possible Venetian cooperation; leaving Genoa (February 10), he (perhaps) passes through Florence, meeting (possibly) Pope Boniface IX there, and Ferrara; continued negotiations with Venice on diplomatic and transportation questions; unable to withstand pressure any longer, John VII joins in signing a treaty between Suleyman and various Christian powers (about February 20), which grants favorable peace and territory, including Thessalonica, to the Empire, all this being done (possibly) without Manuel's knowledge or consent; on his way home after serving Bayazid at Ancyra, Stefan Lazarević of Serbia visits Constantinople, being welcomed there and given the title of Despot by John VII, later also marrying a Gattilusio sister-in-law of John; Bayazid dies (March 8) as a captive during Timur's homeward march; Manuel reaches Venice (late March); complex arrangements for Manuel's transportation consume time, and he leaves Venice (mid-April) for the Morea, accompanied by Manuel Chrysoloras; rejoining his family at Vasilipotamo, Manuel occupies himself with affairs in the Despotate of the Morea; Mechmed, one of Bayazid's sons in Asia Minor, attacks Isa, his brother and rival there; Isa flees to Constantinople and John VII, returning to be defeated again and killed by Mechmed (spring); Manuel's further negotiations with Venice for transportation; arrival of Boucicaut with a Genoese squadron; he goes to meet Manuel and his family at Vasilipotamo; the Genoese and Venetians grant Manuel escort home (May 29), and he departs for Constantinople; he arrives there (June 9?), (possibly) meeting Suleyman(?), and he is received by John VII; breaking his promise to John, Manuel exiles him to Lemnos; John goes to Lesbos and is joined by his father-in-law Francesco II Gattilusio in an attempt to win the aid of Boucicaut and, together with him, then attack Thessalonica; Boucicaut, ending a Genoese raid on Alexandretta, avoids such entanglement, and is then defeated by a Venetian fleet off Modon (October 7); Manuel yields to an accommodation with John, agreeing on succession arrangements and giving John Thessalonica (late October); reception by Manuel of the Castilian ambassador to Timur, Ruy González de Clavijo (late October); Manuel continues contacts and pleas for aid in the West, especially through his ambassadors Alexios Vranas and

Constantine Rhallis Palaeologus, during this time and the next few years; about this time Manuel writes his two brief literary works on the fall of Bayazid.

1404   Treaty of Vasilipotamo (May 5), settling the final withdrawal of the Hospitalers from the Peloponnesus; proposal (spring) by Philippe de Naillac, Grand Master of the Hospitalers, for a general Christian alliance against the Turks, unheeded.

1405   Birth of Manuel's fourth son, the future Emperor Constantine XI (February 8); Manuel's friendly contact with Pope Innocent VII (spring); Manuel's second son, Theodore, sent to the Morea to be educated to succeed Theodore I; death of Timur in Samarkand.

1406   Byzantine treaty with Venice renewed (May 22); about this time, or thereafter, Manuel writes his so-called *Praecepta educationis regiae* and his so-called *Orationes ethico-politicae*, with the accompanying Letter νγ′, all for his oldest son and heir, John (VIII).

1407   Death of Manuel's brother, Theodore I of the Morea; Suleyman crosses to Anatolia (Asia Minor) to begin his assault on the lands there of his brother Mechmed (spring?), enjoying some immediate success; Manuel Chrysoloras is sent West to renew contacts with Latin courts and to investigate chances of aid; he arrives in Venice (December).

1408   Manuel Chrysoloras proceeds to Genoa (April 18) and then to Paris, where he presents Manuel's gift of the manuscript of the Pseudo-Dionysius to the Monastery of Saint-Denys; Manuel II sails to the Morea (summer?), to help strengthen the government there of his son Theodore II; Manuel's initial plans made for rebuilding the Hexamilion across the Isthmus of Corinth; about this time (or soon after) he writes his *Funeral Oration for His Brother Theodore*, and about this time he also writes his Letters μθ′ (?) and να′; death of John VII in Thessalonica (September), having taken the monastic name of Ioasaph; leaving the Morea, Manuel hastens to Thessalonica to install his son

Andronicus as Despot there; Manuel's important *prostagma* on monastic taxation is issued during his stay in this city (December 1).

1409 Manuel returns to Constantinople (beginning of the year?); Manuel Chrysoloras visits England, stopping at London and Salisbury; Mechmed has his brother Musa cross to Europe to draw Suleyman out of Asia Minor; Manuel's sixth son, Thomas, is born.

1410 Manuel's proposal to Venice for an anti-Turkish coalition to take advantage of Turkish wars of succession is evaded by the Venetian Senate (January 10); Musa, with his allies Mircea of Wallachia and (briefly) Stefan Lazarević of Serbia, invades Rumelia; his victory over Suleyman's Beylerbey at Jamboli (February 13); Suleyman returns to Europe and wins a closer alliance with Manuel; Musa is defeated before Constantinople by Suleyman's army (June 15); falling back, Musa is defeated again at Adrianople (July 11); Manuel Chrysoloras travels to Spain and then returns to Italy; to him Manuel II writes (end of year?) his Letter νϛ'; shortly thereafter, he writes his Letter νζ' to Chrysoloras, accompanying a copy of his *Funeral Oration;* Manuel Chrysoloras in Bologna with Pope John XXIII; death of the Patriarch Matthaios (August) and election of of Euthymios II (October) as successor.

1411 Suleyman wastes his advantages while Musa rebuilds his forces; Musa's second invasion, defeating, capturing, and executing Suleyman (February 17); Musa besieges Constantinople and other Byzantine holdings and attacks Serbia; Venice steers a neutral course; Manuel repulses Musa at Constantinople, and his fleet (under Manuel, an illegitimate son of John V) defeats the Turkish ships; Manuel Chrysoloras accompanies Pope John XXIII to Rome (April); Manuel II courts Mechmed of Anatolia; betrothal of John (VIII), Manuel's heir, to Anna of Moscow.

1412 Mechmed is drawn to Europe, but is defeated by Musa (July); new preparations and coalitions against Musa, now including Stefan Lazarević; decline of Musa's support and position; renewal of the Byzantine treaty with Venice (October 31).

1413   Manuel Chrysoloras accompanies John XXIII from Rome to Florence and Bologna; new crossing to Europe by Mechmed (June 15); Musa is defeated, captured, and executed by him (July 5); Mechmed, now uncontested Sultan, makes peace with the Empire, restoring territory to the Empire as of the 1403 treaty.

1414   Marriage of Manuel's heir John (VIII) to Anna of Moscow; leaving John as regent, Manuel sails from Constantinople (July 25), going first to Thasos to put down a rebellion there (summer); (?) Manuel writes his Letter ξ'; he sails on to Thessalonica (autumn), where he winters and attends to local affairs, including those of Mount Athos; Manuel Chrysoloras participates in preparations for the Council of Constance and is present at its opening (November).

1415   Emergence (early winter) of the pretender Mustafa, who crosses to Europe (early summer) and begins to gather support; sailing from Thessalonica (March), Manuel lands at Kengchreai (March 29) near the Isthmus of Corinth, supervises the reconstruction of the Hexamilion there (April 8 to May 2), and begins appeals to Venice for help in maintaining it; Manuel Chrysoloras dies while at the Council of Constance (April 15); as a result of discontent and resistance by the unruly Moreote archons, Manuel is obliged to march against these rebels, defeat them in battle (July 15), and storm their fortresses, conducting operations against them on through the year; he writes his Letter to the Monks David and Damian; he receives the homage of Centurione Zaccaria of Achaia and, through Leonardo Tocco, that of Carlo Tocco of Cephalonia and Joanina; Manuel grants Carlo the title of Despot of Epirus and Leonardo that of Grand Constable; plans are laid for an anti-Turkish league of Aegean Christian powers, but ultimately come to naught.

1416   Nicholas Eudaimonoioannes and John Bladynteros lead a new Byzantine delegation to the Council of Constance, stopping for various negotiations in Venice (February); Manuel leaves the Morea and returns to Constantinople (March), (?) being met by Mechmed at Gallipoli on the way (?); in the midst of a dispute between Manuel and the Patriarch Euthymios, the latter dies (March 29); Manuel convokes a synod to confirm Imperial powers in the Church; Joseph II is then made the new Patriarch of Constantinople (May 12); Venetian naval victory over the Turkish fleet at Gallipoli (May 29); supported by the adventurer Djunaïd and by Voievode Mircea of Wallachia, the pretender Mustafa attacks Rumelia and attempts to seize power there; failing, he and Djunaïd take refuge in Thessalonica; Mechmed's demands for their surrender are put off, and Manuel arranges to imprison Mustafa on Lemnos on terms of a Turkish subsidy to the Empire; the arrangement is settled by John (VIII) during a stop in Thessalonica while on his way to the Peloponnesus (autumn).

1417   John (VIII), in the Peloponnesus, presses the Byzantine offensive against Centurione Zaccaria of Achaia, amid Venetian protests; John's child-bride Anna dies (August); perhaps about this time (October?), Manuel writes his Letter ξβ' to the humanist Guarino, accompanying a copy of his *Funeral Oration* to be translated into Latin.

1418   The future historian Sphrantzes is taken into Manuel's service; continuing his campaigns against Achaia, John (VIII) then leaves the Peloponnesus and returns to Constantinople (summer); his youngest brother, Thomas, is sent to the Morea; Pope Martin V helps encourage Latin aid in defending the Hexamilion and agrees to Latin marriages for Manuel's two eldest sons; attempts are begun to send a Papal legate to Constantinople to study possibilities of Church union; the Byzantine treaty with Venice is renewed (October 30).

1420   Manuel Philanthropinos undertakes a mission to mediate between Venice and Sigismund of Hungary, also visiting Jagiello of Poland; Sigismund plans for a new expedition against the Turks; Pope Martin V's bull (July 12) encourages Latin participation in the proposed expedition; Nicholas Eudaimonoioannes brings the Latin brides for John (Sophia of Montferrat) and Theodore II (Cleopa Malatesta) from Italy (summer).

1421   John VIII is married to Sophia of Montferrat and is designated co-Emperor (January 19); Mechmed requests transportation across the Straits; Manuel resists the pressure of the war party to seize the Sultan; the elaborate reception and escort of Mechmed by the Emperors (winter–spring); Mechmed's return (spring), new negotiations, and the death of Mechmed (May 21); the war party, led by John VIII, presses for use of the pretender Mustafa as the Byzantine candidate for the Turkish succession; Manuel yields to this plan and retires from the government; John assists Mustafa in taking Gallipoli and seizing Rumelia (late summer–autumn); but Mustafa refuses to keep his promise to yield Gallipoli to the Empire, disaffecting and embarrassing the Byzantines.

1422   Mustafa crosses to Anatolia (January 20) but is driven back by Murad II, is defeated and is executed (spring); rejecting peace overtures, Murad begins to besiege Constantinople (June); John VIII leads the defense successfully against an elaborate investment by the Turks (including cannon); accusation and execution of the interpreter Theologos Korax as a traitor; the Turks' general assault (August 24) fails; Manuel returns to active exercise of power, encouraging civil war in Anatolia on behalf of Murad II's younger brother Mustafa; Murad abandons the siege (September 6); the third appointee as Papal legate, Antonio da Massa, succeeds in reaching Constantinople (September 10) and is received by Manuel (September 16); the young prince Mustafa arrives in Constantinople (September 30); amid all these dealings, Manuel suffers a paralytic stroke (October 1), which disrupts the government; John VIII carries on both negotiations, hearing the legate's proposals (October); Patriarch Joseph and his synod prepare the Byzantine answers (October 19), which are formally presented (November

14), ending prospects and illusions of immediate Church union.

1423   Murad II crosses to Anatolia (winter–spring) and puts down the revolt on behalf of young Mustafa, who is executed; renewed Turkish menace to the Empire; the Pope and Venice fruitlessly discuss aid for the Empire; a Turkish army under Turachan breaks through the ineffectively manned Hexamilion (May 21–22), ravaging the Peloponnesus and massacring the Albanians settled there at Tavia (June 5); the Turks besiege Thessalonica; family strife in Constantinople and the flight of Manuel's fifth son, Demetrius, with Hilario Doria and others (summer); unable to maintain Thessalonica, its government, under the ailing Despot Andronicus, negotiates (summer), with the approval of Constantinople, to place Thessalonica in Venetian hands, which is arranged (September); the regular Byzantine treaty with Venice is renewed by John VIII (September 30); leaving his brother Constantine as regent, John VIII sails from Constantinople (November 15) to seek aid personally, especially from Venice and Sigismund; arriving in Venice (December 15), John begins long negotiations.

1424   During John's absence, Byzantine ambassadors arrange a disadvantageous peace with Murad II (February 20/22) on terms of yielding territory and paying tribute to the Turks; John goes to Milan and other northern Italian cities (February to May), finally traveling to Hungary (summer), accomplishing little in discussions with Sigismund; John returns by the Danube and the Black Sea to Constantinople (November 1).

1425   Adopting monastic garb under the name of Matthaios on his deathbed, Manuel expires (July 21?) and is buried in the Church of the Pantokrator amid scenes of deep public mourning.

Introduction

The Subject and Its Sources

The scorn, neglect, and misunderstanding to which the restored Byzantine Empire (1261–1453) and its Palaeologan dynasty have long been subjected are fortunately becoming obsolete attitudes as time passes and more careful study is made. The reasons for such attitudes are too extensive to allow for discussion here, although the chief of them might be a natural distaste for what seems, at first glance, but a period essentially of continuous decline and decay. But at least one reason may well have been the relative dearth of outstanding rulers which the period produced. Of a total of some eleven individuals who bore the consecrated title of *Basileus*, hardly three or four may really be ranked as rulers of genuinely unusual ability or stature. Of itself this is not a bad percentage, but amid their mediocre or even feeble company and amid their unhappy circumstances their reputations have perhaps suffered unjustly.

Yet these rulers deserve detailed study, not only for their own merits, such as they were, but also as indispensable keys to understanding their era. And surely in the entire Palaeologan house no Emperor is more significant, both for his own accomplishments and for his personification of the best and most interesting aspects of his time, than the man to whom this study is devoted. Statesman, soldier, diplomat, administrator, scholar, man of let-

ters, theologian—a person of many talents and interests, excelling
in all, Manuel Palaeologus would have been a man of extraordinary interest whenever he might have lived. Living when he
did, he is all the more fascinating and all the more in need of
thorough study.

It was more than a century ago that there appeared the first—
and still the only—full-length modern work on the entire span of
Manuel's life and activities. This work was Jules Berger de
Xivrey's *Mémoire sur la vie et les ouvrages de l'empereur Manuel
Paléologue.*[1] Its very title indicates its scope: the man and the
Emperor; his activities, personal, political, and literary. A comparison of its length, a scant 181 pages of actual text, with that
of the present study will provide a rough if not fully complete
indication of the vaster resources of material available to us
today which Berger de Xivrey did not have at his disposal.

Indeed, his work was written under what might now seem the
greatest of handicaps. His general source material was limited
to the standard Greek historians and to some scant Western
materials. Few of Manuel's own works had yet been published,
and for these vital sources Berger de Xivrey was obliged to use
the chief manuscript itself of most of the Emperor's writings, the
Parisinus 3041. Little serious study of Manuel had been made
previously, and although the image of this Emperor had been
seen to flit through the pages of classic general histories, such
as those of Edward Gibbon, Charles Lebeau, and, soon after,
George Finlay, there was, relatively speaking, virtually no secondary literature on the subject. Inevitably, these handicaps led
the author into statements, misinterpretations, errors, or oversights that now seem grotesque. Yet, even granting such failures,
Berger de Xivrey handled the material he had with care and
imagination. Many of his observations are penetrating and perceptive and have pioneered in elucidating his difficult subject.
If his study may by now be smugly retired as largely obsolete, it
must still be admired for what it was as an achievement in its
time and noted for what it may yet offer.

Unjustly or otherwise, part of the stature of Berger de Xivrey's
work has been based on the fact that no one has yet attempted

1. *Mémoires de l'Institut de France, Académie des Inscriptions et Belles-
Lettres,* XIX, 2 (Paris, 1853), 1–201.

to supersede it.[2] There have been, however, several important studies of aspects of Manuel's life or activity which are worthy of particular notice. Three subjects have inspired large-scale attention. The first is the Emperor's diplomatic relations, and this subject has evoked two short works. Unfortunately, neither is a major advance. The brief fifty-one-page study in modern Greek by Antonios Mompherratos, *Diplomatic Activities of Manuel II Palaiologos in Europe and Asia*,[3] does gather together a certain range of information, but it is generally superficial. The second work, a short monograph by the Spanish scholar Sebastian Cirac Estopañan, *La unión, Manuel II Paleólogo y sus recuerdos en España*,[4] in spite of its promising title, is essentially a study only of the documents of Manuel's dealings with various Spanish courts and with the Avignonese Anti-Pope. It is useful as far as it goes, but, as a whole, the work has little real scope or interpretative insight.

The second subject is Manuel's celebrated journey to the West. The most extensive study, and still the basic one, on this episode is the long article by the great Alexander Alexandrovich Vasiliev, "The Journey of the Byzantine Emperor Manuel II Palaeologus to Western Europe (1399–1403)."[5] Less detailed and more superficial, but still quite useful, is the briefer study on the same subject by the French scholar Gustave Schlumberger.[6] The third aspect of Manuel's life which has attracted important attention has recently called forth the newest and most significant major work on this Emperor since Berger de Xivrey's study. This is *The*

2. Since the present book was written, T. Khoury has published his article, "L'Empereur Manuel II Paléologue (1350–1425), Esquisse biographique," in *Proche-Orient chrétien*, 15 (1965), 127–144. This includes a brief survey of the major studies on Manuel and his reign, followed by a concise but comprehensive sketch of the Emperor's life. His comments and chronology rarely disagree with my own, but this article will be cited occasionally hereafter when some point requires special attention.

3. Διπλωματικαὶ ἐνέργειαι Μανουὴλ Β΄ τοῦ Παλαιολόγου ἐν Εὐρώπῃ καὶ 'Ασίᾳ (Athens, 1913).

4. Barcelona, 1952.

5. "Putešestvie vizantijskogo imperatora Manuila Palaeologa po Zapadnoj Evropie (1399–1403)," *Žurnal ministerstva narodnogo prosveščeniia* (*Journal of the Ministry of Public Education*), N.S. 39 (1912), 41–78, 260–334 (in Russian).

6. "Un Empereur de Byzance à Paris et Londres," originally published in *Revue des deux mondes*, 30 (1915), republished in the author's collection *Byzance et Croisades: Pages médiévales* (Paris, 1927), 87–147.

Reign of Manuel II Palaeologus in Thessalonica, 1382–1387,[7] by Loenertz' disciple, Father George T. Dennis, S.J. By contrast with the first two of these three subjects, this last has been unjustly neglected. Father Dennis' admirable work has the distinction of focusing attention at long last on this important episode. In addition, in the process of providing the background for his topic, he has actually assembled a good account of Manuel's life from his earliest years through 1387, though with inevitable emphases.

If the aforementioned studies represent the sole works of major scope on Manuel, there is nonetheless a rich literature now of articles and other contributions, bearing directly or indirectly on him, by an imposing number of modern writers. Perhaps the foremost among this group is Father Raymond-Joseph Loenertz, O.P., who knows the history and sources of the Palaeologan period, especially of Manuel's time, as do few other living men. Few aspects of Manuel's life and activity have been left untouched and unclarified by his illuminating scholarship. Great debts are also owed to the pioneering efforts of such distinguished scholars as Peter Charanis and Franz Dölger, as well as Paul Lemerle and Vitalien Laurent. The full roster is inevitably too extensive to be covered in the short survey proper here. But the footnotes and the bibliography will indicate in detail the extent of the vast array of secondary writing, directly or peripherally involving Manuel, which is presently available.

Before the present book could go to press, the final fasicule of Franz Dölger's monumental *Regesten der Kaiserurkunden des ostromishcen Reiches* had appeared.[8] The completion of this landmark in Byzantine studies is itself a cause for rejoicing. As it covers the period of Manuel II's lifetime, moreover, it is a basic reference tool far too important to be ignored, and so appropriate citations of it have been included in the footnotes.

In addition to specialized secondary literature, one should also bear in mind a number of general works by modern writers that provide helpful background. The two prototypes, Edward Gibbon's immortal *History of the Decline and Fall of the Roman Empire* and George Finlay's zealous *A History of Greece from Its*

7. *Orientalia Christiana Analecta,* 159 (Rome, 1960).
8. Part 5: *Regesten von 1341–1453,* with the collaboration of P. Wirth (Munich, 1965).

Conquest by the Romans to the Present Time, B.C. 142 to A.D. 1864, are of course in varying degrees rather obsolete for scholarly purposes, but they are at least always on hand for literary interest. At the end, as it were, of the same great English tradition of literary (and literate) scholarship is Edwin Pears' *The Destruction of the Greek Empire and the Story of the Capture of Constantinople by the Turks.*[9] This book is unfortunately filled with many mistakes and shortcomings, at least for the period of Manuel's life, but it is still useful and is certainly good reading. Remarkable in their way but now rather out of date are Karl Hopf's *Geschichte Griechenlands vom Beginn des Mittelalters bis auf unsere Zeit* (*1821*) [10] and the really obsolete *Essai de chronographie byzantine, 1057–1453* of Edouard von Muralt.[11]

For the general history of Byzantium there is always Vasiliev's *History of the Byzantine Empire, 324–1453*,[12] even though its categorized coverage of material is disconcertingly unwieldy.

More important for purely political history is, of course, the revised and up-to-date English version of George Ostrogorsky's *History of the Byzantine State.*[13] One might note also the popularized and rather unscholarly, but often lively, *La Ruine de*

9. London, 1903. Pears also contributed the chapter (XXI) entitled "The Ottoman Turks to the Fall of Constantinople" to the *Cambridge Medieval History* (Vol. IV, Cambridge, 1923). But since this chapter is largely a derivative, often verbatim, from the aforementioned book, there is little point in employing it independently here. It might be noted, as a symptom of the long neglect of the Palaeologan epoch, that this great cooperative work has no separate chapter devoted to Byzantium from 1261 to 1453.

10. Published as Vol. VIIB in the series *Griechenland*, ed. H. Brockhaus (Leipzig, 1870), or in the Ersch and Gruber *Allgemeinen Encyklopädie der Wissenschaften und Künste*, 86 (Leipzig, 1868).

11. St. Petersburg, 1871, in two volumes; reprint, Amsterdam, 1966.

12. Madison, Wis., 1952.

13. Translated from the second German edition by Joan M. Hussey: American edition, New Brunswick, N.J., 1957. Since the present book was written, the revised third German edition has appeared, still in the series, *Handbuch der Altertums-wissenschaft*, XII: *Byzantinisches Handbuch*, I, 2: Munich, 1963. This latest German edition is naturally the most up-to-date for bibliography; but, for the sake of convenience, most of the citations below to Ostrogorsky's book are kept in the English translation. Also new is Ostrogorsky's Chapter (VIII), "The Palaeologi," in the entirely new Vol. IV, Pt. 1, of *The Cambridge Medieval History* (Cambridge, 1966), 331–387.

Another recent general book may also be mentioned for its valuable reflections on this period, though not in a strictly narrative format: A. E. Vakalopoulos' Ἱστορία τοῦ νέου ἑλληνισμοῦ, Α΄: Ἀρχὲς καὶ διαμόρφωσις τοῦ, Thessalonica, 1961. An English translation of this work is in progress.

Byzance, 1204–1453 by Gérard Walter.[14] Useful, if not always accurate or fully up to date is Averkios Th. Papadopulos' impressive *Versuch einer Genealogie der Palaiologen, 1259–1453.*[15]

For Turkish history, the old classic by Joseph von Hammer-Purgstall, *Geschichte des osmanischen Reiches,*[16] is badly out of date and has been superseded to a great extent by Nicholae Iorga's work of the same title.[17] More recent is the somewhat controversial but trail-blazing *The Foundation of the Ottoman Empire,*[18] by Herbert A. Gibbons, in spite of its unreasonably arbitrary and abrupt ending at the death of Bayazid. Early Osmanli history, however, is still very much in need of an extended and up-to-date scholarly study.

If the secondary literature bearing on Manuel has expanded enormously in the past century, the primary literature has undergone no less significant amplification. Regrettably, there is still no single, fully adequate Byzantine source for the late fourteenth and early fifteenth centuries. The span of Manuel's life coincides exactly with the gap between the ends of the works by Cantacuzenus and Gregoras and the really detailed coverage by three of the four historians of the fall of Constantinople. Tragic as were the events of this crucial period, it is the more sad that they did not produce a major historian. What might a Thucydides have done with the decline of Byzantium! Thus, we are still obliged to draw what we can from the scattered, often contradictory, or at least confusing, allusions and scraps of information in the introductory sections of the three later historians.

But even dealing with these basic sources is not the same as

14. Paris, 1958.

15. Inaugural Dissertation, Munich, 1938; reprint, 1962.

16. The German edition used here is that published in ten volumes in Pest, 1827–35, as reprinted in Graz, 1963; also cited for cross-reference value is the French translation by J. J. Hellert, 18 vols., Paris, 1835–43.

17. Gotha, 1900–10, in five volumes.

18. New York, 1916. Cf. the critique by P. Wittek, *The Rise of the Ottoman Empire* (*Royal Asiatic Society Monograph*, XXIII, London, 1938), 4; Wittek's essay is itself, of course, a provocative contribution. As this book goes to press, a new publication has appeared: E. Werner's *Die Geburt einer Grossmacht—Die Osmanen (1300–1481)*; *Ein Beitrag zur Genesis des türkischen Feudalsimus* (*Forschungen zur mittelalterlichen Geschichte*, 13, Berlin, 1966). This is a comprehensive and interesting study, but its selectively specialized emphases do not really require any revision in the above comment as to the continued need for more broadly focused work in this period of Turkish history.

it was for Berger de Xivrey; for one of them can no longer be accepted as trustworthy. It had long been assumed that the so-called *Chronicon Maius* by the courtier-historian Georgios Phrantzes, or Sphrantzes—as we have now come to recognize the correct spelling of his name [19]—was a more extensive and polished counterpart of the same author's briefer *Chronicon Minus*. As a result, the *Maius* had long been used by scholars while the *Minus*, even when available, was largely ignored. In recent years, however, intense scrutiny and re-evaluation have made clear that the *Maius* is not an authentic work of Sphrantzes, but is, rather, a fraudulent compilation of the sixteenth century, probably by the known forger Makarios Melissenos.[20] The *Minus* is apparently

19. This revision of orthography has been put forth and justified by V. Laurent in his discussion of the problem, "Σφραντζῆς et non Φραντζῆς," *Byzantinische Zeitschrift*, 44 (1951), 373–378; for some further literature on the question, see Dennis, p. 4, n. 6. Also, for a peripheral study, see P. S. Nasturel's article, "Témoinages roumaines sur les formes Sphrantzès et Phrantzès," *Revue des études byzantines*, 19 (1961 = *Mélanges R. Janin*), 441–443.

20. The literature on this question has grown considerably over the years, but several important articles should be noted here. One of the very first important suggestions of the doubtful qualities of the *Maius* was made by J. B. Falier-Papadopoulos in his "Phrantzès est-il réellement l'auteur de la grande chronique qui porte son nom?" *Actes du IVe Congrès international des études byzantines* (=*Izvestija na bulgarskija archeologicheski institut*, 9, 1935), 177–189. (One should note the recent and posthumous republication of most of this scholar's articles on this question in one collection, entitled Αἱ περὶ τοῦ Γεωργίου Φραντζῆ διατριβαί, Athens, 1957.) Further indication of the unreliability of the Maius was given by Loenertz in his "La Date de la lettre ϑ' de Manuel Paléologue et l'inauthenticité du 'Chronicon Maius' de Georges Phrantzès," *Echos d'Orient*, 39 (1940–42), 91–99. And it was again the latter scholar who, in his long and detailed study, "Autour de Chronicon Maius attribué à Georges Phrantzès," *Studi e Testi*, 123 (Vatican City, 1946), 273–311, has provided a devastating and virtually irrefutable demonstration at last of the complete inauthenticity of this forgery. For a discussion of its apparent perpetrator, see Dölger, "Ein literarischer und diplomatischer Fälscher des 16. Jahrhunderts: Metropolit Makarios von Monembasia," in *Otto Glauning zum 60. Geburtstag, Festansgabe aus Wissenschaft und Bibliotek* (Leipzig, 1936), 25–35, reprinted in the author's collection *Byzantinische Diplomatik* (Ettal, 1956), 371–383. The most recent discussion of the two texts and their problems of authorship is the article by their latest editor, V. Grecu, "Georgios Sphrantzes: Leben und Werk—Makarios Melissenos und sein Werk—Die Ausgabe," *Byzantinoslavica*, 26 (1965), 62–73; also, for further comments on the background and authenticity of the *Minus*, the same scholar's paper, "Das Memoirenwerk des Georgios Sphrantzes," *Actes du XIIe Congrès internationale des études byzantines, Ohrid 1961* (Belgrade, 1964), 327–341. For a more general discussion of the entire problem of the authenticity and authorship of these

the only authentic writing of Sphrantzes, and the additional material of the *Maius* must be used, if at all, with the utmost caution.[21] Fortunately, most of its really fundamental information on Manuel, derived from Sphrantzes' personal contact with the Imperial family, is also in the historian's own authentic text.

Still valid, when relevant, are of course the respective works of Ducas [22] and Laonikos Chalkokandyles, or Chalcocondyles.[23] To these has been added an interesting Greek history of the Turkish Sultans, the text of which has recently been published.[24] Unfortunately, however, it has since been demonstrated [25] that this late sixteenth-century text is but a Greek translation and adaptation of the 1573 edition of Francesco Sansovino's Italian *Annali Turcheschi,* which was itself based heavily on Chalco-

works, and for a full listing of the pertinent literature published to 1958, see G. Moravcsik, *Byzantinoturcica,* I (2nd ed., Berlin, 1958), 282–288; see also Dennis, pp. 4–5. At this writing I understand that both the *Maius* and the *Minus* are scheduled for publication shortly in a new edition by V. Grecu, but this was accordingly and regrettably not available for citation here.

21. Since the *Chronicon Maius* has so long been a basic source in the study of this period, it has been deemed advisable in the present work to cite it, third-hand, or worse, as its information may be. To distinguish it effectively from the authentic *Minus,* I have adopted the increasingly common usage of the prefix "Pseudo-"; and to emphasize the distinction further, I have retained the old spelling of the historian's name. The designation "Pseudo-Phrantzes" is therefore intended to signalize the false *Chronicon Maius* (ed. I. Bekker, Bonn, 1838). By way of contrast, the emended spelling of "Sphrantzes" indicates the *Chronicon Minus* (ed. Migne, *Patrologia graeca,* 156, coll. 1025–1080).

22. *Historia byzantina,* ed. V. Grecu (Bucharest, 1958), and ed. Bekker (Bonn, 1834).

23. *Historiarum demonstrationes,* ed. E. Darkó (2 vols., Budapest, 1922–27), and ed. Bekker (Bonn, 1843). As with Ducas, citations below are given throughout to both the new critical edition and also to the old and long-standard Bonn edition.

24. Χρονικὸν περὶ τῶν Τούρκων σουλτάνων (κατὰ τὸν Βαρβερινὸν ἑλληνικὸν Κώδικα 111), ed. G. Th. Zoras (Athens, 1958), cited in the present work as *"Chron. Barb. 111."*

25. By E. A. Zachariades, Τὸ χρονικὸ τῶν Τούρκων Σουλτάνων (τοῦ Βαρβερινοῦ ῞Ελλην. Κώδικα 111) καὶ τὸ ᾿Ιταλικό του πρότυπο (=῾Ελ-ληνικά, Παράρτημα, 14, Thessalonica, 1960). But in his review of both Zoras' edition and Zachariades' thesis, in *Speculum,* 36 (1961), 709–712, G. G. Arnakis is inclined to mitigate the strength of the latter's criticism at least to some extent, and he suggests that this text may still embody very important material. For a previous perspective on this text, see S. Baştav, "Les Sources d'une histoire de l'empire ottomane rédigée par un auteur anonyme grec (1374–1421)," *Türk tarih Kurumu,* Belleten, XXI, 81 (1957), 161–172.

condyles. As such, it has little more basic value than much of the interpolated material in the Pseudo-Phrantzes—much of which is also derived from Chalcocondyles. Nevertheless, it occasionally contains some additional or differing information, and, even if this may be suspect, it is cited below where pertinent for what it is worth.

The most important addition, however, to our Greek source material for this period since Berger de Xivrey's time is undoubtedly the corpus of various short chronicles which have been gathered and published over the years.[26] While these motley texts of varying length and substance are hardly of any literary significance, they are of the most vitally fundamental importance for chronological information and details often unavailable elsewhere. With them alone we are able to correct and go far beyond many of the mistakes or oversights into which Berger de Xivrey fell without them.

A growing amount of documentary material has also become available in quantity, including such things as Imperial chrysobulls and diplomatic correspondence. Such riches are by no means limited to Greek material, for a good deal has now been made available from Western archives. Noteworthy are Genoese documents, but of particular significance are the records of Venetian Senate deliberations. These latter are of enormous value, for they are numerous, orderly, extensively preserved, and invariably well-informed reflections of events of the age, including Byzantine affairs. We are still woefully in need of a thorough publication of the texts of these documents, for the collections or individual publications of texts that have appeared thus far are only a bare beginning.

26. The basic collection is that of S. Lampros, entitled Βραχέα χρονικά (cited as "Βρ. χρ.") and published by K. Amantos ('Ακαδημία 'Αθηνῶν, Μνημεῖα τῆς ἑλληνικῆς ἱστορίας, Α', Athens, 1932–33, Τεῦχος α'). For some useful comments on its contents, see the review by Wittek, *Byzantion*, 12 (1937), 309–323; and by Loenertz, "Etudes sur les chroniques brèves byzantines," *Orientalia Christiana Periodica*, 24 (1958), 155–164. One of the chronicles in this collection (No. 52) has been given a thorough and detailed analysis by Charanis, "An Important Short Chronicle of the Fourteenth Century," *Byzantion*, 13 (1938), 335–362, a kind of treatment which should really be accorded to all these works on a full scale. In addition to those in the Lampros-Amantos collection, a number of other such chronicles of varying value have been published, usually singly. A full listing of these texts will be found in the bibliography at the end of the present study, gathered under the heading "Short Chronicles."

One means of bridging this gap in our source material, by means of extended surveys of the texts in summaries, is at best a poor substitute, of value only in the absence of an immediate alternative. Such a sequence of surveys was provided on a limited scale by Iorga in the first volume of his *Notes et extraits pour servir à l'histoire des croisades au XVe siècle*,[27] which also includes important Genoese texts. A more ambitious and laudable treatment of strictly Venetian material was recently attempted by F. Thiriet in his *Régestes des delibérations du Sénat de Venise concernant la Romanie*.[28] But as striking as Thiriet's work seems at first encounter, its usefulness is seriously impaired by frequent omissions of important deliberations and, even worse, by grave and often inexcusable mistakes, distortions, or oversights in the individual summaries. Further, Thiriet ignores the availability of many deliberation texts, not only in individual publications here and there, but also in such an important collection as that of S. Ljubić in the *Monumenta spectantia historiam Slavorum meridionalium*. It is regrettable that the job was not more thoroughly done, but, even with its flaws, Thiriet's work is still exceedingly useful and important.

In addition to historical writings and documentary materials, a third major category of sources is particularly significant for the Palaeologan era in comparison with other periods of Byzantine history. This is the realm of essentially literary works. Indeed, a rich bulk of such material survives, which will require extensive study and publication for some time to come before the fullest knowledge of the Palaeologan period will be possible. Many of these works, on religious or abstractly speculative subjects, are, of course, of little or no historical value. But panegyrics, orations, and various discourses on a wide range of themes can often be of great importance.

By far the most significant part of this category, however, is correspondence. There are, regrettably, handicaps in the use of such material. Written within a small coterie of the intellectual elite of their day, these letters were cast as exercises in ultra-

27. Paris, 1899, followed by two more volumes, collecting material previously published in *Revue de l'Orient latin*, 4 (1896) to 8 (1900), in serialized format.

28. Three volumes, Paris, 1958–59–61, covering, respectively, the years 1329–99, 1400–30, 1431–63.

refined rhetorical elegance. Their style is usually a supreme distillation of all the obscurity and distortion of grammar, syntax,
and vocabulary in which the late Byzantine writers reveled. As
such, these letters were intended more to provide intellectual
stimulation and to serve as a needed escape from the ghastly
realities of the day than to convey information. Indeed, the rules
of the game often call for *concealing* information, allusions,
names, and facts as far as possible within the stylistic maze. Thus,
even after the modern reader has fought his way through such
essays, he is more likely than not to emerge at the end with a
disappointingly small amount of content or information. Nevertheless, these texts should not be ignored, for here and there
among them one can in fact find some which yield really valuable
tidbits of information. We are thus very much indebted to the
common custom at that time of copying and preserving large
quantities of these letters, as more than merely ephemeral communications.

In this department of correspondence, one of the most important single contributors, at least for our purposes, was Demetrius Cydones. Scholar, man of letters, man of affairs, counselor and intimate of two Emperors (John VI Cantacuzenus and
John V Palaeologus), he was also the teacher and friend of a
third, Manuel Palaeologus himself. Among his surviving literary
works are some four hundred and fifty letters of varying length
and content, to various friends and acquaintances, and of divergent value. Many of them, however, contain information and
allusions of the greatest significance for the student of this
period.[29] For a long time these letters were not available in

29. For a concise estimate of the importance of Cydones and his works,
especially his letters, in the context of the sources for this period, see Charanis, "The Greek Historical Sources of the Second Half of the Fourteenth
Century," *Bulletin of the Polish Institute of Arts and Sciences in America,* 2
(1944), 406–412. Some useful comments on Cydones' letters and their contents may be found in Laurent's "La Correspondance de Démétrius Cydonès,"
Echos d'Orient, 30 (1931), 339–354. The most important discussion of
Cydones' letters for our purposes, however, has been offered by Loenertz,
the leading modern scholar of these texts, in his series of articles entitled
"Manuel Paléologue et Démétrius Cydonès, Remarques sur leur correspondances: Première série," *Echos d'Orient,* 36 (1937), 271–287; "Deuxième
série," *Echos d'Orient,* 36 (1937), 474–487; "Troisième série," *Echos
d'Orient,* 37 (1938), 107–124. These articles contain invaluable observations
on the whole range of this period and are of fundamental importance for its
study. In view of the frequency with which they must be cited, and of the

print. Even up until very recently only a very few of them had
been published.[30] Within the last few years, however, we have
been given a critical edition of these texts, thanks to the patient
toil of Father Loenertz.[31] Their availability at long last is an event

opportunities for confusion that their tripartite division entails, and also of
the large number of other citations necessary to Loenertz' works, it has been
deemed advisable to cite these three articles, not by title, but only by
periodical, number, date, and page. All references, therefore, to Loenertz
in this form are to these three articles. His other contributions are cited
by title.

30. Aside from eight letters edited by C. F. Matthaei in his collection
Isocratis, Demetrii Cydone, et Michaelis Glycae aliquot epistolae, etc.
(Moscow, 1776), 33–46, and then a larger group of thirty-seven included by
J.-F. Boissonade in his *Anecdota nova* (Paris, 1844), 249–326, the only
really important publication of Cydones' letters earlier was a group of fifty
by G. Cammelli in his *Démétrius Cydonès Correspondance* (Collection
byzantine, Paris, 1930). This edition provided the texts, together with
French translations and Latin and French summaries. Cammelli's grasp of
the chronology and events of the period was not always complete, and he
was therefore led into some unnecessary mistakes in analyzing or dating
these letters. But his great contribution was an "Index de la correspondance
complète," which, though often marred by faults in dating and careless
summarizing, provided a listing of all the letters, each with Cammelli's own
consecutive numbering preceding the *incipit* and with a brief (French)
synopsis. The latter are still quite useful.

31. This edition has been organized into two volumes. The first, *Démétrius Cydonès Correspondance*, I (*Studi e Testi*, 186, Vatican City, 1956),
contains the first 131 letters, preceded by Cydones' two orations to John
Cantacuzenus. Volume II (*Studi e Testi*, 208, Vatican City, 1960), contains
the remaining 319 letters. (This second volume had not appeared during
most of the time when the present study was in preparation; I am deeply
indebted to Fr. Loenertz for enabling me to use the material in the volume
in advance by supplying me with proofs of it.) In both volumes a number
of valuable supplementary texts not by Cydones are appended. The foundation for this edition was laid in a previous work, *Les Recueils des Lettres de
Démétrius Cydonès* (*Studi e Testi*, 131, Vatican City, 1947), in which
Loenertz gives a detailed study of the manuscripts, their tradition, contents,
and organization. One of the most important points he demonstrated here
is that the individual sections of the basic manuscript contain letters all, as a
rule, of the same period. In this volume are given also the texts of seven
letters or other little pieces, most of which reappear in his full edition, but
which are provided here with French summaries. The book also includes a
useful alphabetical index of *incipits*. Finally, the work adds (pp. 108–122)
an extended chronological table of the events of Cydones' life. Since these
events also include the principal political events of the period, this table is,
therefore, an indispensable guide for the era's entire chronology, which
Loenertz has done so much to elucidate in all his work. A further example
of his chronological work, incidentally, may be found in his valuable table
of events in the history of the Morea, in his article "Pour l'histoire du
Péloponnèse au XIVᵉ siècle (1382–1404)," [*Revue des*] *Etudes byzantines*,
1 (1943), 153–158.

of immeasurable importance for the study of Byzantium in the fourteenth century. Specifically, these letters are fundamental sources for at least the early sections of the present work.[32]

Of all the source material used for the study of Manuel II Palaeologus, of course, the most fundamental is inevitably the writings of the Emperor himself. A large number of them have survived. For the most part, they are in a style at least as obscure as that of the usual literary products of their age, and generally more so. As a result, they are difficult to read and to use. Admittedly, many of them are of limited or no historical value and concern primarily the student of Byzantine literature and culture as such. But a number of them, as will be seen below, are of great importance as historical sources. There are several discourses that have specific associations with certain events. One such, the Emperor's *Funeral Oration for His Brother Theodore,* is rich in historical information.

But the most important sources among Manuel's works, by and large, are his letters. While those of Cydones are fundamental for the late fourteenth century in general, Manuel's letters are fundamental for the Emperor and his career in particular. Though many of them are nothing more than empty displays of rhetoric, noteworthy mainly for their exasperatingly stilted and studied obscurity, there are yet a surprisingly large number of them which cast fascinating and illuminating light on Manuel's activities. Some of these letters have been used by scholars since they were made available. But, even bearing in mind the for-

---

32. An explanation should be given here of the system of citation used for Cydones' letters in this book. To simplify the diffuse and confusing references that might result, and to aid the reader in making use of Cammelli's synopses while using Loenertz' texts (which are without synopses), I have identified all the letters used by the numbers in the respective numerical systems of both Cammelli and Loenertz. The Cammelli number (that is, from his Index in the back of his publication) is given first, with the initial "C." If the letter in question was also published by Cammelli in the body of his book, I have added in parentheses its number in that sequence; thereafter, it is given the number borne by the text in Loenertz' edition. Thus, for example, "C. 133 (No. 28), L. 222" refers to No. 133 in Cammelli's Index, published as No. 28 in his edition, and now available as No. 222 in Loenertz' full edition. To save space and to avoid confusion, no page numbers in either edition are given; and, in view of their limited contents and (at least in the former case) uncertain availability, the publications by Matthaei and Boissonade are not cited. Allusions to Loenertz' estimated datings of individual letters refer to his edition of the texts themselves, unless otherwise stated.

midable factor of their style, it is astonishing that so many of them contain really valuable material which has gone virtually unnoticed all these years.

In the field of editions, we are at a somewhat greater advantage than Berger de Xivrey, who worked only from manuscript and, at that, from one not containing all the Emperor's surviving works. Now there are at least adequate editions of many of these literary works, including most of the really important ones.[33] But unfortunately there is still much to be done. Many works remain unpublished, and a good critical edition of Manuel's complete works is vitally needed.

Indeed, the very absence of a really satisfactory publication of this important corpus of texts prevents, at this time, the writing of a truly complete study of all aspects of Manuel Palaeologus with the same scope that Berger de Xivrey attempted. The present book is therefore by no means a biography in the conventional sense of the word. Yet, the large accumulation of new secondary literature and the availability of fuller source material during the last century have made the time ripe to some extent for a re-evaluation of at least some facets of this remarkable Emperor's life and reign.

The principal emphasis of the present study is therefore the political aspect. It is not intended to be a history of Byzantium during the seventy-five years of Manuel's life, but rather an examination of Manuel's involvement in political events and his contributions to them; of the problems which he faced and his reactions to them. The basic concern is thus both Manuel in Byzantine politics and Byzantine politics through Manuel; for in him we may observe not only the history of his time, but also the operation of first-class Byzantine statesmanship in action in the days even of the Empire's final decay.

33. Most of the letters in the chief manuscript of Manuel's writings have been published by E. Legrand, *Lettres de l'empereur Manuel Paléologue* (Paris, 1893; reprint, 1962), with a few short works added. The editor promised a commentary, but it never appeared, which is regrettable; for his edition gives only the texts without any synopses or explanations which Palaeologan literary works so badly need. (Rev. George T. Dennis has informed me of his plans to publish a new critical edition of Manuel's Letters, which will, of course, supersede Legrand's publication, once it appears.) The principal collection of Manuel's other writings in print is in Migne's *Patrologia graeca*, Vol. 156. Other editions of specific texts are cited in due course, and may be found in the bibliography.

The pursuit of these goals involves two approaches. The first, the synthesis of all current secondary literature hardly requires any defense or explanation. Since this literature has become so extensive and diverse, the need by this time to pull together the multitude of short articles and studies and to place their contributions in proper context was one of the incentives for writing this book. Of course, in instances where a topic has already been examined thoroughly, most notably in the respective major studies of Dennis and Vasiliev, there is no point in repeating their labors at length; their findings are thus gratefully absorbed with all due credit.

The second approach is the more difficult, and, as it is also more unusual, it merits brief discussion. Plainly, it is desirable to make use as far as possible of all the material in Manuel's own writings bearing on his political activity and on whatever else is relevant. Study of this material soon suggests that discussion of the deeds of an Emperor who was so adept at self-expression, by the standards of his age, can be no better supported or illuminated than by his own words. Such use of Manuel's own words, in translation, has therefore become one of the basic features of the present work.

There is no denying, of course, that this is a dangerous procedure at best. It imposes a great handicap, since Manuel's style is usually so rhetorical and intricate that, even when it has been understood, it is very difficult to transmute it intelligibly into a modern rendering. It is easy to rush to either of two extremes. One is to translate as literally as possible, producing near gibberish, which may reproduce faithfully the author's stylistic traits in his own tongue, but which is virtually unintelligible even with a battery of ponderous explanatory footnotes. The other extreme is to give free paraphrases of the original, smoothing out the author's tortuous twists and turns and reducing his ideas and statements to easy clarity. But the latter course also has great disadvantages, for it is both an injustice to the author and a dangerous oversimplification for the reader, destroying the flavor and spirit, as well as the letter, of the original.

Moreover, since the chief interest in translating these works is not to present them for any purely literary value, real or interpolated, but rather to use them to give insights into Manuel the Emperor and the man, it is desirable to retain as much as possible of his own stylistic qualities. The inevitable compromise attempts its course between Scylla and Charybdis. The translations are as faithful as possible to the original, within, it is hoped, the limits of sensible English. Moderate paraphrase has been employed only where it seemed desirable or unavoidable in the interests of intelligibility. Whatever the success of the attempt, it was one well worth making.[34]

These, then, are the perils of the second approach. It has not been followed at all in the first chapter. There are a good many of Manuel's surviving writings which concern his life before his accession as sole Emperor. But to examine them in detail would expand beyond proper bounds the already distended size of what is, after all, but a preliminary to the real subject, Manuel's career as Emperor in his own right. The first forty-three years of his life are therefore essentially a background to the main body of the subject, albeit a background essential for understanding what followed. This background also happens to cover a period filled with many points of confusion and obscurity, a period that has, in addition, elicited a large and diffuse array of small-scale articles and studies. The necessary concentration in the first chapter is therefore one of synthesis of available material to form as concise and well-grounded a survey as is feasible.

In the following narrative chapters, the employment of Manuel's own writings and of other contemporary documents, when appropriate, is brought into play. The nature of the subject matter has shaped the chapter divisions, and if these divisions are not frequent enough to allow for more compact chapters, length is preferable to Procrustean distortions. The subject matter of the first three chapters has allowed an essentially chronological narrative; indeed, any other approach would be unwise and almost meaningless. In much of the fourth and fifth chapters, however, overlapping sequences of events and simultaneous planes of activity require disjunct and categorized treatment. If

34. It should be added that all reasonable effort has been made to trace Classical or Biblical quotations or derivations. Those that have been traced have been noted in bracketed references. Where the text at hand has reproduced exactly the original passage, the words have been placed within quotation marks. In the case of the Biblical examples, the King James translation has been used to suggest in English the approximate flavor of archaism and authority which the ancient originals might have had for the medieval writer of Greek.

this latter procedure causes some confusion, it is perhaps preferable to even greater confusion. Every attempt has been made to give adequate cross references to enable the reader to keep track of separate or divided discussions of the same material.

Throughout this study, admittedly, the process of expounding the source material thoroughly makes for unfortunately bulky footnotes. But it at least avoids the failing, common in much of the literature on this period, of leaving the reader uninformed of the numerous contradictions and necessary reconciliations in which divergent sources for this period are so often involved. Where the inclusion of long discussions of extended problems or supplementary material have been deemed worth while, they have been added in appendices at the end of the work. And, although the practice may add to bulk and distraction, special effort has been made to relate all the important secondary literature to the author's own findings through the fullest citation at every opportunity.

The sixth chapter is a brief recapitulation. Its purpose is simply to reconsider the broad outlines of Manuel's policies and statesmanship; no new material is introduced. Finally, the supplementary seventh chapter has been added to give the reader some broad idea of Manuel's personal characteristics and, more important, his wide and significant literary activity, insofar as the availability of material and the scope of this book permit.

Such, then, are the aims and methods of the present study. To the degree that it is successful, it is offered as a contribution to the ultimate understanding of a fascinating and complex period and of the remarkable man who was Manuel Palaeologus.

Manuel II Palaeologus (1391–1425):
A Study in Late Byzantine Statesmanship

1. Apprenticeship in Empire, 1350–1391

Few other Byzantine Emperors had a longer apprenticeship or a career prior to accession more thoroughly entangled with the history of their times than did Manuel II Palaeologus. An initial examination of his life up to the beginning of his reign is therefore indispensable for understanding both the development of Manuel's personality and policies and the events which shaped them.

Manuel was born on June 27, 1350,[1] the second son (and apparently the third child) of John V Palaeologus and Helen Cantacuzena. The events surrounding his very birth exemplify the agonies through which the Empire was passing. Gravely decaying under the reign of the inept Andronicus II (1282–1328), then severely ravaged by the revolts of his grandson Andronicus III, Byzantium had won a measure of repose under the latter's rule (1328–1341). But its position had been irrevocably shaken, and, when it was plunged into the new civil wars arising from the usurpation of John VI Cantacuzenus (1347–1354), its future

---

1. Sphrantzes' reckoning of Manuel's age at death, *Chronicon Minus*, ed. Migne, *Patrologia graeca*, Vol. 156, coll. 1031D, would place the date in the year 1348. But R.-J. Loenertz, "Une Erreur singulière de Laonic Chalcocandyle," *Revue des études byzantines*, 15 (1957), 182–83, has clearly demonstrated the proper corrections. A. Th. Papadopulos, *Versuch einer Geneologie der Palaiologen*, 1254–1453 (Inaugural Dissertation, Munich, 1938), p. 52, n. 2, and p. 55, is inaccurate on this point.

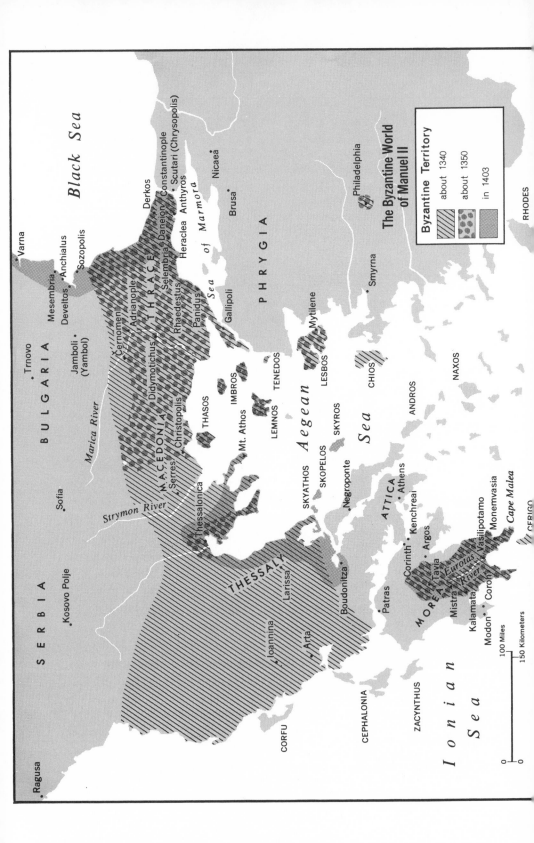

The Byzantine World of Manuel II

Byzantine Territory
about 1340
about 1350
in 1403

as little more than a ruined and dwindling local state was made virtually inevitable.[2] At the very moment of Manuel's entry into the world, his father was absent in Thessalonica, embroiled in the dynastic struggle against his ambitious father-in-law, and it was more than one and a half years before John V saw his new son.[3]

The final triumph of John V and dynastic legitimacy, with the formal abdication of Cantacuzenus in November of 1354, by no means of itself solved the problems of the Empire. Earlier that

2. For the best general accounts of Byzantium in the fourteenth century, see the following: G. Ostrogorsky's Chapter (VIII), "The Palaeologi," in *The Cambridge Medieval History*, Vol. IV, *The Byzantine Empire*, Pt. 1: *Byzantium and Its Neighbours* (new 2nd edition, ed. J. M. Hussey, Cambridge, 1966), 331–387, partially superseding the appropriate section of his *Geschichte des byzantinischen Staates* (*Handbuch der Altertumswissenschaft*, XII: I, 2: 3rd ed., Munich, 1963), trans. (from the German 2nd ed., 1952) by J. M. Hussey as *History of the Byzantine State* (New Brunswick, N.J., 1957), to which latter most citations are made hereafter; A. A. Vasiliev, *History of the Byzantine Empire, 324–1453* (Madison, Wis., 1952; 2-vol. paperback reprint, Univ. of Wis. Press, 1961); L. Bréhier, *Le Monde byzantin*, I: *Vie et mort de Byzance* (Paris, 1947); C. Diehl, *L'Empire oriental de 1081 à 1453* (= *Histoire générale: Histoire du moyen âge*, IX, 1: Paris, 1945); G. Walter, *La Ruine de Byzance, 1204–1453* (Paris, 1958); and H. Hunger's Chapter, "Byzanz in der Weltpolitik vom Bildersturm bis 1453," in the co-operative *Historia Mundi*, Vol. VII (Bern, 1958), 386–444. An old but comprehensive summary may also be found in the early sections of E. Pears' *The Destruction of the Greek Empire and the Story of the Capture of Constantinople by the Turks* (London, 1903). Of two recent books on the same broad theme, Steven Runciman's *The Fall of Constantinople, 1453* (Cambridge, 1965) offers a parallel background account that is much more cursory and, worse, full of inaccuracies. Less carefully documented, and more frankly popular, but with fuller and, surprisingly, far more accurate background sections, is a book by the novelist David Derek Stacton, *The World on the Last Day. The Sack of Constantinople by the Turks, May 29, 1453, Its Causes and Consequences* (London, 1965), rather strangely published in its American edition under the pseudonym of "David Dereksen" with the title *The Crescent and the Cross. The Fall of Byzantium: May, 1453* (New York, 1964).

3. The first allusion to Manuel in any historical text is the reference by Cantacuzenus, ed. Bonn, III (1832), 237–38, to the return of John V to Constantinople in late winter of 1352 and to his departure soon after with his wife and the young Manuel, while the latter's elder brother Andronicus and his sister Irene remained behind. Cf. Loenertz, "Une Erreur singulière," 183; also G. T. Dennis, *The Reign of Manuel II Palaeologus in Thessalonica, 1382–1387* (*Orientalia Christiana Analecta*, 159, Rome, 1960), 11–12; and T. Khoury, "L'Empereur Manuel II Paléologue (1350–1425), Esquisse biographique," *Proche-Orient chrétien*, 15 (1965), 130–31. Cantacuzenus, 253, notes Manuel's presence with his parents at another juncture in the following year.

year the progress of the Turks had been signaled by their seizure of Gallipoli. To be sure, the death of the mighty Stefan Dušan at the end of the following year inaugurated the rapid collapse of the Serbian Empire and, hence, also the removal of that powerful threat to Byzantium. But there was ample pressure to replace it. With the advent of the able Emir Murad I (1362–1389), the Turks embarked upon a tide of conquest in the Balkans that was to sweep away most of the remaining territory of the Empire.[4] Byzantium seemed on the verge of dissolution.

The Empire's grim situation is grotesquely illustrated by the circumstances of the first important reference to Manuel. In a chrysobull dated December 15, 1355, John proposed to Pope Innocent VI a plan to submit his realm to the Roman Church and communion. And in return for military aid from the West for the Empire, specifically, fifteen transport galleys carrying five hundred cavalry, five smaller galleys, and one thousand infantry, John promised to send his second son, Manuel, to the Papacy as a hostage; meanwhile a mission from the Pope would undertake the Latinization of his people, including his elder son. If all these undertakings were fulfilled faithfully, Manuel would be returned to his father. But in the event of various stipulated failures on John's part, the Pope was to retain Manuel as a ward and son, to bring him up in the Latin faith and education, and to marry him off as he wished; Manuel would bear the full title to the Empire, which the Pope might exercise in his name during the prince's minority.[5]

4. Specifically on the confused chronology of the Turkish occupation of Byzantine Thrace, the most recent study is that by I. Beldiceanu-Steinherr, "La Conquête d'Andrinople par les Turcs: la pénétration turque en Thrace et la valeur des chroniques ottomanes," in *Centre de recherche d'histoire et civilisation byzantines, Travaux et mémoires*, 1 (1965), 439–461, arguing that the region was conquered first by independent Turkish commanders, and brought under Murad I's direct control only by 1376–77. For earlier arguments on these chronological problems, see Ostrogorsky, *Geschichte* (3rd ed.), pp. 442–443, and n. 4.

5. No. 3052, pp. 42–43 in F. Dölger's *Regesten der Kaiserurkunden des oströmischen Reiches, 5: Regesten von 1341–1453* (Munich, 1965). The respective Greek and Latin texts of this document are found in A. Theiner and F. Miklosich, *Monumenta spectantia ad unionem ecclesiarum graecae et romanae* (Vienna, 1872), no. 8, pp. 29–33, 33–37, respectively, and the Latin text alone in C. Baronius and O. Raynaldus, *Annales ecclesiastici*, ann. 1355, nos. 34–36 (in the edition available to me, Vol. 25, Bar-le-Duc, 1872, pp. 601–602). For detailed synopses, see O. Halecki, *Un Empereur de*

This fantastic plan was apparently not taken very seriously at Avignon. The answer to John's proposals, dated August 4 of the following year, virtually ignores them.[6] Yet John continued to entertain this scheme. He proposed it anew to Peter Thomas, the Papal envoy sent to survey the possibilities in the East for Church union, but the latter advised against the plan. Nevertheless, in a chrysobull of November 7, 1357, John renewed his proposals, including those involving the seven-year-old Manuel.[7] In spite of some small military aid sent by the Pope, little came of this scheme. But it is ironic to observe that Manuel, who was to have more direct contact with the West than any other Byzantine Emperor, should make his debut in international politics as a proffered hostage and sacrifice to Latin Christendom.

However sincere John's fatuous proposals regarding his sons may have been, he proceeded to prepare them for their princely careers in normal fashion. In August of 1355 John's eldest son and his heir, Andronicus, a little over seven years of age at the time,[8] was betrothed to Maria (Kyratza), a daughter of Ivan

Byzance à Rome, Vingt ans de travail pour l'Union des églises et pour la défense de l'empire d'orient, 1355–1373 (Warsaw, 1930), 24–31; and Appendix IV, pp. 201–202 of J. Smet's edition of *The Life of St. Peter Thomas by Philippe de Mézières* (Rome, 1954); also K. E. Zachariae von Lingenthal, "Prooemion zu Chrysobullen von Demetrius Kydones," *Sitzungsberichte der königlich preussichen Academie der Wissenschaften zu Berlin,* LII (December 1888), pp. 1412–1413; J. Berger de Xivrey, *Mémoire sur la vie et les ouvrages de l'empereur Manuel Paléologue (Mémoires de l'Institut de France, Académie des Inscriptions et Belles-Lettres,* 19, 1853, 2, pp. 1–201), 22–23; cf. Ostrogorsky, *ibid.,* 477; Dennis, 12. See also the reference to a further appeal by John to this Pope in the spring of 1356: Dölger, *Regesten,* no. 3055, p. 43.

6. Text in Baronius-Raynaldus, 1356, 33–34 (Vol. 26, pp. 17–18); cf. Halecki, *Un Empereur,* 53; Smet, 202–203; Berger de Xivrey, 23.

7. Dölger, *Regesten,* no. 3071, p. 48. The text survives only in the Latin version in Mézière's *Life of Peter Thomas,* ed. Smet, 76–80; see also *ibid.,* Appendix IV, p. 205, and Halecki, *Un Empereur,* 62. For an interesting and recently published document concerning Peter Thomas' mission to Constantinople and the union question, see J. Darrouzès, "Conférence sur la primauté du Pape à Constantinople en 1357," *Rev. d. ét. byz.,* 19 (*Mélanges R. Janin,* 1961), 76–109.

8. According to a short chronicle, ed. B. T. Gorianov, *Vizantiiskii Vremmenik,* 2 (1949), p. 286, ll. 208–209, Andronicus was born on April 11, 1348; cf. P. Wirth, "Wan wurde Kaiser Andronikos IV. Palaiologos geboren," *Byz. Zeitschr.,* 55 (1962), 38. His parents had been married in February of the preceding year: Gorianov chronicle, ll. 198–200; Cantacuzenus, III, 11. Cf. Papadopulos, p. 52, n. 2.

Alexander Asan, King of Bulgaria.[9] There was no question as to the destiny of Andronicus as John's successor. Manuel and his subsequent brothers, Theodore [10] and Michael,[11] were, in accordance with late Byzantine custom, given the title of Despot.[12] Manuel is referred to with this title in all documents of this period, such as those noted above, bearing John V's strange proposals to the Pope. In this capacity, for example, the fourteen-year-old prince was present, together with his older brother, at the re-enthronement of the former Patriarch Philotheos on October 8, 1364,[13] after the death of the Patriarch Kallistos on his mission to Serbia.

Manuel's next appearance cast him once more in the role of a pawn in John V's determined negotiations for Church union. In 1366, leaving Andronicus behind as his regent, John became the first Byzantine Emperor—with the possible exception of Cantacuzenus, who visited Dušan on Serbian territory—to pay a state visit outside of the Empire, for the purpose of seeking help. Taking with him the Despots Manuel and Michael, John traveled to the court at Buda of Louis, the Angevin King of Hungary.[14]

9. Dölger, *Regesten*, No. 3047 ("ca. Aug. 17"), p. 41; cf. no. 3044 and no. 3046, both p. 41. The text of the Patriarchal confirmation of the transaction is in E. Miklosich and J. Müller, *Acta diplomata graeca medii aevi sacra et profana* (6 Vols., Vienna, 1860–90), Vol. I, no. 185, pp. 432–433; cf. Halecki, *Un Empereur*, 51.

10. The date of Theodore's birth is unknown, and Papadopulos, 53, simply places it after 1350.

11. Michael Palaeologus is the most obscure of John V's legitimate sons, and he disappears early from the scene. See Papadopulos, 57, for information on him and on sources about him; to the latter should be added the important information in a short chronicle published by Loenertz, "Chronicon breve de Graecorum imperatoribus, ab anno 1341 ad annum 1453 e codice Vaticano graeco 162" (cited hereafter as "*Chron. Vat.* gr. 162"), in Ἐπετηρὶς Ἑταιρείας Βυζαντινῶν Σπουδῶν 28 (1958), no. 11, p. 208. Dennis, p. 27, n. 5, also adds the material concerning the appanage given him by his father; Cydones' Letter C. 148, L. 5, seems to be addressed to him in that status. Michael's involvement with the scheme to put him on the throne of Trebizond is reflected also in F. Thiriet, *Régestes des délibérations du Sénat de Venise concernant la Romanie*, I (Paris, 1958), no. 576, p. 143. See also Appendix IX below.

12. R. Guilland, "Etudes sur l'histoire administrative de l'empire byzantin: Le Despote, Δεσπότης," *Rev. d. ét. byz.*, 17 (1959), 64.

13. Cantacuzenus, III, 363; cf. Dennis, 12.

14. Halecki, *Un Empereur*, 111–113. For comments on the mission in general, see G. Moravcsik, "Vizantiiskie imperatori ich posli v g. Buda" ("Les Empereurs de Byzance et leurs ambassadeurs à Buda"), *Acta historica acad. scient. hung.*, 8 (1961), 239–256: 242–246.

As early as his letter of 1357, John had entertained the idea of going personally to consult the Pope on the matter of Church union and conversion. But in Buda he seems to have been won over to the idea of personal baptism and conversion.[15] He promised further that his two sons, Manuel and Michael, would adopt Latin Catholicism.[16] As security on the promises which the zealous Hungarians had exacted from John in return for talk of a crusade to aid the Empire, it would seem that Manuel and his brother were left behind as hostages.[17]

On his return from Hungary, John V was forced to suffer further humiliation. A few years previously, Bulgaria had been drawn into hostilities with Byzantium and had emerged the worse for them. Now, partly out of a desire for revenge and partly out of a suspicion of any Byzantine entente with Latin Hungary, the Bulgarian ruler Ivan Šišman blocked the passage of John through his realm and forced the Emperor to remain in the Bulgarian city of Viddin, then in the hands of the Hungarians. Fortunately, John's cousin, Count Amadeo VI of Savoy, had entered the scene and had just then, at the end of August of 1366, seized Gallipoli from the Turks to restore it to the Empire. In the early autumn the Emperor's Latin relative was able to make a demonstration against the Bulgarians, not only forcing

15. Dölger, *Regesten,* nos. 3107 and 3108, pp. 55–56. For the negotiations as a whole, see Halecki, *Un Empereur,* 111–137. In greater brevity, J. Meyendorff, "Projets de Concile oecumenique en 1367, Un dialogue inédit entre Jean Cantacuzène et le légat Paul," *Dumbarton Oaks Papers, No. 14* (1960), 153–156; and, less satisfactory, N. Iorga, *Philippe de Mézières, 1327–1405* (Paris, 1896), 330–331. For a comment on the implications of this conference for Balkan ecclesiastical affairs, see P. Wirth, "Die Haltung Kaiser Johannes V. bei den Verhandlungen mit König Ludwig von Ungarn zu Buda im Jahre 1366," *Byz. Zeitschr.* 56 (1963), 271–272.

In connection with Louis the Great's contact with John V, the Latin principle that reunion with Rome by the Greek church must precede any Western help, so often stated in this period, is emphasized again in Pope Urban V's letter of June 22, 1366, to the Hungarian King: text in Theiner and Miklosich, *Mon. spect. ad un. eccles.,* II, no. 142, pp. 74–75. Cf. W. Norden, *Das Papsttum und Byzanz. Die Trennung der beiden Machte und das Problem ihrer Wiedervereinigung bis zum Untergange des byzantinischen Reichs (1453)* (Berlin, 1903; reprint, New York, 1958), pp. 702–705, and note.

16. Pope Urban V speaks of this promise in his letter to John V after the Buda negotiations dated July 1, 1366: text in Baronius-Raynaldus, 1366, 4–6 (Vol. 26, pp. 123–124).

17. This is stated plainly in the text of the chrysobull of 1371 published by Zachariae von Lingenthal, "Prooemion," 1419, especially ll. 36–37; cf. Halecki, *Un Empereur,* 135; Dennis, 12–13.

Šišman to end his blockade of the Emperor, but also extracting some territorial concessions for Byzantium.[18]

Free to move at the end of December of 1366, John spent the winter seeing to the occupation of the restored territories and negotiating with Amadeo on the question of Church union.[19] We do not know when Manuel and his brother were free to leave Buda. The Hungarian King's plans for aid to Byzantium seem to have been abandoned in 1367,[20] and perhaps in any event the presence of Amadeo and of Paul, the Papal legate accompanying him, with John V would have removed the need for hostages in Buda. At any rate, we know that Manuel was present with his parents and his elder brother at the debate which took place in Constantinople as part of the union negotiations in June of 1367.[21]

18. For the Crusade of Amadeo in general see the second chapter, pp. 140–158, of J. Delaville le Roulx, *La France en Orient au XIVe siècle* (Paris, 1886), and the sixteenth chapter, pp. 379–397, of A. S. Atiya, *The Crusade in the Later Middle Ages* (London, 1938); also, less important, Iorga, *Mézières*, 332–337. These authors (Delaville le Roulx, p. 152; Atiya, 389–390; Iorga, 335) follow the inaccurate tradition that Šišman *arrested* John and *confined* him in Viddin. See Halecki, *Un Empereur*, 135 and 140. In his plea for alliance with the Latins rather than with the Orthodox of the Balkans, the so-called *Oratio pro subsidio Latinorum*, ed. Migne, *Patr. gr.*, 154, 975, Demetrius Cydones deplores the "Mysian" (i.e. Bulgarian) insult to the Emperor. Ostrogorsky, *Hist. Byz. St.*, 479–480, suggests that, since the young Andronicus was married to the sister (not the *daughter*, as he actually says) of Šišman, he may well have had some role in the Bulgarian ruler's action against John. Walter, in his journalistic and unscholarly account, p. 273, has accepted the insinuations made against Andronicus as if they are by now proven facts. Note also the account of F. Cognasso, *Il conte verde (1334–1385) (Collina storica, Sabauda,* Turin [1930]), 154–181. For comments and bibliography in general on Amadeo's expedition, see F. Babinger, *Beiträge zur Frühgeschichte der Türkenherrschaft in Rumelien (14.–15. Jahrhundert) (Südosteuropäische Arbeiten,* 34, Munich, 1944), p. 55, and n. 81; note also J. J. Bouquet's article, "Remarques sur l'idée de croisade dans l'expédition d'Amadée VI de Savoie à Constantinople," *Bulletin annuel de la Fondation Suisse,* 7 (Paris, 1958), 17–33. And, more generally, see Iorga's *Geschichte des osmanischen Reiches,* I, 215–235. On the territorial gains involved for Byzantium, cf. A. E. Vakalopoulos, "Les Limites de l'empire byzantin depuis la fin du XIVe siècle jusqu'à sa chute (1453)," *Byz. Zeitschr.,* 55 (1962), 57; on the annexation of these territories subsequently by the Turks, *ibid.,* 58–59. As this book went to press, there appeared E. L. Cox's book *The Green Count of Savoy: Amadeus VI and Transalpine Savoy in the Fourteenth Century* (Princeton, 1967), which I have not yet seen.

19. For the negotiations, see Dölger, *Regesten,* nos. 3113 and 3114, p. 57; also, Halecki, *Un Empereur,* 149–160.

20. So states Halecki, *Un Empereur,* 136.

21. This debate took place soon after the return of the two cousins to Constantinople. Representing the Greeks in this discussion with the legate

Later, jointly with his brother Michael, Manuel was the recipient of a letter from the Pope, dated November 6, 1367, that was virtually identical with one written to Andronicus, urging them all to work toward the desired union.[22]

Primarily as a result of his negotiations with Amadeo of Savoy and the legate Paul, John V had committed himself—or, in the event of his own failure, his son and heir Andronicus—to the undertaking of going to Rome personally to accept the Roman faith. Presumably some time before his departure for this purpose, John seems to have taken one step regarding the arrangement of his family affairs. Since his eldest son was naturally in line for succession and was to be the regent during his impending absence, John provided for Manuel by establishing him as governor in Thessalonica, apparently some time before June of 1369.[23]

Paul was none other than the former Emperor John Cantacuzenus, now the Monk Ioasaph and an indispensable counselor of his son-in-law and erstwhile opponent. (For the role and influence of Cantacuzenus after his deposition, see below, pp. 37–40.) Attention was first called to this episode by Meyendorff, "Jean-Joasaph Cantacuzène et le projet de concile oecumenique en 1367," *Akten des XI. Internationalen Byzantinisten-Kongresses, München, 1958* (Munich, 1960), 363–369. The Greek transcript of this interesting exchange has since been published by him, "Projets de concile oecuménique en 1367" (*D. O. Papers, No. 14*), 169–177, preceded by a synopsis, 164–169; for Meyendorff's own discussion of these particular negotiations, see 156–161. The debate must have taken place at the very beginning of the month, for Amadeo and Paul sailed away on June 4: Halecki, *Un Empereur,* 149; Delaville le Roulx, *La France en Orient,* 157; Atiya, *The Crusade in the Later Middle Ages,* 397; also, Dölger, *Regesten,* no. 3116, p. 57. Atiya is mistaken, by the way, in saying that Amadeo seized the Greek Patriarch and carried him off with the other Greek hostages whom he held. This confusion is apparently due to the fact that the legate Paul had been named the titular Latin Patriarch. The Greek Patriarch Philotheos certainly remained in Constantinople. Moreover, Amadeo did not present himself to the Pope in Rome, as Atiya says. Urban V had only left Avignon in April of 1367 and was at Viterbo before his entry into Rome later in October. Earlier that month Amadeo and Paul were received by him, in Viterbo: cf. Dölger, *Regesten,* no. 3115, p. 57; and Halecki, *Un Empereur,* 161–164; also A. A. Vasiliev, "Il viaggio di Giovanni V Palaeologo in Italia e l'unione di Roma," *Studi bizantini e neoellenici,* 3 (1931), 158–162. For the general Hungarian involvement in these negotiations, see also Moravcsik, "Vizantiiskie imperatori," 246–247.

22. Text published by Halecki, *Un Empereur,* 367–368, no. 8; cf. also *ibid.,* 167; and Dennis, 13.

23. For a discussion of the establishment of this date, see Dennis, p. 13, n. 38. But note that Dölger includes no such hypothetical act at this time in his *Regesten.* Halecki, *Un Empereur,* p. 167, n. 4, assumes that, since Pope Urban V's letter of November 1367 is addressed to "Manueli despoto,"

In the summer of 1369 John embarked for Italy, and, after a stop at Naples, moved on to Rome in August. In October of that year, in a solemn ceremony, John V made a formal renunciation of Greek "errors" and a corresponding profession of the Roman faith. Although this act was purely personal and had no immediate concern with the Orthodox or even the Greek Church as units, it was hoped on both sides that this individual act would be a step toward the ultimate union which had been sought for so long.[24]

However high the hopes that prompted it, John's journey not only failed to produce the Western aid he had sought so desperately, but it also brought him into circumstances of profound humiliation and embarrassment. After various fruitless negotiations,[25] John left Rome in March of 1370, stopped again at Naples, and then began a trip by sea to Venice.[26] At Rome in

Manuel must therefore have been established in Thessalonica by then. But we have already noted the practice of applying this title to an Emperor's younger son, which implies no such specific appointment. For an estimate of the significance of this appointment in relation to the question of succession to the throne, see F. Dölger, "Johannes VII., Kaiser der Rhomäer, 1390–1408," *Byz. Zeitschr.*, 31 (1931), pp. 21–22, n. 2.

24. The basic work on this episode remains, of course, Halecki's *Un Empereur*, especially pp. 188–212; see also the references given by Dölger, *Regesten*, nos. 3120 and 3122, p. 58, and no. 3126, p. 59. Important in addition is the Vasiliev article, "Il viaggio"; but there Vasiliev exaggerated the meaning of John's personal conversion in relation to the problem of actual union of the Churches, as he himself later admitted in his *Hist. Byz. Emp.*, p. 671, n. 282. Cf. also Norden, 708–710; Ostrogorsky, *Hist. Byz. St.*, 480. For Papal documents concerning this affair, see Baronius-Raynaldus, 1361, nos. 1–6; 1370, nos. 1–4 (Vol. 26, pp. 162–165, 170–172); and for Greek texts as well as for Latin, see Theiner and Miklosich, *Mon. spect. ad un. eccles.*, nos. 9–10, pp. 37–43. Chalcocondyles, ed. E. Darkó (2 vols., Budapest, 1922–27), I, 46, ed. Bonn (1843), 50, followed by the Pseudo-Phrantzes, ed. J. B. Papadopoulos (Leipzig, 1935), 57, ed. Bonn (1838), 52, have confused John's voyage with that of Manuel later on: cf. Loenertz, "Jean V Paléologue à Venise (1370–1371)," *Rev. d. ét. byz.*, 16 (1958), 216–232, especially 223–226, for an exegesis of Chalcocondyles; and *id.*, "Autour du Chronicon Maius attribué à Georges Phrantzès," *Studi e Testi*, 123 (Vatican City, 1946), 293–294, for a critique of the Pseudo-Phrantzes text. On Cydones, already a Roman Catholic convert, in this visit, see K. Setton, "The Byzantine Background to the Italian Renaissance," *Proceedings of the American Philosophical Society*, 100 (1956), 55.

25. Halecki, *Un Empereur*, 213–222.

26. *Ibid.*, 227; Loenertz, "Jean V à Venise," 216. On the way, John stopped at Ancona where he was cordially received. This reception is referred to in a letter to John by Cydones, C. 84 (No. 19), L. 349. Cf. Dölger, *Regesten*, no. 3123, p. 58 (a grant made by the Emperor while in Ancona); for a letter of John's regarding the trip to Venice, *ibid.*, no. 3124, p. 59.

Figure 1: *The Citadel of the Thessalonian Fortifications, from the East* (photo courtesy Boissonnas, Geneva; see Appendix XXIV, C, 2, b).

February John had already completed negotiations for a renewal of the regular five-year Veneto-Byzantine treaty.[27] But John's financial situation was still gravely uncertain, and at Venice he opened direct negotiations. His circumstances became so desperate that, although still treated with proper honor due his rank, he was reduced to the status of a prisoner of the Republic for debt.[28]

27. Dölger, *Regesten*, no. 3127, pp. 59–60. Latin text, ed. C. M. Thomas, *Diplomatarium Veneto-Levantinum*, Part II (Venice, 1899; reprint, 1964), no. 89, pp. 151–156. (The Greek text is not preserved.) For instructions to the Venetian negotiators, see Thiriet, *Régestes*, I, pp. 122–123, nos. 480, 482, and 483; for a discussion of the negotiations in general, Halecki, *Un Empereur*, 223–227.

28. This incident has been the subject of great contention. Halecki, *Un Empereur*, 334–343, has proposed the controversial argument that the traditional story, originally set forth by Chalcocondyles, ed. Darkó, I, 46–47, ed. Bonn, 50–51, and the Pseudo-Phrantzes, ed. Papadopoulos, 57, ed. Bonn, 52, so gleefully recounted by Gibbon, *Decline and Fall of the Roman Empire*, ed. J. B. Bury (London, 1902), VII, 90, and accepted by Berger de Xivrey, 35–36, is false. His arguments have been largely discredited by Dölger,

11

In this situation John appealed for aid to Andronicus, his son and regent in Constantinople. The twenty-two-year-old Andronicus, nothing loath to leave his father where he was so that he himself might enjoy further his position of power, declared himself unable to help. Manuel, however, took the burden upon himself and sailed from Thessalonica to Italy to aid his father.[29] He

"Johannes VII.," pp. 22–23, n. 2, and in his review of Halecki's book (*Byz. Zeitschr.*, 33, 1933, 132–136); and by P. Charanis, "The Strife Among the Palaeologi and the Ottoman Turks, 1370–1402," *Byzantion*, 16 (1942–43), 287–291. Cf. Ostrogorsky, *Hist. Byz. St.*, p. 481 and n. 1, who gives good brief summaries of the arguments involved. See in particular Loenertz, "Jean V à Venise," where the sources are examined. Noteworthy among these sources is the Letter C. 81, L. 71, of Cydones, who was with John on his journey. This letter apparently refers to John's being delayed in Venice. According to Loenertz, this letter was written to Constantine Asan, who had been sent home to secure funds for John's return: "Jean V à Venise," 217–218. Loenertz' view is reflected in the more recent accounts of the period written since his argument: such as Ostrogorsky's chapter in *Cambr. Med. Hist.*, Vol. IV (2nd ed.), 1, p. 371, and Khoury, "L'Empereur Manuel II," 134–135. Though recent scholars have not used it seriously for these events, mention might be made of a newly available, if highly suspect source, the Χρονικὸν περὶ τῶν Τούρκων σουλτάνων (κατὰ τὸν Βαρβερινὸν ἑλληνικὸν κώδικα 111), ed. G. Zoras (Athens, 1958; cited hereafter as "*Chron. Barb. 111*"), p. 26. This account makes a merry shambles of this episode, which it places after events of 1387; it mixes in details of Manuel's later trip, makes John Cantacuzenus the voyager, and adds a garnishing of sundry other liberties. But it still conveys the same basic point of the Emperor's dire straits —even describing his very harsh confinement by the Venetians, plainly the result of exaggeration.

29. Chalcocondyles, ed. Darkó, I, 46–47, ed. Bonn, 50–51; Pseudo-Phrantzes, ed. Papadopoulos, 57–58, ed. Bonn, 52–53; also the chrysobull text, ed. Zachariae von Lingenthal, "Prooemion," p. 1420, ll. 5–33; cf. Dölger, *Regesten*, no. 3128, p. 60, for the Emperor's appeal for Andronicus. Halecki, *Un Empereur*, had maintained in his argument that Andronicus was really with his father and thus could not have committed this disobedience. In view of the irrefutable opposition to this opinion, Halecki has since conceded the error of the point, although he has not modified his other views: "Two Palaeologi in Venice, 1370–71," *Byzantion*, 17 (1944–45), 331–335. According to Chalcocondyles, Andronicus pleaded that he was not allowed to use Church funds: cf. Charanis, "Strife," pp. 291–292 and n. 15, who suggests that the Church may in this fashion have encouraged opposition to John, in view of his suspicious doings in Rome. But on the problem of Andronicus' guilt in these matters, see also the next note. Dennis, 90, points out the possibility that Manuel himself may have seized treasures of the Church in order to relieve his father's want in Venice; but the account of Loenertz, "Jean V à Venise," 224–226, makes clear that this is unlikely. Cf. also Zachariae von Lingenthal, "Prooemion," 1414–1415; Vasiliev, "Il viaggio," 190. We also have a letter from Cydones, C. 113, L. 21, to Manuel, written presumably in the summer of 1371, praising the Despot for coming to help his father.

arrived during the winter of 1370–71 and the negotiations continued. The upshot of these negotiations was John's commitment to cede the island of Tenedos to Venice in exchange for financial considerations, which included the return of the Byzantine crown jewels that John had pawned to Venice.[30]

When the miserable John finally left Venice,[31] Manuel was

30. See the passage from the Venetian chronicle of Caroldo, quoted by Halecki, *Un Empereur,* no. 21, pp. 385–386. The account in Halecki's text, pp. 228–231, should be read with the peculiarities of his interpretations borne in mind. Cf. Charanis, "Strife," 288–289; Vasiliev, "Il viaggio," 191. See also Thiriet, "Venise et l'occupation de Ténédos au XIVᵉ siècle," *Mélanges d'archéologie et d'histoire de l'école français d'Athènes et de Rome,* 65 (1953), 224–225; and *id., La Romanie vénitienne au moyen âge* (Paris, 1959), 176–177. The idea of the cession of Tenedos to Venice was not new: it had been bound up in earlier schemes for a projected anti-Turkish alliance, involving John, which never came into being; see Thiriet, "Una proposta di lega antiturcica tra Venezia, Genova e Bisanzio nel 1363," *Archivio storico italiano,* 113 (1955), 321–334.

The crux of the controversies regarding this episode is, again, the Caroldo text, which is also reproduced by Loenertz, "Jean V à Venise," 228–229, where it is analyzed. Subsequently, however, Fr. Loenertz discovered that some changes are necessary in the reading of the crucial passage of this text. In his transcription of this just cited, p. 229, paragraph 6, the second sentence reads: "La qual finalmente fece intender che per il dispoto suo figlio et per diuerse cause la cession de Tenedo non poteua hauer effetto." This is now to be emended to read: "La qual finalmente fece intender per il dispoto suo figlio che per diuerse cause la cession de Tenedo non poteua hauer effetto." This new reading of course necessitates a revision of Fr. Loenertz' own synopsis, *ibid.,* p. 229, which he has suggested should now state: "... Au paragraphe 6 le chroniquer raconte comment l'empereur informa la Seigneurie, *par l'intermédiaire de son fils le despote,* que la cession de Ténédos n'aurait pas lieux pour diverses causes"; in other words, definitely eliminating the suggestion that one reason for the delay in the cession was the interference of "il despoto suo figlio." In addition, the next sentence in the synopsis, in which Fr. Loenertz had previously tried to suggest that "despoto" referred in actuality to the *Emperor* Andronicus, John's son, heir, and regent in Constantinople, would therefore be corrected to read something like this: "Le terme *despote* s'agite manifestement *du Despote Manuel, présent à ce temps en Venise avec son père, pour qui il etait problément intermédiaire diplomatique.*" Also as a result, Loenertz' assumption in this same article, pp. 226–228, would likewise have to be reconsidered and revised; see also below, n. 60. Herself following Fr. Loenertz' suggestions in this line, J. Chrysostomides has explored this entire question in searching detail in her valuable recent article, "John V Palaeologus in Venice (1370–1371) and the Chronicle of Caroldo: A Re-interpretation," *Orientalia Christiana Periodica,* 31 (1965), 76–84. For a discussion of the related problem of the pawning to Venice of the Byzantine crown jewels, see Appendix I below.

31. Halecki, *Un Empereur,* 231–232, maintains that John had left Venice by April of 1371 and gives some source references. But his assumption that

obliged to remain behind, partly to maintain what further negotiations with the Venetians were possible and partly also— again a familiar role—to serve as personal security on John's agreements.[32] John's voyage was apparently a long one, for his return to his capital is not recorded until October 28, 1371.[33] A little while after his return, on the fifth of December to be precise, John is reported to have seized five important Greek nobles. In view of the circumstances, this act may indicate punishment of them for some involvement in Andronicus' refusal to heed his father's pleas.[34] For the moment John seems to have taken no action against Andronicus himself. But in view of Manuel's loyal services, John could not but view his second son with gratitude and growing fervor. Precisely when or how Manuel was able to leave Venice is not certain, but he seems to have been back in Thessalonica by the winter of 1371–72.[35] John, not long after his own return, issued a chrysobull confirming Manuel in his appanage in Thessalonica and also granting him all the lands in Macedonia that he could retrieve from the crumbling Serbian power there and could defend against the Turks.[36]

John reached Constantinople in May is vague and insecurely founded, as well as contrary to other source information that we have; see n. 33 below.

32. Chrysobull text, ed. Zachariae von Lingenthal, "Prooemion," p. 1420, ll. 33–39. Part of this specific passage is quoted and translated by Loenertz, "Jean V à Venise," 219; cf. Dennis, 13–14.

33. Short Chronicle No. 47, p. 81, l. 32, of the collection of S. P. Lampros, published by K. Amantos as Βραχέα χρονικά ('Ακαδημία 'Αθηνῶν, Μνημεῖα τῆς ἑλληνικῆς ἱστορίας, Α΄, Athens, 1932–33, Τεῦχος α΄). Cf. also Charanis, "An Important Short Chronicle of the Fourteenth Century," *Byzantion*, 13 (1938), 340; and *id.*, "A Note on the Short Chronicle No. 45 [*sic*] of the Lampros-Amantos Collection," *Annuaire de l'institut de philologie et d'histoire orientales et slaves*, 7 (1939–44), 449.

34. Βρ. χρ. No. 47, p. 81, ll. 32–34; cf. Charanis, "Strife," 291. But see the skeptical comments of Chrysostomides, "John V Palaeologus in Venice," 76–84.

35. At which time Cydones seems to have written Letter C. 111, L. 79, to him. Cydones wrote Letter C. 82, L. 23, to Manuel apparently about the same time, telling him how his virtue has become such a subject of admiration and discussion. Charanis, "Strife," p. 297, n. 34, however, does not think that Manuel returned from Venice before his father.

36. Dölger, *Regesten*, no. 3130, p. 60; Chrysobull text, ed. Zachariae von Lingenthal, "Prooemioh," p. 1421, l. 23 to p. 1422, l. 20; see also the editor's own commentary, *ibid.*, 1415–1416. Cf. Charanis, "Strife," 293; Dennis, 33; Halecki, *Un Empereur*, 247–248. Manuel sent a gift of money to Cydones in gratitude for the latter's role in drafting the document, and Cydones' reply of self-disparagement, Letter C. 111, L. 79, was answered by Manuel's own Letter ε΄: cf. Loenertz, *Echos d'Orient*, 36 (1937), 278–279.

Figure 2: *John Cantacuzenus, Portrayed as the Emperor John VI and as the Monk Ioasaph.* Illuminated Miniature, Bibliothèque Nationale, Paris, Cod. gr. 1242, f. 123 (photo courtesy Bibliothèque Nationale, Paris; see Appendix XXIV, B, 1).

The event which had permitted the latter stipulation was a crucial one for the history of this period. On September 26, 1371, the Serbian forces under King Vukašin and the Serbian Despot of Macedonia, Iovan Uglješa, were disastrously defeated in a battle on the River Marica (or Maritza) at Černomen, and the two leaders were killed.[37] John V was, of course, still absent at the time of the battle. Byzantine policy seems, at best, to have been confused on the point of helping these Orthodox brethren and was, at worst, perhaps feebly pro-Turkish.[38] This event toppled the last remnant of the once-great realm of Dušan, and Serbia reached the beginning of the end of her independence.

To a limited extent, the results of Serbia's downfall might have benefited Byzantium, for the Greeks under Manuel were able to

37. See pp. 537–538 of an anonymous fifteenth-century *Bulgarische Chronik von 1296 bis 1413*, ed. J. Bogdan in *Archiv für slavische Philologie*, XIII, 4 (1891): the text of the chronicle (hereafter cited as *"Bulg. chron."*) is found on pp. 526–535, but I have been able to use only the Latin translation of it by V. Jagić, appended on pp. 536–543, to which all my citations are made. Cf. Dennis, p. 32, n. 27, for a few other source references. See also: Hammer, I, 169–170, trans. Hellert, I, 225–227; more fully, Iorga, *Geschichte*, I, 236–242; J. K. Jireček, *Geschichte der Serben*, I (Gotha, 1911), 438; P. Lemerle, *Philippes et la Macédoine orientale à l'époque chrétienne et byzantine* (Paris, 1945), 214; D. M. Vaughn, *Europe and the Turk, A Pattern of Alliances, 1350–1700* (Liverpool, 1954), 21.

38. There has been considerable support for the theory that the Byzantines ceded Gallipoli to the Turks at this point, or perhaps allowed them to use it, or at least put up no opposition to their using it. Thus, Halecki, *Un Empereur*, 243–246, and, following him, Lemerle, *Philippes*, p. 214 and n. 3. It has even been suggested that Cydones' so-called *Oratio de non reddenda Callipoli* (Migne, *Patr. gr.*, 154, 1009–1036) was composed for this occasion. Though it belongs more probably to a later period—after all, Cydones was apparently still absent with John before the battle—Loenertz, *Les Recueils des Lettres de Démétrius Cydonès* (*Studi e Testi*, 131, Vatican City, 1947), 112, still dates it thus. And D. A. Zakythinos, "Démétrius Cydonès et l'entente balkanique au XIVᵉ siècle" in his *La Grèce et les Balkans* (Athens, 1947), 47, while discussing this work, also places it in the period of 1371. On all these questions see Charanis, "Strife," 292. At any rate, Gallipoli seems to have been used as some sort of a base by the Turks, since the *Bulg. chron.*, 538, speaks of them as returning there after their victory on the Marica. Charanis suggests that Andronicus may have aided Murad deliberately to secure his hold on the throne. In all events, the entire matter of the Byzantine position at the time of this battle remains extremely obscure and almost impossible to determine accurately. In Letter C. 253, L. 28, Cydones writes to Demetrius Palaeologus, the Grand Domestic on Lemnos, urging him to persuade the Emperor to protect his capital and his realm. Loenertz dates this letter to the summer of 1371; if this date is correct, the reference may be to Andronicus, who may well have needed such encouragement.

enter Serres, the former Serbian capital in Macedonia, in November of 1371 and to extend their authority further into some of the formerly Serbian-held neighboring territory.[39] But this progress was short-lived, for the Turks had no intention of allowing others to reap the fruits of their victory. They themselves pushed into Macedonia, besieging Serres, and may even have attacked Thessalonica itself.[40] The Byzantines may have realized, moreover, that the new Turkish threat called for extraordinary measures. At least Manuel was forced to resort to the expedient of seizing monastery lands to provide for new military grants in the face of the rising danger.[41]

But the real meaning of the Battle of the Marica for Byzantium was not lost on John V, for it was undoubtedly the cause of a

39. The date is preserved in a notice cited by P. N. Papageorgiou, in his "Αἱ Σέρραι καὶ τὰ προάστεια, τὰ περὶ τὰς Σέρρας καὶ ἡ μονὴ Ἰωάννου τοῦ Προδρόμου," *Byz. Zeitschr.*, 3 (1893), p. 316, n. 2. See Dennis, 33 and 65, and Lemerle, *Philippes*, 214–215, who both cite this source evidence. Cf. also Jireček, *Geschichte*, I, 439; Halecki, *Un Empereur*, 427; Loenertz, *Echos d'Orient*, 36 (1937), 278; Ostrogorsky, *Hist. Byz. St.*, 481–482; also, A. E. Vakalopoulos, Ἱστορία τοῦ νέου ἑλληνισμοῦ, Α´: Ἀρχὲς καὶ διαμόρφωσις τοῦ (Thessalonica, 1961), 119; and *id.*, "Les Limites de l'empire byzantin," 56. For the immediate background, see G. G. Soulis, "Notes on the History of the City of Serres under the Serbs (1345–1371)," in Ἀφιέρωμα Μ. Τριανταφυλλίδη (Thessalonica, 1960), 373–379.

40. Dennis, 33, and p. 55, n. 13, asserts that the Turks attacked Thessalonica after Manuel had fled from it. I do not accept the latter part of the assertion, nor do I think that Manuel was anywhere but in Thessalonica from 1371 to 1373. For a full discussion of the entire question, and on the various Turkish seizures of Thessalonica, see Appendix II below.

41. We know this from Manuel's own statement in a *prostagma* of 1408, edited by V. Mošin, *Srpska Kraljevska Akademija, Spomenik*, 91, *Drugi razred*, 70 (1939), 165–167; cf. Ostrogorsky, *Pour l'histoire de la féodalité byzantine*, trans. H. Grègoire (*Corpus Bruxellense Historiae Byzantinae, Subsidia*, I, Brussels, 1954), 161 ff., as well as *id.*, *Hist. Byz. St.*, 482, and especially in his chapter in *Cambr. Med. Hist.*, Vol. IV (2nd ed.), 1, pp. 371–372. See also Charanis, "The Monastic Properties and the State in the Byzantine Empire," *Dumbarton Oaks Papers, No. 4* (1948), 116–117; and I. Ševčenko, "Nicholas Cabasilas' 'Anti-Zealot' Discourse: A Re-interpretation," *Dumbarton Oaks Papers, No. 11* (1957), 159. Dennis, pp. 90–91, n. 30, suggests that Cabasilas' denunciation of the abuses of alienating Church properties might possibly have been directed to some extent against Manuel himself. This suggestion has been welcomed by Charanis, in his review of Dennis' study in *Speculum*, 36 (1961), 476–477. Ševčenko has recently reviewed his stand on this question in "A Postscript on Nicholas Cabasilas' 'Anti-Zealot' Discourse," in *Dumbarton Oaks Papers, No. 16* (1962), 403–408, without presently committing himself as to dating.

basic reversal of his official policy.[42] In the midst of continued negotiations for joint action with the Latin West, John came to the conclusion that all his long hopes for the full help needed from that quarter were after all in vain, and that his only salvation now lay in making the best terms he could with the Turks.[43] Plainly, the realities of the situation after the Battle of the Marica had made it clear that the Turks had grown too powerful to be resisted successfully. Hereafter, John V shed all of whatever initiative or determination he had formerly displayed and slipped into a state of vassalage to the Osmanlis.

Precisely when John's accommodation with the Turks commenced is unknown, but it first came to light in connection with the revolt of Andronicus against his father in 1373. The im-

42. Perhaps the best outline of the course of John's policy toward the Turks may be found in Dennis, 30–37. A puzzling problem is posed by the listing by A. D. Alderson, *The Structure of the Ottoman Dynasty* (Oxford, 1956), Table XXII, of a marriage of a daughter of John V (and Helen Cantacuzena) named Irene to a son of the Osmanli Emir Orchan named Halil (d. ca. 1360) in 1349 or 1359. Now, we know that John V had a daughter of that name, who was apparently born between Andronicus and Manuel, judging from the only reference to her in a Byzantine source (Cantacuzenus, III, 238). She was probably born, therefore, in 1349 and so could have been betrothed as an infant in that year, at a time when John V was not in control of the government, and for reasons similar to the celebrated and humiliating marriage of John Cantacuzenus' daughter Theodora to Orchan himself in 1346. But, on the other hand, we know from the very reference by Cantacuzenus that this Irene was with her family in 1352: see above, n. 3. As to the date 1359 for such a marriage, however, this seems completely incompatible with John's pre-1371 anti-Turkish policies. It is true that the sixteenth-century Turkish history by Mechmet Neshri (available to me only through the Serbian translation by G. Elezović, *Ogledalo sveta ili istorija Mehmeda Nešrije*, in *Srpska Akademija Nauka, Zbornik za istočnjacku istorisku i književnu gradu, Odeljenje društvenih nauka*, I, 3, Belgrade, 1957), p. 34, speaks of a marriage of Murad I to a daughter of the ruler of Constantinople, and of others of that ruler's daughters to some of Murad's sons. But the entire tone of this statement is legendary. Nor does it seem to have any immediate relationship to Alderson's entry. Since Alderson cites no source support for this alleged marriage, I suspect that it should not be taken very seriously until some specific evidence can be examined.

43. Dennis, 34–37; for a thoroughly detailed account, see Halecki, *Un Empereur*, 248–319. Dölger, *Regesten*, no. 3131, p. 60, presumes an embassy to Murad sent by John, and led by Manuel, between late 1371 and 1372, on the basis of the account by Chalcocondyles, which seems to me a very questionable presumption. See also Ostrogorsky, "Byzance, état tributaire de l'empire turc," *Zbornik radova Vizantološkog Instituta* (*Srpska akademija nauka i umetnosti*, Belgrade), 5 (1958), 49–51. On Turkish policy, see H. Inalcik, "Ottoman Methods of Conquest," *Studia islamica*, 2 (1954), 103 ff.

mediate impetus for this affair is not completely clear but the atmosphere is not difficult to imagine. Whether or not Andronicus came under any suspicion in the incident of the Bulgarian blockade of John in Viddin in 1366 is subject to doubt, but there seems little question that the aftermath of the 1370–71 events put him in a bad light. Andronicus must have resented, if not feared, his father's growing favor toward Manuel. Indeed, it is not inconceivable that John was contemplating a revision of the succession to the throne on behalf of his second son.[44]

The sources of conflict and the exact sequence of events are not immediately clear, but historians agree that Andronicus entered into a pact with a son of the Emir Murad named Saudji.[45]

44. Halecki, *Un Empereur*, 302–303, has attempted, as part of his effort to discredit the supposed "legends" of Andronicus' conduct during John's detention in Venice, to throw the blame for Andronicus' disaffection and revolt in 1373 on John's decision to supersede his eldest son's claim to the throne. While much of the background of his argument has been rejected by scholars, this point may not be without some value, to the extent of emphasizing that the igniting spark may well have been provided by John himself. His chrysobull for Manuel, ed. Zachariae von Lingenthal, "Prooemion," p. 1417, l. 23, to p. 1419, l. 8, as Halecki notes, goes on in great length and rhetoric about the difference between judging sons in accordance with nature (φύσις), i.e. natural paternal affection, and according to the virtue (ἀρετή) that they display. Moreover, while the proportion of rhetoric is difficult to establish, it is entirely possible that Cydones, in his Letter C. 111, L. 79, may well reflect, by his use of the words τὸν στέφανον (ed. Loenertz, I, p. 112, ll. 8–11), John's intention to bestow the crown on Manuel.

Certainly a clear-cut knowledge on the part of Andronicus of a genuine threat to his rights of succession would go far toward explaining his subsequent actions. Halecki, 303–304, and Dölger, "Johannes VII.," 22–23, go too far to this extreme, however, by placing the actual elevation of Manuel, really in September, 1373, *before* the revolt of Andronicus, thereby making it the direct cause of the revolt, which came in May of 1373. But we now have the sources to prove the proper chronological relationship. Charanis, "Strife," 293, takes a neutral stand on the matter of Andronicus' motivation, but Dennis, 27, flatly rejects any change in the succession until after Andronicus' revolt itself, which may be the safest interpretation for the time being.

45. Chalcocondyles calls him Σαουζῆς. Ducas, in an earlier reference (ed. V. Grecu, Bucharest, 1958, 37, ed. Bonn, 1834, 16–17), calls him Σαβούτζιος, and then confusedly tells his full story under the name Κουντούζης. (The Pseudo-Phrantzes, completely befuddled, calls him Μῶσης, adding then the proper Τζελέπης, for the Turkish *çelebi*, or "prince.") The *Chron Barb. 111* calls him Σαούς. The Short Chronicle No. 47 calls him, first, ᾽Ισμαὴλ Τζαλαπή, and then, Σαουτζήμπεη. The *Bulg. chron.* uses only a form of *çelebi*, while Clavijo does not give his name at all. Cf. G. Moravcsik, *Byzantinoturcica*, II (Berlin, 1958), 263.

Their pact apparently was, and was certainly construed to be, a joint plot to overthrow their fathers and seize their respective thrones. What is interesting is that, if some of the accounts are to be accepted, the occasion was provided for this stroke by the absence of John and Murad on a campaign together in Asia Minor, leaving their sons behind them as their regents.[46]

The angry fathers cooperated in suppressing the revolt. On May 6, 1373, Andronicus fled and joined the Turkish prince as John assisted Murad and his army in a passage to Europe.[47] On

46. This is the situation as Chalcocondyles describes it in his account of the affair, ed. Darkó, I, 36-46, ed. Bonn, 40-46, followed by the Pseudo-Phrantzes, ed. Papadopoulos, 54-56, ed. Bonn, 49-52. (For discussions of the latter account in connection with the problem of the authorship of this text, see Loenertz, "Autour du Chronicon Maius," 294-296 and 301-302.) The account of Ducas, ed. Grecu, 71-73, ed. Bonn, 43-44, while quite different in many details, does not necessarily rule out altogether the possibility of this situation, nor, for that matter, do any of the others specifically. And one possible source indication of such service by the Emperor is a letter by Cydones, C. 442, L. 194, apparently written to one of the Emperor's retainers, possibly while his master was with the Turks, and perhaps datable to the spring of 1373: such, at least, is the ascription by Loenertz in his edition. Charanis, "Strife," 293, places an accommodation between the two rulers between 1372 and spring of 1373, stating also that Andronicus was left behind as regent. Ostrogorsky, *Hist. Byz. St.*, 482, agrees with this. Dennis, pp. 33-34 and n. 34, states this interpretation but appears reluctant to accept it. Dölger, *Regesten*, no. 3136, p. 61, places the Turko-Byzantine alliance generally in 1373, but *before* John's collaboration with Murad against their two sons (no. 3138, p. 61). In a passage not usually cited, Chalcocondyles, ed. Darkó, I, 47-48, ed. Bonn, 51-52, notes in retrospect that John, on his return from Rome (in 1371), sent his youngest son (Theodore) to serve in Murad's army, and that John did his best to please the Emir, plainly as an acknowledged vassal. This is apparently the basis for the statement, without citation, by H. A. Gibbons, *The Foundation of the Ottoman Empire* (New York, 1916), 149, to this effect. Pears, 194, apparently on the faulty basis of E. Muralt, *Essai de chronographie byzantine, 1057-1453* (St. Petersburg, 1871), p. 699, no. 16, states that, as a part of a recognition of vassalage in 1373 [*sic*], John gave Manuel as a hostage. As is mentioned elsewhere (see n. 40 above and Appendix II below), we apparently have no specific reference in our sources to Manuel for these years, which I believe can be explained only by his continued residence in Thessalonica until perhaps as late as the end of summer, 1373.

47. Βρ. χρ. No. 47, p. 81, ll. 35-39, which also adds that Saudji had been a "fugitive" from his father for ten months and ten days. If this statement is accepted, it would be one of the principal obstacles for adopting the theory that John and Murad had been campaigning together before the revolt, for the disparity in the time between the respective "flights" of the conspiring sons would not correspond with a joint return by the two fathers. Loenertz, "La Première Insurrection d'Andronic IV Paléologue," *Echos d'Orient*, 38 (1939), 342-345, is inclined to question the reliability of this

May 25, perhaps near the town of Derkos, some forty kilometers from the outskirts of the capital, Andronicus fought a battle and lost. On May 30 at Anthyros he surrendered to his father and was taken into custody with his wife Maria.[48] Meanwhile, according to one source,[49] Murad was able by a personal appeal to win over some of his son's forces. At any rate, it was not until September 29 that Murad finally captured his son in the city of Didymotichus. The rebellious prince was blinded—a fatal operation, as it proved, perhaps by design—and his followers were brutally massacred.[50] Finally, having thus exacted his own vengeance, the Emir ordered John to punish his own son likewise in his turn. In spite of a paternal reluctance to do so, John carried out the order

source as a jumbled compilation of unrelated material. A new source on this episode, a confused and mutilated chronicle note of the late fourteenth century in a manuscript in Basel, has been properly identified and published by Dölger, "Zum Aufstand des Andronikos IV. gegen seinen Vater Johannes V. im Mai 1373," *Rev. d. ét. byz.*, 19 (=*Mélanges R. Janin,* 1961), 328–332. This text (p. 328) seems to give May 8 (or 18?) for Andronicus' departure.

48. The Βρ. χρ. No. 47, p. 81, ll. 40–46; Loenertz, "La Première Insurrection," 344–345, suggests that these entries may refer to later events. On the other hand, the new chronicle fragment published by Dölger, "Zum Aufstand," states that during May of this year (the exact date is missing) Andronicus ἔπιγεν [=ἐπήγεν] εἰς τὴν Δέρκον. Dölger suggests (p. 332) that Derkos might thus be accepted as the site of the battle lost by Andronicus—on May 25, assuming that date is accepted. What was the immediate fate of Andronicus? The Chronicle No. 47 goes on to relate (p. 81, l. 48) that "In the year 6882 [1373–74] on September 12th he [the Basileus John] exiled his son to the island of Lemnos." This statement is taken by Loenertz to refer to a later event, as may very well be the case: see n. 179 below. To be sure, there is nothing to confirm the suggestion that John V at first intended to exile the rebellious Andronicus to Lemnos after the 1373 episode. Even so, however, we have no information on the treatment of the discredited prince from the time of his capture in May until after Murad's capture of Saudji later, in September of 1373, at which time the Emir's order to blind Andronicus was given to John. Though it would seem more likely that John imprisoned his son in Constantinople, there is no concrete evidence that obliges us to rule out altogether the relevance of this Chronicle statement to 1373 after all, to the extent of inferring the initial intention of John merely to banish Andronicus. As for the Turkish prince and his fate, see F. Babinger's article, "Sawḏjī (3)," in *The Encyclopaedia of Islām,* IV (Leyden, 1934), 192. Note, however, that Khoury, "L'Empereur Manuel II," 134, fully accepts the assumption that Andronicus and his family were sent to Lemnos as exiles, "jusqu'en 1376," an assumption I find too extreme to accept.

49. Chalcocondyles, ed. Darkó, I, 39–40, ed. Bonn, 43–44.

50. Βρ. χρ. No. 47, p. 81, ll. 50–51; *Chron. Barb. 111,* 25 (which commences here, for our purposes, since the beginning of the work is missing in the manuscript just up to this point). See also the Pseudo-Phrantzes, 51.

on Andronicus, at least to some extent, and also on the latter's young son John.[51]

However debatable may be some aspects of the above reconstruction of events, two undeniable facts emerge from this episode. The first is the acknowledgment by John of some kind of suzerainty of the Turkish Emir, whether specifically before the revolt of Andronicus and Saudji or after it, and with it the concomitant abandonment by John of all hope for or efforts toward obtaining aid from the Latin West. Disillusioned, he had decided by now that the West would or could give nothing beyond promises.[52] Hereafter John was content—when able—to hold on to what he had by making the best bargain he could with his formidable Turkish nemesis. This reversal of policy was the turning point in the reign of John V. Thereafter he virtually ceased to be an active figure in his own government for almost all of the remaining eighteen years of his life.

51. The major Greek historians all agree on this outcome. The notice in the *Chron. Vat. gr. 162*, p. 207, ll. 50–51, states only the barest facts with no details; nor is much more given in the anonymous Ἔκθεσις χρονική (cited hereafter as " Ἐκ. χρον."), ed. S. Lampros (London, 1902), p. 1; fuller and of more value is the entry in the *Bulg. chron.*, 537. The account of Ruy González de Clavijo, *Embajada a Tamorlan*, ed. F. López Estrada (Madrid, 1943), 55; *Dnevnik putešestviia ko dvoru Timura v Samarkand v 1403–1406 gg. (Sbornik russkogo iazyka i slovesnosti Imperatorskoie Akademii Nauk*, XXVIII, 1, St. Petersburg, 1881), ed. (with Russian trans.) by I. Sreznevskii, 84–85; trans. G. Le Strange (London, 1928), 85–86, is very general and is filled with confusion, in which Gallipoli mistakenly figures. The best modern discussions of the source problems are by Loenertz, "La Première Insurrection," and, in less detail, Charanis, "Strife," 293–295. Loenertz, however, attempts to prove that the fighting really took place in Asia Minor and not in Europe. Charanis (p. 295, n. 29) discusses this argument and rejects it, correctly, I believe. Loenertz' pupil, Dennis, 26–27 and 33–34, ignores the issue and accepts the traditional geographical interpretations. Dölger, however, in his recent "Zum Aufstand," 332, has suggested that the new chronicle fragment which he has published strengthens the traditional location in Europe, and he now characterizes Loenertz' geographical reinterpretation as "freilich wenig wahrscheinlich." Loenertz draws also on the Turkish sources, and both he and Dennis add references to Western sources. Note also Dölger, "Johannes VII.," 23–24, and Ostrogorsky, *Hist. Byz. St.*, 482; Berger de Xivrey, 30 ff., is lost in the confusions of chronology of the three Greek historians. Also, Hammer, I, 190–193, or trans. Hellert, I, 254–259; Iorga, *Geschichte*, I, 251–252; Gibbons, 149–150; Pears, 94 (who mistakenly places the revolt in 1374).

52. For a good portrayal of John V's attitudes, see Dennis, 36. In her generally superficial book, Vaughan, 18, mistakenly places John's acceptance of vassalage to Murad in 1363, which is impossible.

The second outcome of this episode was the definite emergence of Manuel as the recognized heir to the throne. After the events of 1373, the replacement of Andronicus was a foregone conclusion. Appearing once more, after some two years' absence from the scene of action, the Despot of Thessalonica was formally proclaimed *Basileus* on September 25, 1373,[53] four days before the capture of Saudji Çelebi and the final collapse of the rebellion. At the age of twenty-three, in spite of his questionable right to the throne [54] and an originally scant expectation of it as a younger son, Manuel was at last the heir to the purple. From this time on, he was to become a figure of pivotal importance in the policies of the Byzantine government.

In the midst of extended negotiations for projects of expeditions to and alliances in the East on the part of the Pope, it was not until perhaps the autumn of 1374 that the West learned,

53. Βϱ. χϱ. No. 47, p. 81, l. 49. With no date, Pseudo-Phrantzes, ed. Papadopoulos, 58, ed. Bonn, 53; Ducas, ed. Grecu, 73, ed. Bonn, 46. In a note to the latter, ed. Bonn, p. 555, the original editor (Bullialdus) preserves an astrological notice which also gives the same exact date. Cf. Halecki, *Un Empereur*, 302, and, in answer to him, Dölger, "Johannes VII.," p. 22, n. 1; also Charanis, "Strife," 293–294 and 295, and *id.*, "An Important Short Chronicle," 340; also Dennis, 27. Halecki (p. 302, n. 1), followed by Dennis (p. 27, n. 7), followed by Khoury, 134, maintain that the actual coronation of Manuel as co-Emperor must have taken place some time later, before March of the following year, on the basis of a statement in a deliberation of the Venetian Senate on March 9, 1374, which speaks of the "despot newly crowned Emperor." But this is not necessarily proof that the coronation itself was later than the autumn date. Though the Short Chronicle and the astrological note do not mention crowning specifically, there is no need to rule out that meaning, as indeed their emphasis on a particular date might suggest. Manuel would still have been "newly crowned" by the following March. (See also Charanis in *Speculum*, 36, 1961, 476.) One difficulty with this Venetian document is that it speaks of a marriage by this "newly crowned Emperor" in question. As Dennis points out clearly in his note, we know of no marriage by Manuel at this time to fit this reference. See Appendix IX below. Since the foregoing was written, critical scrutiny of any "coronation" of Manuel before 1392 has been made by P. Schreiner in pp. 73–75 of his article, "Hochzeit und Krönung Kaiser Manuels II. im Jahre 1392," *Byz. Zeitschr.*, 60 (1967), 70–85; Schreiner also (72–73) rejects the erroneous inference of a supposed marriage contracted by Manuel at this time.

54. This rejection of the custom of primogeniture in succession was unique among the Palaeologi, although it was not without precedent in earlier Byzantine history. John II Comnenus (1118–1143) is reported to have bypassed at least one older son to give the succession to a younger one, Manuel I (1143–1180)—the coincidence of name being also interesting. For the constitutional aspects of primogeniture and John's decision, cf. Dölger, "Johannes VII.," p. 21, n. 2.

with shock and disappointment, that Byzantium had yielded to circumstances and had come to terms with the Infidel.[55] The change in John's policy seems even to have affected his attitude toward Venice, with whom he might still bitterly associate the misfortunes and failures of his Italian journey. During 1375 he hindered with obstacles and delays any renewal of the regular treaty with Venice, and apparently he had to be forced to it in the following year.[56] But he was soon to have need of the Venetians.

The restless Andronicus had not resigned himself to his degradation of 1373. Perhaps deliberately, the operation on his eyes was neither thorough nor total, and after some interval of time his sight, as well as that of his tiny son, was to a degree restored.[57] Andronicus had been imprisoned in the Tower of Anemas, the fearsome complex of dungeons adjoining the Imperial Palace. But apparently his confinement had been relaxed, for he was under guard in the Monastery of Kauleos when, at some time in 1376, he escaped to Galata, together with his wife and son.[58] Free

55. Dölger, *Regesten*, no. 3143, p. 62. For a good outline of the negotiations and of the reactions to the Byzantine change of policy, see Halecki, *Un Empereur*, 304–320; Dennis, 34–37; cf. Ostrogorsky, "Byzance, état tributaire," 49.

56. Dölger, *Regesten*, no. 3150, p. 63; Halecki, *Un Empereur*, 320–322; Dennis, 37; Loenertz, "Notes d'histoire et de chronologie byzantines," *Rev. d. ét. byz.*, 17 (1959), 166. Also, see below, p. 25.

57. John's reluctance to obey Murad's command emerges fairly consistently from the sources. As to Andronicus' recovery of sight, however, there is some confusion. Pears, 94, believes it was never totally destroyed. Gibbons, 150, cites, and Charanis, "An Important Short Chronicle," 353, and *id.*, "Strife," 293, accepts the story that it was the Genoese who helped restore his sight to some extent, and only after his escape to Pera. The account of Clavijo, on the other hand, while rather unreliable regarding most of the revolt of 1373, gives some details on the treatment of Andronicus which may have some value. He says, ed. López Estrada, 55, ed. Sreznevskii, 85–86, trans. Le Strange, 86, that after the blinding of Andronicus, done by means of "hot basins," his wife visited him regularly in prison and managed by the use of medicines to restore his sight in part. (Gibbons, 150, has distorted this story.) This tale, of course, need not rule out further assistance from the Genoese. In all likelihood, a combination of an incomplete operation and some healing may have been the actual case.

58. Chalcocondyles, ed. Darkó, I, 55, ed. Bonn, 60–61; *Chron. Vat. gr. 162*, no. 11, p. 208, l. 40. Ducas, ed. Grecu, 73, ed. Bonn, 45, mentions this prison specifically. The Pseudo-Phrantzes, ed. Bonn, 51, gives its name in a corrupt plural form, Ἀδεμανίδες (but emended to Ἀνεμάδες in Papadopoulos' edition, p. 56), but notes its proximity to the Palace of Blachernae, repeating exactly the phrase of description in the Ἔκ. χρον., 1, and of the

again, the twenty-eight-year-old Andronicus needed only an opportunity and allies to satisfy his vengefulness and ambition. Neither was slow to appear.

The opportunity itself readily arose in the same year. During the summer, after long negotiations and perhaps the pressure of a show of force, John finally signed a renewal of the treaty with Venice, which included also the cession of Tenedos.[59] In his negotiations of 1370–71, John had already committed himself to giving Venice this strategically important island, which commands the approach to the Dardanelles. As a result of either temporizing or hindrance, however, this cession had not taken place,[60] although the Venetians had apparently been allowed to

history of the so-called (Pseudo-)Dorotheos of Monemvasia (in the edition used here, of Venice, 1750), 404. From the latter text (if not from both), the Pseudo-Phrantzes presumably derived the bulk of its account of the entire episode. (Cf. Loenertz, "Autour du Chronicon Maius," 301–302; but note that the Pseudo-Dorotheos eliminates the reference to Blachernae, while the Ἐκ. χρον. does not.) For a further discussion of the Tower of Anemas, see below, n. 67, and Appendix III. A picture of its remains may be seen in Figure 33. Chalcocondyles and Ducas both mention the escape of Andronicus to Galata, but Βρ. χρ. No. 47, p. 81, ll. 52–53, notes the further details, including the monastery from which he escaped. The disparity between the two places of imprisonment may well be explained simply by the account of Clavijo, cited in the preceding note. In relating the sequence of Andronicus' revolts, Clavijo says that John took pity on his son's misery and "ordered him released." This might imply rather an easing of confinement. Halecki, *Un Empereur*, 322, Dölger, "Johannes VII.," 24, and Charanis, "An Important Short Chronicle," 353, state that the Genoese helped Andronicus to escape. The Pseudo-Phrantzes, by contrast, maintains that John released his prisoners—or could it be, again, that he eased their confinement? —as a result of intervention by the Emir in response to pleas from Christian and Osmanli nobles: cf. Dölger, "Johannes VII.," p. 24, n. 2. Possibly the date of this escape can be placed after early March, 1376. For, on the twelfth of that month, the Venetian Senate discussed the possibility of Andronicus as an alternative to his brother Michael as their candidate for the throne of Trebizond: Thiriet, *Régestes*, I, no. 576, p. 143. Such a plan might have been broached to him, as the Senate ordered, if he were lightly confined to a monastery, but it is doubtful that the Venetians could or would have entertained such intentions if Andronicus were by then in Pera in the hands of their Genoese rivals.

59. Dölger, *Regesten*, no. 3150, p. 63. Cf. Halecki, *Un Empereur*, 320–322; Thiriet, "Venise et l'occupation de Ténédos," 225–226; note also *ibid.*, 218–224, for a good summary of the importance of the island and its earlier role.

60. Loenertz, in his "Jean V Paléologue à Venise," 226–228, had suggested the possibility of obstacles allegedly raised by Andronicus during John's difficulties in Venice, and the additional possibility of involvement of the Genoese Lord of Lesbos, Francesco Gattilusio. Indeed, Dennis, 27, had

make use of the island.[61] The cession, now that it was settled, aroused the inevitable concern of the Lagoon Republic's bitter rivals. In order to foil this move, so profitable to Venice and hence so inimical to their own commercial interests and ambitions, the Genoese became the champions of Andronicus, whom they saw as a useful tool.

Support from the Genoese was not enough. The destinies of the Empire were now completely in the hands of the Turks. One cannot but marvel at the diplomatic genius of the Emirs during the early decades of the Turkish conquest of the Balkans and especially at that of Murad I. With sensitivity and skill, the shrewd Turk was able to gauge well his Orthodox opponents, be they Greeks or Slavs, and was ever able to win his successes as much by clever manipulation as by force of arms. If any of the Empire's many foes ever learned to emulate the Byzantines, it was the Osmanlis. As a result, the appearance of Andronicus as a potential instrument suited their aims almost well enough to have been so intended.[62]

accepted outright the culpability of Andronicus in this matter; likewise, Ostrogorsky in *Cambr. Med. Hist.*, Vol. IV (2nd ed.), 1, p. 371. In the light, however, of the correction of the transcription of the Caroldo text, and the new discussions of it, as indicated in n. 30 above, such speculations should now perhaps be abandoned.

61. Thiriet, "Venise et l'occupation de Ténédos," 225.

62. At least one modern writer has gone so far as to suggest that Murad deliberately did not press for the total elimination of Andronicus in 1373 in order to have him available for his own future exploitation. Gibbons is often far-fetched or inaccurate in his interpretations, and he has perhaps overstated this point. But even though he has based his idea on a statement in the Pseudo-Phrantzes, ed. Bonn, p. 51, ll. 21–23 (ed. Papadopoulos, p. 56, ll. 22–24), which is almost irrelevant—it obviously refers to Murad's policy toward his own son and his own state rather than toward Andronicus and Byzantium —it is still a passage worth noting: "If Murad had really desired the death or total blindness of Andronicus, he could easily have secured this result. While punishing his own son, however, he saw to it that Andronicus escaped the consequences of the same crime. Here we have a revelation of the far-sightedness and cold-bloodedness of Murad. He killed his own son, because he feared his rivalry. He spared the son of John Palaeologos in order to perpetuate the rivalry between the emperor and his son. To have killed or incapacitated Andronicus would have been from his viewpoint an act of folly rather than of justice; for Andronicus, brilliant, adventurous, magnetic, was at the same time a worthy exemplar of the name he bore, a name that stood for the acme of unscrupulous conduct and contempt for ties of blood. Murad had only to wait, and history would repeat itself. Internal dissensions in the family of the Palaeologi had made the fortunes of Orkhan. Murad had no intention of getting rid of Andronicus, in whom he saw the means of still further enmeshing the Byzantine emperors." (P. 151.)

Whatever may have been his resentment toward Murad for the latter's role in his punishment in 1373, Andronicus was under no illusions about his need for Turkish support. Contacting the Emir,[63] Andronicus promised subservience and tribute. All too willing to gain this further lever in the affairs of Byzantium, Murad accepted and provided troops. In July, apparently on the tenth or eleventh, Andronicus invested Constantinople, and on August 12 he was able to enter through the important Gate of Pegé.[64] For three days heavy fighting continued within the capi-

63. Chalcocondyles, ed. Darkó, I, 55–56, ed. Bonn, 61–62. This source has Andronicus go in person to the Emir, which is not impossible, but is a bit unlikely; it might, indeed, be a confusion with Andronicus' trip to Murad *after* his seizure (see n. 76 below). Chalcocondyles also puts in Andronicus' mouth a speech in which the prince requests aid in his seizure of power, in exchange for a promise of vassalage and military service, and this offer is accepted. Chalcocondyles mistakenly places these events in the reign of Murad's son and successor Bayazid, who is named as the Emir here (see n. 87 below). In this respect he is followed by the *Chron. Barb. 111*, 29–30 (which confuses the episode still further with the later activities of John VII in the 1390's: see n. 189 below); and by the Pseudo-Phrantzes, ed. Papadopoulos, 59–60, ed. Bonn, 54–55, who also says that Andronicus, after having entered into collusion with one of his wife's relatives in Bulgaria, "fled" to the Emir, together with his son. Nothing is said about the Genoese of Pera. Before the Emir, says the Pseudo-Phrantzes, Andronicus promised annual tribute and other privileges (προνόμια), in return for which the Emir supported him with an army of 6,000 horse and 4,000 foot. Ducas, ed. Grecu, 73, ed. Bonn, 45, says nothing of the Turks, and notes only Genoese aid. The same is true of the *Chron. Vat. gr. 162*, no. 11, p. 208, l. 41. Likewise ignoring the Turks, and contributing no further details, are the Latin sources, citations to which may be found in Charanis, "An Important Short Chronicle," 353, and "Strife," 296, who says that a promise to the Emir of Andronicus' sister in marriage was included in the arrangements, without giving any source support. Dennis, pp. 37–38, n. 49, however, cites two Latin sources for this story, which seems questionable at best; see also Dennis, 29. Cf. Dölger, *Regesten*, no. 3152, p. 64. Ostrogorsky, *Hist. Byz. St.*, 483, seems to believe that Andronicus courted Turkish support only after seizing power, which is plainly wrong. Among the older general accounts from the Turkish point of view, Hammer, I, 217–219, trans. Hellert, I, 295–297, is completely confused by the muddled chronology of the sources, and places the entire episode early in Bayazid's reign; Iorga, *Geschichte*, I, 252–254, covers these events more satisfactorily.

64. Βρ. χρ. No. 52, p. 89, ll. 31–33; also the same text, ed. J. Müller, in his "Byzantinische Analekten" *Sitzungsberichte der philosophisch-historischen Classe der Kaiserlichte Akademie der Wissenschaften in Wien*, IX (1852), p. 392 (59), ll. 15–17; which notes the duration of the siege. Cf. Charanis, "An Important Short Chronicle," 352 ff. Of the other short chronicles, No. 47, p. 81, l. 54, gives the same date but names the Xylokerkou Gate (or Kerkoporta) as the gate of entry; while No. 15, pp. 31–32, ll. 15–16, simply notes his entry "by the aid of the Turks" and the year; and the *Chron. Vat. gr. 162*, p. 208, gives the month of July as the time of entry rather than the

tal.[65] John and his family were able to hold out in the fortress by the Golden Gate, where Andronicus had to besiege them.[66] They were eventually forced to capitulate, and in October Andronicus had the satisfaction of casting his father and his two brothers, Manuel and Theodore, into the very same prison in which he had formerly been held himself, the dread Tower of Anemas.[67] According to Manuel,[68] Theodore was given the op-

correct August. Cf. also Muralt, pp. 705–706, nos. 8 and 9. For the Latin sources, see the citations by Charanis, "An Important Short Chronicle," pp. 353–354, n. 3. The Pseudo-Phrantzes, ed. Papadopoulos, 59–60, ed. Bonn, 55, erroneously turns the Pegé Gate into a palace where he has John and his family seized. On the gate of Pegé itself, see A. van Millingen, *Byzantine Constantinople, The Walls of the City and Adjoining Historical Sites* (London, 1899), 75–77, especially 76.

65. Βρ. χρ. No. 47, p. 81, ll. 54–56, which also states that 160 Genoese fell in the fighting. It is interesting to note that none of the sources which describe the fighting itself mention the involvement of the Turks. This is perhaps explained by Manuel himself, in his *Funeral Oration for His Brother Theodore*, ed. Migne, *Patr. gr.*, 156, 200B; ed. S. Lampros, Παλαιολόγεια καὶ Πελοποννησιακά, III (Athens, 1926), 27. Here Manuel says that, after the city was seized and their own "citadel" was invested, the army of "the Persians" (i.e. the Turks) was approaching. Presumably, therefore, the real fighting was left to the Genoese, and the Turks did not participate in it. Indeed, John and his family may well have preferred surrender to allowing the Turks to intervene directly. Walter, 286, speaks of the participation of Serbian allies of Andronicus under the famous Marko Kraljević.

66. Chalcocondyles, ed. Darkó, I, 56–57, ed. Bonn, 62. Cf. Dennis, 29, who also (n. 10) gives references to Latin sources.

67. Βρ. χρ. No. 15, p. 32, ll. 16–19, names the month and the Tower Anemas. The *Chron. Vat. gr. 162*, no. 11, p. 208, ll. 42–45, mentions no specific prison, but does state that Andronicus also seized his mother and καθεῖρξεν ἐν φυλκαῇ her and the others. But the immediate imprisonment of the Empress Helena seems unlikely, on the basis of Cydones' Letter C. 133 (No. 28), L. 222, a source which will be examined more closely below, p. 39. Ducas, ed. Grecu, 73, ed. Bonn, 45, specifically states that Andronicus imprisoned them in the same "tower" in which he had been held previously; while Chalcocondyles, ed. Darkó, I, 57, ed. Bonn, 62–63, maintains that they were shut up in a small wooden enclosure within a tower. The Pseudo-Phrantzes, ed. Papadopoulos, 60, ed. Bonn, 55, simply says that they were enclosed in "a certain house" and kept under guard. Dennis, p. 29 and n. 2, also gives references to Latin sources. See also Dölger, "Johannes VII.," 24–25; Charanis, "Strife," 296, and "An Important Short Chronicle," 354; Ostrogorsky, *Hist. Byz. St.*, 483; Gibbons, 153; Pears, 94. Loenertz, *Echos d'Orient*, 36 (1937), 284–285, believes that the reference by Cydones in his Letter C. 104 (No. 20), L. 418, to "this tragedy" (τῇ τραγωδίᾳ ταύτῃ), ed. Cammelli, p. 47, l. 23, ed. Loenertz, II, p. 374, l. 20, pertains to the imprisonment of John and his sons. For some observations on the Tower of Anemas, see Appendix III below.

68. *Funeral Oration*, ed. Migne, 200–201, ed. Lampros, 27–29; cf. Dennis, p. 42 and n. 68.

portunity to leave. Already designated by his father before the revolt to succeed Manuel as Despot of Thessalonica,[69] he was to be allowed by an agreement between besieged and besiegers to depart to his realm. But Manuel says that he himself was grievously wounded in the fighting and that Theodore refused to leave his brother, in spite of the wishes of his parents and the alternative of sharing his family's imprisonment.

With the city securely in his hands, Andronicus IV assumed power as Emperor in his own right, although it was not until Sunday, October 18, 1377, a year later, that he legalized his position by having himself crowned *Basileus*.[70] By that time, too, he had a Patriarch of his own choosing; for, taking advantage of the fortuitous death of Philotheos in 1376, he was able to install his own candidate, Makarios.[71]

Immediately after his seizure of power, however, Andronicus' first steps were of necessity to repay two urgent debts. The first was to the Genoese. In a document dated August 23, 1376, eleven days after his entry into the city, Andronicus signed a confirmation of his cession of Tenedos to Genoa.[72] But when the Genoese attempted to take possession of this plum, the garrison of Tenedos refused to honor the cession and instead, in October of

69. This is also mentioned by Ducas, ed. Grecu, 71, ed. Bonn, 44, who states it in conjunction with his reference to Manuel's coronation, which was presumably in 1374 (see n. 53 above).

70. Βρ. χρ. No. 52, p. 89, l. 33, ed. Müller, p. 392 (59), ll. 18–19; cf. Muralt, p. 708, no. 5. Chalcocondyles, ed. Darkó, I, 57, ed. Bonn, 63, says that Andronicus "appointed also his son John Basileus of the Hellenes," which Dölger, "Johannes VII.," p. 24, n. 5, accepts as meaning full coronation with him. But on the other hand, the Pseudo-Phrantzes says (ed. Papadopoulos, 60, ed. Bonn, p. 55) that "Andronicus often considered proclaiming his son John as Basileus. However, it was not possible since the Basileus, his father, was yet living." On this problem, see J. Papadopoulos, " 'Ιωάννης Ζ' ὁ Παλαιολόγος καὶ τὸ χρονικὸν τοῦ Φραντζῆ," *Byz. Zeitschr.*, 32 (1932), 257–259. Also, see n. 200 below.

71. M. Gedeon, Πατριαρχικοὶ πίνακες (Constantinople, 1890), 439; cf. Muralt, p. 708, no. 12.

72. Dölger, *Regesten*, nos. 3155 and 3156, p. 65. The text in the *Liber Iurium Reipublicae Genuensis*, II, no. 250, pp. 819–821, was not available to me; there is, however, another edition, in D. C. Pagano's *Impresse e dominio de Genovesi nella Grecia* (Genoa, 1852), pp. 307–309; and there is an abridgement of it in L. T. Belgrano's "Studi e documenti su la colonia genovese de Pera (Prima serie)," *Atti della Società ligure di storia patria*, 13 (1877), p. 131, no. 24. See Dennis, 38; W. Heyd, *Histoire du commerce du Levant au moyen âge* (2 vols., Leipzig, 1936), I, 518–519, who cites this text; and Halecki, *Un Empereur*, 323; cf. also Charanis, "Strife," 296. This same grant to the Genoese also extended their colony in Galata.

1376, permitted the Venetians, who also had a claim to the island, to occupy it.[73] Andronicus could only vent his rage on Venetians in Constantinople.[74] For Genoa this incident was to be the signal for the long-expected and vicious near-death struggle with Venice known as the Chioggia War.[75]

The second debt had even more ominous implications, for reckoning with the Turks was now no light matter. At some time between his seizure of power and the spring of 1377 (probably in October, 1376), Andronicus went in person to Murad to settle the arrangements between them, and either before then or at that time the Turks' price for their aid was made known and accepted: the cession of Gallipoli. So this vital port, which commands the crossing of the Dardanelles, was yielded up to them,[76] passing forever out of Byzantine hands.

This double dependence upon external support exposed Andronicus and his dwindling realm to humiliation and trouble, as a justly celebrated letter by Cydones makes clear. According to him, the Turks, become more greedy after taking Gallipoli, seek to squeeze even more from the Byzantines; while the Genoese, unreconciled to losing Tenedos and on the threshold of war with Venice, have obliged Andronicus to join with them, with effort and expense he can ill afford, in a projected expedition against Tenedos. And all the while John and his sons languish in prison while the political atmosphere remains precariously unstable and unpredictable.[77] As it happened, moreover, the expedition against

73. Loenertz, "Notes d'histoire et chronologie," 167, and Dennis, 38–39, with the Western sources; also Thiriet, "Venise et l'occupation de Ténédos," 226–227.

74. Dennis, 38–39, with Western references; the seizure and despoiling of Venetians mentioned by Heyd, I, 519, and Charanis, "Strife," 296, apparently are based on these.

75. For the course of the war, called after the town of that name outside Venice where the worst of the fighting was ultimately focused, see Heyd, I, 517–521, in brief. Good accounts of the war at fuller length may be found in W. C. Hazlitt, *The Venetian Republic, Its Rise, Its Growth, and Its Fall, 421–1797*, Vol. I: *421–1422* (London, 1900), 665–717; F. C. Hodgeson, *Venice in the Thirteenth and Fourteenth Centuries* (London, 1910), 504–537; A. Wiel, *The Navy of Venice* (London, 1910), 188–209.

76. See Appendix IV below, for a full discussion of the dating of the cession of Gallipoli and of Andronicus' visit to Murad. This visit, incidentally, may have confused Chalcocondyles and the Pseudo-Phrantzes into thinking that Andronicus went to him before his seizure of power: see n. 63 above.

77. Letter C. 122 (No. 25), L. 167. Cammelli, of course, provides a French translation, and an English rendering of most of it may be found in Charanis, "Strife," 297–298, and Dennis, 38 and 39.

Tenedos was ill-fated from the start. Even before it could get under way, the Venetians organized a counter thrust. In July of 1377 a Venetian squadron mounted a raid on Constantinople and then withdrew to Tenedos.[78] And when the expedition against the disputed island was finally launched in the autumn of 1377, it was a complete failure.[79] After this, Andronicus and Byzantium apparently played no further role in the Veneto-Genoese hostilities.

It must soon have become obvious that the reign of Andronicus IV was a sorry affair. Even at home he must have had difficulty marshaling support; at least one outstanding figure, Cydones, flatly refused to serve him.[80] Certainly, in retrospect, his tenancy of the throne seems to modern historians an unfortunate one for Byzantium,[81] although Andronicus may at least have attempted some honestly constructive measures toward a reform of the currency.[82] But with whatever degree of severity one evaluates this reign, it was neither regrettable nor surprising that it was brief. In truth, his situation was founded upon two weaknesses: that of dependency on external support and that of the danger from his still-living father and brothers. When these two weaknesses coalesced, his position crumbled.

It is at least a credit to Andronicus' honor that he did no more

78. For the details of this incident and its sources, see Dennis, 40.

79. Likewise, again, Dennis, 40; see also Thiriet, "Venise et l'occupation de Ténédos," 227–228; Hazlitt, 667; Muralt, p. 708, no. 6.

80. Cydones' refusal may be found in his actual response to Andronicus, Letter C. 120 (No. 24), L. 154, which Loenertz dates 1377. In the same letter Cydones asks to be allowed to go to Italy. Cf. Loenertz, *Echos d'Orient*, 36 (1937), 283–284. Cydones, of course, may not necessarily have been typical of the attitude of leading Byzantines, since he himself was strongly attached personally to John and Manuel and was pro-Venetian as well. At any rate, perhaps as too eminent a person to be subject to reprisals, Cydones seems to have been left unmolested.

81. The indictment by Dennis, 40, is perhaps the most worthy of quotation: "By the summer of 1379 the brief reign of Andronicus IV could show the following results: he had reduced Byzantium to an even more servile state of subjection to the Ottomans, to whom he had given the strategically located Gallipoli. His alliance with the Genoese had brought him only a Venetian attack (albeit of no great consequence) on his city and the loss of much equipment and many troops in an unsuccessful attempt to dislodge the Venetians from Tenedos."

82. Such is the provocative interpretation of T. Bertelè in his article, "L'iperpero bizantino dal 1261 al 1453," *Rivista italiana di numismatica e scienze affini*, V, 5, 59 (1957), 70–89. But it should be borne in mind that our understanding of the coinage of the Palaeologan period is still somewhat nebulous.

to his family than imprison them, rather more clemency than one might have expected from a Byzantine ruler in general and a Palaeologus in particular.[83] Indeed, considering his relatively restrained treatment of his family and of those who would not support his usurpation, Andronicus might be reckoned, if untalented, selfish, and unstable, at least as a mild ruler. Not that such mildness necessarily made the ordeal of confinement any less unpleasant for the three prisoners, whose anguish and despair, rhetoric notwithstanding, Manuel portrays very vividly.[84] In this condition they remained for "a little less than three years." [85] Possibly there were some efforts to release them.[86] By 1379, pre-

83. There is a statement in the Pseudo-Phrantzes (ed. Papadopoulos, p. 60, ll. 7–12, ed. Bonn, p. 55, ll. 12–15) that "The Emir often informed him that he should slay them and shake them out of the way, if he would wish to be undisturbed in his rule; but he, being cautious, did not wish then to become a patricide and a fratricide." Nor can the questionability of the source invalidate the statement, for it is found in briefer form in Chalcocondyles, ed. Darkó, I, 57, ed. Bonn, 63, from whence it possibly came originally. Such reluctance on the part of Andronicus would be wholly credible, as well as creditable. But one must consider Murad to have been a complete barbarian to accept the idea that he would have made so blunt a suggestion. In view of what we can observe of him, he probably realized how much more valuable to him the continued existence of these potential agents of further discord might be. Hence, it is all the more curious to find Gibbons, the strongest advocate of the Emir's shrewdness in such matters (see n. 62 above), citing this statement with seeming acceptance, p. 153, n. 5; also, Berger de Xivrey, 44.

84. *Funeral Oration,* ed. Migne, 201B–C, ed. Lampros, 29–30; a brief passage of this is translated by Dennis, p. 29, n. 10. In addition, there is another text by Manuel, a letter-discourse to his friend Alexius Iagoup, still unpublished, which contains an enormously valuable autobiographical passage. This passage is translated below, pp. 410–413, and should be consulted for Manuel's particularly interesting comments on his imprisonment in 1376–79. In passing, he describes this imprisonment generally as of three years' duration. He also reveals that he used the opportunity of his confinement to pursue his neglected literary studies, and that the books and study at least managed to preserve his spirits from complete desolation.

85. This is Manuel's own phrase, *Funeral Oration, ibid.,* and likewise in the letter to Iagoup, both cited in the preceding note. The Βο. χο. No. 15, p. 32, l. 19, says simply three years; Chalcocondyles, ed. Darkó, I, 57, ed. Bonn, 63, says that it was only in the fourth year of their imprisonment that they escaped. But Ducas, ed. Grecu, 73, ed. Bonn, 45, and the *Chron. Vat. gr. 162,* no. 13, p. 208, l. 52, say that they were in prison for two years, both obviously in error.

86. In his *Funeral Oration,* Manuel is rather vague on the whole question of their release from prison. We do have one highly romantic tale preserved in a florid and imaginative biography of the intrepid Venetian adventurer and admiral, Carlo Zeno, written by his grandson, Jocapo. This story is

sumably in June, some sort of plot seems to have succeeded, and John escaped with his two sons to Scutari, from which they made their way forthwith to Murad.[87] Of the three powers to which Byzantium had become but a pawn and a victim, it was quite clear which one was now the real master of the Empire's destiny. Nothing displays more clearly the humiliating weakness

summarized below, in Appendix IV, in a related context. The tale is recounted with acceptance by Gibbons, 155–156, and with at least only regretful caution by Wiel, 191–192, while details of it are accepted unhesitatingly by Muralt, p. 707, nos. 6–8, and by Berger de Xivrey, 44–45. A discussion of this source may be found in Hodgson, p. 510, n. 1; see also Dölger, "Johannes VII.," p. 25, n. 1. However much fantasy it may contain, this story plainly reflects some basis in fact, as concluded below in Appendix IV. Certainly the Venetians were anxious to get rid of Andronicus and to restore John and, indeed, had agreed to take steps in that direction: see Hodgson, 513. By its own terms, the Zeno story assumes a time very soon after John's deposition and imprisonment. It is not impossible that there were several other Venetian-inspired plots to release the Imperial prisoners.

87. The *Chron. Vat. gr. 162*, no. 13, p. 208, ll. 52–54, as do all of the other sources, gives no date. Βρ. χρ. No. 15, p. 32, ll. 19–20, adds that they escaped θαυμαστῶς. Ducas, ed. Grecu, p. 73, ed. Bonn, 45, ascribes their deliverance to the aid of "a certain evildoer whose name was indeed Angelos, but whose nickname was Diabolangelos," who, "casting them out from the tower by devices either of an angel or of a devil," got them into a boat. Ducas is also the only writer to note that they fled to Scutari, but he says nothing about going to the Emir. The Pseudo-Phrantzes, ed. Papadopoulos, 60, ed. Bonn, 55, says that "one day the Basileis, outwitting the Bulgarians guarding them," made their escape, but to Bayazid. Chalcocondyles, ed. Darkó, I, p. 57, ed. Bonn, 63, states only the bare fact of their escape, but also wrongly identifies the Turkish ruler involved as Bayazid. To explain this, Berger de Xivrey, 46–47, suggests that Murad was away campaigning in Asia and that his son Bayazid acted in his place; hence, the use of his name in the events of this period by Chalcocondyles and (the Pseudo-)Phrantzes is correct. But there seems to be no support for this proposal, and, indeed, the evidence of the short chronicles refutes it. Whatever information had trickled down to Clavijo a quarter century later is represented only by the statement (ed. López Estrada, 56, ed. Sreznevskii, 85–86, trans. Le Strange, 86) that Andronicus, after his own release from prison, rebelled successfully against his father and imprisoned John in his turn, until "some of his nobles freed him" (*unos caualleros suyos le sacaron*). For these events, see also Berger de Xivrey, 45; Dennis, 41; Muralt, p. 710, no. 7. A letter by Cydones, C. 126, L. 244, which Loenertz dates 1381–82, rejoices over the release of the Emperor from prison and specifically mentions the Tower of Anemas and the flight to "the Barbarians." A passage in another Cydones letter, C. 125 (No. 27), L. 309, which the frequently misguided Cammelli in his edition, p. 63, regarded as applying to John's escape, in reality refers to events of 1385: see below, pp. 51–52, and n. 141. Letter C. 133 (No. 28), L. 222, the most important one for the problems of John's imprisonment and escape, will be considered below, p. 39 and n. 105.

of Byzantium at this time than these alternating coups and countercoups among the Palaeologi.

In these circumstances, Murad could afford to play the role of arbiter. According to one source, the Emir made a show of consulting public opinion in the capital.[88] Whether or not this is true, Murad was careful to consider his own advantage. Exactly why Murad chose to abandon Andronicus and to shift his favor to John and Manuel is difficult to determine positively. It is not impossible to suggest considerations of personality preferences. Also, Murad may well have realized that Andronicus' regime was hopelessly unstable, and hence he may have felt that a more settled and pliant order in Constantinople could be exploited more to his advantage. In all likelihood, however, the offers of John and Manuel must have been sufficient to make him feel that their restoration would be profitable for him. We know, at any rate, that they agreed to pay a large tribute, to provide military forces for regular and annual service with the Emir, and possibly also to cede the city of Philadelphia, the last Byzantine holding in Asia Minor.[89] The vassalage of Byzantium to the Turks was now fully formulated and complete.

88. Chalcocondyles, ed. Darkó, I, p. 57, ll. 14–19, ed. Bonn, p. 63, ll. 10–15, a passage worth quoting: "Sending a messenger to Byzantium, he ["Bayazid"] consulted the Byzantines and their opinion, whom they might wish to be their Basileus, Emmanuel or King Bayazid; for he made trial also in this way of the opinions of the Byzantines concerning himself. But the Byzantines chose Emmanuel, inasmuch as they were then burdened [or, "oppressed"] by the rule of Andronicus." The Pseudo-Phrantzes, ed. Papadopoulos, 61, ed. Bonn, 56, and the *Chron. Barb. 111*, 30, say substantially the same thing. This is accepted by Muralt, p. 710, no. 9, and Pears, 106. Charanis, "Strife," 299, suggests that Murad (and not Bayazid, as Chalcocondyles anachronistically identifies the Turkish ruler) may well have taken such a step "in order to justify his defection from the cause of Andronicus."

89. Chalcocondyles, ed. Darkó, I, 58, ed. Bonn, 63–64, says that Manuel promised a tribute of 3,000 gold pieces, presumably annually, and annual personal military service. Immediately after this episode, he mentions Bayazid's demand, while campaigning with the Byzantine rulers, for Philadelphia, and so the cession may thus pertain to the 1379 agreement: see below, pp. 79–80 and n. 211. The Pseudo-Phrantzes, ed. Papadopoulos, 60–61, ed. Bonn, 55–56, says that Manuel promised to continue the tribute which his brother had agreed upon and also to attend the Emir each spring with a stipulated force of 12,000 foot and horse (was Byzantium possessed of such forces at this time?) for military service wherever he might wish. He further promised to regard all friends and enemies of the Emir, respectively, as his friends and enemies. Ducas says nothing of any such terms or, indeed, of the role of the Turks at all in the restoration. Cf. Berger de Xivrey, 47–48; Cha-

With the active support of the Turks, and with the support of Venice assured, John and Manuel moved on Constantinople. On July 1, 1379, they entered the city by the Charisius Gate.[90] Unable or unwilling to make his stand in the city, Andronicus fled to Galata, taking family hostages with him.[91] A small Genoese garrison had been left behind in the city, and when a Venetian squadron arrived, its leaders were persuaded to assist in routing these Genoese, who resisted fiercely and were not subdued until early August.

The scene of resistance was thereby shifted squarely to Pera, where Andronicus, his captives, and his Genoese allies were besieged by John, Manuel, and John's own allies. Marked by sporadic fighting, this siege apparently dragged on until the spring of 1381 before the final settlement was reached.[92] By May

ranis, "Strife," 299–300; Muralt, p. 710, no. 8; see also Dennis, 41; Ostrogorsky, "Byzance, état tributaire," 51–52. For some reason, Dölger, *Regesten*, has no entry on this pact. It is interesting, if not significant, that the sources seem to indicate Manuel, and not his father, as the negotiator with the Turks for their restoration.

90. The specific date and the gate are reported by the Βϱ. χϱ. No. 52, p. 89, ll. 34–37, ed. Müller, p. 392 (59), ll. 19–24; while No. 15, p. 32, ll. 20–21, states the date and the role of Turkish aid. The notice in the *Chron. Vat. gr. 162*, no. 13, p. 208, l. 55, vaguely says only that John "received the realm" a short time after his flight to Murad. Cf. Charanis, "An Important Short Chronicle," 354–355, and "Strife," 300; Muralt, p. 710, no. 10.

91. Βϱ. χϱ. No. 52, p. 89, ll. 37–38, ed. Müller, p. 392 (59), ll. 24–25; *Chron. Vat. gr. 162*, no. 14, p. 209, ll. 57–58, notes the hostages, who will be discussed below, pp. 38–39.

92. For an account of the fighting between the flight of Andronicus and the settlement of May, 1381, see Dennis, 41–42, 43–44, who gives the Western sources and discusses thoroughly the problems connected with them. The Greek sources completely ignore this extended struggle. Chalcocondyles, ed. Darkó, I, 58, ed. Bonn, 63–64, and, following him, the Pseudo-Phrantzes, ed. Papadopoulos, 61, ed. Bonn, 56–57, are content to let "Bayazid" give the realm to John, and both mistakenly have Manuel crowned while Andronicus and his son become clients or dependents of the Emir; and the Pseudo-Phrantzes even has Andronicus given Thessalonica (a confusion with Andronicus' son John VII, and with Manuel's son Andronicus, both of whom later ruled in Thessalonica); all of this, of course, being completely wrong. Berger de Xivrey, 49, is misled by all this. Ducas, ed. Grecu, 73, ed. Bonn, 45–46, is even more hopelessly garbled. First, he says that after his relatives' escape and comeback, Andronicus had no wish to cause further civil war and, instead, made submission to his father. This tale is accepted blindly by Pears, 94–95, and, with some modifications, by Muralt, p. 710, no. 11. Then, although Ducas correctly notes the appanage created for Andronicus, he erroneously claims that Manuel was crowned Emperor then, and further compounds confusion by stating that at the same time Francesco

of that year it would seem that a truce was drawn up and open hostilities ceased.[93] Although a final treaty with the Genoese remained to be settled, the arrangement between the erstwhile Imperial contenders was ratified by a Patriarchal synod in an act dated May 4, 1381.[94] Meanwhile, the restored Emperors had begun their housecleaning at the end of 1379, securing themselves vis-à-vis the Patriarchate itself by deposing, disgracing, and imprisoning Andronicus' incumbent, Makarios, and replacing him with a new man, Neilos.[95]

Gattilusio was given John's sister (Maria) as a bride. This last point is patently absurd, since (as noted in Appendix IV below) Maria Palaeologina died in 1377. Moreover, we know that this marriage took place in 1354–55, as a reward for the Genoese adventurer's aid against Cantacuzenus. On this see Dölger, *Regesten*, no. 3043, p. 41, with source citations; and W. Miller, "The Gattilusij of Lesbos (1355–1462)," *Byz. Zeitschr.*, 22 (1913), 406–408 (or, as reprinted in his collection, *Essays on the Latin Orient*, Cambridge, 1921, 313–315). Also, see Appendix VII below. On the problem of this passage in Ducas, see Dölger, "Johannes VII.," p. 25, n. 4, who half accepts some of its inaccuracies. As to the Gattilusii, since the foregoing was written Fr. Dennis has published a valuable source on them, "The Short Chronicle of Lesbos, 1355–1428," in Λεσβιακά, 5 (1965), 3–24, including the Greek text (5–7), with a translation interspersed with valuable commentary: in which, specifically on Francesco's Palaeologan marriage, see pp. 8–9.

93. Cydones' Letter C. 63 (No. 8), L. 198, which Loenertz dates in the spring or summer of 1381, speaks of the peace which is restored and of the reconciliation between Andronicus and his father. Cydones also speaks of the important role in this truce and reconciliation played by Triboles, who was later to serve as secretary to Theodore in the Morea, and who was also to be the recipient of Manuel's Letter ϑ'; cf. Loenertz, *Echos d'Orient*, 36 (1937), 285–287; also Dennis, 44–45, and n. 77, where he translates this passage. The Italian sources, perhaps with some bias, suggest that Manuel and his father were obliged to accept terms after failing in their attacks on Pera: thus Muralt, p. 714, no. 15. But, using other Cydones letters (C. 138, L. 219, and C. 206, L. 220), Dennis, pp. 43–44, n. 75, demonstrates that the conclusion of the truce may have followed at least a plausible degree of Byzantine success in arms against the Genoese of Pera. For further reflections on this settlement in the letters of Cydones, see C. 35, L. 201, and C. 379, L. 211: the latter is to John V, rejoicing in the defeat of "the contentious ones."

94. Dölger, *Regesten*, no. 3171, p. 67. Text in Miklosich and Müller, Vol. II, no. 344, pp. 25–27; its terms will be discussed below, pp. 41–42.

95. Gedeon, 440, who seems to think, however, that Makarios may have been on his way out as early as the previous year; cf. Muralt, p. 711, no. 19. On this Patriarch (1379–1388), and commenting on his surviving homilies, the most recent study is I. Dujčev, "Le Patriarche Nil et les invasions turques vers la fin du XIVe siècle," *Mélanges d'archéologie et d'histoire de l'Ecole français de Rome*, 78 (1966), 207–214; on which, however, cf. the very critical remarks of V. Laurent in *Byz. Zeitschr.*, 60 (1967), 166, noting

At this point we would do well to pause and to take note of one extraordinary aspect of this entire period of civil war: the involvement of that remarkable man the Monk Ioasaph, more commonly known by his former name of John Cantacuzenus. Our former conception had this energetic figure sinking after his deposition into the oblivion of an encloistered life, in which he devoted his declining years to writing his theological and especially his historical works. This conception has been exploded by the scholarly investigations of recent years. We now know that he took an active part in state and especially ecclesiastical affairs.[96] His important role in the negotiations for Church union in 1367 has already been mentioned.[97] The restoration of his old supporter Philotheos to a second term as Patriarch (1364–76) may well have signaled or symbolized a return to influence of the deposed usurper. Philotheos himself gives a description of the former Emperor's new status that is rhetorical and perhaps slightly exaggerated, but that is undeniably significant. Cantacuzenus, he says, is now a pillar of the government, its greatest counselor, and a virtual father to the Imperial family. As a result, he is now even more powerful than when he was Emperor in name himself.[98]

After playing a role in the reconciliation of his son Matthew with John V and then spending some time in the Peloponnesus

the more substantial and significant work of H. Hennephof, *Das Homiliar des Patriarchen Neilos und die chrysostomische Tradition. Ein Beitrag zur Quellengeschichte der spätbyzantinischen Homiletik* (Leiden, 1963).

96. For an outline, though not fully complete, of Cantacuzenus' activities after his deposition, see Meyendorff, "Projets de concile oecuménique en 1367: Un dialogue inédit," 149–152. In the wake of Meyendorff, a further review of Cantacuzenus' later career has been published by Lj. Maksimovic, "Politička uloga Jovana Kantakuzina posle abdikacije (1354–1385)" ("The Political Role of John Cantacuzenus after his Abdication"), *Zbornik radova, Vizantinološkog Instituta* (*Srpska akademija nauka i umetnosti*, Belgrade), 9 (1966), 119–193, for the use of which I am largely dependent upon the English summary (pp. 189–193).

97. See above, n. 21.

98. See 1129B–C of the Patriarch Philotheos' *Ant'rrhetici libri XII contra Gregoram*, ed. Migne, *Patr. gr.*, 151; cf. Meyendorff, "Projets de concile oecuménique en 1367," 150, who gives a French translation of this most interesting passage. See below, Appendix IX, for discussion of an allusion in Panaretos (ed. Lampros, p. 284, ll. 6–17) to the encountering, by a Trapezuntine embassy, of Cantacuzenus at the court in Constantinople in April of 1363; that is, even before Philotheos' restoration to the Patriarchate.

with his other son Manuel, as he himself relates,[99] Cantacuzenus took part in the aforementioned negotiations of 1367.[100] His influence was obviously great, for the circumstances of these negotiations make it clear that no decisions could be reached on Papal proposals until his views had been heard on them, such was his position and the importance of his opinions. Not only was he the chief Byzantine spokesman during these negotiations, but, later in that year, in a letter dated November 8, Pope Urban V wrote to him, urging his support in projects for union and noting also his great power.[101] Then in 1375, he was the recipient of another letter, dated January 28, from Pope Gregory XI, who, in his turn, attempted to enlist the aid of Cantacuzenus in the still-hoped-for project and went so far as to invite him to come to Rome.[102]

Active as Cantacuzenus was in ecclesiastical affairs, he appears to have had some involvement in political developments also. There is even a slight possibility that he was influential in the abandonment of Andronicus in favor of Manuel in the 1370's.[103]

99. Cantacuzenus, IV, 49, pp. 356–360; cf. Meyendorff, "Projets de concile oecuménique en 1367," 151.

100. Meyendorff, "Projets," 161–164.

101. Text, Baronius-Raynaldus, 1367, no. 8 (Vol. 26, pp. 144–145, written at the same time as those to John and his sons mentioned above, p. 9. Cf. Meyendorff, "Projets de concile oecuménique en 1367," 152; see also Halecki, *Un Empereur*, 167–168, and Berger de Xivrey, 34.

102. Text, Baronius-Raynaldus, 1375, nos. 2–3 (Vol. 26, pp. 246–247). This letter is part of a group including letters also to John V and to Manuel, who was by now "imperator" and is addressed as such. Cf. Halecki, *Un Empereur*, 309–311. Berger de Xivrey, who missed the significance of these appearances of Cantacuzenus, embarks on an extraordinary flight of imagination, pp. 40–42, n. 3, in which he concludes that Cantacuzenus accepted the invitation and did go to Rome (or wherever the Pope was). Halecki, *Un Empereur*, 311, lays this theory gently to rest and also points out the relationship of the invitation to Cydones and to the latter's trip. Cf. also Loenertz, *Echos d'Orient*, 36 (1937), p. 485, n. 4. It is a pity that Berger de Xivrey did not have as a source the *Chron. Barb. 111*, 26, where he would have found to his delight the statement that John V sent John Cantacuzenus to the West. But he could have gained little comfort from this passage in actuality, for it is an unbelievably jumbled confusion of the Western journeys of John V and Manuel II.

103. The Pseudo-Phrantzes, ed. Papadopoulos, p. 59, ll. 14–15, ed. Bonn, p. 54, ll. 16–17, in its account of Andronicus' supposed visit to Murad to obtain his aid in 1376, has Andronicus protest his and his son's claims by right of birth. "But," continues the prince's complaint (in indirect discourse) in this account, "the father and grandfather [πάππος] wishes to do them injury and to give [the throne], as we said, to the later-born [son]." Granted that this source is suspect and the entire episode unlikely. But the

We hear nothing of him during the usurpation of Andronicus IV, and perhaps he was left alone, as Cydones seems also to have been. But he could only have been regarded with suspicion, for he makes his next appearance as one of the captives—along with his daughters, including the Empress Helena—who were taken by Andronicus on his flight to Pera in 1379.[104]

The reasons for this situation are given in an important letter of Cydones to the Empress Helena herself.[105] In this letter, Cydones reminds the Empress of her suffering during the civil wars; how she was torn between her love for the contending members of her family, and how her pleas for those imprisoned were interpreted harshly as preference for them; how, after the escape of her husband and sons in 1379, she and her father were suspected of collusion in this and were therefore both seized and confined; and how in this state she had to endure grave discomforts and hardships amid barbarian jailers during the ensuing fighting, when Pera, to which they had been taken, was besieged. Plainly, then, Cantacuzenus and his daughter were arrested on suspicion—perhaps justified in this case, for all we know—of helping the prisoners to escape, and they were then held as hostages after the return of John V and his sons.[106] Presumably, they were

point here is how one translates the verb. If one takes the singular form of βούλεται at normal face value, one would assume a singular subject, John V, both as πατήρ of Andronicus and as πάππος of the future John VII. Such would be the usual reading. Yet, it is tempting to wonder if we might not take the sentence as involving a common Atticism, the use of a singular verb form for a plural subject. This would make Andronicus the sole pivot of relationships, with John V only as the πατήρ and with none other than Cantacuzenus himself as the πάππος. In all likelihood, the grammatical grounds for such an interpretation are too weak to allow it any real security. Still, even in the text of a sixteenth-century forger, there is perhaps some value in pointing out this tantalizing possibility, however slender.

104. *Chron. Vat. gr. 162,* no. 14, p. 209, ll. 57–58: "And the lord Andronicus, taking his consort, Maria, [his] grandfather [πάππον] Cantacuzenus and his mother Helene, departed to Galata."

105. C. 133 (No. 28), L. 222, which Loenertz, *Echos d'Orient,* 36 (1937), pp. 281–282, n. 8, and in his edition, dates after 1392. Manuel himself also read this missive, and in his own Letter χγ′ expresses his appreciation to Cydones for it.

106. Manuel, *Funeral Oration,* ed. Migne, 205D, ed. Lampros, p. 34, ll. 11–17, says that his brother Theodore refused to leave for his new realm in the Peloponnesus until "he should also see his mother, with her own father and her sisters, returned back home from their prison, in which they were held by the Latins." This is the only source which mentions the captivity of Helena's sisters; all the others speak only of her and her father.

not released until the truce of 1381, but, whenever it was, Cantacuzenus then returned to Constantinople.[107] We know that shortly thereafter John was in the Peloponnesus counseling his son, the Despot Matthew, for Cydones notes this in a letter written, apparently in 1381–82, to the latter, whom he also apprises of the coming of Theodore Palaeologus.[108] According to Manuel,[109] it was on the advice of John Cantacuzenus as well as on the invitation of Matthew that Theodore was urged to go to the Peloponnesus. John Cantacuzenus was in the Morea when he died, on June 15, 1383.[110] Only then did this brilliant and remarkable man finally depart from the stage of Byzantine history.[111]

Not long after the truce of May, 1381, the Chioggia War as a whole ended with the signing, on August 23, 1381, of the Treaty of Turin, drawn up under the aegis of Amadeo VI of Savoy.[112] By

107. *Chron. Vat. gr. 162*, no. 14, p. 209, ll. 59–60: "And soon, not long after, they made peace, Cantacuzenus returning to the City."
108. Letter C. 139 (No. 29), L. 241; Loenertz in his edition dates this text autumn of 1382.
109. *Funeral Oration*, ed. Migne, 208C, ed. Lampros, p. 36, ll. 2–4. On Cantacuzenus in the Morea at this time, see Loenertz, "Pour l'histoire du Péloponnèse au XIVe siècle," [*Rev. d.*] *Et. byz.*, 1 (1943), 162–165. D. A. Zakythinos, *Le Despotat grec de Morée*, I (Paris, 1932), 114 ff., while he notes the earlier Papal letter to Cantacuzenus, seems quite unaware of the former Emperor's final presence in the Morea with his son.
110. Βρ. χρ. No. 52, p. 89, ll. 50–51, ed. Müller, p. 393 (60), ll. 13–15; cf. Charanis, "An Important Short Chronicle," 358; also A. G. Mompherratos, Οἱ Παλαιολόγοι ἐν Πελοποννήσῳ (Athens, 1913), 6.
111. John Cantacuzenus is badly in need of a good up-to-date study. J. Parisot's *Cantacuzène, homme d'état et historien* (Paris, 1845) is now hopelessly inadequate, especially as he is totally unaware of this very period of Cantacuzenus' life after the mid-1360's. The myth of this restless man's "retirement" from public affairs after his abdication has most recently been perpetuated by Ostrogorsky, in *Cambr. Med. Hist.*, Vol. IV (2nd ed.), 1, p. 367.
112. The text in *Liber Iurium Reipublicae Genuensis*, II, no. 256, pp. 858–906, was not available to me; but there is another edition of the text, ed. S. Ljubić, in *Monumenta spectantia historiam slavorum meridionalium*, 4 (Zagreb, 1874), no. 241, pp. 119–163. The terms of the treaty were first drawn up in Buda, dated February 13, 1381 (p. 148); a congress of signatories convened in Turin on August 8 of that year (p. 119 ff.), and the actual signing of the treaty was dated August 23 (p. 163). (Many modern writers mistakenly give August 8 as the date of the signing: e.g., Muralt, p. 715, no. 10.) See pp. 132–133 of the Ljubić text for the section dealing with the question of the Byzantine throne. Cf. Dennis, 46–47; Thiriet, "Venise et l'occupation de Ténédos," 228–229; *id.*, *La Romanie vénitienne*, 178; Ostrogorsky, *Hist. Byz. St.*, 483–484 (whose statement of the year as 1382 is apparently a misprint: it is corrected in *Geschichte*, 3rd ed., 449); Vasiliev, *Hist. Byz. Emp.*, 627–628.

the terms of the Treaty, the Genoese and the Venetians were obliged to reconcile themselves to the respectively unpalatable aspects of the Byzantine internal settlement of the previous May; and the crucial problem of Tenedos was attended to by calling for the dismantling of its fortifications, the uprooting of its population, and the total abandonment of its use by either Genoa or Venice, while the island was to be neutralized under the supervision of the Count of Savoy himself.[113] The actual disputes between Byzantium and Genoa were finally settled in a treaty of November 2, 1382, which restored peace and imposed guarantees on the settlement of May, 1381.[114]

For our purposes this latter settlement is of greatest importance. The agreement of May, 1381, had two basic features. In the first place, Andronicus was removed from the explosive proximity of his family and was given an appanage which had Selymbria as its capital and which included further the towns of Daneion, Herakleia, Rhaidestos, and Panidos—thus forming a chain of coastal points along the Thracian shore of the Marmora. Thither Andronicus withdrew with his wife and son.[115] But the

113. The actual execution of these agreements regarding Tenedos is an elaborate story in itself. The Venetian *bailo* sent to supervise the matter, Zanachi Mudazzo, encouraged by the resistance of the islanders, delayed and hindered the fulfillment of the terms. Only after he had been brought to heel with the cooperation of Genoa and Savoy could the inhabitants of the island, in spite of their protests, be evacuated to Crete and Negroponte in the winter of 1383–84. For an exposition of the Venetian deliberation documents on this course of events, see Thiriet, *Régestes*, I, pp. 148–163. For further discussion of them and of the subject as a whole, see *id.*, "Venise et l'occupation de Ténédos," 229–237; cf. also Ostrogorsky, *Hist. Byz. St.*, 484. There were even several unsuccessful attempts on the part of the Byzantines to have the island restored to their authority: cf. Dölger, *Regesten*, no. 3178, p. 69, and Thiriet, *Régestes*, I, no. 637, p. 156 (January 26, 1383); and such discussion was to recur for several decades thereafter. The actual status of Tenedos, however, continued to be disputed among all parties involved, and there were movements in 1397 to refortify it, jointly or unilaterally, as a measure of defense against the Turks: *ibid.*, pp. 216–218 (nos. 924, 926, 928, and 931). At any rate, Venice continued to use the island herself to one extent or another, agreements to the contrary notwithstanding: cf. Thiriet, "Venise et l'occupation de Ténédos," 237–245; also, Heyd, I, 523–524.

114. Dölger, *Regesten*, no. 3177, pp. 68–69; text in Belgrano, no. 26, pp. 133–140; also in L. Sauli, *Storia della colonia dei Genovesi in Galata* (2 vols., Turin, 1831), II, no. XV, pp. 260–268. See Dennis, 50–51; also, Charanis, "Strife," 300; Gibbons, 162–163; Heyd, I, 524–525; Muralt, p. 719, no. 5 (who gives the date as November 4).

115. The only source to record this stipulation is Ducas, ed. Grecu, 73, ed. Bonn, 46. In spite of its location in the midst of this historian's fantastic

second feature of this settlement was even more crucial: the thirty-three-year-old Andronicus and his line were recognized as the legitimate successors to the throne. This represented a drastic step backward for John V and a relinquishing of his resolution of at least ten years to make Manuel his successor.[116]

As far as can be judged, Manuel was apparently serving with Murad at the time of the conclusion of the May, 1381, agreement, or just after it.[117] Therefore, he may well have been absent when the resettlement of the succession, so detrimental to him, was made. We have no way of knowing whether he was aware that this crucial alteration of his status was contemplated. Nor do we know what his reaction was when his new position, or loss of position, was made known to him in whatever fashion.[118] Indeed, almost every aspect of this important juncture in Manuel's life is shrouded in obscurity, thanks to a total lack of any clear information. But, for all we do not know and for all the questions yet unanswered, the facts that we can ascertain about Manuel's course of action speak volumes to us.

In our ignorance of so many of these events, we have no idea

jumble of the events of 1379–81, it seems to be well-founded and reliable in the light of our other knowledge. Dölger, "Johannes VII.," p. 26, n. 2, suggests that the statement by (the Pseudo-)Phrantzes, ed. Papadopoulos, 61, ed. Bonn, 56–57, that Andronicus received Thessalonica as a Despotate is a confusion with the later investment of his son John; it is probably also a confusion with Manuel's own son Andronicus, who was the Despot of Thessalonica in later years. For a discussion of the seat of the appanage, see F. Dirimtekin, "La Forteresse byzantine de Selymbria," *Actes du Xe Congrès Internationale d'Etudes Byzantines, 1955* (Istanbul, 1957), 127–129.

116. On this settlement in general, see Dennis, 45; Charanis, "Strife," 300; Dölger, "Johannes VII.," 26; Ostrogorsky, *Hist. Byz. St.*, 484.

117. Such is the apparently sound conclusion of Dennis, 47–49, on the basis of Cydones' Letters C. 132, L. 218; C. 138, L. 219; and C. 206, L. 220, which are dated by Loenertz to May–June of 1381. Also, Letter C. 365, L. 208 (which Loenertz can only date 1380–82), may well refer to the absence of Manuel (and not of John V, as the note by Loenertz in his edition, II, 86, suggests). Cydones himself seems to have been involved in some negotiations on Lesbos in this period: cf. Letter C. 404, L. 202; and, following that, Dölger, *Regesten*, no. 3173, p. 67 (dated 1382); also Dennis, "Short Chronicle of Lesbos," 11. In a group of short chronicle entries edited by M. Gedeon in Ἐκκλησιαστικὴ ἀλήθεια, 23 (1903), there is one (p. 382, φ. 162) which speaks of Manuel entering Constantinople on September 17 of the year 6890, eleventh indiction. This would be our year 1381, save for the fact that the Byzantine year 6890 was a *fifth*, not an eleventh, indiction year; and just why Manuel would be arriving then is difficult to say. In all likelihood the statement of year is defective, and this entry probably applies to a later time: see n. 175 and n. 179 below.

118. Cf. Dennis, 49.

what Manuel's status was to be in the light of the newest revision of the succession. It is not completely improbable that he
was intended to resume his former position as Despot of Thessalonica, but we can by no means be sure of this.[119] It seems

119. Dennis, 45–46, and also 79, concludes that Manuel was not intended
to return to Thessalonica, on the basis of two arguments: that when Manuel
did go there, (1) he had to leave for it secretly, and (2) he was not expected
there when he arrived. Both these arguments seem to be reasonably well
justified themselves as statements on the basis of fairly explicit sources. But
I am not so certain that "these two facts are inexplicable if Manuel, at the
time of the agreement of 1381, had by an express clause, or even by a tacit
understanding, recovered his rights to Thessalonica" (p. 46). The second
argument is by no means conclusive, since it could have been the specific
time of his arrival, and not the ultimate prospect of his coming at one point
or another, that was unexpected. The first argument is less easy to explain
away, but at the same time it proves nothing conclusively. It is not impossible, again, that it was intended for Manuel to go to Thessalonica, but not
so soon, and that his departure required secrecy because it was earlier than
his father had wished or envisioned.

Certainly, Thessalonica would be the logical place for Manuel, and one
is tempted to suspect such an intention also from the change in Theodore's
assignment from Thessalonica, to which he was supposed to go in 1376
(as noted above, p. 29), to the Morea, where he did go in 1382. It could be,
of course, that the urgency of the advice of Matthew and John Cantacuzenus,
of which Manuel speaks (see above, p. 40), impelled this change. But one
must always bear in mind that Manuel may simply have been trying to justify
with this statement Theodore's right to take over this long-time stamp'ng
ground of the Cantacuzeni. At any rate, it would seem that the date of this
transfer may have been about the time of the new settlement with Andronicus. For, at some time after his release from prison with his father and
brother, Theodore issued a *prostagma* in his capacity as Despot of Thessalonica. Although we cannot be certain of the exact date or circumstances of
this document, it must have been delivered between 1380 and 1382. On this
see Loenertz, "Un Prostagma perdu de Théodore Iᵉʳ Paléologue regardant
Thessalonique (1380/82?)," Ἐπ. Ἑτ. Βυζ. Σπουδ., 25 (1955), 170–172;
cf. Dennis, p. 42 and n. 69, for the other literature on this problem.

Thus, Theodore's transfer could have been decided upon at about the
same time as the deprivation of Manuel of his right to the succession—and
for only one reason. In view of the parceling out, deliberate or otherwise,
of the remaining segments of the Empire at this point to the various members
of the Imperial family, it is not unrealistic to think that Theodore was transferred to the Peloponnesus deliberately to make way for Manuel's return,
sooner or later, to Thessalonica.

But, amid all these problems, we simply do not know the true course of
events. On the basis of the scant material at hand, I would by no means
regard Dennis' interpretation as the only tenable one. He also suggests, as a
result of this speculation, that, if no particular compensation were set aside
to offset Manuel's loss of the promise of the throne, there might have been
some kind of personal conflict between Manuel and his father, as a background to this whole episode and as a preparation for the ill will of 1387.
This suggestion seems even more farfetched, for all its ingenuity. But, again,
we simply do not know.

fairly clear that he was back in Constantinople some time in the summer of 1382 and possibly at the time when the negotiations with the Genoese were under way.[120] It is certain that he was in the city when Theodore departed for the Morea, which seems likely to have been in autumn of 1382; for he himself describes the difficulty with which he and the rest of his family bade goodbye to his brother.[121] It was therefore apparently later in the

120. So Dennis, 50, concludes.

121. Manuel, *Funeral Oration,* ed. Migne, 208C, ed Lampros, p. 36, ll. 5–7; and, in the passage immediately following, Manuel reports Theodore's departure. The precise date of the young Despot's departure, however, is difficult to ascertain. Two of the short chronicles speak of his arrival in the Peloponnesus: Bρ. χρ. No. 27, p. 46, ll. 21–22 (p. 516, ll. 3–4, in the edition of the same text at the end of the Bonn edition of Ducas), puts it in the year 6896 (1387–88), while No. 19, p. 36, l. 16, places it in 6891 (1382–83). Loenertz has newly collated these two related texts, together with a third, in his synthesis published as "La Chronique brève moréote de 1423," in *Mélanges Eugène Tisserant,* Π (= *Studi e Testi,* 232, Vatican City, 1964), 399–439 (cited hereafter as "*Chron. br. mor.*"); these two passages are harmonized (No. 13, p. 406), with the discrepancy of date explained as an error, and with 6891 accepted as the right date. There is also a chronological entry quoted by G. Gerola, "L'effige del despoto Giovanni Cantacuzeno," *Byzantion,* 6 (1931), p. 385, n. 3; itself using the reckoning in years of the Christian Era, it gives Theodore's arrival as in 1381.

Chalcocondyles, ed. Darkó, I, 48, ed. Bonn, 52, relates (immediately after telling of John's vassalage to Murad in the early 1370's) that "afterwards" Theodore was sent to Peloponnesus to replace the dead son of Cantacuzenus; and that, on the way, Theodore stopped at Thessalonica, where Manuel was already established, and where the two brothers agreed on revolt against Murad. But no date is given, and in view of Chalcocondyles' general chronological confusion the whole statement is of little value especially since we have Manuel's own statement that he himself was in Constantinople when Theodore departed.

We have noted above (n. 106) Manuel's own reference to Theodore's desire to stay in Constantinople until his mother, aunts, and grandfather were released from captivity—which apparently came to pass in the spring of 1381—and until his father's situation was fully settled. He could have tarried on to await the completion of peace negotiations. In view of the fact that Cantacuzenus was in the Morea before Theodore, and in view of Manuel's apparent absence with Murad in 1381 or 1382, it is likely that Theodore did not leave until the autumn of 1382. Such is the conclusion of Loenertz, "Pour l'histoire du Péloponnèse," 163, and of Dennis, 43 and 58–59; cf. also his p. 115; and, most recently, Loenertz' commentary to his *Chron. br. mor.,* pp. 418–420. But it might well be noted this dating remains extensively conjectural. Mompherratos, Παλ. ἐν Πελ., 6, and Zakythinos, *Le Despotat grec,* I, 119 and 125, ignore the question of when Theodore arrived and simply reckon his reign as having begun in 1383. Loenertz assigns the date 1382–83 to Cydones' Letter C. 188, L. 251, to Theodore, praising the latter for his success in the Morea. Cf. also C. 190, L. 425.

autumn of 1382 [122] that Manuel left the city—suddenly, it would seem, unexpectedly, and in secrecy.[123] His destination was Thessalonica, and, being able upon his arrival to secure the obedience of this city,[124] he thereupon began his second period of rule there.

It was a strikingly different rule from Manuel's earlier one in the 1370's, and its importance as a phase in the course of his life cannot be underestimated.[125] In the earlier period, Manuel held

122. This is the conclusion of Dennis, 57–60, who suggests the time just before or just after the signing of the treaty of November 2, 1382. In view of what sources can be marshaled at this moment, it is as sound as is possible for the present. Dennis' interpretations and chronology for this episode are followed closely by Khoury, 135.

123. That Manuel left secretly, as well as unexpectedly, was the conclusion of Loenertz, *Echos d'Orient*, 36 (1937), 476, and was accepted by Charanis, "Strife," 301. Dennis, 60, asserts this, primarily on the somewhat vague but reasonably tenable basis of allusions by Cydones in Letters C. 420, L. 203; C. 220, L. 243; and C. 105, L. 247, all written to Manuel in Thessalonica, and which Loenertz dates either to the autumn of 1382 (perhaps a bit early) or to autumn and winter 1382–83. Cydones' Letter C. 186, L. 214, may possibly relate to this period also. Dennis, 108, also makes clear his interpretation of Manuel's departure as a definite demonstration of his displeasure with the settlement of 1381–82.

124. Cydones makes this plain in his Letter C. 105, L. 247, ed. Loenertz, II, p. 150, ll. 12–15, which Dennis, 62–63, also translates; cf. Dennis, 61, who emphasizes what he considers the extra-legal nature of Manuel's assumption of power in Thessalonica, which, of course, presupposes that he was not duly assigned to it by his father (see n. 119, above).

125. This entire episode has formerly been the source of much confusion, primarily as a result of the short and garbled accounts of the Greek sources. The *Chron. Barb. 111*, 26, in spite of its questionable character, places the episode correctly in chronological context, though it is inaccurate in some details. But this text, for what it is worth, has only recently been published and had not been used by former modern writers, who were dependent on the standard Greek historians. Of these, while Ducas ignores the whole episode, Chalcocondyles, ed. Darkó, I, 42 and 48, ed. Bonn, 46 and 52, relates the events in a context that would seem to place them in the 1370's. Confused by this, the Pseudo-Phrantzes, ed. Papadopoulos, 52–54, ed. Bonn, 47–49, makes the episode Manuel's first appearance in history, placing the events before those of Andronicus' revolt of 1373, which is in turn placed before John's journey to Italy—quite a stretch of the imagination! This chronological hash misled many modern writers at first, including Berger de Xivrey, 26–30; Hammer, 165–166; Muralt, p. 701, no. 16; Gibbons, 151–152; and, to a lesser extent, O. Tafrali, *Thessalonique au 14e siècle* (Paris, 1913), 281–285. Only in the work of more recent scholars, most notably Loenertz, in general, and such others as Charanis (e.g., "Strife," 300–301) and Lemerle (*Philippes*, 217–219), has the proper place of this episode begun to emerge clearly. Now, with the appearance of Dennis' important work, we at last have a deservedly careful account. Especially in its pp. 53–155 will the student of

the city as the legal and faithful deputy of his father, bearing only the noncommittal title of Despot. And even later, on through the civil wars of 1376–81, everything Manuel did was as a loyal and devoted son, completely identified with the interests of his father and—barring the minor exception of his richly appreciated aid to John during the latter's detention in Venice in 1370–71— apparently with little or no personal initiative of his own. Not only did he display emphatic initiative now, but also blunt independence. Retaining the prerogatives of the title of *Basileus* and of issuing chrysobulls,[126] he reigned as if he were an independent sovereign in his own right. Indeed, his course of action amounted to a virtual defiance of his father.

This fact is most clearly evident in the basic sphere of his external policy and principal activity. John, as a vassal of the Emir, was committed by definition to peace and amity with the Turks. Quite on the contrary, Manuel's conduct from the outset was based on overt hostility to the Turks.

Manuel's ultimate aims are difficult to discern, but his immediate goal seems to have been the re-establishment of Byzantine authority over Macedonia and Thessaly.[127] One cannot but admire his boldness—if not his rashness—in the face of the growing might of the Turks, who clearly would not tolerate any pushing back of their own tide of conquest. But, in spite of this danger, Manuel's moves were crowned with initial success. From a few letters of Cydones we can follow how, apparently not very

this epoch find the most thorough and extensive discussion of it. The only course possible here is to summarize the bulk of his findings and acknowledge freely the debt to him.

126. For a discussion of the chrysobulls which Manuel issued in this period, see Dennis, 99–102; cf. Dölger, *Regesten*, nos. 3173a, 3175a, 3175b, 3180a, and 3181c, pp. 68–70. In the light of Dennis' work, however, see the subsequent comments of Ostrogorsky, *Geschichte* (3rd ed.), pp. 450–451, and n. 4; of Vakalopoulos, *A History of Thessaloniki*, trans. T. F. Carney (Thessalonica, 1963), 62–63; and of Khoury, pp. 135–137.

127. At least part of such an aim would seem to have been achieved, nominally, at any rate, through diplomatic means; for, early in his reign, Manuel secured submission and recognition of Byzantine suzerainty from Alexius Angelus, the Caesar of Thessaly, and the same also from Thomas Preljubović, the Despot of Epirus. Whatever superficial and theoretical value these steps may have had, they apparently never provided Manuel with any practical advantage or support. For discussion of these matters, see Loenertz, "Notes sur le règne de Manuel II à Thessalonique—1381/82–1387," *Byz. Zeitschr.*, 50 (1957), 390–394; and Dennis, 103–108; also, Vakalopoulos, 'Ιστ. τ. ν. ἑλλ., I, 162–165.

Figure 3: *View of the Land Walls of Thessalonica, from the Outside* (photo courtesy Boissonnas, Geneva; see Appendix XXIV, C, 2, a).

long after Manuel's arrival in Thessalonica, news began to trickle in of this success.[128]

The principal effect of his victories, presumably in the late fall and early winter of 1382, was twofold. In the first place, the important Macedonian town of Serres was fully restored to Byzantine control.[129] Secondly, the mere occurrence of Byzantine

128. Dennis, 61–64, projects this picture splendidly on the basis of Cydones' Letters C. 220, L. 243; C. 411, L. 244; C. 105, L. 247; and C. 304, L. 249; with translations of extensive passages.

129. The accounts of Chalcocondyles and the Pseudo-Phrantzes portray this as the seizure, or attempted seizure, of a town already in Turkish hands, and most previous modern writers have accepted this. Thus, Loenertz, *Echos d'Orient*, 36 (1937), 278 and 478. Formidable arguments for the occupation of this city by the Turks prior to 1382 are presented by F. Taeschner and P. Wittek, "Die Vezirfamilie der Gandarlyzāde (14./15. Jhdt.) und ihre

victory over Turks sent a thrill through the spirits of those—from Cydones himself down to the humblest Macedonian refugee— who had previously known only the despair of Turkish triumph and the humiliation of Byzantine submission. Over the winter and on into the spring of 1383 a stream of enthusiastic volunteers seems to have poured into Thessalonica to join Manuel's brave counterblow against the enemy.[130] With the support now of these greatly augmented forces, Manuel renewed operations, and during the campaign season of 1383, he was able to achieve at

Denkmäler," *Der Islam*, 18 (1929), pp. 72–73, n. 1, on the basis of Turkish sources; and by Lemerle, *Philippes*, 214–219, on the basis of Greek sources. But Dennis, 65–68, partly with the help of passages in Cydones' letters cited above, argues that this important fortress had simply been under continued siege and that Manuel was able to relieve it, not seize it. In his review of Dennis' study for *Speculum*, 36 (1961), 476, Charanis has challenged Dennis' conclusions on this point, reasserting the former interpretation of an actual Turkish capture and a full recapture by Manuel. Most recently, Ostrogorsky, "La Prise de Serrès par les Turcs," *Byzantion*, 35 (1965), 302–319, has argued in detail that Serres was never taken by the Turks in the period of 1371–83, and that they acquired it at no time before their documented capture of it on September 19, 1383. There the controversy rests at the moment, and it would seem best to assume no more than a relief, and not a reconquest, of the town by Manuel in 1382. In general on Serres, there is a book by E. G. Strates, Ἱστορία τῆς πόλεως Σερρῶν ἀπὸ τῶν ἀρχαιοτάτων χρόνων μέχρι τῶν καθ' ἡμᾶς . . . (Serrai, 1926), which was unavailable to me and whose usefulness I therefore cannot judge. More recently, however, there is Ostrogorsky's new general study on the city in the post-Dušan epoch, *Serska oblast posle Dušanove smrti* (*Posebna izdanja Vizantološkog instituta*, 9, Belgrade, 1965), supplemented by H. Miakotine's "Analyse de l'ouvrage de G. Ostrogorski sur la Principauté serbe de Serrès," in *Centre de recherche d'histoire et civilisation byzantines, Travaux et mémoires*, 2 (Paris, 1967), 569–573.

In addition, since the foregoing was written, there has appeared the study by I. Beldiceanu-Steinherr, "La Prise de Serrès et le Firman de 1372 en faveur du monastère de Saint-Jean-Prodrome," *Acta historica*, 4 (1965), 15–24, which, in effect, seconds Ostrogorsky's argument on this point by asserting that the document mentioned in her title is a forgery and that there is consequently no reliable documentation for an Osmanli occupation of Serres before 1383.

130. Dennis, 64, 70–72. Noteworthy among the sources indicating this influx is Cydones' Letter C. 395, L. 250, written supposedly in the spring or summer of 1383, recommending to Manuel one Theodore Cantacuzenus, who was eager to join the venture in Thessalonica: cf. Dennis, 71–72, with partial translation. Cf. also Letter C. 418, L. 248, for reflections on the extent of the emigration to Manuel. Further, see C. 219, L. 259, for an additional example of Cydones' hope in the significance of Manuel's actions for restoring "the freedom of the race of the Romans." Cf. Dennis, 70.

least one naval victory and another combined land and sea victory over the Turks.[131]

But the flush of victory was short-lived, and within a scant year the tide was turning. Once the Turkish military machine was fully set in motion even Manuel's bravest efforts could be no match for it, especially under the leadership of the formidable Khairaddin Pasha, whom Murad sent to subdue his rebellious Byzantine vassal.[132] By the end of the summer the Turkish counteroffensive had gathered thrust, and on September 19, 1383, the fortress of Serres—significantly, the focus of Manuel's first victories—was taken.[133] Following this there soon came another Greek defeat at a place called Chortiatou.[134] In the letters of Cydones we can follow the rapid plunge of Manuel's fortunes.[135] And, as the final months of the year drew on, the last and longest phase of Manuel's reign in Thessalonica began, commencing with

131. Dennis, 72–73, on the basis of a statement by Manuel himself, in the text, ed. B. Laourdas in " 'Ο «Συμβουλευτικὸς πρὸς τοὺς Θεσσαλονίκεις» τοῦ Μανουὴλ Παλαιολόγου," Μακεδονικά, 3 (1955), p. 300, ll. 23–32; and of Cydones' Letter C. 226, L. 312.

132. See Taeschner and Wittek, 73 ff.; cf. Dennis, 73–74. Chalcocondyles calls him Χαρατίνης (as does Cydones in his Letter C. 250, L. 318); the Pseudo-Phrantzes calls him Καραλί-πασιᾶ, and the *Chron. Barb. 111*, Καράπασα: cf. Moravcsik, *Byzantinoturcica*, II, 337 and 151; also A. Nimet, *Die türkische Prosopographie bei Laonikos Chalkokandyles* (Dissertation, Hamburg, 1933), 84–85.

133. The same precise date is given with unusual unity by no less than five of the short chronicles: Βρ. χρ. No. 16, p. 33, l. 5; No. 20, p. 37, l. 4; No. 21, p. 38, l. 5; No. 22, p. 41, l. 1; No. 32, p. 61, l. 1; also, the year is given by No. 48, p. 83, l. 9; and a false dating, 6926 (1417–18), is given by No. 28, p. 53, l. 23. Cf. Dennis, 6 and 75; and Charanis, "An Important Short Chronicle," 360; see also Ostrogorsky, "La Prise de Serrès par les Turcs," cited in n. 129 above.

134. Dennis, 75–76.

135. In Letter C. 418, L. 248 (Partial translation, Dennis, 74–75), written presumably in late summer 1383, Cydones expressed to Rhadenos, his former pupil and now the friend and counselor of Manuel, his concern over the increasing "storm" threatening the large Byzantine commitment in the Thessalonian venture. In C. 168, L. 289 (partial translation, Dennis, 75), Cydones laments specifically and by name the disasters of Serres and Chortiatou and despairs for Manuel amid such distress. Cf. Loenertz, *Echos d'Orient*, 36 (1937), 478. Further, in C. 148, L. 282, Cydones bewails at length the trials and sorrows of his "fatherland," Thessalonica. Cammelli had suggested that this letter referred to the situation after the Serres disaster, and Loenertz himself seems to agree by dating the letter to the autumn of 1383. Cf. similarly Letter C. 350, L. 272, to an unspecified friend, in the same tone; and, more vaguely, C. 356, L. 276, to Manuel.

the investment of the city itself by Khairaddin in the autumn of 1383.[136]

Manuel's activities in Thessalonica must have been a bitter blow to his miserable father. We know from at least one letter by Cydones that the rush of volunteers to Thessalonica was viewed at court with great disfavor, and that the mere suspicion that someone was going to join Manuel was a grave matter.[137] Certainly Manuel's performance, especially the more successful it was, put John in an awkward position in view of his and his Empire's (and therefore Manuel's) obligations of vassalage to the Turks.[138] John's whole policy since his reversal after the Battle of the Marica had been built on the assumption that the only hope for Byzantium's survival, at least for some time, was in appeasement of the Turks. All things considered, this view was probably correct, and the turn of the tide against Manuel only seemed to prove it, particularly with the serious threat it came to pose against the important city of Thessalonica.

John's indubitable anger over these events might have been mitigated if his own situation at home had settled down as originally hoped. But he was to be bitterly disappointed here, also. The disaffection of Manuel had been the price of the settlement of 1381. But, not only had this settlement driven the cheated Manuel into defiance, it had not even satisfied its chief beneficiary, Andronicus IV. By abandoning Manuel, John lost his one buttress, only to be left doubly exposed. For the restless Andronicus refused to remain satisfied with the settlement of 1381.

Soon after the departure of Manuel for Thessalonica, Cydones had foreseen the difficulty. He wrote to Manuel that there was greater need than ever for the latter in the capital—this, in view of the continued quarrels, undoubtedly of the two Emperors,

136. See Dennis, p. 76 and n. 66, for an establishment of the dating of the siege. On the siege in general, see also Vakalopoulos, Ἱστ. τ. ν. ἑλλ., I, 166–168.

137. In Letter C. 90, L. 264, which Loenertz dates in summer of 1383, Cydones warns his friend John Asanes that in his absence the latter's enemies, seeking to slander him before John V, have been accusing him of intending to go to "the new empire"—that is, Manuel's independent venture—in Thessalonica. Plainly, this must have been a serious charge and, as Dennis, 59, suggests, shows that such intentions must have been fairly common. See also Dennis, 109.

138. Cf. Dennis, 63–64 and 108–109.

father and son.[139] We have no precise information on the relationship between John and Andronicus during this period, but that
it must have involved friction and bitterness is clearly shown
when, apparently in the spring of 1385, open hostilities broke
out. Desiring a fortress outside his enclave, Andronicus sent his
son to Murad to request it. Either failing in this effort or not
awaiting its resolution, Andronicus moved on his own initiative,
seizing the fortress near the town of Melitias, perhaps the very
one he had requested. John must have viewed this as something
more than an isolated move of aggression, for he personally led
out a force to retaliate. There was a fierce battle which finally
turned against Andronicus, who withdrew to Selymbria.[140]

In two letters written soon after this episode, Cydones laments
this shameful "rebellion" which, he says, would not have taken
place had Manuel been home. He also mentions John's narrow escape from death in battle, with God's aid.[141] It was, however,

139. Letter C. 420, L. 203, ed. Loenertz, II, pp. 80–81, ll. 20–24. In
C. 220, L. 243, Cydones comments more generally on the dangerous and
unpleasant circumstances in the city. Loenertz dates both to the autumn of
1382. Cf. Dennis, 60. Muralt, p. 728, no. 3, on vague authority, speaks of
Genoese attempts to reconcile John V with his son.

140. Βρ. χρ. No. 15, p. 32, ll. 23–25, names the town and describes the
conflict; it gives no date, but says that it occurred "in a few days" before
Andronicus' final illness and death. There is a fascinating if fragmentary
postscript appended to the text of the treaty of November 2, 1382, published
in Belgrano, 139–140, and reedited by Loenertz, "Fragment d'une lettre de
Jean V Paléologue à la commune de Gênes, 1387–1391," *Byz. Zeitschr.*, 51
(1958), 37–38, which recounts the same events and adds information about
the mission of Andronicus' son to the Turks, all from the fragment of what
is plainly part of a bill of complaint to the Genoese by John V himself. See
Loenertz' own comments, "Fragment d'une lettre," 39–40, and Dennis,
109–110. Dölger, "Johannes VII.," 26, thinks that the reference to the future
John VII may actually imply the obtaining of an appanage for him. He also
takes seriously a statement—which is not in (the Pseudo-)Phrantzes, as he
says, but in Chalcocondyles, ed. Darkó, I, 58, ed. Bonn, 64—that Andronicus
and his son dwelt "for two years" at the Turkish Porte. But this statement
does not in its context merit acceptance, unless to indicate vaguely that
Andronicus, while ruling from Selymbria, was apparently dependent upon
Murad's support.

141. Letter C. 118, L. 308, speaks of the conflict in terms general enough
so that it might well have been written before the news of the actual battle
at Melitias. But C. 125, L. 309, specifically mentions the battle and John V's
preservation through it, curiously enough, in words very similar to those
describing the same thing in the Genoese document cited previously. Cf.
Dennis, 110–111, who translates all of the first letter and part of the second.
See also Loenertz, *Echos d'Orient*, 36 (1937), 477–478, and *id.*, "Fragment

Andronicus, all of thirty-seven years of age, who did not long survive this latest conflict. A short time after his defeat, he fell ill in his capital of Selymbria and died on Wednesday, June 28, 1385.[142]

From John V's point of view, the revolt of Andronicus and the continued defiance of his son, John (VII), with the support of the Genoese,[143] would thus have voided the treaties of 1381 and 1382 and, with them, the restored succession of Andronicus and his line. These events by themselves, then, would have automatically left the way clear for the succession of Manuel. But the situation had been vastly complicated by Manuel's independent action in Thessalonica and its inevitable outcome. We cannot be certain what definite plans John V made for the succession after 1385, but, if events will show that he was to retain the idea of passing it on to Manuel, they will also reveal the great degree of bitterness, disillusionment, and damage which Manuel's enterprise brought to all parties involved—except, of course, to the Turks.

The key to the problem was the fate of Thessalonica as a result of Manuel's actions. The siege was to be a long one. Apparently in the fall of 1383, at the outset of the Turkish investment of Thessalonica, Khairaddin issued an ultimatum to the Thessalonians, to choose between tribute on one hand or pillage and massacre by the Turkish army on the other.[144] Manuel, whose

d'une lettre," pp. 39–40 and n. 8. Note also, in general terms, Cydones' Letter C. 275, L. 306, which Loenertz dates to some time in 1385, before the death of Andronicus.

142. Βϱ. χϱ. No. 15, p. 32, ll. 25–27, gives the date as June 8, but this may be a confusion with the indiction number of the year, which is also 8; but No. 52, p. 89, ll. 29–40, ed. Müller, p. 392 (59), ll. 25–27, gives the full, and correct, date now accepted by scholars; cf. Muralt, p. 274, no. 20. This date is verified by two other short chronicle notices, as published by M. Gedeon ('Εκκλησιαστικὴ ἀλήθεια, 23, 1903), p. 381 (φ. 108) and p. 382 (φ. 141), both giving the same date in full (save for the day of the week), the latter with exaggerated expressions of praise. (The first of these two Gedeon entries is cited by Amantos in his preface to the Βϱ. χϱ., p. ϑ'; also in the comments of Dennis, pp. 111–112 and n. 25, and by Charanis, "An Important Short Chronicle," 355. All of these short chronicles, except Gedeon's first one, state that Andronicus was buried in the Monastery of the Pantokrator in Constantinople. For confusion in a different source regarding the place of his burial, see Appendix VII below.

143. For the subsequent activities of John VII from this time on, see below, p. 69 ff.

144. Dennis, 78–79.

position in this city of obstinately independent citizens seems to have been a good deal less than absolute, took the occasion to draw up and present an elaborate *Discourse of Counsel to the Thessalonians When They Were Besieged*. In this document he pointed out that the real alternatives they faced were total subjection to the Turks or total destruction by the Turks: he urged the citizens to be willing to fight for their freedom, but also to place hope in some sort of negotiations with the Turks.[145] Whatever negotiations may have been carried on by Manuel with the Turks are unknown to us, and, from the silence of the sources and the course of events as they came to pass, we can only conclude that if there were any they came to nothing.[146]

Manuel seems to have been able to keep in check, at least for a while, any misgivings his subjects may have had, and together they settled down to the protracted beleaguerment. From the period of this siege we have a number of letters by Cydones to Manuel, reflecting the former's growing concern about the dangers the siege posed to Manuel and to Byzantium.[147] Manuel

145. The full text is available to us as edited by Laourdas, " 'Ο «Συμβουλευτικὸς πρὸς τοὺς Θεσσαλονίκεις» τοῦ Μανουὴλ Παλαιολόγου," Μακεδονικά, 3 (1955), 295–302. An excellent synopsis of the text is given by Dennis, 81–84, who also discusses its circumstances and contents, 79–81 and 84–85; cf. Khoury, 136. Loenertz, "Notes sur le règne," 394–396, had attempted to date this *Discourse* at the time of Manuel's arrival, in 1381/82 [*sic*], but the acceptance by Dennis (who ignores this unlikely supposition) of autumn 1383 is not only convincing but might also seem to imply the approval now of Loenertz himself. For further discussion of the dating, see Laourdas' own comments, 290–293. Manuel sent a copy of this work to Cydones, accompanied by his letter ια'. This letter contains some interesting reflections on the *Discourse* and is translated below in another context, pp. 415–416. It was answered by the glowing praises of Cydones in his own Letter C. 187, L. 262. Cf. Dennis, 79–80, who translates a passage from the latter; and, on this exchange in general, Loenertz, *Echos d'Orient*, 37 (1938), 113–114.

146. See Dennis, 85. It is possible that some aspects of such negotiations may be reflected in some later references: see below, pp. 56–57 and n. 156.

147. Letter C. 221, L. 283, is in general terms, expressing concern over the woes of his country and offering a prayer for Manuel. In C. 141 (No. 41), L. 291, Cydones voices his unhappiness over being unable to forget his friend, surrounded by enemies. In C. 213 (No. 48), L. 299, he concerns himself more with the hardships of Thessalonica itself, citing Biblical and Classical parallels, and offering the assurance that its Protector, St. Demetrius, will save it. For a partial translation of this last letter, see Dennis, 77–78. Cammelli, in his edition of this last text, claims that it refers to a supposed siege in the 1390's—on which, see Appendix II below—but Loenertz,

himself could not remain idle, however, and, in one of his letters to a subordinate of the Emperor, Cydones asks him to pass the letter on to Manuel unless he is too busy with his concerns for the defense of the city.[148] But in addition to his cares for the defenses and his administrative needs,[149] the Emperor involved himself in elaborate diplomatic activity.

One of the Emperor's first attempts to win allies and support for himself in his increasingly threatened position was an alliance with his brother Theodore and Nerio Acciajuoli (then Lord of Corinth) against common enemies. While Manuel cooperated to the extent of sending a contingent of his cavalry to aid Theodore in 1385, the alliance seems to have brought little advantage or

Echos d'Orient, 36 (1937), 482–483, disposes of that suggestion, and in his own edition dates it himself 1383–86.

In C. 276, L. 80, Cydones is still praying for divine help to Manuel, but his anxiety seems to be much stronger. Grave concern also shows clearly in a letter of similar tone, C. 212, L. 320, which Loenertz dates 1383–84, winter–spring. Then, in C. 167 (No. 39), L. 273, written to someone other than Manuel, Cydones is gravely alarmed over Manuel's situation, which is such, says the writer, that his friend does not know what to do. Plainly foreseeing disaster in the future, Cydones insists that Manuel's failure is the result of factors not his fault, and that the young Emperor deserves praise for what he has tried to do. A passage from this letter is translated by Dennis, 119 and 162. This letter is interesting also because it contains a specific reference to the death of Francesco Gattilusio of Lesbos, which occurred on August 6, 1384: see Miller, "The Gattilusij of Lesbos," 411 (319); also Dennis, "Short Chronicle of Lesbos," 13. The letter, therefore, was written after this date, and Loenertz in his edition goes so far as to date it August, 1384.

A good insight into the rush of refugees, who—reversing the previous influx in the phase of success—were deserting Thessalonica now that the tide had turned, is provided by C. 150, l. 324. In it Cydones writes to Rhadenos, urging him to escape also. Cf. Dennis, 97–98. In general terms, note also Letter C. 306, L. 271.

There is also one problematical letter connected with this period. With C. 61 (No. 7), L. 328, Cydones, in writing to a friend in Thessalonica, encloses a translation of some work to be used to combat something. In his edition of the text Cammelli dates the letter to 1354 and considers the something to be combated to be the doctrines of Palamas, suggesting further that the text might have been by Barlaam. But Loenertz in his own edition thinks the something is Islam (specifically, the Koran) and the work one by Ricoldus, dating the letter to 1386. Certainly the latter dating is more reliable than Cammelli's, in view of the letter's location in the manuscripts. At least we are safe in assuming that, whatever its concerns, it does date from the period of the 1383–87 siege.

148. Letter C. 286, L. 329; cf. Dennis, p. 97, n. 49.

149. For a good discussion of some aspects of Manuel's administration in Thessalonica, see Dennis, 96–102.

aid to him.[150] Realizing the need for something more, Manuel and also Theodore turned to Venice. An emissary was dispatched on behalf of both with requests for military and financial aid, which the Senate heard and in effect rejected on April 18, 1385. The Senate did, however, entertain sympathetically Manuel's corollary request that Venice use her good offices to effect a peace, or at least a truce, between the Emperor and Murad.[151] But nothing seems to have come of such promises.

While no more productive of any help to Manuel, the most interesting of Manuel's diplomatic activities at this time are those involving Pope Urban VI. In spite of the handicap from which he suffered as a result of the Great Schism of 1378, the Roman Pope maintained a genuine interest in continuing the work toward a union of the Churches. He was therefore readily receptive when Manuel made overtures to him in hopes of winning Western aid by means of this elusive procedure. At the end of winter in 1385 an embassy was sent from Thessalonica to Italy.

We are completely ignorant of its activity, but it must have been fruitful to some extent, for a little more than one year later a Papal legate was sent East. By mistake the legate went first to Constantinople, and there he received a decidedly chilly reception. He moved on to his main destination, however, and by the autumn of 1386 was in Thessalonica. We have no specific evidence of any agreement or performance or even of Manuel's own personal bearing in the matter. But there is at least a possibility that some sort of union, at least of the Church at Thessalonica, was concluded with the Latin Church. Manuel's position may well have been so desperate that he was willing to agree to almost anything. Yet, whatever aid any such step was supposed to bring him never appeared, and this latest attempt to induce western support for the oppressed Byzantines through this ecclesiastical maneuver was a complete fiasco.[152] With this

150. See Dennis, 114 ff., especially 119–123, for a good account of this alliance and its course. See also Vakalopoulos, 'Ιστ. τ. ν. ἑλλ., I, 155.

151. The text of this important deliberation is published by Dennis, 163–164, and also on pp. 437–438 of Vol. II of Loenertz' edition of Cydones' correspondence; cf. Thiriet, *Régestes*, I, p. 168, no. 693; and Dölger, *Regesten*, no. 3181b, p. 70. For the best summary of this negotiation and its implications, see Dennis, 123–126.

152. Dölger, *Regesten*, no. 3181a, p. 70, for Manuel's embassy to Rome. For the entire course of these involved negotiations, see Dennis, 136–150,

failure also came the end of Manuel's diplomatic efforts to secure support for, if not survival in, his position in Thessalonica—all fruitless.[153]

Meanwhile, the situation of Thessalonica had become increasingly difficult. There continued to be some efforts to come to terms with the Turks. While, as noted,[154] we are ignorant of any specific embassy to Khairaddin or to Murad himself which Manuel may have sent when the siege began, there may be some reflection of such things in references, in letters of both Cydones and Manuel himself, to Murad's treachery and false promises.[155] Following the apparent failure of Manuel's effort of 1385 to induce the mediation of Venice, the initiative was taken up by his father. At some point in this or the following year, John V sent a representative to attempt negotiations between the Turks and

who is forced to rely heavily upon a number of letters by Cydones, which he marshals and enumerates fully, often giving translations of extensive passages. In spite of the limited evidence, Dennis concludes explicitly that there was an actual agreement of union. But it is perhaps unwise to be so positive on this point. Charanis (in *Speculum*, 36, 1961, p. 476) stresses that the inconclusive evidence in Cydones' letters is insufficient foundation for Dennis' emphatic assertions. More recently, and apparently only on the basis of Dennis, Vakalopoulos, 'Ιστ. τ. ν. ἑλλ., I, 166, has asserted also that Thessalonica accepted union with Rome; but this scholar has ignored the dangers of this issue; cf. again the comments of Charanis, *The American Historical Review*, 67, 2 (1962), 686–687. Aside from Cydones' letters there are few other documents for this episode, since the all-important Papal Registers for Urban VI are missing for most of the period of 1383–86: see Halecki, "Rome et Byzance au temps du grand schisme d'Occident," *Collectanea theologica*, 18 (1937), 477–481. On pp. 481–494 of this article, Halecki attempts to review the Papal relations with the East during the incumbency of Urban VI (1378–1379), but he does not seem to be aware of the Thessalonian project. Indeed, on p. 496, he goes so far as to deny that Manuel ever had any intention of emulating John V's actions of the 1360's. At best, the problem remains mysterious and uncertain.

153. To this discussion of Manuel's diplomatic contacts during this period should be added the brief and—in this context, at least—very minor incident of a protest by the King of Aragon, Peter IV, to Manuel over the seizure of property of a Catalan merchant in Thessalonica. The text of Peter's letter may be found in A. Rubió y Lluch, *Diplomatari de l'Orient Catalá (1301–1409)* (Barcelona, 1947), no. 598, pp. 634–635. For a thorough analysis of the affair, see Dennis, 130–131; cf. Dölger, *Regesten*, no. 3183a, p. 71 (where the King is identified as Peter III).

154. See above, p. 53 and n. 146.

155. Cydones' Letter C. 402, L. 285, apparently to Rhadenos and assigned to autumn of 1385; and Manuel's Letter η′ to Cydones, written perhaps at the time of the Papal embassy, 1385–86; cf. Dennis, 128–129.

Manuel.[156] But we know nothing of any results from this step.

By the turn of the year 1387, it must have become evident to all parties that the loss of Thessalonica was imminent, and in both Constantinople and Thessalonica steps were taken to deal with this eventuality. In the capital, John's bitterness over the behavior of his son—whatever may have been his own role in provoking it—and over its results was coming to a head. At a time when Manuel was needed by John as his heir and as the buttress to his throne in his old age and feebleness, it must have been all the more galling for him to witness Manuel's reckless independence and near rebellion.

Faced with the likelihood of losing the second city of his realm—all the more important in view of the Empire's dwindling territory—John held his son in disgrace and even went so far as to consider drawing up a formal, written reprimand of his son. Still important in court circles, Cydones expressed the hope, in a letter to a monastic friend ascribed to the spring of 1387, that he himself would not be called upon to draft it, as he had drafted a quite different document for Manuel previously—that is, in 1371–72.[157]

Meanwhile, Manuel himself was preparing for the worst. In his efforts to decide on a course of action, he wrote to his old master and friend for advice. Cydones replied, first revealing that John V had held a meeting of advisers on Manuel's fate; but, since Cydones himself had been excluded as a partisan of Manuel, he was ignorant of its deliberations or decisions. He then points out three courses which Manuel might follow: to go to the Peloponnesus, to go to the West, or to return to Con-

156. Dölger, *Regesten*, no. 3181, p. 70, and Dennis, 129, both on the basis of Cydones' Letter C. 250, L. 318. Does John's embassy suggest the possibility of any last shred of good relations between father and son? Or was it simply the old Emperor's effort to try to salvage something for the good of his realm? Dennis, 129–130, also points out the possibility of a reference in Letter C. 154, L. 335, to a further attempt by Manuel himself, in a trip out of the city, to negotiate in person with the Turks. But, as he admits, it is impossible to make this interpretation with any certainty. Indeed, as one reads in it Cydones' warning that all may be lost and that the addressee, Rhadenos, should himself flee, the whole text becomes the more puzzling. Cf. Loenertz, *Echos d'Orient*, 37 (1938), 110 and 115–116, who by no means exhausts the problem.

157. Letter C. 119, L. 346; cf. Dennis, 112, 152. For this document of 1371/72, see above, p. 14 and n. 36.

stantinople. Rejecting the first two, which would only bring Manuel to grief, Cydones urges the third course, asserting that John needs his son, would pardon him, and would restore him to the succession, requiring of his son only his disassociation from allegedly evil advisers.[158] (Such a rosy outlook, however, hardly tallies with Cydones' own description of the disgrace Manuel was in while John was contemplating a reprimand, as just mentioned.)

At about the same time, Cydones wrote another letter to Manuel's companion, Rhadenos, deploring the long-feared fall of his native city. He renews his warning that, if Manuel goes to the Peloponnesus, he will only fall into strife with his brother there, and he again rejects the course of flight to the West as an exile and outcast. Instead, he repeats his advice that Manuel should come to Constantinople trustingly, bringing only a reduced group of retainers to eliminate his bad advisers—and, we might suspect, to reduce the perhaps formidable strength of his following.[159] But Manuel's course, for uncertain reasons,[160] was not to follow Cydones' advice.

158. Letter C. 161 (No. 30), L. 342. Dennis, 113 and 151–153, gives a full analysis of this text with a partial translation. Cf. Charanis, "Strife," 301–302; and Loenertz, *Echos d'Orient*, 37 (1938), 115–118, who even goes so far as to suggest that this and the letter next cited were not sent. In his edition, Loenertz dates from this same period, spring 1387, Letter C. 258, L. 348, to Manuel, complaining that the woes of the nation prevent him from writing and bring him pain.

159. Letter C. 157 (No. 31), L. 332; see Dennis, 88 and 153–154, for analyses and partial translations; and Loenertz, *Echos d'Orient*, 37 (1938), 115–118. On the basis of this letter, Dölger, *Regesten*, no. 3185, p. 71, assumes an actual summons by John V to his son to return to Constantinople, which seems unwarranted. Dennis himself, 151, prudently notes the problem that the probable size and strength of Manuel's following must have posed. There must have been something to the talk of a possibility that Manuel might go to the Morea. For we have a deliberation of the Venetian Senate for June 1, 1387 (text, ed. Loenertz, p. 438 of Vol. II of his edition of Cydones' *Correspondance;* summary by Thiriet, *Régestes*, I, p. 175, no. 729), agreeing to provide transportation for Manuel and a suite of twenty to Constantinople from the Morea, should he be found there. For the knowledgeable Venetians to assume that Manuel might go to Constantinople at this point, and might be in the Morea in the first place, suggests food for thought. Cf. Dennis, p. 153, n. 4. On the basis of Cydones' warnings to Manuel against going to the Morea, Cammelli, in his edition of Letter C. 162 (No. 34), L. 275, has made the fantastic suggestion that this text refers to an actual arrival of Manuel there, and to a subsequent struggle with Theodore. This is in absolute defiance of both good sense and the sources. Loenertz, *Echos d'Orient*, 36 (1937), 272–273, puts this text where it belongs, about 1359–61,

The end soon came for Thessalonica. On Saturday, April 6, 1387, Manuel left the city by ship, and on Tuesday, April 9, the Turks entered its gates.[161] Instead of accepting his friend's recommendation, Manuel sailed to Lesbos, where Francesco II Gattilusio's government refused to allow him and his band to enter the city of Mitylene.[162] So it was that, as the heat of summer drew on, Manuel and his followers had to pitch tents under the blazing sun and make do as best they could. In these circumstances Manuel penned one of the most bitter of his writings, the long *Discourse in Letter Form to Cabasilas*,[163] in which he

in reference to the conflict between Matthew and Manuel Cantacuzenus. Cammelli also suggested that Manuel's alleged evil counselors may also be referred to in Letter C. 163 (No. 36), L. 161, but Loenertz, *ibid.*, 285, believes—probably more rightly—that this was addressed to someone other than Manuel and in the early 1380's.

160. Dennis, 154–155, suggests a few possibilities, but they are no more than that.

161. This date is given in an entry of the *Chronicon breve thessalonicense*, ed. Loenertz in Vol. I of his edition of Cydones' *Correspondance* (a text cited hereafter as *"Chron. brev. thess."*), p. 175, no. 6. For a justification of the use of this source for this dating, see Appendix II below. The short chronicle, ed. Müller, p. 394 (61), ll. 1–2 (from the same manuscript as Bϱ. χϱ. No. 52, but omitted from the Lampros-Amantos publication), gives the date of the fall simply as April, 1387, adding that the city had been besieged for four years; cf. Muralt, p. 729, no. 14. A deliberation by the Venetian Senate of July 22, 1387, speaks of the city as being already in Murad's hands. This document, omitted in Thiriet's *Régestes*, is published by Dennis, 164, and on pp. 438–439 of Vol. II of Loenertz' edition of Cydones' *Correspondance*. It is also stated in a life of St. Athanasius of Meteora, ed. N. Veēs, Βυζαντίς, 1 (1909), 259, that the saint predicted the taking of Thessalonica would come three years after his death in 1383. For a discussion of these sources and of chronological problems connected with this date, see Charanis, "An Important Short Chronicle," 359–361, and Dennis, p. 155, n. 11; also Loenertz, *Echos d'Orient*, 36 (1937), 477–478; cf. Khoury, 137. In addition, for a discussion of the question of a later recovery of Thessalonica by the Greeks, and another Turkish capture of the city in the 1390's, see also Appendix II below.

162. In his account of Manuel's flight from Thessalonica to Lesbos, Chalcocondyles, ed. Darkó, I, 48, ed. Bonn, 53, says that the Lord of Lesbos refused to allow him to land at all; but we know that this was not true. The author does state, however, that John V refused to allow Manuel into Constantinople, and this is now shown to be substantially correct by the letters of Cydones (to be discussed shortly). The Pseudo-Phrantzes, ed. Papadopoulos, 52–53, ed. Bonn, 47–48, gives the same account as Chalcocondyles. Cf. Dennis, pp. 156–157 and n. 17, as well as his subsequent "Short Chronicle of Lesbos," 17.

163. Text (not included in Legrand's publication), published by Loenertz, "Manuel Paléologue, épître à Cabasilas," Μακεδονικά, 4 (1956), 38–46. In

describes to his friend his miserable situation and pours out his feelings at length. The objects of his principal anger were the citizens of Thessalonica, who were, he believed, the real cause of his failure, by clinging to their rights, by accusing him of tyranny, and by hindering him in every way.[164] Accustomed as they were to civil strife, jealous of their communal rights, alarmed by the devastation of their outlying lands, pinched by the ruin of their commerce, and oppressed by the burdens of the military forces among them and by the demands of defense, the Thessalonians were in all likelihood hardly eager to support Manuel wholeheartedly. There is no doubt that their pressure was the immediate cause of his giving up the struggle, fleeing, and allowing the city to yield.[165]

From Manuel's point of view, the project for which he had risked so much, and which had become such a patriotic struggle, was not necessarily lost entirely with the investment of the city, for it could very well have held out longer. Quite probably he was right, to a certain extent, for the city was open to the sea throughout the siege, and it might well have resisted for a considerable time—after all, it fell not by storm but by capitulation—had it not been for the factor of popular disaffection.

And so, not yet thirty-seven years of age, his title to the throne and his entire future still gravely in doubt, Manuel camped in

one of his worst chronological misinterpretations, Berger de Xivrey, 80–81, imagines that this work was written between 1393 and 1396, during, he assumes, an enforced escape to Lesbos from Constantinople under pressure of attacks by John VII and the Turks. Dölger, "Johannes VII.," p. 27, n. 4, does not entirely escape this error. The mistake is laid to rest by Loenertz, *Echos d'Orient*, 37 (1938), 113–115. Cydones was able to read this work, and in a letter to Manuel, C. 107 (No. 21), L. 380, dated by Loenertz 1387–88, he praises it highly; cf. Loenertz, *ibid.*, 118–119. Presumably it was to this same Cabasilas (perhaps the well-known Nicholas Chamaëtos Cabasilas, the Mystic: see Loenertz' introduction to his edition of Manuel's text, p. 37) that Manuel also wrote three other letters. Letter ς' plainly was written during the siege of Thessalonica, and in the course of it Manuel echoes Cydones' hopes that St. Demetrius and God Himself will aid the city. Letter ζ' and Letter ιε' are of uncertain date and are in substance merely rhetorical apologies for failure to write.

164. Manuel, *Discourse to Cabasilas*, ed. Loenertz, pp. 38–39, ll. 21–28; see Dennis, 85–86, for a translation of most of this passage. See also Loenertz, *Echos d'Orient*, 37 (1938), pp. 114–115 and n. 5.

165. Chalcocondyles, ed. Darkó, I, 42, ed. Bonn, 46, specifically makes their "stubborn" or even "presumptuous" (αὐθαδέστερον) treatment of him the cause of his flight.

discomfort on Lesbos and nourished his bitterness. Fortunately, from this period we have a few letters by Cydones which give some valuable scraps of information as to the subsequent events. In one letter,[166] written during that summer, Cydones complains to Rhadenos of their lack of contact with him, save a little note telling him no more than he already knew. For it was Cydones himself, he says, who had written to the Lord of Lesbos to beg for Manuel's reception. Belying his former optimism, Cydones now warns that Manuel and his companions must not look forward to a return to the capital soon, for John V has decided not to allow his son into the city. And Cydones goes on to predict that Rhadenos will soon find himself at the Turkish Porte.

What this obscure final comment meant is more plainly revealed in a subsequent letter, also to Rhadenos.[167] Cydones reviews the hardships which Manuel and his company are suffering, now that they have moved to an island bare of necessities and fit only for a pirates' lair. But if this is bad enough, worse awaits them on the mainland, for the barbarians are trying to entice them with money and grain, and with ambassadors who speak of relief and friendship. These fair words, says Cydones, are only nets with which to ensnare the helpless, and they should not trust them but should beware of becoming deserters to the Turks. Such words of friendship, he points out, are only pretense and are only temporary, and hold ruin in store.

This letter makes vividly clear Manuel's new course. The barren island mentioned is almost certainly Tenedos, now deserted under the terms of the Treaty of Turin in 1381. Why he moved there is uncertain, but it well may also have been at the instigation of the ambassadors of whom Cydones speaks. These, from Murad, of course, were trying now to persuade Manuel to come to the Porte in person. That the Emir should have been willing to forgive Manuel's recent campaigns against him is not difficult to understand. A prince of Manuel's ability merited cultivating, especially if, in doing so, the Porte would add to the

---

166. C. 145, L. 350; cf. Dennis, 157. According to Loenertz, *Echos d'Orient*, 37 (1938), p. 118, n. 1, the correct sequence of Cydones' letters bearing on this phase of events should be: C. 145 (L. 350), C. 425 (L. 351), C. 159 (L. 352), C. 440 (L. 353), C. 142 (L. 354), and C. 156 (L. 355). The second and fourth of these, which are not discussed below, are simply complaints to Rhadenos of his failure to write.

167. Letter C. 159, L. 352; cf. Dennis, p. 158, n. 23.

internal frictions of Byzantium as well as avoid driving Manuel toward further opposition to Turkish interests.[168]

More difficult would be Manuel's position. As the recent hero and rallying figure of Byzantine opposition to the Turks, it must have been a cruel dilemma for him to have to face the idea of reconciliation with the enemy. His preceptor and friend, Cydones, long a staunch foe of accommodation with the Turks, did not disguise his disappointment and alarm at the news that Manuel was going to see Murad, and he wrote renewed warnings to Manuel's aide and companion, Rhadenos.[169] (It is curious, by the way, if not also significant, that none of any letters written by Cydones to Manuel himself survive from this period.)

But to Murad Manuel did go, as we know, apparently in the late summer or autumn of 1387. The Greek historians have pictured this visit as the reckless flight of a desperate man who simply flung himself upon Murad's mercy, hoping for the best.[170] Thanks to the evidence from Cydones, we now know that this was not the case, but that Manuel, apparently without any move on his own initiative, was first approached by Murad's ambassadors. We also know now that he had full assurance—false, Cydones suspected—of a favorable reception before he decided to go.[171] But it must be made clear that, if Manuel's journey to

168. Cf. Dennis, 157–158, for parallel observations.

169. In this Letter C. 142, L. 354, Cydones expresses his regrets about the planned trip and his fears of what the Turks might do, once Manuel and his comrades are in Murad's hands. In C. 156, L. 355, he renews his insistence that "there is nothing to be gained from the unbelievers," who are bent solely on enslaving the Byzantines. Cf. Dennis, p. 158, n. 23.

170. Chalcocondyles, ed. Darkó, I, 42–43, and 48, ed. Bonn, 46–47, and 52; and the Pseudo-Phrantzes, ed. Papadopoulos, 53–54, ed. Bonn, 48–49; who are followed by such modern writers as Berger de Xivrey, 28–29, and Gibbons, 152, and even Vasiliev, *Hist. Byz. Emp.*, 587. The account in the *Chron. Barb. 111*, 25–26, is virtually the same as that of the two other Greek historians. Of the two modern historians of the Turks, Hammer, I, 193–194 (trans. Hellert, I, 259–260), rightly joins the story of Manuel's flight to Murad with his account of the siege and fall of Thessalonica; whereas Iorga, *Geschichte*, I, falls afoul of the confusion in Chalcocondyles and reports the flight to Murad (p. 249) as quite separate from, and earlier than, his account of the fall of Thessalonica (p. 255). On Manuel's dealings with Murad after his escape from the city, Dölger has no entries at all in his *Regesten*.

171. Loenertz, *Echos d'Orient*, 37 (1938), 118, was the first to maintain this point, obviously on the basis of the Cydones letters just used, though he made no specific citation or detailed presentation of them. In this he was followed by Charanis, "Strife," 302. Now Dennis, 156–158, has analyzed these documents thoroughly, using Loenertz' new edition of them, which

Brusa was not a bold and sudden act of abject supplication, it was nevertheless an act of deep humiliation. It must have been a bitter pill for Manuel to swallow, to have to bow before the victor. It also meant a rejection of all of Manuel's course of resistance to the Turks and his total reversion to the official Byzantine policy of appeasement and submission. This was a double victory for the wily Emir, who at once had won Thessalonica and Manuel himself.

As our historians relate, Manuel was well received and apparently made a good impression upon the Emir, who, we are told, spoke cordially and affably with him. But in his letters Cydones continued to be unhappy. There was ground for it, to be sure, in the premature death of Rhadenos during the sojourn in Brusa, and Cydones laments to Manuel in one letter this grief that they could both share. In the same letter, moreover, he grieves for his country and hopes for the restoration of Manuel to his former dignity.[172] In another letter from the same time, Cydones continues to see only ill coming from Manuel's presence among the Turks and only grim prospects for the capital. But he still maintains that Manuel is now the Empire's only hope, and he expresses the fervent wish that Manuel will return home safely.[173] And in still another letter, Cydones tries to encourage Manuel to have hope in spite of his present reverses [174]—a sure indication of how humiliated and self-debasing Manuel must have felt at the Porte.

Murad, we are told, sent Manuel back to his father with a

makes them at last available. His results are followed by Khoury, 137. Beyond all this, Loenertz, in "Pour l'histoire du Péloponnèse," p. 167 and n. 6, also goes so far as to suggest that, for his submission to Murad, Manuel was invested as a vassal with the city of Christopolis. Since a ship from that city did play a role in the events of 1390 (see below, p. 77), it is not inconceivable that Manuel held it. But this must remain only conjecture.

172. Letter C. 185 (No. 45), L. 363. Loenertz, *Echos d'Orient*, 37 (1938), 120–121, had previously assigned this letter to the time of Manuel's exile to Lemnos, but he has since corrected this ascription, in *Recueils*, p. 118, n. 1, and in his edition.

173. Letter C. 153, L. 365. In his edition, Loenertz dates to about this same time Cydones' Letter C. 419, L. 364, to Theodore Palaeologus, bewailing the evils by which "the Romans" are besieged and expressing hope in God's aid.

174. Letter C. 279, L. 367. Dennis surely means the last of the three letters cited in his p. 158, n. 24, to be this, instead of the (C. 158, L.) 370 cited there, perhaps by printer's error.

warm recommendation of conciliation. Whatever the case, now that Manuel was openly reconciled with the Emir and had been converted to his father's policies of appeasement, there were no longer any major obstacles to the return of Manuel to Constantinople. Moreover, John V would have been unlikely to oppose Murad's obvious wish for the reception of Manuel back in the capital, even if he had desired to do so. Cydones made no effort to conceal his joy, once Manuel was back in Constantinople.[175] But the mere fact that Cydones was obliged to write to Manuel indicates the difficulty and suspicion involved in trying to see him personally. And Cydones actually says that the danger of spies and informers at court forces him to hope for association without fear only later. But at the same time, he is still certain that Manuel will inherit the throne.[176]

Plainly, then, Manuel upon his return to Constantinople was still held in some sort of disfavor or distrust, and his future was in doubt. Aside from Cydones' never-ending optimism on the matter, we have no way of knowing the nature of feelings between father and son, nor of when and how and in what spirit they

175. Letters C. 158, L. 370, and C. 164, L. 373, which Loenertz dates to the autumn of 1387. Among the short chronicle entries published by Gedeon ('Εκκλησιαστικὴ ἀλήθεια, 23, 1903), there is one (p. 382, φ. 162) which reads as follows, in translation: "On the 17th of September of the 11th indiction entered the holy and just Basileus the Lord Manuel Palaiologos into the holy city, the new Jerusalem [i.e., Constantinople], in the year 6890." At a glance this entry might seem worth taking at face value, accepting September 17, 6890 as applying to our year 1391. Such an application does not, however, make much sense (see above, n. 117). More important, the indiction number given does not fit this year: 6890 was a fifth, not an eleventh, indiction year. On the other hand, if we accept the indiction number as stated, and assume that the number for the year is perhaps incomplete, we might then read the date as September 17, 6898, in a year which *was* an eleventh indiction; in other words, September 17, 1387. This is an eminently plausible date for Manuel's arrival in Constantinople after leaving Murad's court. For a possible obstacle to this interpretation, however, see n. 179 below. Most recently, Khoury, 137, has committed himself to a general dating of "1387 (automne-hiver?)" for Manuel's return.

176. Letter C. 173, L. 368. The same tone may be found in C. 144 (No. 35), L. 381, in which Cydones, flattered that Manuel wishes to see him and hoping for more opportunity to meet, still fears slanderers at court. He trusts that, with the help of Cydones' own efforts, John V will heed the voice of "nature" and will yield to his normally warm feeling for Manuel. Originally, Loenertz, *Echos d'Orient*, 37 (1938), 122, placed this letter at a time of Manuel's supposed return after the Battle of Kossovo; but he has since (*Recueils*, p. 118, n. 2, and in his edition) abandoned this gravely questionable dating.

met. But apparently John V bore some kind of grudge, or at least thought that Manuel should receive some form of punishment. It was therefore decided that he should be exiled to the island of Lemnos, which was seemingly, in the age of the Palaeologi, a common place of exile for persons of important rank. Cydones grieved but was still undaunted. In one letter,[177] regretting that he has just seen Manuel but has been unable to speak with him, he notes the decision that his young friend must go into "forced leisure" on Lemnos. But he still hopes for reconciliation between father and son. In another letter,[178] presumably written just before Manuel's departure, Cydones wishes the prince a smooth voyage to Lemnos and, again, hopes that in spite of court slanderers John will hearken to the call of "nature" and will restore his son to favor. Undoubtedly, then, the question of whether or not John would restore Manuel to the succession had not been settled—at least, not as far as Cydones knew or told—at the time when Manuel was about to leave for Lemnos.

And to Lemnos he went, perhaps as early as the autumn of this busy and fateful year of 1387.[179] For us, as it must have seemed to him in his own way, this period of exile is a great

177. C. 169 (No. 32), L. 372.
178. C. 151 (No. 33), L. 374. On this and the preceding letter, see Loenertz, *Echos d'Orient*, 37 (1938), 120–122.
179. There is an entry in one of the short chronicles, Βρ. χρ. No. 47, p. 81, l. 48, part of a group of notices concerning the revolt of Andronicus in 1373. This reads: "In the year 6882 [1373–74] on September 12 he [the Basileus John] exiled his son to the island of Lemnos." This statement may or may not actually bear on events of 1373: see n. 48 above. If it does not, it is just possible that the confused chronicler may actually have preserved a true date which, belonging to the year 6896 (1387–88), applies to the one case known to us of John V exiling a son of his to Lemnos. Thus, Loenertz, *Echos d'Orient*, 37 (1938), 119–120, and also in his "La Première Insurrection d'Andronic Paléologue," 343, believes that his statement may well give us the date of the beginning of Manuel's exile. It is not an impossible date, though September 12 would seem a bit early in the year in view of all that came to pass before it. More seriously, there is the chronicle entry edited by Gedeon, which might plausibly give us the basis for dating Manuel's *arrival* in Constantinople from Murad's court as September 17, 1387: see n. 175 above. Accepting one of these chronicle datings would thus exclude the other; unless, having already made adjustments in the Chronicle No. 47's date, we amend it further to, say, September 22. This alteration might provide a logical resolution of the entire question, though it remains entirely conjectural, of course. Charanis, "Strife," 302, makes no mention of these references and settles generally for the period of late 1387 to early 1388 for the time of Manuel's departure for Lemnos.

blank in his life. No writing whatsoever from his pen survives from these years. We know that he wrote letters at least to Cydones, but none are preserved in the manuscript which contains most of his still-extant letters, the preparation of which he seems to have supervised himself. He may have refused deliberately to save anything from this period, which could only have had painful memories for him. Our only real sources for information about Manuel's exile, indeed, are Cydones' letters to his friend. Many of them [180] contain only vague rhetoric and trivia of little value or meaning. One of them, actually to Manuel's companion Chrysoberges,[181] also contains the continued hope that Manuel will yet be restored to favor. We have a little personal note in one letter [182] in which Cydones chides Manuel for giving himself up to hunting, and urges him to return to his studies— which were presumably one of Manuel's scant sources of spiritual sustenance during his exile. And another [183] apparently refers to an illness from which Manuel has recovered.

Two further letters are examples of Cydones' efforts to keep Manuel abreast of current news. Certainly there was enough afoot to justify these efforts. For in this period the Turks took a great step forward in their reduction of Serbia. Cheered by a Serbian victory over the Turks at Bileće on August 27, 1388, Cydones wrote to Manuel expressing regret that the latter had not been free to lead the Greeks and to make the victory complete.[184] But the outlook was to darken quickly, for in the spring of the following year Murad mounted the counteroffensive which culminated in the epic and epochal Battle of "the Field of Blackbirds," Kossovo Polje, on Tuesday, June 15, 1389. The effect

180. Such as C. 311, L. 397; C. 147, L. 379; C. 362, L. 390; C. 114, L. 391; C. 109, L. 392; C. 202, L. 401; C. 197, L. 424; and C. 106, L. 393.
181. Letter C. 143, L. 387; there is also a suggestion of the same sentiment in C. 109, L. 392 (ed. Loenertz, II, pp. 345–346, ll. 34–43).
182. Letter C. 234, L. 388.
183. Letter C. 387, L. 395.
184. Letter C. 166, L. 398. This interpretation of the letter was posed by Loenertz, *Echos d'Orient,* 37 (1938), 122, and was questioned by Charanis, "Strife," pp. 302–303, n. 56. But since such an interpretation has no real effect on the actual point of Charanis' main position there (regarding the time of Manuel's return from Lemnos), no valid objection to accepting Loenertz' interpretation seems to exist. Cf. Loenertz' reply to Charanis, *Recueils,* p. 119, n. 2. For this battle, see Jireček, *Geschichte der Serben,* II, 118–119; Gibbons, 169.

of the Battle on the Marica seventeen years earlier was completed by this death blow to Serbian independence. But it cost Murad his life at the hands of his Serbian assassin and thus brought to the Osmanli throne his terrible son Bayazid. It is possible that another of Cydones' letters refers to this disaster.[185]

In the midst of these gripping events, the role or even the position of Byzantium is virtually unknown. In such circumstances it is all the more frustrating that what we know least about Manuel's exile is when it ended. It is not impossible that, concerned over his position after the great Turkish victory, John called his son back to Constantinople in 1389 and was fully reconciled with him. Indeed, this assertion has been made. But it is simply not possible to be certain that it is correct.[186]

185. Letter C. 195, L. 396, as is the interpretation of Loenertz in his edition, and Dennis, 158. For the Battle of Kossovo in general, see Hammer, I, 205–215, trans. Hellert, I, 277–291; Iorga, *Geschichte*, I, 260–264; Jireček, *Geschichte der Serben*, II, 119–121; Gibbons, 173–178; Pears, 107–108. An interesting Slavic source account is found in the *Bulg. chron.*, 538; and a good Greek account in the *Chron. Barb. 111*, 27–28; also Chalcocondyles, ed. Darkó, I, 49–50, ed. Bonn, 53–54, followed in even greater chronological confusion by the Pseudo-Phrantzes, ed. Papadopoulos, 85, ed. Bonn, 81; Ducas, ed. Grecu, 35–37, ed. Bonn, 15–16. Cf. also N. Radojčić, "Die griechischen Quellen zur Schlacht am Kosovo Polje," *Byzantion*, 6 (1931), 241–246, and H. Grègoire, "L'Opinion byzantine et la bataille de Kossovo," *ibid.*, 247–251.

186. Loenertz, *Echos d'Orient*, 37 (1938), 122, first suggested that Manuel may have been summoned back to Constantinople after Kossovo, in interpreting Cydones' Letter C. 144 (No. 35), L. 381 (see above n. 176), which he then associated with a supposed reconciliation between father and son in 1389. Charanis, "Strife," pp. 302–303, nn. 56–57, rejected this suggestion and interpretation of the letter. He maintained that Manuel did not return until March of 1390, on the basis of Ignatii of Smolensk (see below, p. 72 and n. 193). He also reinterprets this letter in relation to C. 39 (No. 3), L. 371, which he dated himself to 1374.

Time has mitigated many of the points of dispute, for Loenertz, who had shrugged off Charanis' arguments (*Recueils*, p. 118, n. 3, and p. 119, n. 3), has since revised his dating of C. 144 (No. 35), L. 381, to 1387, thereby removing one of the original bases of dispute; and he has also, on sound bases, dated C. 39 (No. 3), L. 371, to 1387–88, with no reference to the points under discussion. He now offers, however (*Recueils*, p. 119, n. 3; followed by Dennis, p. 158, n. 27), as a proof of Manuel's return to Constantinople in 1389, a document published by R. Cessi, "Amadeo di Acaia e la rivendicazione dei domini Sabaudi in oriente," *Nuovo Archivio Veneto*, N.S. 37 (1919), 18–19. This text is a letter, dated October 21, 1389, from Theodore Palaeologus to Amadeo VI of Savoy, and in it Theodore speaks of doing things "which I would be able to do on behalf of our lord and brother the Constantinopolitan lord emperor" ["ego posim facere pro domino et

Whenever and on whatever basis Manuel did return to Constantinople, John V was soon to have need of his son if only for support against Manuel's nephew, John VII, as the specter of civil war rose again.

John Palaeologus, son of Andronicus IV, had maintained both the territorial position and the dynastic claims of his deceased father. From the outset there was friction, and the Genoese, ready to continue their support of the dissident factions of the reigning house of Byzantium in hopes of advancing their own interests, did their best to foster it. John V himself charged that the Genoese of Galata saluted his nephew, during a passage

fratri nostro domino imperatori constantinopolitano"]. Although this reference would seem indeed to impute to Manuel a position of importance and esteem in the capital, it is not necessarily enough to justify the sweeping assumption that therefore Manuel was really back in Constantinople and was fully reconciled with his father at that moment. (Nevertheless, this argument seems to be the basis for the assertion by Khoury, 137, that Manuel's exile ended in the summer of 1389, "avant le 21 octobre.") Nor is the ascription by Loenertz of Cydones' Letters C. 200 (No. 22), L. 410, and C. 95 (L. 82) to 1389–90, after a supposed return by Manuel, entirely free from a good deal of doubt. The same is true of Cydones' curious little account, not really a letter (published by Loenertz, *Recueils*, pp. 105–106, and then as L. 411), of a strange dream, which allegorizes a reconciliation between John V and Manuel: in autumn of 1389, claims the editor, but not necessarily with decisive foundation or authority.

On the other hand, the testimony of Ignatii of Smolensk, as we shall see below, by no means excludes the possibility that Manuel did indeed return from exile before March of 1390. To be sure, there are other source leads that might suggest this, but they must be used very critically. Loenertz, *Echos d'Orient,* 37 (1938), 124, in connection with dating Manuel's Letter ιγ΄, notes that Chalcocondyles (ed. Darkó, I, 55, ed. Bonn, 60) speaks of the presence of Manuel and also of John VII serving in the army of Bayazid after the Battle of Kossovo (in which regard, cf. Dölger, *Regesten,* no. 3190, p. 72). He therefore assumes that this also is an indication of Manuel's return from exile by then. But there is no way to be sure of the period to which this statement refers, and, even if there were, Chalcocondyles' chronology is so demonstrably unreliable for this epoch that so vague a reference holds all the less reliability.

Nor can we take any more seriously the fact that the *Chron. Barb. 111,* 27, just before relating events of Kossovo (and immediately after the hilarious hash about the visit of "Cantacuzenus" to the West: see above, nn. 28 and 102), states that "the Basileus John sent his son the lord Manuel to Sultan Murad that he might stay with him as *bailo* [μπαΐλον], as the Basileis had as a custom." This statement goes on to say that John sent his other son Theodore to the Morea: hence, this whole passage probably refers to the period of 1380–82. Thus, our sources are simply too vague on the return of Manuel from exile on Lemnos to justify a confident interpretation, which must await the availability of more specific evidence.

to or near Pera, with the full acclamations due an Emperor; while, says John V, when he himself passed by the shore of Pera—apparently when returning from his campaign against Andronicus in 1385—these citizens insultingly refused to tender him the same honors. And these same Peraiotes, John maintained, continued to be involved in plots against him.[187]

The Genoese were ready to support the young pretender even further. There is now good reason to believe that John actually went to Genoa in person, in early 1390 or before, and was negotiating some kind of support from the old allies of his house. It seems certain that he returned from Genoa on the eve of his new move with at least some Genoese backing.[188] It was more

187. Dölger, *Regesten*, no. 3184, p. 71. The entire accusation is in the fragmentary text of the letter of John V to the Genoese, in Belgrano, 139–140, and ed. Loenertz, "Fragment d'un lettre," 37–38; see also Loenertz' own comments, 140, and Dennis, 110 and 112. On the other hand, Muralt, p. 728, no. 3, on only the vaguest authority, speaks of Genoese efforts to reconcile John V with his grandson on November 2, 1386.

188. Establishment of this episode involves one of the most frightful source confusions for the entire period of Manuel's lifetime. In the first place, we have the concrete statement of the Βϱ. χϱ. No. 15, p. 32, l. 28, which portrays John VII as "coming back from Genoa by land" (ἐπανελθὼν ἀπὸ τῆς Γενούας διὰ ξηρᾶς) for his enterprise against his grandfather, with Bayazid's aid. Aside from the geographic puzzle that this statement presents, the testimony of this important source is too generally reliable to be discarded out of hand. Charanis, "An Important Short Chronicle," 356, and "Strife," 303–304, has accepted this statement and has also used here the tale of Chalcocondyles, ed. Darkó, I, 77–78, ed. Bonn, 83, of Manuel's supposedly treacherous dispatch of John to Genoa. He has also linked the Chalcocondyles story with Manuel's last days in Thessalonica and thereafter, which seems particularly unwarranted. All of Charanis' conclusions on these points have been rejected by G. Kolias, " Ἡ ἀνταϱσία Ἰωάννου Ζ' Παλαιολόγου ἐναντίον Ἰωάννου Ε' Παλαιολόγου (1390)," Ἑλληνικά, 12 (1952), p. 44, n. 2, who vaguely consigns the Chalcocondyles story to some later period in the 1390's, during Bayazid's siege, and in conformance with the similar ideas of such scholars as Lampros and Dölger.

This entire problem is discussed at length in my own article, "John VII in Genoa: A Problem in Late Byzantine Source Confusion," *Orientalia Christiana Periodica*, 28 (1962), 213–238. My conclusion there is that the controversial Chalcocondyles tale is almost completely worthless as it stands and reflects rather some elements of a journey by John VII to Genoa before or by 1390, as the Short Chronicle statement seems to make clear. Among the indirect supports for this conclusion are several Latin documents (published for the first time as appendices to my article), which demonstrate that: (1) an emissary of John V was in Genoa early in 1390, very possibly for at least the partial purpose of protesting over Genoese troublemaking on John VII's part (cf. Dölger, *Regesten*, no. 3191, p. 72); and (2) John VII's mother

important support, however, that finally gave the young John the opportunity for nothing less than the seizure of the throne by a coup of his own.[189]

Bayazid was more than willing to follow the policies of his father to profit from the divisions and quarrels within the Byzantine Imperial house. His aim was clearly the ultimate annexation of Constantinople and its scant remnants of Empire. The

traveled through Milan and Venice in the summer of 1390 on her way home, presumably to rejoin her son, by then on the Byzantine throne, after having accompanied him previously on his mission to Genoa for aid. The evidence for John's trip to Genoa in or before 1390 is still largely circumstantial, and more source material, probably archival, needs to be brought to light before it can be proved finally and conclusively. But I believe that these conclusions offer a working basis for resolution of this thorny question.

189. The revolt of John VII in 1390 is virtually ignored by the principal Greek sources, but we have valuable information in two short chronicles to be cited below. There is also a rather crude and oversimplified account, confusing elements of the events of 1376–81, in the *Chron. Barb. 111*, 29–30. The same confusion of events of the two episodes appears also in the accounts by Chalcocondyles and the Pseudo-Phrantzes of the 1376 revolt: cf. Loenertz, "Autour du Chronicon Maius," 295–296.

Fortunately, however, we have one major source of the foremost quality, in the account of a pilgrimage by the Russian Archimandrite Ignatii of Smolensk. The author was an eyewitness to the events he describes, and he set them down with great detail and clarity. His narrative forms the basis for any account of the events, and, unless otherwise stated below, all facts incorporated in the account below are drawn directly from it. I was unable to use the text in the original Russian (*Khoždenie Ignatiia Smolnianina*, ed. S. V. Arseniev, *Pravoslavnyi Palestinskii Sbornik*, 12, IV, 3, 1887), but there are several translations. The only complete one, and the best known as well as the most widely used, is in French, by S. F. Khitrovo, *Itinéraires russes en Orient* (Geneva, 1889), 129–157; 140–142 for the section involved here. This translation has been criticized by R. Salomon, "Zu Ignatij von Smolensk," *Beiträge zur russichen Geschichte Theodor Schiemann zum 60. Geburtstage von Freunden und Schülern dargebracht* (Berlin, 1907), 241–270, who discusses this text and its background in detail and provides literal German translations of the sections on John VII's revolt (pp. 256–258) and Manuel's coronation (pp. 260–265). There is also a modern Greek translation of a few sections of the work by K. Meliaris, " Ὁδοιπορικὸν τοῦ Ῥώσσου Ἰγνατίου Σμολιάνιν (1389–1405)," Νέα Σιών, 32 (1937), 24–37, 97–98. Another translation into the same language has been made of the section on John's revolt by Kolias, " Ἡ ἀνταρσία Ἰωάννου Ζ′ Παλαιολόγου (1390)," 39–41; but, since his rendering was made not from the original Russian but from the German of Salomon, to whom Kolias is generally much indebted, it is of limited value by itself. Kolias' article, however, is noteworthy as the most extensive and, if not without some points of dispute, the most important single study on this episode.

Also important are M. Silberschmidt, *Das orientalische Problem zur Zeit*

untried and ambitious young pretender could well serve as a feeble front for the subversion of the city.[190] The fact that the young John had a legally defensible claim to the throne enabled Bayazid to pose as the defender of dynastic legitimacy. The fact that John had in addition a faction in the city favorable to him— whether by virtue of his rights or simply out of dissatisfaction with John V—was a further advantage.[191]

So it was that, with Bayazid's blessing and a military force of Turks, the young John advanced on the capital. He seized outlying fortresses and, during Holy Week of 1390, took up positions before the Land Walls.[192] At this juncture, on Holy Thursday, March 31, Manuel arrived from Lemnos to aid his father. This is the first concrete reference to Manuel that we have since his exile. Whether Manuel had already been released from his exile prior to these events, or whether this return itself marked the end of it, and, if so, by what previous arrangements, is not

der türkischen Reiches nach venezianischen Quellen (Leipzig, 1923), 66 ff.; Dölger, "Johannes VII.," 26–28; Charanis, "Strife," 303–304; Ostrogorsky, *Hist. Byz. St.*, 486–487. While Hammer has been misled by source difficulties to confuse this episode with Andronicus IV's coup (see n. 63 above), Iorga, *Geschichte*, I, 278–279, has the events in the right place. The out-of-date treatments by Pears, 95–96, and Gibbons, 197, are not fully reliable; but Muralt, p. 737, no. 7, and p. 738, no. 1, has at least placed the date correctly even if he also (p. 737, no. 6) mistakes the activities of Manuel at this time.

190. Cf. Kolias, 41–43; Dölger, "Johannes VII.," 26–27. Note, however, that in his *Regesten*, no. 3190, p. 72, Dölger has Bayazid accepting a renewal of his father's treaty with John (and Manuel), "after June 15" of 1389, i.e. after Kossovo.

191. That John did have an active faction favoring him can be seen clearly in the course of events and in the account by Ignatii. Cf. also Kolias, 43. Dölger, "Johannes VII.," 27, suggests that Bayazid's excuse for supporting John's usurpation was the refusal of Manuel to fulfill his duties as a vassal. But any such refusal refers to a later episode, as far as one can gather from the unreliable chronology of the Greek historians. Moreover, as Kolias points out, p. 44, n. 2, Manuel was apparently not in a position of authority—even if of freedom—to deliver such a refusal at this time. The account by K. Hopf, *Geschichte Griechenlands vom Beginn des Mittelalters bis auf die neuere Zeit*, II (=Ersch and Gruber, *Allgemeine Encyklopädie der Wissenschaften und Künste*, 86, Leipzig, 1868), 54–55, creates some chronological confusion of its own. It should also be noted that the whole section of Berger de Xivrey, 51–78, dealing with events of the 1380's and 1390's is no longer acceptable chronologically.

192. Ignatii specifically mentions Turkish participation and John is also described as "receiving aid and an army [φοσσάτον] from the Emir Bayazid" in Bℓ. χℓ. No. 15, p. 32, ll. 28–30.

definitely known.[193] Two days later, on Saturday, April 2, a plot on behalf of the pretender was uncovered, and fifty conspirators were seized. Their prompt and severe punishment, in the old Byzantine tradition of judicial mutilation, indicate how seriously the threat was regarded. Likewise indicative are the additional facts that all but one of the gates of the city were sealed, and that provisions sufficient for two years were gathered.[194]

But the extent of the support for the pretender was soon made clear. About midnight of Wednesday, April 13, some people from the suburbs of the city were able to open the unsealed gate, the Gate of Charisius—the same gate through which John V and Manuel had returned in 1379—and to admit the pretender's followers into the city. The only exception, a notably prudent and natural one, was that the Turkish allies were not allowed into the city. Powerless to resist, John V and Manuel took refuge in the fortress of the Golden Gate, the very fortress in which they had been besieged in 1376.[195] The nobles, meanwhile, fled to Hagia Sophia to trust in the usurper's clemency. With the field thus cleared for him, John VII made his triumphant entry

193. As noted in the previous discussion of this problem (n. 186), Charanis has maintained that the statement by Ignatii does describe Manuel's actual recall from exile. On the surface of the matter, it might well seem to be the case. But there is nothing inherent in Ignatii's statement—and nothing in any other source—to make it definite that this is true. To be sure, we do have a Genoese expense account entry for Pera of March, 1390, ed. Iorga in *Notes et extraits pour servir à l'histoire des croisades*, I (Paris, 1899), 40–41, which refers to expenditures "pro adventu domini chir Manoli, imperatoris," but the exact date of the month is not made clear, and assuming that it may well refer to March 31, it adds nothing specific to our knowledge. Kolias, p. 45, n. 3, points out that the interval between the appearance of the young John with his forces before Constantinople and the arrival of Manuel would have been too brief to allow much communication to Lemnos; and therefore that Manuel's recall, if this was his recall, must have been negotiated by some arrangement prior to this time. But, again, we can only be certain of what the sources tell us. Anything more is, even at its best and most ingenious, still only conjecture.

194. Cf. Kolias, 45–46.

195. Βρ. χρ. No. 15, p. 32, ll. 30–33, simply gives the date April 14 of this year and specifically states the fortress as the place of refuge. No. 52, p. 89, ll. 41–43, ed. Müller, p. 393 (60), ll. 1–4, gives the date, the indiction number, the further fact that this was in the week of St. Thomas, and also the name of the gate; cf. Muralt, p. 736, no. 7. On the establishment of the dating, see Dölger, "Johannes VII.," p. 27, n. 3, and Charanis, "An Important Short Chronicle," p. 356, n. 1. See also Kolias, 46–47. For discussions of the gate of entry and the fortress, see Salomon, 259; and Kolias, respectively, 54–55, and 55–57.

Figure 4: *Constantinople, the Golden Gate from the Southwest* (photo courtesy M. Auger, 1949; see Appendix XXIV, C, 3).

into the city in the early hours of the morning of April 14, 1390, and received from the populace a tumultuous acclaim, whether sincere or encouraged by his armed supporters.[196]

196. Ignatii's vivid description is worthy of quotation: "Tolling bells resounded through the entire city: the soldiers illuminated the entire city with torches, while their cavalry and infantry at the same time ran through the city with their weapons naked in their hands and with the arrows readied in their bows, shouting, Πολλὰ τὰ ἔτη 'Ανδρονίκου ['Many be the years of Andronicus,' or 'Long live Andronicus']. And all the multitude, men, women, and little children, all the citizens responded in a loud voice, Πολλὰ τὰ ἔτη 'Ανδρονίκου. And whoever did not immediately shout this cheer, him they goaded angrily with the sword. And it was remarkable to see and to hear the excitement throughout the city. Some trembled with fear, others rejoiced; and nowhere were any slain to be seen, so great was the fear struck by those bearing swords. And when the day broke, at dawn, there were a few conflicts; and there were only a few wounded. And about evening all hailed the young emperor, the son of Andronicus, and the city calmed itself and the sorrow was changed into gaiety." Cf. Kolias, 47–48.

The traditional acclamation is interesting in that it is recorded so precisely and that it should refer to Andronicus instead of his son. Salomon, 259–260, and Kolias, 57–61, each discuss this matter and suggest that the text may be defective. The latter scholar offers the emendation: "Πολλὰ τὰ ἔτη [τοῦ υἱοῦ] 'Ανδρονίκου." But the application at this time of the name of

History had repeated itself. As had his father Andronicus IV before him, John had also, through a coup and factional division, seized the power and rank to which he believed himself entitled by birth. John extended the parallel by initiating the newest round of the current Patriarchal leapfrog: arranging for the deposition of the incumbent Antonios, on July 30 John restored to the throne Makarios, who had been made Patriarch for the first time under Andronicus, and was now again elevated as a pawn in the latest chapter of the same dynastic struggle.[197]

The reign of John VII, however, proved to be even less stable and of even briefer duration than that of his father. Even before his coup, the possibility of his usurpation was foreseen by the shrewd Senators of Venice. But they also realized the uncertainty of the situation. In a deliberation of April 9, 1390, the Senators instructed their ambassadors, who were charged with pressing negotiations for renewal of the regular Veneto-Byzantine treaty, with alternate provisions for the possibility that "the son of Andronicus" might be installed in Constantinople, and also for the further possibility that "the son of Murad" might hold the city.[198] At any rate, the Venetians had no desire this time to oppose the deposition of John V and Manuel and were instead willing to negotiate normally with John VII. So it is that the treaty of June 3, 1390, was signed by that Emperor and not by his grandfather.[199] No one seemed to question the assumption

Andronicus to John VII, even without using it as a patronymic, may have represented an effort, deliberate or otherwise, at avoiding confusion of him with his grandfather. One Genoese text of September 28, 1390 (ed. Belgrano, p. 151), refers to an embassy "ad dominum Imperatorem Chirandronicum," who was obviously John VII.

197. See Miklosich and Müller, Vol. II, p. 142. *Ibid.*, no. 417, pp. 142–147, for the synodal decision of August, 1390, on Makarios, recalling the background of his off-again, on-again Patriarchate and exculpating him from all former charges. Cf. Muralt, p. 737, nos. 10–11; Gedeon, Πατριαρχικοὶ πίνακες, 448. Antonios had been elevated to the Patriarchal throne under John V, after the death in 1388 of Neilos, the successor to Makarios after the latter's first Patriarchate. To John V's and Manuel's credit, after their restoration Makarios was apparently not replaced immediately in his turn again, either until his death, or at least until after a decent interval. At any rate, by the summer of 1391 the cycle was completed with the reinstatement of Antonios for his own second Patriarchate (1391–1397): Gedeon, 448–450.

198. Thiriet, *Régestes*, I, no. 772, p. 186. Cf. Vasiliev, *Hist. Byz. Emp.*, 586.

199. Dölger, *Regesten*, no. 3192, pp. 72–73; Greek text, Miklosich and

that John VII had a legitimate right to sit on the throne of Byzantium.[200]

But such superficial success was not enough, for there was a fatal flaw in John VII's position. He had failed to eliminate the opposition of his grandfather and uncle, being even less successful in this respect than his father had been in 1376. The old Emperor and his loyal son had taken refuge in their fortress. John V chose to remain there, perhaps because of the feebleness of age as an obstacle to flight. There is, however, the likelihood it had been agreed by father and son that this remaining foot in the door, as it were, was too precious a position to be lost. At any rate, Manuel was able to escape and seek aid.[201]

Müller, Vol. III, no. 33, pp. 135–143; Latin, Thomas, *Diplomatarium Veneto-Levantinum*, II, no. 135, pp. 224–229; Italian summary (R. Predelli), *I libri Commemoriali della Republica di Venezia, Regesti,* III (Venice, 1883), no. 347, pp. 207–208. But none of these publications takes proper note of the correct signer: see Silberschmidt, 75–77; Dölger, "Johannes VII.," p. 27, n. 5. (But the assumption by Silberschmidt, 72, that the negotiations with Venice discussed by the Senate on October 4, 1390 [Thiriet, *Régestes,* I, no. 780, p. 188] were in the name of John VII is surely incorrect, though it is still accepted by Dölger in his *Regesten,* no. 3192a, p. 73.) In various official references to John VII the Venetians were content to accord him the full Imperial title without dispute: see, for example, the Senate's deliberations concerning John VII's mother in Barker, "John VII in Genoa," 237–238. Even after John VII had been expelled from the capital, the Venetians were reluctant to become involved in any of this internal quarrel, as can be seen in the Senate's deliberation of October 4, 1390: text, Iorga, "Veneţia in Marea neagră," *Analele Academiei Române, Memoriile Secţiunii istorice,* II, 36 (1913–14), no. 20, p. 1105; cf. Thiriet, *Régestes,* no. 780, p. 188, whose summary is inadequate.

200. Kolias, p. 48, n. 2, and also p. 49, n. 2, believes that John VII assumed power already bearing the title of Emperor, and that we hear nothing of a coronation of him because John felt there was no need of one. (This theory discounts the more simple explanation of the shortness of his time in power; after all, it took his father a good thirteen months to have himself crowned after his own coup in 1376: see above, p. 29.) Here again is raised the issue of whether or not Andronicus IV crowned his son with himself in 1377 (see above, n. 70); but, as plausible as Kolias' position may be on this point, he goes too far in his distinction between the titles of βασιλεύς and αὐτοκράτωο in the coronations of Manuel. On the questions regarding the respective coronations of Andronicus IV and John VII, see also A. Christophilopoulou, Ἐκλογή ἀναγόρευσις καὶ στέψις τοῦ βυζαντινοῦ αὐτοκράτορος (Πραγματεῖαι τῆς Ἀκαδημίας Ἀθηνῶν, 22, 2, Athens, 1956), 197–199.

201. Cf. Kolias, 46–47, who does not consider the possibility of any positive motive for John V's remaining behind.

Realizing how much depended on routing out this last dangerous pocket of resistance, John VII applied his full energies to a
close and vigorous investment of the fortress.[202] But John V was
able to maintain his position. And even the Genoese, the usurper's strongest allies, thought it wise to maintain contact with
the old Emperor, for there seem to have been some specific negotiations between them.[203]

Manuel's exact course of action is not fully clear. Our chief
source tells us only that, during the summer, Manuel twice returned to the city with an army of "Franks," but was unable to
accomplish anything. Whatever the source of this aid, he ultimately was able to gain the assistance of the Hospitalers, the
Knights of St. John on Rhodes.[204] On the twenty-fifth of August,

202. Kolias, 49. *Ibid.*, n. 1, he suggests that the disputed question of
whether or not John VII really did use κανόνια in this siege deserves further
investigation as a possibly notable early use of firearms.

203. An expense entry for Pera dated August 8, 1390 (Belgrano, no 32,
p. 151), speaks of "expensis factis ... quando dominus Potestas ivit ad
Creseam pro ponendo acordium inter Imperatores." "Creseam" is undoubtedly a corruption of the Greek for the Golden (Χρύση) Gate, in the fortress
of which John V was blockaded; and the "Imperatores" must have been at
least John V and John VII. Was the "acordium" some kind of truce the
Genoese were attempting to bring about? An entry for September 22 (*ibid.*)
speaks of two emissaries sent also "ad Creseam" to deal with Manuel, of
course after his arrival with aid for his father. Another entry for the same
date (*ibid.*) speaks of expenses for transporting "dominum Potestatem et
suum Consilium ad Creseam ad salutandum dominum imperatorem Calo-
janem," presumably John V. And a fourth entry, for September 28 (*ibid.*)
speaks of two representatives being sent "ad Cresseam [*sic*] ad dominum
Imperatorem." Again, this Emperor was presumably John V, especially since
John VII is referred to separately in the same entry, and as "dominum
Imperatorem Chirandronicum" (see above, n. 196). These contacts were
noted by Loenertz, "Fragment d'une lettre," 39, who even went so far as
to suggest that it was then that John V drew up his bill of complaints against
the Genoese for their violations of the 1382 treaty. But he has since abandoned this idea: see Barker, "John VII in Genoa," p. 231 and n. 2.

204. Ignatii says that Manuel went to Lemnos when he escaped from the
city. On the other hand, Βρ. χρ. No. 15, p. 32, ll. 32–34, after mentioning
the besieging of John V in his fortress ("by his grandson and the Galatenoi":
the Genoese of Galata perhaps being the source of the mercenaries hired by
John VII, according to Ignatii), then says that Manuel, seemingly directly,
sailed to Rhodes "to the Brothers" (εἰς τοὺς Φρερίους). Kolias, p. 47, and
n. 3, and pp. 49–50, believes that Manuel first did go to Lemnos, and that
he went to Rhodes only later. He notes that Ignatii distinguishes between
the "Franks," on the one hand, who aid Manuel in his first two counter-
attacks, and the Hospitalers, on the other hand, whom he calls "Romans"—

Manuel appeared before the city with a small fleet, including two galleys from Rhodes, one each from Lemnos, Christopolis, and Constantinople, and four other smaller vessels.[205] He managed to penetrate into the harbor of his father's stronghold and thus to relieve the besieged John V. The fighting seems to have been redoubled outside the walls. Finally, by means of a sudden sally from the fortress of the Golden Gate on Saturday, September 17, 1390, which surprised John VII unarmed at mealtime, the usurper was driven out of the city.[206] The Genoese seem also to have resisted, and we hear of the futile involvement of Gattilusio,

perhaps to emphasize their religious affiliation by identifying them specifically with the Latin or Roman Church—noting particularly the crusading symbol, the embroidered white cross they wore on their breasts. Kolias seems to have the weight of the evidence on his side (note, for instance, the presence of a Lemnian vessel in Manuel's fleet), and in this position he is supported by Ostrogorsky, *Hist. Byz. St.*, 487. Interesting evidence of Manuel's transactions with the Hospitalers for their aid may apparently be found in a document of November 21, 1398, issued by Manuel in Constantinople; cf. Dölger, *Regesten*, no. 3272, p. 85. This text, published by Loenertz, "Jean V Paléologue à Venise," 231–232, catalogues various precious objects belonging to the Emperor which were returned by an agent of the Knights of Rhodes. Loenertz suggests plausibly, 226, that these objects may have been given as security against aid from the Hospitalers in 1390. There is perhaps an additional reflection of a sense of Byzantine obligation to the Hospitalers, presumably for their aid in 1390, in a reference by Manuel in his *Funeral Oration*, in connection with the later sale of Corinth to them. Here (ed. Migne, 244–245, ed. Lampros, p. 69, l. 70 to p. 70, l. 11) Manuel notes their being "amicably disposed toward us."

205. Βρ. χρ. No. 15, p. 32, l. 35–37.

206. In addition to the description by Ignatii (which includes the date), there is the account of Βρ. χρ. No. 15, p. 32, ll. 37–39, which gives no date, but which notes that Manuel disembarked all his forces but those of the Knights of Rhodes; and No. 52, p. 89, ll. 44–46, ed. Müller, p. 393 (60), ll. 5–8, gives the precise date and day of the week. Cf. Kolias, 50–51; Charanis, "An Important Short Chronicle," 356–357; Muralt, p. 738, no. 1. A Peraiote expense entry for September 22, 1390 (Belgrano, p. 151), makes mention of the "galeas domini Chirmanoli," doubtless meaning the ships which Manuel had brought back with him in aid. Another such entry (ed. Iorga, *Notes et extraits*, I, p. 49) refers to expenditures "factu in conducendo duos Caschadini[?], qui fuerunt missi pro domino potestate ad galeas domini Chir Manili." Such a dispatch must have been made to Manuel while he was still at his fortress before the final victory. These same entries (ed. Iorga, *ibid.*) note visits by the Podestà of Pera (August 3) and by men sent by him (July 10) "ad dominum imperatorem," who is possibly John VII. John seems to have fled to Pera after his expulsion, if not to carry on the fight, at least for refuge. For we have another expense entry (Iorga, *Notes et extraits*, 50), for September 21, 1390, "in ratione diverssarum expensarum, casu visitacionii domini Calojane."

apparently Francesco II of Lesbos, who may already have become John VII's father-in-law as well as ally.[207] But the game had been played out, and the brief reign of John VII at this point was abruptly ended.

The young John was driven back into dependency upon Bayazid, who seems to have been willing enough to maintain this useful tool in his train, but who apparently made no effort to sustain John in Constantinople or to restore him upon his ouster. Thus, in this latest stage of civil war, the direct support of the Emir was not the decisive factor on the side of the ultimately triumphant party, as it had been in 1379. But if John V and Manuel had managed to win without Bayazid's active help, their victory was still owed to him in the negative sense that he did not actively oppose them and at least tacitly approved. Bayazid may well have felt that the failure of John VII to secure himself effectively in the city had shown the pretender to be unworthy of the Emir's continued support.[208] At any rate, Bayazid, we may be sure, must have felt confident that he could bend the restored John V and Manuel to his wishes sufficiently to tolerate their return. Perhaps at least part of his price was a fulfillment by Manuel of Byzantine obligations of military serv-

207. For a discussion of the marriage of John VII to the daughter of Francesco II Gattilusio, and the question of its chronology, see Appendix V below. John's indebtedness to the Genoese of Pera is noted further in one small fashion, however, in an expense account entry for October 17, 1390, citing the debt of a small sum by "Calo Jane, filius quondam bone memorie domini Chir Andronici Palaeologi imperatoris": Iorga, *Notes et extraits*, 41. *Ibid.*, 47, Iorga notes the receipt of a slightly larger sum "in [nomine de?] domino Chir Andronicho Palaeologo." This is not, of course, Andronicus IV. But Iorga (*ibid.*, n. 2) is quite wrong in suggesting that this person was Manuel's son Andronicus, the future Despot of Thessalonica—who not only was not yet born at this date (see Appendix XIII below), but whose parents were not even yet married! It is likely that this corrupt text refers rather to John VII, *son of* Andronicus Palaeologus, perhaps in connection with the very same debt noted above, in n. 206. On the use of the name Andronicus elsewhere for John VII, see above, n. 196.

208. This plausible interpretation is suggested by Kolias, 49. It might be noted that Alderson, *The Structure of the Ottoman Dynasty*, Table XXIV, has Bayazid married to a daughter of John V (and Helen Cantacuzena) in 1389. If this date were taken flexibly, it might suggest some kind of accommodation by John with the Emir or perhaps even some kind of condition of Bayazid's support for the threatened or deposed old Emperor. But Alderson gives no citation for this union, and I have found no reference to it in any source I have used, certainly not in Greek ones.

ice, which were presumably neglected during Manuel's exile and earlier, in view of John V's age and ill-health.

For Manuel himself the events of 1390 had been decisive. Whatever had been the occasion and nature of the reconciliation between him and his father, the civil strife of April–September 1390 had given him his golden opportunity, as he himself must surely have been aware, to prove once and for all his loyalty and indispensability to John V during the latter's declining years, especially amid such perils.[209] The bonds that had linked them so strongly from 1371 to 1379 were forged anew, even more strongly. Whether by formal acknowledgment or by tacit agreement, it was quite plain now that John V fully accepted his able son as his heir and successor.[210]

The price to be paid, however, for this restoration as heir apparent was the onerous task of serving the military vassalage of Byzantium to the terrible Emir. And so it was that Manuel found himself, apparently in the fall of 1390, leading a contingent of troops in the army of Bayazid, side by side with his rival, John VII. As if this were not embarrassing enough, Manuel was forced to participate personally in the reduction of Philadelphia, the last independent Byzantine city in Asia Minor. Its formal cession had already been wrung from Manuel and his father previously, but it had refused to surrender. To Manuel fell the humiliating duty of assisting in the forcible seizure of this stubbornly loyal stronghold.[211]

209. Cf. Kolias, 47, 49, and 51.

210. Ducas, ed. Grecu, 77, ed. Bonn, 48, specifically says, in connection with Bayazid's demand in the winter 1390–91, that John V intended Manuel to succeed him as Emperor.

211. Chalcocondyles, ed. Darkó, I, 58, ed. Bonn, 64 (followed closely by the *Chron. Barb. 111*, 30), relates the cession, the refusal of submission, and the taking, with the aid of Manuel and John, of Philadelphia immediately after the account of events of 1376–81. This may suggest a confusion of a possible formal cession of the city in 1381 (see above, p. 34 and n. 89) on the one hand, with, on the other hand, the actual taking of the city in 1390, which latter date fits in with the context of the events which the historian describes thereafter. From the researches of Wittek, *Das Fürstentum Mentesche, Studie zur Geschichte Westkleinasiens im 13.–15. Jhdt.* (*Istanbuler Mitteilungen, 2*, Istanbul, 1934), 77–81, and Charanis, "Strife," 304–306, has emerged a reliable reckoning of the dating of the campaign against, and the taking of, Philadelphia. Their findings are accepted by Ostrogorsky, *Hist. Byz. St.*, 487, and Dölger, *Regesten*, no. 3191a, p. 72 (Muralt, p. 737, no. 6, under March of 1390, has badly confused the nature of this campaign, amid his jumble of sources.) The taking of Philadelphia by the Turks is also men-

Manuel, it is assumed, remained with Bayazid during the winter of 1390–91. It soon became quite evident that the Emir regarded him not only as a vassal but also as a hostage.[212] The fortress by the Golden Gate had twice served as a vital bastion for John V, and the old Emperor had taken care to keep it in good repair, if not also to strengthen it at this time. Seizing his opportunity to weaken the Byzantine position in Constantinople, Bayazid sent word to John that Manuel would be imprisoned and even blinded unless these fortifications were demolished. Faced with such an ultimatum, John V had no choice but to comply, at least to some extent.[213] This frightful humiliation proved the final blow for John. Prematurely aged and broken by his long miseries, physically weakened by a life of something less than moral perfection, the old Emperor retired to the gloom of his palace, and there, not yet having reached his sixtieth birthday, he died on Thursday, February 16, 1391.[214]

tioned by Ducas, ed. Grecu, 39–41, ed. Bonn, 19, in a context which makes dating difficult; but it is placed squarely in the reign of Bayazid and of no one else, thus refuting the dating of the event to 1381, under Murad, made by Gibbons, 154, and Pears, 106–107; or to 1379 by Muralt, p. 710, no. 12. Curiously, however, Khoury, 138, puts this episode in the summer–autumn of 1389, rather than in 1390, as is now generally accepted; since John VII was presumably in Genoa in late 1389, this dating is almost certainly untenable, regardless of the additional dilemma of Manuel's whereabouts in late 1389 (on which question, see n. 186 above). That "the Basileis of the Hellenes" mentioned in the source account of this campaign are indeed Manuel and John *VII*—not John V—cannot be doubted for this juncture; cf. Kolias, p. 53, n. 1.

212. Ducas, ed. Grecu, 75 ff., ed. Bonn, 46 ff., simply says that Bayazid, while casting his eyes covetously now on Constantinople, commanded the military service of John; though the campaign he then describes would seem rather to be the operations of 1391. Ignatii, continuing directly at the end of his account of John VII's expulsion, says that Manuel went to Bayazid to "pay his respects," and that the Emir, while he had him in his hands, sent his demands to John V. This account ignores the factor of the military service, but it does encourage the suspicion—whether justified or not, perhaps depending on one's interpretation of the reason for Bayazid's demand (see Appendix VI)—that Bayazid intentionally sought to use Manuel's presence in his power as a lever for concessions from Byzantium. Cf. Kolias, 51–52.

213. For a full discussion of the sources and problems concerning this point, see Appendix VI below.

214. An effusively laudatory short chronicle entry among those edited by Gedeon gives this year and the correct indiction, but states the date as February 15: Ἐκκλησιαστικὴ ἀλήθεια, 23 (1903), p. 382, φ. 191. Βϱ. χϱ. No. 15, p. 32, ll. 43–44, states the same date; but February 16, which is currently accepted as the correct date, is given, with the day, by No. 29, p. 54, ll. 23–24; while No. 52, p. 89, ll. 47–48, ed. Müller, p. 393 (60), ll. 9–12,

So passed away one of these personalities of history who are doomed to preside over tragic disaster not entirely of their own making.[215] At his birth, Byzantium was still a major power in the East; at his death, it was but a wretched fragment, seemingly

furnishes the fullest dating information of all these texts. On the confirmation of this date, see Charanis, "An Important Short Chronicle," 357–358 (though he omits the Gedeon notice and the passage in No. 15); also, Kolias, 52; and Muralt, p. 739, no. 9, which is corrupted by apocryphal additions (see Appendix IX below). For some unexplained reason, Dölger, "Johannes VII.," p. 28, n. 4, has transformed the date into June 28, 1391; but in his *Regesten*, p. 80, he accepts February 16.

John's age is the subject of some source confusion. The Βρ. χρ. No. 47, p. 80, ll. 11–12, places his birth in the year 6840 (1331–32), with which the other sources generally agree. But this text is garbled, either in the original manuscript or as a result of an error in the edition; for it gives both the month of November and the date June 17. Charanis, "An Important Short Chronicle," 344, has accepted November, which would make the year 1331. Papadopulos, *Versuch*, 46, however, has established the date of John's birth as June 18, 1332, on the basis of Nicephoras Gregoras, X, iii, ed. Bonn, p. 482, ll. 1–3; cf. Berger de Xivrey, p. 64 and n. 2. This latter dating receives significant confirmation in another of the short chronicle entries edited by Gedeon (*ibid.*, p. 382, φ. 312, the last of three), which also gives June 18 in 6480 (that is, 1332), adding that this date was the feast of St. Leontios, which is correct. Such accuracy and detail are not to be dismissed lightly. And, in fact, if John was born then, he would still have been nine years old when his father, Andronicus III, died in June of 1341: the source statement of which Charanis had used in defense of the November 1331 dating, though, as is self-evident, it can just as well support the later dating. It therefore seems likely that John V Palaeologus was indeed born on June 18 (which, after all, is not too far from the Chronicle No. 47's June 17), 1332; which would have made him less than fifty-nine years old at the time of his death. It is true that the Gedeon notice which records John's death also states that this Emperor had lived for fifty-nine years and seven months. If this statement was accepted, it would then indicate a birth date of June in 1331. Since none of our other evidence would seem to support that early a dating, we might rather assume that here the chronicler erred in reckoning John's age by one year too many.

As to John's moral character, many sources, and Chalcocondyles in particular, give him a bad reputation indeed. Some of this reputation is probably exaggerated, but just how lurid the myths and legends were can be observed, for example, in the history of the so-called (Pseudo-)Dorotheos of Monembasia (edition of Venice, 1750), 492. For a discussion of John V's place of burial, see Appendix VII below.

215. Cf. Charanis, "Strife," p. 286, no. 2, and p. 306. The severe stricture of Gibbons, 198, is more cruel than just. Even the great Edward Gibbon, who recounts with unholy glee the last miseries of the Empire (an account no longer acceptable for accuracy but still worth reading for literary satisfaction), is willing to concede in arch fashion, *Decline and Fall*, VII, 40, that the death of John V might, in the interests of charity, be ascribed to the shock of Bayazid's order.

on the brink of final dissolution. At a time when Byzantium needed a ruler of the caliber of John Cantacuzenus—as the latter himself in his ambitious acts was the first to insist—it received instead John Palaeologus. Kind, simple, and earnest by nature, John V was a man of mediocre ability and weak moral fiber. Yet he was not without awareness of the dangers he faced and not without some conception of how to cope with them.

His efforts to win aid for the Empire by a policy of rapprochement with the Latin West foreshadowed exactly what was later to become his successor's fundamental policy. Though he followed this course consistently and honestly at first, by 1371 he had reached the conclusion that it was doomed to failure, at least in the circumstances which he faced. He thereupon reversed himself, concluding that the only hope for his state was the opposite course—accommodation with and appeasement of the rising Osmanli power. This course, also, he endeavored to follow consistently and honestly, if despairingly, in spite of the recurrent and heartbreaking civil strife and the independent enterprise of Manuel, all of which exposed his realm the more to the tender mercies of the Turk. His final humiliation, a blow alike to his concern for his remaining realm and to his sorely tried paternal affection, was an ironic epitome of all he had suffered. Outclassed as a statesman in his early years by his usurping father-in-law, he now sank to his grave to pass on the remnant of of his patrimony to his more able and more fortunate successor Manuel, who in ability and understanding was far more the grandson of John Cantacuzenus than he was the son of John Palaeologus.

As for Manuel himself, the news of his father's death reached him while he was with Bayazid. Realizing how critical was the element of haste, Manuel managed to effect a secret escape from the Emir's entourage.[216] By March 8, 1391, he reached Constan-

216. Ducas, ed. Grecu, 77, ed. Bonn, 49. Cf. Muralt, p. 739, no. 10; Hammer, I, 222–223, trans. Hellert, I, 303–304; Iorga, *Geschichte*, I, 279–280; Pears, 109; Gibbons, 198. See also Kolias, 53, who perhaps goes a bit too far in his assumption that Manuel was held as a virtual prisoner beyond John's fulfillment of Bayazid's demand. This need not be carried to such lengths, since Manuel in Bayazid's entourage was as good as Bayazid's prisoner anyway. Moreover, Manuel cannot have been too carefully confined, else he would not have been able to hear the news of his father's death— news which the Emir might well have wished to keep secret for his own purposes—nor even to make his escape successfully.

tinople.[217] Once in the city he met with no opposition, as far as we know or might suspect. If there was such a contest, then Manuel had won his race for the succession with the puppet John VII and his sinister manipulator Bayazid. And so, by the end of winter of 1391, having not yet completed his forty-first year, Manuel II Palaeologus at last sat on the throne of Constantine as Emperor in his own right.

217. This date results from an entry of that date in an account of expenses of the Commune of Pera, published by Belgrano, no. 36, p. 161. The reference is to expenses incurred on that date in connection with "the arrival of the lord Chirmanoli emperor of the Greeks when he came from Turchia into Constantinople." Other such entries published by Iorga, *Notes et extraits*, I, 45, speak also of "expensiarum factarum in adventu domini Chir Manoli, imperatoris," but under the date of March 18; and, before that, an entry for March 17 speaks of expenses "pro duobus barchis, que portaverunt dominum potestem in Constinopoli, ad dominum Chir Manoli, imperatorem." As Iorga suggests, p. 41, n. 1, these entry dates may refer to the time of the reimbursement for the expenses rather than to the actual occasion of the expenses. If this warning is correct—and, from the contradictory nature of many of these entry dates at various times, it would certainly seem to be correct, and justified—one should therefore use such dates with some caution, and should avoid relying too heavily on such entries for decisive chronological support. Another such Genoese entry, ed. Belgrano, p. 162, for April 8, 1391, similarly notes expenses for the formal visit of the Podestà of Pera to the Emperor Manuel. Note also another entry, ed. Iorga, *ibid.*, under the date February 25, "pro duobus barchis, que portaverunt dominum potestatem in Constantinopoli, ad dominam imperatricem." The editor mistakenly identifies the Empress in question as Manuel's *wife*. But this is impossible, and in all likelihood this visit was to Manuel's *mother*, to pay respects after the death of John V. The *Bulg. chron.*, 538, by the way, puts the death of John V and the succession of Manuel in the year 6880 (1371–72): the unreliability of this statement need not be dwelt upon.

2. The Failure of Appeasement, 1391–1394

By his escape from Bayazid's camp, Manuel Palaeologus had managed to secure his position on the throne in Constantinople itself in the late winter of 1391. But this accomplishment alone did not settle the question of succession. The aged Cydones, just returned from a trip to Venice, might with pardonable satisfaction and joy hail the accession of "the philosopher king," [1] whom he had so long regarded as his country's last hope. But, however much other Byzantines may have shared his enthusiasm, the choice of their ruler was no longer theirs alone.

The hasty return home would have meant nothing for Manuel's success until Bayazid's attitude had become clear. The Emir's will was now what regulated the fate of the wretched Empire. According to our meager information, Bayazid was enraged by Manuel's escape from his entourage upon hearing the news of John V's death. If this is true, it may well indicate that the Emir did indeed have hopes of putting John VII on the throne as his own candidate. In these circumstances, he might well have

1. Letter C. 214 (No. 47), L. 430, one of Cydones' shortest letters, which Loenertz dates to 1391, after March 8. In it Cydones pleads the fatigue of his recent journey and looks forward to seeing Manuel when the former has recovered his strength. Cf. Loenertz, *Echos d'Orient*, 36 (1937), 281. Cydones himself uses the Platonic phrase τὸν φιλόσοφον Βασιλέα as a complimentary epithet for Manuel often in his letters: for example, C. 219, L. 259, and C. 216, L. 438.

accepted Manuel's escape as a challenge and marched against him forthwith to chastise such presumption. But Bayazid was apparently too deeply committed at that moment to his campaigns in Asia Minor and perhaps did not wish to distract himself with an attack on Constantinople, whose defenses he was possibly reluctant to essay at this point. At any rate, he may have felt that, regardless of this frustration of his own chance to pick the new Emperor, his obvious mastery of the situation was sufficient to make it a matter of little difference who reigned in the capital.

Therefore, Bayazid decided to let matters stand as they were. He sent his terms to Manuel, who was undoubtedly called upon to maintain his status of vassalage and service to the Emir. Bayazid demanded further the establishment of a *kadi* in the capital in order that Muslims might have their own judge in litigation among them there; also, the establishment of a quarter in the city for Turkish merchants. The payment of an annual tribute was, of course, insisted upon. And, finally, Manuel was conceded the right to rule at least within the city, but at the same time Bayazid made it clear that all territory beyond its walls belonged to the Turks.[2]

2. The Greek historians are extremely confused in their narratives and chronology for the whole period of the 1390's. Ducas is the only one to give an account of the death of John V and of the flight and accession of Manuel. For the events thereafter, however, there are points of confusion. Ducas' account, ed. Grecu, 77 ff., ed. Bonn, 49 ff., makes at least some statements which can be accepted as having reasonable plausibility: (1) Bayazid was angry over Manuel's escape; (2) Bayazid sent an embassy to Manuel with his demands; (3) he demanded the establishment of a kadi; (4) he occupied territory outlying the capital. (Cf. Muralt, pp. 739–740, no. 11.) From Ducas' ensuing description of Bayazid's overrunning of the land and investment of Constantinople, writers such as Muralt, p. 744, nos. 10 and 12; Hammer, *Geschichte*, I, 223–224 (trans. Hellert, I, 304–305); Gibbons, 198; Pears, 109–111; also to a lesser extent, Vasiliev, *Hist. Byz. Emp.*, 629, and, most recently and most surprisingly (apparently following Iorga, *Geschichte*, I, 288), Khoury, "L'Empereur Manuel II," 138, have erroneously concluded that Bayazid's siege of Constantinople began at this time. As a result of recent researches, and from our other source material, we now know that this was not at all the case. Cf. Charanis, "Strife," 306–307. But, at any rate, at least the burden of Ducas' information would still appear to merit some credence. Note also the arrogant restriction of Manuel's rule to within the city alone, which Ducas ascribes to the Emir.

There is confirmation of at least his implication that the Turks occupied the lands outside the capital, in Cydones' Letter C. 58 (No. 5), L. 442. In this, he describes the hardship and misery he found in Constantinople upon

For the time being, then, Bayazid was willing to grant Manuel his ephemeral rights. The Emperor of Constantinople would pay his way well enough as a vassal. Manuel himself had no choice but to continue his father's now-standard Byzantine policy of appeasement and subservience to the Turks. Thus it was that, barely on the morrow of his accession to the throne as sole Emperor, Manuel was summoned back to Bayazid's camp to suffer once again the harsh strains and humiliations of yet another campaign as a vassal of the Turks.

returning from a journey, all as a result of the greed of the Turks, who had seized land and levied an impossible tribute. He also states clearly the utter dependence on the Emir, for his support, by the contending claimants to the throne. See Charanis, "Strife," 308–309, for a partial translation of this invaluable text. For its further use, see below, pp. 87–88. Similar if less specific allusions may be found in Letters C. 59 (No. 6), L. 443; C. 228 (No. 49), L. 436; and C. 229 (No. 50), L. 431, all dating also from this same period.

We have seeming confirmation of the installation of a kadi in Constantinople within a year or so of this time, in an entry in the Genoese expense accounts for Pera, published by Belgrano, "Studi e documenti su la colonia genovese di Pera (prima serie)," no. 38, pp. 171–172, which records expenditures of May 24, 1392, "pro zucharo pro recipiendo Cadi turchorum in Palacio." A similar entry is found for October 17, 1391 (Iorga, *Notes et extraits*, I, 52). But we should be cautious in making this interpretation, for we have another such entry of October 16, 1391, which notes, "Expense facte pro cadi Turchorum, qui moram facit in Constantinopoli, quando venit visitando dominum potestatem" (Iorga, 47). That the kadi should be described as making a "delay" ("moram") in Constantinople does not suggest that he was permanently located there. Another Genoese entry, *ibid.*, 43, for the date October 28, 1390, mentions a debt "pro expensis factis in barch[a] pro cadi." This need not be the same kadi, nor do these different entries disprove the possibility of one being in the city after Manuel's accession. But it is clear that we cannot use these entries to prove the point either way. In addition, one should bear in mind that further on Ducas (ed. Grecu, 87, ed. Bonn, 56) states that one of Bayazid's conditions for acceding to John VII's agreement with Manuel in 1399 was that John install a judge for the Turks in Constantinople. Here Ducas does not use the word καδῆς as he does the first time, but, this discrepancy aside, we might infer that Manuel did not fulfill this demand by Bayazid in 1391, if it really was made then, but that it was only left to John to carry out this demand after 1399. Such is the conclusion of Dölger, "Johannes VII., Kaiser der Rhomaer," 31. (Note the uncritical acceptance by K. Lippmann in his old study, *Die Konsularjurisdiktion im Orient, Ihre historische Entwicklung von den frühesten Zeiten bis zur Gegenwart* [Leipzig, 1898], 19–20, of the establishment of a Turkish kadi in Constantinople in 1391.)

In addition to these sources, we have a badly confused entry in Baronius-Raynaldus, *Annales ecclesiastici*, 1393, no. 7 (Vol. 26, p. 540). This states Bayazid's demand for a Turkish quarter and also for a mosque therein; and it also speaks of the exaction of a tribute of 10,000 gold pieces annually. Unfortunately, this reference is included unjustifiably in connection with an

Manuel left Constantinople on June 8, 1391.[3] On July 4 of that year the Venetian Senate took note of the news that the Emperor was going to fight in Bayazid's army.[4] In his absence, Manuel had apparently left his mother, Helena Cantacuzena, as his regent.[5] He himself, shouldering the burden of his obligations, had gone off on a campaign that was to take him deep into Asia Minor with the Turkish army.[6] In a letter written to Theodore Palaeolo-

alleged commencement of the siege of Constantinople in 1393 after the Hungarian victory at Nicopolis Minor; but it is quite likely that its information refers instead to 1391. Such terms of a tribute (also 10,000 gold coins) and establishment of a kadi and mosque in Constantinople, are also stated by Cantemir in his old work, *The History of the Growth and Decay of the Othman Empire,* trans. Tindal (London, 1734), 52–53, but he places this step after Nicopolis, and his chronology is difficult to understand accurately. Perhaps he used the same basic information, derived from Turkish sources, as did Dölger, *Regesten,* nos. 3263–3264, p. 84, in positing a peace treaty between Manuel and Bayazid in 1396–97, including establishment of the kadi at that time—certainly an unlikely chronology in view of our other evidence.

3. Among the chronicle entries published by Gedeon in Ἐκκλησιαστικὴ ἀλήθεια, 23 (1903), is one (p. 381, φ. 140) which reports that "On the 8th of June the Basileus the holy Lord Manuel crossed over to Anatolia, on the feast of the holy Megalomartyr Theodore." The fixing of the date to the feast of (the translation of) St. Theodore (Stratelates) is correct; and even though this entry lacks a statement of year, it may plausibly be accepted as referring to 1391: Loenertz, in Vol. II his edition of Cydones' correspondence, p. 443, n. 1, in connection with some Venetian Senate deliberations.

4. Text on p. 443 of Vol. II of Loenertz' edition of Cydones' correspondence, with the correct date; text also in Iorga, "Veneţia in Marea neagră," 1106, giving the incorrect date of July 14, which is followed in the French summary of Thiriet, *Régestes,* I, no. 797, p. 191; but cf. also Jireček in a review (of Iorga's *Geschichte*) in *Byz. Zeitschr.,* 18 (1909), 584, with the correct date. On June 11, the Senate had arranged for a change of its ambassador and *bailo* in Constantinople (Thiriet, I, p. 191, no. 795), and was now uncertain as to whether or not to carry out this change. Cf. Silberschmidt, *Das orientalische Problem,* 74 (with the correct date); Loenertz, *Echos d'Orient,* 36 (1937), 281.

5. In a deliberation of July 24, 1391, the Venetian Senate finally arranged for a change of *bailo* in Constantinople and gave instructions that, in the event of the Emperor's absence, the departing *bailo* was to address himself to the Empress—unquestionably Helena: Thiriet, *Régestes,* I, no. 798, p. 191. Cf. Silberschmidt, 74; Loenertz, *Echos d'Orient.* Also, an entry in a Genoese expense account for Pera (Iorga, *Notes et extraits,* I, 46) for August 14, 1391, notes the debt to a certain individual "pro expensis factis per ipsum in barchis, quando dominus capitaneus cum sociis irit ad visitandum dominam imperatricem." This Empress plainly was Helena, regent for her son.

6. Loenertz, *Echos d'Orient,* 36 (1937), 281. Charanis, "Strife," 307 ff., settles the chronology and character of this campaign.

gus, dated the autumn or winter of 1391,[7] Cydones describes the dismal situation of Constantinople, oppressed by "the barbarians," its defenses reduced, and its citizens selfishly striving against one another, while the Emperors—Manuel with his rival and, again, undesired comrade-in-arms, John VII—are obliged to fight with "the barbarians" in Phrygia and Pontus.

From correspondence also comes our most important picture of this campaign. But this time the correspondence is Manuel's own. In a series of letters to his friends, Manuel laid bare his feelings and his experiences as he suffered through this ordeal. For some reason contrary to what one might expect in view of the terrible memories it must have held for him, Manuel favored this episode and preserved no less than eight or nine letters of this period when he later gathered a selection of his correspondence for preservation. As a result, we have a priceless set of sources. And, regardless of what factual information may be drawn from them, their greatest value is in their extraordinarily moving and vivid revelation of the miseries of Byzantium and of the sensitive reaction to them of its sovereign, which is unmatched in the annals of Byzantine literature and history. It is a sequence that demands, at long last, a full exposition.

The first of the series in the order in which Manuel preserved them is one that, we may conclude, was written fairly close to the beginning of his absence. Addressed to Cydones, it readily sets the tone of the entire sequence:

Truth to tell, those of my friends who are skilled in writing, who write to me twice and even thrice, hardly ever have an answer from me. Yet, in your case, while you keep your own hand at rest, you command me to write just as if you had written yourself. As to the first point, indeed, the explanation is not to be put down to contempt, or that I think little of giving pleasure to my friends. Never thus may I be found neglectful toward my friends! Rather, there is another reason: even when at leisure words are not readily at my fingertips, as they say, since I have never joined the company of

7. Letter C. 58 (No. 5), L. 442. In his edition, Cammelli makes the grievous mistake of dating this letter and the events that it describes to the incongruous context of 1353. The total incorrectness of this ascription is pointed out by Loenertz, *Echos d'Orient*, 36 (1937), 282, and more emphatically by Charanis, "Strife," p. 308, n. 74. Cammelli's edition of course adds a full French translation; Charanis gives a partial translation into English of this important text.

rhetoricians in the haunts of the Muses; while now, in addition, there is a multitude of troubles, and many preoccupations and crises—as you can imagine! For, to see the Romans and myself, neglecting our own interests, fighting in the land of the Scythians [Tartars] against the Scythians, and serving as a commander to our own enemies—would this not puzzle any Demosthenes and deprive him of all power of speech? So much, then, for the first point. But, as for the second, it is very much a work of your Sirens; for when they sing, they subdue their hearers not only by delighting them but also by making them better men [cf. *Odyssey*, XII, 188]; and when they do not do this, they are more likely to enthrall those who have had some experience of them. For those who are love-stricken long the more for their loved ones when they are absent. As a result, since I have received your customary letter when I am eagerly desirous of it, though in the midst of war and turmoil and though about to mount my horse and there-upon to be occupied in arms, putting aside these things just now, I have not hesitated to write to you, so as to give you a pretext for writing yourself. But do you really yearn to learn what circumstances we are in? I know you do, and your yearning I would fulfill if the situation did not so completely prevent it. But this much only I have concluded must be said: that we exchange fears for fears, and dangers for dangers, and toils for toils, by comparison the lesser for the greater —that is, those that we suffer now with the Persians [Turks] for those that we, being then viewed with suspicion, would suffer if we should not fight in alliance with them—and these things we exchange as if they were but coins, as your comrade Plato says.[8]

8. Letter ιδ′, ed. E. Legrand, *Lettres* (Paris, 1893; reprinted, 1962), 18–19; fully translated here. A free translation in French of a very brief passage from this letter may be found in Berger de Xivrey, *Mémoire*, 66–67. That Manuel's use of the word Σκύθαι in this and the following letter refers to the Tartars is suggested by Moravcsik, *Byzantinoturcica*, II, 282 (though his citations are inaccurate).

The reference to Plato at the end of this letter is not without stylistic interest. It involves the bulk of the last sentence of the letter (after the semi-colon in the above translation): ὅτι φόβους πρὸς φόβους, καὶ κινδύνους πρὸς κινδύνους, καὶ πόνους πρὸς πόνους ἀνταλλαττόμεθα, μικροὺς τῇ παραθέσει πρὸς μείζους, τοὺς νῦν μετὰ τῶν Περσῶν πρὸς τοὺς ἀπὸ τούτων, εἰ μὴ συμμαχοίημεν, ὑφορωμένους, ὥσπερ τὰ νομίσματα, ὁ σὸς ἑταῖρος Πλάτων φησίν. Compare that with the following antecedent passage in Plato's *Phaedo*, 69A: (῍Ω μακάριε Σιμμία, μὴ γὰρ οὐχ αὕτη ᾖ ἡ ὀρθὴ πρὸς ἀρετὴν ἀλλαγή,) ἡδονὰς πρὸς ἡδονὰς καὶ λύπας πρὸς λύπας καὶ φόβον πρὸς φόβον καταλλάττεσθαι, καὶ μείζω πρὸς ἐλάττω, ὥσπερ νομί-σματα.... The obvious and pointed paraphrase of this passage, doubtless made by Manuel from memory rather than direct reference in his circum-stances at that moment, must readily have been recognized with appreciation by Cydones, a fellow-admirer of the great philosopher.

The perennial custom of using classical names for contemporary peoples or places is not the only stylized characteristic of this letter, which is typical of Byzantine epistolography. The stilted rhetoric and the extreme striving for literary elegance will be obvious. The continued protestation of inability to write or apologies and justifications for not doing so are frequent themes, most especially in the letters of Manuel. It is undoubtedly a mannerism to some extent. Yet, one cannot dismiss it entirely as such, for in Manuel's case there were undoubtedly many distractions with which he had to contend. We can understand his problem particularly in connection with this campaign. Indeed, all of the next letter, to Cabasilas,[9] is an elaborate if empty rhetorical discourse on obstacles to his own regular correspondence. There is virtually nothing in it to identify it clearly, but it seems safe to assume that it belongs to our sequence of letters written during the 1391 campaign.

The next letter, to Cydones, is probably the best known of this series. In spite of its crabbed and tortured style, it is also perhaps the most vivid and the most striking: [10]

Much land did your letter traverse and far beyond the mountains it went, and, after crossing rivers, it found me at last in a quite small plain. As this plain is encircled by continuous mountains—precipitous, a poet would have said—it scarcely suffices as a camp for the army. In addition, it both seems and is extremely wild; and, save for a little wood, and water not altogether clear, it can furnish us with none of the essentials. For it is uninhabited, as a result of the flight of its inhabitants from it to clefts and woods and tops of mountains, as they tried to escape from what they have not been able to escape: a slaughter that is most savage and most inhuman and without any formality of justice. Every mouth that is opened toward pleading some defense the sword anticipates, as it were, stopping it up. And, in truth, neither unripe age nor feminine weakness and nature are spared. Nor, therefore, could those no longer able to turn their feet to flight—either because of old age or because of illness—escape this murderous blade. And, quite the most insufferable thing, he among the priests of

9. Letter ιε', ed. Legrand, 20–21. For the identity of this Cabasilas, see above, pp. 59–60 and n. 163.

10. Letter ις', ed. Legrand, 21–25, fully translated here. There is a nearly complete translation into French by Berger de Xivrey, 55–59, and in English by Charanis, "Strife," 310–311; also, a very brief passage in Vasiliev, *Hist. Byz. Emp.*, 587–588.

the Persians [Turks] who is revered, be it said even villainous, is called a "mavlonas." Indeed, this most revered salutation is no more common for them, among the people of the same race, than among the Tribalians [Serbians], Mysians [Bulgarians], and Illyrians [Albanians], who, supposing that they exact judgment for what they have suffered long ago from this nation and proclaiming that they avenge Christ, actually kill all those whom they chance to meet thereafter. Even thus they do, but it is not seemly for me to speak of these things; perhaps you may hear them from others.[11]

So much, then, for the details of this slaughter.

But as for the plain in which I am now, it did indeed once have some name when it prospered under the Romans, while they frequented and dominated it. But now, in seeking to learn this name, it is just as if I were to seek for wings on a wolf, as they say, in the absence of someone to inform me. While it is certainly possible to see here many cities, yet, they do not include that by which cities are truly adorned, and without which they are not rightfully called cities —people. And so the majority of them lie as but a pitiable sight for those to whose ancestors they belonged as a possession in olden times. But not even the names remain to these places as a result of their previous destruction. In truth, when I asked what the cities were named, and whenever those of whom I enquired would reply that "We destroyed these places and time has destroyed their names," forthwith was I aggrieved; but yet in silence I mourned for a while, since I was still able to be discreet. But should someone take away the names that the cities once possessed and then apply some barbarous and uncouth ones, henceforth lamenting with an outcry, I was not able to conceal my feelings, though for many reasons—as you can imagine—I all but wished to do so.

And since, therefore, I have not been able to inform you plainly where on earth we are—for, as to places to which a name remains not, what contrivance is there to make them clear in letters?—the second best course I may attempt to follow is to enable you, as far as is possible, with the aid of other places whose names have not been destroyed, to imagine also those in which I am occupied.

Do you know of the city of Pompeios [Pompeiopolis], that beautiful, marvelous, and great city—but rather the city that once was such, for now scarcely anywhere do remains of it appear—lying on a bank of the river with a bridge of stone and once adorned with porticos marvelous in their majesty, beauty, and skill? This city, whose founder was called "Great" by the Romans, and whose own title as

11. For an attempt to interpret this enigmatic passage, see Appendix VIII below.

such was confirmed by many trophies—testified, when flourishing, no less by the monuments I have described, that he was indeed great. Then, leaving behind this city, and after it that of Zeno [Zenopolis], and with Sinope on one hand to the left side and with the Halys on the other, we marched on for many days, just as if we were using the sun as our guide. For it is necessary to take note of its arising and then to advance accordingly in a straight line if we would intend, as they say, not to become experienced in error.

Do you wish to learn to what end it pleases him who leads the army to do these things? He supposes that he would either enslave or win as an ally a certain satrap [emir], by name Peitzas, who is master of land bordering on both Sinope and Aminsos, and of some few small towns and of a number of men easily reckoned. And, further, once he has taken Sinope, as if by envelopments, he will either render subordinate to himself, or else, after he has bound Spentares—this is the ruler of Sinope—by such oaths as the latter would see fit to approve and to abide by, he will then by means of such trophies frighten the man who rules Sebasteia with the Scythians [Tartars]. And, when he should achieve these things according to his intent, thereupon, as he says, he will himself go back homeward, and I will do the same myself, with God's help.

It is not, of course, an easy matter to bear such things; nor to bear the scarcity of provisions, and the strong wintry weather, and the disease which, since it has taken hold of many of my men, has also—as you can imagine—stricken my soul. And there are other concerns also; so many that the convention of letters excludes them from enumeration. Indeed, since I have now been absent for such a long time, there are so many concerns of this kind that it is likely our affairs at home are in jeopardy. But it is particularly unbearable that, while I am occupied here, it is not possible to see or to hear or to do anything from which my spirit might manage to derive some cultivation and refinement. Unbearable it is, also—amid these activities in which I neither was reared nor am accustomed nor was born to rejoice—to have to abstain from those of my occupations that are altogether more important. And this era lost in total violence concedes no surcease of what conduces toward this situation. So must one, for the time being, condemn the era while letting alone the very individual one ought to blame.

And this is but the worst of the evils which brought me to this position, these evils that bloom and swell within me like diseases and wounds, today even more than formerly. Wherefore, a sensible person who partakes of these troubles will not, having now experienced the diseases, expect deliverance, since he was not delivered formerly when doing these things while healthy. But, oh that God would allow those who are delivered from a surely most evil mode of life to enjoy pure health the rest of the time! For many reasons, therefore, it is better to anticipate reaching this state, and then, holding out these hopes to ourselves, to undertake what actions might seem to contribute to them.

I know I am exceeding the measure of a letter. But perhaps I did not exceed your longing to learn of my circumstances. Thus, while another person will suppose that he is hearing Thersites haranguing when he reads my letter, yet, you would, for your part, regard it as laconic. But, O worthy one, do not pursue unattainable goals, such as having me tell all of the unpleasant things I have come to experience. So numerous also are become their ramifications that they are themselves constraints on me to keep silent. Into such a sea, then, you needs must sail your ship, but I ought not send my vessel thus out to sea. And the more so, since there is no end to it within my sight. But it is best to imagine that my ship, should it sail along the coast and reach a harbor before sunset, gains an anchorage there. For these reasons, therefore, neither did I speak on all matters nor did I remain silent on all matters. And I also considered this an especially just discharging of my obligation; for there is an obligation on those of us bound by love to take up the task of making known our circumstances to each other in these letters whenever we should not be together, yet not to extend the narrative with what would have aggrieved you. Following this principle, then, I leave off writing; but also for the further reason that I can all but see those who are summoning me to our ruler. For perhaps he wishes to drink a toast again and to force me to take my fill of his wine in plenty out of all sorts of golden bowls and drinking cups, supposing with these gestures to soothe my despondency over what things I have described; which circumstances themselves would fill me with sorrow, even were I otherwise in good spirits.[12]

12. Loenertz, *Echos d'Orient*, 36 (1937), p. 281, n. 6, maintains that the foregoing letter was answered by Cydones' Letter C. 217, L. 432, which he dates in his edition to November, 1391. Cydones' letter is a florid affair, praising the style—or, should one say, the successful obscurity?—of Manuel's letter, describing the woes and hardships being endured by Constantinople, and expressing the hope that the Emperor will at last bring help to "the Romans." This same general theme—the hope that Manuel, the nation's one remaining bulwark, will soon return to bring salvation—may be found also in similar form in other Cydones letters: C. 241, L. 444, and C. 227, L. 429, which Loenertz dates summer–autumn of 1391; and also C. 216, L. 438, and C. 247, L. 447, which he thinks may date from 1393, but which seem also to fit readily into the period of 1391. Also to this exchange of correspondence belongs Letter C. 218, L. 445.

The next letter, to Pothos, is again an elaborate but general exercise in rhetoric by Manuel, on the difficulty he faces in answering letters. But we might note in passing its conclusion:

For the sake, then, of what is in your prayers—to see me swiftly returning home safe and receiving as a reward for toils and dangers the safety of our homeland, as far as is possible—receive now this letter which comes to you.[13]

As the campaign waxed on, its hardships for Manuel and his company increased. These privations are notably portrayed in the next letter, to Constantine Asan:

What letters you desire I am well aware. For, were I myself remaining at home, while you yourself were away from me, I would be eagerly desirous of them, even as I know you to be indeed desirous of the same things. Those suffering from these ills are in need of identical medicines. And these requisites are but long letters with long narrative; for this alone serves, as it were, to bind friends separated by distance. To be sure, there are many things that afford me numerous pretexts to protract my letters. But at the same time, these very things that cause me to have so much to write do not allow me an opportunity to write. For, in the respects in which this situation supplies raw material, it does not permit me to be at leisure, deluging me with troubles that would rival snowstorms. Hear, however, what is certainly like to a riddle, but is nonetheless most true; from this I believe you should well be able to see for yourself, at least in imagination, the rest of my circumstances. As to the one part of this paradox, none of our enemies attacked this army, for it has not been so much as seen from afar. Nor did they even send forth "a sound from the holy precinct," which is customary, both among others of our neighboring enemies who are by no means stronger than we are and, especially, also among the Scythians [Tartars], who imitate bitches. For when the latter are afraid, while they may be fleeing in terror themselves, they cease not in their effort to frighten others. Thus now do the once marvelous Scythians tremble, while allowing the ravaging of their land with impunity.

As for the other part of this paradox, the scarcity of market goods has come to exceed all ability of an enemy to harm us. For some days now we have been seeking barley as if for wings on a wolf, as they say; since one would more readily find a white Ethiop than this necessity. And while it is certainly possible to find it somewhere now, yet, whoever should chance on this good fortune is forthwith prosperous

13. Letter ιζ', ed. Legrand, 26–27; translated here are ll. 26–32.

and is celebrated. And grass there is in no wise, nor any other greenery from which a horse that is famished is likely to be nourished. For this earth is on every side without moisture, being like as sand. Wherefore the majority of our horses, once they are worn out, are become worthless to us. And so one was obliged to sell some of his horses just to purchase barley. But then he learned that he would have to accept only five pieces of silver himself for each of his horses, but that he would have to pay five plus forty if he had to give but one horse his fill of barley. The unhappy fellow who calculates that the proper nourishment for one horse for each day would cost nine horses, and who raises an outcry as he marches past the horses that are being slaughtered, has become an image of common talk to an extent that has never occurred before, I believe, not even among people besieged in their cities, much less in an army which was besieging cities. And as for you, well do I know that you will laugh at these things, and yet be stung to the soul by what trials it is necessary for me to suffer likewise with the others.[14]

The next letter, to Cydones, continues in much the same vein, although not without some additional bitterness and recrimination against detractors or restless elements at home:

To be sure, you are the sort of person who understands how to judge occasions and places, and, in general, what significance the said circumstances have in times which bring so many difficulties. But I, on my part, am ever in arms and in expectations of wars; and I am also involved, moreover, in monstrous hunger and in cold and in crossing rivers, and in passing over mountains that are not even able to sustain wild animals, and in other circumstances more unpleasant than these, which have need of an historian, not of a letter-writer. But these hardships are, of course, in common with all the army. What is indeed unbearable for me is that I am fighting beside these people and on behalf of these people when to add to their strength is to diminish our own. If, therefore, I had thought you would reckon as an injustice my not having sent letters to you for such a long time, I would in fact be doing you an injustice. Is this not so? If you are indeed, on your part, as I have just described you, I am, in my turn, in a state of affairs with which God alone could deal. Even if there were otherwise perhaps some leisure for me to write, there would have hindered my hand, as well you know, the fact that I have nothing to write except what it were perhaps better not to write. And certainly now my obstacles to leisure and my troubles are no less than

14. Letter ιη′, ed. Legrand, 27–28, fully translated; a brief passage has been put into French by Berger de Xivrey, 69.

before. But the fact that I can rejoice in having people to whom I am able to write causes all the other matters to be put second, and causes me to write to you more eagerly. This I am doing even now in a little tent, and by night, as if concealing myself, and exchanging for going to sleep—which serves no less than even nourishment itself, I know, to strengthen an exhausted body—this writing. As for those to whom it is not bearable that I should be engaged in literary pursuits when sitting at home, they would quickly make a great outcry could they but see me doing these things here. For, with regard to all the evils which they are presently experiencing, and have experienced, they need only blame themselves. Yet, they would as easily blame my literary pursuits for making rivers flow backward, since they do not consider me guiltless of such charges, and you equally as well, for obvious reasons. But I am returning to you safe and as swiftly as possible, with God's help, and restoring to our homeland all those whom I was leading when I departed from home. And since we are dealing with unpleasant troubles which far surpass in this respect the preceding ones in former times—for this was agreed by all those now in such advanced age—we probably enjoy our cheerfulness the more when suddenly becoming free of them. Verily, the situation is naught else but that the Comic Poet [Aristophanes], if he were present to observe it, would, I believe, compose a drama, just as he once did the *Plutus,* now with Fortune appearing as blind in representation of our dangers and toils and numerous expenses. Since he [Bayazid] admits that furnishing him these things [i.e. Byzantine aid] has provided him with a considerable advantage in the balance against his enemies, he promises that there will be great rewards from him for us. But, while we may as yet be discreet, for him to take away nothing else of what is still ours may itself be justly considered a great reward. If our circumstances are going to appear changed for the better, it will simply be attributable to God alone: may He, being good and encompassing all things in His hands, loose us from this evil and bring us back in the swiftest possible way to the good fortune of our ancestors! [15]

The implication of the foregoing letter is clearly an expectation on the part of Manuel that the campaign will end and he will return home not long thereafter, bringing with him at least some advantage accrued to Byzantine interests as a result of it all.

15. Letter ιθ′, ed. Legrand, 28–30, fully translated here. A rendering of a very brief extract from this letter may be found in French in Berger de Xivrey, 59; and in English in Charanis, "Strife," 109–110, and Vasiliev, *Hist. Byz. Emp.,* 587. But no one has fully exploited this difficult and important letter in full. See also below, pp. 419–420.

But, assuming that these letters are indeed in proper chronological sequence in our manuscript, we may infer that he miscalculated his prospects, at least as regards his returning home soon; for the next few letters reveal him apparently still on campaign, or at least delayed on the way home. These remaining letters, three of them, offer less that bears directly on these events, but they do contain some interesting minor details. The next in the sequence [16] describes a difficult passage of the River Halys and also a stop at Ancyra. This latter allusion is of special interest, because it was undoubtedly during this stop that Manuel had the opportunity to enter into a disputation with a Muslim scholar that resulted in the Emperor's important polemical work *Dialogue Which Was Held with a Certain Persian, the Worthy Mouterizes, in Angkyra of Galatia.*[17] The next two letters,[18] both brief and

16. Letter χ', ed. Legrand, 30–31.

17. This lengthy work, consisting of twenty-six Dialogues plus a *Prooimion,* is of great value for its insight into the religious perspectives of the times as well as into many of the customs of the rising Turkish nation. In the introductory letter to his brother, Theodore, for whom the work was prepared, Manuel describes (ed. Migne, *Patr. gr.,* 156, coll. 126–129) the occasion of its genesis.

Despite its importance among Manuel's works, this major composition is only now being published in its entirety. Suddenly, after such long neglect, no less than two publications involving it are appearing. One is a complete critical text, with notes and commentary, by E. Trapp, *Manuel II. Palaiologos, Dialoge mit einem "Perser"* (*Wiener byzantinische Studien,* 2: Vienna, Graz, & Cologne, 1966). The other is but an extract, including, however, not only text and notes but also a French translation, all prepared by T. Khoury, as *Entretiens avec un musulman, 7e controverse* (*Sources chrétiennes,* 115: Paris, 1966). Neither of these publications had reached me by this writing and therefore, though I have included them in my cumulative Bibliography below, I have been unable to use them in preparing this book. Previously, the only segments of the total work available in published form were the *Prooimion,* with its introductory epistle, and the first two Dialogues, in Migne, *Patr. gr.,* 156, coll. 126–173. Otherwise, until now, the only good idea of its contents to be obtained was in L. Petit's valuable essay on Manuel and his writings in the *Dictionaire de théologie catholique,* IV, 2, pp. 1929–1930. For an allusion to the work as a reflection of the Byzantine attitude toward Turkish power, see C. Turan, "The Ideal of World Domination among the Medieval Turks," *Studia islamica,* 4 (1955), 87; while this theme has been expanded upon more fully since then by C. J. G. Turner in pp. 348–352 and 372–373 of his article, "Pages from Late Byzantine Philosophy of History," *Byz. Zeitschr.,* 57 (1964), 346–373. In general, cf. also Charanis, "Strife," 309.

Only as this book goes to press has there appeared an article prompted by the Trapp and Khoury publications cited above: E. Voordeckers' "Les 'Entretiens avec un Perse' de l'empereur Manuel II Paléologue. (A propos de deux éditions récentes)," *Byzantion,* 36 (1966 [1967]), 311–317.

18. Letters χα' and χβ', ed. Legrand, 31–32, and 32, respectively.

both to Cydones, are of interest simply in that they speak of a plague that we know raged in the capital during the year 1391.[19]

As a group, however, this sequence of letters gives us a clear portrayal in Manuel's own words, stilted as they often may be, of his situation and of his own attitudes. He realized, as he points out in that one memorable passage, that helping the Turks grow stronger by campaigning for them only helped Byzantium become weaker. But he also understood that, under current conditions, there was little else he could do. Plainly, in these early years of his reign, Manuel had completely, if reluctantly, accepted his father's policy of appeasement and was trying to follow it as faithfully as John V had done. As for Bayazid, he may have been willing to allow Manuel the honor of the Imperial title, but he took a sardonic delight in making clear to the Emperor that it was an empty honor by subjecting Manuel to every indignity and humiliation while he had him under his thumb. Manuel's own descriptions of his misery win our renewed admiration for his ability to continue to follow his commitment to the policy of accommodation with the Turks, regardless of all the extremes of physical and mental anguish it brought him personally.[20]

Yet, for all the bitterness we can see accumulating in his

19. The plague is dated to this year in Βρ. χρ. No. 27, p. 46, l. 24 (p. 516, l. 9, in the back of the Bonn edition of Ducas). Loenertz, "Pour l'histoire du Péloponnèse au XIVᵉ siècle," 155, and, following him, Charanis, "Strife," 311, perhaps as a result of a misprint, mistakenly cite Letter κ' as the one that refers to this plague, when it is really Letter κα' which does so. At any rate, the former wisely points out the link between Cydones' Letter C. 229 (No. 50), L. 431, and Manuel's Letter κα' (which he cites correctly in his edition of Cydones' text). The letter by Cydones was written to Manuel in October–December of 1391, according to Loenertz' dating. Aside from its reference to the plague, it is very much in the tone of those other Cydones letters cited in n. 12 above. Loenertz, *Les Recueils des Lettres de Démétrius Cydonès*, 121, dates Manuel's Letter κβ', along with a number of its successors, to 1392–96. In view of the reference to the plague also in Letter κβ', however, I would suggest placing it with Letter κα', so similar to it, about 1391 or early 1392.

20. Cf. Charanis, "Strife," 309: "These letters reveal the delicate nature of their author and the spiritual agony which he experienced for having to serve the barbarian. Manuel was spiritually never reconciled to the servile policy that he was forced to follow toward the Turkish Sultan. He could stand the fatigue and the privations that this policy imposed upon him, but he could not bear the thought that he was contributing to augment the power of the Turks." Cf. also Vasiliev, *Hist. Byz. Emp.*, 587–588.

letters, there is no indication that Manuel had any intention of not continuing the official course of appeasement by the time this nightmarish campaign ended. Its duration was long. According to a Genoese document, he was apparently back in the capital only in early January of 1392.[21] It was only on February 16 of that year that the Venetian Senate took notice of his return.[22] But by this latter date there had already occurred an important event in both the life of Manuel and the history of Byzantium.

In February of 1392 Manuel, in his forty-second year and apparently not previously married,[23] took as his wife and Empress Helena, daughter of the Serbian prince Konstantin Dejanović, or Dragaš.[24] To what extent this unique marriage of a Byzantine

21. An entry in an account, published by Belgrano, no. 38, p. 169, of expenses for the colony of Pera for January 7, 1392, lists an expense for vessels "pro eundo ad visitandum dominum Imperatorem in Constantinopolim in festo vigilie Epifanie Domini per dominum Potestatem con comitiva." Cf. Iorga, *Notes et extraits*, I, 53. There is another reference (Iorga, *ibid.*) to expenses dated "the last day of January," 1392, "pro barchis que portaverunt . . . ambaxatores communis ad dominum imperatorem."

22. Text of this notice as published by Loenertz, pp. 445–446 of the second volume of his edition of Cydones' correspondence. Cf. Thiriet, *Régestes*, I, no. 808, p. 193; also Jireček review, *Byz. Zeitschr.*, 18 (1909), 584–585. On March 8, the Senate instructed its agents to congratulate Manuel on his accession and to renew negotiations concerning debts and arrangements for Tenedos: Thiriet, no. 809, p. 193; cf. Silberschmidt, 75–76. Halecki, "Two Palaeologi in Venice, 1370–1371," 334–335, speaks of a Venetian document of 1391 which expresses congratulations to Manuel on his accession and which attempts to renew the good will which, the Venetians affirm, had flourished between the *Serenissima* and Manuel's house. Unfortunately, he is unable to quote or cite specifically, and no such text as he describes has yet been published or discussed elsewhere. (He also attempts to use this reference to good will between the Venetians and Manuel's house as an argument in favor of his rejection of John V's "imprisonment" in 1370; but such use is unwarranted since, as we have seen, there were later instances of Venetian support or aid for John V and Manuel to which the Venetians could be referring.)

23. For a discussion of Manuel's marital status and also of the related problem of the last years of his mother, see Appendix IX below.

24. On Helena Dragaš, the only single study is D. Anastasejević's article "Jedina vizantijska carica Srpkinja" ("The Only Serbian Byzantine Empress"), *Brastvo*, 30 (*Društvo Sv. Save*, 50, Belgrade, 1939), 26–48. Although it contributes no startling or unusual information, this article does bring together the already known and available information on her. It suffers, however, in the light of subsequent researches, which have revised and settled questions of dating, especially of the marriage, and of the events of Serres. But, on the other hand, it is useful for discussion of her Serbian background, pp. 26–28. On her father, there is a book by J. Hadji-Vasiljević, *Dragaš i Konstantin Dejanovići* (Belgrade, 1902), which was not available to me. On the question

ruler with a Serbian princess may have implied an alliance by
Manuel with the powerful ruler of a large Macedonian realm is
difficult to determine, since the source accounts linking it with
demonstrably later events are incorrect, at least so far as such
a specific link is concerned.[25] At any rate, it was to be a fruitful

of her father's name, however, there is now the article by Ostrogorsky,
"Gospodin Konstantin Dragaš" ("Le Sieur Constantin Dragaš"), in *Zbornik
Filozofskog Fakulteta,* 7/1 (Belgrade, 1963), 287–294 (in Serbo-Croatian,
with a French summary).

Sphrantzes (*Chronicon Minus,* ed. Migne, 156), 1052–1053, in relating
Helena's death on March 23, 1450, gives only the monastic name which she
took, Hypomene (see also Appendix IX), and it is only in the Pseudo-
Phrantzes, 210, that her original name is incorrectly given as Irene. Hence
the unwarranted confusion among modern writers who have often accepted,
or at least partly credited, this actually quite inauthentic invention or mistake
of the spurious text. This fact also renders unnecessary the ingenious suggestion of Anastasejević, p. 39, that Irene could have been an earlier monastic
name, taken before a final vow under the name of Hypomene. She is named
as the nun Hypomene in a diptych, the text of which is in the *Parisinus gr.
2509,* f. 232ᵛ: published by F. E. Brightman, *Liturgies Eastern and Western*
(Oxford, 1896), 551–552. Since this diptych was made in the reign of the
Patriarch Joseph II (1416–1439) we have a *terminus ante quem* for her
taking the veil. If the dating of the manuscript containing this text to about
1430 is correct, she may well have become a nun within several years after
Manuel's death in 1425.

We do not know her age at the time of her marriage, but, in view of the
fact that she survived her husband by a full twenty-five years, she must have
been a good deal younger than he. We know little of her personally, although
it is plain that she was an important stabilizing influence among her quarrelsome sons in the last decades of the Empire. Again, as with Manuel's mother,
the dowager, even when a nun, was not completely secluded and isolated
from court life.

The *Chron. Vat. gr. 162,* no. 15, p. 209, ll. 65–66, speaks of Helena as "one-
eyed, but prudent by nature" (τῆς μονοφ θάλμου, τῆς φύσειφρονίμον).
This strange assertion is inexplicable, and is supported by no other source.
There seems to be no indication of such a deformity in the famous portrait
of her with Manuel and three of their sons in the manuscript of Dionysus
the Areopagite, now in the Louvre. (For Helena and this manuscript portrait, see Anastasejević, p. 33, and Vasiliev, *Hist. Byz. Emp.,* 586–587; see
also below, pp. 263–264.) This statement is therefore probably best set
down as some kind of mistake.

25. Chalcocondyles, ed. Darkó, I, 75, ed. Bonn, 81, followed by the
Pseudo-Phrantzes, ed. Papadopoulos, 62–63, ed. Bonn, 58, and the *Chron.
Barb. 111,* 35, maintains that the betrothal of Helena to Manuel was the outcome of a pact among the Christian princes after the meeting at Serres. But
we know from our other sources that the latter event belongs to a later year,
as will be shown below (see nn. 46 and 47), whereas this marriage is irrefu-
tably datable to some two years earlier. The account by the aforementioned
historians cannot be trusted: cf. Loenertz, "Pour l'histoire du Péloponnèse,"
180. But it is not impossible that some alliance was nevertheless envisioned

Figure 5: *Manuel, with His Wife and Three Oldest Sons.* Illuminated
Miniature, Musée du Louvre, Paris, *Ivoires* A 53, f. 1 (photo courtesy M.
Chuzeville, Paris; see Appendix XXIV, A, I, 3).

and presumably happy marriage for Manuel. On the seventh or eighth of February, Helena made her entry into the capital.[26] On the tenth of February the wedding was celebrated, and on the following day Manuel and his new Empress were crowned together by the Patriarch Antonios.[27] In view of the unstable state

even in 1392. Berger de Xivrey, 77, accepts this false story, although he dates the whole affair to 1391, and in this he is mistakenly followed by A. T. Papadopulos, *Versuch einer Genealogie der Palaiologen, 1259–1453*, 55. Muralt, p. 752, no. 22, confusing everything, dates this false association 1395. Even Anastasejević, pp. 28–30, cannot escape the pitfalls of these source confusions, in spite of the best critical intentions. And, more recently, Dölger, *Regesten*, no. 3237, p. 80, persists in accepting the Pseudo-Phrantzes' statements at face value.

26. The Genoese expense account, Belgrano, 169, notes, for this hyphenated double date, expenses for some things "which were cast over the head of the lady Empress in her entry which she made into Constantinople." ("Pro Jocabo de Terdona domicilo domini Potestatis, et sunt qui proiecti fuerunt super capud domine Imperatricis in eius adventu que fecit in Constantinopoli," 16 *hyperpyra*.) It is difficult to explain the structure of the words "et sunt qui" in this passage. Conceivably the text is corrupted or barbarized —plainly, the Latin of these entries is generally far from pure—and either a word has been fragmented or distorted or left out. On the other hand, however, such wording does occur elsewhere occasionally in these entry passages; perhaps it is a standard phraseology in which one might read an additional "pro" before "qui" and hope for the best. What these "things" were is difficult to say in this context. They could have been coins. The custom of showering coins over the monarch's head is noted in the description, cited below, in Ignatii of Smolensk's account of the coronation: cf. Salomon, "Zu Ignatij von Smolensk," 270. But they would have had to be coins of extremely small value to have been covered by the expenditure of 16 *hyperpyra*. These "things" might also have been flowers. Then, too, they might have been *confetti*, in the literal sense of the Italian word, from which is derived the modern Greek word and custom of κουφέτα—that is, sweetmeats, candied fruits, nuts, and so on, which are given or thrown at weddings. (For such a use of the word "confetti," meaning simply "sweetmeats" without such specifically festal significance, in connection with the reception of John VIII in Venice in 1423, see the extract from a contemporary text quoted by Iorga, *Notes et extraits*, I, pp. 349–350, n. 2.) Since Helena's "adventus" was for her wedding, this sort of reception would not at all have been out of place. The "domicilus" cited might then have been involved with the preparation of such things. This same "Jocabo de Terdona" is mentioned elsewhere in these Genoese expense accounts, in connection with the procuring of wine: Iorga, *Notes et extraits*, pp. 42, 43, 44 (twice), 45, 48–49, and 49 (twice again, once "pro confectis et vino"). He may have been some sort of supervisor of provisioning for the Podestà. All things considered, I think this explanation of the passage, as referring to some kind of "confetti," is the most plausible until there is evidence to the contrary.

27. The Genoese expense account, Belgrano, 169, notes for the tenth of February the transportation of the Podestà of Pera and his company to the city for the nuptials of the Emperor ("Pro avaris barcarum que porta-

of Manuel's circumstances, the taking of a wife might have seemed a somewhat dubious luxury for him. But he understood clearly that the possession of heirs, which this marriage soon brought him, was a decided advantage to his position in his

verunt dominum potestem et comitivam ad festum nupciarum domini Imperatoris.") The celebration of the coronation on the next day, February 11, is attested by two independent sources. One is a chronicle notice among those published by Gedeon (p. 382, φ. 190), which is extensively detailed and essentially accurate; this source seems not to have been used in modern discussions of the event. The other source for this date is a long and detailed description of the ceremony by the eyewitness Ignatii of Smolensk: trans. by Khitrovo, *Itinéraires russes en Orient,* 143–147, and by Salomon, 260–265. In his comments (265–270), Salomon adds extended commentary on the coronation ritual. Strangely enough, Christophilopoulou, Ἐκλογή, ἀναγόρευσις καὶ στέψις τοῦ βυζαντινοῦ αὐτοκράτορος, totally ignores this coronation, in spite of Ignatii's priceless description of the ceremonial. There is also another source on this coronation of 1391, published by Ch. Loparev in his article, "K chinu tsarskago koronovaniia v vizantii," in a Festschrift in honor of D. T. Kobeko (St. Petersburg, 1921), pp. 1–11; this study of Byzantine coronations was not available to me, but, according to a notice in *Byz. Zeitschr.,* 22 (1922), 601, Loparev transcribes this fragmentary Greek text on his pp. 9–11. For some general comments, however, on the coronation ceremony in the time of Manuel, see A. Heisenberg, *Aus der Geschichte und Literatur der Palaiologenzeit* (*Sitzungsberichte der Bayerischen Akademie der Wissenschaften, Philosophische-philologische und historische Klasse,* Abhand. 10, Munich, 1920), 89 ff., and 111.

Cf. also Kolias, " Ἡ ἀνταρσία Ἰωάννου Ζ'," 53, who (as noted above, p. 75, n. 200) makes too much of the idea of this coronation as a legalization of Manuel's claim to the full Imperial title and ignores the more important association of the event with Manuel's marriage to Helena. For this coronation not only celebrated Manuel's sole accession to the throne, but it also served the purpose of crowning the new Empress.

That the marriage and the coronation took place respectively on two successive days can hardly be doubted, in view of the failure of our respective sources for each event to mention the other—a secure assumption particularly in the case of the manifestly detailed and complete description by Ignatii. Unfortunately, however, we lack the ultimate confirmation of a separate Genoese expense entry involving the coronation; even though we know from Ignatii that Genoese representatives were present at the latter ceremony. The date of the marriage possibly may not, of course, have been the actual one given by the Genoese document, but it could not have been later than February 10, when the expenditure was made good (if not actually incurred) by authorities of Pera; whereas Ignatii's account plainly gives February 11 (correctly given as a Sunday, the Feast of the Prodigal Son, which is when this movable Feast fell in 1392), and its accuracy has never been questioned. As for the Gedeon entry, though it does give the year as 6901, first indiction, which would be 1393, this can perhaps be safely regarded as an error by one year, for the entry otherwise corroborates Ignatii by giving the same date of February 11, adding the fact that it was the Feast of St. Vlasios in the normal Church calendar, which is correct, and which did fall on Sunday, February

rivalry with his childless young nephew, as is shown in a later literary work by the Emperor.[28]

Manuel was intended by Bayazid to campaign again during the season of 1392, this time in an unusual capacity. For the first time the Turks mounted a war fleet, and the command of it was to be given to Manuel, who was to participate thus in an assault by sea and by land on Sinope. At least such was the report which, by April 26, 1392, reached the Venetians, who were gravely concerned as to any possible ulterior designs on their own Levantine holdings.[29] Two other Latin documents,

11, in 6900, indiction 15 (1392). The distinction between the separate dates for the marriage and the coronation has not been noted by Loenertz, "Une Erreur singulière de Laonic Chalcocandyle," p. 182, n. 3. Iorga, *Geschichte*, I, 280, mistakenly places the coronation of Manuel and Helena in 1391, immediately following his father's death.

Since the foregoing was written, P. Schreiner has published his exhaustive and valuable study, "Hochzeit und Krönung Kaiser Manuels II. im Jahre 1392," *Byz. Zeitschr.*, 60 (1967), 70–85, in which he reviews the bride's background (70–72), takes note of the difference in date (72), gives a new edition of the rare Greek account of the coronation ceremony (75–79) which had previously been published by Loparev, as mentioned earlier in this note, and then discusses (79–81) and translates into German (81–85) the account by Ignatii of Smolensk.

28. Loenertz, "Une Erreur singulière," 183, on the basis of Manuel's unpublished Περὶ γάμου. Loenertz, *ibid.*, 182 and 183, reviewing the faulty reckoning of Sphrantzes, places the birth of the Imperial couple's first son, the future John VIII, on December 17, 1392. Cf. Loenertz, *Recueils*, 121; also Khoury, 139. There is corroboration of this date in another source, though Loenertz did not cite it. One of the short chronicle entries edited by Gedeon (p. 382, φ. 190, second entry) reports that "On the 18th of the month of November, [on the feast] of the holy megalomartyr Sebastian, there was born the most fortunate Basileus and son of the Basileus the Lord Manuel." No year is given, so that the statement might refer to either of Manuel's two sons who became Emperor—John VIII or Constantine XI. Since we know that Constantine was born in *February* (of 1405: see Appendix XV below), the reference cannot be applied to him. On the other hand, since the Feast of St. Sebastian occurs on *December* 18, not November 18, it obviously must refer to the birth of John. The difference between December 17 as in Sphrantzes and December 18 in the chronicle is not much of a problem.

29. The text of this deliberation is on pp. 446–448 of Vol. II of Loenertz' edition of Cydones' correspondence; and in Iorga, "Veneţia in Marea neagră," 1107–1108; cf. Thiriet, *Régestes*, I, no. 813, p. 194. In a further deliberation, of April 30 (text, Loenertz, *ibid.*, 448–449; cf. Thiriet, no. 813, p. 194), the Venetians noted that "the lord emperor of Constantinople, as is clear from all indications, is ever ready for all commands of Bayazid." In view of their interests in the area, they therefore took steps to investigate these rumored naval movements; cf. Jireček review, *Byz. Zeitschr.*, 18 (1909), 585; cf. also Silberschmidt, 78–82, and Vasiliev, *Hist. Byz. Emp.*, 629–30, who also yield

however, make it clear that in July of 1392 Manuel was in Constantinople. Therefore, it is not definitely known whether he really did participate in such an expedition.[30]

The spectacle of the successor of Constantine as a military vassal to the Turk could not fail to make a deep impression on other Christians, especially of the Orthodox Faith. And, indeed, we have an extraordinarily vivid reflection of the attitudes such a decline really did breed and of the Byzantine reaction to them in a Patriarchal letter written, apparently in 1393, to "The most noble great King of Moscow and of all Russia" (μέγα ῥὴξ Μοσχοβίου καὶ πάσης Ῥωσίας), that is, the Grand Prince of Moscow, Vasilii I (1389–1425). The occasion for this long letter was a

themselves to fantasies about a merging of Greek and Turkish aims and policies.

30. A deliberation of the Venetian Senate, dated July 20 (text, in Loenertz' Cydones edition, II, 449–450; cf. Thiriet, *Régestes*, no. 280, p. 196), speaks of dealings with Manuel and his mother. Silberschmidt, 82 and 86, and Charanis, "Strife," 307, have held that this text indicates that Manuel was in the city then and did not go on this expedition. On the other hand, Loenertz, *Echos d'Orient*, 36 (1937), pp. 281–282, n. 8, suggested that this text, "ne suppose pas nécessairement que Manuel était déja de retour." This latter assumption is indeed conceivable in view of the wording of the document, if one studies it with all possibilities in mind. (Thiriet's summary is not really adequate.) But the controversy is futile, since we have another document, which seems to have gone generally unnoticed, but which settles the immediate problem clearly. In the Genoese expense account for Pera is the entry (Belgrano, p. 173) for July 19 for expenses incurred "pro barchis missis in Constantinopolim ad dominum Imperatorem . . . pro aliquibus negociis Comunis." Plainly, then, Manuel was in the city perhaps as late as the middle of July of 1392. And he was probably also in the capital at least until about May 24 of that year, on the basis of another entry, also apparently unnoticed previously, in the same expense account (Belgrano, p. 171): "Pro quibusdam grecis, pro equis ductis pro parte domini Imperatoris ad dominum Potestatem more consueto ad festum [Pentecostes] parii equorum." Another entry (p. 172), for June 2, speaks of the Emir ("dominus Jhalabi"—clearly, a corruption of "çelebi," or "prince") as being still in Brusa.

All these scraps of information, of course, do not entirely rule out the possibility of Manuel's participation in the projected campaign with Bayazid *after* (though not, in all likelihood, *before*) July of 1392; indeed, Khoury, "L'Empereur Manuel II," 138, attempts to resolve the problem by having Manuel serve with the Turkish fleet during April and return on May 24. I prefer to let the point remain in uncertainty for the moment. The involvement of Manuel's mother in the Venetian document itself implies that she was probably on the scene as a regent-designate, since she had served in this capacity at least one other time during this period: see Appendix IX below. Hence, the Venetian reference to her implies their expectation that they might have to deal with her as an alternate to Manuel himself, presumably in his absence.

quarrel within the Church of Russia. In connection with enforcing his judgment in such matters, the Patriarch Antonios proceeds to remind the apparently recalcitrant Prince of the latter's obligations of obedience:

... for, since Our Moderacy [ἡ μετριότης ἡμῶν] holds you as a genuine son and friend and welcomes any advantage for your soul and your honor and your realm, as many reasonable and just and canonic things as Your Nobility [ἡ εὐγένιά σου] seeks from us, that many things we are constrained to do, even as we now do. For we are guardians of the sacred laws and canons, and we are obligated in this respect to all Christians, especially rather to great men and rulers of nations and local rulers, such as is Your Nobility. Even how all these things have become canonical and lawful Your Nobility is about to discover from this letter we have written. And since we are a universal teacher of all Christians we are constrained that, if we should hear of anything whatsoever done by Your Nobility which harms you spiritually, we should write this to you as your father and teacher with admonition and advice, in order that you may rectify this. And you are also constrained as a Christian and a son of the Church that you should make rectification.

Wherefore, then, do you despise us, the Patriarch, and wherefore are you not rendering honor which your ancestors, the great kings, used to give, but despise both us and the men whom we send to you; and they have no honor nor the position which the men of the Patriarch always held? Do you not know that the Patriarch holds the position of Christ and sits on the very throne of the Master? You despise not a man, but Christ Himself, since he who honors the Patriarch honors Christ Himself. For, not because we have lost our places and lands, through the common sins, ought we even now to be despised by the Christians. Even if we are despised in earthly rule, yet, Christianity is proclaimed everywhere, and we hold the same honor which the Apostles and their successors held. For those men had not human glories or earthly realms; rather, indeed, they were persecuted and insulted by the unbelievers, and daily they died. But their splendor and their power which they held among Christians was beyond all honor.

For this reason, my son, we write and we advise and we counsel Your Nobility that, as if honoring Christ Himself, thus may you honor the Patriarch and his words and the letters and the communications and the men he sends. For this does you good in your soul and in your honor and in your rule. And if you despise and dishonor God, beware lest He Himself be His own Avenger. "For it is a fearful thing," He says, "to fall into the hands of the Living God." [Hebrews x, 31] And again through the Prophet He says: "Behold, ye despisers, and wonder, and perish." [Acts xiii, 41] These things we in our turn are obliged to recommend and to teach to Your Nobility, and you on your side owe it to hearken as a son of the Church and to correct the matter.

Up to this point the letter presents a Patriarchal claim of ecclesiastical sovereignty which, save for the reference to the current temporal decline, would not be particularly remarkable at any period. It is what immediately follows, however, that makes this document exciting. For the Patriarch then proceeds, at a time of the Empire's greatest humiliation, to expound the claims of the Byzantine throne to universal sovereignty in terms that would be noteworthy in any period, but which are really fantastic in this one:

But also, concerning our most powerful and holy Autokrator and Basileus, we hear of certain words spoken by Your Nobility, and we are aggrieved. For you hinder, so they say, the Metropolitan from commemorating the sacred name of the Basileus in the diptychs, a matter which would be at any time impossible; and that you say that "We have a Church, but we neither have a Basileus nor do we reckon one." Now these things are not good. The holy Basileus holds a great position in the Church, for the Basileus is not thus also as are the other rulers and sovereigns of localities, since from the beginning the Basileis confirmed and established their piety in all the inhabited world. The Basileis brought together the ecumenical synods. And they themselves established and enacted to be ratified the matters concerning the correct dogmas and the matters concerning the polity of the Christians that the sacred and sanctified canons now say. Many times did they contend against the heresies; and Imperial regulations, with the synods, formed the chief sees of the archpriests and the divisions of their provinces and the partition of their territories. For which reasons they hold both great honor and position in the Church.

For even if, with the acquiescence of God, the Gentiles have encircled the realm and land of the Basileus, yet, up to this day, the Basileus has had the same election by the Church and the same prayers, and with the same great myrrh is he annointed and is he elected Basileus and Autokrator of the Romans, that is, of all Christians. And the name of the Basileus is commemorated by all patriarchs and metropolitans and bishops in every place in which there are any who call themselves Christians—which honor, indeed, no one of the other rulers or local authorities holds at any time. And such power has he from all men that even the Latins themselves, they who have no sort of communion with our Church, even they themselves give to him the same honor and the same subordination which they gave even in the early days when they were united with us.

To a much greater extent do the Orthodox Christians owe these things to him. Simply for the reason that the Gentiles have encircled the land of the Basileus, it is yet not necessary for the Christians to despise him. But rather, let this teach them, and let it make them more moderate; since, if the great Basileus, the lord and ruler of the inhabited world, he who is invested with such power, has come into such hardship, what would certain other particular local rulers and rulers of few subjects suffer, as Your Nobility and the place there often suffer, and are besieged by the unbelievers, and are taken captive? Thus, it is not just for Your Nobility to despise us for this reason.

But we, both Our Moderacy and the holy Basileus, write to you according to the ancient usage. The honor which the great kings before you held, the same we give to you in our letters and in our communications and in our embassies. Therefore, it is not a good thing, my son, that you should say that "We have a Church, but not a Basileus." It is not possible among the Christians to have a Church and not to have a Basileus. For the Basileus and the Church have great unity and commonality, and it is not possible for them to be divided from each other. The Christians reject alone those Basileis who were heretical, who were raging against the Church and were introducing dogmas corrupt and alien to the teachings of the Apostles and of the Fathers. But our most mighty and holy Autokrator, by the grace of God, is most Orthodox and most faithful champion and defender [δεφένστωρ] and guardian of the Church, and it is not possible to be an archpriest and not to commemorate him.

Hearken to the foremost of the Apostles, Peter, saying in the first of the General Epistles [Peter I, ii, 17]: "Fear God, honor the Basileus." He does not say, "the basileis," in order that one should not assume those self-styled basileis scattered among the nations, but "the Basileus," making clear that there is one universal Basileus. And what were his reasons? Even though the one who was then the ruler was an impious man and a persecutor of the Christians, yet, as a Saint and Apostle, foreseeing what was to come—that the Christians were going to have one Basileus also—he taught that they honor the impious Basileus in order that they learn from this how it is necessary to honor the pious and Orthodox one. Now, if certain others of the Christians also attribute to themselves the title of Basileus, yet all those things are contrary to nature and illegal, and done rather by usurpation and force; for what Fathers, or what sort of synods, or what canons speak of them? Yet, they shout up and down, complaining about the natural Basileus, whose legislations and regulations and *prostagmata* are acceptable to all the inhabited world, and of whom alone—and not of any other—do Christians everywhere make commemoration.

I therefore write, my son, to Your Nobility, and I counsel . . . [The remainder is lost.] [31]

31. Text in Miklosich and Müller, *Acta et diplomata graeca*, II, no. 447, pp. 188–192; the passage translated here begins on p. 189 and runs to the end of the text, the paragraph divisions being completely my own throughout, in the absence of any in the published text. The latter part of this text is frequently quoted. An abridged translation in English of excerpts from it may be found in Vasiliev's "Was Old Russia a Vassal State of Byzantium?" *Speculum*, 7 (1932), 358–359, where it is used in connection with relations between Byzantium and Russia. More recently, in the same connection, W. V. Medlin in his *Moscow and East Rome, A Political Study of the Relations of Church and State in Muscovite Russia* (*Etudes d'histoire économique, politique et sociale*, 1, Geneva, 1952), 69–71, has given some translations of large passages from this text, together with valuable references for its ideas back to the ninth-century law code of Basil I, the *Epanagogé*. There is another partial translation of a passage by Charanis, "Coronation and Its Constitutional Significance in the Later Roman Empire," *Byzantion*, 15 (1940–41), 64–65, where its reference to coronation is exploited. Another English rendering of excerpts from this celebrated text may be found in Ostrogorsky, *Hist. Byz. St.*, 491–492; while some larger selections are to be found in Stacton's *The World on the Last Day*, 113–114 (="Dereksen," 119–120). Ostrogorsky has also since made use of the text also on p. 9 of his article, "The Byzantine Empire and the Hierarchical World-Order," *Slavonic and East-European Review*, XXXV, 84 (December 1956), 1–14. The most extensive English translation, however, may be found in the selection of documents translated by E. Barker under the title *Social and Political Thought in Byzantium* (Oxford, 1957), 194–196; but even this rendering includes only the portion directly concerned with the Imperial office.

The original ending of the document, with its date, is lost, and hence we have no absolutely certain way of dating it by itself. The editors, however, have placed it among texts for the year 1393. This placement is probably correct, since the document concerns disputes between the Churches of Kiev/Moscow and Novgorod (which the Muscovite Prince was then attempting to dominate), a dispute which figures in other corresponding texts undeniably dating from this year, 1393; cf. Dölger, *Regesten*, no. 3241, p. 81. This dating has been rejected by Ostrogorsky, *Hist. Byz. St.*, p. 492, n. 1, but for no other reason than the reference to the people who "have encircled" (περιεκύκλωσαν) the Emperor's realm. This allusion to encirclement, however, need not be taken as referring specifically to any siege of Constantinople, which, as Ostrogorsky correctly notes, did not begin until 1394. The allusion seems to refer rather to the swallowing up of all the Empire's lands around the area of the capital by hostile peoples. To be sure,

That such a sweeping pronouncement of the Imperial claims should be made at all is interesting for Byzantine political thought and its study. That it should be made by the Patriarch, and not by the Emperor himself, is particularly noteworthy for the study of Byzantine Church-State relations. But that it should be made so baldly by anyone at a time when the power of the Emperor was all but destroyed and his status one of humiliation and shame is really extraordinary. This document gives some idea of the growing prestige of the Patriarch in relation to the Emperor, when the latter's position was crumbling, and suggests something of the moral momentum which helped the Patriarchate survive the collapse of the Empire and live on so influentially beyond its wreckage. For our purposes, however, this document demonstrates two important points: first, that the prestige of the Empire was almost destroyed by the Emperor's compromised role as a vassal to the Turk and as an all but ruined ruler; second, that the Byzantines themselves were painfully aware of these attitudes, but only clung the more stubbornly to their old claims of universal Christian (i.e. Roman) sovereignty, at least in terms of official posture.

After the uncertain episode in 1392, we hear no more of Manuel's participation in any campaigning with Bayazid. Indeed, the rest of the year 1392 and virtually all of 1393 are, for the most part, a blank for us as far as Manuel's activities are concerned. We have no concrete information as to any of Manuel's doings during this period of approximately fifteen months. Presumably, Manuel continued his policy of loyal vassalage to Bayazid, whatever the form. Yet, we now do have one remarkable statement by the Emperor himself of a turn of events which may well demonstrate that not only was Manuel not idle during this period, but he was involved in constructive activity with serious repercussions.

the text says nothing directly on the matter, but the fact that, after the siege began, the Emperor was in the slightly more flattering position of at least opposing the Turks would have entitled him to some sympathy from the Orthodox. And, as we shall see, the Russians were willing then to give besieged Byzantium some help, under those circumstances. But if the letter was written, as it seems likely, in 1393, then the outrage and disgust and scorn of his coreligionists and supposed subjects would be all the more understandable, in view of the Emperor's miserable subjection and servile vassalage to the hated Infidel.

In the course of his *Moral Dialogue, or, Concerning Marriage,* which is cast in the medium of a discussion between Manuel and his mother, the name of Manuel's nephew and rival is brought into the conversation. Continuing on the subject of John VII, Manuel proceeds to say:

. . . For you know how, when deceivingly speaking of having conceived repentance for what had been done, and while he was vehemently singing the praises of peace to those whom he was addressing, and while he was promising that he would be in the position of a son to me and in loyalty for the rest of time, all these things he did then as if in secret, but he purposely made them evident to the hateful unbelievers while they were observing peace and treaties with us. These things he did, then, in order that, by embroiling them with us, he should stir up this war and should indeed, in this fashion, climax the enmity which he nourished against us for a long time. You know further, O Mother, that I trusted this proposal at that time: for that which we wish to believe, as they say, we are only too ready to believe. Gladly giving my first-born son as in the place of a first-born son to him—for I did well to put the common good before my own child—in exchange for him, I then received him back himself in his turn. And verily, in the need for hostages I did not spare of my loved ones, nor did I take into account by any means that there would be produced from this transaction as many dreadful consequences as have been produced. And there was involved also a substantial amount of money to provide securities, and many other things, as is known both by the leading citizens of the Romans and by those of the Latins who were of their council and by as many ambassadors as then came to him. And these facts, I believe, give you good proof, O Mother, of the subject of which you have spoken. . . .[32]

32. This text, the Διάλογος ἠθικὸς ἢ Περὶ γάμου, is unfortunately still denied us in a complete published edition. This passage alone, however, has been made available by Loenertz, "Une Erreur singulière," 183–184, who deserves full credit for focusing attention on its important meaning. Cf. also his *Recueils*, 121. Berger de Xivrey, who lists this work in his catalogue of Manuel's writings as No. 16, has erroneously estimated its date as "before 1389" (p. 61, n. 2, and p. 189). On the basis of content and context, Loenertz, "Une Erreur singulière," 183, has justifiably dated the conversation it purports to present, if not also the composition of the work itself, as between the beginning of Bayazid's siege of Constantinople in the summer of 1394 and the death of the Empress Helena (Manuel's mother) in the autumn of 1396. The work cannot have been written much later than 1396, because Manuel sent a copy of it, together with his Letter ξδ' to Cydones during the latter's final visit to Venice. Loenertz, *Recueils*, 122, has dated

The meaning of this statement is fairly clear, even if its style is not. Manuel must have entertained the hope that he might end the discord in his family by means of a reconciliation with his nephew and an exchange of reciprocal adoptions. Such a move, even if made only after a display of initiative on the part of John, would have been wise and statesmanlike in the fullest degree. From what Manuel says, it would seem that even the Genoese of Pera (i.e. the "Latins" with their "βουλή") found the project acceptable and cooperated toward its execution. But then, whether with premeditated treachery, as Manuel maintains, or whether simply as a result of a change of heart or of a desire to secure advantage with Bayazid, lest such a scheme backfire, John VII chose to reveal the agreement to the Emir and proceeded to incite him against Manuel. In view of the reference to peace with the Turks and to Manuel's possession of at least one son, there can be little doubt that such an episode must have taken place during the year 1393.[33]

It has been suggested that Bayazid's rage after the revelation of this attempted reconciliation was a cause—if not *the* cause— of the grim events at Serres which followed. Certainly the Emir would resent strongly Manuel's efforts to undercut one of the most useful Turkish advantages: the quarreling and factionalism

this journey during 1396–97, and has set Cydones' death in the winter of 1397–98. Recently, V. Laurent, "La Date de la mort d'Hélène Cantacuzène, femme de Jean V Paléologue: Une précision," *Rev. d. ét. byz.*, 14 (1956), 200–201, has suggested that this treatise, or at least Letter ξδ', was written just before the death of Manuel's mother, supposedly in November– December, 1396. Manuel's Letter ξδ' is itself of great interest, for more than the fact that it is possibly the Emperor's last missive to his old master and friend. In view of its remarkable bearing on their relationship at the end of Cydones' life, it is translated below, p. 418.

33. See Loenertz, "Une Erreur singulière," 184; his reconstruction of this episode is followed by Khoury, 138–139. It is just barely possible that some traces of this episode are reflected in Chalcocondyles' strange story about an alleged reconciliation between Manuel and John VII: see Barker, "John VII in Genoa," 216–223, 235; but cf. Dölger, *Regesten*, nos. 3235–3236, p. 80, where that source's statements are still given weight.

It is quite understandable that John VII, having failed in his coup of 1390, chafed in his inferior position in Selymbria while Manuel continued to occupy the throne with the approval of Bayazid. Such a turn of events as this would have served his interests well, for the purpose of turning the Emir against Manuel and securing a transfer of active support back to the pretender. Hence, it is not very difficult to recognize a considerable degree of credibility in Manuel's charges of willful and malicious treachery on the part of John.

of the Byzantine Imperial house.[34] Such supposed provocation may well have supplied strong impetus. But we must bear in mind a broader background as we confront one of the most fantastic and gripping spectacles in the history of the Osmanli conquest of the Balkans.

We are fortunate in having an account of this episode in Manuel's own words, which, supplemented by the information available in other sources, provides a vivid picture of what happened. In his important *Funeral Oration for His Brother Theodore Palaeologus*, Manuel recounts the struggles of his brother against the unruly and quarrelsome *archons* (or magnates) of the Morea. The cause of their rebelliousness, he says,[35] was none other than the machinations of "the most hostile beast" (ὁ δυσμενέστατος θήρ), "that Persian, *Pagiazites* I mean," or "the Satrap," as the Classics-minded Emperor calls Bayazid (Παγιαζίτης). As always, Bayazid was undoubtedly ready to take advantage of local situations for his own purposes. But it is to the foolish and treacherous actions of "the renegade Christians" (τοὺς αὐτομολοῦντας Χριστιανούς) that Manuel ascribes the terrible outcome.[36] And so, addressing the Peloponnesians in his *Oration*, Manuel writes:

. . . But since the plots against you by these devils, though doing their all, came to naught, and since at the same time the barbarian force in Europe, having trouble on all sides, seemed unable readily to enter the Isthmus and to do this continually and thereby to gratify the Satrap's wishes, they [the "renegades"], therefore, being in distress themselves, proposed to him that he should cross the Hellespont from Asia to Thrace and, having traversed it, should sojourn in Macedonia. And he should from thence, through ambassadors, summon my

34. This is the position of Loenertz, "Une Erreur singulière," 184. Anastasejević, "Jedina vizantijska carica Srpkinja," 28–29, notes the similar circumstances of the other major vassals assembled by Bayazid at Serres, for all of them were faced by accusations of one sort or another from their own dissident elements. Into this picture the troublemaking of John VII would fit perfectly. And we shall see clearly from the course of events and also from Manuel's own account how important and sinister a role John did play in what followed.

35. Ed. Migne, 217B, ed. Lampros, p. 46, ll. 3–11.

36. *Ibid.*, ed. Migne, 217B–221A, ed. Lampros, p. 46, l. 12 to p. 50, l. 3, in which he deplores at length the folly and maliciousness of these—as he regards them—selfish traitors and malcontents. Characteristically, Manuel names no names; also, in view of his intended audience in this case, this was prudent discretion.

brother to come to him, and should threaten him in indirect fashion with all kinds of ills, should he not come in obedience—but openly he should promise many great advantages, some through his ambassadors and some in a long letter. And these advantages should be in the form of his promises both to aggrieve him as little as possible and to honor him as much as possible, to send him away as swiftly as possible, and never again to annoy him in any regard whatsoever.

These things, on their part, they proposed to the Satrap. The latter, in his turn, was persuaded, and he did all things even more maliciously than they were advising him to do. . . .[37]

Manuel stresses the role of these traitorous subjects of Theodore as the cause for Bayazid's summons. As one-sided as this interpretation may seem, it is well-grounded to the extent that we know that the other Christian princes who were called together were also summoned, in one way or another, on the grounds of complaints against them by their own countrymen before Bayazid.[38] The arrogant Emir undoubtedly felt, therefore, that he had a good opportunity to demonstrate his power by assembling all his Christian vassals at once in order to sit in judgment of them.

So it was that in the autumn of 1393 or the winter of 1393–94 [39] Theodore obeyed the summons. Manuel's description, for the purposes of his *Oration*, is given from the point of view of Theodore, but it obviously reflects his own as well. Theodore suspected treachery, says Manuel, but heeding his duty and thinking only of the good of his country and his people,[40]

. . . he went to the Satrap, not having let him [Bayazid] be confident in advance that he would come. On the contrary, he had ruled out his coming, so that he should make an even more pleasing appearance, since he was not at all expected, and that in the unexpectedness of the event he would gratify him the more; and also that he should demonstrate to him that he had come by his own decision, while not being deceived by his flatteries and threats. Accordingly, he found him in Pherres [Serres], and me with him also, since I had arrived before him. In fact, I had come five days before, since a rather urgent necessity then brought me there for the purpose of rescuing my subjects from dangers, although this had been absolutely forbidden by

37. *Ibid.*, ed. Migne, 221A–B, ed. Lampros, p. 50, ll. 4–19.
38. Cf. Anastasejević, 28–29; and above, n. 34.
39. For the establishment of this dating, see below, n. 47.
40. Ed. Migne, 221B–224A, ed. Lampros, p. 50, l. 19 to p. 52, l. 8.

me—I mean the presence of both of us before him at the same time. For it seemed not safe that our sojourn be in this wise with him who had for so long been striving to inflict unjust murder upon us. But, nevertheless, the fearsome thing came to pass, since I was expecting him [Theodore] to remain yet at home, and he, in his turn, was assuming the same about me. So, as if by agreement, we were setting forth from home on the same day—if I have remembered rightly— and even, if you will, at the same hour. But there happened something even worse. For round about the Persian were those who were in any way whatsoever leaders of the Christians—at least those who were accustomed to come to him [i.e. his vassals]. That man had, in fact, carefully collected them, since he wished to obliterate them all utterly. And it seemed necessary for them to come, even to accept rather the danger of doing so, than not to heed his command. Now, it was indeed a step full of danger to go to him, especially at the same time, they all reckoned reasonably. For they were not ignorant of the man or of his intentions concerning them. But, on the other hand, not to yield to his commands was a step full of much greater danger. For neither would he bear the insult of their disobedience, nor would he be still in not enduring it, but he would indeed want to destroy them completely, and he would be able to do what he wanted. So, for these reasons, preferring one evil to another, they took to the road entrusting their fate to God and journeying with hopes.

Now verily, their conviction concerning myself and my brother, that we would not come at that time, together, to that most-dread-beast—for they did not suspect that this occurred not by chance, nor indeed that it was by our deliberate intention—had dissipated the bulk of their fear and had encouraged them to come, since just suspicion was driven away. For they knew that he, mouth agape after the manner of Hades, was aiming to swallow them all; and they knew that he would probably fear lest his design turn out to the contrary for him, should he strike shamelessly against them all when he did not also have us in his hands. But when they came themselves and saw my brother with me before the Persian, and when they realized that the outcome had gone beyond their expectations, struck speechless for a long time, they uttered not a word to each other. But even when at length they recovered themselves, they were scarcely able even to let out a sound. Then, giving forth this first exclamation, they all cried, "We have breathed our last!"

These men, then, had already been gathered together at this time with us—and see how all these elements rushed together, and how they did draw up our fears, as one might say, to the very summit of the peak!—when, newly from Selymbria, there came also the Basileus, my nephew. And this confused me further, to such an extent that I all but gave up entirely and felt the need of a will and testament, as is requisite for those who have given up all hope of life. So were we as "sheep in the midst of wolves"—such, then, being the saying [Luke x, 3] delivered by the Savior to the Disciples—though trampling on the heads of our enemies, the very image of serpents and scorpions, and sustaining no harm from them, walking rather in the faith of Him Who has the power to save. That beast, then, received my brother neither gladly—for he bore "malice thereafter in his breast till he should satisfy it" [*Iliad* I, 82–83]—nor, so it seemed, unpleasantly. For he felt ashamed, even if not for his promises to my brother, yet, at least for seeming unable while in my presence to restrain, even for a while, the venom within him, but having rather to spew it forth straightaway.

Therefore, being thus disposed, he formed a plan—I do not say under whose influence, be it even under that of the devil whom he bore in his soul—both to slay us and all our house, and at the same time to slay the rulers of the faithful [i.e. of the other Balkan Christians]. For, since he had wanted this for a long time, he supposed it necessary to accomplish such purification then in order that, as he alleged, once he had purified the land of the thorns—meaning us, of course—it would be possible for his children not to bloody their feet in dancing triumphantly over the Christians. So was he for his part planning such things; yet, to the True Lord—Who is not as an hired shepherd—these same plans concerning His sheep did not seem good. For he [the Emir] ordered his general, who was but a eunuch, to kill us by night and by no means to do otherwise; and if not, he threatened to condemn him to death. Yet God commanded him by no means to do this deed. So it was, I imagine, like unto that which once came to pass for the sake of Sarah [cf. Genesis xx]. And when the murderer [Bayazid] learned this presently, instead of dealing evilly with the disobedient man, he even acknowledged gratitude to him for his admirable hesitation, alleging that, straightaway he had given his order, he was stricken by extreme repentance—which certainly derived from none other than God.[41]

Amid the coating of rhetoric, the outline of events is strikingly clear. Bayazid called his vassals together, tricking them into coming by making them assume that they were not all coming at the same time. Only when they actually had all come together did they realize to their horror that they had put themselves as a

41. *Ibid.*, ed. Migne, 224A–225D, ed. Lampros, p. 52, l. 8 to p. 55, l. 16.

group completely in his power. Our other sources [42] generally bear out this account and add a few more details. We learn that the other important Christian rulers of the Balkans included the two Serbian lords, Stefan Lazarević, whose father had been killed on the field of Kossovo, and Konstantin Dejanović, or Dragaš, Manuel's father-in-law. Manuel makes clear, especially by his reaction to the sight of him, the role of John VII, his nephew, at this gathering, as Manuel's own nemesis, if not accuser. But he portrays Theodore's opposition simply as an ill-defined group of "renegade Christians." From our other sources we learn that Theodore, too, had one specific detractor, in the person of Paul Mamonas, the scion of the powerful family which resented the Despot's efforts to wrest the important fortress of Monemvasia from their independent control. The appeal of this proud baron to Bayazid provided the Emir with a lever for extending his authority into the Peloponnesus by right of adjudication.[43] One source also adds the detail that Ali, the son of Khairaddin, was the eunuch who, out of either fear or prudence, put off carrying out Bayazid's treacherous command until the latter had changed his mind.[44]

It is this last aspect of the affair that is so remarkable. Bayazid's scheme for murdering his vassals—or at least the Palaeologi—may at this point have been the focus of a premeditated plan. But it would seem more likely, from his quick change of mind, that it was simply a whim, a savage, blood-curdling whim. How terrifying must have been Bayazid's ruthlessness and unpredictability can be read between the lines of Manuel's continued narrative:

42. Chalcocondyles, ed. Darkó, 74–75, ed. Bonn, 80–81; followed by the Pseudo-Phrantzes, ed. Papadopoulos, 61–63, ed. Bonn, 57–58 (which omits many details, including the presence of John VII), and the *Chron. Barb. 111*, 34–35. For a valuable Slavic source, see n. 46 below.

43. On Mamonas and the Monemvasian question, see Loenertz, "Pour l'histoire du Péloponnèse," 175–176; Zakythinos, *Le Despotat grec de Morée,* I, 125–128, especially 128, and also 153. See also Miller, "Monemvasia During the Frankish Period," *Journal of Hellenic Studies,* 27 (1907), 234–235 (or, as reprinted in his collection, *Essays on the Latin Orient,* 236–237); and, less satisfactory, *id., The Latins in the Levant: A History of Frankish Greece (1204–1566)* (London, 1908), 367.

44. Chalcocondyles, ed. Darkó, 74–75, ed. Bonn, 80–81. Cf. Taeschner and Wittek, "Die Vezirfamilie der Gandarlyzāde (14./15. Jhdt.) und ihre Denkmäler," 87–88.

So it was; and the Ethiop was not able to wash the blackness from his soul. But first he spewed forth his wrath by means of the outrages he committed upon our followers, cutting out the eyes of our admirals [?], and cutting off hands, and bringing some of those in authority into great disgrace. And when in this fashion he had put at rest his unreasonable spirit, thereafter he very simple-mindedly attempted to reconcile me—whom he was injuring and had dishonored with myriad injustices—greeting me with gifts and sending me homeward, just as they do who soothe with sweetmeats children who weep following their punishment. His reasoning was plain: for it was in order that he might thereafter secure my brother. It seems, in fact, that he did not consider it safe to extend his hands to both of us. Which, indeed, he could then have done; but at the same time, since he had been blinded by God, he did not know he could do this—just as he did not perceive this else, that he would no longer have my friendship. But he believed that he was deceiving me with words of utmost stupidity, even while he was, on one hand, committing such great outrages upon our followers and was, on the other, still holding my brother in his hands and was also demanding of him the best cities, as if they were some inheritances, and was commanding in addition things which no intelligent person would command even of men captured in war.[45]

As Manuel indicates, Bayazid thus restricted his violence to senseless punishments inflicted on at least the Greek nobles with the Emperor. Manuel's revulsion speaks for itself. Whatever further adjudications Bayazid may have been disposed to give by this time, the congress of vassals broke up, and its participants looked to their own safety.[46] Not so Theodore, however, whom

45. *Funeral Oration*, ed. Migne, 225D–228A, ed. Lampros, p. 55, l. 17 to p. 56, l. 9.
46. Manuel speaks of no further activity of the group as a whole, and, although his silence is not irrefutable, it may mean something. Our three other Greek sources—that is, Chalcocondyles, ed. Darkó, 75, ed. Bonn, 81, and his two satellites, the Pseudo-Phrantzes, ed. Papadopoulos, 62–63, ed. Bonn, 58, and especially the *Chron. Barb. 111*, 35—maintain that, in the course of this Balkan "summit conference," the Christian princes recognized the common threat which Bayazid posed for all of them and agreed to cooperate secretly to betray the Emir; and at least one token of this agreement, so this story goes, was the betrothal of Manuel to Helena Dragaš; cf. Dölger, *Regesten*, no. 3237, p. 80 (dated "ca. 1393"). The association of this last event with the episode of Serres has already (see n. 25 above) been shown to be false. This, however, does not prove that no such agreement of cooperation was made. Quite the contrary, there may well have been some such arrangement to cause Chalcocondyles to confuse Manuel's earlier mar-

Bayazid detained, since he had decided now to concentrate his attentions on Greece. The captive Despot was then brought on the Emir's campaign into Thessaly. The cession of some Morean fortresses, including the disputed Monemvasia, was extracted from him, and further pressure was put on him by one of Bayazid's creatures (whom Manuel calls "Moures") to yield up more, including Argos. Theodore pretended to comply, but soon succeeded in making good his escape from the Turkish camp, then situated by the River Sperchios. He managed to hasten to the Morea in person just in time to foil his own unwilling cessions. Thus was Bayazid cheated at his own game. But he made little attempt personally at immediate reprisals. He was later to satisfy himself with sending a punitive expedition into the Peloponnesus.

riage with these later events. Loenertz, "Pour l'histoire du Péloponnèse," 180, however, rejects the idea of any entente. At any rate, we have no other information, and, as subsequent events were to show, no such course of cooperation was followed. The *Chron. Barb. 111*, 35, also speaks of John VII (who is identified as Manuel's brother, and is described as a "bailo" with Bayazid) as going over to the side of the Christian princes in conjunction with their entente. This statement is probably a confusion with other events, perhaps of the Chalcocondyles story of the reconciliation of Manuel and John, and of the later 1399 reconciliation.

This extraordinary gathering, however, may not have disbanded so abruptly and ominously for all of the vassals. At least one of the Balkan princes, Stefan Lazarević, seems to have emerged in great favor with Bayazid. Indeed, quite a different story is found in the life of the Serbian prince written by Konstantin the Philosopher, ed. V. Jagić, *Glasnik Srpskog učenog društva*, 42 (1875), 244–328. This text completely ignores the presence of all the other princes. According to its narrative, ed. Jagić, 266–269 (abridged text with German translation by M. Braun, *Lebenschreibung des Despoten Stefan Lazarevićs* [The Hague, 1956], 9–10), some of Stefan's nobles reported to Bayazid that Stefan was involved in dealings with Sigismund of Hungary, to the detriment of the Turks. Informed of this, Stefan permitted his mother to go herself to Bayazid and plead for her son. Stefan then went in his own turn to the Emir (location unstated), and was received with forgiveness and great cordiality. Cf. S. Stanojević, "Die Biographie Stefan Lazarevićs von Konstantin dem Philosophen als Geschichtsquelle," *Archiv für slavische Philologie*, 18 (1896), 420. In comparing this less bizarre account to Manuel's, it should be noted that Stefan always seems to have been a favorite of Bayazid's among the Christian vassals; and that Konstantin's biography, whatever sources he may have used, cannot have quite the same validity as Manuel's own narrative.

On this entire gathering in general, the old account by Hammer, I, 245–247 (trans. Hellert, I, 340–342), is unreliable and badly confused in chronology. Cf. also Vaughan, *Europe and the Turk*, 34; and Khoury, 139; Runciman and Stacton ("Dereksen") both curiously overlook this dramatic episode, which could have added further color to their narratives.

But for the moment he contended himself with the annexation of the Latin Duchy of Salona and, apparently, also the city of Thessalonica, withdrawing then from Greece.[47]

Meanwhile, Manuel had made his hasty departure from Serres. (One is tempted to wonder what irony he must have seen in the occurrence of this incredible gathering in the city which had been in the past such a pivotal point in his fortunes during his administrations in Thessalonica.) Even if we dismiss as hindsight some aspects of his descriptions, quoted above, of his reaction to Bayazid's fantastic performance, it is easy to recognize how much it must have jolted Manuel. Surely he realized by now that, with such an Emir as Bayazid to deal with, the recent policy was no longer possible. With Murad it had sufficed, for Murad was shrewd enough to cultivate situations advantageous to him as alternatives to force. Bayazid was a different man. He did not lack some of his father's diplomatic cleverness, but he was far more arrogant and impatient. If Murad was no less savage and ruthless at times than his son, such traits were the more notice-

47. Manuel, *Funeral Oration*, ed. Migne, 228A–233B, ed. Lampros, p. 56, l. 10 to p. 63, l. 11. At one point in his narrative (ed. Migne, 232A, ed. Lampros, p. 60, ll. 6–9) Manuel refers to his mother in such a fashion as to imply that she was still in close personal contact with him, if not also continuing to participate in the government. In all likelihood Manuel had again left her as his regent in Constantinople when he went to Serres. See Appendix IX below. Chalcocondyles, ed. Darkó, I, 61–64, ed. Bonn, 67–69, gives essentially the same account, with fewer details and some differences. Cf. Loenertz, "Pour l'histoire du Péloponnèse," 178–185; also, Zakythinos, *Le Despotat grec*, I, 154–155.

The occurrence in this context of the annexation of Salona in Thessaly provides at last a definite resolution of the problem of dating the "Congress of Serres," which has long been a point of dispute. The chronology of the regular sources is little help, for, while the Pseudo-Phrantzes places the gathering at Serres just before the Battle of Nicopolis (1396), Chalcocondyles (and the *Chron. Barb. 111*) in greater confusion places it immediately after this battle, and he narrates Bayazid's Thessalian campaign separately, as a mere comparison of citations will reveal. Berger de Xivrey, 73–77, estimated the date at 1391. Following Muralt, p. 752, nos. 21 and 23, Gibbons, 200, set it in 1395 and then, pp. 229–230, placed Bayazid's Thessalian expedition in 1397; and on this latter count he is mistakenly followed by Atiya, *The Crusade in the Later Middle Ages*, 464, and by Delaville le Roulx, *La France en Orient*, 350. Hopf, *Geschichte Griechenlands*, 61, and Silberschmidt, 89–96, put the gathering at some time before the campaign of Nicopolis in 1396. Zakythinos, *Le Despotat grec*, I, 152–154, followed by Charanis, "Strife," 313, had settled on May of 1394. Earlier, Jireček, in his review in *Byz. Zeitschr.*, 18 (1909), 585–586, had shrewdly placed the

able in the latter because Bayazid had a far less stable character. The calculating Murad would never have given way to whim as did Bayazid at Serres. Yet, for all the differences between personalities, one must bear in mind also the differences between prevailing conditions. Murad had been the great builder of the Osmanli state, and its position was fully confirmed only by the battle which had cost him his life. By contrast, Bayazid was the reaper of his father's harvest and could now afford the greater haughtiness, pretensions, and irresponsibility which he displayed. There need no longer be any polite veneer over Turkish aims and power. Now Bayazid could set his aim openly on "the head and Basilissa of all cities." [48]

Apparently not long after his return home, Manuel was faced with an ultimatum from Bayazid. According to one story, Bayazid summoned the Emperor to his court once again. This time Manuel ignored the order. Bayazid then sent his Grand Vizier, Ali Pasha. This same man who had saved Manuel's life at Serres announced the Emir's renewed demands, but privately he warned

episode generally in the winter of 1393–94. Most recently, however, has come the fundamental discussion by Loenertz, "Pour l'histoire du Péloponnèse," 172–181, which has finally laid the matter to rest with reasonable certainty. Loenertz reproduces the text (pp. 177–178) of a letter written by Nerio (Ranier) Acciajuoli, the Duke of Athens, to his brother Donato, which refers to the recent taking of Salona by the Turks. (This text may also be found in Rubió i Lluch, *Diplomatari de l'Orient Català*, no. 644, pp. 673–674; and appended to F. Gregorovius, Ἱστορία τῆς πόλεως Ἀθηνῶν κατὰ τοὺς μέσους αἰῶνας, trans. Lampros, Vol. II, Athens, 1904, 652.) The date of this letter is February 20, 1394, which would therefore make it about this time that Theodore made his escape. The gathering at Serres, immediately preceding, would thus have taken place in the autumn of 1393 or the winter of 1393–94, as Loenertz proposes. In this same Acciajuoli letter reference is also made to what seems to be a Turkish attack on Thessalonica at this time. This is a confused and thorny problem: see Appendix II, B, below; but such a seizure after Serres would be quite understandable.

Finally, in his narrative Manuel maintains (ed. Migne, 236A–D, ed. Lampros, p. 64, l. 1 to p. 65, l. 7) that Bayazid turned his attention from the Morea out of frustration over not having his path into the Peloponnesus swept clear for him as he had intended; and he adds, with evident disbelief, the report that the Emir abandoned his project in Greece because he was called to aid the Sultan of Egypt against the aggressions of Timur. Cf. Loenertz, "Pour l'histoire du Péloponnèse," 179–180, who suggests that the latter report may have had some validity; and see below, p. 124, n. 3, for possible evidence to this effect. Also, for the expedition which Bayazid later sent to the Peloponnesus, see below, p. 127.

48. This is the phrase of the *Chron. Barb. 111*, p. 30, ll. 33–34.

Manuel not to go. Manuel, so the tale goes, put off the summons again.[49]

By this time Manuel had come to the inevitable conclusion: no further trust could be placed in a course of vassalage to the Turks. Bayazid's retaliation would be swift and firm. Byzantium was now faced with the alternatives only of resistance or total capitulation. The policy inaugurated by John V, reluctantly accepted and continued by Manuel II, had finally ceased to work. Appeasement had failed.

49. This story appears in Chalcocondyles, ed. Darkó, I, 76–77, ed. Bonn, 82–83, and also in the *Chron. Barb. 111*, 35. Loenertz, "Pour l'histoire du Péloponnèse," 180–181, disparages it, but I can see no immediate or overwhelming reason for rejecting its essence. Cf. Taeschner and Wittek, 88. Dölger, *Regesten*, no. 3234, p. 80, accepts the Chalcocondyles story, but chooses to apply it with some uncertainty to the year 1391, in the light of that historian's badly garbled chronology.

3. The Quest for Aid, 1394–1402

The events of Serres in the winter of 1393–94 had forced Manuel to abandon the policy which he had reluctantly inherited from his father. Manuel's refusal to heed any of Bayazid's new demands was his public acknowledgment of his new position. Bayazid required no additional prompting. Once Ali Pasha's embassy had proved fruitless, Bayazid dispatched no more messengers, but rather an army. And so in the year 1394, presumably in the spring, began the Turkish siege of Constantinople, which was to last for some eight years.[1]

This siege involves, directly or indirectly, a great many problems, and our knowledge of it is gravely limited. What we can ascertain must be pieced together painfully from confused and fragmentary sources with cautious awareness of uncertainty. But certain outlines do emerge after careful study. This is particularly the case with the help of what Venetian documents survive and are available to us, for they shed some very valuable light on this epoch, especially concerning the beginning of the siege.

Two of these documents, both dating from the period when Bayazid must have been pressing the siege in earnest, offer particularly interesting information. The first reports a deliberation of the Venetian Senate for May 21, 1394. The *Sapientes* in-

1. For a full discussion of the problems of dating the beginning and the duration of the great siege, see Appendix X below.

structed their agents to sympathize with Manuel, now that his citizens were in "great perplexity," "because of the ill disposition of Basitus." Manuel was to be assured of the *Serenissima's* good will and to be urged not to leave his city, lest this lead to the final disaster and the complete triumph of the Turks over his realm. Manuel was also to be urged to write to the Pope, the Emperor (of Germany), and other Christian rulers, to ask their aid against the infidel; the Republic would give its full assistance to the forwarding and support of such requests. These instructions, however, were then delayed until further information could be obtained on the intentions of "Baisitus," when Venetian interests could be looked after.[2]

The second document covers another deliberation, of July 24, 1394, which considered the news from Constantinople and the requests of the Emperor brought to the Senate by their agent. In their answer, Manuel was to be urged again not to leave the city, in view of the harm that it might bring and especially in view of the fact that "Basaitus" was now involved with "the emperor of the Tartars," and hence the situation was not yet fully clear. Moreover, aid from the West was sure to be forthcoming, the *Sapientes* thought. Should Manuel, however, wish to leave the city, the Republic would provide transportation for him to Venice, which would receive him cordially, or, as an alternative, to the island of Lemnos ("insula Staliminis"). Also, Manuel was again urged to write to the Pope, to the (Holy Roman) Emperor, and to various other rulers, to request their aid. Finally, as to Manuel's proposal to sell the island of Lemnos itself to Venice, the *Sapientes* declared themselves not in a position to assume responsibility for it.[3]

2. Text, ed. Iorga, "Veneţia in Marea neagră," 1111–1113; cf. Thiriet, *Régestes des délibérations du Sénat de Venise concernant la Romanie,* I, no. 851, p. 202; also, Silberschmidt, *Das orientalische Problem,* 85–87. See also Loenertz, "Pour l'histoire du Péloponnèse au XIVe siècle," 181.

3. Text, ed. Ljubić, in *Monumenta spectantia historiam slavorum meridionalem,* IV, no. 473, pp. 332–334; cf. Thiriet, *Régestes,* I, no. 860, pp. 203–204; Silberschmidt, 87; and Muralt, *Essai de chronographie byzantine,* p. 749, no. 32; also Dölger, *Regesten,* no. 3246a, p. 82. For additional comments on both documents, see Halecki, "Rome et Byzance au temps du grand Schisme d'Occident," 496–497. The "imperator Tartorum" is of course Timur, and this reference to the distraction which he provided Bayazid at this time may bear out the suggestion that it was a possible reason for the Emir's abandonment of his campaign in Greece: see above, p. 121, n. 47.

There are several points of obvious interest in these two deliberations. First, it is noteworthy that Manuel should have felt so pressed financially as to contemplate selling the important island of Lemnos, one of the few remaining Byzantine territorial holdings outside the walls of the capital. (Of course, after the unhappy experience of his exile there, Manuel may not have regretted personally the idea of parting with the place!) Far more striking, however, is the fact that Manuel should consider—initially, at least, even before the beginning of the siege, as far as can be judged—the idea of fleeing Constantinople. How serious was this plan and how far the advice of the Venetians served to discourage it are impossible to ascertain on the basis of these two references alone. But it is significant that the realization of the possible consequences of the failure of the old appeasement policy and of the rupture of relations with Bayazid should have prompted even the idea of flight for Manuel, even though we know that his nerve never did fail. Also significant, moreover, is the repeated urging of Manuel to appeal to the West for aid. We do not know whether the Venetians were the first to suggest this scheme, or whether their encouragement merely reflected an idea already entertained by the Byzantine government. But, as we shall see, it was to become the foundation of Manuel's new policy.

For the time being, at any rate, Manuel settled down to bear the shock of Bayazid's first full onslaught against Constantinople. Certainly, by autumn of 1394 the siege had begun in earnest. And Manuel's countermeasures had begun in earnest also. A deliberation of the Venetian Senate for December 23, 1394, reveals two aspects of these measures. In addition to reassuring Manuel that transportation by ship out of Constantinople would be provided for him should the situation become critical, the Senate dispatched a shipment of grain (1,500 *modii*) to fulfill the Emperor's request, in view of the great hardship within the capital. Moreover, the Senate deferred any decision on a proposed league against the Turks until it might have time to consult with expected ambassadors from France, Burgundy, England, and Hungary.[4] Of these early overtures for a league more was to

4. The text, ed. Ljubić, no. 482, p. 338, covers only the discussion of the last matter; Thiriet, *Régestes*, I, no. 868, p. 205, gives a summary of the

come, but only later. For the time being, Manuel had to sustain his situation as best he could.

There is only one of Manuel's surviving letters which refers directly to the Turkish siege at this time. Addressed to Cydones, it is essentially a piece of rhetorical fluff. But it does give us some slight impression of Manuel's frame of mind during the siege, certainly a healthy contrast to the bitter depressions of his letters during the humiliations of 1391:

Since you yourself are not allowed by your illness to behold him for whom you long—that is me, I mean—you take refuge in sailing the next best course, and you request me to write, choosing to forget all the hindrances there are to my doing this. There were even some of those present who accused you of importunity, little knowing, I suppose, how to love. But I, on my part, avoid thinking as they do, to such an extent that, even though formerly I was not ignorant of the greatness of your affection, I recognize it now more than ever and I acknowledge my gratitude to you for it. For, if this feeling on your part were not so great and urgent, you would not then be seeking eagerly after letters which are entirely destitute of Greek elegance— you, yet, who so closely pursues them! Nevertheless, wishing both to be obedient to you, and not to be disobedient to Solomon—who ad-

entire deliberation. See also Silberschmidt, 87 and 100; and Dölger, *Regesten*, no. 3248, p. 82.

Though the documents of this period do not seem to specify names, one is disposed to wonder if, in any of these negotiations with Venice during 1394, the Byzantine agent was none other than Manuel Chrysoloras. If with tenuous documentation, it has been argued and generally accepted that during 1394–95 this eminent scholar made his first voyage to Italy at the behest of his friend, the Emperor Manuel, to seek Western aid for Byzantium: see G. Cammelli, *I dotti bizantini e le origini dell'umanesimo*, I: *Manuele Crisolora* (Florence, 1941), 25–28, with discussion of the evidence and arguments for the point; more recently, in I. Thomson, "Manuel Chrysoloras and the Early Italian Renaissance," *Greek, Roman and Byzantine Studies*, 7 (1966), 63–82: 76–77. If this tradition is correct, we may wonder how early in this period, immediately after the breach with Bayazid, Manuel II began his appeals to Western powers; although, in this case, Chrysoloras' mission may have been restricted simply to Venice. The tradition also includes the understanding that Chrysoloras was accompanied in this 1394–95 mission by Demetrius Cydones, a point that is itself problematical, and has been disputed by such scholars as Loenertz. If Cydones was in fact with Chrysoloras at this time, however, it would mean that Manuel II's correspondence with his old friend during the early phases of the Turkish siege was an overseas one. Cf. Setton, "The Byzantine Background to the Italian Renaissance," *Proceedings of the American Philosophical Society*, 100 (1956), 56, who accepts the verity of Cydones' journey at this time.

vises [cf. Ecclesiastes iii: 1 and 17; and vii: 6] that it is necessary to apportion one's time to one's duties—I write, indeed, as if in discharging an obligation; for even a trifle can be no trifling pleasure to friends. But, for the moment, I am going forth to give aid, with God's help, to a certain fortress that is being besieged—small, to be sure, and little able to profit our enemies if it should be taken, though it would provide them with honor and delight. But be of good cheer! For, as God previously turned back their satrap empty-handed whenever he attacked it, this same thing will he now do.[5]

The first onslaught by the Emir was a failure. In spite of his large army and his siege engines, Bayazid was unable to pierce the still formidable fortifications of Constantinople. Instead, he was forced to settle down to a long blockade that at least reduced the city to considerable hardship.[6] But, after the first shock, the Byzantine position seems to have been a little less desperate, even though the blockade was maintained. Bayazid himself turned his mind to other things. By the beginning of 1395, if not the end of 1394, Bayazid sent his general Evrenos-Bey on a punitive raid into the Peloponnesus.[7] An even greater distraction for Bayazid personally was his campaign against Bulgaria and, especially at this time, Wallachia. It was in the latter that Bayazid fought the bloody Battle of Rovine on May 17, 1395.[8] The immediate significance of this battle for Byzantium

5. Letter κθ', ed. Legrand, 36–37, fully translated here. It is impossible to date this letter precisely, save for the fact that, in the supposedly chronological order of the manuscript, it appears before a letter referring to the disaster of Nicopolis and to Cydones' departure for the West in 1396 (see below, pp. 134–136), and that it was plainly written while Cydones was still in the city. Hence, it must have been written between 1394 and 1396. In view of the allusion to active hostilities under Bayazid's personal command, the most likely date is probably 1394 or, at least, early 1395.

6. Ducas, ed. Darkó, I, 79, ed. Bonn, 50; who also sets the number of Bayazid's forces at "over ten thousand men." According to Konstantin the Philosopher, ed. Jagić, 270 (cf. Stanojević, "Die Biographie Stefan Lazarevićs von Konstantin dem Philosophen als Geschichtsquelle," 421), the unsuccessful Bayazid turned his arms instead on Galata; but, see n. 29 below.

7. For this, see Loenertz, "Pour l'histoire," 155, 185–186; also Zakythinos, *Le Despotat grec de Morée*, I, 155; and Mompherratos, Οἱ Παλαιολόγοι ἐν Πελοποννήσῳ, 10; cf. also Muralt, p. 753, no. 25. Nor was this the end of Bayazid's punishment of the Despotate, for two years later, in 1397, his generals Iakoub Pasha and Timourtash led another raid which sacked Argos: see Loenertz' *Chron. br. mor.*, no. 19, p. 406, and his commentary, p. 424.

8. This date has been advanced over the traditional one of October 10, 1394, by Dj. S. Radojičić, "La Chronologie de la bataille de Rovine," *Revue*

was in the death then of Konstantin Dejanović, Manuel's father-in-law. Ironically, the Serbian prince was not killed fighting against the Turks, as one might like to hear, but rather in the Emir's ranks, together with his fellow vassals the celebrated Marko Kraljević, who was also killed, and Stefan Lezarević, who escaped. Later in this year, in October, Manuel and his wife Helena jointly bestowed grants, respectively, of 100 and 500 *hyperpyra*, upon the Monastery of (St. John the Baptist in) Petra, in the capital, to make provisions for the memory of the Empress' father.[9]

There is no doubt that the blockade of Constantinople remained in force, even if no longer an intense siege. At least one assault by the Turks is recorded for September 29, 1395.[10] Yet, Bayazid himself seems largely to have withdrawn from personal prosecution of the beleaguerment, and, while the evidence is still very vague, there is some possibility that Manuel may have been under somewhat less pressure during at least some parts of the year 1395.[11]

historique du sud-est européen, 5 (1928), 136–139; and the revision has been accepted by such scholars as Loenertz, "Pour l'histoire du Péloponnèse," 186, and Ostrogorsky, *Hist. Byz. St.*, 489–490. The battle is described, but without date, by the *Bulg. chron.*, 538–539. On the battle, see also Jireček, *Geschichte der Serben*, II (Gotha, 1918), 130–131; and Iorga, *Geschichte des osmanischen Reiches*, I, 275–276, who give the old date; cf. otherwise Babinger, *Beiträge zur frühgeschichte der Türkenherrschaft in Rumelien (14.-15. Jahrhundert)*, 14–15.

9. Text in Miklosich and Müller, *Acta et diplomata graeca*, II, no. 499, pp. 260–264; cf. Dölger, *Regesten*, no. 3257, p. 83; Radojičić, "La Chronologie," 138; Anastasejević, "Jedina vizantijska carica Srpkinja," 32; Babinger, 14; note also the use made of this text by Radojičić in his "Listina manastira Petre od oktobra 1395 god. kao izvor za chronologiju bitke na Rovinama," *Bogoslovjle (Organ pravoslavnog bogoslovskog Fakulteta y Beogradu)*, 2 (1927), 293–301.

10. Βϱ. χϱ. No. 45, p. 77, ll. 8–11, a curious note in an otherwise useless chronicle for this period. In a Russian chronicle for this time, in the *Sofiiskaia pervaia letopis (Arkheograficheskaia komissiia, Polnoe sobranie russkikh letopisei*, 5, 1851), p. 246, there is a note for the Byzantine year 6903 (1394–1395), lacking any more specific date, which speaks of an unsuccessful Turkish attack on Constantinople led by John VII. It is not impossible, though hardly certain, that these two assaults were one and the same: cf. Barker, "John VII in Genoa: A Problem in Late Byzantine Source Confusion," p. 224, n. 2.

11. Manuel's negotiations seem to have eased off with Venice, for his only transaction during this period, in what documents are currently available, is a renewal of the regular treaty. A difficulty in the unsuccessful negotiations for this renewal is noted in a deliberation of the Senate of March 12,

But Manuel was by no means inactive during this period. The league proposed against the Turks was no idle talk, but was the first indication of a major project in the making. And Manuel was in the thick of its preparations. The background of diplomatic negotiations for this grand alliance, to become the so-called Crusade of Nicopolis, is a long and complex story.[12] Our principal concern here is the direct involvement of Manuel and Byzantium. Some of the Byzantine sources are aware that Manuel played an important role in the formation of the league, a role that can easily be overestimated.[13] To be sure, the key figure in this ex-

1395: Thiriet, *Régestes*, I, no. 871, p. 206; see also Silberschmidt, 110–111; and Dölger, *Regesten*, no. 3252, p. 83. But it should be borne in mind that we can draw the conclusion of this easing off only from the lack of any available source information to the contrary. No other Venetian documents involving Manuel have been noted for this period by any of the scholars who have edited, summarized, or cited these texts. It remains to be seen whether there are indeed any other such documents. It might be pointed out here also, as mentioned previously (above, p. 60, n. 163), that the proposal of Berger de Xivrey, 80–81, of a temporary sojourn by Manuel on Lesbos under pressure of attacks on Constantinople during these years is completely unfounded and unacceptable.

12. Atiya, *The Crusade of Nicopolis* (London, 1934), 33–49, for a summary of the league's background. But one must scrutinize critically this author's treatment of the Byzantine involvement, especially in his use of the Venetian sources. Also still important is Bk. III (pp. 209–258) of Delaville le Roulx, *La France en Orient au XIVe siècle*, especially pp. 220–245, for the background; likewise, A. Brauner's old monograph, *Die Schlacht bei Nikopolis, 1396* (Inaugural Dissertation, Breslau, 1876), 8–24; Mompherratos, Διπλωματικαὶ ἐνέργειαι Μανουὴλ Β΄ τοῦ Παλαιολόγου ἐν Εὐρώπῃ καὶ ᾿Ασίᾳ (Athens, 1913), 10–15; L. Kupelwieser, *Die Kämpfe Ungarns mit den Osmanen bis zur Schlacht bei Mohács, 1526* (Vienna, 1899), 12 ff.; also Vaughan, *Europe and the Turk*, 34 ff. A full exploitation of the Venetian sources for this background may be found in Silberschmidt, 97–120, and 158 ff. See also the summary in Stanojević, 421–423. For the background from the point of view of Papal involvement, see Halecki, "Rome et Byzance au temps du grand Schisme d'Occident," 494–504.

13. The account of the Crusade of Nicopolis by Chalcocondyles, ed. Darkó, 68–71, ed. Bonn, 73–77, makes no mention of Manuel in the launching of the project, but places the initiative solely on the shoulders of Sigismund of Hungary. Likewise, in essence, the *Chron. Barb. 111*, 32–33. The account by the Pseudo-Phrantzes, ed. Papadopoulos, 63–65, ed. Bonn, 58–60, is essentially the same, but differs in some details, including reference to ambassadors sent to conclude a pact with Manuel, though only after the expedition was well under way. This late involvement is also implied by the passing reference in Froissart, *Chroniques*, IV, 1, ed. J. A. C. Buchon (3 vols., Paris, 1836), III, 244. By contrast, Ducas, ed. Grecu, 79–81, ed. Bonn, 50–53, traces the origin of the expedition to the initiative of Manuel, who, after the beginning of Bayazid's siege, was supposedly so desperate

pedition was King Sigismund of Hungary, its prime mover. But Manuel's role need not be underestimated. His critical situation entitled him to the sympathy of the Crusaders, and—more important—his valuable strategic position made him a significant partner in the venture, even if he could not really contribute much to it materially.

We have several Venetian documents that indicate Manuel's involvement in the organization of the league. The Lagoon City had been the natural choice as focal point for the negotiations and embassies which were to prepare the Crusade. But, in a series of responses of December 9, 1395, to the Greek ambassador, the Venetian Senate pointed out that it would be better for Venice not to become an open partner in the land expedition, though she would cooperate fully by maritime means. The other responses by the Senate, however, give us further clues as to Manuel. The *Sapientes* point out that there is no need to encourage Manuel to remain in his capital; implying thereby that Manuel had given up any plan whatsoever that he may have had to leave Constantinople and had determined to maintain his position—especially, one presumes, in view of the aid promised by the imminent Crusade. In addition, the replies continue, Manuel's request for a shipment of needed grain (7,000 to 8,000 *staria*) is acknowledged. Finally, reference is made to a loan which Manuel hopes to negotiate with the *Serenissima*, for which he is offering as securities certain holy relics.[14]

for aid that he wrote to the Pope, the King of "Phrangkia," and the "Krales of Oungria." To be sure, this would seem to fit the suggestion of the Venetian Senate in 1394; and, further, Manuel may well have followed such advice, as is concluded by Dölger, *Regesten*, nos. 3249–51, pp. 82–83. Atiya, *The Crusade of Nicopolis*, pp. 173–174, n. 1, moreover, uses a French source to suggest that at least one embassy from Manuel may have been on such business in France in 1395; and Delaville le Roulx, *La France en Orient*, p. 228, n. 1, similarly cites the presence of a Byzantine emissary in Burgundy in the same year.

It would be easy, therefore, especially from the statement by Ducas, to conclude that the initiative for the Crusade was primarily Manuel's. And this has indeed been the assumption of Brauner, 8; cf. Delaville le Roulx, *ibid.*, and Mompherratos, 10–11. This assumption has been challenged, however, by Atiya, 34–35, who is undoubtedly correct in his insistence that Manuel's pleas could only have been of secondary importance, and that the interests and outlook of Sigismund were the principal factors. Note, however, that even Atiya's handling of the Byzantine role is often inaccurate, as is particularly the case with the faulty citation in his p. 175, n. 31.

14. Thiriet, *Régestes*, I, no. 892, p. 210; unfortunately, the text itself has not been published.

In a deliberation of February 17, 1396, the Venetian ambassadors to Bayazid were instructed to take up certain matters with the Emir, including some attempt at mediation between Bayazid and Manuel. These ambassadors were then to proceed to Constantinople and were to discuss with Manuel—who, it is mentioned, had come to some sort of agreement with the Genoese of Pera—the overtures for peace with Bayazid. As to other negotiations with Manuel, in addition to pressing for a renewal of the last Byzantine treaty (of John VII) with Venice, the ambassadors were told to refuse the relics offered as securities for a loan. This refusal was to be made on the grounds that the transfer of such revered objects might cause too violent a popular reaction in Constantinople.[15] This latter Venetian document would require little comment were it not for the strange scheme for patching up a peace with Bayazid. We have no way of knowing whether or not Manuel took any such scheme very seriously. But it is difficult to understand how the clever Venetians could have done so either, save that the Republic of St. Mark was always anxious to settle a peaceful status quo in the Levant for the benefit of her commercial interests. At any rate, whatever form such efforts, if any, finally took, they plainly came to nothing.

In the winter of 1395–96, an alliance against the Turks was formally concluded in Buda between the Hungarian King, Sigismund, and Byzantium, the latter being represented in the person of Manuel Philanthropenos. The negotiations were completed by February. On the twenty-eighth of that month, it was announced to the Venetian Senate from his letter that this Byzantine ambassador would return by way of Venice, and arrangements were made to convey him home, now that the alliance was agreed upon.[16] On March 1, 1396, the Senate was officially informed of

15. Partial text, ed. Iorga, "Veneţia in Marea neagră," 1115–1116; cf. Thiriet, *Régestes*, I, no. 896, p. 210. See also Silberschmidt, 109; Dölger, *Regesten*, no. 3256, p. 83. That Manuel himself was to have no qualms about giving out relics from Constantinople we shall see later in connection with his trip to the West. The reference to an agreement with the Genoese may reflect a league of which King Sigismund speaks after Nicopolis: see Appendix XI, especially p. 484. From another Venetian Senate deliberation we can infer something of Manuel's financial difficulties at this time. On June 30, 1396, it was decided that the *Signoria* would assume the cost of repairs on the house of the Venetian vice-*bailo* in Constantinople, even though this obligation would normally be the Emperor's, who will therefore owe the amount (150 *hyperpyra*) to Venice: Thiriet, *Régestes*, I, no. 911, p. 213.

16. Text of this deliberation, ed. Ljubić, no. 508, pp. 359–360. The

the impending arrival of the Byzantine representative and was likewise apprised of the accord with Sigismund. This accord, it was stated, obliged the Emperor to arm ten galleys, paid for by Sigismund at a cost of 30,000 ducats, for use in the Danube area in the coming campaign. Moreover, in view of these agreements, Venice promised to abandon her efforts toward a reconciliation between Manuel and Bayazid, as projected during the previous month.[17] On the same day, however, the Senate revoked the foregoing instructions. The Venetian Captain of the Gulf was instructed to report to Manuel that Venice had learned from Philanthropenos of the agreements with Sigismund. For Manuel's "comfort and consolation," eight galleys were to be sent with provisions for the city. An embassy was to be sent, after all, to attempt to effect peace between the Emperor and "Basitus," and it is hoped that this Venetian demonstration of support for Manuel will serve to impress the Turk.[18] Why the Venetians

ambassador's name is given as "Hemanuel Philotropimos." This document is noted only in passing by Thiriet, *Régestes*, I, p. 211, n. 1. On the Philanthropenos mission, see also Dölger, *Regesten*, no. 3255, p. 83. For a general discussion of Hungarian-Byzantine relations before and after Nicopolis, see Moravcsik, "Vizantiiskie imperatorii ich poslj v.g. Buda" ("Les empereurs de Byzance et leurs ambassadeurs à Buda"), 249, 250.

17. Text, ed. Ljubić, no. 519, p. 360; cf. Thiriet, *Régestes*, I, no. 900, p. 211. See also Delaville le Roulx, *La France en Orient*, 243. Muralt, p. 756, nos. 17 and 18, has not even the most basic understanding of Manuel's true involvement in Sigismund's expedition. On the ships which Manuel provided, see also Appendix XI below.

18. Text, ed. Ljubić, no. 520, pp. 360–361, which is perhaps incomplete, since there are suspicious discrepancies between it and the summary by Thiriet, *Régestes*, I, no. 901, pp. 211–213. The latter, however, omits the important reference to the restored plan to attempt mediation between Manuel and Bayazid. On the other hand, he adds the statements that the renewal of the Veneto-Byzantine treaty was to be urged; and that the Venetian commercial interests in the Levant were to be looked after, while the Venetian squadron was to be ready to aid Constantinople in case of its danger. Indeed, the latter statements sound more germane to the deliberation of May 18, 1396, in which the Venetian naval armaments and cooperation with Sigismund's expedition were reviewed. At the same time, the Senate added that assurances were to be given Manuel, and it issued directives to its agents in the East in the light of likely conditions: ed. Ljubić, no. 517, pp. 374–376. On the earlier of these deliberations, cf. also Mompherratos, Διπλ. ἐν., 15; and, in much greater generalities on the Venetian policy uncertainties, Hazlitt, *The Venetian Republic*, I, 737–738. Philanthropenos, incidentally, was presumably provided with transportation back to Constantinople. For, in a deliberation of April 9, 1396 (ed. Ljubić, no. 513, pp. 363–364), while pointing out to Sigismund their zeal on behalf of the alliance, the *Sapientes* referred (p. 364) to their care in providing for this return trip of the Byzantine ambassador.

chose to persist in their plan to mediate between the Empire and the Emir, once the alliance had been concluded and the plans for the expedition had been set in motion, is difficult to understand, except in terms of the usual Venetian readiness to play all sides at once for the best possible advantage. We have no way of knowing Manuel's outlook on the matter, but there can be no doubt that any such talk of peace with Bayazid was wasted breath.

Regardless of any agreements or desires, Manuel was hardly in a position to participate actively in the military operations of 1396. Rather, he was obliged simply to sit on the sidelines, blockaded in his capital, a helpless spectator. Events soon ran to their disastrous climax. By the early summer there had come together a vast host of Hungarian, French, Wallachian, German, and English forces, with additional volunteers or mercenaries of Styrian, Bohemian, Polish, Spanish, and Italian origins, all totaling upward of 100,000 men.[19] Ravaging its way across the Danube, the Crusader army seized successfully and brutally the fortresses of Viddin and Rahova and, by September, had settled down to besiege the Danubian stronghold of Nicopolis. Before its walls on Monday, September 25, 1396, a combination of hopeless disorganization among the Crusaders, the usual foolhardy recklessness of French chivalry, and the ruthless strategy of Bayazid, all contributed toward the crushing defeat of the Christian army. The Emir relished his triumph amid a hideous orgy of massacre of captives, while pitiful remnants of the host endeavored to make their escape, not always with success or good fortune. Not the least among the fugitives were King Sigismund and Philibert de Naillac, Grand Master-elect of the Hospitalers, who, with a few lesser leaders, managed to escape by way of the Danube and then proceeded ingloriously by ship to Constantinople.[20]

19. For a discussion of the numbers and groups of the crusading army, see Atiya, *The Crusade of Nicopolis*, 66–71; also *id., The Crusade in the Later Middle Ages*, 439–440; on the reliability of the figures, cf. R. Rosetti, in the *Analele* of the *Academiei Române, Memoriile Sect. Ist.*, III, 25 (=*Memoriile*, 16, 1943), 727–746, which I have not seen personally. On a supposed message sent by Manuel to encourage the Crusaders on their way, see Dölger, *Regesten*, no. 3262, p. 84.

20. On this campaign and battle, the basic work is Atiya, *The Crusade of Nicopolis*, especially Chaps. IV–VI (pp. 50–97); to which some details are added by R. Rosetti, "Note on the Battle of Nicopolis (1396)," *The Slavonic Review*, 15 (1936–37), 629–638. The corresponding chapter

As despairing as was the reaction in the West to this terrible disaster, what must Manuel have felt! The one great Western exertion that stood a good chance of bringing him substantial relief had collapsed in a nightmare of bungling, bloodshed, and devastating failure. It is unfortunate that the one surviving reflection of any length by Manuel himself on these events should be so encrusted with obscure hyperbole. But, even as it stands, there is ample indication of the unhappy Emperor's state of mind in this letter to Cydones, written after the latter's last departure for Italy, about the time of the battle:

No sooner had you put to sea, when the King, forthwith landing in the harbor, did gladden us as much by his appearance as did its manner fill us with grief, we who had been yearning for him. It was ordained, so it seems, for these things to happen and for you to depart on the very same day, in the midst of winter, you, disregarding illness and old age, to emulate the birds in their migrations, whose spreading of wings often does not wait on their thoughts. I know not what I am to make of this: whether it is a result of by no means good fortune or of an extremely well-disposed Divinity. For, certainly, what actions have been taken toward the common interest would have been very much the better had you been able to give your assistance to them with your discourse and your understanding and all your other faculties—nor do I speak out of partiality. Accordingly, your not being present was a stroke of fate far from good, and altogether malicious, since you alone have passed beyond the view of this brave and good man, and savior of his portion of enslaved Christians, for whom you were longing, perhaps, no less than anyone else. Well do I know, therefore, that your soul will be filled with sorrow and despondency, and that my comments on this misfortune—how could one sufficiently bewail it?—will be as arrows shot at you. But then,

(XVIII, pp. 435–462) in Atiya's *The Crusade in the Later Middle Ages* is a useful condensation of his full study. Another good study is G. Kling, *Die Schlacht bei Nikopolis in Jahre 1396* (Inaugural Dissertation, Berlin, 1906); still useful is Delaville le Roulx, *La France en Orient*, 246–299; likewise, Brauner, 24–50; Kupelwieser, 15–30; and J. Aschbach, *Geschichte Kaiser Sigismund's*, I: *Sigismund's frühere Geschichte bis auf die Eröffnung des constanzer Conciliums* (Hamburg, 1838), 86–111. In less detail, see Hammer, I, 236–244, trans. Hellert, I, 325–338; Iorga, *Geschichte*, I, 291–296; Gibbons, *The Foundation of the Ottoman Empire*, 201–211; and G. Beckmann, *Der Kampf Kaiser Sigmunds gegen die werdende Weltmacht der Osmanen, 1392–1437. Eine historische Grundlegung* (Gotha, 1902), 6–8; also, Ostrogorsky, *Hist. Byz. St.*, 490; Mompherratos, Διπλ. ἐν., 16–17. Though it is not absolutely complete, the extensive bibliography appended to Atiya's detailed study will serve to indicate further material on this by-no-means-neglected episode.

when I behold myself and all who have some share of intelligence, speaking ill of mortal life as never before and disgusted that they did not just give up the ghost after the first outcry, when the un-looked-for turn of events became known—when I see this, therefore, your voyage, which previously I could not approve, now, changing my tune, I hold as the work of a far-seeing and protecting God.

After all, if we who are healthy are inclined to be no stronger than those who are ill, reckoning ourselves half-dead when smitten by the unexpected, and if we cry out continuously against living, what would have been your case were you to be present and to see and to hear all this, since you have been struggling with lengthy illnesses and are indeed not yet completely free of them? For, to prudent men, life is not worth living after that calamity, and after that deluge—not, to be sure, that deluge of the whole world, but one worse than that, inasmuch as it carried off men better than those of yore!—after this crash, echoing with its savagery and ill omen, after these thunderclaps one upon another, all, terrifying circumstances. And so they have all come together at this juncture, as if they were so many very dense clouds of evil. And not in a rush of wind and in a thrust of swollen sin was this come to pass, but beyond all anticipation, when the sky was bright, and when calm was expected by those who, as it were, expected to complete their voyage with a fair wind, by those whose haven was all but at hand! All these woes just recited have, therefore, set upon us with such great violence as to have torn out by the roots—so far as is within human calculation—all hope for anything better.

Indeed, to hope to find release from these, the evils which are so long oppressing our race; and to hope to check those who, themselves enslaved once upon a time, are now enslaving others; and, to get to the point for those already informed, to hope to reverse for the better our entire situation; and then suddenly to see everything go in the opposite fashion—what sort of Herakleses, or what giants, would this not have cast down? The will of what adamant souls would it not have laid low? Yet, He has suffered us to remain firm: for God, having wounded, will heal. It is really better for those of good hope to speak and to believe thus, since God, being good, and He alone—since only one is good [cf. Mark x: 18; Matthew xix: 17]—will not in the end, I believe, want to be wholly wroth with those who have stumbled, nor to let loose continuously the rod of the unbelievers upon the portion of the just, I mean on that of the faithful. . . .

(Continuing, Manuel expands further upon the conviction that God will at last punish evildoers, and he riddles his assertions with Scriptural quotations or allusions. Then the balance of the letter is led into a lengthy development, again laced with Scripture, of a further idea: that the false and evil teachings of Islam must be clearly revealed for what they are, so that the sinful Muslims may not, after all the crimes they have committed, defend themselves on the Day of Judgement with the excuse that they did not know that these teachings, which they followed faithfully, were false and evil. The letter ends, finally, on a note of hope and trust in God.) [21]

It is unfortunate that this letter is such a jungle of studied obscurity, and that Manuel felt himself obliged to take refuge in what must have been stereotyped Byzantine rationalizations and religious self-assurances in the face of the terrifying successes of "the unbelievers." But, even in this state, the letter indicates the ordeal through which Manuel and his subjects felt themselves passing, and it gives us an idea of how they must have reacted to it. Regrettably, Manuel gives us no specific or factual statements on the events themselves, although his allusions to the disaster are quite obvious. Obvious also is his reference to "the King" who sailed into Constantinople. Sigismund had been brought to the city by a Venetian squadron, and there he conferred with Manuel. Understanding was reached on both sides that the King would prepare another expedition for the following spring.[22] He

21. Letter λα', ed. Legrand, 39–44: translated here are ll. 1–60. Manuel's only other apparent reference directly to the Battle of Nicopolis comes in passing in his *Funeral Oration* for Theodore. Speaking of his brother's great difficulties in the Morea, Manuel notes the Byzantines' hard circumstances as a result of such things as their own weakness and the conquest of "All the Albanians ['Illyrians'] and Bulgarians ['Mysians'] and Serbians ['Triballians']." He then continues, noting "on the other hand, the great army which was struck down at Nikopolis—I mean that collected from the Paionians [Hungarians] and Kelts, and the western Galatians, at all of whose names alone I shudder as at an entirely barbaric thing. And, as the allies, or some of them, were also defeated by a most evil fate both on land and on sea, for my part, the troubles seemed to me to have come to an extreme of the dreadful consequences in so great a concourse of our evils, since these were thus for such a long time." (Ed. Migne, 261A–B; ed. Lampros, p. 84, ll. 14–21.) Since this passage was written long after the hope of substantial aid from the West had begun to wear thin, Manuel could find cynical satisfaction in his snobbish affectation of deploring the intrusion of "barbaric" Latin names into his otherwise "pure" Greek. Cf. Berger de Xivrey, 71.

22. Chalcocondyles, ed. Darkó, I, 70–71, ed. Bonn, 76, relates that Sigismund sailed to Constantinople, "and holding converse with the Basileus of Byzantium, and negotiating with him as many things as he wished, he left, sailing away homeward" (ἐς λόγους δὲ ἀφικόμενος τῷ Βυζαντίου βασιλεῖ, καὶ χρηματίσας αὐτῷ ὅσα ἐβούλετο, ᾤχετο ἀποπλέων ἐπ' οἴκου). There is no doubt that Sigismund stopped at Constantinople, for Johann Schiltberger,

then resumed, under particularly ignominious circumstances, his homeward voyage in Mocenigo's ships through the Adriatic.[23]

But while the West—and subsequent historians—were distracted by the dramatic task of ransoming the nobles whom

captured after the battle, specifically says in his celebrated *Reisebuch,* ed. V. Langmantel (Tübingen, 1885), p. 4; trans. J. B. Telfer (Hakluyt Soc., London, 1879), p. 4, that Sigismund sailed to the city. We have further, if less contemporary, confirmation of Sigismund's presence in Constantinople from the eighteenth-century *Chroniche di Ragusa* of Giunio Resti (*Mon. spect. hist. slav. merid.,* XXV, Zagreb, 1893), 182, who says that, after the battle the King "fled to Costantinopoli of Thrace, from which, sailing to, etc." But dwarfing all such references in importance is the ultimate confirmation of a letter, dated November 11, 1396, written by Sigismund from Constantinople. This letter also casts interesting light on the situation immediately after Nicopolis. For the full text, with translation, and a discussion of this valuable document, see Appendix XI below.

There is every reason to suppose that the rest of Chalcocondyles' statement is essentially correct; for, once there, Sigismund only naturally would have conferred with Manuel. Berger de Xivrey, 84, however, had brushed aside this statement (ignoring its confirmation by Schiltberger) and had come to the conclusion that Manuel's refernce in Letter λα′ to a ῥήξ does not apply to Sigismund but rather, he says, to King James I of Cyprus. And as a basis for this conclusion he uses Manuel's fulsome and virtually meaningless Letter λβ′ to one Manuel Raoul, apparently an official of this ruler. But such support is hardly defensible; and we know, moreover, of no visit by the King of Cyprus to Constantinople at this time, nor was he among those present at Nicopolis. Berger de Xivrey's contention has been raised (in connection with the chronology of Cydones' last voyage) and derided by G. Mercati, pp. 117–118 and n. 3 of his "Tre piccoli scritti di Caleca e la fine di Demetrio," in *Notizie di Procoro e Demetrio Cidone, Manuele Caleca e Teodoro Meliteniota ed altri appunti per la storia della Teologia e della letteratura bizantina del secolo XIV* (*Studi e Testi,* 56, Vatican City, 1931).

Part of Berger de Xivrey's argument is based on Manuel's phrase "in the midst of winter" (χειμῶνος μεσοῦντος). The date of Sigismund's letter, which presupposes a sojourn already of at least a few days on his part in Constantinople, only confirms the difficulty of this expression, for, since Sigismund did demonstrably arrive in early November, this time could hardly be called "the midst of winter" unless it was, as Mercati drolly suggests, "un inverno precoce." But, even setting aside any theories that the climate of the city was once much harsher, it is perhaps possible, knowing Manuel's style, to dismiss this seeming incongruity as simply a far-fetched rhetorical device. At any rate, there can be no doubt that Manuel refers to Sigismund's arrival.

Finally, that plans were laid by the two conferring sovereigns for another expedition by Sigismund about spring is clear not only from the plain statements in the King's letter. For in a Patriarchal text of January, 1397, only a scant month or so later (see below, pp. 150–151, for a translation), the prelate tells with full conviction of Sigismund's intention to launch a new expedition by the following March: "For he departed from us [about a month previously] with such statements and commitments. . . ."

23. Schiltberger, ii, ed. Langmantel, p. 7, trans. Telfer, p. 6, says that

Bayazid had spared among his captives for that lucrative purpose,[24] Byzantium was to suffer the more immediate and more ominous consequences of the disaster at Nicopolis. As early as October 29, 1396, the prudent Venetian Senate had realized the danger which threatened Constantinople. Provisions were made, with an allotment of 5,000 ducats, to maintain a fleet for the defense of the city.[25] Such foresight was to prove justified.

If the Turkish blockade of Constantinople had been somewhat relaxed prior to the Crusade of Nicopolis, it was probably eased even more during that episode. But, once Bayazid had been freed from such distractions, he moved to press the siege of the city with renewed vigor.[26] By winter the outlook must have become

when Sigismund sailed through the Hellespont, the Turks took their captives from the battle, who had been confined in Gallipoli, and arrayed them along the shore, mocking and reviling the Hungarian King even if they could not halt or harm him. For Sigismund's voyage, see Atiya, *The Crusade of Nicopolis*, 98–99; Delaville le Roulx, *La France en Orient*, 287–289; Kling, 106–107.

24. For the ransoming of the captives of Nicopolis, see Atiya, *The Crusade of Nicopolis*, 99–112; Delaville le Roulx, *La France en Orient*, 300–334; Mompherratos, Διπλ. ἐν., 17–23.

25. Text of this deliberation, ed. Ljubić, no. 535, pp. 386–388; cf. Thiriet, *Régestes*, I, no. 971, pp. 214–215. See also Silberschmidt, 166–167. The Senate had, on the previous day, discussed requirements for the safety of Venice's own possessions in the light of the new situation: ed. Ljubić, no. 534, p. 386. Even further, the *Serenissima* was moved to investigate the possibility of joint moves with Genoa for the common good (November 24, 1396: Thiriet, no. 918, p. 215), leading then to further attempts to get Genoa to agree to a joint renunciation of the terms of the Treaty of Turin, and to rearm Tenedos (January 30, 1397: Thiriet, no. 924, p. 216; and February 8: Thiriet, no. 926, pp. 216–217). But this project came to naught (March 9: Thiriet, no. 928, p. 217), leaving Venice to take the initiative itself regarding the island.

26. In their confused chronology, all of the Byzantine historians say nothing of the commencement of Bayazid's siege of Constantinople until after the events of Nicopolis. Thus Ducas, ed. Grecu, 81 f., ed. Bonn, 53 f.; Chalcocondyles, ed. Darkó, I, 77 ff., ed. Bonn, 83 ff., followed by the Pseudo-Phrantzes, ed. Papadopoulos, 65 f., ed. Bonn, 61 f., and the *Chron. Barb. 111*, 35 f. In all these cases the question is complicated by the interpolation of the conferences of Serres at this point. Possibly, the explanation is that the historians mistook a renewal of the siege in 1396, after Nicopolis, for the actual initiation of the siege in 1394, after the conference at Serres. Be it noted that the *Bulg. chron.*, 540 f., although completely independent of these later Greek sources, makes the same error of placing Bayazid's siege only immediately after, and as a result of, the Battle of Nicopolis. But it should by no means be concluded, at the other extreme, that the blockade of Constantinople was completely interrupted or withdrawn. Apparently Bayazid

clear, for by January 2, 1397, the Venetian Senate was convinced of "the aggressive intentions of Bayazid against the *partes Grecie*" and ordered appropriate armament of its squadrons.[27]

Within at least a few months after the Crusade, Bayazid had reinvested the city closely and had prepared to take it by assault. Once again the Emir called upon Manuel to yield up the city and to restore the rights of succession to John VII. The latter demand was apparently enough to cause considerable sentiment within the capital for surrender—or at least considerable dissatisfaction with Manuel.[28]

Manuel and his supporters were hard-pressed. The new expedition promised by Sigismund was still a long way off; in fact, it was never to come. Bayazid was set on his goal, and he per-

was supervising the siege himself when he received word of the crusading army's advance: Konstantin the Philosopher, ed. Jagić, 270; see also Atiya, *The Crusade of Nicopolis*, 62–63.

Nor is it correct to assume (as does Atiya, 63) that the Emir completely raised his siege when he departed forthwith. However they may disagree as to the number of years the siege lasted, it is almost unanimously agreed by the sources cited in Appendix X that it was a continuous period of time which, by all correct computation, would include the year 1396. Especially important in this respect is the Patriarchal document of 1400/01 (Miklosich and Müller, II, pp. 463–467), which correctly reckons the years of the siege, and which states expressly that there was no interruption. Moreover, to prove specifically that the blockade was maintained to some degree during the time of the Crusade of Nicopolis, we have the further testimony of King Sigismund himself, in his letter which is discussed in Appendix XI. From our evidence, therefore, the middle course is apparently the safest: the blockade was maintained without real break from its beginning in 1394, but was probably relaxed slightly in 1395–96, to be renewed as an active siege again, in the literal sense of the word, after the Battle of Nicopolis. Thus, the elaborate and clever explanations by Gibbons, 234–235, of why Bayazid did not follow up his great victory and destroy the last remnant of Byzantium are somewhat pointless.

27. Thiriet, *Régestes*, I, no. 922, p. 215.

28. All of the Greek sources cited in n. 26 speak of John VII in connection with the siege at this juncture. Ducas in particular quotes Bayazid's demand and speaks also of the disaffection and difficulty within the capital. To be sure, such use of John VII as a front for Bayazid's goal could have occurred, and presumably did occur, in the earlier phase of the siege. But John was certainly available at this time as a tool which the Emir could not have failed to use. Ducas seems to suggest that Bayazid used the claim on Constantinople for John as an alternative to depriving the latter of Selymbria: see J. W. Barker, "John VII in Genoa," 215 f., 220 f. Delaville le Roulx, *La France en Orient*, 354–355, who also stresses the reinvigoration of Bayazid's offensive against Constantinople after Nicopolis, places heavy emphasis on the use of John VII by Bayazid at this time.

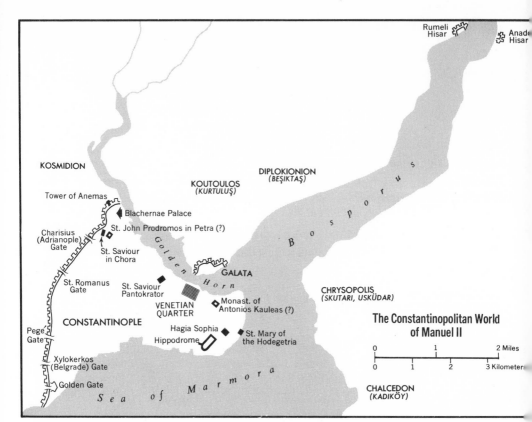

The Constantinopolitan World of Manuel II

sonally directed a sequence of fierce assaults on the city. The Byzantines set great store by pious rituals and divine protection. More tangible defense, however, was provided by the still-magnificent fortifications of Constantinople, which not only served as an obstacle well-nigh insurmountable to the Turks at this time, but also afforded a position from which the defenders were able successfully to hurl back the attackers. Nothing daunted, Bayazid gazed from afar upon the distant glory of Hagia Sophia and proclaimed it worthy to become his palace after his expected victory; whereupon his nobles, following their master's example, proceeded to choose and parcel out among themselves the various churches of the city, all fully anticipating their triumph. But, apparently stymied by the fortifications of Constantinople itself, the Turks began to concentrate their attentions more upon Galata. Even here, however, Bayazid's special siege engines were unequal to their task. Moreover, "the Franks" of Pera also repulsed all attacks valiantly, with the generous help of the Constantinopolitans, who fought side by side with their Latin brethren, present adversity having banished ancient hostility.[29]

Although our knowledge of these events is restricted, it seems

29. Virtually all of the foregoing information is derived from the *Bulg. chron.*, 540–542. It might seem unwise to accept so wholeheartedly the testimony of this text, which is usually so very unreliable on most matters Byzantine. But actually the chronicle's disproportionately long account of these events is in striking and significant contrast to the rest of its dealings with Byzantium. The narrative is lively and is filled with far too many temptingly acceptable details to be wholly imaginary. Rather, it suggests reliable sources and perhaps even eyewitness testimony. Our other sources say virtually nothing of the specific events at this juncture, so there is nothing to contradict these statements. And, indeed, the statements do seem to fit quite well into the context of what little other information we have or can reconstruct. It should be noted, moreover, that this Bulgarian source is much closer in date of composition to the events than most of our other historical sources, perhaps a further endorsement of its probable reliability in this case.

In addition, it seems on at least one count to be confirmed by a curious little Greek text that is perhaps closest of all to these events in date of composition. This is the anonymous *Narrative about the Marvellous Happening Wrought by the All-Holy Mother of God in the Days of the August Basileus Lord Manuel Palaiologos*, etc., formerly attributed to John Chortasmenos, and ed. by P. Gautier, in his "Un Récit inédit du siège de Constantinople par les Turcs (1394–1402)," *Rev. des ét. byz.*, 23 (1965), 100–117. In this text (which Gautier dates between 1405 and 1411) is described the virtually identical scene to be found in the *Bulg. chron.*, wherein Bayazid arrogantly surveys the besieged city, parcels out its buildings to his lieutenants, and selects Hagia Sophia for himself (p. 108, ll. 14–35). This text gives little precise chronological information: it specifically places this scene *after* the time when Timur had returned from Syria and was beginning to menace Turkish power directly, and also, by implication, while Manuel was away in the West. Thus, this text might suggest a time more around 1401 or 1402 for this scene, which might or might not then cast some reflection of our use of the parallel information in the *Bulg. chron.* for the period immediately after Nicopolis.

Also close to these events, however, is the testimony of Clavijo, ed. López Estrada, 58, ed. Sreznevskii, 89–90, trans. Le Strange, 89–90, who speaks of sieges of Pera at two different times, on one occasion—the most serious—for six months by 400,000 men and 60 galleys. Unfortunately, this text gives no more details. But it might be safe to assume that the six-month siege may well have been that of 1396/97, with the less serious one coming later, when Pera was demonstrably still threatened by the Turks.

Further indication of the Turkish threat to Pera is provided by the *Chronica Caroli sexti*, or *Chronique du Religieux de Saint-Denys*, XX, iii, ed. M. G. Bellaguet, Vol. II (Paris, 1840; reprint, 1965), p. 690. This indication comes in a vague reference to the time of Marshal Boucicaut's expedition of 1399, but that may suggest the second siege of Pera. At any rate, fully likely that this fighting and the brunt of Bayazid's renewed siege fell in midwinter of 1396–97.[30] Such dating is rendered tenable by two decrees of the Venetian Senate. On January 26, 1397, the *Sapientes* issued two responses to ambassadors of King Sigismund, in which they assured the monarch of their support amid his expenses and further hopes of action. Asserting that they did not wish "to desert Christianity nor the city of Constantinople," the Senate authorized the arming of eight more of its galleys to defend the area from the Turks; and they would

the allusion to the drawing of help for the capital through Pera—in the role of a food depot—is clear: "... hostilesque [Turci] continuantes discursus, Peram, villam maritinam, Januensibus subditam, ex qua Constantinopoli victualia suppetebant, viribus expugnassent, nisi ville marescallus prefatus succurrusset." On the other hand, we have the assertion by Konstantin the Philosopher (ed. Jagić, 270; ed. and trans. Braun, 13–14) that *before* the Battle of Nicopolis, Bayazid, unsuccessful in his siege of Constantinople, vainly attacked Galata also: cf. Stanojević, 421. But I do not think this assertion should oblige us to date to the pre-Nicopolis siege the testimony of the *Bulg. chron.*, which seems so distinctly related to the post-Nicopolis period. Rather, Konstantin's statement may possibly refer to an earlier assault on Pera, perhaps even the other of the two Clavijo mentions (even though our present sources do not speak of such danger to Pera before Nicopolis as they do after it); or else, more likely, the statement is a reversal of the usual practice in our sources, and places *before* the Battle of Nicopolis events which really transpired afterward.

Following Muralt, p. 757, no. 6, and using utterly irrelevant citations from Ducas and Chalcocondyles, Gibbons, 234, and also Pears, 110 and 136, seem to place about this time the building by Bayazid of the fortress known as Anadolu-Hisar. Intended as a base of operations for use in attacks against Constantinople, this castle was erected on the Asiatic shore of the Bosporus, across from the site of the later Rumeli Hisar built by Mechmed II on the European side. In his book *The Fall of Constantinople, 1453*, 66, Runciman makes the curious assertion that Byzantine protests against the building of Rumeli Hisar in 1452 were based in part on the claim that, in accordance with previous treaty agreements, Bayazid had *asked the permission* of Manuel to build Anadolu-Hisar. *Post facto* evidence of this kind would be of questionable value by any standards, but Runciman seems, without actually citing it specifically, to derive his assertion from a passage in Ducas (ed. Grecu, p. 297, ll. 22–25; ed. Bonn, p. 239, ll. 3–7) that in fact refers to Sultan Mechmed I (1413–1421), not Bayazid; Runciman's assertion therefore has no valid bearing on Bayazid's construction of his castle, which certainly could not have been built *with Manuel's permission!* A portion of Anadolu-Hisar still stands, unfortunately nowhere near as well-preserved as its magnificent counterpart across the Straits: cf. E. A. Grosvenor, *Constantinople* (2 vols., Boston, 1895), I, 222–223; see also S. Toy, "The Castles of Bosporus," in *Archaeologia, or Miscellaneous Tracts Relating to Antiquity*, II, 30 (1930), 215–228.

30. At best, this attempted dating is no more than conjectural; but in the

seek to have the Genoese contribute five of their own vessels likewise.[31] More to the point, on February 4, the Senate instructed one of its commanders to sail to Constantinople to express to Manuel the concern of Venice over the defeat at Nicopolis, to assure him that the Christian rulers of the West would soon come to his aid, and to inform him that Venice and Genoa were each sending five galleys. Further, this commander was to give comfort to the citizens of Pera as well, and to keep watch on its security as well as that of Constantinople. Finally, there were two significant provisions for alternate situations: the commander was given instructions made conditional on whether Constantinople alone should be "in the hands of the Sultan," or whether both Constantinople and Pera "might be taken."[32] The meaning

light of the information cited in the following two notes, it is possible to suggest some chronological feasibilities. Chalcocondyles, ed. Darkó, I, 71, ed. Bonn, 76–77, says that the Turks' campaign of immediate reprisal against Hungary after Nicopolis was curtailed by an attack of gout suffered by Bayazid. However true this statement may be, it is clear that Bayazid did at least make some inroads into Hungarian territory from the account by Schiltberger, iii, ed. Langmantel, pp. 7–8, trans. Telfer, p. 6. This writer says nothing to indicate that Bayazid thereupon turned his attention back to Byzantium. But, conversely, he says absolutely nothing that would rule out the possibility of this next step. Even if Chalcocondyles (who wrote some seventy years after this time) is correct about the Emir's gout, such a malady need not have lasted too long, nor at any rate have hindered him from ordering the stepping up of the siege and even his supervising it himself. Modern writers are wont to give the impression that after Nicopolis Bayazid was essentially occupied with the treatment and ransoming of his prisoners. But there seems to be no evidence of his extensive personal involvement with the dealings concerning them until the late winter or the spring of 1397. There is every reason to suppose that he was almost entirely free during the winter for a project such as a siege, an activity which, moreover, need by no means have been restricted to the customary campaign season. Cf. also Silberschmidt, 172 ff., who has come to essentially the same conclusion; see also Mompherratos, Διπλ. ἐν., 24–25.

Note that Dölger, *Regesten*, nos. 3263–3264, p. 84, citing a Turkish source, places in the period "autumn 1396–autumn 1399" a supposed peace mission by Manuel to Bayazid, and the successful conclusion of a treaty, by whose terms the oft-mentioned Turkish *kadi* was admitted into Constantinople. I would hardly accept such a dating, which seems so out of harmony with the other evidence at hand.

31. Text, ed. Ljubić, no. 548, pp. 398–400; cf. Thiriet, *Régestes*, I, no. 923, pp. 215–216, whose summary is rather weak; also, Silberschmidt, 178; Muralt, p. 758, no. 13; Stanojević, 425.

32. Thiriet, *Régestes*, I, no. 925, p. 216; cf. Silberschmidt, 179–180, 181–182. It is a great pity that the text of this, as well as of many other Venetian

of these instructions is incontestable: at the time they were issued, both Constantinople and Pera were seriously threatened and were—one of them or both—in real danger of falling to Bayazid. Plainly, both were under siege, the very siege our source describes, one which must have been an active siege during this period.

If Manuel's position was direly threatened from the outside, it was no less grim within his city. In spite of some shipments of grain and food from without, the blockade still imposed great famine and privation of necessities on the citizens of Constantinople, who suffered grievously.[33] Hand in hand with such hard-

documents for this period, has not been published. The Venetian actions in this case were plainly prompted, at least in part, by exactly the sort of embassies sent to Venice and Genoa which are mentioned by Sigismund in his letter of November 11, 1396 (see Appendix XI): cf. Silberschmidt, 177 ff. For further comments on Venice and action vis-à-vis Byzantium at this juncture, *ibid.*, 166–168. This deliberation of February 4 also includes instructions for conveying some "French barons" from a Dalmatian port to Gallipoli or Constantinople. These nobles can only have been the representatives who, having consulted with Sigismund, were to negotiate the ransom of captives from the Battle of Nicopolis: cf. Atiya, *The Crusade of Nicopolis*, 101 ff., who has not used this document.

33. Most of our Greek sources have something to say on this subject, and, though their comments are sometimes placed in a context explicitly or implicitly connected with an earlier phase of the siege, they could refer to this period just as well. At any rate, such statements undoubtedly characterize the situation throughout most of the siege as a whole. Chalcocondyles, ed. Darkó, I, p. 77, ll. 17–18, ed. Bonn, p. 83, ll. 12–13, speaks of the long years the siege endured, "in which years many of the city departed, both having been killed by the famine, and departing to the barbarians." The *Chron. Barb. 111*, p. 35, l. 35, also observes that during the blockade "many people died from the hunger." The *Chron. Vat. gr. 162*, no. 17, p. 210, ll. 76–77, notes awkwardly that the blockade was so severe "as a μουζούρι [*modius?*] of grain to become (worth) 100 aspers, and it was not found." But Ducas, ed. Grecu, p. 79, ll. 11–14, ed. Bonn, p. 50, ll. 13–17, is not only more stylish but also more vivid: "There was indeed a severe famine within the city, of grain, of wine, and of oil, and of all other kinds of things. And, in addition to a want of bread and of all other materials used by cooking people, since there was a lack of wood, they threw down the magnificent homes and burned the beams." Later on, in connection with the compromise of 1399, Ducas speaks further (ed. Grecu, p. 85, ll. 6–9, ed. Bonn, p. 55, ll. 14–17) of these hardships: "For, a *modius* of grain cost more than twenty *nomismata*. And where were *nomismata?* As for wine, it was likewise. And there was a lack of other essential nourishments. Out of necessity, the common people were inclining to faithlessness and to betrayal of homeland." And in a Venetian document of September 10, 1401, notice is taken of the fact that a *modius* of grain in "Romania" cost twenty-four *hyperpyra:* Iorga, *Notes et*

ship went constant disaffection against Manuel. Unpredictable enough were those who were always ready to grumble against those in power during straitened circumstances.[34] But those who favored the claims of John VII constituted a graver danger. Bayazid's propaganda advantage in his opportunity to exploit the pretender was a great one. Throughout the siege there was undoubtedly a strong faction within the walls that agitated for the admission of the supposedly rightful claimant to the throne.[35] To this unpleasant situation was added the sorrow of personal bereavement; for, not long after the Battle of Nicopolis, probably

extraits pour servir à l'histoire des croisades, I, 114. The going price for grain in at least the early Palaeologan period was originally about one *nomisma* per *modius,* itself a doubling of what the price had been in an earlier age: G. I. Brătianu, *Etudes byzantines d'histoire économique et sociale* (Paris, 1938), 159. A propos Ducas and the scarcity of money, see Zakythinos, *Crise monétaire et crise économique à Byzance du XIIIe au XVe siècle* (Athens, 1948), 41.

34. Ducas, ed. Grecu, p. 81, l. 29 to p. 83, l. 5, ed. Bonn, p. 53, ll. 5–17: "And the multitudes of the City, being overwhelmed by the famine, were broken in spirit and were minded to yield the City. But when they called to mind the things which had been done in Asia by the Turks, the ruin of the cities, the desolation of the holy precincts, the trials and calumnies at every hour prompting abjuration of the Faith, hastily they changed their minds, saying: 'Let us not grow weary; let us put our hope in God; yet a little let us endure and, who knows, if God, overlooking our sins as he once did for those Ninevites, will then have pity and will save us from this beast.' But the more the tyrant beheld how much the Citizens were resisting and were not giving in to his wishes, the more he became wroth and the more he became angry against the City." From which point Ducas moves into Bayazid's use of John VII's claims and the support for the pretender within the city, indicating significantly how readily the Emir was able to sow dissension thus among those already weakened by their hardships.

35. After telling of Bayazid's demand that John VII be allowed to reign in the city in the place of Manuel, Ducas, ed. Grecu, p. 83, ll. 18–24, ed. Bonn, p. 54, ll. 10–19, writes: "Then the Basileus Manuel saw the populace wavering in dissensions—some of them were mutinous and grumbling, others actually became very bold and shouted out: 'Let John be brought in and let the scandals be ended!' The Basileus Manuel, being thoughtful and experienced, seeing the vulgar people murmuring and making the accusation that 'he does not make place for his successor on the throne but, wishing to rule as an usurper, he cares not for the common good,' planned a most wise and exceedingly sagacious plan." This plan, Ducas continues, was Manuel's reconciliation with John and departure on his journey to Europe (both actually in 1399). Ducas thus makes this popular dissatisfaction and support for John VII the principal inspirations for Manuel's journey. Without question this implication is an exaggeration and a distortion. But it may well contain a grain of truth, to the extent of suggesting the seriousness of factional, if not popular, support for the pretender under Bayazid's pressure.

in November of 1396, Manuel's beloved mother died.[36] Just before her death, the Empress Helena had joined with her son in approving of the sale of Corinth by the Despot Theodore to the Hospitalers,[37] the first step in a nearly disastrous attempt to introduce Latin buttressing to the constantly overrun and unstable Morea.

Manuel's situation had become grave indeed by the end of winter in 1397. On April 7 of that year, the Venetian Senate took note of some overtures by Manuel (reminiscent of similar ones made in July of 1394) to place Constantinople in the hands of Venice in case he should be obliged to leave it, and to cede to Venice, on certain conditions, the islands of Imbros ("Embri") and Lemnos ("Emni"). The Venetian commander was instructed to brush aside such offers politely and to assure Manuel that aid from the West would soon come. (Manuel was also to be informed specifically of the activities of Sigismund, should the Emperor inquire after the King of Hungary. Obviously, there was still some hope on the part of the Byzantine government for the promised help from Sigismund, although by now the outlook for his expected expedition may have diminished.) If Manuel and the Genoese of Pera were intending to come to terms with the Turks, the commander was to do his best to dissuade them or at least to discourage independent negotiations. As usual, however, the chary *Sapientes* appended instructions for alternate circumstances, in this case in the event that John VII should be on the throne and should be unwilling to surrender the city to "Basitus." In that event, the Venetian agents were to salute John with due honor and were to negotiate with him for a treaty renewal.[38] No mention is made of how John might be on the

36. For the dating of the death of Helena Cantacuzena, see the end of Appendix IX.

37. This sale is noted by Manuel in his *Funeral Oration*, ed. Migne, 244B–254A, ed. Lampros, p. 69, l. 24 to p. 70, ll. 14 ff.; he also makes mention here of his mother's approval. For a full discussion of this transaction, see Loenertz, "Pour l'histoire du Péloponnèse," 186 ff.; cf. also Delaville le Roulx, *Les Hospitaliers à Rhodes jusqu' à la mort de Philibert de Naillac, 1310–1421* (Paris, 1913), 77–80, and Zakythinos, *Le Despotat grec*, I, 156–159, for a fuller background; also Mompherratos, Οἱ Παλ. ἐν Πελ., 13–15. For the dating of the episode and its relation to the death of the Empress, see V. Laurent, *Rev. d. ét. byz.*, 13 (1955), 137.

38. Partial text, ed. Ljubić, no. 553, pp. 402–404; cf. Silberschmidt, 184–185; Muralt, p. 759, no. 19; Stanojević, 425–426. The otherwise admira-

throne in Manuel's place; nor is there any suggestion that, should Manuel have been replaced by force, Venice would assert or champion his rights. Taken at face value, this instruction seems to imply rather a peaceful arrangement, assuming John's defection from Bayazid. If this inference is correct, the instruction represents a startling bit of prescience, since this is exactly the sort of settlement which was to come to pass two and a half years later. Such an instruction may suggest that the reconciliation eventually effected between Manuel and John VII may have been contemplated long before its final adoption.

In another deliberation of this same date, April 7, 1397, in the course of extensive instructions to its admirals in the Levant, the Senate also ordered the dispatch of three galleys to Constantinople "for the comfort of the lord emperor and of the Genoese of Pera" and for the safety of the area, with the dispatch of additional galleys also being arranged. Renewed caution, however, was to be urged regarding the question of inclination on the part of Manuel and the Peraiotes to come to terms with "Basitus." [39]

From these documents, it is plain that Manuel was contemplating desperate measures. Hope for real help from the unreliable

ble summary by Thiriet, *Régestes,* I, no. 932, p. 218, makes inexcusable errors on the important passage concerning John. Thiriet identifies him, in a compound mistake, as John VIII, the *grandson* [sic] of Manuel. He also misunderstands the allusion to Bayazid, interpreting the latter's role as a *supporter* of John. This deliberation is obviously the origin of the bald statement made by Heyd, *Histoire du commerce du Levant,* II, 264, and Silberschmidt, 178, with no direct citation of any authority (dutifully followed by Delaville le Roulx, *La France en Orient,* 356, Mompherratos, Διπλ. ἐν., 27, and the uncritical Vaughan, 35) that Manuel offered to hand Constantinople over to Venice. Curiously, Dölger makes no reference in his *Regesten* to these proposals by Manuel.

The Senate, incidentally, persisted at this time in its policy of playing on all sides in the hope of stabilizing the delicately balanced status quo, essential for Venetian interests. In another deliberation of April 7, 1397 (Thiriet, no. 931, p. 218), the *Signoria* instructed its envoys to inform Sigismund of its efforts to protect Constantinople and to dissuade Manuel and the Peraiotes from concluding a separate peace with the Turks. But the Senate emphasized also the strains on Venice, and its possible obligations to negotiate separately itself with Bayazid if its efforts are not supported soon by Sigismund. Actually, on May 31, 1398 (Thiriet, no. 942, p. 220), the Senate was considering such separate negotiations. And by October 19, 1398 (Thiriet, no. 952, pp. 221–222), the possibility was still entertained that such a peace could be concluded.

39. Text, ed. Ljubić, no. 554, pp. 405–407; this document is not mentioned or discussed by Thiriet.

Sigismund had probably been all but abandoned by Manuel. Whether he actually would have carried out a renewed version of the old plan for flight from Constantinople or whether he would even have countenanced the admission to power of his nephew at this point cannot be ascertained from our limited evidence. The fact remains that he resorted to neither course of action, at least for the moment. The reason why would apparently be that for the time being Bayazid had given up his intensive prosecution of the siege.

When this relaxation took place is not readily determined. There is nothing in the Venetian deliberations of April 7 to testify conclusively that the siege operations were still going on, but it seems likely from the tone of the deliberations that the situation which prompted them was still one of serious conflict. At any rate, either before or after this date, Bayazid seems to have given up any hope of an immediate seizure of Constantinople. Our source for the fighting speaks of the decisive role of an influx of grain and other supplies from Trebizond, Amastria, various islands, and even Venice and Mitylene, which enabled the defenders to throw back the Turks decisively.[40] Whether or not this account is true, Bayazid himself may have become discouraged with his failure to win his objective by means of direct assault, and he may also have come to realize the inability of his siege engines to cope with Constantinople's strong fortifications—at least at this point. Moreover, he may also have felt the need to turn to other business, such as the ransoming of his captives from Nicopolis. Whatever the precise details, it was probably by spring of 1397 that the Emir withdrew his active and personal prosecution of the siege.

It should by no means be concluded, however, that Bayazid

40. Once again, the *Bulg. chron.*, 542. It is at this point that the text states the duration of the siege as seven years, a time which would hardly fit the text's own ascription of the beginning of the siege to after Nicopolis. Further, the statement of this duration at this point in the narrative might suggest that the fighting which the text has described should be construed to refer to the actual beginning of the siege in 1394. But the linking of Pera with Constantinople as a target also for Bayazid's assaults seems to fit too clearly the period of 1396–97 instead. Clavijo, ed. López Estrada, 58, ed. Sreznevskii, 90, trans. Le Strange, 90, ascribes the Turkish failure to effective defense by the Genoese and to unskillful siege operations by the Turks. Muralt, pp. 758–759, no. 15, imaginatively concocts a truce granted by Bayazid.

abandoned completely his investment of Constantinople. While he may have given up the full operations of sustained assault, his forces nevertheless maintained their blockade and harassment of the city. And, if Manuel's position became a little less desperate in immediate terms during 1397, he was still in very grave difficulty. Nor was the danger to disappear in the months to come. Venice was still to talk of possible peace with Bayazid, in an embassy instructed on June 17, 1398, to give encouragement to Manuel while reminding him of the Commune's expenses on his behalf.[41] But the Lion of St. Mark also remained mindful of Constantinople's continued danger. On September 7, 1398, for example, the Senate ordered its Captain of the Gulf to be ready to defend the city in the event that the Turks might attack it by sea with a squadron from Gallipoli.[42]

Less able than ever to rely on his own virtually nonexistent resources, Manuel could only continue to look to Christendom without for help. The spectacular failure of the Crusade of Nicopolis had all but extinguished the last spark of crusading ardor, and it was not until some forty-eight years later, in the Crusade of Varna, that another—and the last—such expedition was to be mounted against the Turk. But it was Manuel's misfortune that his time of greatest need was at the outset of this interim period. Sigismund's *idée fixe* about a new expedition against the Turks under his command was to remain a vain chimera. But to Manuel the disastrous Nicopolis venture did not seem to be the anticlimactic epilogue to the crusading era we now know it to have been. Even though unsuccessful, the venture was at least a demonstration of what Christendom could do if it really set its mind to the Turkish problem and heeded the plight of Byzantium. Now that Manuel's government was fully committed to a policy of hostility and resistance to the Turks, external military aid became a fundamental concept and goal of his policy.

We have noted the Venetians' constant advice to Manuel to write to the rulers of the West to request aid and their constant assurances that such aid would be forthcoming. But, although Manuel appealed for aid in the period up to 1396, it was only in

41. Partial text in Iorga, "Veneţia in Marea neagră," no. 57, p. 1118. This deliberation is not noted by itself by Thiriet.
42. Thiriet, *Régestes*, I, no. 949, p. 221.

the years after Nicopolis that he began an all-out quest for help from abroad as the cornerstone and sole hope for his policy of resistance to the Turkish menace.

Of Manuel's personal messages of appeal, almost nothing survives to us. But we do have several of these appeals sent in the name and interest of the Empire by no less than the Patriarch Antonios. The role of the spiritual head of Orthodoxy in these appeals is a point of no little interest. The principal explanation for his inolvement is, of course, the question of Church union, which was inevitably and regularly linked with a good deal of the talk of aid to Byzantium. This fact in itself is important to keep in mind. It is also noteworthy that these surviving documents are concerned not with the Latin West, but with Central and Eastern Europe. In this brief spurt of dealings with this seemingly peripheral zone of appeal, we may see some interesting indications of the temper and outlook of Byzantium in some of its darkest hours.

One of these documents is a Patriarchal *pittakion* dated January, 1397, presumably while Constantinople was still bearing the brunt of Bayazid's renewed siege operations. It is addressed to "the most noble, most celebrated, most prudent kral and sovereign of all Poland, of Litvo-Russia, and of the Littoral, and of many other places" (πάσης Πόλτζης, Λιτβορωσίας, Παραθαλασσίας καὶ ἄλλων πολλῶν τόπων), that is, Jagiello, Grand Duke of Lithuania (1377–1434), and King of Poland (1386–1434) under the title of Vladislav V. Much of this document concerns ecclesiastical affairs, especially concerning relations with Orthodox Russia. But Jagiello was greatly interested in the idea of Church union, and the Patriarch sought to channel his zeal. One portion of this letter therefore gives us a passage that was perhaps typical of the kind of plea for aid sent out during this period, especially in its clear statement of the one Byzantine prerequisite to serious consideration of union with the Latins:

. . . You write concerning the union of the Churches, and we ourselves also wish for and agree to this. But this cannot be done at the present time. For there is war with the unbelievers, the routes are closed off, we are in straitened circumstances, and how is it possible, conditions being as they are, for any representatives to go forth from us in order to convene a synod there? But if God should grant peace, and if the roads should be open, we ourselves will be ready for this on our own initiative. But until this should come to pass, we strongly urge that Your Nobility should, in the season of spring, join with the most noble King of Hungary [Οὐγγρία], and that you should come forth even yourself on behalf of the Christians, both with your army [μετὰ φωσσάτου σου] and with your resources, for the destruction of the unbelievers. And then, when the road is open, with ease will there be the union of the Churches, even according as Your Nobility, and we ourselves, agree to this. But the most noble King of Hungary, if God may allow, will bestir himself from the month of March on. For he departed from us [i.e. about a month previously, after Nicopolis] with such statements and commitments, and there is no reason for you to understand otherwise.[48]

This passage makes clear that the Byzantines regarded union as the cart and aid as the horse, and that they had very strong opinions as to which should come first. Not, of course, that it was anything new for the Byzantines to hold out promises of Church union as bait for help or for some other consideration from the Latin West. It is also noteworthy here that at this time the Byzantines clearly regarded Sigismund of Hungary as the natural leader around whom any further military action was to be organized, and that they fully expected a new expedition for their aid in the coming spring, as the Patriarch states, on the basis of the King's promises of this made but a month before.

Jagiello himself was king of a country of the Roman communion, although, prior to his union with Jadwiga in 1386 and his conversion then from paganism, he had been on the verge of adopting the Orthodox faith. Hence, the words of the leader of Orthodoxy might carry only indirect weight. But the prestige of the Patriarchal hand was somewhat greater among the Orthodox; hence the interest in similar appeals to the one independent Orthodox state then with a promise of future greatness.

At the same time as the first of our Patriarchal documents was written, that is, January of 1397, another *pittakion* was addressed to "the most sanctified Metropolitan of Kiev [Κνέβος] and of all Russia ['Ρωσία]," Kyprianos. Again, much of the document con-

43. Miklosich and Müller, II, no. 515, pp. 280–282; the passage translated here is on pp. 280–281. For background on this letter, see Halecki, "La Pologne et l'empire byzantin," *Byzantion*, 7 (1932), 41–67, especially p. 49; and *id.*, "Rome et Byzance au temps du grand Schisme d'Occident," 527. On this ruler in general, note the article of J. Skrzypek, "The Southeastern Policy of Poland from the Coronation of Jagiello to the Death of Hedwig and the Battle on the Worskla (1386–1399)," in *Archiwum Tow. Nauk.we Lwowie*, II, xxi, 1 (1936), written in Polish and unavailable to me.

cerns ecclesiastical affairs, but it is all related to Jagiello's urging of projects toward union and the Metropolitan's support for them. Therefore, a significant portion of this text is likewise relevant to the pressing question of aid, with its inevitable pendant of Church union:

. . . But concerning the union of the Churches and their concord of thinking, it is also our prayer that this will come to pass, were it not for the fact that neither the situation at the moment, nor the place in which Your Sanctity writes that the synod should be brought together, is permissible. After all, while the problem demands that the synod be an ecumenical one, not a local one, yet the occasion allows neither any of the patriarchs or their deputies, nor any of our archpriests, nor even any of our familiars to come out of their localities. For the war is encircling us, closing off all entries to you, and it is stirred up against us to the greatest degree. Wherefore, indeed, even were there peace, the land of Russia is entirely unsuitable for an ecumenical synod. What I mean is that, while it might be possible, though difficult, for envoys from this city to go forth and to reach you, yet, to convey such from Egypt to you is an impossibility at the present time. But if, rather, the most noble kral [i.e. Jagiello] wishes to effect some results noble and worthy of his honor, and of his position, and of his rule, then let the questions of the union of the Churches, to which there are now many obstructions, be put aside, and let him join with the most noble king of Hungary, and let him struggle even himself on behalf of the name of Christ and toward the destruction of the unbelievers, who are attempting to swallow up all the inhabited world. When this has come to pass, then we ourselves also will have our freedom to move about wherever we may wish and to summon others to us. And then is there going to be the synod, wherever it may seem advantageous. Indeed, for him who cooperates with the most noble kral there will be crowns and rewards from God and from us praises and thanksgivings. Indeed, no one other than Your Sanctity is better able to do this, since, as you write, the kral is very much your friend. Hasten, then, concerning this very matter, in order that it may be done first.[44]

44. Miklosich and Müller, II, no. 516, pp. 282–285; the passage translated here is on   pp. 282–283; cf. both Halecki articles, "La Pologne," and "Rome et Byzance." For a discussion of the Kievan Metropolitan who was the addressee of this and (until his death in 1406) of the other Patriarchal messages discussed in this book, see A. E. Tachiaos, "'Ο μητροπολίτης 'Ρωσίας Κυπριανὸς Τσάμπλακ," Πανεπιστημίου Θεσσαλονίκης, Ἐπετηρὶς Θεολογικῆς Σχολῆς, 6 (1961), 161–241.

Such an address was in effect but an indirect appeal to the Russians for help, since it involved simply encouragement to the King of Poland by means of ecclesiastical inducements. For "the kral" was, of course, not the ruler of Russia, but Jagiello of Poland-Lithuania, the addressee of the previous letter. The two letters are linked, since Kyprianos of Kiev had been negotiating with Jagiello on the question of Church union, and the Patriarch's appeal to each was for Jagiello to come to the aid of Byzantium. Needless to say, the appeal was productive of nothing tangible.

Unfortunately, we lack any further texts of communications with Russia at this point, and hence we do not know precisely what specific appeals may have been made directly to the Muscovite state. But it seems quite certain that such appeals for aid were sent thither, and that at least financial assistance was sent to Byzantium.[45] If there were any hopes for active Russian

45. Dölger, *Regesten*, no. 3267, p. 85. Vasiliev, "Putešestvie vizantiiskogo imperatora Manuila II Paleologa po Zapadnoi Evropie (1399–1403)" ("The Journey of the Byzantine Emperor Manuel II Palaeologus to Western Europe"), *Žurnal ministerstva narodnogo prosveščeniia* (*Journal of the Ministry of Public Education*), N.S. 39 (1912), 47–49 (or, in its offprint form, 9–11), gives a detailed account of the supposed appeal and the supposedly generous Russian response. But his sources for these statements, notably the nineteenth-century historians Karamzin and Tatishchev, are not fully trustworthy. Cf. Vasiliev's comments in his later article, "Was Old Russia a Vassal State of Byzantium?" *Speculum*, 7 (1938), 357. (For another apparent source reporting Russian contributions at this time, see Muralt, in the notes to p. 762, no. 8. More evidence in this line may perhaps be found in L. V. Cherepnin, "Otraženie meždunarodnoi žizni XIV-nachala XV v. v moskovskom lietopishanii" ("Les Relations internationales au bout du 14ᵉ et commencement du 15ᵉ siècles au lumière du Annaliste de Moscou"), *Meždunarodnie svjazi Rossii do XVII v.* (Moscow, 1961), 225–256, which is, however, unfortunately not available to me. But there seems to be at least some confirmation for these assumptions in a reference to be found in a subsequent Patriarchal document (see below, pp. 202–203), mentioning aid from the Russians—some already sent, some still being collected at that time. Cf. Dölger, *Regesten*, no. 3268, p. 85. Gibbons, 232, also on the questionable basis of Karamzin, dates to this time the surely later marriage of the future John VIII, Manuel's eldest son, to the Russian Princess Anna (see below, p. 345), the dowry she brought being allegedly the point of greatest interest to the hard-pressed Byzantines. This same writer refers to a mutilated text which survives to us: Miklosich and Müller, II, no. 686, pp. 566–570, dated October 1397 (and not 1396, as this edition mistakenly gives it); cf. Muralt, p. 760, no. 1. This document is a Patriarchal inventory of the treasury of Hagia Sophia. Gibbons, 232–233, implies that this inventory was made with an eye to current heavy expenses and needs. We have no immediate information, however, on any use of Church properties and treasures by Manuel at this time.

aid, however, they were no more realized than those for another expedition under Sigismund.

Much more significant, in terms of subsequent events, were contacts with Western Europe. It was, after all, the Western princes to whom Manuel had been referred by the Venetians originally. From the outset it was plain that the most important of Manuel's contacts among these rulers would be with the French King, especially in view of the significant French contributions to the Crusade of Nicopolis. Unfortunately, that very disaster had dampened French ardor for further operations on that scale. Nevertheless, the court of Charles VI was still more than cordial to the direct overtures which proceeded from Manuel.

By summer of 1397 Bayazid's active offensive against Constantinople had apparently ended. But the blockade of the city was no less disastrous. Still convinced of the urgency of Western aid—which the Venetians continued to forecast—Manuel decided to make a strong direct plea. In this year Nicholas Notaras was sent on an embassy to France and England.[46] He was followed by Theodore Palaeologus Cantacuzenus, the Emperor's uncle, on a mission that occupied the latter months of 1397 and much of 1398. The latter reached Paris in mid-October, bearing a letter to King Charles VI from Manuel, dated July 1, 1397. Since the contemporary French chronicler who quotes it obviously had the original document before him—he describes it in detail—we can presumably rely upon the text which he transmits to us. According to him, the letter was bilingual, with a Greek text on one side and the Latin on the other. The former is lost, for it is only the Latin which is transcribed. In view of its importance, it is worth quoting in full, in English translation from the Latin:

46. Du Cange, in his *Familiae augustae byzantinae* (*Historia byzantine*, Pt. I, Paris, 1680), p. 242, cites a receipt by François d'Aunoy, Charles VI's treasurer, for a grant by the King of 1,000 gold pieces for aid to "the Christians," to "Nicolas de Natala," on his way through France to England in 1397. On this and other such references, see below, n. 49. Cf. also Dölger, *Regesten*, no. 3269, p. 85 (where the ambassador is referred to as "John Notaras": again, see n. 49 below), and no. 3271, p. 85; also, *ibid.*, no. 3265, p. 84, for reference to an earlier embassy allegedly sent by Manuel to Charles VI in late 1396, after Nicopolis. During the course of his mission, incidentally, on April 8, 1397, Notaras was granted the rights and privileges of a Venetian citizen by the Doge; for the text of this award, see Appendix XII below.

To the most serene and excellent Lord Charles, King of the Franks, our most dear brother, Manuel, in the Divine Christ Emperor and Moderator of the Romans, Palaeologus, health and happy attainment of your wishes.

Because we know, brother, the very great power which is held by that impious tyrant, the Turk Basita, lord of the Turks, enemy to Jesus Christ and to the entire Catholic faith, which power also is daily increased; and since we know also our own and our people's misery and poverty, which we have suffered for a long time previously, and are still suffering, for about three years in particular, because of the war wherein we are now engaged, directed against us by the said Turk Basita, who strives with all his strength and power to subject to his lordship this, our city, and the Christians of these regions, and to efface utterly from the land the name of Christ, not sparing by day and night in any particular the labors and expenses of his own self or of his subjects; and in the knowledge, further, of how great an injury would befall all Christendom if the said Turk Basita should obtain his will concerning the aforesaid city (may that never come to pass!); and perceiving especially that without doubt this city is in no wise able to endure to the coming summer, during which we expect and hope to have the aid of the Christians, with the intervention of God's grace and of your most serene royal majesty, wherein we trust manifoldly and effectively:—Therefore, we appoint as ambassador our vigorous and most beloved uncle, a noble and prudent man of our state, wise and experienced as well, the lord Theodorus Palealogus Canthacosino [*sic*], the bearer of these presents, whom we send forth to your aforesaid royal majesty; to whom let your majesty wish, and let it be pleasing to you, to accord full faith in all proposals by him to your majesty verbally on our behalf, as if your majesty should hear those things in speech from our own mouth. Moreover, we firmly believe your same royal majesty is ready to take action in all respects in which we are in need from your majesty, because we have seen you, in the past year, with no request made of you but by your own free will, out of reverence for God, send a great force of your people for our liberation and that of the Christians of these regions; which aim would rightly have been fulfilled, but that an unexpected situation should have befallen by reason of our since. We are, indeed, at present in greater need of aid than we were then, by reason of the exhaustion to which we have come as a result of the said war, according as your said royal majesty can be informed by your barons and nobles, who saw all and are fully informed concerning the state and condition of these regions.

Given in the city of Constantinople in the year of the Lord the one thousand three hundred ninety-seventh, on the first day of the month of July.[47]

Charles VI welcomed this letter, much flattered and impressed by such a complimentary appeal to him. The King's uncles, the Dukes of Berry and Burgundy, supported the idea of a new expedition, and the Duke of Orleans begged for the command of it. Charles was reluctant, however, and opposed any immediate military aid. But he promised such assistance, if possible, in the following year; a promise which he was to fulfill. Meanwhile, he showered the Byzantine embassy with gifts and honors.[48]

Charles's enthusiasm and promises were apparently sincere. On June 28, 1398, the King wrote to the Doge, Antonio Venerio, the Council, and the Commune of Venice. In his letter he told of what he had heard from Theodore Cantacuzenus, and he regretted that the disunion of the Church and his own heavy expenses at that moment prevented an immediate response. But he revealed that he had given the Byzantine ambassadors the sum of 12,000 gold francs, and he urged that the Venetians support the Byzantine cause vigorously.[49]

47. The text of this document is in the *Religieux de Saint-Denys*, XVIII, viii, ed. Bellaguet, II, 558–560; it is reproduced in Appendix XIII below, together with the chronicler's observations on it. Cf. Dölger, *Regesten*, no. 3269, p. 85.

48. *Religieux de Saint-Denys, ibid.*, p. 562. For another source, see n. 67 below. Cf. Vasiliev, "Putešestvie Manuila," 44–45 (6–7), and Delaville le Roulx, *La France en Orient*, 358; also Silberschmidt, 190. Unfortunately, Vasiliev's account of the pleas and projects for aid to Manuel in this period is somewhat jumbled chronologically. Mompherratos, Διπλ. ἐν., 27–29, places this embassy mistakenly in 1399. Cf. also Delaville le Roulx, *La France en Orient*, 355–356, who thinks that ambassador Cantacuzenus was accredited to England as well. But, save for the reference in Du Cange, cited below in n. 49, there seems to be little basis for this assumption. See, further, Walter, *La Ruine de Byzance*, 292–293.

49. Text in Thomas, *Diplomatarium Veneto-Levantinum, 1351–1454*, II, no. 149, p. 261; Italian summary (Predelli), *Commemoriali*, III, no. 120, p. 260; cf. Vasiliev, "Putešestvie Manuila," 46 (8). Du Cange, *Fam. aug. byz.*, p. 238 and n. a, cites references from the treasury receipts of François d'Aunoy (see above, n. 46) to three grants to Theodore Palaeologus (Cantacuzenus): 300 gold pieces on January 29, "1397" (properly 1398, in the normal modern reckoning of the new year); 400 pieces on April 18, 1398; and 2,000 on May 24, 1398: all for his and his companions' expenses on their way to England in search of aid. Although there is apparently no other evidence in this direction, this statement might support Delaville le Roulx's

As the embassy began its homeward journey, Charles wrote another letter, dated July 22, 1398, also to the Doge, the Council, and the Commune of Venice, in much the same vein. Charles regretted anew his own difficulties which distracted him from devoting his energies to aid Byzantium. He expressed the hope that there would be a better opportunity for active succor in the following year. Charles also requested that the Venetians receive well the Byzantine ambassador Notaras.[50] By the end of summer the embassy reached Venice on its way home, and on September 17, 1398, the Senate authorized transportation homeward for Theodore Cantacuzenus.[51] More than a month previously, meanwhile, on August 8, the Senate had ordered the conveyance of the sum of 7,000 ducats sent from France for the Basileus,[52] which sum may well have represented part or all of the very grant which Charles had given to him through Theodore Cantacuzenus.

assertion (see preceding note) that Theodore was accredited to England as well as to France. Berger de Xivrey, pp. 85–86 and n. 142, has cited these references, and that to Nicholas Notaras (see n. 46). But he has confused them badly: Notaras' name is garbled into John, apparently on the basis of unreliable references in other French sources (likewise Dölger, *Regesten*, no. 3269, p. 85); and, perhaps through typographical errors, three numbers are distorted—April 18 becomes April 28, the last of the three grants is reduced from 2,000 to 1,000 gold pieces, and page 242 becomes 241. Berger de Xivrey adds that, in spite of an intense personal search, he was unable to find these treasury documents; thus, he says, we must simply take Du Cange's word for them. On Nicholas Notaras, cf. J. W. Barker, "John VII in Genoa," pp. 229–230 and n. 3.

50. Text, ed. Thomas, *Diplomatarium*, no. 150, pp. 262–263; Italian summary (Predelli), *Commemoriali*, III, no. 126, p. 262; cf. Vasiliev, "Putešestvie Manuila," 46 (8). Charles VI seems to have been involved in some further projects of aid to the East being discussed vaguely among the Genoese and the Venetians: (Predelli), *Commemoriali*, III, nos. 145–146, p. 267, for November 14, 1398.

51. Thiriet, *Régestes*, I, no. 951, p. 221. It is not certain whether or not Notaras and Cantacuzenus carried out their missions jointly, but in view of Charles VI's reference to the former, and then the Venetian provision for the latter at a plausible interval, it might be presumed that they at least returned home together. Cf. Delaville le Roulx, *La France en Orient*, 356–357; Silberschmidt, 190–191. On November fifth previous (1397), Manuel is reported to have asked Venice to provide transportation for his ambassadors, at his expense: (Predelli) *Commemoriali*, III, no. 72, p. 248. Whether or not this request has anything to do with Notaras and Theodore Cantacuzenus or whether it refers to other emissaries is not clear.

52. Thiriet, *Régestes*, I, no. 946, p. 221. Is it this instance of French aid which is reflected in the fantastic entry for (December?) 1396 by Muralt, p. 757, no. 8?

While there was this promising prospect of help from French sources, Manuel was to press his cause in other areas. Not the least among the Western princes to whom the Venetians had been urging Manuel to write was the Pope. Unfortunately for Manuel, the Great Schism had complicated the picture gravely, not only in terms of direct relations with the respective Popes of Rome and Avignon themselves, but also in terms of dealings with different kingdoms which differed in their recognition of the rival claimants to the tiara.

The Roman Pope, Boniface IX, was actually very eager to make efforts toward possible union of the Churches, partly for the enhancement of his own prestige. For some time after the setback of Nicopolis, however, there was apparently no direct contact between the Byzantine Emperor and the Pope, although Venice seems to have adopted the role of intermediary between them for a while.[53] Partly as a result of Venetian encouragement, Boniface decided to throw his weight behind renewed efforts to aid the Empire. On April 1, 1398, Boniface issued a bull urging the Christian powers of the West to furnish military or at least financial contributions toward a new crusade against the Turks on behalf of Manuel and his subjects. For this purpose he appointed Paul, the titular Bishop of Chalcedon, and his own Benedictine chaplain, Augustine de Undinis, to enlist aid for the project.[54]

Presumably encouraged by this important Papal step, Manuel hastened to secure direct relations with the Roman See through the person of Hilario Doria, the Genoese husband of Zampia, his illegitimate daughter.[55] Doria's mission was apparently to cooperate with Boniface IX in whatever ways would expedite the obtaining and dispatch of aid to the beleaguered capital. To carry out this task, the Emperor's son-in-law labored diligently. In the wake of such direct Byzantine contact with the Papacy through Doria, Boniface was moved to further efforts.

53. Halecki, "Rome et Byzance," 504 ff.
54. Text, Baronius-Raynaldus, *Annales ecclesiastici*, 1398, no. 40 (Vol. 27, p. 40); cf. Halecki, "Rome et Byzance," 506–509; Vasiliev, "Putešestvie Manuila," 44 (6).
55. Dölger, *Regesten*, no. 3270, p. 85; Halecki, "Rome et Byzance," 509; also Vasiliev, *ibid.;* Delaville le Roulx, *La France en Orient*, 356; cf. also, in general, Mompherratos, Διπλ. ἐν., 26. For Doria's matrimonial relationship with Manuel's family, see Appendix IX below.

Over the date of March 6, 1399, he issued a bull that, specifically mentioning Doria's mission, renewed the call for action against the Turks in the hope of relieving Constantinople and thereby of contributing to the longed-for goal of Church union. The Pope therewith authorized the collection of funds for a project of military aid to the Emperor, offering the renewal of indulgences for the remission of sins.[56]

The Bishop of Chalcedon was again assigned, together with the Genoese Antonio Grillo and Niccolò Lomellini, to the task of implementing the Papal bull, and with him Doria was also assigned. In the Italian cities success was meager, in view of local distractions and entanglements. Lucca and Siena (each?) contributed the somewhat less than spectacular sum of 500 gold ducats. But no amount was too small for the hard-pressed Byzantines. We have the text of a letter by Manuel himself to the Archbishop of Siena, dated September 22, 1399, in which the Emperor thanks the Sienese for their contribution of 500 Florentine ducats and urges arrangement for their prompt relay.[57] In general, however, the Italian cities could or would give no real assistance.[58]

Unfortunately, also, as the mission to the states recognizing the Roman Pope continued, friction developed between Doria and the Papal agents. In Genoa there had been unpleasant moments over Doria's demands for Papal reimbursement for the expenses of the Byzantine mission.[59] Then, in the summer of 1399, when the joint mission proceeded to England, further discord hampered the collection of funds.[60] In spite of this, however,

56. Partial text in Baronius-Raynaldus, 1399, nos. 1–4 (Vol. 27, pp. 41–43). Cf. Halecki, "Rome et Byzance," 508–509, who cites an edition of the full text not available to me.

57. Dölger, *Regesten*, no. 3275, p. 86; Latin text, published by Lampros with comments, " Ἐπιστολὴ Μανουὴλ Παλαιολόγου πρὸς τοὺς Σιεναίους," Νέος ἑλληνομνήμων, 6 (1909), 102–104, and the text alone republished in the same editor's Παλ. καὶ Πελ., III, pp. 120–121. In the text, Manuel speaks of the mission of Nicholas Notaras and also of the services of Lomellini; cf. Dölger, *Regesten*, no. 3271, p. 85.

58. Vasiliev, "Putešestvie Manuila," 44 (6); Delaville le Roulx, *La France en Orient*, 357.

59. Halecki, "Rome et Byzance," 511.

60. *Ibid.*, 511–512; Vasiliev, "Putešestvie Manuila," 46–47 (8–9); cf. Dölger, *Regesten*, no. 3273, p. 86 (for the dispatch of Doria), and no. 3276, p. 86 (a subsequent message sent in late summer of 1399 to Richard through Peter Holt, Prior of the Knights of St. John for Ireland: see n. 100 below).

there seemed some hope for financial aid from Richard II, who made provisions for an extensive collection and ordered an immediate dispatch of 2,000 pounds as an advance payment to be made through the Genoese agent Reginaldo Grillo. But this latter sum never reached Manuel, and a later investigation of the collection after Richard's dethronement revealed extensive abuses.[61] The Papal-Byzantine mission continued on, however, even though efforts to foster interest and contributions in Germany and Scandinavia brought little success.[62]

If the West did not fulfill Manuel's hopes for extensive financial aid, it was at least able to provide some small degree of military assistance. Pleas for such assistance were inevitably the basic theme of Manuel's diplomatic ventures at the time, and we can see some evidence of a response. One minor response came from the King of Aragon, Martin I. It is presumed that Manuel sent one of his pleas thither,[63] and, as a result either of such a plea or of the initiative of the individual involved, the King wrote a letter of presentation to accompany one Dalmacius (Dalmau) Darnius, who was going to Constantinople to fight in the Emperor's service.[64]

Much more significant, however, was to be help from France. As we have seen, in 1398 Charles VI had held out the hope of an expedition in the following year. For once a Latin promise to

61. Vasiliev, *ibid.*, and 264–265 (44–45). This agent, through whom the advance was to have been conveyed to Manuel, seems to have absconded with the sum, as Manuel himself later suggests (see Appendix XVI below). Is his name, as given, a confusion with the Genoese Antonio Grillo, or was he a relative or associate of the latter? Certainly we know that many members of a Grillo family were active as commercial and diplomatic agents throughout the fourteenth century (as one may see, for example, in the pages of Heyd). But this particular Grillo seems to be otherwise unknown.

62. Halecki, "Rome et Byzance," 512; Vasiliev, "Putešestvie Manuila," 64–65 (26–27).

63. Cf. Vasiliev, "Putešestvie Manuila," 47 (9), who suggests this on the basis of an obscure statement by an Italian source.

64. Text of this letter in Rubió i Lluch, *Diplomatari de l'Orient Català*, no. 651, p. 679. Cf. S. Cirac Estopañan, *La unión, Manuel II Paleólogo y sus recuerdos en España* (Barcelona, 1952), 55. C. Marinesco, "Du Nouveau sur les rélations de Manuel Paléologue (1391–1425) avec l'Espagne," *Studi bizantini e neoellenici*, 7 (1953 =*Atti dello VIII Congr. Intern. di Studi Biz.*, 1), 421, suggests the likelihood that this Darnius was intending to join Boucicaut's imminent expedition. But there seems to have been a certain number of Westerners fighting in Constantinople during Bayazid's siege, probably on an individual basis; see Appendix XVII below.

Figure 6: *Jean II le Meingre, Maréchal de Boucicaut, with His Wife, Antoinette de Turenne, Venerating the Madonna and Child.* Illuminated Miniature, *Heures du Maréchal de Boucicaut,* Musée Jacquemart-André, Paris, Dedication Page, f. 26ᵛ (photo courtesy Bulloz, Paris; see Appendix XXIV, B, 2, a).

Manuel was not an idle one. In the spring for 1399, Charles organized a force which he placed under the command of Jean le
Meingre, better known as the Marshal Boucicaut.[65] No happier
choice could have been made, for Boucicaut was a brave and
capable leader, of decisive and praiseworthy character, and well
acquainted with affairs in the East as well. Among his numerous
adventures prior to this time, Boucicaut had fought in the Battle
of Nicopolis, had been taken captive by Bayazid, and had played
a role in the ransoming of his fellow captives. In this last capacity he had stopped at Constantinople,[66] and presumably he
had met the Emperor then. When the 1399 expedition was organized in response to Manuel's pleas for help, Boucicaut was
reportedly delighted to accept its command.[67]

On June 26 the expedition set forth from Aigues-Mortes: 400
men-at-arms of honorable families, 400 armed attendants, and a
number of archers, all totaling an estimated 1,200, in two galleys
and four other vessels.[68] The expedition made stops at Naples,
Capri, Messina, the island of Sapienza off Modon, Chios, Mitylene on Chios, Negroponte, and Tenedos, swelling its strength
along the way with the addition of Venetian, Genoese, Rhodian,
and Lesbian galleys. The passage through the Straits having been
essayed, the flotilla, fully united at Tenedos, sailed on to Constantinople.[69] Insignificant as this force might be in relation to

65. On this man we are fortunate in having a contemporary biography,
the celebrated *Livre des faits du bon messire Jean le Maingre, dit Bouciquaut,
Mareschal de France et Gouverneur de Jennes*, ed. J. A. C. Buchon, pp.
563–695 in Vol. III of his edition of Froissart (Paris, 1835). This text gives
invaluable information on these events.

66. *Livre des faits*, I, xxvii, p. 600; cf. Mompherratos, Διπλ. ἐν., 25.

67. *Livre des faits*, I, xxix, p. 601, which mentions the previous mission
of "Catacuseno" from Manuel to the West.

68. *Ibid.*, pp. C01–602; *Religieux de Saint-Denys*, XX, iii, ed. Bellaguet,
II, p. 690, which gives the same total of men but which states, probably in
error, that Boucicaut departed in May. Cf. Delaville le Roulx, *La France en
Orient*, 359–364; Vasiliev, "Putešestvie Manuila," 50–51 (12–13). Also G.
Schlumberger, "Jean de Chateaumorand, un des principaux héros français
des arrière-croisades en Orient à la fin du XIVᵉ siècle et à l'aurore du XVᵉ"
(included in the author's collection, *Byzance et croisades: Pages médièvales*,
Paris, 1927), 300; and *id.*, "Un Empereur de Byzance à Paris et Londres"
(originally published in *Revue des deux mondes*, 30, 1915; republished in
the same collection), 94 (or, in the separate offprint version, Paris, 1916, p. 7).

69. *Livre des faits*, I, xxix–xxx, pp. 602–603. Cf. Delaville le Roulx, *La
France en Orient*, 364–368; *id.*, *Les Hospitaliers*, 275–276; Schlumberger,
"Chateaumorand," 300–301; *id.*, "Un Empereur," 94 (7–8). Also, Berger de

full Byzantine need, it was nevertheless welcomed joyously by Manuel and his desperate subjects, who promptly paraded the new arrivals in a festive review.[70]

The little army was soon put to work. Under the joint leadership of Boucicaut and Manuel, the immediate neighborhood of the city was cleared of enemies, an attack, though unsuccessful, was mounted on Nicomedia, and a number of towns on the neighboring Asiatic shores were assaulted or harassed.[71] But such activity, although vigorous and sweet after long years of despair, represented, after all, little more than ephemeral raiding of superficial value. It must soon have become apparent to all concerned that much more was needed. From the point of view of the Greeks, the task called for a far vaster effort than this small expedition could provide. And from Boucicaut's point of view it was plain that his relatively small band of restless cavaliers—not to say cutthroats—had reached the limit of their usefulness. Provisions were too scanty and prospects for plunder or reward were too restricted to support them in further operations. The resourceful French commander soon came to a decisive conclusion: in order to obtain really substantial aid, Manuel must go and make a personal appeal before the French King.[72]

Whatever Manuel's initial reaction to such a plan may have been is not known. But it must have been obvious to him that the Byzantine internal situation as it stood would not permit its

Xivrey, 88–90; Mompherratos, Διπλ. ἐν., 30–32; Gibbons, 236–237; and, very carelessly, Muralt, p. 763, nos. 9–12. For the role of Venice, see Silberschmidt, 194–196; for the involvement of Francesco II Gattilusio of Lesbos, see Miller, "The Gattilusij of Lesbos," 414–415 (321–322), and Dennis, "The Short Chronicle of Lesbos," p. 18, n. 41.

70. *Livre des faits*, I, xxx–xxxi, p. 603; *Religieux de Saint-Denys*, XX, iii, p. 690. Cf. Delaville le Roulx, *La France en Orient*, 369.

71. *Livre des faits*, I, xxxi–xxxiii, pp. 603–606; *Religieux de Saint-Denys*, XX, iii, p. 690. Cf. Delaville le Roulx, *La France en Orient*, 369–375; Berger de Xivrey, 90–91; Mompherratos, Διπλ. ἐν., 33; Gibbons, 237; Muralt, p. 764, nos. 13–17. On the expedition in general, see also K. Rados, Τὸ ναυτικὸν τοῦ Βυζαντίου, ὑλικόν, ὀργάνωσις, τακτική, ἱστορία (Athens, 1920), 138–140; and Walter, 294–295.

72. *Livre des faits*, I, xxxiii, p. 606; according to which there was also entertained a scheme to offer the suzerainty of Byzantium to Charles VI. Cf. Muralt, pp. 764–765, no. 1; Gibbons, 238–239. But this scheme, if there really was such, was to meet with no more success than John VII's even more extreme proposal of 1397, of which mention is about to be made. To promise help to Byzantium was one thing; to assume direct responsibility for its survival was quite another, despite the glory.

execution until the dynastic breach in the Imperial house was healed. The key to the next step, therefore, became John VII. This prince had lapsed into a state of torpor in the years since his active collaboration with the Turks in the siege of Constantinople, earlier in the 1390's. In the period after the Battle of Nicopolis, he continued to be maintained as a façade for Bayazid's designs on the blockaded capital. But by 1397 John had tired of this farce. Taking advantage of the homeward passage of the ransomed captives of Nicopolis, John drew up a remarkable document for them. In it he authorized Jean, Comte de Nevers, the future Duke of Burgundy, and Henri de Bar as his agents, with Francesco II Gattilusio (by now John's father-in-law) as his intermediary, to offer to Charles VI the cession of his rights to the Byzantine throne in return for an annuity of 25,000 gold florins and a castle in France. This document is in two parts: the first is dated July 15, 1397, in "Saura" (Selymbria?); and the second and principal part is dated "insule Mathelini" (i.e. Mitylene on Gattilusio's island of Lesbos) on August 15, 1397—that is, exactly at the time the returning captives were there. But, in spite of its dubious attractions, this offer presumably met with little interest on the part of the French King and his advisers, who were already in friendly contact with Manuel. And so this curious document seems to have been ignored.[73]

73. Dölger, *Regesten*, no. 3194, p. 74. The first important notices of this document were taken by Delaville le Roulx, *La France en Orient*, p. 378, n. 1; and Miller, "The Gattilusij," 414 (321). Subsequently, Lampros published the complete text in Νέος ἑλληνομνήμων, 10 (1913), 248–251. See also Dölger, "Johannes VII., Kaiser der Rhomäer, 1390–1408," 29–30; Silberschmidt, 197; Ostrogorsky, *Hist. Byz. St.*, 493; cf. Zakythinos, *Crise monétaire*, 97. The most recent comments on this transaction are by P. Wirth in his article, "Zum Geschichtsbild Kaiser Johannes' VII. Palaiologos," *Byzantion*, 35 (1965 [1967]), 592–594, 599–600, expressing some doubts as to its import. Wirth also points out, *ibid.*, 593, that the place-ascription "Saura" for the first part of the document need not necessarily have been a reference to Selymbria, as assumed by Lampros and everyone else since, but rather to Saray, a kind of reception-center maintained by the Turks during this period for foreign ambassadors: such an identification might suggest that it was there (and not in Selymbria) that John VII met the French nobles, but the point is neither certain nor crucial. For the marriage of John VII, see Appendix V below. The attempt by Muralt (p. 761, no. 8) to make sense of the perilous sources for John's activities, using the incorrect tales of Bayazid's occupation of Selymbria for the year 1397, should be discounted. On the question of John's continued residence in Selymbria during these years, see Appendix XIV below.

But, if John's scheme had failed, he was still a very present factor on the scene and had to be taken into account, of necessity, before any further move could be made by Manuel and Boucicaut. With John still hostile and a tool at the disposal of the Turks, Manuel could hardly leave his post. It is a tribute to the quick-wittedness of the French commander that he readily recognized the nature of the situation and acted accordingly. Sailing forthwith to Selymbria, Boucicaut constrained John to return with him to Constantinople on December 4, 1399. Confronted thus with each other, uncle and nephew were content to come to terms. It was agreed that Manuel would depart for the West with Boucicaut. In his place in Constantinople John would rule, and then, after Manuel's return, John would be granted the city of Thessalonica (at that time in the hands of the Turks) as an appanage.[74]

At long last, the Imperial family feud, dating back more than two and one-half decades, had been ended in a patriotic compromise, and the basis had been laid for a final settlement. This important step taken, Manuel was then free to heed seriously the urgings of Boucicaut that the Emperor should journey westward. Before long this proposal was accepted. Indeed, it was presumably agreed upon in principle before the reconciliation with John, on which it depended. Before the year 1399 had ended, Manuel had embarked on the most remarkable and celebrated episode of his life.

No single phase of Manuel's career has been so extensively studied as his journey to Western Europe.[75] It is not strange

---

74. For a full discussion of the sources and problems of this reconciliation, see Appendix XIV below.

75. Amid the rich modern literature on this episode, by far the most important work is Vasiliev's "Putešestvie Manuila," already cited extensively. It is true that its language (I myself, in my present ignorance of Russian, was obliged to have it read to me) and its relative unavailability may render it inaccessible to some. Its one serious flaw is the omission of all attention to the documents on the negotiations with Aragon, but only because these documents were published some time after the article was written. Otherwise, its shortcomings are essentially minor. With allowance for occasional supplementary material when needed, it is still today the basic and indispensable study on the subject. Less searching but still valuable are Schlumberger, "Un Empereur de Byzance à Paris et Londres"; and, perhaps to a somewhat lesser degree, M. Jugie, "Le Voyage de l'empereur Manuel Paléologue en Occident (1399–1403)," *Echos d'Orient,* 15 (1912), 322–332. While the bulk of his focus is not fully germane to our topic, one should

that this subject should be so attractive. The very idea of a ruler of the fabled and seemingly remote Byzantium emerging from the exotic East and visiting such familiar European cities as Venice, Milan, and, especially, Paris and London; associating with rulers and nobles whom history (and Shakespeare) has rendered so vividly close to us; in short, appearing in a setting that is so vitally a part of our own Western background and tradition, especially for the purpose of begging aid for his once-great Empire—it is all a spectacle that exerts the most exciting and romantic fascination on us.

But, if such a reaction is natural for us today, it was in its own day even more distinct among those peoples whom Manuel visited. In spite of the long process of decline through which Byzantium had been passing while the Latin West had been surging ahead on its own, the glory of the successors of Constantine had not been forgotten. Indeed, Byzantium, to the West, had always appeared as a realm of almost fairy-tale splendor and grandeur, a reputation that the ordeal of the Crusades, tragic decay, and a degradation before the Turkish advance had not entirely dimmed. Added to the awe inspired by Manuel's rank and traditions was the sympathy toward the sorely oppressed Emperor which, in spite of the disinclination or inability of Latin Christendom to back it up with effective action, was sincere.

note pp. 767–769 of H. C. Luke's article "Visitors from the East to the Plantagenet and Lancastrian Kings," *Nineteenth Century*, 8 (1930), 760–769. In addition to these individual and specialized studies, one should bear in mind the discussions of the subject in general works, in particular that by Berger de Xivrey, and, to a lesser extent, that by Mompherratos. All of these will be cited in due course wherever possible. A stimulating if questionable thought on Manuel's journey is contributed by Runciman, in his *The Fall of Constantinople*, 13 (in the midst of a very general and uneven sketch of Manuel's life and reign): "When he journeyed westward in search of aid, he chose a moment when the Papacy was discredited by the Great Schism, and he made his appeal to lay potentates, hoping thus to escape ecclesiastical pressure, i.e. toward Church union." Some reflection reduces the validity of this observation, however, since Manuel hardly "chose" the occasion for his visit in any objective sense. The avoidance of pressure upon him as regards union schemes must therefore be regarded as a fortuitous byproduct of circumstances rather than a function of Manuel's personal attitudes or official policies toward reunion of the Churches, as Runciman seems to suggest. Among other general works of this kind, sketches of Manuel's journey and its implications may also be found in Khoury, 139–140, and Stacton, 115–116 (="Dereksen," 121–122).

In all, Manuel made a vivid impression on the minds of his Western hosts, at least as a person—so much so that it is to the Western sources that modern scholars have been obliged to turn for the most important and most extensive information on the course of Manuel's great journey.[76]

Whether the initial idea was Boucicaut's or Manuel's own, the Emperor had committed himself, by December of 1399, to a new implementation of his basic policy. If Byzantium was to continue its resistance to the Turks on the assumption of support from the West, the quest for this aid must now be pursued by means of the most imposing method possible: the personal diplomacy of Manuel himself.[77] Once this decision was made, Manuel and Boucicaut acted upon it with characteristic decisiveness. Provisions were made for the defense of the city under John VII,[78] and Boucicaut, his job in Constantinople accomplished, gathered the bulk of his force for withdrawal. Less than a week after the entry of John into the city, on December 10,

76. It is certainly true that the Greeks themselves were vividly aware of Manuel's important journey, and there are few Greek sources for the period which do not speak of it. But many of them do no more than make bare allusion to the fact that Manuel did make his journey: thus, of the short chronicles, the *Chron. Vat. gr. 162*, no. 17, p. 210, ll. 77–79; and the Βο. χο. No. 15, p. 32, ll. 50–52, which gives at least the year of his departure; likewise the short chronicle entries cited below in n. 79, which also add the exact date of the departure and the transportation by Venetian ships. Nor are many more details given in the brief relevant passage by Ducas, ed. Grecu, 85, ed. Bonn, 56. Likewise the Pseudo-Phrantzes, ed. Papadopoulos, 66–67, ed. Bonn, 61–62, and the *Chron. Barb. 111*, 36 (the latter of which even identifies the traveling Emperor as "John Palaeologus"!). The same lack of detail exists to a similar extent in Chalcocondyles, ed. Darkó, I, 78–79, 90, ed. Bonn, 84–85, 96–97, save that in between these passages the historian takes the opportunity to launch himself into a long and celebrated digression describing Western Europe, at least as the Greeks knew it. Even more curious is the contribution of the late sixteenth-century *Historia politica et patriarchica Constantinopoleos* (Bonn, 1849), 4, a strange tale which will be noted later (see Appendix XVIII below).

77. That Manuel's journey was a serious diplomatic mission and not merely a groveling for charitable handouts should become clear as we examine Manuel's own letters below, if not also from the dignified and lavish receptions given him wherever he went. Cf. Vasiliev, "Putešestvie Manuila," 53 (15).

78. For a discussion of the arrangements for John's assumption of power in Constantinople and of how he and the city fared during the absence of Manuel, see below, pp. 200 ff.

1399, Manuel sailed with Boucicaut out of the capital for the Peloponnesus aboard Venetian galleys.[79]

The only direct reference in any of Manuel's writings to his departure for the West is in his *Funeral Oration for His Brother Theodore*. Its appearance there is unfortunate, to the extent that it is cast into a background for the outlook of Theodore who, alarmed by the progress of the Turks, was in the midst of an abortive attempt to buttress his position in the Morea by allowing the Hospitalers to extend their control in his realm. The passage therefore serves the double purpose of showing Theodore's frame of mind in the face of Manuel's departure and of defending Theodore's unpopular move. But, in spite of this slanted and somewhat irrelevant context, the passage is still interesting as some indication of Manuel's own outlook on his reconciliation with his nephew and his trip to the West:

The dreadful situation waxed, and the barbarian did not accept a truce, but was uncontrollable in his hostilities against us. And there was no one either to check this man or to give aid to my brother. For he could have confidence in me alone, who suffered variously with his own troubles. And our strength had thus sunk in the long period of the war, so that in this respect it seemed that we had reached the extremity of our dreadful circumstances, and that no hope whatsoever was left remaining for one experienced in human reckonings. Indeed, there arose both for me and for him a double fear: each for himself and both for each other. For, as with even the finest of runners, the difficult progress all but removed all hope of salvation. But it seemed good both to me and to my advisers, and in addition to the more prudent of our allies, to betake myself to Italy ['Ιταλία], and then even to Transalpine France [Γαλλία ἡ κάτω], and to Britain [Βρεττανία] itself. It seemed reasonable, after all to persuade in person those who have the power to defend us, to be willing to use their strength, and not to give way to delayings and neglectings—

79. The exact date and the involvement of Venetian transportation are given only by the Βρ. χρ. No. 18, p. 35, ll. 14–16, and by the virtually identical short chronicle entries (β′, γ′, and δ′) published by Lampros (under the title of "Χρονικὰ σημειώματα περὶ Μανουὴλ καὶ Ἰωάννου Η′ Παλαιολόγου") in his Παλ. καὶ Πελ., III, 360–361. Cf. Vasiliev, "Putešestvie Manuila," 55–56 (17–18); Berger de Xivrey, 94; also, Schlumberger, "Un Empereur," 96–97 (10); Delaville le Roulx, *La France en Orient*, p. 379 and n. 2; Mompherratos, Διπλ. ἐν., 36; Silberschmidt, 197; Muralt, p. 766, no. 11.

since this is the accustomed thing for them to do. Accordingly, when all had agreed to my plan—for, just as it was communicated by me at the outset to the foremost of our own authorities and of our allies, so it was thereafter communicated by them to the appropriate persons—the resolution was put into effect. Since I will speak no more concerning myself, I will not protract my discourse by tarrying with the other details and with those involved with that long absence abroad.

Nor verily did I permit the ship of state to sail however it might chance or to be steered by one of those minor persons among those sometimes placed in command, as if of some small merchant vessel, either by appointment or by chance. Yet, since my son was not at an age at which to rule, I then reconciled my nephew to myself by the best of good fortune, and I set him at the helm until, if the Diety should wish, I was to return. Therefore, because he had been much smitten by this—by my going away, I mean—my brother was even more despondent than formerly, since the outcome was certainly for him a veritable orphanhood. For, while the voyage was indeed long, the absence abroad was, in its turn, much longer. And to such an extent was my outlook in uncertainty that my very return was but something to be wished for, though after a long time.[80]

80. Ed. Migne, 240C–241B, ed. Lampros, p. 68, l. 1 to p. 69, l. 5; the paragraph division is my own. The passage immediately following ours portrays Theodore's precarious situation during Manuel's fruitless absence and the Despot's effort to find "a cure" for his troubles by involving the Hospitalers. For this project, see below, pp. 232–233. It is interesting that Manuel avoids virtually all mention of Boucicaut in the passage given here. Only the slightest suggestion of the role of the Marshal and his expedition may be seen in his deliberately vague reference to "the more prudent of our allies" (τοῖς φρονιμωτέροις τῶν συμμαχούντων), and to "our allies" (τῶν συμμάχων) who are indicated by context as remaining behind. For the other Greek sources to have ignored or overlooked Boucicaut's role is perhaps not inexplicable (see Appendix XIV below). But certainly Manuel should have known better. What is the explanation? If, as has been maintained by at least one scholar, Boucicaut had been the supporter of John VII in the Thessalonica affair of 1403 (see below, pp. 242–243), it might have been that Manuel deliberately left out the important role of his old comrade out of pique; but, since this suggestion about Boucicaut in 1403 is almost certainly incorrect (see below, p. 244, n. 75), such an argument would plainly have no value. Was the real reason, then, that in this topical context Manuel chose not to complicate his discourse, as he himself promised? Or was it that in this rhetorical idiom the pedantic imperial stylist chose not to sully his "pure" Greek with such non-Hellenic names and facts? This is a problem on which it is impossible to reach definite conclusions, but on which it is interesting to speculate. Gibbons, 240, describes a fatalistic conversation between Manuel and Theodore before the Emperor's departure

In addition to the extensive personal suite necessary for his journey,[81] Manuel had brought with him on the first leg of the trip his family: his wife, the Empress Helena, and the two sons she had borne him by then, the future John VIII and Theodore.[82] These he intended to leave behind, not in Constantinople, but with his brother in the Morea. That he should take this step suggests vividly the kind of faith he put in John VII's loyalty, regardless of all the oaths and promises exchanged.[83]

In the Peloponnesus the progress of Manuel's journey was delayed. Negotiations had been entered into with Venice that had to be settled before the Emperor could leave. Manuel was concerned about the safety of his family even in the Peloponnesus, unsettled as it was, for he had asked the Venetian Senate for guarantees of refuge for them. On February 27, 1400, the Senate responded with a promise that, in case of Turkish invasion of the Morea, the Imperial family, and Theodore himself as well, would be allowed to take refuge in the Venetian ports of Coron

to Venice, for which he gives no real source, and which I therefore assume to be largely imaginary. Otherwise, the only apparent basis for this interpolation would be a less embellished, but equally fanciful, entry by Muralt, p. 766, no. 12, with utterly irrelevant source citations.

81. Manuel's retinue must have been large, befitting his rank. Of several allusions we have to its size (see below, pp. 228–229, and p. 232, n. 60), the largest figure quoted is in the fifties. Many references to Manuel's journey, and in particular to individual people in his service during it, are to be found in the fascinating Satire of Mazaris, published by Boissonade, *Anecdota graeca*, III (Paris, 1831), 112–186, and by A. Ellissen, *Analekten der mittel- und neugriechischen Literatur*, IV (Leipzig, 1860), 187–250. Vasiliev, "Putešestvie Manuila," 56–58 and 74 (18–20, 36), has used these references extensively. Be it said, also, uncritically. Much of the prosopographic material in this text is undoubtedly well-founded; but in view of the scurrilous nature of many of these references, and in view also of our lack of any other material with which to check them specifically, at least some caution must be exercised in handling them. Unfortunately, this entire problem calls for much more discussion than space permits here, and which I hope rather to attempt in subsequent work on this remarkable text. For other comments on members of Manuel's retinue, especially regarding those involved in negotiations with the various Spanish rulers, see Cirac Estopañan, *La Unión*, 54.

82. For a discussion of Manuel's family as it was in 1400 and of his later children, see Appendix XV below.

83. As pointed out by Dölger, "Johannes VII.," 32, and Ostrogorsky, *Hist. Byz. St.*, 493. Indeed, according to Ducas, ed. Grecu, 85, ed. Bonn, 55–56, Manuel had serious misgivings as to John's loyalty and ambitions and simply took the risk hoping for the best.

and Modon; provision was also made for housing them in these circumstances or for transporting them to Venice.[84]

These matters at last settled, Manuel took leave of his family at Modon and sailed from there, still with Boucicaut, aboard a Venetian vessel headed for the Lagoon City.[85] The Senate prepared for him: on April 4, 1400, the *Sapientes* assigned 200 ducats for his expenses.[86] Other necessary arrangements were made, and Manuel arrived (presumably) not long after.

From here on the familiar story is easily told. In Venice the Byzantine sovereign was received and housed with honor. Following promising discussions with the Venetian leaders,[87] he proceeded on his way across Italy, while Boucicaut was sent on ahead to Paris to prepare the way in France. After a brilliant reception in Padua, where he stayed eight days, Manuel proceeded by way of Vicenza and Pavia to Milan, where he was welcomed proudly by Gian Galeazzo Visconti. There the Emperor was able

84. Iorga, *Notes et extraits*, I, pp. 96–97; Thiriet, *Régestes*, II (Paris, 1959), no. 978, p. 10; cf. Dölger, *Regesten*, no. 3279, p. 86. See also Vasiliev, "Putešestvie Manuila," 58–59 (20–21); Silberschmidt, 198. Apparently Manuel occupied himself during his stop in the Peloponnesus with further negotiations. For a deliberation of the Venetian Senate for March 26, 1400, speaks of a projected alliance being discussed with the Genoese and the Hospitalers to guard Constantinople: Thiriet, no. 981, p. 10; see also below, pp. 204–205 and n. 5.

85. Ducas, ed. Grecu, p. 85, ll. 17–19, ed. Bonn, p. 56, ll. 4–6, says: "Having left them behind in Methone [Modon] and having sent back the triremes [on which he had come from Constantinople?] he himself, in one of the great ships [of Venice?], sailed to Venice...." The Pseudo-Phrantzes, ed. Papadopoulos, 66, ed. Bonn, 62, says instead that Manuel left his wife in Sparta (Mistra) with his brother. This is probably a generalization or a confusion of the apparent fact that Helena, with her children, proceeded to Mistra, where they took up their residence with Theodore. See Vasiliev, "Putešestvie Manuila," 59 (21); in general, with inaccurate chronology, Muralt, p. 766, no. 14.

86. Iorga, *Notes et extraits*, I, 97; according to his citation, the sum was assigned "pro honorando dominum Chiermanoli, imperatorem Constantinopolitanum." Cf. Vasiliev, "Putešestvie Manuila," 60 (22); Silberschmidt, 197. It might be noted at this point that this form of Manuel's name, or other forms like it, were commonly used in the West, especially during the Emperor's journey there. They are, of course, simply corruptions of the Greek expression Κῦρ (for κύριος) Μανουήλ, or κυρ ʼΕμμανουῆλος, or the like.

87. Apparently one of the matters discussed, either during or after Manuel's stay in Venice, was a league involving various Levantine Christian powers, with Genoa and possibly Venice, directed against the Turks: see below, pp. 204–205 and n. 5.

to enjoy the company of his friend the celebrated Manuel Chrysoloras, who had been enticed thither from his triumphs among the Greek-intoxicated Florentines. Visconti, happy to acquire such an opportunity for a display of prestige, spoke freely of aid to Manuel, promising to go to Constantinople himself if other rulers would cooperate with their aid. Moreover, he provided the Greek mission with generous gifts, money, horses, guards, and guides for the journey to France—by what route we do not know precisely.[88]

The question has been raised as to whether or not Manuel met with the Roman Pope, Boniface IX, during this phase of his journey.[89] Although it is impossible to answer this question, it is quite likely that at least Manuel's presence in Italy inspired the Roman Pontiff to issue his bull of May 27, 1400. This proclamation renewed the plea for a crusade or for financial contributions to one, with the usual promise of indulgences.[90]

Undoubtedly buoyed up in spirits by the grand receptions and promises given by the Italians, Manuel moved on to even greater encouragement. By the end of May the Emperor was well on his way to France. King Charles VI and his council, feeling deeply honored by the coming of this august visitor, prepared his way with all due pomp. When the Emperor reached Charenton out-

88. Vasiliev, "Putešestvie Manuila," 59–63 (21–25). See also Schlumberger, "Un Empereur," 99–104 (12–16); Berger de Xivrey, 96–98; Delaville le Roulx, *La France en Orient*, 379–380; Mompherratos, Διπλ. ἐν., 36–37; Jugie, 326–327; and the chronologically inaccurate Muralt, p. 716, no. 15. For Chrysoloras in Milan, see Cammelli, *I dotti bizantini e le origini dell' umanismo*, I: *Manuele Crisolora* (Florence, 1941), 98 ff.

In connection with Chrysoloras at this time, an effort has recently been made to link his famous teaching activities in the West with his sovereign's policy aims. Thomson, "Manuel Chrysoloras and the Early Italian Renaissance," 76–79, has suggested that, with the Emperor Manuel's approval or encouragement, Chrysoloras accepted the teaching opportunities offered him in Florence and elsewhere with at least the partial aim of inspiring sufficient pro-Greek sympathy in the West to induce Latin help to Byzantium against the Turks. It is an interesting idea, but I am not much convinced by Thomson's arguments, which are based on not a shred of concrete evidence and remain pure speculation.

89. Halecki, "Rome et Byzance," 514; Vasiliev, "Putešestvie Manuila," 64 (26); but strongly to the contrary is Gibbons, 240–241. See also Appendix XIX.

90. Partial text in Baronius-Raynaldus, 1400, no. 8 (Vol. 27, pp. 68–69); summary in Iorga, *Notes et extraits*, II (Paris, 1899), 81. Cf. Halecki, "Rome et Byzance," 514–516; Vasiliev, "Putešestvie Manuila," 64 (26).

Figure 7: *The Reception of Emperor Charles IV [Manuel?] on the Road to Saint-Denys by Officials of Paris.* Illuminated Miniature, *Grandes Chroniques de France*, Bibliothèque Nationale, Paris, *Ms. fr. 6465*, f. 444ᵛ (photo courtesy Bibliothèque Nationale, Paris; see Appendix XXIV, A, II, 3, a).

Figure 8: *The Meeting of Emperor Charles IV [Manuel?] by King Charles V before the Walls of Paris.* Illuminated Miniature, *Grandes Chroniques de France*, Bibliothèque Nationale, Paris, *Ms. fr. 6465*, f. 446ʳ (photo courtesy Bibliothèque Nationale, Paris; see Appendix XXIV, A, II, 3, b).

Figure 9: *The Arrival of Emperor Charles IV [Manuel?] at Saint-Denys.* Illuminated Miniature, *Grandes Chroniques de France*, Bibliothèque Nationale, Paris, *Ms. fr. 6465*, f. 444ʳ (photo courtesy Bibliothèque Nationale, Paris; see Appendix XXIV, A, II, 3, c).

side Paris on June 3, 1400, he was met by a reception of the greatest possible splendor, which was personally presided over by the King himself. The French were enormously impressed by the noble appearance, the dignity, and the physical agility of the fifty-year-old Emperor, who was then conducted to the quarters set aside for him in the old Louvre and fêted royally. Lodged at French expense, Manuel rested. Soon he met with the King and the Royal Council, who were sympathetically disposed by the Emperor's recital of his troubles and needs. Agreeing that Christian princes should aid one another against the infidel, the King and his advisers decided to provide Manuel with another force of 1,200 men, again paid for a year's service and commanded by Boucicaut.[91]

It was about at this point that Manuel penned the first of his series of letters written during his Western sojourn. We are indeed fortunate in having these six letters preserved to us, for they reveal vividly the Emperor's feelings and expectations during his journey, at least in its early phases. The first of these surviving letters is addressed to Manuel Chrysoloras who, be it remembered, was still in Italy at the time and had only recently seen his sovereign. The fairly brief communication suggests the breathless joy Manuel must have felt at the crest of his promising reception in Paris:

Often have I wished to write to you. But the fact that I did not yet have such things to write by which you would be pleased held back my hand. For the route was troublesome, and the events along it were not particularly pleasant. And, in addition, there was the change of the language, which did not allow the contacts we wished with men who are quite admirable and quite desirous of pleasing me.

91. *Religieux de Saint-Denys*, XXI, i, pp. 754 ff., for the famous contemporary description of his arrival and reception (translated below, p. 397); and Vasiliev, "Putešestvie Manuila," 65–69 (27–31); cf. Schlumberger, "Un Empereur," 104–109 (16–22); also Berger de Xivrey, 99–100, 103; Jugie, 327–329; Mompherratos, Διπλ. ἐν., 37–38; Delaville le Roulx, *La France en Orient*, 380–381; Muralt, p. 769, no. 44. As we shall see in the letter translated below, p. 187 (see also n. 118), Manuel specifically states that Boucicaut was singled out for the command in preference to the king's kinsmen. These princes of the blood had sought such an appointment previously, in 1399 (see above, p. 156), but Boucicaut was obviously better qualified. Of Manuel's arrival and residence in Paris, there are some possible Western artistic reflections: see Figures 7, 8, 9, 13, 14, 15, and 16, and the notes on them in Appendix XXIII below.

But now that I am in France [Γαλάτια], my hand raced on of its own accord, and it hastens to reveal to you by letter what things could perhaps be commnuicated better orally, for they surpass the limits of a letter. And while this hand has been aroused and now grasps at writing, yet, it then seemed that it would be attempting the unattainable if it wished to go over each detail. Many, indeed, are the favors that have come to me from the most illustrious king, and many from those in some way related to him by birth, and not a few also from all those in authority. All of which surely bears witness to their nobility of soul and love for us and an extensive kind of zeal for the Faith. But I wish to speak in brief: unless the customary envy of evil fortune should oppose, and unless some dreadful kind of unexpected obstacles should suddenly appear, there is great hope of my returning speedily to our homeland, for which, as I know, you on your part are praying, and against which on their side our enemies are praying.[92]

During this initial phase of Manuel's residence in Paris, his hosts took every opportunity to entertain and honor him. He was showered with rich gifts and grants. He was included in the royal hunts and at the most lavish and elegant festivals or celebrations of the court. All the while, his Greek customs and mode of worship fascinated the French.[93] But not all of Manuel's time was spent on such diversions and trivia, for the Emperor did not limit his appeals to the countries in which he was staying at a given time. The purpose of his visit continued to be diplomatic. Although there survives to us no great body of diplomatic correspondence with various European princes from this period, we do have a series of such documents regarding relations with the

92. Letter λζ′, ed. Legrand, 50–51, fully translated here. French translation by Berger de Xivrey, 102–103, reproduced by Schlumberger, "Un Empereur," 111 (23), and partially by Delaville le Roulx, *La France en Orient*, 382, and Jugie, 329. Russian translation, complete, by Vasiliev, "Putešestvie Manuila," 70 (32). Vasiliev argues, pp. 70 and 71 (32, 33), that this letter was written between Manuel's sympathetic hearing, with the agreement that rulers should help each other, and the specific decision to send a force for his aid. The distinction is perhaps hair-splitting, but it seems plausible.

93. Vasiliev, "Putešestvie Manuila," 71–74 (33–36); who stresses the possible significance of the fact that Manuel was seated next to the Papal legate at a banquet in honor of the marriage of the son of Louis de Bourbon on June 24. See also Schlumberger, "Un Empereur," 112–118 (24–29); Berger de Xivrey, 103–106; Mompherratos, Διπλ. ἐν., 38–39; Muralt, p. 769, no. 47.

courts of Spain. This series is of great interest not only for its own sake, but also as a representation of what similar relations the Emperor doubtless maintained with other courts.

Manuel apparently opened contact with Aragon at least not long after his arrival in France. For we have a letter from King Martin I, dated July 28, 1400, to a "Vezcomte" of Rhodes inquiring into the authenticity of a holy relic sent to him by "lo emperador de Constantinoble." [94] Whatever the results of such initial contact, they must have been encouraging to Manuel, for in the late summer or early autumn of that year he dispatched an important embassy to Spain. By October Manuel's ambassador, Alexios Vranas, had appeared before the King and had set forth his case. Martin was plainly sympathetic, for on October 15 he wrote a letter to the Archbishop of Saragossa recommending to the latter's care and attention "Allexi Vernan embaxador del muyt alto e excellent princep Emanuel," who was on his way similarly to solicit aid from the Kings of Castile and Navarre.[95]

Martin, in fact, went so far as to write a letter, dated one day previously (October 14), to King Henry III of Castile, urging him to give the requested aid to the Greek Emperor.[96] Then, on October 16, Martin wrote to Manuel himself, thanking the Emperor for the relics—plentiful Constantinopolitan export commodities, which Manuel was ready to use liberally as ice-breakers for his diplomacy—and for the accompanying chrysobull brought to him by Vranas. The King expressed his sympathy and promised to give his aid, the scope of which would be discussed when Vranas returned from Castile.[97] And, on the same date, the King addressed a letter to John VII to reassure him and to inform him of the pledge to Manuel.[98] The particular chrysobull which Manuel sent to Martin with the relics does not survive, but we have an undoubtedly similar one, dated August 30, 1400, written

94. Rubió i Lluch, no. 656, pp. 683–684; cf. Cirac Estopañan, *La unión,* 63.

95. Dölger, *Regesten,* no. 3281, p. 87; text, Rubió i Lluch, no. 658, p. 685; cf. Marinesco, "Du Nouveau," 421–422; Cirac Estopañan, *La unión,* 55.

96. Marinesco, "Du Nouveau," p. 422 and n. 3.

97. Text, Rubió i Lluch, no. 660, pp. 686–687; cf. Marinesco, "Du Nouveau," 422, and Cirac Estopañan, *La unión,* 56 and 63–64. For comments on Manuel's use of relics in general in his dealings with Spain, see Cirac Estopañan, *La unión,* 60 ff.

98. Text, Rubió i Lluch, no. 659, pp. 685–686; cf. Marinesco, "Du Nouveau," 422; Cirac Estopañan, *La unión,* 56. See also below, p. 205.

in the Louvre at Paris, and addressed to King Charles III of Navarre. In it the Emperor certifies certain relics conveyed by Vranas and describes his need for aid. This particular document was delivered to Charles, with the relics and the requests, when Vranas moved on to Navarre, presumably in early 1401.[99]

If Manuel was content to negotiate with such courts as those of Spain through embassies, he was interested in visiting at least one more country himself. Early in the summer of 1400 Manuel opened negotiations on the possibilities of going to England. His principal intermediary was Peter Holt, Prior of the Hospitalers in Ireland, who was also in favor with King Henry IV. In a letter dated July 11, 1400, from London, Holt replied to Manuel's overtures for a visit to England by pointing out the awkward factor of bad relations with France, even though there was now peace, and noting also the King's distraction with a Scottish rebellion. Nevertheless, Holt promised to do what he could before the King.[100] Apparently the results of such initial action were favorable, for Holt continued his intermediacy, going to Paris and seeing to the necessary arrangements in the early autumn of 1400.[101]

There is no doubt that a passage from France to England was a delicate matter at this time—one has but to think of Israel and her Arab neighbors in our own day—but for a distinguished outsider such as Manuel it was not impossible. Manuel plainly considered the trip worth his while, especially as he soon found out

99. Dölger, *Regesten*, no. 3282, p. 87. The text of this interesting chrysobull is given by Marinesco, "Du Nouveau," pp. 422–424 (Greek). Both forms of the text are also published by Cirac Estopañan, *La unión*, 102–103, with translations, 104–105; for comments on the background of this particular mission, *ibid.*, 57–58 and 64–65; for comments on the document itself, *ibid.*, 91, 95, 96, 99 ff., and 108–109.

100. Latin text of this letter published by F. C. Hingeston, *Royal and Historical Letters During the Reign of Henry the Fourth, King of England, and of France, and Lord of Ireland*, Vol. I: *A.D. 1399–1404* (=*Rerum Britannicarum medii aevi scriptorum*, 18, London, 1860), no. 17, pp. 39–40. Cf. Dölger, *Regesten*, no. 3280, p. 87; Vasiliev, "Putešestvie Manuila," 74–76 (36–38); also, Delaville le Roulx, *La France en Orient*, 381. That Manuel should conduct such dealings through the agency of a Hospitaler is perhaps a further demonstration of his contacts and good relations with the Knights of St. John. Note, also, that Manuel had previously been using Holt as an intermediary, as early as late summer of 1399, when he addressed a letter to the former English King, Richard II, through Holt: Dölger, *Regesten*, no. 3276, p. 86.

101. Vasiliev, "Putešestvie Manuila," 76–77 (38–39).

that he could not accomplish much more in France at that moment; for the late summer of 1400 had brought Manuel his first confrontation with reality in France. During August and September poor King Charles VI slipped into the first spell of his insanity suffered during Manuel's visit. As this spell lasted until the beginning of the following year, with only brief interruptions, the time seemed as propitious as any for the Emperor to move on to England. Therefore, in October of 1400, Manuel proceeded to Calais with Holt for the passage to England.[102]

The actual crossing of the Channel was not made until December, presumably because of the Scottish situation. Manuel was welcomed at Canterbury on December 13, and on December 21 another triumphant reception brought him to London. Lodged at royal expense, Manuel spent Christmas with the court, treated with great honor. Henry IV, on his throne only since September of 1399—and rid of his predecessor, Richard II, only since February of 1400—was eager to enhance his still shaky position with the prestige of his distinguished guest. Manuel was heard with the greatest sympathy, and Henry assured him strongly that he would aid the Empire.[103]

After the apparent setback in France, this new encouragement filled Manuel with renewed delight. This spirit is amply reflected in the second of our letters from Manuel on his journey. Probably written at the beginning of 1400, from London, it also is addressed to Manuel Chrysoloras:

> I presume that you received the letter which conveyed my beautiful message to you; and that you then remained forthwith in suspense and expected a second to arrive after that, informing you that our good luck was continuing, and straightway then a third, yet much better than the second, and then another, better than all, and perhaps also longer and fuller, each of the newer ones always excelling their predecessors a bit. But then, perhaps even the contrary was not

102. *Ibid.*, 77–78 (39–40).
103. *Ibid.*, 260–262 (40–42); Schlumberger, "Un Empereur," 118–121 (29–32); Berger de Xivrey, 106 ff.; Mompherratos, Διπλ. ἐν., 40–41; Delaville le Roulx, *La France en Orient*, 381–382; Luke, 768; Jugie, 329; Muralt, p. 794, no. 20. According to E. J. King, *The Grand Priory of the Order of the Hospital of St. John of Jerusalem in England. A Short History* (London, 1924), 46–47, Manuel's place of residence during his stay in England was the Hospitalers' Priory at Clerkenwell, outside London. (This author, however, seems to be unaware of the role of Prior Peter Holt in the visit.)

unreasonable: for, after that first letter, you were to see not many or long letters, but myself, their dispatcher, no longer consoling you with mere hopes, but gladdening you with the sight itself of the hoped-for results.

But now that some time has passed and some others of my many letters have come to you from us, but without any mention whatsoever of an army and of other aids by which the city is to be saved for us, I expect that you bear in your mouth the expression "Our treasures are ashes" [Lucian, *Zeuxis*, 2]. And, indeed, this probably was your reaction. But I on my part kept silent, not because I was deceived by my hopes, but because I was satisfied with what I had sent, and I was informing you by my silence that I had nothing new to say. This, then, was indeed the excuse for my silence. As to the excuse for the present letter, there are, to be sure, the many letters that have come to us from many quarters conveying extremely fine and optimistic messages. Most of all, however, there is the ruler with whom we are staying at present, the King of Britain the Great [Βρεττάνια ἡ μεγάλη]—which is, as one may say, the second universe. He overflows with many merits and is bedecked with all kinds of virtues. Indeed, by those who do not see him he is marveled at in his fame; while to those who once behold him he brilliantly attests that fame cannot really be a goddess, inasmuch as she is not able to display the man in the greatness that actual experience presents.

This man is at once most illustrious in form and most illustrious in judgment; at once with his might he astonishes all, and with his sagacity he wins himself friends; and he extends a hand to all, and himself furnishes every sort of assistance to those who are in need of aid. And now, following in his nature, he established a virtual haven for us in the midst of a twofold tempest—both of the season and of fortune—in himself and in his gestures toward us who have come into his port. And he appears very pleasant in his conversations, gladdening us in all ways and honoring us as much as possible and loving us no less. And, while he has gone to excess in all his negotiations, he seems even to blush a little, supposing himself, alone of all, to fall short of what is needed, so magnanimous is this man. So, if in observing a custom of letters it is necessary to compress my discourse, since this man is both worthy in beginnings and also worthy in completing the course—even becoming better each day—and since he contends eagerly at all times to excel himself in the projects concerning us, he therefore appeared much more noble with respect to the completion, since he has put forth both a capstone to the problems and a rivaling with himself in them. For he furnishes us with a military assistance of men-at-arms [ὁπλιτῶν] and archers and money, and ships which will convey the army wherever it is necessary.[104]

The modern reader may well smile to think that Manuel's extravagant description was inspired by Henry IV of England. But, as sincere as Henry may have been in his frequent talk of a crusade to the East, and as genuinely interested as he may have been in Manuel's plight, he was hardly in a position to provide Byzantium with even the little military aid he had promised, in view of his unstable domestic situation and of the revolts by the Scots and, later, the Welsh. Nevertheless, he was able to make good on some financial commitments. Henry ordered an inquiry after the money that Richard II had ordered collected as a result of the Papal mission of 1399. When the abuses of it were thus revealed, King Henry made good to Manuel, through Holt, the sum of 3,000 marks which had been promised by Richard through the unreliable Grillo, as well as the 4,000 pounds accumulated in the collection.[105] In a letter written in Latin and dated in London on February 3, 1402, Manuel expressed his gratitude to Henry for the latter's generous gift in fulfillment of Richard's unrealized grant.[106]

As with the French, Manuel made a profound impression upon the English, who were also fascinated by him personally and by the appearance and customs of himself and his followers. Nor was there any lack of sympathy for the sufferings of his oppressed

104. Letter λη΄, ed. Legrand, 51–52 (a fragment also ed. Migne, *Patr. gr.*, 156, 181–182), fully translated here. Partial French translation by Berger de Xivrey, 108; reprinted by Schlumberger, "Un Empereur," 121–122 (32–33), and Jugie, 329–330; and a short extract in Walter, 298. Partial translation in modern Greek by Mompherratos, Διπλ. ἐν., 41; partial Russian rendering by Vasiliev, "Putešestvie Manuila," 263 (43); partial English translation by Luke, 769. (Note also a line translated in English in *Hist. Byz. Emp.*, p. 633, by Vasiliev, whose account there, pp. 632–634, of Manuel's journey is a good, if very brief, summary of his long earlier study.)

105. Vasiliev, "Putešestvie Manuila," 264–265 (44–45); cf. Gibbons, 242.

106. Dölger, *Regesten*, no. 3283, p. 87. The text of this letter (published by Hingeston, no. 25, pp. 56–57) exists only in Latin and presumably was simply drawn up for him by a Latin scribe as a purely diplomatic document. As a result, it does not really fit into our series of Manuel's personal letters. But, in view of its interest, and to make it more readily available, this text, with a translation, is given below as Appendix XVI. On Richard's original promises and the Grillo affair, see above, p. 160, and n. 61. Also on this letter, see Vasiliev, "Putešestvie Manuila," 265 (45).

subjects and realm.[107] Manuel did not tarry long in England, however. That his departure after less than two months there might imply any disillusionment with English promises is not impossible, in view of a subsequent statement by him. But there is also some indication that he may have hastened back to France as the result of some good news, which proved false.[108] Whatever the cause or occasion, Manuel left the island kingdom in mid-February of 1401. Still full of promises that may have been wearing thin, Henry bestowed more gifts and money on Manuel and provided for his honorable escort to the sea. With a final display of sympathy and honor, the English bade farewell to their remarkable visitor.[109]

Crossing the Channel to Calais, Manuel retraced his steps to Paris, arriving at the end of February, in time to find Charles VI at the beginning of that monarch's latest period of sanity. Together the two sovereigns attended a Latin liturgy at Saint-Denys, causing shock among some of the French, who were scandalized that their King should thus associate himself with

107. The chief contemporary (and eyewitness) English source for Manuel's visit to the island is the *Chronicle* of Adam of Usk, ed. E. M. Thompson (2nd ed., London, 1904), 56–57, trans. *ibid.*, pp. 219–220. It is here we find the striking and oft-quoted comment on Manuel's situation as a sympathetic Westerner observed it: "I thought within myself, what a grievous thing it was that this great Christian prince from the farther east should perforce be driven by unbelievers to visit islands of the west, to seek aid against them. My God! What dost thou, ancient glory of Rome? Shorn is the greatness of thine empire this day; and truly may the words of Jeremy be spoken unto thee: 'Princes among the provinces, how is she become tributary!' [Lamentations, i: 1.] Who would ever believe that thou shouldst sink to such depth of misery, that, although once seated on the throne of majesty thou didst lord it over all the world, now thou hast no power to bring succour to the Christian faith?" (Thompson's translation.) See Vasiliev, "Putešestvie Manuila," 266–267 and 272 (46–47, 52); and cf. *id.*, *Hist. Byz. Emp.*, 634; see also Stacton, 116 (="Dereksen," 122).

108. Vasiliev, "Putešestvie Manuila," 267–271 (47–51), cites one source statement that Manuel left England because of the arrival of news of a great defeat of the Turks. He analyzes this passage in great detail and suggests plausibly that this statement may refer to the capture and sack of Sivas (Sebasteia) in August of 1400, by Timur; further, that the form of this news as it reached him prompted Manuel to hope for relief to his realm and impelled him to plan his return; but that it had become clear by the time he had reached Paris that the situation of Constantinople was eased in no appreciable way as a result.

109. Vasiliev, "Putešestvie Manuila," 271 ff. (51 ff.); Schlumberger, "Un Empereur," 122–123 (33–34); Berger de Xivrey, 108–109.

Figure 10: *The Royal Abbey of Saint-Denys, Paris, West Façade* (photo courtesy Archives Photographiques, Caisse Nationale des Monuments Historiques, Paris; see Appendix XXIV, C, 4).

a schismatic, but winning admiration among others for the King's tolerance and zeal for encouraging understanding and union between the Churches.[110]

Manuel's hopes remained strong. Presumably he continued to press his case before the French court. He seems also to have joined in French diplomatic efforts during the summer of 1401 to contact Timur and to spur on the Tartars against Bayazid.[111] We know, at any rate, that he continued his negotiations with other Christian powers. The surviving records of the negotiations indicate some degree of Manuel's unabated hopes.

To John I of Portugal Manuel sent out, on June 15, 1401, a gift of relics, accompanied by his solicitations.[112] More interesting, however, is the opening of negotiations with the Avignonese Anti-Pope. But Benedict XIII, besieged in his palace by his opponents, could offer little concrete help when Vranas was allowed through the lines to confer with him in July of 1401. Nevertheless, the beleaguered Pontiff was liberal in his promises of indulgences to those, in lands which recognized his authority (Aragon, Cyprus, Scotland, and Savoy), who would give aid. And he promised more attention to the matter when his own affairs should be more settled.[113]

A more specific indication of what progress Manuel must have thought he was making during early 1401 may be found in further negotiations with Aragon. Carrying out his promise of the previous year, Martin I settled down to a consideration of the details of specific aid, presumably in consultation with Vranas. In a letter to Manuel of February 3, 1401, the King repeated his thanks for the relics sent him and promised to contribute six armed galleys to the cooperative expedition—as soon as the contributions of the other Christian rulers were ready.[114] Under the

110. *Religieux de Saint-Denys*, XXI, vi, p. 774. Cf. Vasiliev, "Putešestvie Manuila," 275 (54); Berger de Xivrey, 110–111; Schlumberger, "Un Empereur," 124–125 (34–36); Jugie, 330; Mompherratos, Διπλ. ἐν., 41–42; Muralt, p. 774, no. 26.

111. For this, see Appendix XVIII below.

112. So says Vasiliev, "Putešestvie Manuila," 280–281 (60–61), following Hopf, *Geschichte Griechenlands*, 65; cf. Dölger, *Regesten*, no. 3284, pp. 87–88; but this assertion and the evidence for it have been questioned by Marinesco, "Du Nouveau," pp. 425–426 and n. 1.

113. Dölger, *Regesten*, no. 3285, p. 88; Cirac Estopañan, *La unión*, 58–59; Vasiliev, "Putešestvie Manuila," 281 (61); Halecki, "Rome et Byzance," 518.

114. Text, Rubió i Lluch, no. 664, p. 689; cf. Marinesco, "Du Nouveau," 426; Cirac Estopañan, *La unión*, 56, 63–64.

same date, Martin wrote another letter, to Charles VI, informing the French King of these promises of aid to the Emperor.[115]

Thus, through well past the first half of 1401 Manuel still seemed to have good prospects of cashing in on the Western promises, even, it appears, those of Henry IV of England. We can see just how optimistic Manuel was in this period in the next of his letters, written from Paris to the Priest—later Patriarch (1410–1416)—Euthymios. Its tone leaves no doubt whatsoever of Manuel's active involvement in plans and his real hopes for them:

While I have received from you many letters which were surely produced in collaboration with the Muses—for they were really of worthy language and thought, and of a level of intellect to express such affection as is proper, and of an ability to advise such things as would be useful—and while I was wishing to reply with ones equal, and this often, as you can imagine, yet, never once was I able to draw myself to what was needed. The reason is not my genuine inability to reply on exactly the same level. To be sure, this were likely to be the reaction of those who, priding themselves in their skill of letters, avoid being put to a test. But, as competing is altogether unattainable, this fact itself consoles me, since, likewise, I am by no means distressed at not being able to fly. Not because I feared defeat in comparison with you, then, did I deprive you of the news. Yet, if one wished to learn what was hindering me, he would find an entirely reasonable justification. For numerous distractions, sufficient to disable the mind's eye, and an indescribable multitude of practical affairs, such as is capable of dulling not only such as me but even someone sharp with words: all these I have. And verily also, as Plato has pointed out [*Phaedo*, 85A], "no bird sings" while it is grieving.

Indeed, as long as my negotiations had reached merely a point of fine-sounding assurances—and these from men who readily do this—and since I knew that your salvation was dependent on deeds, not words, I had become entirely numb, hand and tongue and mind, especially when I was anxious to raise a song of triumph. Furthermore, I feared lest, once I involved myself with lamentations, I might forget to what degree I should have been attempting to sing to you of better news; for some slight suspicion might more readily have dragged a soul, which was trembling for our race, down to the former lamentations, than would worthy promises toward the opposite reaction. But now that your hopes have been brought to fulfillment;

115. Text, Rubió i Lluch, no. 663, pp. 688–689; cf. Marinesco, "Du Nouveau," 426; Cirac Estopañan, *La unión*, 56, 63.

and now that from all quarters my transactions have been falling together favorably, since the commanders have begun to take hold
of their tasks with vigor, as a result of which there should come into
being what people call "in actuality" [cf. Aristotle, *Metaphysics*, VIII,
vi, 5–10]; and now that nothing is still lacking other than to go from
hence to you on the day appointed for the return—for it was necessary
that there be fixed a day and some place in which then the portions
of the British [Βρετάνοι] and all the other allies will be collected together:—now that all these things have come to pass, forthwith, then,
I have hastened to write. And while I have many things to say for
your delight, I will say one in place of all, since the circumstances
that are impelling me to be active do not allow me to delay very
long. That is: I expect that I will arrive not long after this optimistic
message itself. And you will see, with the aid of God's Mother, a
variegated army following me, one no less selected than collected
from every side, one which is able to accomplish well that for which it
comes—to sum up the whole matter, one far exceeding, I believe, your
own hopes.[116]

The foregoing letter is a most valuable witness of Manuel's
situation at this point. Plainly, there had been periods of uncertainty and even of wavering hope. Even at this time Manuel
readily understood the meaninglessness of Latin promises. But
definite progress had been made. This letter was plainly penned
when Manuel was certain that all the promises made to him,
even those of the English (whom he particularly mentions),
were on the threshold of immediate and complete fulfillment. His
hoped-for expedition was, it seemed, at last all but ready to depart.

Manuel's next letter, also to Euthymios, after an apparent lapse
of some time, is very brief. But it suggests no serious waning of
the Emperor's good spirits:

116. Letter λθ΄, ed. Legrand, pp. 53–54, fully translated here. A greatly
abridged translation in French by Berger de Xivrey, 109–110, is reproduced
by Schlumberger, "Un Empereur," 123–124 (34); and a brief passage from this
is in Walter, 299. Partial translation in Russian by Vasiliev, "Putešestvie Manuila," 275–276 (55–56). These translators have rendered the participial clause
καὶ μηδενὸς προσδέοντος ἔτι, ἢ τοῦ τὴν κυρίαν ἐλθεῖν τῆς ἐνθένδε πρὸς
ὑμᾶς επανόδου (ll. 31–33), taking τὴν [ἡμέραν] κυρίαν as an object accusative, in the sense of "all that is lacking is to choose the time, etc." But it
seems more correct to regard the case as an accusative of time, a rare example of a Greek modernism which crept into Manuel's style, usually so self-
consciously "Classical." On Euthymios and Manuel's letters, see Mercati,
Notitzie, pp. 516–517.

I know that my progress gladdens you, since you are cordially disposed toward me. To be sure, this made even the son of Laertes to long for the smoke [i.e. rising from his homeland: cf. *Odyssey*, I, 57–59]. Wishing, then, to delight you in all ways, since I have already gladdened you in your hopes on behalf of our race, I gladden you now also with this product of my hand. And in order that you may rejoice thrice over, know that my body is well, and that perhaps even my soul will at some time be in a good state, since you are indeed interceding on its behalf with Him Who died for those that are condemned.[117]

The next letter of the series, to Demetrius Chrysoloras, returns in even greater degree to the mood of enthusiasm and striking conviction regarding the projected expedition:

Well, now, you are the fastest man from the starting gate, as they say, in the race to find the pretext for my silence up to now, and you are also competent to carry out the judgment that has been made against it. I assume, then, not only that you do not wish to bring a charge against me, but that you will speak what is required in my defense. And as proof of this is the fact that, often when you yourself have written and have received no reply whatsoever from me, you neither stopped writing thus nor indeed did you think it necessary to ask the reason for my silence. This would mean that you understand precisely the obstacle to my tongue and hand, even before you were to learn anything from me concerning these problems. This is by no means behavior for all men, but is seemly only for such men as you yourself are; for you are clever, and you know me, and you understand the times, and you are not entirely inexperienced of these Western regions, and not entirely unknown to you is the matter of my critical circumstances, of which there is much discussion before those who are reviewing them. And if these things are so, and our good Demetrius displays a nature beyond mere skill, and if his sagacity of Nestor vanquishes the prophetic power of a Chalchas, as is probable, it is quite clear that he will understand that which impels me to write now, so that what I might say to him would be all but beside the point. But, even so, something gratifying will be said

117. Letter μ′, ed. Legrand, 54, fully translated. Partial Russian translation by Vasiliev, "Putešestvie Manuila," 276 (56). But does the lukewarm tone of this short note, amid the enthusiasm of its predecessor and successor, suggest that at least it might be out of a strict chronological sequence? Or is it simply an example of the kind of short memo Manuel might have dashed off in an odd moment, suggesting a genuine lapse of time between λθ′ and μα′?

to those who will be hearkening, inasmuch as it brings tidings in which they will take pleasure.

I know that your salvation required practical measures, not just promises. While having some very fine-sounding assurances, yet, being very fearful for the outcome—inasmuch as it requires so much time, in which many things could happen—these, my circumstances, I was making known to you by another's hand through letters. But just now the matters at hand have been advancing in accordance with my way of thinking, and, indeed, the ambassadors who have been sent everywhere have accomplished what we are praying for. The commander has been proclaimed—this is the Marshal, to my delight, in preference to many of those kinsmen of the King who were voted for [118]—and he is now in charge of the operations. And nothing is lacking except to collect the forces that are being prepared for us by not a few sovereigns, in the place that has been designated for them; and to distribute the pay to the soldiers here, who are very free with their money when it is in hand, especially since the band which is to receive the pay is so eager that they would even concede their pay if someone would only give them just means for their arms. For these reasons, then, both my tongue and my hand, freed from my suspicion over our prospects as if from chains, forthwith move quickly, as you can imagine, to the tasks that they have been eager to perform. And now, seeking delight for you, and at the same time discharging a debt for my previous silence, I have sent the present letter, the work at once of a hand unlearned and of a tongue more unlearned, but at the same time of someone beloved by you. As you rejoice, then, expect us swiftly, perhaps not long after the present letter itself. And you will see those who shall be beyond your hopes, at least by no means less, but who will be able to do that for which we come—if He Who is our Master, as we struggle on behalf of those for whom He Himself died, joins with us in our efforts.[119]

118. There seems no other way to explain Manuel's word μανισκάλκος than by the word *maréschal,* as is the conclusion of Berger de Xivrey, 70–71, followed by Walter, 299. Indeed, the word as it stands in the manuscript could probably be emended with safety to read at least as μαρισκάλκος. We have seen that the *Maréschal* Boucicaut had already been named as commander of the planned expedition, and the reference is unquestionably to him. In this case, we have here apparently the only direct allusion to Boucicaut by Manuel in any of his writings. It is also interesting to note Manuel's reference to this preference for Boucicaut, to his obvious pleasure, even before the King's relatives, as the choice for this command: see above, n. 91.

119. Letter μα΄, ed. Legrand, 55–56, fully translated here. The Russian translation by Vasiliev, "Putešestvie Manuila," 277 (57), is greatly abbreviated,

But Manuel's high hopes were not to continue. While he was kept in touch with events in the East,[120] his negotiations in the West dragged on inconclusively, with his prospects proving more illusory than he had expected. Manuel had not forgotten Italy, and his pleas there continued. But when, for example, the Emperor's kinsman, Demetrius Palaeologus, was sent to Florence with an appeal for aid, he received a discouraging reply. In a letter of August 20, 1401, the Commune of Florence wrote to Manuel, expressing its sympathy, but pointing out that their city was distracted by its own threat of an "italicus Baisettus" (i.e. Visconti) and, hence, at this time was not free to give help. The Florentines added, however, the cheerful hope that they might give aid later, if the Pope were to grant indulgences, and if circumstances were to become more favorable.[121]

Even more discouraging must have been the delays in regard to the most important project, the launching of the expedition which Manuel had been awaiting confidently and excitedly for so long. The condition of King Charles and his government was, in reality, hardly conducive to effective action. Nor was the cooperation from the other rulers as thorough as Manuel had

while the rendering in French by Berger de Xivrey, p. 71, n. 1, of a very scant passage, is rather inexact. If we accept the hypothesis that the manuscript order of Manuel's letters is basically chronological, this letter to Demetrius Chrysoloras would therefore have been written at least no earlier than the second one to Euthymios. But the manuscript order alone cannot be absolutely convincing evidence. Actually, the contents, the spirit, and much of the sentence structure of his letter to Chrysoloras are so similar to those of the first letter to Euthymios that there seems reasonable ground for regarding them as having been written at the same time. Indeed, were it not for its reference to "your hopes on behalf of our race," and its apparently happy tone, one might well be tempted to relegate the first letter to Euthymios to a later time, perhaps after the planned expedition had collapsed and after Manuel's outlook for returning was uncertain. But we have nothing tangible with which to resolve this question. Perhaps Manuel's enthusiasm and hope did last long enough after all—through the middle of 1401—to allow him to write these letters even in their present manuscript order.

120. At least once, on May 6, 1401, the Venetian Senate decided to communicate the latest news of affairs in "Romania" to Manuel: Iorga, *Notes et extraits*, I, 110; Thiriet, *Régestes*, II, p. 18, no. 1016. Cf. Vasiliev, "Putešestvie Manuila," 283 (63). It is obvious, as well, that Manuel was in reasonably regular contact with his own friends and informants at home, at least through his secretarial staff, as he suggests in the last of his letters presented above.

121. Text in Lampros, Παλ. καὶ Πελ., III, 124–125; cf. Dölger, *Regesten*, no. 3286, p. 88; Vasiliev, "Putešestvie Manuila," 282–283 (62–63); Walter, 299–300.

thought it would be. On August 26, 1401, King Martin I of Aragon wrote to Manuel, acknowledging a letter from the latter brought by Alexios Vranas, calling upon him to contribute the ships he had pledged for the expedition. Martin pleads, however, that the lateness of the season does not allow him time to ready his galleys. On the same day he also wrote another letter of the same tenor to King Charles VI.[122] Nevertheless, Martin continued to give encouragement, and on August 28, he issued an order to his officials that provided a safe conduct for Vranas and commanded all due respect and assistance to be given the Byzantine embassy in its continuing journeys.[123] The actual collapse, for all intents and purposes, of the projected expedition is further suggested by the appointment of Boucicaut, instead, as the French governor of newly subject Genoa, in which capacity he entered that city on October 31, 1401.[124]

Perhaps only now did Manuel begin to realize how misplaced his confidence had been, for all his high-flown verbiage to his friends. The Latins had been free with their promises, and even Manuel had exercised some caution and critical skepticism. But by now the usual "when the others are ready" clause that qualified the specific pledges of aid had begun to show its significance. Perhaps many of the pledges, even with such qualifications, might have been fulfilled if there had been some direction to the scheme for aid. Rightly, that direction should and would have come from the French court, as long as Sigismund of Hungary remained out of the picture. But France was in no position to give direction or leadership now that her government was increasingly paralyzed by the recurrent and increasingly hopeless madness of Charles VI and by the concomitant struggles for power among the factions of his family. As for the cooperation that Manuel had specifically expected from the English, on that count another link was soon enough added to the growing chain of disillusionment. By the spring of 1402, perhaps after the news of the Welsh revolt in the preceding year, Manuel reached the

122. Texts in Rubió i Lluch, no. 665, p. 690, and no. 666, p. 691, respectively; cf. Dölger, *Regesten*, no. 3287, p. 88; Marinesco, "Du Nouveau," 424; Cirac Estopañan, *La unión*, 56.
123. Text, Rubió i Lluch, no. 667, p. 692; cf. Marinesco, "Du Nouveau," 427; Cirac Estopañan, *La unión*, 56; also, Dölger, *Regesten*, no. 3287, p. 88.
124. *Livre des faits*, II, iii–vi, pp. 614–616; cf. Delaville le Roulx, *La France en Orient*, 402–405.

conclusion that, for all his promises and good will, Henry IV of England could not be relied upon for any real aid. To this effect, at least, he wrote to his nephew in Constantinople.[125]

Manuel was too perceptive a person to have persisted in his delusion too long. Exactly when the light of reality began to dawn upon him is not certain; nor can we know precisely how he reacted to the realization. One last letter of his series from Western Europe, notably brief, is a small exercise in obscurity that cannot be dated precisely as to its period of composition. All one can be sure of is the Emperor's exhortation to his friend Manuel Pothos to encourage the waverers at home. And, at the same time, Pothos has plainly been urging Manuel to come home, something the Emperor is only too eager, if not also ready, to do. This emphasis on the idea of Manuel's returning is perhaps significant. Also significant, however, is not what the letter does say, but what it does *not* say: there is only the very vaguest mention of the aid that Manuel had been hoping and expecting to bring back with him almost immediately. This vague allusion might place it in the period when Manuel expected to return soon with his relief force. Yet, this relative silence and absence of confidence on the one subject which had been the sole and spectacular theme of all (save one, perhaps) of his other letters in the series, as well as this talk of returning, are perhaps reasonable grounds for suggesting that this last letter may possibly belong to at least the beginning of Manuel's phase of disillusionment:

Certainly the fine letter sent by you is enough to stir up one who is delaying [i.e. coming home]. But this is like inviting a Lydian into a plain, as they say. Cease, now, such exhortation of those who are already speeding to do this, and take hold of the tasks that will be as a salvation in our troubles. But yet, I have made the same mistake as you, by goading you on to what you have already been doing. Nevertheless, I myself will add something on your behalf to your eagerness for my return—if it were indeed possible to add something that is itself pleasing both to me and at the same time to you and to the city. Play the man and become better than yourself, not only to do your own tasks better, but also to exhort the more sluggish to this, in order that our toil may be fruitful; and that you do not perish

125. Dölger, *Regesten*, no. 3289, p. 88. For more on this notice to John, see below, p. 213. Walter, 299, quotes a message sent by the English to Manuel which I presume to be a product of his own imagination.

needlessly while those who will be fighting on your behalf are before your very gates. May that not come to pass! [126]

Whatever other letters Manuel wrote in this later phase of his sojourn in the West have not survived, although presumably he must have maintained at least some correspondence with his friends.[127] It is difficult to imagine that any letters written in his

126. Letter μβ', ed. Legrand, 56–57; Russian translation of a brief passage by Vasiliev, "Putešestvie Manuila," 277 (57). The proverb "Λυδὸν εἰς πεδίον [προσκαλεῖν]" has the meaning of inviting someone to do what he requires no invitation to do, what he most naturally does of his own accord. This proverb is used by Libanius, Epistle 617 (532); cf. also E. L. Leutsch and F. G. Schneiderwin, *Corpus Paroemiographorum graecorum* (Göttingen, 1839; reprint, 1965), I, pp. 191–192, n. 65. Manuel himself used this expression again in his *Funeral Oration for His Brother Theodore*, ed. Migne, 221B, ed. Lampros, p. 50, ll. 20–21. It has been commonly claimed that Manuel's extant letters from Western Europe were all written in the early part of his visit, and that none survive from this later period when he realized the hopelessness of his mission: thus, Vasiliev, *ibid.*, and *Hist. Byz. Emp.*, 634. But, on the basis of the arguments advanced above, there seems possible doubt about this claim, and I for one am inclined to think there is some likelihood that this Letter μβ' actually does date from this later period. It is, at any rate, the last of Manuel's letters which we can ascribe with certainty to his European sojourn.

The next letter preserved in the manuscript order (μγ') is simply a discourse to Demetrius Chrysoloras, urging the latter to concentrate on his studies and to forget delusions of military glory: cf. Berger de Xivrey, 67. It is not impossible that this letter was written in Europe also, but there is no way of being positive. If it does belong to that period, it would be a good reflection of the Emperor's attempts to take refuge from his disillusionment in his own literary distractions.

Certainly the next letter, μδ', and those after it, were plainly written after Manuel had returned home. (Cf. Letter με', ed. Legrand, p. 64, ll. 68 ff.) It is in this next letter (μδ'), incidentally, that we have Manuel's only remaining allusion, and a very general one, to his European journey: ed. Legrand, p. 60, ll. 50–55. This letter is also a valuable reflection of Manuel's state of mind on his return from the West, and the bulk of it, including the interesting allusion just mentioned, is translated below, pp. 403–405.

127. It might be worth noting here, in the vein of Manuel's exchanges of correspondence, a letter by Isidore, presumably the future Metropolitan of Kiev and Cardinal. It is addressed to a Byzantine of importance who had been visiting various Western European nations on important business and had been received with high honor. The surviving text, in the Vatican Library, does not name the addressee, and the consensus of scholarly opinion in the past has been that it was written to Manuel Chrysoloras around 1408–10: cf. Mercati, *Scritti d'Isidoro il Cardinale ruteno e codici a lui appartenuti che si conservano nella Biblioteca Apostolica Vaticana* (*Studi e Testi*, 46, Vatican City, 1926), 21–22.

Recently Zakythinos, "Μανουὴλ Β' ὁ Παλαιολόγος καὶ Καρδινάλιος Ἰσίδωρος ἐν Πελοποννήσῳ," *Mélanges offerts à Octave et Melpo Merlier,*

phase of high enthusiasm would have held any less bitter
memories than those written in his phase of disillusionment. But,
at any rate, whatever there may have been of the latter, he apparently preferred not to preserve them, for there are no such
letters in the manuscript in which he collected his correspondence. There do survive, however, two other literary works
which the Emperor wrote during his long second residence in
Paris. One is a good-humored description of a tapestry which
hung in the Louvre when he was housed there.[128] The other work
is of more significance. During his second sojourn in Paris, a
French theologian presented to Manuel a little work outlining
the Latin point of view on the old and thorny question of the
Procession of the Holy Spirit, long a bone of bitter contention
between the Eastern and Western Churches. A Byzantine to the
core and an Emperor-theologian in the best East Roman tradi-

III (Athens, 1957), 52–53 (or, in offprint, 8–9), published this text and
argued instead that this letter was written to Manuel II in Europe, before
June of 1403. If this hypothesis were correct, this letter would indeed be of
value to us, especially in the light of some of its contents. Unfortunately,
however, there would be too many obstacles to this explanation of the letter,
not the least being the presumed writer's extreme youth at this conjectured
time. Far more decisive, however, is the obstacle of Isidore's reference in the
letter to the recipient's ability to converse with his Western hosts "now in the
speech of the Romans, now in that of the Italians" (l. 16). Now, we know
quite well—indeed, from Manuel's own statement in his first letter from
Paris: see above, p. 174—that the Emperor knew no Western languages.
Fortunately, in a correction inserted at the end of the article, Zakythinos
concedes the error of his hypothesis and notes the newly estimated ascription
of the letter to 1416–18, with the addressee identified as Nicholas Eudaimonoioannes. He does this, however, on the basis of information provided
by Loenertz and not in view of any of the intrinsic objections to his original
hypothesis. For more on this letter, see also below, p. 327, n. 54.

128. Ἔαρος εἰκὼν ἐν ὑφαντῷ παραπετάσματι ῥηγικῷ, text ed. Migne,
Patr. gr. 156, 577–580; complete Russian translation by Vasiliev, "Putešestvie
Manuila," 278–280 (58–60). Cf. *id., Hist. Byz. Emp.*, 634; also no. 7, p.
1927, of Petit's article on Manuel in *Dict. d. théol. cath.*, IX. Berger de
Xivrey, 100–101, and, following him, Schlumberger, "Un Empereur," 109–
110 (22), and also Jugie, 328, all refer to this work in the context of the
longer second residence there. This suggestion seems more plausible, for
Manuel had far more leisure to write—recall his hyperbolic references earlier
to his constant proccupation with diplomatic affairs—and he probably welcomed, if not deliberately sought, such refined and congenial distractions
from his enforced inactivity then. K. Krumbacher, *Geschichte der byzantinischen Litteratur* (Munich, 1897), 491, suggests that Manuel's model
for this work was Libanius' Ἔκφρασις ἔαρος συγγραφικῷ χαρακτῆρι
(ed. Foerster, Teubner, VIII, 479–482).

tion, Manuel ignored the niceties of tact in a Latin country, even when he was desperately seeking help from Latins, including the Pope(s). Forthwith, he penned a long and unequivocal exposition, in some one hundred and fifty-six chapters, of the Greek point of view on this and other questions, including the Papal primacy.[129] Manuel was willing to talk about Church union, but, when it came down to specific issues, he was as irascibly stubborn in his beliefs as any other devout adherent of the Orthodox faith.

Time must surely have hung heavily on the Emperor's hands, and, as his second residence in Paris wore on, his outlook may well have begun to seem bleak indeed. It has been suggested that Manuel deliberately protracted his stay in Paris to evade the unpleasant task of returning empty-handed to his all-but-conquered realm.[130] But, from what we know of Manuel, we must conclude that he surely had too much of a sense of responsibility to have abandoned his unhappy land and his family as well. Certainly, such an allegation would rather have been an unjust calumny to him. And, indeed, we can see that this interpretation is as false as it is unfair in the light of two facts.

In the first place, we know that Manuel did contemplate returning after the phase of disillusionment had set in, with its knowledge of the unlikelihood of obtaining aid after all. On January 29, 1402, the Venetian Senate wrote to Manuel ("in partibus Flandrie") to inform the Emperor that the latest news from Constantinople made it imperative that Manuel should return to the capital. The *Sapientes* therefore urged him to gather what aid he could from the Western princes and hasten home speedily.[131]

129. This work has not been published. For a brief discussion of it, see Petit's article in the *Dict. d. théol. cath.*, no. 5, pp. 1931–1932. See also Vasiliev, "Putešestvie Manuila," 280 (60), Berger de Xivrey, 111–112, and Jugie, 330–331, all of whom cite the famous and caustic comments on this work by Leo Allatius. See also Schlumberger, "Un Empereur," 125–128 (36–38); Muralt, p. 774, no. 27. Jugie, *ibid.* (followed by Schlumberger, 128 [38]), suggests that a discourse on the Dormition of the Virgin attributed to Manuel (Petit's no. 7, p. 1928) was also written by Manuel at this time, favoring the Franciscans in a current dispute with the Dominicans.

130. Thus, Ostrogorsky, *Hist. Byz. St.*, 494: "It almost looked as though Manuel felt that he could not face the return, for he broke his journey in Paris and stayed there for nearly two years, although he could have no illusions about the possibility of getting any help." (Trans. Hussey.)

131. Thiriet, *Régestes*, II, no. 1039, p. 23.

Manuel apparently accepted the suggestion—if not immediately, at least within two months. For, in the spring of 1402, Manuel requested of Venice that she intercede, together with the Genoese, with the French and English Kings on behalf of Manuel's pleas for aid; that Venice also provide six galleys to join others from Genoa in helping to defend Constantinople; and that Venice consider the question of his return by way of Modon. In a reply of May 8, 1402, the Senate was evasive. The *Sapientes* pointed out that Venice had already made such intercession once before with success (in 1399, leading to Boucicaut's expedition), but could have no effect before the rulers of England and Germany; while Manuel and the Genoese were themselves in a better position now before the French King than was Venice, whose activity would only be superfluous. The Senate also refused to send any further forces to Constantinople, in view of the needs of the Venetians' own Levantine holdings; but, the Senate added, if the French King and the Genoese should advance any definite aid, Venice would make some further contribution as well. Finally, as to Manuel's projected return voyage, the Senate warned of the plague in the area of Modon. On May 20, the Senate further decided that, because of the plague, the Emperor should proceed not by way of Modon, but by way of Corfu.[132]

In the light of such haggling and discouragements, Manuel seems to have abandoned any ideas of returning home at this point. But these documents do demonstrate clearly that he was quite ready to accept the Venetian suggestions and to consider going back to Constantinople, empty-handed or not, if any critical developments seemed to make this return necessary.

In the second place, we know that Manuel continued to press his negotiations for aid from various Western sources. It is certainly natural to assume that, by this time, Manuel had become disillusioned, or at least skeptical of all the promises and hopes which had initially made him so exultant. But, regardless of what

132. Icrga, *Notes et extraits*, II, 118; Thiriet, *Régestes*, II, no. 1055, p. 27. Cf. Dölger, *Regesten*, no. 3288, p. 88; also, Vasiliev, "Putešestvie Manuila," 284 (64), who suggests that the reference to the Genoese position vis-à-vis France was a sarcastic allusion to the submission of Venice's old rival to French suzerainty, of which the Venetians disapproved and were suspicious. What is really interesting is Manuel's plea for intercession with the French court. Had Manuel's standing there deteriorated so, as his visit wore on, that he really needed such intercession on his behalf?

Figures 11 & 12: *Seal on One of Manuel's Chrysobulls (to Pope Benedict XIII), Obverse and Reverse.* Cathedral of Palma, Majorca (photo courtesy Museos de Arte, Barcelona; see Appendix XXIV, A, III, 1).

realities Manuel may have realized, and regardless of what his personal feelings may now have become, Manuel did not change his official policy. Indeed, as we shall see, Manuel never really did abandon his official policy of the quest for aid at any time hereafter, in spite of various circumstances. And certainly at this time Manuel had little choice but to stay on in the West as long as he could, until his efforts brought some result. The record clearly shows, therefore, that Manuel, at least outwardly, never fully gave up hope of winning some kind of assistance, even in the latter phase of his second sojourn in Paris.

A number of testimonies to this continued activity survive to us. In spite of his obligations to the Roman Pope, Boniface IX, Manuel maintained contact with the Anti-Pope Benedict XIII, for what little it was worth. On June 20, 1402, in Paris, Manuel

195

Figures 13 & 14: *Gold Medallion of Constantine the Great [Manuel?]*, *Obverse and Reverse*. Bibliothèque Nationale, Paris, Cabinet des Médailles (photo courtesy Bibliothèque Nationale, Paris; see Appendix XXIV, A, II, 1, a).

Figures 15 & 16: *Gold Medallion of Heraclius [Manuel?]*, *Obverse and Reverse*. Bibliothèque Nationale, Paris, Cabinet des Médailles (photo courtesy Bibliothèque Nationale, Paris; see Appendix XXIV, A, II, 1, b).

issued a chrysobull for the Avignonese Pontiff, certifying a relic he was sending to him, with renewed hope for his aid.[133] Benedict seems to have made some small efforts to encourage help for Manuel.[134] And, still anxious to explore any possibilities for seeming assistance, Manuel renewed his appeals to Venice. But the Venetians persisted in their unwillingness to commit themselves. On July 6, 1402, the *Sapientes* responded again that it was useless for them to intervene on his behalf with the French King, since the latter had already promised aid to the Byzantines. Further, they added, the Venetian expenses to help "the Christians of Romania" had already been so heavy that Venice would contribute more—once again the standard qualification, so familiar by now—only if France and Genoa would make some genuine effort of their own.[135]

Thus, on through this phase of disillusionment and seeming hopelessness, Manuel continued to the bitter end to hope and to work for some sort of help from the Latin powers. Certainly, Manuel must have looked upon remaining in Paris, not as an

133. Dölger, *Regesten,* no. 3290, pp. 88–89. The parallel Latin and Greek texts have been published by Marinesco, "Du Nouveau," 427–430; and also by Cirac Estopañan, "Ein Chrysobulles des Kaisers Manuel II Palaiologos (1391–1425) für den Gegenpapst Bennedikt XIII (1394–1417/23) vom 20. Juni 1402," *Byz. Zeitschr.,* 44 (1951), 89–93, with full commentary (and facsimile); and included again in his *La unión,* 100–101 (with Spanish translation, 101–102); for comments on this embassy, *ibid.,* 59, 62–63; for comments on the document itself, 90–91, 95, 97–99, and 108–109. The beautiful seal of this document is reproduced as Figures 11 and 12.

134. Marinesco, "Du Nouveau," 430.

135. Iorga, *Notes et extraits,* I, 119; Thiriet, *Régestes,* II, no. 1063, p. 29; cf. Dölger, *Regesten,* no. 3291, p. 89; and Vasiliev, "Putešestvie Manuila," 285 (65). Apparently Manuel had also had some requests sent to Venice through an embassy of Boucicaut's, which was bound for there; for, on the preceding day, July 5, 1402, the Senate took note of the Genoese embassy's request for the dispatch of three Venetian galleys to the "partes Romanie" and for the arming of three more galleys "pro conducendo ad ipsas partes dominum imperatorem." But these requests were countered by another complaint about the Venetian burden of expenses in this sphere, and the Senate would agree only to replacing its two galleys in "Romania" (at Constantinople?) with two others: text, Delaville le Roulx, *La France en Orient,* II, *Piéces justicatives,* no. 24, pp. 97–98. M.-M. Alexandrescu-Dersca, on p. 19 of her background material in *La Campagne de Timur en Anatolie (1402)* (Bucharest, 1942), converts this request into one by John VII. But this is plainly wrong, for in this context the "dominum imperatorem" is surely Manuel, still in the West.

abandonment of his country, but rather as a kind of dogged staying at his post in his own way.

Yet, it must have seemed a depressing task as the summer of 1402 drew nigh. Manuel had ceased to impress the French, who had come to regard him as a kind of permanent fixture; and so we hear little of him in French sources during this second sojourn in Paris.[136] More crucial, judging from his appeals for the intercession of Venice, the demoralized French court apparently all but forgot him. Yet, while there seemed little to be gained for the moment, there is no telling how long Manuel would have remained in Paris, or at least in the West in general, if he had not been called back in the late summer of 1402 by the news of a sudden and dramatic event that altered his entire outlook.

But even that remarkable event, the Battle of Ancyra, could not alter one basic fact: in its own turn, the quest for aid had failed. Manuel's original policy, appeasement of and collaboration with the Turks, the relic of his father's government, had been proved worse than useless by 1394. But Manuel's alternative, his policy of resistance on the basis of hoped-for support and aid from the Latin West, seemed no more effective, even when implemented to the ultimate degree by Manuel's barely precedented and remarkable journey of personal diplomacy. This failure, certainly not his own fault, did not prevent Manuel from maintaining at least the essence of this policy hereafter, as we shall see. But, as we shall also see, he must have been aware to some extent that his quest for aid was fundamentally doomed to disappointment.

136. Cf. Vasiliev, "Putešestvie Manuila," 275 (55); *id., Hist. Byz. Emp.,* 634; for more on Manuel's second residence in Paris, see Schlumberger, "Un Empereur," 128–130 (38–40); Delaville le Roulx, *La France en Orient* (I), 382–383.

4. Byzantium in the Turkish Time of Troubles, 1399–1413

It was a grim outlook that Constantinople faced during the time Manuel was to spend in his fruitless mission in Western Europe. John VII had no illusions about the difficult responsibility placed on his shoulders. Indeed, he had refused to accept it unless he was left with some forces to defend Constantinople. Boucicaut had recognized readily the justice of this demand and had taken steps to fulfill it. Out of the ranks of his force the Marshal picked a small detachment of 100 men-at-arms, 100 armed attendants, and a number of archers, who were to be left in the city under the command of the Seigneur Jean de Chateaumorand. Boucicaut also left behind for these men the provisions necessary for their stay there and also their monthly pay for that period, placed in the hands of "bons marchands." The Venetians and the Genoese, in recognition of these arrangements, each contributed on their part four galleys for the defense of the city. Accepting the support provided by these concessions, John took up the government of Constantinople as Manuel and Boucicaut sailed away for the West in December of 1399.[1]

1. *Livre des faits,* I, xxxiii, ed. Buchon, p. 607; in much less detail, the *Religieux de Saint-Denys,* XX, iii, ed. Bellaguet, II, 690–692, who speaks of only 100 men left behind with Chateaumorand. Cf. Schlumberger, "Jean de Chateaumorand, un des principaux héros français des arrière-croisades en Orient à la fin du XIVᵉ siècle et à l'aurore du XVᵉ," 304–305; Berger de Xivrey, *Mémoire sur la vie et les ouvrages de l'empereur Manuel Paléologue,*

Meanwhile, there was Bayazid to consider. His role at this point is ambiguous. On one hand, his continued hostility against the city seems undeniable. And yet, if our information is correct, John appears to have been obliged to come to some sort of understanding with Bayazid in order to take up his position in Constantinople. Even before John's assumption of power in the city, there was fear that he had connived with Bayazid to surrender it, once it was in his hands, to the Turks in exchange for the rule of the Peloponnesus.[2] That John would not do such a thing Manuel could only pray. As it happened, John did not. But he was plainly under some constraint to come to terms with his old master and supporter, the Emir. If one source is correct, John was obliged to agree to Bayazid's demands that a Turkish judge be established in the city—perhaps in final fulfillment of a condition that Manuel had not carried out as agreed in 1391—and that Selymbria and, indeed, all the territory outside the city be surrendered to the Turks.[3]

93; Delaville le Roulx, *La France en Orient au XIVᵉ siècle*, I, 379; Walter, *La Ruine de Byzance*, 301. The number of at least the Venetian, and perhaps also the Genoese, vessels on guard at the capital may have varied. In July of 1402 the Venetian Senate referred to having only two of its galleys at Constantinople: see above, p. 198, n. 135.

2. Ducas, ed. Grecu, 85, ed. Bonn, 55; cf. Dölger, "Johannes VII., Kaiser der Rhomäer," 32. It might be pointed out, à propos this suspicion, that the Peloponnesus was no more a Turkish possession at this time than Thessalonica was Byzantine. If the rumor was true, then John VII had a curious talent for inspiring both sides to offer him territory that was not then their own!

3. Ducas, ed. Grecu, 87, ed. Bonn, 56–57, is the only Greek historian to give any information at all on events of John's regime in Constantinople. On the question of the judge (here Ducas does not use the word "kadi"), see above, p. 86, n. 2; cf. also Dölger, "Johannes VII.," 31; and Alexandrescu-Dersca, *La Campagne de Timur en Anatolie (1402)*, 17. But Dölger, *Regesten*, no. 3195, p. 74, as discussed below in n. 7, suggests a pact between John and Bayazid in or about the summer of 1401. Hopf, *Geschichte Griechenlands*, 65, had suggested that Bayazid, under pressure of his distractions with Timur, restored Selymbria to John in 1401; and in this view he was followed by Delaville le Roulx, *La France en Orient*, 386. But Loenertz, "Pour l'histoire du Péloponnèse au XIVᵉ siècle," 144–145, has demolished this claim, which has nonetheless still been accepted by Alexandrescu-Dersca, 18, even though she notes thereafter the failure of the very negotiations which would have effected any such cession (see below, p. 212, and n. 16). Ducas, *ibid.*, maintains that John was crowned *Basileus* upon his assumption of the government of Constantinople for Manuel. Christophilopoulou, Ἐκλογή, ἀναγόρευσις καὶ στέψις τοῦ βυζαντινοῦ αὐτοκράτορος, 202–203, in her reference to this transition, says nothing of such a ceremony,

Bayazid may well have been willing to come to a temporary or quasi settlement with John at this juncture because of other distractions or because he fully expected that he could bend John to his wishes—perhaps even to the point of making him yield the coveted city. On the other hand, Bayazid may simply have taken this opportunity to extort whatever he pleased on the basis of his commanding position. Whatever the circumstances, however, it seems readily plain that the blockade was maintained, to one extent or another.

That the Turkish threat was as grave as ever, regardless of any possible concessions to Bayazid, is clearly indicated by an important Patriarchal document of this time. Written to the Metropolitan of Kiev by the Patriarch Matthaios, it sets forth vividly a complete picture of the situation at the end of 1399:

Most sanctified Metropolitan of Kiev and of all Russia, in the Holy Spirit most beloved brother of Our Moderacy, and fellow minister: grace and peace from God be unto Your Sanctity. Your Sanctity knows that our most mighty and holy Autokrator, the lord Manuel, and Our Moderacy, wrote and dispatched emissaries some time previously to Your Sanctity and to our most noble son, the most glorious great King of all Russia, and the remaining kings, in order that, according as you aided us with what contributions you sent a little time previously—since that proved to be an encouragement for the city and aid for the Christians and for the Great Church—you might thus again send some of your own and some of the joint contributions of other Christians and might aid us, who are under the constraint of the blockade and the struggle with the enemies besetting us.

But now, some considerable time after the departure of those emissaries from here, with support and aid of Him Who puts all at peace, Christ our God, the holy Basileis made peace with each other and united just as father and son. Nature acknowledges itself, and no more is there dissension in them, neither contentiousness nor struggle. And on his part the holy Basileus, the lord Manuel, departed to the regions of France [Φραγγία] for aid and military alliance for the city and the Christians. And in his turn, meanwhile, the holy Basileus, the lord John, his nephew, returned here from Selymbria with the most mighty and holy Despoina, his mother, and all his

and, indeed, in view of John's background (cf. above, p. 75, n. 200), and in view of the city's desperate situation, it would seem superfluous and unlikely. Muralt, *Essai de chronographie byzantine*, pp. 761–762, no. 8, and p. 762, nos. 3 and 4, has made a complete mess (dated 1398) out of the Greek sources for John's establishment in Constantinople.

magnates [ἄρχοντες], and he received the realm from the hands of our most mighty and holy Autokrator, his uncle, and is sovereign and Basileus of the Christians, by grace of God. And he has undertaken the struggle against the unbelievers and attends to all matters concerning the guarding and safety of the city and of the Christians.

Lest ever these matter be heard of in your country otherwise than as they transpired here, it seemed good to us that, both through our trusty agents and through our letter, we inform you of all the things that have happened. We were therefore intending to dispatch a letter bearer with a view merely to confirming the facts, for we have neither other reports nor information besides what we wrote to you through our emissaries who preceded. But, for your greater honor, we chose and dispatched as emissary the most sanctified Archbishop of Bethlehem, a most beloved brother in the Holy Spirit and fellow minister of Our Moderacy, as one well-known in your region and a friend of Your Sanctity, that he himself may collaborate as much as possible in order that our emissaries who were dispatched previously may ascertain if God granted anything and if it has been gathered together for the sake of the Christians; and that he may also be joined with them, and that they may bear it here posthaste, since we are in great need. For this, our enemy and opponent, hearing of the union of the holy Basileis, and that our most mighty and holy Basileus, the lord Manuel, is arming himself from the regions of France for the sake of guarding the city, rages and arouses himself against us.

Accordingly, we have need of a subsidy and of many expenditures for our guarding, even much more now than previously. And, while we indeed hope for many and great things also from those regions, yet, to be sure, we do not wish Your Sanctity as well to be without some share in this noble enterprise, to the end that you may have the prayers of the Holy Fathers. O most beloved brother, if indeed you ever exerted yourself, as a man who loves the Romans, exert yourself now and instruct and recommend counsel to all that they should do according as we suggest and require. And assure them that giving for the sake of guarding the holy city is better than liturgies and alms to the poor and ransoming captives; and that he who is doing this will find a better reward before God than him who has raised up a church and a monastery or than him who has dedicated offerings to them. For, this same holy city is the pride, the bulwark, the sanctifying, and the glory of the Christians everywhere in the inhabited world. How many monasteries could one found or how many captives could one ransom that would be equal to the monasteries of the city or to the inhabitants within it? He is the founder and ransomer of all of these who would be guided by God and would make alms and contribution for the sake of aid for the city and the Christians. And Your Sanctity again will be as an agent, exciting them to it.[4]

The Patriarch takes great pains in this document to make clear that John VII had fully accepted his responsibility to defend Constantinople. Our other available evidence indicates that this assertion was indeed true. However questionable John's previous activities may have been, he seems to have made an honest attempt to do his job as he had promised, in spite of the pressures of Bayazid. This position is reflected in a decision of the Venetian Senate of March 26, 1400. One of their commanders is instructed to stop at Constantinople and to warn John against the "fallacious promises" of the Turk. At the same time, he is to assure John of the support and friendship of Venice in his defense of the city. Report is to be given of some negotiations carried on by Manuel with Genoa and the Hospitalers to have them help guard Constantinople. Meanwhile, John is to be urged to follow strictly his uncle's instructions to preserve the city and the Empire.[5] We

4. Text, Miklosich and Müller, *Acta et diplomata graeca*, II, no. 556, pp. 359–361, fully translated here; the paragraph divisions are my own. Cf. Dölger, "Johannes VII.," 32; Muralt, p. 771, no. 65, gives a brief summary. This document bears no precise date itself, but it was obviously written not long after the departure of Manuel. The manuscript contains two fragmentary marginal notes which are included in the published edition. They may be reconstructed thus:

1

[T]οῦτο ἤργησε
[μ]ὲν μεταφρά-
[-σθ]η δὲ καὶ ἐγρά-
[-φ]ησαν ἄλλα
[ἀν]τὶ τούτων καὶ
[ἐ]στάλησαν ὡς κό-
[-βα?]ν ἀποκρισιάρι-
[-οι] ὁ Βηθλεὲμ
['Ρ]αοὺλ καὶ ὁ Καν-
[-τ]ακουζηνός.

1

This was cancelled, although it was translated, and meanwhile others were written instead of this and there were sent to (Kiev?) as emissaries Raoul of Bethlehem and Cantacuzenus.

2

[Οὕ]τω γὰρ ἔδοξεν
[αὐ]τοῖς καλὸν ἀπὸ
[συ]μφώνου καὶ
[ἐ]γένετο.

2

For thus it seemed good to them in agreement and it was done.

5. Thiriet, *Régestes des délibérations du Sénat de Venise concernant la Romanie*, II, no. 981, pp. 10–11; cf. Dölger, "Johannes VII.," 32; Silber-schmidt, *Die orientalische Problem*, 197; Alexandrescu-Dersca, 17. Appar-

shall see presently one other indication that John was kept in touch with the course of Manuel's diplomatic efforts to obtain aid from the West. But, for the moment, we have one such illustration that belongs specifically to this time. On October 16, 1400, after he had written to Manuel, pledging his cooperation in the projected expedition to be sent to aid Byzantium, King Martin I of Aragon also wrote to John VII himself to inform Manuel's regent of this pledge and to assure him that help would be coming.[6]

It may have been that John's sincerity in his efforts was a disappointment to Bayazid, who had probably hoped that the young Emperor would at least serve as his pliant puppet. At any rate, the Emir seems soon to have hardened his policy and demanded that John surrender the city. According to our source, his message from Adrianople left no doubts as to his designs: "If I have indeed put the Basileus Manuel out of the City, not for your sake have I done this, but for mine. And if, then, you wish to be our friend, withdraw from thence and I will give you a province, whatever one you may wish. But if you do not, with God and his great Prophet as my witness, I will spare no one, but all will I utterly destroy." [7] In spite of their weakness, the Byzantines gave

ently the Venetians themselves were willing to join in such cooperative ventures, for, on February 16, 1402, the Senate decided to open negotiations with the Hospitalers, the Genoese of Chios, and the Duke of the Archipelago, for a naval league against the Turks: Iorga, *Notes et extraits à servir pour l'histoire des croisades XVe siècle*, I, 115; cf. Thiriet, *Régestes*, II, no. 1042, p. 24. In addition, on March 22, 1401, the Senate had ordered moves designed to lead to a formal treaty of peace and assistance between the Byzantine Empire, Venice, and Genoa, for the good of the Christian East: Iorga, *Notes et extraits*, I, 105–106; Thiriet, *Régestes*, II, no. 1007, pp. 15–16.

6. Text, Rubió i Lluch, *Diplomatari de l'Orient Català*, no. 659, pp. 685–686; see above, p. 176.

7. Ducas, ed. Grecu, p. 89, ll. 11–15, ed. Bonn, p. 59, ll. 4–9. It is impossible to say precisely when Bayazid delivered his ultimatum, if it was delivered, and in this fashion; but in the context of other evidence it was probably fairly early in John's regime. Pears, *The Destruction of the Greek Empire*, 137, puts it in 1402, but this is surely too late, especially in view of Bayazid's growing distraction with Timur after the fall of Sivas (August, 1400). But the entire outlook of Bayazid during and after the reconciliation of John VII and Manuel is a puzzle. Is it possible that the Turk actually did not understand its real purpose and the true reason for Manuel's departure until after a while? Dölger, *Regesten*, no. 3195, p. 74, employs the unreliable testimony of the Pseudo-Phrantzes to affirm, if hesistantly, a pact made by John VII with Bayazid "ca. 1401 sommer"; but, in relation to other evidence, this idea seems untenable.

a reply to the Turkish messengers that, if our information is reliable, reflects the highest honor on them: "Withdraw, report to your lord: we are in poverty and there is no great power whereunto we may flee, except to God Who aids the powerless and Who overpowers the powerful. So if you wish anything, do it." [8]

Whether or not Bayazid responded to this reported defiance with any attempts at actual storming of the city is not known. But certainly his pressure must have increased. On April 23, 1401, the Venetian Senate took special pains to have one of its commanders appear before John VII and assure him of Venetian support.[9] But, on August 10, the Senate took notice of the fact that its commander had been prevented from carrying out this order as a result of the operations of a Turkish fleet from Gallipoli. In view of this situation, the Senate took steps to send aid to Constantinople, especially since it appeared by now that Manuel was at last going to receive from the Kings of France and England the aid he had been seeking.[10]

Manuel was indeed still hoping during the summer of 1401 that the promised expedition would be launched, as we have seen. But, as the Emperor's absence lengthened and as the hoped-for aid did not come, the situation in Constantinople grew worse. In spite of the fact that Bayazid was obliged to turn his attention after a while to the growing threat posed by the aggressions of Timur, the pressure on the city grew increasingly harsh. Famine and despair gripped it. Many of its citizens were pushed to the extreme of slipping out of the city by night by lowering themselves over the walls and surrendering to the Turks.[11]

8. Ducas, ed. Grecu, p. 89, ll. 17–20, ed. Bonn, p. 59, ll. 11–15; cf. Pears, 138. It is interesting, if perhaps not necessarily significant, that Ducas gives this response not as that of John VII himself, to whom the ultimatum had specifically been directed, but as that of the Greeks in general, or their leaders.

9. Iorga, *Notes et extraits,* I, 109–110; Thiriet, *Régestes,* II, no. 1015, p. 18.

10. Thiriet, *Régestes,* II, no. 1023, pp. 19–20.

11. *Livre des faits,* I, xxxiv, p. 607; cf. Gibbons, *The Rise of the Ottoman Empire,* 343; Alexandrescu-Dersca, 16–17. Ducas, ed. Grecu, p. 91, ll. 23–28, ed. Bonn, p. 61, ll. 11–19, inserts into the midst of his account of Bayazid's reaction to Timur's invasion a passage which would seem more relevant simply to the general picture of the sufferings within Constantinople: "And with the Basileus the poor Citizens, raising their hands to God, were beseeching with many tears, saying, 'O God and Lord of compassion, pity us, Thy helpless servants, and grant to this threat against us and to this, Thy house, and the holy things therein, Thy solicitude, care, and consideration; so that,

Chateaumorand's small garrison did what it could to ease the situation by keeping guard on the defenses and even by sallying forth beyond the walls for some small raiding and plundering.[12] But such sorties were of little real value in the face of the total threat, and even Chateaumorand's force itself was not entirely free from privation.[13]

In the circumstances, it is not surprising that spirits wavered and suspicions flourished. There was talk of secret bargains with the Turks.[14] The Patriarch Matthaios himself was accused of clandestine negotiations with the enemy to preserve his position, if not to betray the city as well. In answer to such allegations and in view of current conditions, the Patriarch had drawn up for him a special exhortation which is of great interest. While it undoubtedly leans heavily on the familiar theme of tribulation as punishment for sins, it nevertheless suggests the degree to which popular morale (if not also morals) had deteriorated under the grinding hardship and disruption of the siege.

having become free of this tyrant, we may glorify Thee, the Father and Son and Holy Spirit, Who is One God through the ages, Amen.'" The Byzantines had not forgotten that time after time, especially in recent years, their city had been spared capture—by divine intervention, as they confidently presumed.

12. *Livre des faits*, I, xxxiv, p. 607; cf. Schlumberger, "Chateaumorand," 305–312; Delaville le Roulx, *La France en Orient*, 385–386. During his stay in Constantinople, Chateaumorand seems to have been delegated some sort of responsibility in the government of Pera. For we have a document of May 23, 1402, in which Chateaumorand is included among others nominated by Boucicaut—who was by then the French Governor of Genoa—as a syndic of the colony: Iorga, *Notes et extraits*, I, 65–66.

13. Schlumberger, "Chateaumorand," 307–308, who cites some notarial documents. Cf. Zakythinos, *Crise monétaire*, 110.

14. Note in this connection the report of the Anonymous Narrative (Διήγησις) on the supposedly miraculous delivery of the city, ed. P. Gautier, "Un Récit inédit," *Rev. des ét. byz.*, 23 (1965), p. 108, l. 34 to p. 110, l. 10, that "the inhabitants of Constantinople," in the hopes of obtaining better terms from Bayazid now that Timur was menacing him, "sent to him as an embassy some of their distinguished men" (πέμπουσιν αὐτῷ πρεσβείαν ἄνδρας τῶν παρὰ σφίσιν ἐνδόξων). Since the author of this hyperbolic text never mentions John VII and is deliberately vague on points of fact, it is difficult to conclude from his wording if he refers to an official "embassy" sent by the Byzantine government or to an informal delegation sent by private individuals. Thus, it is possible that this reference may reflect something of the embassy of late summer 1401, discussed below, or another similar diplomatic move. On the other hand, this text's emphasis on the abject helplessness of the Byzantines and their lack of any bargaining position might discount that possibility and suggest rather an earlier plea, perhaps of the sort, clandestine or otherwise, that the Patriarch mentions in the document to be considered next.

All of the citizens, magnates, consecrated men—both celibate priests (ἱερομονάχοι) and monks—and the entire Christ-named people of the Lord, children in the Lord of Our Moderacy: grace be unto you all, and peace. I assume it is well known to you all that, through our sins and because we have all turned attentively to wicked ways, we have enkindled against us the wrath of God to such a degree that he has seized our flesh and marrow and bones, and has brought such affliction upon us, and has brought on the disfigurement and desolation of all of this great city. For lo, for six years we are besieged by famine, and by wars without break, and by captivity of friends and kinsmen; by slaughter, also, and by daily dangers; and simply by everything in which God's scimitar is flashed against the sinful and against those who have, by their monstrous deeds, provoked His All-Holy Name.

It is therefore necessary to review the cause of so much evil, through which the former beauties of this great city—once a paradise of luxury—have now become as a plain of destruction; and to find how a multitude of sins forced God's infinite love of mankind and great goodness toward displeasure and anger; and thus to repent and to lament in the presence of the Lord Who made us, and by repentance and confession to correct our former sinnings, and thus to turn aside from us so much displeasure of God against us.

We are shot through with these same sins and even greater ones, since we are wrongdoers and liars and perjurers, and unblushing practitioners of every kind of wickedness, attackers of our brothers in their misfortunes, exasperating their troubles, quick to set upon their portion and to trample down and to devour the poor, lovers of quarreling, to such an extent as to excel each other in wickedness. He who does misdeeds still does misdeeds; he who commits wrongs still commits wrongs; he who utters blasphemies still utters blasphemies. Lusts, adulteries, perjuries, rapes, robberies, murders—they are all perpetuated by us carelessly each day. There is no fear of God; there is no amendment in us up to now, nor one trace of repentance. And a sign of these ways is the increase of God's wrath and scourge.

For if we were repentant, as is proper, and if we effected correction of our trespasses with abstinence and confession and repentance of our wicked ways, God would certainly change his purpose and avert His anger from us, since He is a lover of mankind and is by His nature well disposed to this. For He says through the Prophet: "Thou shalt cry, and ye shall eat the good of the land: but if ye refuse and rebel, ye shall be devoured with the sword: for the mouth of the Lord hath spoken it." [Isaiah, i, 19–20]

Since, therefore, not only a sword devours us, but also a dread siege and a most harsh famine, and wars and sinking and inroads of other races, and countless dreadful things, it is certain that we wish not the will of God, neither do we hearken to the Lord. And, for this reason, not only are we deprived of "the good of the land," but we also suffer all these things because of our sins. Accordingly, many of the things that are perpetuated by us each day are hateful to God and are destructive deeds, because of which the wrath of God comes to the sons of disobedience. But, above all, and rather as if both the end and the beginning of all things, stand our envy against each other, and our malice also, and our slander, and our loss and lack and need of love. That envy and need of love are, as it were, wicked descendants of all the evils, our Lord and God makes clear, saying, "And because iniquity shall abound, the love of the many shall wax cold." [Matthew, xxiv, 12] And therefore, since love now does not dwell anywhere among us, it is certain that iniquity abounds in us.

And that love is not wholly true and firm among us I know you also will agree. But, nevertheless, I will instill in you a clear indication drawn from my own case. This is presently the fourth year since —by which judgments God knows—I was raised to this Ecumenical Throne and was entrusted by God with the care of your souls. Therefore, with His grace and with the prayers of our Sacred Fathers, I was zealous to aggrieve or to do evil to or to abuse no one in any way, as far as it was in my power. But, nevertheless, it has not escaped the notice of most of you how much I have been falsely accused and slandered. But I was bearing it all bravely, being assured that I was not only being done no injury by these things, but that I was even being done the greatest benefits. For, "Blessed are ye," says Christ, "when men shall say all manner of evil speaking against you falsely for my sake." [Matthew, v, 11]

Pondering this in my heart, accordingly, I prayed from my soul— and I still pray—for those who accuse me falsely. But now, since some go on to the chief question itself, that of my faith, and denounce my action, it would cause at once ruin to the Church of God, as well as harm to me, if I should pass over this situation in silence. Thus, since by my silence I would appear to be agreeing with it, I judged it to be necessary to speak out on it and to make clear to all the details of the false accusation.

The claim is that I, having sent a certain person to the Emir ['Αμιρᾶς], arranged for myself to have security from him on my own account if the great city itself should indeed ever be taken. Which act I judge as nothing other than open betrayal of Christ Himself.

For, [there is the admonition of] the blessed Paul, who says, "Now ye are the body of Christ, and members in particular" [Corinthians, xii, 27], and he says this to a small number of the faithful. If this is so, therefore, he who gives over to the unbelievers this great city, in which are bound up the confidence and the hopes of all Christians, not only those still free, but those also who by God's concession have been drawn down into slavery; and which city is a veritable head and source and root of the faith of us Christians—he, then, who wishes to betray this city is very clearly all but zealous to betray Christ Himself. And he betrays it most clearly who at once furnishes encouragement to the unbelievers that they will seize it by his seeking his own safety from them, and who at the same time furnishes utter despair to his fellow citizens. And thus, I clearly hold such conduct as betrayal of the city; so that, a short while ago, I pronounced once, twice, and thrice a burden of fearful excommunication against the envoys who were sent, should they ever make such demands which could be absolutely ruinous to the city.

How much harm, then, is going to be produced hereafter when such talk is sown in the souls of those who are hearkening that they have as their own bishop and leader a traitor and not a shepherd? And how much harm for me, were I admitting such a charge by my silence?

I therefore speak, and I utter a curse on myself that, if I have indeed ever made any such an attempt, or if my thinking ever took this form, or if, indeed, I dispatched anyone to the Emir on account of these things, or if I entrusted someone already there with arranging a security from the unbeliever for me, I may be banished from the communion of Christ in the coming age; which would be to me the most grievous of all distressing penalties.

But if certain men have unjustly and slanderously fabricated these charges against me—either for my injury or for ruin of the Church of Christ—Our Moderacy pronounces against them the most grievous, horrible, continuous, and unpardonable excommunication from the Holy and Life-Giving and indivisible Trinity, which neither a priest nor a bishop, neither a confessor nor a patriarch, will have license to pardon, unless they, coming before Our Moderacy, whom they falsely accused, confess this in full, adding also for what reason they contrived such things.

And I expect all of you, most beloved children in the Lord, to repent and to withdraw from these wicked deeds and pursuits, and to cleanse out with confession and tears the uncleanness that has been entering into our souls, and thus, to summon our mankind-loving God to mercy. Indeed, come hither all, O brothers: let us fall down and let us weep in the presence of the Lord Who made us. Let us establish a common mourning, every age and nature, every class and every occupation. Let us gain our own souls with compassions and mercies for beggars. With mercy let us obtain mercy. Let us remove from us the just wrath of God. Let us wish to see Him, even as He has become angry, so also as he has become reconciled. Let us purify ourselves from all pollution of flesh and spirit. Let us be merciful to ourselves. Let us imitate the great goodness of God, Who "maketh his sun to rise on the evil and on the good, and sendeth rain alike to all, the just and the unjust." [Matthew, v, 45] Let us become worthy, compassionate, merciful, because our Father is merciful to the ungrateful and wicked. Let us be humble in the presence of the Lord; for "the sacrifices of God are a broken spirit: a broken and contrite heart, O God, thou wilt not despise." [Psalm li, 17] Let us approach His presence with confession. Thus may we show proof of both the correction and the care for our souls.[15]

As serious as would be any possible accusations against the Patriarch, even more serious would be any suspicions against John VII. In the long run, as we shall see, any such suspicions would have been correct, to a degree.

The preceding document speaks of no less than three embassies that were sent to Bayazid. Plainly, some sort of contact was maintained with the Emir, though for what purposes is not fully clear. We do have specific evidence of one particular embassy, although it was probably later than any to which the Patriarch referred. Apparently there was hope for a while that, in the face of Timur's onslaughts, Bayazid might be constrained to make

15. Text, Miklosich and Müller, II, no. 626, pp. 463–467, fully translated here; the division into paragraphs is entirely my own. Cf. Schlumberger, "Chateaumorand," 308–309; Muralt, p. 777, no. 52. See also Hunger, "Das Testament des Patriarchen Matthaios I. (1397–1410)," *Byz. Zeitschr.*, 51 (1958), 291. The document bears no specific date, but its reference to the year as being the fourth of the incumbency of Matthaios (who ascended the Patriarchal throne in November of 1397) enables us to place the document with reasonable certainty in the year 1401. This estimate, of course, renders valuable also the reference to the duration of the siege up to that time as having been six years: see Appendix X below. The style of the text is much more self-consciously literary and elegant than is customary with these documents. This quality is perhaps explained by the superscription of the document, indicating that it was drafted for the Patriarch by the *Protekdikos* (Chief Justice) Eugenikos. (This individual is also mentioned in another Patriarchal document: Miklosich and Müller, II, no. 678, pp. 556–558.) For another interesting and even more extreme example of this kind of homiletic "for our sins" self-reproaching, see L. Oeconomos, "L'état intellectuel et moral des Byzantins vers le milieu du XIVe siècle d'après une page de Joseph Bryennios," *Mélanges Ch. Diehl*, I (Paris, 1930), 225–233.

concessions. On September 10, 1401, the Venetian Senate heard reports from a Genoese, newly arrived from Romania, that John, in concert with the Genoese of Pera and the Venetians of Constantinople, had sent an embassy to the Turks. On August 6, the report went, the Archbishop of Gothia (John Holobolos) and a member of the Melissenos ("Molissinus") family representing Byzantium, one Quilico dei Taddei representing the Genoese, and Francesco Foscarini, the *Bailo* of Constantinople, representing the Venetians there, had set forth from the city for Brusa, where they had discussed, if not negotiated, peace with the Turks. The terms that they proposed included the offer of an annual amount of 5,000 *hyperpyra* from Genoa, "not as tribute but as a gift"; while the Byzantines, on the other hand, were supposed to receive back "all the maritime castles and places that they were holding before the war." According to the informant, who had left Constantinople on August 24, these terms then had yet to be ratified by Bayazid, who, it was said, was in difficult circumstances.[16] But we have no evidence of any useful or practical results actually produced by such supposed negotiations.

Indeed, quite the contrary, for we have every indication that Bayazid did not relax his grip on the city. This may be assumed

16. Dölger, *Regesten*, nos. 3196–3197, p. 74; text, Iorga, *Notes et extraits*, I, 112–113; this important document is overlooked by Thiriet. See Alexandrescu-Dersca, 18–19, who goes on to suppose (p. 19, and n. 1) that this effort was abandoned by the Byzantines because of the advice of ambassadors from Timur. (The visit to Constantinople of these ambassadors is reported in this same Venetian document: see below, Appendix XVIII.) Cf. the most recent comments by the skeptical P. Wirth, "Zum Geschichtsbild Kaiser Johannes' VII. Palaiologos," 598–599, and 600.

The text makes the curious observation that the allied ambassadors left Constantinople "pro eundo ad *matrem Zalapi,* que erat in Burssa, pro tractando pacem." Alexandrescu-Dersca assumes that this person was the mother of Bayazid. But the Emir himself is rather referred to elsewhere in this text, and repeatedly, as "Basaithum." It seems more likely that "*Zalapi*"—obviously a corruption of the Turkish word *çelebi*, "prince"—refers to someone else. As we shall see later (below, n. 39), the Venetians had already opened negotiations with a Turkish prince whom they called "*Zalapi*." Subsequently, this name was to be used regularly for Suleyman, Bayazid's son, who seems then to have been our "*Zalapi*" in question here. Assuming a consistent use of this name by the Venetians, therefore, the "*matrem Zalapi*" in this text might be Bayazid's *wife*. But even this distinction hardly helps much, for it still does not explain why such negotiations would have been left to a mere woman, especially by Bayazid.

certainly from a plea by John VII himself. By the spring of 1402, Manuel, who had by now begun to realize the emptiness of the promises of aid he had received, had concluded that at least Henry IV of England would give no real help at that time. Manuel, therefore, had John informed of this fact. We know he did so because we have a letter sent by John to Henry, begging the latter for at least some aid. This letter deserves to be quoted in full, for it illustrates a number of important points: first, even allowing for some exaggeration to strengthen the plea, that Constantinople was at the time of this writing (June 1, 1402) in a position as threatened as ever, if not more so; second, that Manuel was by this time quite aware of the realities of his prospects for aid, at least in this one specific instance; third, that John kept, or was kept, in apparently regular contact with his uncle's activity in the West; and, finally, that John himself was laboring in all earnestness to do what he could to save Constantinople. The letter reads as follows:

> To the Most Serene Prince and most powerful Lord, Henry, by God's grace, King of England, our exceedingly most dear cousin, John, in Christ our God faithful Emperor and Ruler of the Romans, Palaeologus: health in Him through Whom kings reign.

In the great perils presently facing us we are in need of essential aids. And for that reason, we ask and seek of your renowned royal Majesty, as far as he shall deem us worthy, in the name of the Savior Jesus Christ and on account of the fame that your royal Excellency has throughout the whole world, to contribute to the aid and support of this our city of Constantinople, which, indeed, for a long space of time, and in poverty from the wars it has been and still is presently waging with the infidel Turks, persecutors of the Christian name, and at last diminished in men and power and in every faculty whatsoever, lies prostrate, not strong enough to strike at enemies any longer; on the contrary, neither able to defend itself on its own. It is in danger of submitting to the yoke of these infidel Saracens, unless by your power and that of the other Christian Kings and Princes, with the intervention of Divine Grace, it is raised up from the danger of disaster.

And if, by chance, your royal Highness is not at present able to bestow as much support and aid as he desires—as my most serene and excellent Lord and Father, the Lord Emperor, writes to us—

at least let your royal clemency deem it good to expend support and succor and to contribute some men-at-arms and money, in such portion that the said city may be able to be preserved from the aforesaid dangers and incursions of enemies, until the large and more fully appointed provision is made by your Majesty together with the other Christian Kings and Princes. Because, if—may it be avoided!—the said city would be let slip from the hands of the Christians, which city may be called the House of God, it would lead to damage and disgrace of the whole faith of the Christians, and it is to be feared that the name of Jesus Christ would be abolished and lost from these regions of the East.

Moreover, renowned King, because warm praise is due the upright, we neither ought nor are able to pass over in silence those who are distinguished by deeds of bravery and who cease not daily to perform praiseworthy acts; especially when some of your excellent men, sojourning in the defense of this city, are deservedly to be extolled for their deeds with worthy praises. For this reason, since their good deeds have been interposed, we pay tribute to you by rendering most worthy gestures of thanks, since they contributed expert and intrepid attention to full defense of this city from enemies, and to our advantage and honor, striving as the best of men, while nothing was omitted which has any bearing upon the good and secure state of us and of our said city and of its citizens. Truly, it is nothing new of most illustrious England to produce such fruit.

May your renowned royal Highness prosper and increase your designs in what you wish, happily, for a very long time.

Given in the Constantinopolitan city, in the year from the Nativity of the Lord the One Thousandth Four Hundredth second, on the first day of June.[17]

John had been given a task of the utmost difficulty, and he had discharged it fairly. As the months of 1402 drew on, it probably seemed as if the task was really hopeless. In spite of his distractions with Timur, Bayazid had by no means loosened his hold on Constantinople. Oppressed in all ways, the city could not endure much more on its own. The hoped-for foreign aid had not materialized, and Manuel's prospects as he bided his time in Paris could hardly have appeared bright at this juncture. In these circumstances it is perhaps not fitting to judge John very harshly

17. Dölger, *Regesten*, no. 3198, p. 74. The full text and source of this document, with a discussion of its contents, may be found in Appendix XVII below.

for concluding that he had no choice but to come to terms with Bayazid at last.

There can be no doubt that John VII made an agreement to surrender Constantinople to the Emir when the latter had ended his conflict with the invading Timur.[18] And, indeed, a delegation of Byzantine nobles is reported to have been on its way to the Emir in Asia, bearing the keys to the city.[19] The surrender was never to be effected, however, thanks to one of the most dramatic strokes of fate in late Byzantine history.

Bayazid had seemed to be at the peak of his dazzling career. It appeared to be only a matter of time before he achieved the great triumph of winning the Queen of Cities itself, thereby fulfilling the Turkish destiny as heir of the Byzantine Empire. But

18. Clavijo, ed. López Estrada, 28 (cf. ed. Sreznevskii, 40; trans. Le Strange, 52): "The old emperor [Manuel] being in França, the young emperor [John] had an agreement when Morat [i.e., Bayazid] and Tamurbeque wished to come together in their battle, that if the Turk conquered Tamurbeque, to surrender to the Turk the city of Constantinople, and to become his tributary." Since Clavijo's sources of information on John VII were not only fairly reliable but also friendly, it seems likely that such a statement, in a sense somewhat unfavorable to John, is indeed correct, especially since we have apparent confirmation of it (see next note). Dölger, *Regesten*, has no entry on this point. Alexandrescu-Dersca, whose presentation of events of this period seems very confused chronologically, claims (p. 17) to find confirmation for this agreement by John VII in the Patriarchal letter to the Metropolitan of Kiev, which is translated above, pp. 202–204. But that document was almost surely written at the beginning of John's regency, whereas the promise to Bayazid was made in all likelihood much later, closer to the showdown between the Turk and the Tartar at Ancyra. More to the point, moreover, the text itself contains nothing to support her claim, as the reader may see. The important question, however, is the meaning of the apparently focal element in Clavijo's statement of the impending battle. Is Clavijo exaggerating by seeming to make Bayazid's victory in the battle a condition of the surrender? In view of the other statements by Clavijo and other evidence, is it possible that John was engaged in an effort to play Bayazid and Timur one against another? Or, on the other hand, was the implication simply that Bayazid could attend to the city once he was freed of the preoccupation of dealing with Timur? The entire question of John's stance is further complicated by the problem of his relations with Timur. For further discussion of these matters, see Appendix XVIII below.

19. *Chron. Vat. gr. 162*, no. 18, p. 210, ll. 82–84: "And those in the City being famished, the people fled. And certain of the leaders took the keys of the City and carried them into Kotyaïos to the Sultan, to surrender the City." This obviously independent source thus gives important confirmation of the essence of Clavijo's statement (see preceding note) on John's agreement with Bayazid. Indeed, it might perhaps indicate that the Byzantines fully expected Bayazid to win his clash with Timur. Dölger takes no notice of this source statement in his *Regesten*.

it was at just this point that the ruthless Emir met his match in the even more ruthless lord of Samarkand. The friction of respective frontier interests, aggravated by haughty exchanges between two arrogant personalities, had impelled the mighty Timur-i-lenk, or Tamerlane, to hurl himself upon the startled Osmanlis. After the brutal seizure of Sivas (Sebasteia) in August of 1400, the Tartar had diverted his attention to older centers of Islamic power and glory: Baghdad, Damascus, and Egypt. But the ultimate clash with Bayazid was unavoidable. The reckless Emir wavered between activity and debauchery and finally allowed himself to be maneuvered into disaster. On July 28, 1402, near Ancyra, the ancient Angora, the Turkish army was utterly defeated and Bayazid himself was captured.[20]

At one stroke the entire situation of Byzantium was altered. "And the leaders who had taken the keys [of the city, to give

20. The Greek historians all give accounts of this remarkable sequence of events. The most extended is Chalcocondyles, ed. Darkó, I, 95–147, ed. Bonn, 102–158, followed by the *Chron. Barb. 111*, 37–39, and, in confused brevity, the Pseudo-Phrantzes, ed. Papadopoulos, 72–73 and 87–89, ed. Bonn, 67–68 and 83–85. Also Ducas, ed. Grecu, 87–89, 89–91, 91–99, ed. Bonn, 57–59, 59–61, 61–67. For an Eastern point of view, see the account by the Arab, Ahmed ibn Muhammad, called Ahmed ibn Arabshah, *Timur the Great Amir*, trans. J. H. Sanders (London, 1936), 170 ff.; cf. also the account by Clavijo, ed. López Estrada, 89–94, ed. Sreznevskii, 139–147, trans. Le Strange, 129–136. The date of the battle is also given by a number of the short chronicles, correctly by the *Chron. brev. thess.*, no. 10, p. 175 (adding that the day was a Friday, which it was), and the Βρ. χρ. No. 6, p. 9, ll. 3–4; but incorrectly by No. 15, p. 32, ll. 45–49, and by the *Chron. Vat. gr. 162*, no. 18, p. 210, ll. 84–88. The most recent study of Timur, and the only full-length treatment in English of his entire career, is now H. Hookham's *Tamburlaine the Conqueror* (London, 1962). This author gives a compact and eminently readable account of Timur's involvement with Bayazid in pp. 212–221, though it is not without a few questionable statements regarding Manuel; for her discussion of the date of the Battle of Ancyra, see p. 251. For extended discussions of the conflict, campaign, and battle, see Alexandrescu-Dersca, 30–79 (also 116–119, for a full investigation of the sources on the dating of the battle); and G. Roloff, "Die Schlacht bei Angora (1402)," *Historische Zeitschrift*, 161 (1940), 244–262. In general, see also R. Grousset, *L'Empire des steppes: Attila, Gengis-khan, Tamerlan* (Paris, 1939), 528–533; Hammer, *Geschichte des osmanischen Reiches*, I, 257–316, trans. Hellert, II, 1–95; Iorga, *Geschichte des osmanischen Reiches*, I, 305–322; and, more briefly, Gibbons, 243–254; Pears, 138–144; Delaville le Roulx, *La France en Orient*, 391–394; Muralt, p. 781, no. 26. See now, also, the most recent comments of E. Werner, *Die Geburt einer Grossmacht—Die Osmanen (1300–1481). Ein Beitrag zur Genesis des türkischen Feudalismus* (*Forschungen zur mittelalterlichen Geschichte*, 13, Berlin, 1966), 170–179.

them to Bayazid] turned back rejoicing," we are told.[21] But with joy also came shock. The clash between Turk and Tartar had been expected to be great and important.[22] And certainly the Byzantines had every reason to hope for the defeat of Bayazid, if not to work for it as well. Indeed, there is strong evidence that John had also been involved in some kind of understanding with Timur.[23] But it must have seemed incredible, nonetheless, that the dreadful Bayazid—who had been surnamed *Yildirim*, "Lightning," for his quick and decisive blows in the past—had become a captive and, soon after, a harmless corpse. The event threw the entire Levant into confusion. As ever, the Christians unfortunately could display no consistent policy. The Venetians, interested in Gallipoli, seem to have taken seriously the idea of blocking the Straits to cut off the Turkish passage.[24] But such an

21. *Chron. Vat. gr. 162*, no. 19, p. 210, l. 90.

22. Aside from the realities involved, it is interesting to note two Greek sources which report, in the best superstitious fashion, great portents that foreshadowed the battle: Ducas, ed. Grecu, 93–95, ed. Bonn, 63–64 (cf. Marino Sanuto, *Vite di duchi di Venezia*, ed. Muratori, *Rer. Ital. Script.*, 22: 791); and a curious eyewitness testimonial by a monk named Dionysos appended to the otherwise essentially Thessalonian fourteenth-century *Chron. brev. thess.*, no. 10, p. 175.

23. For a discussion of Byzantine relations with Timur, see Appendix XVIII below.

24. Venice was anxiously concerned over the effect of the events at Ancyra. Even before the battle, on May 8, 1402, the Venetian Senate had considered proposals to send a squadron to protect Venetian holdings, to take advantage of the situation while Timur engaged Bayazid, and to bring encouragement to Constantinople; but these proposals were rejected after two considerations: Thiriet, *Régestes*, II, no. 1056, p. 27. Then, on September 22, having heard the news of Ancyra, the Senate discussed sending its fleet to the Straits, and decided to investigate the possibility of buying the much-coveted Gallipoli: Thiriet, no. 1070, p. 30. On the next day, however, the Senate revoked this decision and agreed to wait and see how the situation would develop: Iorga, *Notes et extraits*, I, 122; Thiriet, no. 1071, p. 31. On October 30, 1402, the Senate instructed its commander in Crete, Tommaso Mocenigo, to investigate seriously the possibility of seizing Gallipoli, "pro bono christianitatis": Iorga, 124; Thiriet, no. 1078, p. 32. Apparently this project did not advance very far. And the Venetians were ready enough to come to peace terms with Timur, for, on October 17, 1402, the Senate issued orders to open negotiations with Tartar agents in Ephesus: Thiriet, no. 1076, p. 31. More to the point is a letter by Giovanni Cornaro, a Venetian commander, written from Constantinople on September 4, 1402 (text in Sanuto, 474–475, reproduced by Alexandrescu-Dersca, 125–128). He speaks of Venetian movements, upon the news of the Turkish defeat, to close the Straits: cf. Alexandrescu-Dersca, 83. But this letter already indicates the collapse of such efforts at that time.

idea was in vain. Once the fleeing Turkish forces crowded to the crossing, the Genoese, joined ultimately by the Greeks and the Venetians themselves, aided in ferrying the shattered army across the Straits.[25]

Perhaps a partial explanation for the lack of any coordinated policy among the Christians at this point was a fear on their part that the terrible Timur, after his astonishing victory, might then contemplate hostilities against Europe—a fear heightened by Timur's brutal wresting of Smyrna from the Hospitalers in December of 1402. But actually the whirlwind was to depart even more quickly than it had appeared. In early 1403, Timur began his homeward march, on which the once mighty Bayazid was to die, a humiliated captive. Timur reached Samarkand that spring, and there he was to die himself two years later.[26]

In the meantime, John VII was left in an awkward and exposed position. The sweeping change of outlook brought by the prostration of Bayazid was, as John himself must have understood plainly, more than he could cope with on his own. His experience, his strength, and his authority were inadequate to the task now facing whoever must guide the Empire through the new crisis. There could be no doubt that the situation required Manuel's presence once more. Presumably in agreement with the allies, Chateaumorand was dispatched to France to give a personal report of the state of affairs and, doubtless, also to speed Manuel

25. Sanuto, 791, and, at greater length, 796, where an eyewitness account is given. According to this account, the Venetians were at first ready to cooperate in barring the passage. Cf. Gibbons, 261; Alexandrescu-Dersca, 83–84; Delaville le Roulx, *La France en Orient*, p. 390 and n. 2. The Byzantines themselves may have intended originally to fulfill a promise to Timur to block the Straits, for the *Chron. Barb. 111*, 40, speaks of "Roman" ships on guard there. According to Clavijo, ed. López Estrada, 94, ed. Sreznevskii, 147, trans. Le Strange, 136, after the Genoese and Greeks had aided the Turks to cross to Europe on their ships, in violation of an agreement by them with him, Timur regarded the Greeks as treacherous and hostile, and thereafter mistreated Christians in general out of anger for this; cf. Gibbons, 261. But apparently there was at least some abuse of this job of transport, for there was some pillaging and even enslaving of some of the Turkish refugees, at least by the Genoese, if not by others, as is reflected in a Genoese document published by Iorga, *Notes et extraits*, I, 74–75, and even more in the account of Ibn Arabshah, 185–186.

26. Chalcocondyles, ed. Darkó, I, 147–158, ed. Bonn, 158–168; Ducas, ed. Grecu, 99–111, ed. Bonn, 68–78. Cf. Alexandrescu-Dersca, 85 ff.; Hammer, I, 316–338, trans. Hellert, 96–124; Gibbons, 257–260; Pears, 146–147; Delaville le Roulx, *La France en Orient*, 395.

homeward. For the time being, John would manage as best he could amid the treacherous currents. With the help of at least one illness—of either the genuine or the diplomatic variety—he tried to stall for time.[27]

Chateaumorand probably left early in August, and after a swift journey he reached Paris some time during the following month.[28] Reports and rumors of the momentous events had already reached Manuel and the French,[29] but the valiant soldier was able to give a more full and official report. There was no

27. In the letter cited above in n. 24, Giovanni Cornaro relates (Sanuto, 795C; Alexandrescu-Dersca, 127) that in early September the Emperor was confined to his bed and was paying no attention to affairs of state. Out of this, Berger de Xivrey, 121–122, had developed the theory that John, to gain time, had pretended that Manuel had returned but was indisposed. But the Emperor referred to was incontestably John, not Manuel; Berger de Xivrey's groundless elaboration is rightly discarded by Alexandrescu-Dersca, p. 127, n. 7. Not that some other writers are any less confused about Manuel's presence in Constantinople at this time. Thanks to such source confusions as Chalcocondyles' apparent statement (ed. Darkó, I, 90, ed. Bonn, 96–97) that Manuel returned home before the Battle of Ancyra, and to the misinterpretations of modern writers, a number of historians have been regrettably misled. Pears, 112, seems to accept this incorrect placement of Manuel's return as before Ancyra; Runciman, *The Fall of Constantinople, 1453*, 13, is the most recent perpetuator of the error; while Stacton, *The World on the Last Day*, 116 (="Dereksen," 122), is ambiguous on this point. Muralt, p. 780, no. 23, p. 781, no. 1, and p. 782, no. 5, followed by Gibbons, 259–260, avoid this specific mistake, but they are quite wrong in affording Manuel a speedy enough return to enable the Emperor to be on hand for Timur's orders and alarums.

28. The exact dates of Chateaumorand's journey are not known. Schlumberger, "Chateaumorand," 312, logically suggests August as the month of departure; and, in all likelihood, it was not very long after the battle. Chateaumorand's absence from Constantinople is reflected in a document of Pera of October 28, 1402: Iorga, *Notes et extraits*, I, 66. Not that this reference tells us much, for actually Chateaumorand had long been in France by that time. Delaville le Roulx, *La France en Orient*, cites (I, p. 396, n. 1) and then publishes (II, pp. 76–77; also published by Schlumberger, "Chateaumorand," 314) parts of an inventory of the Duc de Berry listing relics from Constantinople given him by Chateaumorand in September of 1402. Hence we can presume his arrival in that month. Cf. Vasiliev, "Putešestvie vizantiiskago imperatora Manuila Palaeologa po zapadnoi Evrope (1399–1403)," 286 (66). We are not told whether or not the soldiers whom Boucicaut left in Constantinople returned with Chateaumorand, but it is likely, especially in view of his rapid journey, that they remained behind until later: see below, n. 69.

29. Vasiliev, "Putešestvie Manuila," 286–287 (66–67); cf. Berger de Xivrey, 112–113; Schlumberger, "Un Empereur de Byzance à Paris et Londres," 132–133 (42–43).

doubt as to what must be done now. On October 9, 1402, the Venetian Senate had sent off a letter to give Manuel its confirmation of the news of Bayazid's defeat and to urge that Manuel return to his own realm as soon as possible.[30] By this time Manuel hardly needed such urging. The great news had removed all remaining doubt about ending his fruitless sojourn in the West and had made clear that his presence was now required at home in view of the change of circumstances that had come to pass. But, at the same time, it should be made clear that, contrary to frequent modern assumptions, Manuel did not rush home. As a matter of fact, after he had heard the news of Ancyra, a good ten or eleven months passed before the Emperor actually set foot in Constantinople.

Plainly, Manuel's return was as much a part of his diplomatic activities as the rest of his journey. First, there were affairs to settle in France. Even now, of course, no real aid was to be given, but the Emperor was showered with parting gifts and demonstrations of honor. Chateaumorand was wisely designated to command the 200 men provided to escort Manuel. Only on November 21, 1402, did the Emperor and his entourage leave Paris for the first leg of the long journey home.[31] Ambassadors to announce Manuel's departure from Paris were sent ahead to at least Venice, where the Senate gave its responses to the inquiries of Manuel's envoy on December 29, 1402. The *Sapientes* stated that they had no news from Romania, and they pledged the Emperor a cordial welcome to Venice, but they urged that he hasten home quickly.[32]

The route that Manuel followed out of France is no better

30. Iorga, *Notes et extraits*, I, 122; Thiriet, *Régestes*, II, no. 107, p. 31; cf. Vasiliev, "Putešestvie Manuila," 286 (66); Mompherratos, Διπλωματικαὶ ἐνέργειαι Μανουὴλ Β΄ τοῦ Παλαιολόγου ἐν Εὐρώπῃ καὶ 'Ασίᾳ, 42; Delaville le Roulx, *La France en Orient*, p. 396, n. 1.

31. *Religieux de Saint-Denys*, XXIII, x, ed. Bellaguet, Vol. III (Paris, 1841), p. 50. Cf. Vasiliev, "Putešestvie Manuila," 228 (68); Berger de Xivrey, 114; Schlumberger, "Un Empereur," 133–134 (43–44); Jugie, "Le Voyage de l'empereur Manuel Paléologue en occident," 331; Mompherratos, Διπλ. ἐν., 42; and (wrongly placing the departure in early summer of 1402), Muralt, p. 780, no. 23. Schlumberger, "Chateaumorand," 313–316, suggests that the French knight may have entertained Manuel as his guest at his chateau. See also the end of Appendix XIX.

32. Dölger, *Regesten*, no. 3292, p. 89; Iorga, *Notes et extraits*, I, 126; Thiriet, *Régestes*, II, no. 1088, p. 34; cf. Vasiliev, "Putešestvie Manuila," 289 (69).

known than the one he took into that country.[33] The first stop of which we know definitely was at Genoa. Either before or upon Manuel's arrival there, he was separated from Chateaumorand, who had been charged by Boucicaut on January 6, 1403, with a mission in the Levant on behalf of Genoese interests.[34] The French governor of Genoa was now, of course, none other than Boucicaut himself, ruling the once strife-torn city with just and stabilizing efficiency, and with the added grace provided by his beautiful and beloved wife, Antoinette de Turenne. This old comrade gave Manuel a particularly grand reception to the city on January 22, 1403, and the Emperor was housed and fêted grandly at Genoese expense.[35]

Once again, however, Manuel demonstrated that he was interested in more than entertainments. Even while in Genoa he began negotiations with an eye to the future. An embassy was sent to Venice. On January 31, 1403, four points which the Greek ambassador had raised were answered by the Senate. The first two were fairly routine: the Senate approved of Manuel's intention to come to Venice after leaving Genoa; and, as for the galleys requested by the Emperor for his homeward journey, in view of the uncertainty of the situation in the East at that moment, such matters could not be decided until Manuel actually reached Venice. This latter reply was to prove a foreshadowing of trouble to come. The remaining two matters, however, are more significant. Manuel had asked the Senate to authorize the Venetian ambassador then in Genoa to discuss Byzantine affairs with the Genoese while the Emperor was there. To this the Senate replied evasively that it had to await news from Romania before such a decision could be made. Manuel had offered to

33. See Vasiliev, "Putešestvie Manuila," p. 289 (69), and n. 3, who examines the possibility of a route through German territory. Cf. Schlumberger, "Un Empereur," 135 (44–45).

34. Delaville le Roulx, *La France en Orient*, p. 425, n. 4; and Vasiliev, "Putešestvie Manuila," 288 (68), who presume that this date means that Chateaumorand had gone on ahead of Manuel to Genoa; while Schlumberger, "Chateaumorand," 316, supposes merely that the parting of paths came only when the two arrived together in Genoa subsequently.

35. Vasiliev, "Putešestvie Manuila," 290–292 (70–72); Berger de Xivrey, 115–116; Schlumberger, "Un Empereur," 135–137; Delaville le Roulx, *La France en Orient*, 424–425; Jugie, 332; Mompherratos, Διπλ. ἐν., 42–43. We have at least one expense entry referring to Manuel's stay in Genoa: Iorga, *Notes et extraits*, I, 130–131.

mediate disputes between Genoa and Venice: the Venetians expressed their thanks, but pointed out haughtily that Venice was strong enough to maintain its rights.[36]

These latter two points are of great significance, for they allow us to see plainly that Manuel was busy formulating a policy to fit the new circumstances. His offer of mediation was no gesture of mere courtesy. It was rather intimately linked with the proposal to enable discussion of his Empire's situation with the Venetians and the Genoese together in Genoa. Manuel's western journey may have made him skeptical about Latin promises of aid, but such an enlightenment did not by any means end his quest for that aid. On the contrary, Manuel had promptly seen in the blow that Ancyra had dealt to the Turks a great opportunity and the best reason for working the harder for a strong alliance against the unbelievers. He realized that the keystone of any such alliance must be the joint and active participation of both Venice and Genoa, reconciled and no longer wasting their energies fighting each other. Hence, his desire to effect their full reconciliation and to engage them quickly in discussions.

No factor other than Manuel's interest and efforts in this vein of continuing the quest for aid could explain satisfactorily the length of time that Manuel spent in Italy on his return trip. It is particularly important to bear this fact in mind at this point, for, after his ceremonious departure from Genoa on February 10, 1403, we have no precise information as to Manuel's route or whereabouts during the thirty-two-day interval before his next documented stop, in Venice. It has been suggested with good likelihood, however, that he made his delayed progress to the Lagoon City by way of Florence and Ferrara. And, as a possible reason for this southward inclination, it has been supposed that in the former city the Emperor met and conferred with Pope Boniface IX.[37] Meanwhile, as Manuel was making his leisurely way to Venice, the Senate, on February 12, 1403, began discussing measures to receive him and to transport him home.[38]

Unfortunately for Manuel, momentous steps were being taken

36. Iorga, *Notes et extraits*, I, 131; Dölger, *Regesten*, no. 3293, p. 89; the summary by Thiriet, *Régestes*, II, no. 1092, p. 35, is quite inadequate. Cf. Vasiliev, "Putešestvie Manuila," 292 (72).

37. On this problem, see Appendix XIX below.

38. Iorga, *Notes et extraits*, I, 131; this deliberation has been overlooked by Thiriet. Cf. Vasiliev, "Putešestvie Manuila," 295 (75).

in his absence and, perhaps also, to some degree, in his ignorance. The immediate problem centered about the importunities of one of Bayazid's sons and successors, Suleyman Çelebi, who had taken over control of the European section of the Turkish lands. Anxious to secure his position, the Turkish prince eagerly sought from the outset to cultivate good relations with the once all-but-conquered Byzantines. This eagerness had been demonstrated vividly when, on December 7, 1402, the Venetian Senate heard an emissary sent by Suleyman. Part of the reason for the embassy was the wooing of the Venetians with promises of commercial concessions. But the bulk of Suleyman's communication concerned Manuel. The prince asked Venice to urge Manuel to return to Constantinople immediately, since, the prince insisted, he wished "to be his son and not to depart from his [Manuel's] will, not doubting that they will be rightly in concord. . . ." The Venetians replied that Manuel was on his way home at that moment and that these matters would be discussed with him upon his arrival in Venice. For the present, with an allusion to their suspicions of John VII, they noted "that they may be able at once to be in concord and to hinder those things which are begun by his nephew and the Genoese," as they had already informed Manuel.[39]

Ever eager to stabilize the Levant and then to exploit it for their commercial advantage, the Venetians were naturally anxious to pursue these possibilities. A deliberation of February 26, 1403, reveals that Manuel was in continual contact with the Venetians and was discussing his plans with them. It is interesting to note the relative weight given to the successive aspects of his intentions as revealed to the Senate. Manuel's greatest concern

39. Partial text and summary, Iorga, *Notes et extraits*, I, 125–126; cf. Thiriet, *Régestes*, II, no. 1038, p. 33; see Vasiliev, "Putešestvie Manuila," 289 (69). Suleyman had been in contact with Venice at least once before, for on August 19, 1400, the Senate considered with pleasure the overtures of Suleyman (called *Zalapi*, a name which they used hereafter regularly to designate this particular prince, or *çelebi*), then governor of a small principate from the old city of Ephesus (then called Theologo or Altoluogo). He asked for friendship and cooperation between himself and the *Serenissima*. As early as this date Venice foresaw the possibility of a struggle for power among the sons of Bayazid after his death, and were anxious to be in a good position if it should come. Summaries of this deliberation in Iorga, *Notes et extraits*, I, 102, and Thiriet, *Régestes*, II, no. 988, p. 12; cf. Alexandrescu-Dersca, 24–25.

is with the situation in the Morea. The news is that the Despotate is in great confusion as a result of the illness of his brother and of the controversial encroachments of the Hospitalers.[40] Manuel, therefore, requests transportation thither, where he proposes to spend a month to settle the explosive affairs there. Next, he notes that while in the Peloponnesus he will take counsel with representatives of the various Balkan Christians (Wallachians, Albanians, Serbians, and others), "to whom he has sent his ambassadors." And also while he is there, he will await an ambassador of Suleyman for negotiations with him.[41] Manuel's concern for the welfare of the important Despotate was natural. But it is interesting that he should be as much concerned in negotiations with his Christian brethren in the Balkans—with a view toward an alliance against the Turks?—as in meeting with representatives of Suleyman. Indeed, the relatively casual way in which the latter point seems to be included makes one wonder if Manuel was aware of the negotiations that his nephew John, Venice herself, and other allies, had already been conducting, and if he really took negotiations with Suleyman very seriously himself.

As for Suleyman, the prince had been too impatient to await the return of Manuel himself. Presumably at some time in midwinter, Venice had authorized agents to negotiate with the Turks in conjunction with the Genoese of Chios, Duke Jacopo I Crispo of Naxos, the Hospitalers of Rhodes, and John VII, who had all formed a league in order to deal jointly with the Turks. In spite of whatever efforts he may have made to stall for time, John was pressured or enticed into joining such negotiations. Stefan Lazarević of Serbia was also brought into the dealings. Thanks to Suleyman's eagerness, it was not long before terms were reached.[42] At some time about February 20, 1403—in other

---

40. For this situation, see pp. 232–233 below.

41. Dölger, *Regesten*, no. 3294, p. 89; Iorga, *Notes et extraits*, I, 132; cf. Thiriet, *Régestes*, II, no. 1097, p. 36. Manuel also suggests that, for the good of Christendom, the Straits should be blocked against Timur; the prospect of a Tartar invasion of Europe was still a very real fear. Again, however, the Venetians evaded proposals of cooperation with Genoa. On the transportation, see pp. 228 ff. below.

42. An interesting exposition of the preliminary negotiations, by the Venetian agent, Pietro Zeno, Lord of Andros, himself, is presented by Iorga, *Notes et extraits*, I, 126–130; cf. Alexandrescu-Dersca. 105.

words, a good month before Manuel even reached Venice—the treaty was accepted. It is a striking illustration of what the Battle of Ancyra had done to upset the Turkish power vis-à-vis the Christians in general and the Byzantines in particular. A number of sections of this treaty deal with the Latins of the league and with Stefan, granting wide commercial privileges to the Venetians and making various adjustments with the other parties. But it was undoubtedly the Greeks who received the most crucial concessions. Suleyman swears peace and friendship with John VII ("Caloiani") and the Greeks. To them he restores the city of Thessalonica ("Salonichi"), with its environs and fortresses, and also the Chalcidice and the islands of Skopelos, Skyathos, and Skyros, as well as an extensive tract comprising the Thracian coast from Mesembria to Panidos ("Pauido"), that is, a large tract of the coast of the Black Sea and the entire coastal enclave of Marmora. He abolishes all former tribute paid by Byzantium to the Turks and any other imposts or duties; and he makes provision for Turkish commercial activity in Constantinople on terms favorable to the Greeks. He orders the release of all Greek prisoners (and those of the other league powers) in his or in his subjects' prisons, and he promises aid to Constantinople in case of any attack by Timur. He also makes the interesting agreement that his vessels will not enter the Straits, neither the Dardanelles nor the Bosporus ("ni de sova ni de soto") without the permission of the Emperor and of all the league.[43]

43. This treaty apparently survives only in an Italian translation of the Turkish original: this Italian version may be found in Thomas, *Diplomatarium Veneto-Levantinum*, II, no. 159, pp. 290–293; and appended to Iorga's "Privilegiu lui Mohamed al II-lea pentru Pera (1-iu Junie 1453)," *Analele Academei Române, Memoriile secțiunii istorice*, II, 36 (1913–14), 85–88. (For other editions of the text, see Alexandrescu-Dersca, p. 106, n. 1.) An excellent discussion of this treaty is given by Heyd, *Histoire du commerce du Levant*, II, 267–269; and also by Alexandrescu-Dersca, 105–107; see also Delaville le Roulx, *Les Hospitaliers à Rhodes*, 290–291. On the territorial arrangement, see Vakalopoulos, "Les Limites de l'empire byzantin depuis la fin du XIVe siècle jusqu'à sa chute (1453)," 59–60. Cf. Ostrogorsky, *History of the Byzantine State*, 495; and Iorga, *Geschichte*, 328–329, who precedes this treaty with mention of Suleyman's matrimonial link and personal interview with Manuel, which undoubtedly came later (see p. 253 and n. 88 below).

Much needless chronological confusion has developed about this treaty, thanks in large measure to Dölger. In his "Johannes VII.," p. 33 and n. 4, in chronological estimates that are no longer workable for this period, he arbitrarily calls this pact "the Treaty of Pera" and dates it June 3, 1403; he

John VII must have taken a certain satisfaction in being a party to such terms. In the first place, it obviously brought great relief to be able to see Byzantium not only freed from the crushing and nearly disastrous situation before Ancyra, but now actually in a very favorable and influential position in relation to the Turks. In addition, John must have relished specifically the restoration of Thessalonica to the Empire, which would pave the way for the fulfillment of the projected final settlement with his uncle when Manuel returned. But the implications of this treaty went much further, and in such light Manuel himself would have to evaluate it.

Manuel's own bearing with regard to this treaty is an enigma. In view of his apparently frequent, if not regular, contact with affairs at home, it is not impossible that Manuel was aware of the negotiations being conducted with Suleyman. On the other hand,

asssumes that it was Manuel who was the Byzantine party to it, after John had left Constantinople; and he states that John VII is not mentioned in the treaty. And, since then, Dölger, *Regesten*, no. 3201, p. 75, though recognizing John VII's involvement with the treaty, still dates it June 3, 1403. Meanwhile, at least two scholars have run afoul of Dölger's example. Khoury, "L'Empereur Manuel II," 141, appears to follow Dölger's chronology, for he implies that the treaty post-dates Manuel's return to Constantinople, and he states that it was Manuel who signed this agreement with Suleyman, which was certainly not the case. More recently, Wirth, "Zum Geschichtsbild Kaiser Johannes' VII. Palaiologos," 594–596, and 600, has restated and reformulated the arguments for John VII, not Manuel, as the Emperor involved with the treaty; but in spite of his correction of Dölger on that point he needlessly handicaps himself by retaining Dölger's dating of the treaty.

On John's role, there is no question: "lo gran imperador Caloiani, imperador de Griesi" is stated at the outset as the Byzantine party to the pact. As for the date, the June 3 confusion is perhaps the result of Iorga's edition of the text. The treaty text itself, as we have it, contains no date. In the Thomas collection, the text is placed between documents specifically dated April 22, 1403, and July 24, 1403; but this seems entirely arbitrary, unjustified by any citational evidence provided; at least Thomas labels our text itself with no more than "A.d. 1403." Iorga on the other hand, labels his edition with the date "before [*inainte de*] 3 June 1403"; and for this estimate he refers (both here and in his *Geschichte*, I, p. 329, n. 4) to C. Hopf's *Geschichte der Insel Andros* (without page citation), which I have been unable to locate, but apparently involving evidence dealing with the Lord of Andros as another party to the treaty.

Ironically, it is Iorga himself who has provided the best resolution of the problem of defining how much "before 3 June 1403" the treaty should be placed. Previous discussions at least having come to agree on the year 1403 in general (see those by Heyd, p. 268, n. 1; and Iorga, *Notes et extraits*, I, p. 58, n. 3), Iorga was the one who alone has taken note of a decisively

the only allusion we have by Manuel to any dealings whatsoever with the Turks at this time comes in the noncommittal and
seemingly casual reference of February 25, discussed above, to
meeting ambassadors of Suleyman in the Morea—an allusion
which indicates that Venice had informed him at least of Suleyman's overtures, but which, of itself, suggests no specific awareness of the treaty negotiations then being completed. Could the
Venetians have suppressed all news or denied the Emperor full
information on these negotiations until later? This is not inconceivable, although the silence of available sources gives no real
clue. We cannot even be certain as to when Manuel did hear
about it. But it is entirely possible that it was only when
Manuel reached Venice—*after* the treaty had been signed—that
he received at last any full, perhaps his first, information on these
negotiations and their important outcome.

In March of 1403 the final preparations were made for Man-

important Genoese expense notice, which he published in his *Notes et
extraits*, I, pp. 58–59: "Item, die xxª Februarii [1403] pro Lavignino de
Murta, notario, et socio, scribis Curie Peyre, et sunt pro eorum labore et
mercede, per eos passis, tam in scribendo et extrahando instrumentum pacis
inite inter Serenissimum imperatorem et Commune nostrum cum liga, ex
una parte, et illustre dominum Mosorman Jhalabi, Turchorum dominum in
Grecia, ex alia, etc." The date of the entry is the date of the expense reimbursement and not necessarily of the occasion on which it was incurred, but
it does give us a *terminus ante quem* that is incontestable, and totally eliminates the need for any further use of the June 3 date, either "on" or merely
"before." Needless to say, the "Mosorman Jhalabi" of the entry is simply
one of the many variants of the name "Musulman Zalapi," or other such
corruptions by which Suleyman Çelebi was known to Westerners.

Since the foregoing was written, and as this book went to press, a new
article appeared by Father Dennis, "The Byzantine-Turkish Treaty of 1403,"
Orientalia Christiana Periodica, 33 (1967), 72–88. Father Dennis has nothing
to say (corresponding to my own ideas) about Manuel's subsequent attitude
towards this treaty, but he does agree with my view that Manuel knew
nothing about it when it was being concluded, and he presents a position
and extensive comments which I find fully in agreement with my own. In
addition, he is able to offer fuller documentation, not only reprinting the
treaty's Italian text (with detailed English synopsis), but also publishing
some Venetian material bearing on the involvement of Pietro Zeno of Andros
in the negotiations and signing—which latter occurred, he makes clear, at
Gallipoli. This Dennis article is now, therefore, the fullest and most up-to-
date establishment of this transaction's history and chronology, rendering my
own foregoing discussion somewhat superfluous. Also newly available, moreover, are the general comments on the situation of the Balkan Christian
powers after Bayazid's fall in Werner's *Die Geburt einer Grossmacht*,
213–218.

uel's actual arrival in Venice. On March 13 the Senate took note of his request for money and official reception ceremonies. On March 16 the Senate selected three of its members "for going to greet the Emperor of Constantinople, coming hither." [44] Manuel apparently arrived soon after March 21 [45] and was accorded the usual distinguished welcome. By that time the news of the completion of the treaty negotiations was fully known in Venice itself. For, on March 24, 1403, the Senate discussed the necessity of ratification of treaties recently concluded with two sons of Bayazid, one "in partibus Grecie" (Suleyman) and the other "in partibus Turchie" (Isa or Mechmed?), and it appointed Giacomo Suriano as its ambassador to accomplish this and other tasks. [46]

At least by this time, then, Manuel must have known definitely of the treaty. His reaction, if any, is not recorded. Indeed, there is no mention of any discussion of it by Manuel in the available Venetian documents. Nor, for that matter, was there seemingly any discussion of much else, except only the question of arranging for the Emperor's return. Unfortunately, the settlement of that question was a long-drawn-out affair which must have tried Manuel's patience.

Actually, the arrangements for Manuel's transportation had been in progress for some time even before his arrival and had been initiated as long before as February 12, 1403. [47] Then, on February 26, when the Senate heard the announcement of Manuel's plans, it began to make some specific provisions. Manuel had pointed out that the Genoese (or at least Boucicaut) had promised to provide three galleys to help convey him to Constantinople. As for this and talk of dealings with Genoa, the Senate archly observed that Manuel "is a most wise prince and is especially esteemed in that realm even though he was always friendly to our state and his nephew to the Genoese." The Senate agreed, however, to provide armed vessels to transport Manuel with a retinue of twenty-five to thirty persons, while the remainder of the Imperial entourage would have to travel in unarmed ships. This convoy would leave Venice on March 4 and would serve

44. Iorga, *Notes et extraits,* II, 89; cf. Vasiliev "Putešestvie Manuila," 298–299 (78–79).

45. Vasiliev, "Putešestvie Manuila," 298–299 (78–79).

46. Iorga, *Notes et extraits,* I, 133–134; cf. Thiriet, *Régestes,* II, no. 1104, p. 37, which is less adequate.

47. See above, p. 222 and n. 38.

only for the voyage to Modon, after which three galleys might be sent for his subsequent use.[48] Manuel, however, seems to have complained about these terms, for on March 2, the Senate hastened to amend its decision to suit him. It was decided that its armed vessels could now provide for forty of Manuel's followers, leaving the rest to the unarmed galleys. These vessels would leave after the following Wednesday (March 7). Venice would send three galleys—Manuel had requested four, one armed at his expense—to Modon for the remainder of the voyage, though the Senate now claimed that Manuel's idea of going on to Constantinople by sea was something new.[49] On March 5, the redoubtable Carlo Zeno was given detailed instructions for taking Manuel to Modon to meet and take aboard his family and to settle affairs in the Morea.[50] To round out the arrangements, instructions were given on March 6 for the reception of Manuel in Modon,[51] and on the same date money was allocated for Manuel's reception at Pola, Coron, and Modon.[52]

Unfortunately, this arrangement collapsed. One reason may simply have been the fact that Manuel did not reach Venice soon enough. But another reason was that the Venetians had by then become concerned over the movements of a Genoese expedition under Boucicaut against Cyprus. On March 9, therefore, Zeno and the squadron originally intended for Manuel's voyage were instead dispatched to the Ionian Sea to join other Venetian squadrons in keeping check on Genoese movements.[53]

48. Iorga, *Notes et extraits*, I, 132; cf. Thiriet, *Régestes*, II, no. 1097, p. 36; Vasiliev, "Putešestvie Manuila," 295–296 (95–96); see also above, pp. 223–224 and n. 41.

49. Iorga, *Notes et extraits*, I, 132–133; cf. Thiriet, *Régestes*, II, no. 1098, p. 36; Vasiliev, "Putešestvie Manuila," 296–297 (76–77). Also discussed was a proposition to ship Manuel and his company directly to Constantinople on five or six galleys and have done with the whole business at one stroke. But presumably this nonstop scheme found no favor among the *Sapientes*.

50. Text in C. Sathas, *Documents inédits relatifs à l'histoire de la Grèce au moyen âge*, I (Paris, 1880), no. 5, pp. 5–6; summary in Thiriet, *Régestes*, II, no. 1099, p. 36; cf. Vasiliev, "Putešestvie Manuila," 297–298 (77–78), and Dölger, *Regesten*, no. 3294, p. 89.

51. Text in Sathas, *Documents inédits*, II (Paris, 1881), no. 319, p. 107; cf. Vasiliev, "Putešestvie Manuila," 298 (78).

52. Iorga, *Notes et extraits*, I, 133; cf. Vasiliev, "Putešestvie Manuila," 298 (78).

53. Vasiliev, "Putešestvie Manuila," 298 and 301 (78 and 81); Delaville le Roulx, *La France en Orient*, I, 422–423. Thiriet, *Régestes*, II, no. 1100, p. 36, has perhaps misread the instructions to Zeno.

As a result, the whole arrangement had to be worked out all over again. The Senate began anew, on March 11, by allotting two galleys for the voyage of Manuel,[54] who only reached Venice later that month. Presumably after Manuel's arrival, however, there developed the idea of killing two birds with one stone, by combining Manuel's voyage, at least as far as the Peloponnesus, with Suriano's mission to the Turkish princes. After his selection for this mission on March 24, Suriano had been busying himself with preparations. On April 5 he was assigned a priest for his entourage.[55] And on April 9 the Senate drew up Suriano's instructions. The ambassador is to sail in a squadron of three galleys commanded by Leonardo Mocenigo, and with him at the same time will go Manuel. Suriano is to be taken to Gallipoli to seek Suleyman, with whom he will discuss confirmation and observation of the terms of the recently negotiated treaty. Suriano is then to try to meet likewise with the son of Bayazid ruling in Brusa (Isa or Mechmed?), if this is possible. From there he will go to Constantinople to negotiate with the Emperor. Presumably Manuel will be installed in the city by then. The ambassador is to offer felicitations to the Emperor, discuss the long-deferred treaty renewal, and press for the payment, at least in part, of the Byzantine debt of 17,163 *hyperpyra* to Venice. But the shrewd Venetians, foreseeing the possibility that John VII might refuse to yield the throne and might then still be in possession of it, provided alternate instructions. If Manuel's nephew has maintained himself in Constantinople, Suriano is to negotiate no less courteously with him. John is to be informed of Venice's sympathy and friendship for him and his realm, and that the Venetian transportation of Manuel had not implied any specific hostility toward John's regime. The Venetian squadron is not to intervene in any dispute between John and Manuel; while the latter may be allowed the presence of the Venetian ships at his disposal for no more than eight days.[56]

54. Iorga, *Notes et extraits*, I, 133; cf. Vasiliev, "Putešestvie Manuila," 298 (78).
55. Iorga, *Notes et extraits*, I, 134; cf. Vasiliev, "Putešestvie Manuila," 299 (79).
56. Iorga, *Notes et extraits*, I, 136–137 (date incomplete); Thiriet, *Régestes*, II, no. 1107, p. 38; cf. Vasiliev, "Putešestvie Manuila," 299–300 (79–80). As to Venetian speculations on John VII's intentions, note the apparent contacts of John with Venice in April of 1403, cited by Dölger, *Regesten*, no. 3200, p. 74.

Once these interesting instructions were given, the arrangements for the joint departure of Manuel and Suriano, with their respective followings, were doubtless brought to swift completion. Within a few days, loaded with gifts and with at least outward signs of honor, Manuel sailed from Venice in Mocenigo's squadron. With Manuel was Manuel Chrysoloras, who had joined the Emperor's train at some point in the latter's travels through northern Italy, and who was now accompanying his sovereign on the homeward trip.[57] We do not know the specific date of departure, but by April 13 or 14 Manuel had sailed by Ragusa. Originally, this Dalmatian Coast republic had made great plans to welcome the Imperial party during a projected stop there. But, as it happened, no such stop was made there at all.[58] Within a few days the squadron reached Modon. There the Emperor was welcomed by his wife and children,[59] who had apparently been apprised of his coming. After this reunion with the family he had not seen for just a little more than three years, Manuel moved to take up the task of rejoining his own people and looking to their needs. The most immediate problems were in the Morea itself, and to the Byzantine Despotate Manuel therefore turned his attention first. From Modon the Venetians conveyed Manuel, his family, and his retinue to Vasilipotamo.[60]

57. Cammelli, *I dotti...Manuele Crisolora*, 128 ff.; Thomson, "Manuel Chrysoloras and the Italian Renaissance," 80. Apparently during the following summer the Italian humanist Guarino followed Chrysoloras to Constantinople to become his disciple: Cammelli, 131 ff. For some recent comments on the relations between the great Greek scholar and his Italian pupil, see M. Baxandall, "Guarino, Pisanello and Manuel Chrysoloras," *Journal of the Warburg and Courtauld Institutes*, 28 (1965), 183–204.

58. On Manuel's departure from Venice, see Ducas, ed. Grecu, 85, ed. Bonn, 56; also Sanuto, 780–790. Not even the latter gives any exact date, but, for some unstated reason, Vasiliev, "Putešestvie Manuila," 300 (80), sets April 5 as the *terminus post quem*. Obviously, however, it must have been after April 9, in view of the Senate's deliberation of that date. On the projected stop at Ragusa, the relevant documents were first made available, with a full commentary by M. A. Andreeva, "Zur Reise Manuels II Palaiologos nach Westeuropa," *Byz. Zeitschr.*, 34 (1934), 37–47, and 351. This episode gives us a very valuable chronological guide. For, although Andreeva (see p. 47) accepts Vasiliev's date of April 5, the indication of bypassing Ragusa on April 13 or 14 suggests the necessity of a later·date for Manuel's departure from Venice.

59. Ducas, ed. Grecu, 85; Vasiliev, "Putešestvie Manuila," 300 (80). Among the children was apparently a new son, Andronicus, whom Manuel had not seen until then: see Appendix XV below.

60. Vasilipotamo, or Vasilopotamo, which is another name for the River Eurotas, was apparently also a landing on the mouth of that river on the

And from this point within the Despotate the Emperor had at last direct access to the Morea and its problems.

Certainly the Morea had need of his steadying influence. During Manuel's absence his brother Theodore had made a desperate attempt to bolster his realm. Internally, the Morea was wracked by the centrifugal strife and divisiveness of the restless local magnates, the ἄρχοντες, who resented bitterly any curbs by a central authority, and who conspired with external powers of the Peloponnesus and beyond. Against these elements Theodore waged a fluctuating struggle. To external foes Theodore was even more vulnerable, and the Morea was repeatedly raked by devastating raids sent by Bayazid. Lacking resources of his own and unable to count on real help from Constantinople, Theodore had resorted to the idea of introducing a Latin power as a bulwark. We have already noted that in 1396 Theodore had negotiated the sale of Corinth to the Knights of St. John on Rhodes.[61] The Hospitalers, all too conscious of their avowed role of advancing the cause of Christendom in the Levant, saw in this entry into the unstable Peloponnesian scene a ready opportunity to build themselves a valuable base for wider operations and they were therefore eager to extend their influence in the area. Regardless of personal feelings, Theodore was willing to acquiesce in this extension as a last resort to shore up the battered Despotate.

At the time Manuel was leaving for the West the issue was brought to a head. During the spring of 1400 the negotiations were carried out. In a short time the Hospitalers began expanding their control over the territory as far as the capital, Mistra (Sparta), while the Despot removed his court to Monemvasia. Unfortunately, the scheme did not work. Indeed, it only produced further trouble. The volatile local populace, ignorant or

Gulf of Laconia. On May 14, 1403, the Venetian Senate took note of the fact that Manuel had been unable to pay the expenses of this transportation thither, and therefore the officials involved were granted reimbursement from the *Signoria*. The respective summaries of this deliberation by Iorga, *Notes et extraits*, I, 134, and Thiriet, *Régestes*, II, no. 1114, p. 39, differ on the size of the Imperial suite: the former puts it at eight persons, the latter at fifty-eight persons, including Manuel and his family. Only publication of the text itself will settle the problem. In another reflection on the Imperial voyage, on the previous day, May 13, the Senate exempted from normal customs duties some cloth which Manuel had taken home with him: Iorga, 138; Thiriet, no. 1113, p. 39. On all this, cf. Vasiliev, "Putešestvie Manuila," 300 (80); see also Mompherratos, Οἱ Παλαιολόγοι ἐν Πελοποννήσῳ, 22.

61. See above, p. 146 and n. 37.

unconcerned about the larger issues, viewed with alarm and rage the establishment of the hated Latins in authority over them. The results were riots and violent popular resistance. In short order the situation had deteriorated hopelessly, and the Despotate verged on internal chaos. Theodore's only hope to restore order was to renounce the cession and attempt to reclaim the strife-torn realm in loyalty to himself. The Byzantines had reserved the right of retrocession, and negotiations were therefore entered into to buy back the disputed territory from the Hospitalers. The negotiations were extremely lengthy and difficult and, only later, with the Treaty of Vasilipotamo of May 5, 1404, was the final agreement reached on the complete withdrawal of the Hos-pitalers from the Peloponnesus.[62]

Thus, when Manuel appeared on the scene in late April of 1403, he found a grim and unsettled situation in the Morea. We have seen already that, even before he had reached Venice, he was gravely concerned over this situation, and that he intended to hasten to the Peloponnesus to settle affairs there. Regrettably, we have no record of his activities there, once he arrived, or of what he may have accomplished. But we can have no doubt that Manuel involved himself actively in the situation, and that, in all likelihood, he made important contributions to reaching the ultimate settlement of a year later. And, as for Manuel's avowed intentions, both to sound out the other Christians of the Balkans and to meet the emissaries of Suleyman, we likewise have no information. But it is entirely possible that he attended to such matters to some degree.[63]

62. For source information, see Chalcocondyles, ed. Darkó, I, 91–92, ed. Bonn, 97–98, and the Pseudo-Phrantzes, ed. Papadopoulos, 67–69, ed. Bonn, 63–64. For critical analyses of these sources, see Loenertz, "Autour du Chronicon Maius attribué à Georges Phrantzès," 290–293; Loenertz has also contributed a new source in his *Chron. br. mor.*, No. 22, p. 406, with his commentary, pp. 426–427. See also the *Chron. Barb. 111*, 37–38. Rich and extended information may be found at length in Manuel's own *Funeral Oration* for Theodore, and this is fully exploited by Loenertz in "Pour l'histoire du Péloponnèse au XIVe siècle," 190–196, which is the most thor-ough and up-to-date account of the episode. See also Delaville le Roulx, *Les Hospitaliers*, 277–281, 301; Zakythinos, *Le Despotat grec de Morée*, I, 159–160; Miller, *The Latins in the Levant*, 368–369; Mompherratos, Οἱ Παλ. ἐν Πελ., 21–23; Muralt, p. 780, nos. 20–22, p. 784, no. 8. Cf. also Alexandrescu-Dersca, 106.

63. If we were to regard the supposed marriage of Suleyman with an illegitimate daughter of the Despot Theodore as having taken place not long after Manuel's return to Constantinople, we might construe this occurrence

Meanwhile, to the Venetians Manuel's homeward voyage must have come to seem a poor investment for them. Their prime interest was their Levantine commerce, and their concern was therefore to do their best to safeguard such interests. The practical Venetians had probably been willing to finance Manuel's trip on the assumption that his speedy return to his realm and his resumption of the reins of government would help to hasten a settling of the situation in the East after the disruption of Ancyra. But Venice seems to have taken a dim view of Manuel's desire to tarry in the Peloponnesus over affairs there, and the *Serenissima* apparently grew impatient as that sojourn drew on. On May 2, 1403, the Senate issued a directive to Suriano, who was apparently waiting in the Morea while Manuel was occupied there. The ambassador was ordered to proceed with his mission to the Turkish princes in order to secure the needed treaty ratifications, lest the Venetian interests suffer from such delays. And special attention was given to making clear that Suriano's association with the transporting of Manuel did not imply Venetian favor in any possible struggle impending between John VII and his uncle.[64]

as possible evidence that Manuel met with an embassy from Suleyman while in the Peloponnesus, agreed on the union then, and brought the girl home with him from there. Unfortunately, as discussed below (see n. 88 and n. 142), it seems more likely that such a marriage occurred in 1409 or later, and, if Manuel ever brought the girl to Constantinople himself, it may well have been from his visit to the Morea in 1408, not in 1403. Nevertheless, despite the absence of concrete evidence, we may not be overly incorrect in continuing to suggest the possibility that Manuel met with Turkish representatives in the Morea at this time.

64. Iorga, *Notes et extraits*, I, 138; Thiriet, *Régestes,* II, no. 1111, p. 39. Cf. Vasiliev, "Putešestvie Manuila," 301 (81), who interprets the last clause as meaning that the Venetians wished to avoid appearing to favor Manuel in opposition to the Turks, lest it jeopardize their treaty with the latter. But this seems incorrect, both in terms of what the document seems to be saying (as far as Iorga's and, now, Thiriet's summaries reveal), and also in the context of the treaty, to which Venice was a party as a member of the league with Byzantium. We have evidence of Suriano's activity later on in this same month in an entry in an expense account of Pera for May 18, 1403: "Expensis in communitate cum ambasator Venetorum [Suriano?], in pannis de Florentia xiiij et de Janua, pro vestibus quinque exeniatis in dicta ambasata, tam prefacto domino Criihi, quam aliis ex suis . . ." (Iorga, *Notes et extraits,* I, 61). "Dominus Criihi," as we shall note below (n. 82), was a corrupted Western name for Mechmed. Suriano was then on his way to see Mechmed, who by this time had apparently overcome his brother in Anatolia (see below, p. 248).

In these circumstances, Manuel's preparations for the final leg of his homeward journey, to Constantinople itself, might well have lapsed into an unpalatable round of acrimonious haggling in the usual Venetian fashion were it not for the timely arrival of someone by now an old hand at coming in the nick of time to help Manuel. Boucicaut's Genoese expedition to Cyprus passed by Modon, and when it sighted that post the gallant Frenchman was ready for a fight if the Venetians should be pugnaciously inclined. Fortunately, good sense was exercised by Carlo Zeno, whose squadron was at Modon, and Boucicaut was instead welcomed cordially.[65]

Going ashore, the Governor of Genoa was met by ambassadors from Manuel. The Emperor had heard of Boucicaut's coming and had sent the fervent request that the latter not depart without seeing him. Manuel was still in the Morea, twenty miles inland, the message continued, and, if Boucicaut would wait, the Emperor would come to him. Highly flattered, Boucicaut moved quickly to meet Manuel more than halfway. Taking with him Chateaumorand, who had joined him by this time, Boucicaut took a ship to Vasilipotamo, where he awaited Manuel. Hearing of the Emperor's approach, Boucicaut went out and met the Emperor and his family. There was an exchange of cordialities, and then Manuel proceeded to the point by requesting that Boucicaut provide him with transportation to Constantinople. Boucicaut forthwith ordered four galleys to be set aside for this purpose, under the well-advised command of Chateaumorand, and promised to escort the Emperor as far as he could himself.[66]

This was a shrewd move on Manuel's part. It not only provided an irresistible opportunity for Boucicaut to embarrass the Venetians—a not unpalatable prospect for him, we may be sure—but it was also an ideal way to eliminate any difficulties with the Venetians themselves over transportation. In the latter respect the move worked splendidly. The Venetians suddenly discovered their obligation to the Emperor. Carlo Zeno, who had been grudgingly authorized to provide no more than three galleys for

65. *Livre des faits*, II, xii, pp. 622–623; it is interesting to note that the *Vita Caroli Zeni* virtually ignores this incident. See also Delaville le Roulx, *La France en Orient*, I, 424; Vasiliev, "Putešestvie Manuila," 301–302 (81–82).

66. *Livre des faits*, II, xiii, p. 623; cf. Vasiliev, "Putešestvie Manuila," 302 (82); Delaville le Roulx, *La France en Orient*, I, 425–426.

Figure 17: *Jean II le Meingre, Maréchal de Boucicaut, Alone, Venerating St. Catherine.* Illuminated Miniature, *Heures du Maréchal de Boucicaut,* Musée Jacquemart-André, Paris, f. 38ᵛ (photo courtesy Giraudon, Paris; see Appendix XXIV, B, 2, b).

Manuel's voyage to Constantinople, realized that his country's honor was at stake unless he could match the Genoese generosity. Hastily he called an assembly of his fellow commanders on May 29, and it was agreed that the initiative should be taken to furnish Manuel with *four* Venetian galleys. At the same time, Zeno wrote home to inform the Senate of his independent action. And later, on July 10, the Senate reviewed the incident and registered its approval of Zeno's patriotic intitiative.[67] Thus did Manuel both cut through inevitable Venetian delays and red tape and also secure a brilliant escort home. Only a minor triumph of diplomacy, perhaps, but it was in the best Byzantine tradition, and it must have given the distracted Emperor a good chuckle.

In a short time Manuel was able to make his final preparations, and at some time in early June he boarded the joint fleet for the last phase of his homeward journey. At Cape Malea ("Sanct-Angel"—Sant' Angelo, as the Venetians called it), Boucicaut bade farewell and proceeded on to Rhodes.[68] Meanwhile, Manuel was escorted on through the Dardanelles as far as Gallipoli, where John VII had come out to meet him. And from there they proceeded to Constantinople, apparently on June 9, 1403.[69] After an

67. *Livre des faits*, II, xiii, p. 623; the text of the Venetian Senatorial deliberation is published by Delaville le Roulx, *La France en Orient*, II, no. 27, p. 114; cf. Thiriet, *Régestes*, II, no. 1122, pp. 40–41. See also Vasiliev, "Putešestvie Manuila," 302–303 (82–83); Delaville le Roulx, *La France en Orient*, I, 426; for this entire episode, see also Schlumberger, "Chateaumorand," 318.

68. *Livre des faits*, II, xiii, p. 623; cf. Delaville le Roulx, *La France en Orient*, I, 426; Vasiliev, "Putešestvie Manuila," 303 (83); Schlumberger, "Chateaumorand," 318.

69. Konstantin the Philosopher (ed. Jagić, 279; ed. and trans. Braun, 21) refers to Manuel's return, interestingly enough to Gallipoli specifically, and not to Constantinople. Of the Greek historians, only the Pseudo-Phrantzes, ed. Bonn, 62 (but *not* ed. Papadopoulos, 67), gives a date for Manuel's return: but its statement of September 13, 1405, may be ignored completely, even though Muralt, p. 781, no. 1, has used the date with equal absurdity for 1402; while recently, on the basis of a Sphrantzes/Pseudo-Phrantzes/Short-Chronicle variant, Wirth, "Zum Geschichtsbild Kaiser Johannes' VII. Palaiologos," 595, and 599, has argued for a retention of the September 1403 dating of Manuel's return, which I find unacceptable. Two of our published short chronicles refer to the return of Manuel. One of them, the *Chron. Vat. gr. 162*, no. 19, pp. 210–211, ll. 90–92, simply speaks vaguely of his return from "Phrangkia" after hearing of Bayazid's defeat, and of his assuming the rule of "the City." But the Βρ. χρ. No. 15, p. 33, ll. 34–36, says that he returned in June of 6910 (1402). The year is plainly a mistake, but that the

absence of more than three and one half years, Manuel's long journey was ended, and he was once again in his capital.

On his return, Manuel faced two major problems. The most immediate one was the final settlement with his nephew, John VII, who had quite literally been "holding the fort" all this time— and, from outward appearances, fairly well at that. This settlement could be a serious problem. After all, John was no mere deputy or appointee left behind as regent. He was Emperor in his own right, bearing the title and rank of *Basileus* by virtue of both a fully legal hereditary claim and a coronation at one time or another. Although his reign in Constantinople from December of 1399 to June of 1403 was theoretically at Manuel's sufferance, it was nonetheless a legitimate reign as *Basileus,* in which capacity John issued, if not his own chrysobulls, at least his own coinage.[70]

month is correct is borne out by a number of important Pera expense account entries published by Iorga, *Notes et extraits,* I, 62. One, for June 15, 1403, speaks of expenses for one man, "patrono unius bregantini armati pro eundo obviam dominum imperatorem." Another, for June 23, mentions reimbursement for another individual, "pro armamento cujusdam fuste, pro obviam dominum imperatorem. . . ." A note for the same date indicates the trip by John VII to Gallipoli to welcome his uncle, by referring to expenses by certain persons "quando fuerunt missi cum domino imperatore Calojane super galeam usque Galipolim, ubi tunc existebat dominus imperator Chir Manoli. . . ." See also Vasiliev, "Putešestvie Manuila," p. 303 (83) and n. 4. In fact, however, a more specific and, apparently, more reliable date for Manuel's return seems now to be supplied in a statement by one of the members of the Emperor's train, Metropolitan Makarios of Ancyra, that Constantinople was reached on June 9. This statement has been quoted by P. Gautier, in his article, "Action de grâces de Démétrius Chrysoloras pour l'anniversaire de la bataille d'Ankara (28 juillet 1403)," *Rev. d. ét. byz.,* 19 (1961), 345–346; cf. Khoury, p. 140 and n. 37. The disparities between this date and those of the Genoese accounts present no real problem, since such entries were often dated at the time of reimbursement, not of the expenses themselves.

Another entry for June 15 reflects the presence of Chateaumorand, in speaking of money for one man, "pro conduci facere galeotam unam, domino Chatemorantis donatam per dominum imperatorem, videlicet Constantinopoli, in Peyram. . . ." Chateaumorand eventually rejoined Boucicaut at Rhodes (*Livre des faits,* III, xiv, p. 624; cf. Delaville le Roulx, *La France en Orient,* I, 427–428) after he had gathered some ships. Though we have no specific evidence, it is possible that it was at this time that the French garrison left by Boucicaut in 1399 was removed from Constantinople: see n. 28 above. On this mission Chateaumorand probably tarried a while in Pera, for another expense entry, for August 15, 1403, speaks of expenses made "pro domine Johanne de Castromorandi" (Iorga, *Notes et extraits,* I, 63).

70. We have no actual chrysobulls by John VII from this time. We do have a few coins, although the problem of his coinage is a controversial one. There is at least one authentic coin, a silver one, of John himself. This was published by H. Goodacre, "Notes on Some Rare Byzantine Coins," *Numismatic Chronicle,* V, 11 (1931), 156. Although its reverse bears an image

In view of his previous conduct, John might well have broken his agreement and might have tried to hold onto the throne of Constantinople, as the Venetians very shrewdly thought he would. But evidently John made no attempt to resist the return of Manuel, and the exchange of rulers seems to have been completely peaceful. That this should have been the case has interesting implications. Perhaps, after his three and one-half trying years in Constantinople, John had had enough of the capital—perhaps also *vice versa*—and was quite content, if not eager, to relinquish its burdensome responsibilities. The terms of a final settlement had been agreed in advance, and the return of Thessalonica to the Empire by the recent treaty with Suleyman had made fulfillment of that settlement a matter of nothing but the last formalities. John had lived up to his part of the bargain: all that was necessary was for Manuel to do likewise.

But Manuel did not. Exactly what were his motives or reasons are difficult to determine fully. On the surface it would seem like base betrayal, inconsistent with what we know of Manuel's character. There are two possible reasons, however. The one given in our source is that Manuel was angry with John for having agreed to surrender the city to Bayazid.[71] This is not im-

identified as Saint Demetrius, the Patron Saint of Thessalonica, Goodacre assigns this coin to the period of 1399–140(2) regency; cf. the same writer's *A Handbook of the Coinage of the Byzantine Empire* (London, 1957), 350. Another apparently authentic coin of John VII is more obviously from this period. A bronze, it bears the image of Manuel II on the obverse, and on the reverse it shows John VII and Manuel's Empress Helena, according to the accepted identifications. On this coin, see W. Wroth, *Catalogue of the Imperial Byzantine Coins in the British Museum*, Vol. II (London, 1908; reprint, 1966), 369, who rejects the idea that "the John represented may possibly be John VIII the *son* of Manuel II," and who ascribes it definitely to John VII's regency; cf. Goodacre, *Handbook*, 349. A specimen of this coin was published by Bertelè, "Monete bizantini inedite o rare," *Zeitschrift für Numismatik*, 36 (1926), 1–36. A total of six other coins of similar types have been ascribed to John VII by T. Gerasimov, "Edna medna moneta Joan VII Paleolog (1400–1403)" ("Monnaies de cuivre de Jean VII Paléologue"), *Izvestija Arkheologicheskaia Institut, Bulgarska Akademija na Naukite*, 20 (1955), 585–586; and in "Les Monnaies de Jean VII Paléologue (1400–1408)," *Byzantinoslavica*, 17 (1956), 114–119. But Dölger and Laurent respectively (in *Byz. Zeitschr.*, 49 [1956], 539) have questioned Gerasimov's ascriptions and suggest that these coins should rather be assigned to John VIII, Manuel's son and successor.

71. After describing John's agreement with Bayazid, Clavijo (ed. López Estrada, 28; cf. ed. Sreznevskii, 40, trans. Le Strange, 52) relates: "For the which [i.e. John's agreement] the old emperor, when he had returned to Constantinople, over what his nephew had agreed was very angry with him, and he ordered him that he never more appear before him, and that he

plausible, for, while one can understand the desperation to which John may well have felt himself driven in promising this, one can also appreciate that this agreement was indeed treason and a categorical violation of the terms on which John had been left behind. From Manuel's point of view, this agreement would have proved that the rumors about John's conniving with Bayazid were true after all. Such a reason might well have seemed enough for Manuel to justify his violation of the arrangement for the settlement with John.

But it is perhaps plausible to suggest another reason. Let us recall that Manuel's efforts had been devoted to organizing Western aid against the Turks. We do not know his original attitude toward the overtures of Suleyman and the idea of a new understanding with the Turks. It is not impossible that Manuel may initially have opposed such an understanding. From what we know, he himself had nothing whatsoever to do with the crucial treaty of February, 1403. Moreover, as we have seen and will presently see even more, Manuel's efforts toward arousing the West certainly continued without interruption after Ancyra and his return. And, as we shall also see, he recognized at least once the possibilities which the post-Ancyra situation gave for smashing the Turks. Was this his sole aim? Certainly his experiences with the Turks in the past ten years since Serres would not have encouraged him to return to friendship and accommodation with them. If this was his frame of mind, therefore, Manuel might well have resented John's entire policy regarding the Turks, not only before Ancyra, but after the battle as well. By coming to terms with the Turks, and by assisting them in other ways, John would thus have compromised Manuel's own policy of military alliance against them. It may perhaps have been as much for this transgression as it was for John's earlier willingness to surrender to Bayazid that Manuel broke his promise to his nephew. By this reasoning, John had been entirely too pro-Turkish, after as well as before Ancyra, to satisfy Manuel.[72]

depart from his land. And he gave him the island of Lemnos ['escalime,' i.e., 'Stalimene,' or Lemnos: Le Strange mistakenly identifies this with Mitylene, for which Clavijo uses a quite different word], and he deprived him of this said city of Thessalonica ['Saloni']." See also below, n. 73.

72. In the passage translated in the previous note, Clavijo speaks only of Manuel's anger over John's agreement with Bayazid. If Manuel's reason did not extend further, it is possible that Clavijo omitted mention of more because he either had not heard of it or did not understand it. Such an argu-

As little as we know of Manuel's precise reasons for spurning John, we are no more enlightened as to the procedure by which it took place. All we can gather is that Manuel angrily banished John to Lemnos and deprived him of the promised appanage of Thessalonica. It is noteworthy that we hear nothing at this time of any popular reaction on Constantinople in John's favor. This fact might suggest that the very malcontents who had grumbled under Manuel for John's restoration had become disenchanted with John after they had actually had to put up with him. And,

ment, of course, is hardly conclusive. Certainly in view of Manuel's former unhappy dealings with his nephew, and his continued suspicion of John VII when he departed in 1399, the very idea of the latter's agreement with Bayazid could well have touched an extremely sensitive point in Manuel's reflexes and, indeed, might have been all he would need to feel that John was treacherously up to his old tricks.

But let us reflect again on Manuel's activities. Since 1394, Manuel's policy had hinged entirely on the hope, desire, and quest for concerted military action by the West against the Turks. The disaster of Nicopolis had not daunted him one bit in that outlook. If his subsequent personal mission to the West had been a disappointment and a decidedly sobering experience, it had still not altered this basic policy. We have seen that Manuel continued, all through his homeward journey, his negotiations and pleas for the same thing—military action against the Turks, especially now that the defeat of Ancyra had so disorganized them. His only reference to treating with the Turks, in his message which the Venetians considered on February 26, 1403, is much too vague to tell us much, but it is also vague enough to suggest that the idea meant little to Manuel himself. We can only speculate as to whether or not Manuel met with Turkish agents in the Morea (see n. 63 above), but we know nothing about this for certain. Yet, that is all we hear of the idea of Manuel himself negotiating with the Turks. Hence, it seems quite plausible to suppose that Manuel did not originally wish to commit himself to friendship with the Turks at all. I therefore submit that this attitude—and its corollary rejection of all John had done in establishing friendly relations with the Turks—may well have been a reason for Manuel's summary treatment of John and for his violation of their compact. It should be made clear, however, that this suggestion remains no more than a hypothesis.

Another explanation has been suggested by Alexandrescu-Dersca, 109. She maintains that Manuel, on his return, was anxious to please Timur, who was angry with the Byzantines for their pro-Turkish policy after Ancyra in violation of their promises to him. Manuel therefore felt himself obliged to repudiate the regime which had adopted that policy, and so he pretended to exile his nephew, the guilty culprit in Timur's eyes, to Lemnos, to defer the assignment of Thessalonica to him only until later. But there is probably even less defense for this hypothesis than for my own. Among other flaws: it is plain that, by the time Manuel returned, the fright over Timur was all but over and could have exerted little influence on Manuel's policy by then; also, Clavijo makes it indisputably clear that Manuel was angry personally and that John was cheated. If nothing else, however, at least even this theory catches the idea of Manuel's reaction against John's pro-Turkish policy.

For new light on this question, see the end of Appendix V below.

to be sure, we hear no more of popular clamor for John hereafter. On the other hand, this absence of popular reaction might
also indicate that John's ouster was effected either by stealth or
by deception. But we cannot determine clearly from our present
evidence whether John's expulsion was managed by trickery or
by force.[73]

Manuel must certainly have realized, however, that the matter
could not end here. Either after or instead of going to Lemnos,
to which he had been sent, the angry John made his way to his
father-in-law, Francesco II Gattilusio of Lesbos. Together, about
the middle of September, they set out with a flotilla of two gal-

73. Ducas (ed. Grecu, p. 111, ll. 14–16, ed. Bonn, p. 78, ll. 13–16) says:
"And his nephew withdrew from the rudder of the realm, and he was sent
to the island of Lemnos; and Manuel was acclaimed as sole Basileus by the
palace and the populace." This statement seems to make clear that Manuel's
return to the throne was peaceful and popularly acceptable. But the verb
πέμπεται is not strong enough to indicate how forcible John's dispatch to
Lemnos may have been. It apparently provided the basis for the assumption
by Vasiliev, "Putešestvie Manuila," 303 (83), and Dölger, "Johannes VII.,"
33, that John was first sent to Lemnos to await the next step, and that only
thereafter was it made clear that he would not be given Thessalonica as
promised. This is certainly a reasonable possibility: although Dölger is incorrect in his statement that Thessalonica was restored to the Byzantines only
after John had been sent to Lemnos. Moreover, such a possibility might be
supported also by the clear sequence of events to be noted in the passage
by Clavijo translated in n. 71: Manuel returned and was angry; Manuel
banished John; Manuel "gave him" ("dióle") Lemnos (for his realm *à la*
Napoleon as "King of Elba"?); Manuel deprived him ("quitó le") of
"Saloni." If this sequence reflects literally the actual chronology, John may
have been banished first, and may even have accepted it, only later to realize
that he was not to receive the expected appanage. Walter, 305, makes the
ingenious but entirely unfounded suggestion that Manuel banished John,
with reproaches, to Lemnos at the very time the latter met his uncle at
Gallipoli. But this writer's entire understanding of these events warrants
little trust. Konstantin the Philosopher, ed. Jagić, 279–280, ed. and trans.
Braun, 22, speaks only in general terms of John's obedient relinquishing of
the throne and departure to his realm in Thessalonica after it was restored
by Suleyman: cf. Stanojević, "Die Biographie Stefan Lazarevićs von Konstantin dem philosophen als Geschichtsquelle," 430.

The exact date of John's departure from Constantinople, in whatever
fashion, is not known. Significantly, we have no less than four references in
Peraiote expense accounts of this period to gifts ("exenia") of various things
made to John VII: Iorga, *Notes et extraits*, I, 56 (June 26, 1403), 65
(June 28), 63 (July 19), and 64 (July 27). These various dates, of course,
are not reliable or consistent enough to pin-point the end of John's presence
in Constantinople or its area. Such gifts from the Genoese to John were not
unique either. There is record of another presentation to him on January 28,
1403: *ibid.*, 59.

leys and five galliots to try to seize Thessalonica by force or, at least, to make a demonstration before it. At the same time, they sent a message to Boucicaut who, after his expedition to Cyprus, had moved on to make a move against the Muslim stronghold of Alexandretta in Syria. John reminded Boucicaut that the latter had been a witness to the sworn agreement that uncle and nephew had made. He requested that Boucicaut, when he left Alexandretta, join Gattilusio and himself at Lemnos, where they would await him, so that they could then all go on to seize Thessalonica. An answer from Boucicaut soon reached Mitylene, although its contents are not recorded. But its tenor must have been negative, for Boucicaut was too busy to have any truck with such a scheme.[74]

Of any actual attack by John and Gattilusio on Thessalonica we have no knowledge, and in all likelihood it never took place; for in less than a month a settlement had been reached. Exactly why is not clear. Perhaps Manuel allowed his wrath to cool. Perhaps the threat of the proposed attack on Thessalonica had something to do with it. Probably Manuel realized that a fulfill-

74. Clavijo, ed. López Estrada, 27 and 28, ed. Sreznevskii, 39 and 40–41, trans. Le Strange, 51 and 52–53 (which last is again marred by a confusion between "escalime," Lemnos, and "metalin," Mitylene). Clavijo arrived in Mitylene in early October, shortly before which John and his father-in-law had left on their expedition. Clavijo left on October 6, 1403, at which time the message from Boucicaut had just come but was not yet revealed. But the Castilian heard news that Boucicaut had already sailed from Syria for an unknown destination. Actually, Boucicaut had started back toward Genoa, but ran into trouble off Modon, where he fought a battle with a Venetian fleet on October 7, 1403. For a full presentation of this story, see Delaville le Roulx, *La France en Orient*, I, 428–457. Miller, "The Gattilusij of Lesbos," 415–416 (322–323), and Dölger, "Johannes VII.," 33, in their respective accounts make the assertion that John and his father-in-law actually made an attack on Thessalonica, "early in 1403," or "zu Anfang des J. 1403," which is violently inconsistent not only with the facts but, in Dölger's case, with his own narrative (since he states that the treaty which returned Thessalonica to Manuel was not negotiated until June of 1403, an incorrect statement in itself). Both scholars err also in stating that Clavijo met John VII personally on Lesbos: the Castilian himself says that John and Gattilusio were away on their expedition when he touched at the island. The latest discussion of the perplexing events and chronology of this 1403 episode, by Wirth in his "Zum Geschichtsbild Kaiser Johannes' VII. Palaiologos," 596–597, and 600, is compromised in my outlook by commitment to the untenable datings of the 1403 treaty to June 3 and Manuel's return to September, and, more generally, by a somewhat fragmented approach to the problems of and sources for the history of John VII in his nonetheless laudable efforts to bring Dölger's article on that Emperor up to date.

ment of his original promise was, after all, the only sensible solution to the long-smoldering feud in the Imperial family.[75] At any rate, before the beginning of November, 1403, Manuel had agreed on an arrangement to share with John the Imperial title and succession.[76] More immediately important, he granted John

75. Miller, "The Gattilusij of Lesbos," 415–416 (322–323), makes no effort to explain the reason for Manuel's final decision. Dölger, "Johannes VII.," 34, however, makes this assertion: "But apparently it was again Boucicaut who, after October 1403, was the intermediary of a renewed understanding between Manuel and John." And this suggestion is blindly accepted as fact by Walter, 305. It is an imaginative suggestion, to be sure. Unfortunately it has no definite basis in fact. Nothing in Clavijo gives any statement or hint of such a further role on the part of Boucicaut, and the author of the *Livre des faits* is completely unaware of the entire episode. An argument *ex silentio* is of course always dangerous, and it is true that Boucicaut's biographer overlooks the request by John and Gattilusio, which plainly *was* made. But that by itself was a small incident in the midst of Boucicaut's busy expedition; for the writer to overlook it would be quite understandable. On the other hand, to pass over such an episode as a new reconciliation between Manuel and John would have been a different matter indeed. What could have demonstrated better the honor and gallantry of *le bon messire* than a second intervention in this nasty family quarrel, this time to insure the fulfillment of a sworn pledge as well as to preserve peace? Not only, moreover, is there not a shred of evidence to support Dölger's suggestion, but all of the facts we have available emphatically rule it out. As we know from the passage in Clavijo which is cited in the next note (and which Dölger did not use), the final settlement was reached before the beginning of November. We know very well from Boucicaut's well-documented movements that he could not possibly have been involved personally in these affairs. For after he left Syria he sailed into the battle off Modon, on October 7, and from there he returned to Genoa, by October 29. It is not inconceivable that he might at least have written a letter or sent some kind of diplomatic communication to Manuel, but even this is questionable. There is thus almost no likelihood that Boucicaut had anything to do with the final settlement between John VII and Manuel.

76. Clavijo was in Constantinople at the end of October and the very beginning of November 1403. In recounting his visit there, he indulges in a digression on the revolts of John V's eldest son, Andronicus, and then proceeds (ed. López Estrada, 56; cf. ed. Sreznevskii, 86, trans. Le Strange, 86–87): "And after his days [i.e. after John V's death] he left the empire to this Chirmanoly, his [Andronicus'] brother, who now holds it. And his [John V's] elder son left a son named Dimitri, and it is he they say now who had a right to the empire and to a joint rule as emperor. And they are now agreed in this manner: that both be called emperors and that after his days of him who now rules the empire [i.e. after Manuel's death], that the other be emperor; and after his days that it return to be the son of him who now rules; and after, the son of the other. And in this manner are they agreed; the which [pact] I hold that the one will not preserve with the other." The identification of the son of Andronicus as "Dimitri," or "Demetrius," is very strange. Apparently Clavijo was confused in his information, for the

the promised appanage. Presumably not long after, and perhaps from Lemnos, John was conducted to Thessalonica by Demetrius Lascaris Leontaris—who was to become in time one of Manuel's most trusted henchmen. There John was installed as "Basileus of all Thessaly." [77] Leontaris remained as his administrator and, doubtless, also as liaison man and overseer for Manuel.

Established in his appanage at last, John VII settled down to a quiet existence, ruling in his own right independently, causing no trouble, and turning his attention to the setting up of pious foundations for the benefit of his restless soul.[78] With this move, Manuel at long last all but ended the tragic rivalry and division that had wracked his family and exposed the Empire to danger with only brief interruptions for three decades.

While and after this matter was attended to, Manuel faced the second and larger problem that he found on his return to Constantinople. This was the question of his entire external policy in the light of the outcome of Ancyra. By the summer of 1403 the threat of Timur had evaporated. At the time the Castilian ambas-

prince can be none other than John VII, as Le Strange correctly recognizes. And this agreement has all the earmarks of being a new compact and part of one which had just settled the dispute that the unrealizing author had previously described. It is surprising that this important passage has not been noticed and used before for its proper meaning. (Save that it is the only explanation for the curious reference by Van Millingen, *Byzantine Churches in Constantinople* [London, 1912], 230, to "the Despot Demetrius," who is plainly John VII. No explanation whatsoever is given for this identification, but it must reflect an acquaintance of some sort with this passage in Clavijo, since John VII is called "Demetrius" in no other source that I have seen.)

77. Ducas, ed. Grecu, 113, ed. Bonn, 79. The Ἐκ. χρον. not only ignores the ill feeling between Manuel and John, but makes the granting of the appanage a reward for a good job well done as ruler in Manuel's absence: "But his nephew was in all respects most able and devout, wherefore also after (the Basileus' return) from Italy he [Manuel] gave him Thessalonica" (p. 1, l. 17 to p. 2, l. 1). See also Βρ. χρ. No. 15, p. 33, ll. 56–58, which mentions the granting of Thessalonica to John, "who was reigning as formerly until when the Basileus of the Heavens took him to His realm, in which there is glory through the ages, Amen." Cf. Mompherratos, Διπλ. ἐν., 53. The *Chron. Vat. gr. 162*, no. 19, p. 211, ll. 92–93, says that Manuel sent "Andronicus"—a confusion in this source of John VII either with Manuel's brother or with his son—to Thessalonica, "δεσπόζειν" (significantly, not "βασιλεύειν") it.

78. See the excellent discussion of his reign in Thessalonica by Dölger, "Johannes VII.," 34–36. For John's pious grants, see Dölger's *Regesten*, nos. 3202–3206, 3208–3211, pp. 75–78. On his death, and for Leontaris in Thessalonica, see below, pp. 278–279.

sador to Samarkand, Ruy González de Clavijo, passed through Constantinople, at the end of October, and had an audience with Manuel,[79] Timur had returned to Asia and seemed but a strange and apocalyptic phantom to the Byzantines. It was rather with the Turks that Manuel had still to contend.

It is easy enough to point out the striking relaxation of the Byzantine position as a result of Ancyra, and it is surely all but superfluous by now to dwell upon the old saw that Timur's victory gave Byzantium more than fifty years of additional life. Certainly, indeed, once he had heard the news of the death of Bayazid early that year in March, it is understandable that Manuel should seek some satisfaction in literary form over the dramatic downfall of his former nemesis and hated adversary.[80] But the end of Bayazid and the disruption of the Turkish state hardly solved everything. If the remnant of the Empire was no longer fighting desperately for its very life, the Turks were still very much present, and their strength, actual and potential, was still impressive. It must have been clear to anyone of Manuel's intelligence that it would only be a matter of time before the Turkish power, if left alone to work out its problems, would be once again fully organized and marshaled—and aggressively on the march.

To meet this situation, Manuel was obliged to review his former policy. That policy, we need hardly be reminded at this time, had been of necessity uncompromising hostility to the Turks, based on the active hope and quest for military and financial aid from the West. How much of this policy was still applicable?

79. Clavijo and his embassy were received by the Emperor and his family. His description of the audience (ed. López Estrada, 34–35, ed. Sreznevskii, 50–51, trans. Le Strange, 61) is very valuable. With the Emperor were his wife, the Empress Helena, and "three very little sons." This statement is important, for it proves that Manuel's son Andronicus must have been born while Manuel was absent in the West. See Appendix XV below. Clavijo estimated the age of the eldest at about eight years. John was actually almost eleven years old at that time, and Theodore was probably not more than seven or eight, while Andronicus could not have been much more than three. On this interview and embassy, see also Cirac Estopañan, *La unión, Manuel II Paleólogo y sus recuerdos en España*, 67–68. On Clavijo's visit to Constantinople in general, see *id.*, "Tres monasterios de Constantinopla visitados per Españoles en el año 1403," *Rev. d. ét. byz.*, 19 (=*Mélanges R. Janin*, 1961), 358–381.

80. For a translation of Manuel's two little works in this connection, see Appendix XX below.

Part of the answer to that question was no longer under Manuel's control. New Byzantine policy had already been shaped in advance in the last six months of John VII's regime. Whether Manuel liked it or not—and which reaction it was we can only conjecture—the treaty of February 1403, between the Christian powers and Suleyman, had drastically altered the Empire's course. It had, to be sure, brought a superficial peace and a not unimpressive territorial restitution to the Empire. But its deeper implications may be seen in the fact that the treaty, and John's involvement with other Turkish affairs, now committed Byzantium and Manuel to two important paths: in the first place, to the principle of some degree of outward friendship and cooperation with the Turks; and, in the second place, to a role in the unavoidable struggle for succession among the sons of Bayazid. For better or worse, Manuel found himself faced with the task of allying himself with one or another contender. For the period now under consideration, the respective histories of the Byzantines and the Osmanlis become more inextricably intertwined than ever.

As with the formulation of policy, the context of events had begun to take shape even before Manuel had returned. The sudden eclipse of Bayazid had left the Turkish state in a chaotic condition. No single period of Osmanli history demonstrates better the palpable practicality of the brutal Turkish custom, later to become virtual law, that the designated successor to the throne must murder all his brothers to avoid the dangers of civil war. Unfortunately, no single successor to the throne had been marked out. Of Bayazid's sons, after the disappearance of the eldest, Mustafa, at the Battle of Ancyra, there were no less than four who were eligible for power. Three had escaped from the battle. The oldest of these, Suleyman, had gone to Brusa. But before the pursuit of Timur's victorious army, which captured and sacked the city, the prince fled across the Straits and established himself in the still-intact European portion of the Turkish lands, Rumelia. Meanwhile, Mechmed, one of the younger of Bayazid's sons, had fled to his enclave of Amasia, where he maintained himself while another son, Isa, was able to establish himself in Brusa. Still another of Bayazid's younger sons, Musa, was captured in the battle and was for a while held prisoner. Subsequently, after the death of Bayazid (March 8, 1403) on Timur's homeward march, Musa was allowed to escort his father's remains back to Brusa for burial. For these four men, and for the Turks, there was to be no rest until one of them alone had finally emerged in supreme power.[81]

The first phase of the struggle had already been accomplished. Mechmed's ambitions were made plain from the outset. Asserting his claims to all of Anatolia, he challenged Isa. Driven from Brusa, Isa sought refuge in Constantinople, and, willingly or otherwise, John VII acceded, although the degree of outright Byzantine cooperation is unclear. Isa attempted to regain his position in Anatolia, but he was again defeated by Mechmed and was dispatched from the scene. Thus, by the time Manuel was personally in command of Byzantine policy again, one of the competitors had already been eliminated.[82] Mechmed was master

81. This entire period of civil war over the Turkish succession (1402–13) is extremely complex and difficult. The three Greek historians devote much attention to it and give a good deal of useful information: Ducas, ed. Grecu, 101–102, 111–113, ed. Bonn, 70–72, 78–97; Chalcocondyles, ed. Darkó, I, 147–148, 154–155, 159–172, ed. Bonn, 158, 165, 169–183; and the Pseudo-Phrantzes, ed. Papadopoulos, 70, 88–93, ed. Bonn, 65, 84–89; and also the *Chron. Barb. 111*, 40, 43–45. Accounts by modern writers are few, confused, and scanty. Still useful, though not always up-to-date on some points, are Hammer, I, 325–329, 335–337, 338–360, trans. Hellert, II, 105–109, 120–122, 124–158, and more helpful, Iorga, *Geschichte*, 322, 325–360. The cursory account by Pears, 149–152, is not worth much; Muralt's entries are few and utterly confused. See also, however, the useful articles on "Sulaimān Čelebi" by E. Rossi, and on "Muhammad I" and "Mūsā Čelebi" by J. H. Kramers, in *The Encyclopaedia of Islām*. Most recently, there are now also the comments of Werner, *Die Geburt einer Grossmacht*, 180–213.

82. Ducas, ed. Grecu, 113, ed. Bonn, 80. Chalcocondyles, ed. Darkó, I, 159–160, ed. Bonn, 169–170, followed by the Pseudo-Phrantzes, ed. Papadopoulos, 90, ed. Bonn, 86; and also Konstantin the Philosopher, ed. Jagić, 280, ed. and trans. Braun, 23, have Isa defeated and executed by Suleyman's later Anatolian expedition. This apparently erroneous version of events is most recently accepted by Runciman, *The Fall of Constantinople*, 43, compounding the problem by giving 1405 as the date; even more confusing, and without explanation or documentation, F. Taeschner, in his chapter, "The Ottoman Turks to 1453," in *Cambr. Med. Hist.*, IV (2nd ed.), 1, p. 767, has Isa defeated and slain by Musa. For other accounts, see Iorga, *Geschichte*, 336–337; Hammer, I, 341–343, trans. Hellert, II, 130–135; cf. also Wittek, "De La Défaite d'Ankara à la prise de Constantinople," *Revue des études islamiques*, 12 (1938), 19–20. Konstantin the Philosopher actually does later (ed. Jagić, 284–285) describes Suleyman's later campaign in Anatolia against Mechmed as being against Isa: cf. Stanojević, 434 ff. At least this source's dissent from Ducas may therefore be safely discounted. Suleyman is also given responsibility for Isa's death in the account by Ibn Arabshah, 186–187, of the struggle of Bayazid's sons. But his entire account is highly biased, and not overly reliable.

More crucial information is contained in a report of the clash of Isa and his brother in the course of a letter by the Ragusan government to King

of Anatolia, with Musa still an uncertain factor vaguely under his wing, and he could now lay firm claim to bear the title of Sultan.[83]

Sigismund of Hungary, ed. J. Gelcich and L. Thallóczy, *Diplomatarium relationum reipublicae ragusanae cum regno Hungariae* (=*Raguza és magyarország összeköttéteseinek oklovéltára*, Budapest, 1887), no. 92a, p. 123. In this letter, dated August 11, 1403, the Ragusans relate: "... Diebus his a nonnullis nostris mercatoribus nobis supervenerunt litere, continentes, principem Celopiam contra fratrem obtinuisse victoriam et hinc inde interfectum. ..." Now, since the name "Celopia" is commonly applied in these as in other documents to Suleyman, as a corruption of his title of *Çelebi* ("Prince"), this text might seem to support the reports that it was *Suleyman* and not Mechmed who disposed of Isa. But in the very next letter of this pair, ed. Gelcich and Thallóczy, no. 92b, p. 124, dated August 23, 1403, the Ragusan authorities inform Sigismund: "... Nuperius per literas nostrorum mercatorum habuimus ... principem vero Celopiam ingentibus continuo augere potenter, *fratrem vero in his citramarinis partibus* defecisse potencia." In other words, the "Celopia" (i.e. "Prince") who is growing stronger, by implication *in ultramarinis partibus* in Asia Minor, is obviously Mechmed; whereas "his brother in these regions this side of the sea" (i.e. in Rumelia) is Suleyman. Only later does the Ragusan use of "Celopia" in their documents refer to Suleyman, with a different name then applied to Mechmed.

That this interpretation is correct is further supported by another set of sources, which also provides valuable chronological evidence for the dating of the struggle between Mechmed and Isa. In the Genoese expense accounts for Pera, published by Iorga, *Notes et extraits*, I, 61, an entry of May 19, 1403, speaks of an ambassador "transmis[s]um in Turchia pro negociis Communis, de mense Januarii proxime preteriti, ad presenciam domini Esebey, *tunc dominatis in Turchia* ...," and of expenses then "pro una veste exeniata prefato domino Esebay." Thereafter, another entry, for May 18, 1403, speaks of expenses for the same ambassador, "transmissum ad presenciam domini Chiriihi, *dominantis in Turchia*, pro factis Communis, videlicet pro pace tractanda cum ipso domino Criihi. ..." And another entry, for June 15, 1403 (*ibid.*, 61–62), reports expenses made by a Genoese ambassador, "missum ad dominum Criihi *in Turchia dominantem*, pro pace tractanda pro Communi nostro ...;" another entry for the same date (*ibid.*, 62) refers again to Genoese "ambassiatoribus domini Criichi, *in Turchia dominantis*. ..." One of the surnames given to Mechmed was Kürüshdji," "Wrestler," and so in Western sources such extreme corruptions as "Chiriihi" or "Criihi" are commonly used for his name. These references indicate that it was probably between January, when Isa was *tunc dominans in Turchia*, and May, when Mechmed was (*nunc*) *dominans in Turchia*, that their clash occurred. Whether the first clash only, or both, is not clear; but Iorga suggests in his comments (p. 61, n. 2) that the May date refers only to the time after Isa's first defeat. This is plausible, if we assume that the Genoese would have hastened to send an ambassador immediately to the victor. Conceivably, therefore, the June date might possibly refer to an embassy sent after Mechmed's second and final victory over Isa; although this conjecture is far less safe. At any rate, at least Isa's first defeat and his refuge in Constantinople, if not also his second defeat, had already occurred by the time Manuel had returned to the city in mid-June of 1403.

83. It was an occasional practice in the past to regard the Osmanli use

We know of no moves on Manuel's part at this time regarding Mechmed. But the closer proximity of Suleyman required that Manuel's course be decided upon promptly. According to our information, Manuel made at least one decisively anti-Turkish move promptly upon his return. Able at last to rid himself of this stigma of former Turkish domination, Manuel expelled the Turkish quarter, the establishment of which had been imposed by Bayazid.[84] But Turkish power had no intention of drying up and disappearing. Manuel knew that he must come to terms with it. Whether or not he originally approved of John's policy of good relations with at least some elements among the Turks, Manuel recognized that he would have to make the best of the situation and choose allies among the contending Bayazidlings.

Fortunately, Byzantium now had some advantages in such a policy, for the first time in dealing with the Turks since their rise. The very struggle among the rival brothers gave Manuel an opportunity at least to attempt to play one off against another. This trick was hardly unfamiliar to Byzantine diplomacy, of course. And if the Empire had in better times had more strength and resources of its own with which to back up such manipulations, this course still offered fruitful possibilities for winning Byzantine advantage now. Indeed, the various Turkish princes themselves at one time or another all recognized that the support and alliance of Byzantium could be a vital factor in their struggles.

of the title "Sultan" as beginning primarily in the time of Mechmed I. Indeed, the *Chron. Barb. 111,* 55, so much as states that Mechmed I was the first to bear it. This assumption is quite untenable now, and Atiya, *The Battle of Nicopolis,* 157–160, has given some ample demonstrations that the title was used as early as the time of Orkhan (1326–1359) and was very common by the time of Bayazid. However, the Greek sources for the period discussed thus far have usually employed the title ἀμηρᾶς, from "Emir," and it has been deemed appropriate to adopt this usage. The grander term "Sultan," however, may suggest something of the new tone of the reign of Mechmed I, who was indeed the ruler to set the Osmanli state at last on its organized program of true empire. Therefore, though the distinction is admittedly a somewhat artificial one, this latter title will be used hereafter to designate Mechmed I and his successors.

84. For source citation, see Alexandrescu-Dersca, 109, who mistakenly assumes that this move was one of several allegedly made to placate the anger of Timur. But, as we have pointed out elsewhere in this regard (see above, the end of n. 72), Timur had passed out of the picture and was no influence on Byzantine policy by the time of Manuel's return. Muralt, p. 781, no. 1 (for the year 1402!), also asserts this move on Manuel's part, but himself cites no relevant sources.

We have seen that the short-lived Isa had already had recourse to Byzantine aid, if inconsequentially. But far more important was the readiness of Suleyman to reach a friendly accommodation with Byzantium.

Conscious of the internal weakness of his position in Rumelia,[85] Suleyman had been seeking to strengthen himself by firm ties with Byzantium. The basis of the rapprochement had already been laid in the treaty of February 1403, with John VII as one of the parties to it. But Suleyman would be anxious, naturally, to cement his tie personally with Manuel himself, whose approval and relations obviously carried the greater weight. According to two sources, Suleyman went so far as to go to Constantinople to ally himself with Manuel; but this visit may actually have come later.[86] Indeed, from all outward evidence, it would seem as if

85. Such is the plausible interpretation of Wittek. In his *Rise of the Otto-man Empire* (*Royal Asiatic Society Monographs*, 23, London, 1938), Wittek outlined the provocative interpretation of the growth of the Turkish state in terms of the activity of the Ghāzīs, the fanatic Muslim warriors whose sense of struggle for the glory and expansion of the faith became identified with the expansion of Osmanli power. (I do not have available to me an earlier and broader presentation of this thesis by Wittek in his "Die Glaubens-kämpfer im Osmanenstaat," in *Ostersche Genootschap in Nederland, Verslag van het achtste Congres*, Leyden, 1936, pp. 2–7; cf. the summary in *Byz. Zeitschr.*, 36 [1936], 493.) In his subsequent article, "De La Défaite d'Ankara à la prise de Constantinople," Wittek projects this interpretation into a more specific epoch, and the 1403–13 phase becomes crucial. As far as Suleyman himself is concerned, Wittek seems to maintain (17–19) that (in addition to has alleged character failings) this prince antagonized the Ghāzīs, warlike frontier elements particularly important in Rumelia, by his favor to Christians, especially Greeks, and by his lack of aggressive impulse. As a result, Suleyman was in a very awkward position as far as his internal support was concerned; hence his efforts to strengthen his external position all the more, creating a kind of vicious cycle.

86. Ducas, ed. Grecu, 111–113, ed. Bonn, 78–79, describes an entry into Constantinople by Suleyman and an interview between Manuel and the prince (whom most of the Greek sources name as "Μουσουλμάν," or "Μουσουλμάνης"), as having occurred immediately after the Emperor's return. Konstantin the Philosopher, ed. Jagić, 279, ed. and trans. Braun, 21–22, describes a conclusion of amity at Gallipoli immediately upon Manuel's return from the West: cf. Stanojević, 430; Hammer, I, 341, trans. Hellert, II, 129–130; and Iorga, *Geschichte*, I, 328. But both sources associate this meeting with the treaty of February 1403, which they portray as an agreement with Manuel, and the terms of which at least Ducas exaggerates. Hence, their entire chronology for this episode may be suspect; for, of course, the treaty was drawn up before Manuel returned (but then, would this visit have been to John, at the time of the treaty's settlement?), and the personal visit to Manuel seems rather to be the one that other sources place a little

Manuel's total commitment to Suleyman was not forced for some years after the former's return from the West.

Nevertheless, Suleyman was ultimately obliged to demonstrate his dependency on Manuel. Fostering his own ambitions in Anatolia, Suleyman crossed to his brother's territory in 1407 and seized Brusa.[87] Such success, however, was only temporary. Musa, for the time being acting on the side of Mechmed, opposed Suleyman and was encouraged by Mechmed to strike out on his own in Rumelia. Musa took up this idea and hied himself to the northern frontiers of Rumelia to win support from the neighboring Christian states which were more-or-less vassals to the Turks. Outflanked by this diversion, Suleyman was forced to abandon his Anatolian designs in order to cope with the new threat. Thus, by 1409, Suleyman was required to give up his larger schemes and to face a direct challenge in his own territory.

By this time it was obvious that Suleyman needed all the support he could find. Having already cultivated the Byzantines in the 1403 treaty, he now sought more direct personal ties. In the face of Musa's challenge, he went directly to Constantinople

later, in 1409 or 1410. (And Konstantin the Philosopher actually does speak of the later meeting as a separate and second one: see n. 143 below.) See also n. 88.

87. This dating can be corroborated usefully by an important passage in a text apparently not much used before: one of the letters of the Ragusan authorities to King Sigismund of Hungary, ed. Gelcich and Thallóczy, *Diplomatarium*, no. 109, pp. 170–171. In this letter, dated June 14, 1407, the Ragusans report (p. 171): "... His diebus recedentem ad hoc littora quamdam galeam Venetam de levantinis partibus accessisse, cuius rectores, prudenter tentati Calopiam Teucrorum principem in partibus illis ultramarinis fratri suo insidiato, ipsumque fugare per moncium cacumina ambobus cum debili hominum potencia constitutis nos allocuti sunt. Novimus atque volante fama ambassiatam vestre maiestatis ad dictum dominum Calopiam missam iam pluribus retroactis temporibus, dum sibi supplicaretur per aliquos dicte maiestatis emulos eam in longum pertrahi debere, ut conceptus maiestatis vestre felices frustratis temporibus impediantur, sagaciter fraudis dulcedine retardari." It seems plain that here, once again, the name "Calopia" refers to Mechmed as the "prince in those regions beyond the sea [i.e. Asia Minor]," rather than to Suleyman: see above, n. 82. In view of the date of the Ragusan report, we might estimate that Suleyman's crossing to attack Mechmed must have been, at the latest, by early spring of 1407. Cf. Hammer, I, 345–347, trans. Hellert, II, 135–139; Iorga, *Geschichte*, I, 339–341.

and addressed himself as a devoted son to the Emperor Manuel. Lest this filial profession be insufficient, he offered as hostages for the good faith of his alliance with the Byzantines a young brother and a sister of his, and he also took as a wife a member of Manuel's family.[88]

88. Ducas, ed. Grecu, 111, ed. Bonn, 78–79; Chalcocondyles, ed. Darkó, I, 161, ed. Bonn, 172; Pseudo-Phrantzes, ed. Papadopoulos, 90–91, ed. Bonn, 86–87; *Chron. Barb. 111*, 43. All of these sources agree on one thing: that Suleyman went into the capital and established personal amity with Manuel. The last three of these sources all relate this unprecedented act as being the result of Musa's attack on Rumelia. It seems likely, therefore, that Ducas' relating the incident to the treaty of 1403, or at least to Manuel's return to Constantinople, is but part of his general confusion of chronology for these events, as discussed in n. 86. All the other sources speak of Suleyman's marriage.

Chalcocondyles identifies the bride as an unnamed daughter of (Hilario) Doria, and hence the granddaughter of Manuel through his own illegitimate daughter, Zampia, Doria's wife: see Appendix IX below. Both the *Chron. Barb. 111* and the Pseudo-Phrantzes, however, differ from Chalcocondyles, and both identify the bride as an unnamed illegitimate daughter of Manuel's brother, the Despot Theodore. Ordinarily, the testimony of Chalcocondyles might take precedence in such a choice, but it is significant that both of these satellites should diverge from their usual source. Perhaps they had other information. And since we have other testimony (see below, p. 368 and n. 120) that a daughter of Doria was supposedly married later to a Turkish prince, though a different one, it may well be that Chalcocondyles fell into confusion as a result of this parallel. Certainly it is generally accepted that it was Theodore's daughter whom Suleyman married at this time: cf. A. T. Papadopoulos, *Versuch einer Geneaolgie der Palaiologen*, 56 and 57. (If it were she, indeed, she was possibly brought back from the Morea after her father's death by Manuel at the end of his 1408 visit: see n. 142 below: also n. 63 above.)

On the other hand, two different marriages are made out of these references by Iorga, *Geschichte*, who first (p. 328) refers to the marriage to Theodore's daughter as having occurred "später," after the treaty of 1403; and then (p. 350) speaks of a second marriage thereafter, in 1410, confusing Chalcocondyles' reference to Doria and the relationship to Manuel. Ducas, on the other hand, says nothing of any marriage, but he alone quotes an alleged promise by Suleyman to regard Manuel as his father, in words strikingly similar to those of his ambassador to Venice in December of 1402: see above, p. 223. Ducas also speaks of the giving of hostages. He does not give the name of the boy, but he identifies the girl as Φατμαχάτουν. This alleged name is perhaps a jumble of two, for Alexandrescu-Dersca, p. 109 and n. 5, derives from the Turkish sources the names Kāsim and Fātima, respectively. (On the other hand, Moravcsik, *Byzantinoturcica*, II, 331, indicates that it could reflect the genuine name Fātma-qatun.) Subsequently, Ducas tells their fate: he says (ed. Grecu, 135–137, ed. Bonn,

Thus, regardless of any possible initial reluctance to come to terms with the Turks, Manuel did at length take such steps. And by 1410, through this double alliance with Suleyman, personal and political, Manuel had fully committed himself to taking sides in the wars of Bayazid's sons, as those wars drew on. In many ways it was an advantageous course, as it is so often assumed, and as results ultimately proved, at least to some degree. But it was also virtually the only course, for Byzantium had no choice but to become involved in this struggle.

Yet, if Manuel had yielded to this necessity and had at length entered into a policy of qualified accommodation with the Turks once more, he had by no means abandoned his recent policy of seeking aid from the West. Quite the contrary, Manuel was as convinced as ever of the need for their help, in spite of the failure of his personal diplomacy among the Western rulers. This is a point which has not been readily understood. It has been common to notice Manuel's involvement in the Turkish civil wars, and to assume that, after the Battle of Ancyra had halted Turkish aggressiveness against Byzantium, Manuel simply devoted himself exclusively to alliances thereafter with one or another of Bayazid's sons. It has also been common to emphasize the disappointment that had been the prime result of the Western journey.[89] To be sure, as we shall readily see shortly, Manuel's

98–99) that, while Manuel returned the girl (now identified significantly only as Φατμά) to Brusa to be raised, he had the boy educated as a Christian with his own son John and eventually baptized before his death. Dölger, *Regesten,* no. 3201, p. 75, accepts Ducas' chronology and makes the handing over of these two hostages a concomitant of the 1403 treaty.

Chalcocondyles, ed. Darkó, I, 167, ed. Bonn, 178, also speaks of Turkish hostages, although he presents them as given not by Suleyman but by Musa (see n. 154 below): he speaks of "the youngest of the sons of Bayazid" who went to the Greeks and died among them, having accepted the Christian faith (cf. Muralt,, pp. 800–801, no. 6, who places his death in 1417). He identifies this son as Isa ('Ιησοῦς; the *Chron. Barb. 111,* 48, calls him 'Εσαί) but this entire reference is probably another confusion on Chalcocondyles' part, and in all likelihood it alludes to the very same prince Ducas mentions. Sphrantzes, *Chron. Minus,* 1025C (Pseudo-Phrantzes, ed. Papadopoulos, 70; also 90; ed. Bonn, 62; also 86), however, identifies him as 'Ιωσούφ[ης], who became a Christian under the name of Demetrios. See Moravcsik, *Byzantinoturcica,* II, 141 and 142; cf. Berger de Xivrey, 137–139; also Iorga, *Geschichte,* 350; Muralt, p. 786, no. 5 (under 1405) is completely jumbled. In addition, note Ch. Diehl, *Figures byzantines,* II (Paris, 1938), 272–273.

89. Cf. Jugie, 332: "A few galleys, some rich presents, some pleasant

personal experiences with the Latin rulers on that journey certainly did affect and modify his outlook. But Manuel was too much aware of the ultimate realities of the Byzantine situation to think that his realm could really survive on its own resources, regardless of the current divisions among the Turks. Indeed, Manuel's prime consideration all through these years after Ancyra was exactly a program of continued agitation for help from the West; full commitment to collaborating with Turkish factions came only later on, when the state of the Turkish civil wars finally made it unavoidable.

We are obviously not in a position to know all of Manuel's diplomatic activity during this time. But it is plain that there must have been a great deal of it—indeed, a steady continuation of what there had been previously. We can also see that, even while on his way home, Manuel had initiated further embassies to Western courts to continue the quest for aid. Once again, the documents of the Aragonese chancery give us invaluable illustrations of what this activity was.

It was undoubtedly while still on his homeward journey, perhaps while still in the Peloponnesus, that Manuel sent another of his family ambassadors, one Constantine Rhallis Palaeologus, to Western Europe. On June 26, 1403, King Martin I wrote to the Prior of Catalonia to provide for this ambassador's passage through areas of his realm.[90] Meanwhile, the indefatigable Alexios Vranas was still traveling back and forth between Spain and France on his mission: on the same date, June 26, Martin ordered a safe conduct and all necessary provisions for Vranas' passage to France.[91] Constantine Rhallis, however, remained on

mementoes, such was all that Manuel brought back from his long voyage to the West. It was little, without doubt, but Tamerlane had provided the splendid supplement which had guaranteed to old Byzantium fifty years more of existence."

90. Text, Rubió i Lluch, no. 675, pp. 697–698; cf. Marinesco, "Du Nouveau sur les relations de Manuel II Paléologue (1391–1425) avec l'Espagne," p. 432, and n. 4. On the basis of one of several letters written by Martin I of Aragon on February 28, 1403, Marinesco, p. 431, followed by Dölger, no. 3295, p. 89, note the passage of a Byzantine ambassador on his way to the court of Henry III of Castile. No name is mentioned, but one might suspect that it is this same Constantine Rhallis Palaeologus.

91. Rubió i Lluch, no. 576, p. 698; cf. Cirac Estopañan, *La unión*, 56–57, and 57. In a letter dated the following day, June 27, 1403, Martin rejoices with Manuel over the defeat of Bayazid and the return to obedience of the

Spanish land for the time being. His mission was to assist in the collection of aid for which Benedict XIII, the Avignonese Anti-Pope, had called on Manuel's behalf.[92] On September 25, 1404, King Martin provided a cordial letter of safe-conduct to Constantine and his son Theodore for this work.[93] The gathering of financial aid was carried on, but apparently it was hampered by difficulties. For, on the same date, September 25, Martin issued a decree in response to complaints from the Byzantine ambassadors, taking action against flagrant abuses in the collection of money.[94]

Apparently Greek emissaries had been filling Spanish ears with tales of renewed Turkish oppression, although Byzantium was no longer urgently in danger. For, on April 3, 1405, the King of Aragon issued a special decree: all his civil and religious officials were called upon to give all due attention and support to the Byzantine emissaries, as if they were the King's own men, that they might gather men and other necessities in view of the allegedly crucial situation in the East, and in view of Benedict XIII's preachings for a crusade.[95] Not restricting its efforts to Aragon, the Byzantine embassy pursued its mission elsewhere in the Iberian Peninsula. On April 24, 1405, King Martin provided a letter of recommendation for Theodore Rhallis Palaeologus to the King of Navarre.[96]

Meanwhile, during this period there was another Byzantine ambassador active in Aragon, either as part of the Rhallis em-

former Byzantine lands: Rubió i Lluch, no. 677, p. 699; cf. Marinesco, "Du Nouveau," 432; Cirac Estopañan, *La unión*, 57. And on April 1, 1404, Martin also addressed a letter to Timur, congratulating him on his victory: Rubió i Lluch, no. 679, p. 700.

92. Marinesco, "Du Nouveau," 430–431.

93. Rubió i Lluch, no. 681, p. 702; cf. Marinesco, "Du Nouveau," 432; Cirac Estopañan, *La unión*, 57; also Dölger, *Regesten*, no. 3297, p. 90, on the entire mission.

94. Rubió i Lluch, no. 682, p. 703; cf. Marinesco, "Du Nouveau," 432; Cirac Estopañan, *La unión*, 57.

95. Rubió i Lluch, no. 684, pp. 705–709; Marinesco, "Du Nouveau," 433.

96. Rubió i Lluch, no. 685, pp. 709–710; cf. Marinesco, "Du Nouveau," 433. At this time, i.e. during 1405–06, Constantine Rhallis himself seems to have been in France, where his publication of the Papal bulls and his collection of aid under the sponsorship of the French government seem to have been hampered by Constantine's ignorance of the local language: see Berger de Xivrey, 140–142; cf. Dölger, *Regesten*, no. 3298, p. 90.

bassy or on a separate commission from Manuel. For, in a letter of November 24, 1404, King Martin ordered his governor of Roussilon and Cerdagna to assist one "Angel" (i.e., Angelos) in his mission for the Emperor and to take stern measures against abuses in the collections.[97] The collections continued through these years, but so did the abuses, for, on August 23, 1406, the King wrote to certain officials to condemn more frauds in the gathering of the aid.[98] And on through 1407 such further actions against these abused continued as the Byzantine embassy carried on its work.[99] But the work dragged on for several years, and, as late as 1409 and 1410, we find Constantine Rhallis still active in the areas of Spain and France.[100]

Unfortunately, aside from a few specific figures, we have no complete knowledge of the final or total results of this long embassy. But the records of it demonstrate that, in the decade after Manuel traveled to Europe himself, his agents continued the quest for aid without cessation.

Manuel's hopes for Western action covered other fields and were concerned more with projects for military action. The Emperor did not neglect to press his cause further with the Papacy, in spite of the Schism and the delicate problem of union. The death of Boniface IX on October 1, 1404, did not end the Roman Papacy's interest in sponsoring aid to the East in the ultimate hope of union. His successor, Innocent VII, was eager to continue that course. Apparently Manuel sent an embassy to him not long after the Pope's accession, for, on May 25, 1405, he addressed a bull to the Emperor in reply. Tactfully avoiding questions of union itself, Innocent deplored the ravages of Timur and the continued oppression by the Turks. In the most cordial terms possible, the Pope promised to call for a new crusade and discussed arrangements for preaching it in Eastern and Central Europe.[101] But, unfortunately, these Papal moves meant little.

97. Rubió i Lluch, no. 683, p. 704; cf. Marinesco, "Du Nouveau," 432; Cirac Estopañan, *La unión*, 57; and Dölger, *Regesten*, no. 3302, p. 91.

98. Rubió i Lluch, no. 693, pp. 715–716; cf. Marinesco, "Du Nouveau," 433.

99. Marinesco, "Du Nouveau," 433–434.

100. *Ibid.*, 434–435.

101. Text, Baronius-Raynaldus, *Annales ecclesiastici*, 1405, nos. 1–4 (Vol. 27, pp. 126–128). Cf. Halecki, "Rome et Byzance au temps du grand

Innocent himself died in the following year, and, amid the deepening complexity and acrimony of the Great Schism during this period, the divided Papacy was to play little further role in Eastern affairs.

Schisme d'Occident," 519–520. For further use of this document, see also E. Goeller, "Zur Geschichte Manuels II. von Byzanz," *Römische Quartalschrift für christliche Altertumskunde und für Kirchengeschichte,* 15 (1901), 189 and 190. Cf. also Muralt, p. 786, no. 10, who speaks of an actual call for a crusade on June 25, 1405. For some curious reason, Dölger completely ignores Manuel's incontestably genuine bull to Pope Innocent VII in his *Regesten.* On the other hand, Dölger does (no. 3296, p. 89) take quite seriously the account given by Adam of Usk (ed. Thompson, pp. 96–97; trans. pp. 272–273) of "solempnes ambassiatores" who appeared before Boniface IX in Rome in spring of 1404 "ex parte imperatoris Constantinapolitani" to demand the restoration to the Empire of the Kingdoms of Lombardy and Naples, wrongfully usurped by the German Emperor; or, this failing, that their master be allowed to press his claim by a personal combat to be fought between them in Rome. Though Adam was in Rome at the time and professes to have met these ambassadors personally, his entire story is too absurd to be taken at face value, though what reality it may dimly reflect is difficult to determine.

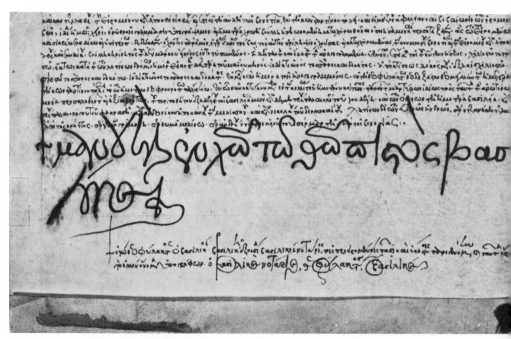

Figure 18: *Manuel's Formal Signature: The Byzantine Treaty with Venice of May 22, 1406.* Archivo di Stato, Venezia, *Miscellanea, atti, diplomi e privilegi,* 928 (see Appendix XXIV, A, III, 3).

Not that occasional inclination for military activity in the East was entirely lacking. The idea of an active league against the Turks came to the fore occasionally. As early as the spring of 1404, the Knights of St. John on Rhodes were willing to foster such a project. Philibert de Naillac, the Grand Master of the Hospitalers, sent out negotiators to various powers, including Byzantium, toward this end. And this idea continued to be raised by the Hospitalers in subsequent years. Unfortunately, nothing came of it.[102] Not that the idea was to end here, as we shall see. But appeals for such projects fell on deaf or distracted ears. Moreover, among the powers whose cooperation would have been essential, that of such a key one as Venice was most unlikely.

More than ever, amid the Turkish upheavals the aim of the Serene Republic was, quite literally, to "mind their own business." It is true that on September 6, 1403, the Senate was willing

102. Delaville le Roulx, *Les Hospitaliers*, 302–303.

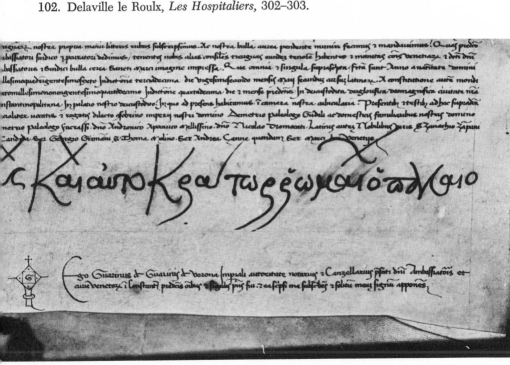

to send a small force to Constantinople to defend the city in the event of any Turkish attack against it,[103] even though such an attack was quite unlikely by this time. Much more important to the Venetians was the regularization of the situation in the East after the upheavals of 1402 for the good of their commercial interests. This aim applied to the Byzantines as well. No treaty between Venice and the Empire had been signed since that of 1390 (with John VII), which had long ago expired. On May 27, 1404, the Senate discussed the need for sending a new agent to Constantinople and for renewing the treaty with the Emperor: for that purpose Paolo Zeno was chosen.[104] On July 19 Zeno received his instructions: he was to congratulate Manuel on his return home and to press for the renewal of the treaty; he was to raise the question of the Byzantine debt to Venice, urge Venetian rights in this and other matters, and avoid any dispute over the island of Tenedos, if such should arise.[105] But it was precisely this last issue that delayed agreement on the treaty, and a long sequence of haggling ensued.[106] Only a full two years after the

103. Partial text, Iorga, *Notes et extraits,* I, 140, overlooked by Thiriet. The Senate also deplored the abuses committed during and after the Turkish crossing of the Straits after Timur's victory.

104. Thiriet, *Régestes,* II, no. 1158, pp. 46–47.

105. *Ibid.,* no. 1165, p. 48; Iorga, *Notes et extraits,* I, 142.

106. The Venetian envoys in Constantinople apparently met with stiff resistance. By the beginning of the following year a Byzantine envoy, John Moschopoulos, had gone to Venice, and on January 13, 1405, the Byzantine demands for Venetian renunciation of all claims to Tenedos were rejected: Thiriet, *Régestes,* II, no. 1175, p. 50; cf. Dölger, *Regesten,* no. 3303, p. 91. On January 30–31, new proposals were presented, modifying the Byzantine stand as to Tenedos, but introducing a host of other problems, including disputes over the respective inheritances of Theodora Ghisi (who had died in Constantinople, having willed land on Negroponte to the Emperor, who now claimed it) and of John Lascaris Kalopheros (a Greek citizen of Venice and an old friend of Cydones whose estate was disputed). The Senate promptly proceeded to haggle away in their best fashion: Iorga, *Notes et extraits,* I, 144–146; Thiriet, no. 1176, pp. 50–51 (on another proposal in this deliberation, see below, p. 272 and n. 128). After the whole complex of issues had dragged on longer, the Hospitalers decided to add their contribution with a request to construct their own fortification on the disputed island; this happy idea received a somewhat less than cordial reaction: Thiriet, no. 1194, p. 54. More than a year after the last reported discussion, Byzantine ambassadors were still, or again, present in Venice, themselves pushing for some decision; and the best solution seemed to be simply to put off the question of Tenedos until the next treaty renewal: Iorga, 149–150; Thiriet, no. 1203, p. 56. More aspects of the Tenedos question were debated, but inconclusively, on March 30, 1406: Iorga, 150–151; Thiriet, no. 1208,

matter was initiated was the treaty finally settled and dated May 22, 1406.[107] Amid such prolonged bickering over routine problems, we hear nothing of any serious negotiations between Venice and Manuel.[108]

Nonetheless, negotiations, not only with Venice but with a number of other powers, were to be increased considerably as a result of Manuel's most elaborate and formal diplomatic venture of this period. The Emperor was apparently anxious to continue, as far as possible, the personal contacts which he had established with the courts of Europe during his own journey. Manuel also wished to make another attempt to arouse the West to the fact that the Byzantines still needed aid. But it is apparent that the element of personal contact was itself a strong factor in the embassy which Manuel sent. For these purposes he needed a man who was both close to him and also known and respected in the West. With these qualifications in mind, he could not have made a better choice than Manuel Chrysoloras. Chrysoloras was not only a personal friend and adviser to Manuel, but he was also a distinguished man of letters. In the 1390's he had won a matchless reputation among the Italian humanists. His role in reintro-

pp. 56–57; Muralt, p. 787, no. 5. See also Thiriet, "Venise et l'occupation de Ténédos au XIVe siècle," 242–243.

107. Greek text of this treaty in Miklosich and Müller, III, 144–153; the abbreviated Latin instrument of renewal in Thomas, *Diplomatarium*, 301–302; summaries by Iorga, *Notes et extraits*, I, 151–152, and (Predelli) *Commemoriali*, III, no. 16, p. 313. (For a reproduction of part of this treaty, see Figure 18; cf. Appendix XIV: A, III, 3.) Cf. Dölger, *Regesten*, nos. 3310–3311, pp. 92–93. On May 29, the Senate had word of the adoption of the treaty and arranged for ratification: Thiriet, *Régestes*, II, no. 1216, p. 58; Iorga, *Notes et extraits*, 152. On July 24, 1406, Paolo Zeno returned with the ratified treaty: Thiriet, no. 1230, p. 62.

108. On September 29, 1406, a Byzantine representative discussed a minor dispute over an alleged breach of the treaty, regarding rights of Byzantine citizens: Iorga, *Notes et extraits*, I, 153. Also, on July 23, 1407, the Emperor's inability to maintain the residence of the Venetian *bailo* of Constantinople as he was expected to do is noted: Thiriet, *Régestes*, II, no. 1271, p. 71. Previously, on March 1, 1407, instructions were given the Venetian ambassador to Suleyman to proceed, after negotiations with the latter, to Constantinople to discuss various minor questions and disputes: Iorga, 155–156; Thiriet, no. 1248, p. 66. Similar instructions were given on July 20, 1408, to Piero Zeno, who was being sent to Suleyman as an ambassador; and, indeed, in this case the Venetian envoy was specifically told not to become involved in any commitments or entanglements regarding the Emperor: Iorga, 162–164; cf. the inadequate summary of Thiriet, no. 1311, p. 78. For the significance of this deliberation's reference to Manuel, see n. 132 below.

Figure 19: *Manuel Chrysoloras*. Pen Drawing, Musée du Louvre, Paris, Département des Dessins, no. 9849 (reproduced from Giuseppe Cammelli, *I dotti bizantini e le origine dell'umanesimo, I. Manuele Crisolora* [Florence, 1941], frontispiece; see Appendix XXIV, A, 3).

ducing Greek among them in the West was enormous. Having returned from Italy with Manuel in 1403, Chrysoloras had been in Italy twice since then, in 1404 and 1405–06.[109] And, since he had but recently returned to Constantinople from these trips, he was readily available.

Taking up his commission, Chrysoloras left his homeland, apparently for the last time, toward the end of 1407. On December 8 and 13 of that year the Venetian Senate discussed and rejected certain requests that Chrysoloras brought from the Emperor, none of which, however, were of far-reaching import.[110] From Venice Chrysoloras proceeded across Northern Italy. On April 18, he was in Genoa, preparing to pass on to France.[111] He must have moved on soon, for he was in Paris in 1408.

Just how much his mission was intended to maintain the Emperor's friendly relations with his personal contacts in the West may be observed in the most famous memento of Chrysoloras' visit to Paris. For he brought with him as a gift from the Emperor a manuscript of the works attributed to Dionysius the Areopagite, which was bestowed appropriately upon the Royal Abbey of Saint-Denys outside Paris. Its most important feature for our purposes is the celebrated painting it contains (see Figure 5). One of the great masterpieces of Byzantine Imperial portraiture, this superb miniature portrays the Emperor Manuel, his Empress

109. Cammelli, *I dotti . . . I, Manuele Crisolora,* 139–142, who gives the scanty documentation. But we know very little about these trips. They might have been made for personal reasons, at least in part. But on January 3, 1406, Chrysoloras was a witness to an agreement in Venice: (Predelli) *Commemoriali,* III, no. 14, pp. 312–313; and in this document he is described as an "ambasciatore dell' imperatore di Constantinopoli." For a portrait of Chrysoloras, made during the 1406 trip, presumably in Florence, see Figure 19; cf. also Appendix XXIV (B, 3) below.

110. Dölger, *Regesten,* no. 3318, pp. 95–96. In view of the relationship of virtually all of these requests to another subject, these deliberations will be discussed below, pp. 273–275, and notes 130–131. On this part of Chrysoloras' mission see also Cammelli, *Crisolora,* 144–145; Marinesco, "Manuel II Paléologue et les rois d'Aragon, Commentaire sur quattre lettres inédites en Latin, expédiées par la chancellerie byzantine," *Académie Roumaine, Bulletin de la Section Historique,* 11 (1924), 193–194. More generally on the entire span of Chrysoloras' activities in the West in 1407 and thereafter, see Thomson, "Manuel Chrysoloras and the Early Italian Renaissance," 80–81.

111. Cammelli, *Crisolora,* 146, who also quotes (n. 1) the relevant Genoese state document, which is reproduced also by Iorga, *Notes et extraits,* I, 161–162.

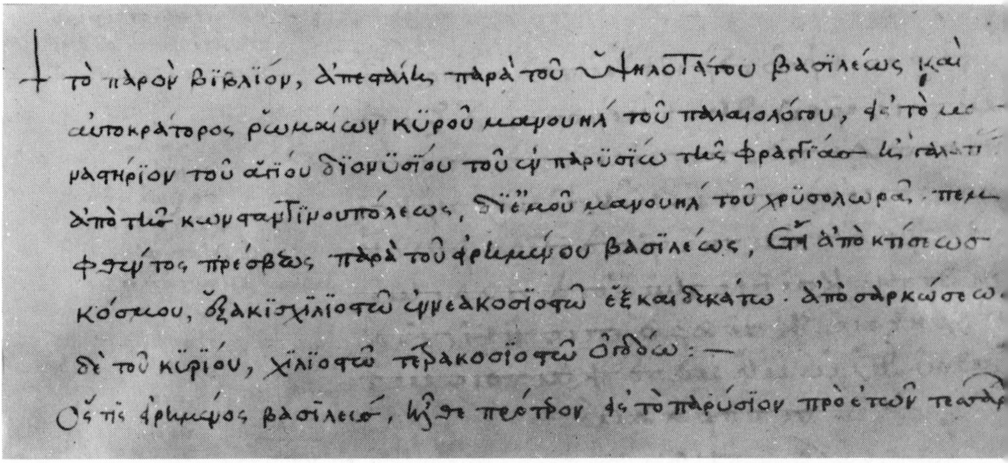

Figure 20: *Autograph Inscription by Manuel Chrysoloras in the Manuscript of the Works of Dionysius the Areopagite Brought as Manuel II's Gift to the Royal Abbey of Saint-Denys*. Musée du Louvre, Paris, *Ivoires A 53*, f. 237ᵛ (photo courtesy M. Chuzeville, Paris; see Appendix XXIV, B, 4).

Helena, and their three oldest sons, John, Theodore, and Andronicus. The ambassador's own dedication, inscribed in the manuscript, reads as follows:

The present book was sent by the most exalted Basileus and Autokrator of the Romans, lord Manuel Palaiologos, to the Monastery of Saint Dionysios in Paris of Phrangia, or Galatia, [France] from Constantinople through me, Manuel Chrysoloras, who has been sent as ambassador by the said Basileus, in the year from the Creation of the Universe, the six thousandth nine hundredth sixteenth, and from the Incarnation of the Lord, the thousandth four hundredth and eighth; the said Basileus himself came formerly to Paris four years before.[112]

112. Manuel had actually left Paris some *six* years before, in November of 1402. This important manuscript is now in the Louvre in Paris (Ivoires A53). A facsimile of Chrysoloras' inscription is reproduced as Figure 20. A transcription of its text may be found below, in Appendix XXIV (B, 4). Cf. Cammelli, *Crisolora*, 146, who also gives (n. 2) the Greek text of this inscription; cf. also Berger de Xivrey, 148–151, and Schlumberger, "Un Empereur," 145–147 (54–56), who give the same translation of the inscription. For the portrait of Manuel and his family in this manuscript, see Figure 5, and cf. below, Appendix XXIV (A, I, 3). Generally on Chrysoloras' mission, see Dölger, *Regesten*, no. 3319, p. 96. Strange as it may seem, in view of Chrysoloras' important gift to the Royal Abbey, the *Religieux de Saint-Denys* makes no reference to it. Indeed, this text's only allusion to any aspect of this journey by Chrysoloras to the West is only a fortuitous one to his involve-

264

Following his Emperor's footsteps, Chrysoloras passed over in the following year to England, where he visited at least London and Salisbury.[113] And then, in 1410, Chrysoloras went to Spain. His coming there had been anticipated and in a way that again stressed his role as the personal envoy of Manuel to Western rulers. Moreover, together with its total background, this visit by Chrysoloras marks another phase of Manuel's ventures in what might be called "reliquary diplomacy." Under the date August 17, 1405, King Martin I of Aragon had drafted three letters concerning some relics in Constantinople that he wanted. The first of these letters was addressed to the Emperor Manuel himself, urging the request and introducing the royal emissary on this quest, a Catalonian merchant named Pere de Quintana. The second letter, in essentially the same vein, was to the Patriarch of Constantinople. And the third letter contained a safe-conduct and commission for Quintana, who was to bear them all East.[114] Manuel's reply is dated October 23, 1407, in Constantinople—written, if not to be carried by Chrysoloras himself, at least to be dispatched at the beginning of the latter's mission. The Emperor regrets the disruption of the Aragonese embassy caused by the death of Quintana at sea; but he assures the King that the relics will be sent, in the hands of the Imperial ambassador, Chrysoloras.[115] This ambassador was in Spain in 1410,[116] and there he doubtless fulfilled this charge. Unfortunately, we have no acknowledgment on the part of the Aragonese King—at least none currently available.[117]

ment in 1414 with preparations for the Council of Constance: see below, pp. 321–323, n. 40. (But for a different, and vague, citation on Chrysoloras' presentation, see Muralt, p. 790, no. 5.)

113. Cammelli, *Crisolora*, 146.

114. The texts of these letters are in Rubió i Lluch, respectively no. 686, p. 710; no. 687, p. 711; and no. 688, pp. 711–712; cf. Marinesco, "Manuel et les rois," 194, and *id.*, "Du Nouveau," 435; also, Dölger, *Regesten*, no. 3308, p. 92.

115. There are three publications of this text: in Rubió i Lluch, no. 694, pp. 716–718; in Marinesco, "Manuel et les rois," 198–200 (cf. 195, and *id.*, "Du Nouveau," 436); and in Cirac Estopañan, *La unión*, 115–116 (cf. 114 and 64). See also Dölger, *Regesten*, no. 3317, p. 95.

116. Cammelli, *Crisolora*, 146.

117. We do have, however, two letters from Martin to Manuel, one of June 25, 1409 (Rubió i Lluch, no. 696, p. 719), and another of June 26, 1409 (*ibid.*, no. 697, pp. 719–720), both recommending to the Emperor the same subject of the King. The latter of the two bears the notation that it was not sent.

From Spain, Chrysoloras returned to Italy in 1410 and went to Bologna. Here he found the curia of the third Papal line, which had been contributed to the Great Schism by the Council of Pisa in 1409. And here Chrysoloras began the second phase of his embassy. As this phase carried him beyond the chronological period under consideration here and into a project that will be taken up fully only in the next chapter, discussion of the remainder of Chrysoloras' long mission will be completed further on.[118] But attention to the first phase of this mission should not end simply on this note. Lest the foregoing outline make it appear that the embassy of Chrysoloras was solely concerned with such maintenance of friendly personal relations with the Western rulers, we should consider an important letter by Manuel himself, one of the few of those surviving that are indisputably relevant to this period. It is addressed to Chrysoloras, and it was in all probability written at the end of 1410 or thereafter:

Having received your letter, I was indeed pleased—for I suppose there is none of your writings that is not among my delights. But at the same time, when I had opened it and had straightway read it—for I had every reason to expect that I would meet with such words with which I might lighten my dreadful burdens—accordingly, going through it swiftly, I was both aggrieved, as you can imagine, and I also pronounced all its contents but an empty bliss that had formerly been imagined by everyone. For there was nothing in it whatsoever of the news which was hoped for. And, further, even if it had held great promises, that still would not have been enough. For now there is need of deeds which will bring help and not of words and promises, as were customary in the past. For those at the peak of their sickness—such being our circumstances now—there is need of curing medicines, not of fine assurances which always contain postponements.

But what you state the exalted ruler has said and the manner in which he concedes it—he, if you will, whose duty requires him both to be concerned about and also to provide for all needs—this rather diminishes than augments our optimistic hopes. For, your explanation, I mean that "the situation here is still in need of improvement," will not excuse him for having done nothing whatsoever of what he should. Even if it may be that his waves of trouble have not been completely smoothed, yet, indeed, in comparison with his former storm and deluge, they are now in an unbroken calm. At least it would

118. See below, pp. 321–322.

have been proper, I think, for him to have shown himself, by some small and easy tokens, to be willing to rescue someone who has made a claim on him at this time from the impending enemies of our common faith. And a small contribution from him would certainly seem considerable to us, partly because our circumstances are so very straitened, and partly because we would consider it a sign that better things will then follow; and, in addition, because of the expectation it would inspire in the calculations of our enemies—for verily would it be not so much a stimulant to us as a blow against them. Now the fact that, after all this time, no aid whatsoever amid these our troubles has come from anywhere affords them the greatest audacity against us; but, likewise, the opposite situation would produce the opposite effects. It would be possible to prolong this letter, but to you it suffices to say so much. For I know well that you will take thought how some succor might come hither from there at the right time; for nothing, however fine, is of any value when it is too late. But if—may it not be so!—the bases of our hopes should be gone, at least bring yourself back and restore yourself to your homeland and to him who loves you—I mean, of course, me—which will verily be no small thing to us.[119]

Bearing in mind that this letter was probably written during, if not after, the violent conflict between Suleyman and Musa, with Byzantium fully involved, one can see that it is of extraordinary interest and significance. For one thing, it makes crystal clear the fact that a very important part of Chrysoloras' mission was the continued appeal for aid from Western rulers. The letter indicates that in at least one case not even promises of aid were as easy to obtain as in the past. But it also gives us some priceless insights into Manuel's own attitudes by this time regarding that very quest, his own established policy.

There is no need at this point to re-emphasize that Manuel had continued his policy of seeking aid from the West in spite of the easing of Byzantine circumstances after Ancyra. This letter certainly illustrates that fact clearly. But, at the same time, it shows vividly how Manuel's personal attitude had been modified by his bitter experience with the West, especially during his own journey there. Even when obtainable, words alone were not

119. Letter νς', ed. Legrand, 84–85, fully translated here. It is amazing that this important text has been virtually ignored heretofore. For a discussion of its date and of certain problems of its contents, see Appendix XXI below.

enough: he had realized this himself in 1401, as we have seen in his letters then. But by this time he understood the more how free the Latins could be with words alone and how wont they were to neglect following them with deeds. Nothing could demonstrate more fully Manuel's realism and his grasp of the problems with which he was dealing than this understanding of the nature of the Westerners of his time. In this light, we can see more than mere Byzantine snobbery in another interesting reflection by Manuel on the Latin character. This passage is in his *Funeral Oration for His Brother Theodore,* which is roughly contemporary with the preceding letter:

. . . For the men of the Western regions, French [Γαλάται], and Spaniards ['Ισπανοί], and British [Βρεττανοί], and, to generalize, all the rulers of the Latins and the nations under them, though not easily aroused, by and large, *can,* however, be aroused; and when they are, it is recklessly, having seized on some small pretext. And, once they have been set in motion, they are difficult to hold in check thereafter. But they are capable of many things once they are willing; and this fact past time has often demonstrated clearly. . . .[120]

There can be little doubt that by this time Manuel had a sound understanding of all aspects of the Latin psychology.

It is a point of considerable significance for understanding Manuel's policies that, in spite of his personal attitudes toward the realities of Byzantine prospects with the West, the Emperor continued his government's fundamental course of action. Indeed, it was actually in the wake of the initial phase of Chrysoloras' mission that Manuel made his most serious diplomatic effort toward a project of Western action. At the beginning of 1410, Manuel submitted a major proposal to Venice. His ambassador laid before the Senate the suggestion that, in view of the struggles between the Turkish princes, the time was ripe to destroy the power of the Turks and to deliver Byzantium from their influence. Byzantine resources would hardly suffice alone, and other European powers would be invited to participate in this worthy venture. From Venice were asked a mere eight galleys which, together with two Greek galleys, would patrol and block

120. Ed. Migne, 249B, ed. Lampros, p. 74, ll. 10–16. These words were prompted by discussion of the introduction of the Hospitalers into the Peloponnesus by Theodore and of their great eagerness to extend their control there. On the date of this text, see Appendix XXII below.

the passage across the Straits. But the Venetian reply of January 10, 1410, was evasive. The Byzantines were given the familiar reply that Venice would join in this admirable enterprise only if all the other Christian powers would contribute.[121]

Manuel's proposal, unsuccessful as it was, is of great interest. It matters little that Manuel was not the only one, or the first one, to contemplate a Christian league against the Turks after Ancyra. It is, of course, true that the Hospitalers had broached a similar idea some six years earlier.[122] And it is true that King Sigismund of Hungary had not yet given up his hopes of leading another expedition against the Turks; although by now he had taken up the popular theory that the key to the whole problem of the Turkish menace was a Christian seizure of Gallipoli, toward which goal he had appealed in vain to Venice for cooperation.[123] What matters for us, however, is not the originality of Manuel's proposal, but rather the fact that he should have made it at all. It indicates that Manuel by no means looked upon his rapprochement with Suleyman about this time as anything permanent or binding, especially in the fluctuations and uncertainties of the wars of Bayazid's sons. Manuel saw plainly that the true enemy

121. Dölger, *Regesten*, no. 3327, p. 97; Iorga, *Notes et extraits*, I, 179–180; Thiriet, *Régestes*, II, no. 1362, pp. 88–89; it is unfortunate that the actual text of this deliberation has not been published. Cf. Vaughan, *Europe and the Turk*, 42. In the same deliberation the Senate also discussed a number of other matters raised by the Byzantine ambassador. It rejected complaints about the transportation of Turks in the area of Gallipoli in Venetian ships, in evasion of Greek customs duty; replying that such activities were beyond the *Signoria's* control, and that, in accordance with their treaty, it was up to the Emperor to guard against that evasion. There was more discussion of the controversy over the inheritance of Kalopheros; steps were taken to deal with brawls in Constantinople involving Venetians; and provisions were made that the Venetians there supply themselves with needed grain (to prevent a drain on the city's own resources?). For reference to still another matter discussed in this deliberation, see n. 144 below. As an interesting background to this 1409–10 proposal by Manuel, note the Emperor's communication to Venice in January of 1407, cited by Dölger, *Regesten*, no. 3315, p. 94. In it, Manuel is quoted as urging the Venetians to reconcile themselves with the Genoese as good Christians so that they can then together come to his aid against the Turks.

122. See above, p. 259.

123. In their deliberation of October 23, 1408 (Thiriet, *Régestes*, II, no. 1323, pp. 80–81), the Venetian Senate responded to Sigismund's overtures with the usual formula that only if others would participate would Venice participate also. On the idea of Gallipoli as the requisite focal target for Christian arms, see Vaughan, 45–46.

still was and always would be the Turk. This proposal shows, moreover, that Manuel grasped the central fact of the post-Ancyra situation: that the turmoil among the Turks after the defeat of Bayazid and during the struggle for his throne provided the best and perhaps the last real chance for Christendom to break the power of the Turks and turn back their advance, if not to drive them out of Europe.[124]

Whatever further steps Manuel may have taken to promote his idea, we hear nothing more of it in available sources. Indeed, as promising as it may have seemed as an idea, it was doomed to failure in reality. There may have been some who recognized its feasibility, but none of the Western rulers could or would act upon it, even if they understood it. The Christian powers were unable even to attempt to organize any coordinated effort. The very powers that might have given leadership were distracted by their own problems. France had no power to help herself, let alone others: now that King Charles VI had slipped hopelessly into his insanity, the realm was wracked by the struggles for

124. Cf. the comments of Halecki, "The Last Century of the Crusades—From Smyrna to Varna (1344–1444)," *Bulletin of the Polish Institute of Arts and Sciences,* 2 (1945), 304, in the course of his criticism of Atiya's premise that the expedition of Nicopolis in 1396 was the last of the true medieval crusades: "It has been rightly said that it was only the crushing defeat which the Turks suffered in 1402 from another Asiatic power, from Tamerlane, which prolonged for fifty years the existence of the Byzantine Empire. These fifty years also gave to Christian Europe a last series of opportunities to check the Turkish advance, and that is one more reason why the expedition of Nicopolis cannot be considered the last crusade. It is, however, true that none of these opportunities was sufficiently utilized, thus permitting the Turks to restore their aggressive power until the final blow of 1453." Cf. the same author's "Angora, Florence, Varna, and the Fall of Constantinople," *Akten des XI. Internationalen Byzantinistenkongresses München 1958* (Munich, 1960), 216–217. On the other hand, in his recent book, *The Fall of Constantinople,* Runciman penetratingly observes (pp. 42–43) that even had a Christian alliance been effected it could only have accomplished a limited success: "... though the dynasty might have perished, a Turkish problem still would have remained. Historians who blame the Christians for missing a heaven-sent opportunity forget that there were already hundreds of thousands of Turks settled firmly in Europe. It would have been a formidable task to subdue them and almost impossible to expel them. Indeed, Timur's intervention had added to their strength; for families and even whole tribes fled before his armies to the safety of the European provinces. . . . Bayezit had left large armed forces there to guard the frontiers and police the provinces. The Ottoman dynasty had been humiliated at Ankara, and their military machine had been weakened. It had not been destroyed."

power among his kinsmen, and it fell a ready prey at length to the English. Henry IV of England, who had never felt secure enough at home to carry out his dreams of an Eastern crusade, was succeeded by his son, "the warlike Harry," the brilliant soldier-King Henry V, whose energetic but brief reign (1413–1422) was devoted to the renewal of the Hundred Years War. Even Sigismund himself, who had once been regarded as the leader of the fight against the Turks, was preoccupied with his own numerous adventures, especially his election to the throne of the Holy Roman Empire and then the settlement of the Great Schism.

And Venice itself, which would have to be the essential maritime cornerstone of any cooperative venture, was much too anxious about preserving its commerce to be willing to enter any great undertaking against the Turks, unless its own advantage would seem fully guaranteed. It is true that Venice, once its relations with Suleyman had deteriorated, and once it no longer seemed possible that it could derive advantage from him, was willing to consider in 1409 the possibility of replacing him with his brother Mechmed, to whom it would offer assistance in seizing Rumelia.[125] But such schemes obviously had no bearing on any major effort by Christendom and were reflected upon solely for Venice's own selfish advantage.

So it was that, while Manuel may have realized fully all the realities and possibilities and necessities of the situation in the East during the Turkish "Time of Troubles," his efforts to induce the Latin West to act upon them were of no avail. Byzantium was forced to rely on its own scanty resources and to make what it could out of existing circumstances, primarily by diplomatic means. That is to say, Byzantium had no real choice but to become deeply involved in the wars of Bayazid's sons, since an alternative course of all-out hostility to the Turks in general was closed to it as a result of Western indifference. Whatever success

---

125. Deliberations of March 26, 1409: Iorga, *Notes et extraits,* I, 169–171; cf. Thiriet, *Régestes,* II, no. 3147, p. 85. The stipulation was made that the Emperor was to be consulted if the move to replace Suleyman was to be carried out. The only other dealings between Manuel and Venice between these contacts and 1411 seem to have concerned trivia. On January 11, 1410, for example, the Senate discussed a strong complaint against Manuel for alleged violation of the treaty, specifically, his arrest of a Venetian citizen: Thiriet, *Régestes,* II, no. 1364, p. 89.

Manuel was able to derive from this "Time of Troubles" was to come solely from his own diplomatic skill in handling the Turks and not from any Western help.

Meanwhile, during the course of this period of intricate diplomacy, Manuel had additional concerns regarding his own affairs. The focal point of these concerns were two deaths in his family. The first was that of his brother, the Despot Theodore I of the Morea, in the year 1407.[126] His final illness had apparently been a long one, for Theodore (who had no legitimate male heir) had the time to summon his nephew and namesake, Manuel's second son, to come to the Morea as his successor.[127] This summons may have come as early as 1405. On January 30/31 of that year, in a deliberation on matters connected with the renewal of the treaty with Byzantium, the Venetian Senate considered a request by Manuel that he and his family be provided with transportation either to his possessions in the Morea or to Venetian colonies (Modon and Coron?) if he should wish.[128] Such a request may very well have been prompted by Theodore's suggestion that his successor designate be sent to him. After this, however, we hear no more of transportation negotiations with

126. The year of his death, 6915 (Sept. 1406 to Aug. 1407), is given in the short chronicle published at the end of the Bonn edition of Ducas, p. 517, ll. 7–8; and republished as Βρ. χρ. No. 27, l. 37, p. 47. Cf. Loenertz, "Pour l'histoire du Péloponnèse," 156; Zakythinos, *Le Despotat grec*, I, 164–165. But the precise date, or even the month, of his death is not known, although Hopf, 70 (followed by Mompherratos, Οἱ Παλ. ἐν Πελ., 29), asserts that it occurred in the summer of 1407: presumably his authority for this assertion must be in the Venetian documentation which he cites, for certainly none of his other sources (n. 79) are so precise. And, indeed, Theodore's death must have occurred *by* the summer of 1407, for on August 27 of that year reference was made in a deliberation of the Venetian Senate to the "dominum Despotum de novo creatum," obviously the newly designated Theodore II: ed. Sathas, *Documents inédits*, I, p. 20, l. 3; cf. Thiriet, *Régestes*, II, no. 1282, p. 73. In his collation of the *Chron. br. mor.*, No. 21, p. 406, and in his commentary, pp. 425–426, Loenertz, however, has suggested that a dating of June 24 for the death of Theodore II in 1448 may actually apply as well, or instead, to the death of Theodore I in 1407. Such a dating is perfectly plausible, though it must remain a conjecture at present in the absence of further corroboration. As was the custom, Theodore became a monk before he died, adopting the name Theodoret.

127. Chalcocondyles, ed. Darkó, I, 193, ed. Bonn, 206; cf. Zakythinos, *Le Despotat grec*, I, 165–166, whose use, however, of Manuel's Letter ϑ′ in this context is incorrect, as the latter is earlier and refers to other matters.

128. This request was approved: Iorga, *Notes et extraits*, I, 145; Thiriet, *Régestes*, II, no. 1176, p. 51. For the remainder of this deliberation, see above, n. 106.

Manuel. The Emperor certainly must have been too busy to consider further the idea of making the trip himself at this time. But it does seem likely that the young Theodore, who must by this time have been a little over ten years old, was sent on ahead to profit from the precepts of his uncle while the latter was yet alive.[129]

The actual death of Theodore I in 1407, however, revived the question of a personal trip by Manuel himself. To be sure, part of the reason may have been the warm affection that Manuel professes to have existed between himself and his brother, and the latter's death certainly seems to have been a sad blow to him. But the motive was more than personal. Manuel had always taken an active interest in the welfare of the important Despotate. Not the least demonstration of how Manuel ranked its importance is perhaps the seniority he assigned it in the appanage distribution for his sons. John V had preferred to send his second son to Thessalonica and was content to give the Morea to his third son. For Manuel, by contrast, it was exactly the opposite. It was his own second son, Theodore, who was sent to rule the all-important Despotate.

Manuel was doubtless concerned to assure the smooth succession of his son, and to try to check any possible outbreaks of disorder among the turbulent barons of the Morea. With these needs in mind, Manuel opened negotiations with Venice. These negotiations were carried on by none other than Manuel Chrysoloras, in Venice at the beginning of his Western mission for the Emperor. On December 8, 1407, the Senate considered a number of Byzantine proposals concerning matters in the Morea, including the question of Venetian provision for escort of the Emperor home from the Morea. As usual, the Senate haggled and evaded.[130] On December 13, however, after renewed press-

---

129. Such is the inference of Chalcocondyles, ed. Darkó, I, 202, ed. Bonn, 216, who states that the young Theodore was raised and educated (ἐξετρέφετο ἅμα καὶ ἐπαιδεύθη) by his uncle.

130. Iorga, *Notes et extraits*, I, 159–160; Thiriet, *Régestes*, II, no. 1290, pp. 74–75; cf. Dölger, *Regesten*, no. 3318, pp. 95–96. See above, p. 261, n. 108. Cf. Zakythinos, *Le Despotat grec*, I, 166, who ignores the matter of naval escort and also another matter. This latter was the proposal, evaded of course, that the Venetians contribute toward the building of the Hexamilion, the wall across the Isthmus of Corinth. As we shall see (below, p. 311 ff.), this project was not to be carried out until Manuel's later visit, in 1415. But it is interesting and significant to find that Manuel was considering this idea at this early date.

Figure 21: *Mistra, the Palace of the Despots: General View from Above* (photo courtesy Ljubica Popović, 1961; see Appendix XXIV, C, 5, a).

Figure 22: *Mistra, the Palace of the Despots: The Façade and the Fore-court* (photo courtesy Ljubica Popović, 1961; see Appendix XXIV, C, 5, b).

Figure 23: *Mistra, the Palace of the Despots: The East Wall of the Throne Room* (photo courtesy Ljubica Popović, 1961; see Appendix XXIV, C, 5, c).

ing of the matter by Chrysoloras, the Senate yielded to some extent, in view of the importance of Manuel's visit to the Morea: the possibility was conceded that the required escort might be provided.[131] Once this and other such arrangements had been made, Manuel probably felt that conditions at home were still calm enough to allow him a quick visit to the Morea. There he seems to have sailed, probably in the summer of 1408.[132]

131. Iorga, *Notes et extraits*, I, 160; the summary by Thiriet, *Régestes*, II, no. 1291, p. 75, is inadequate; cf. Dölger, *ibid.* It is noteworthy that Manuel only requests an escort back to Constantinople, and not the actual transportation there itself and back. This distinction probably explains why we have no reference in Venetian documents—at least in those thus far available—to the actual voyage of Manuel to the Morea.

132. Sphrantzes, 1025C (Pseudo-Phrantzes, ed. Papadopoulos, 70; ed. Bonn, 65) and Chalcocondyles, ed. Darkó, I, 202–203, ed. Bonn, 216, are the only historians to speak of this visit as distinct from that of 1415. Loenertz, "Pour l'histoire," 156, dates the visit 6916 (1407–08). Hopf, 70, and Iorga, *Geschichte*, 345, have also maintained that Manuel went to the Peloponnesus at this time, but in 1407. But this assumption of date is based on the supposition that Manuel's request for escort home from the Morea proves that he was already there when Chrysoloras submitted the request in December of that year. Actually, however, our evidence indicates the contrary; for Manuel was in Constantinople on October 23, 1407, the date of his letter to King Martin I of Aragon announcing the mission of Chrysoloras (see above, p. 265), since the text states plainly that it was "given" in that city on that date. Moreover, the Venetian Senate's deliberation of July 20, 1408, implies that Manuel was still in Constantinople about that date (see above, n. 108). Now, we know that Manuel's absence from Constantinople extended at least to the end of 1408. We might be tempted to suppose that Manuel left the capital together with Chrysoloras in late autumn or early winter; but it seems very unlikely, even aside from the indication of the Venetian deliberation of July 20, 1408, that the Emperor would, or did, prolong his visit to Greece more than a year, as he would have had to do to fit the old interpretation of his departure. Rather, Manuel's visit gives the impression of having been a very short one. In view of the evidence, the middle of 1408 would seem to be a more logical date for his departure. Loenertz, "Pour la chronologie des oeuvres de Joseph Bryennios" *Rev. d. ét. byz.*, 7 (1940–50), p. 24, n. 2, had argued for 1407 in dating thus a letter by Vryennios to Manuel, which, he proposes, was written to the Emperor while the latter was absent in the Morea after Theodore's death. As Mompherratos, Οἱ Παλ. ἐν Πελ., before him, Zakythinos, *ibid.*, avoids the whole question of a visit by Manuel to the Morea at this time. But the latter, in his article "Μανουὴλ ὁ Παλαιολόγος καὶ ὁ Καρδινάλιος Ἰσίδωρος ἐν Πελοποννήσῳ," 6, on the basis solely of the panegyrics published by Lampros, and ignoring the other aforementioned evidence, reaches the same conclusion as to the date of this visit: 1408. And, indeed, for what it is worth, we have the cryptic statement in Βρ. χρ. No. 19, p. 36, l. 29, that "In the 6916th year the Basileus Lord Manuel came to Corinth." Loenertz, in his compilation of his *Chron. br. mor.*, No. 23, p. 407, which includes this text, and in his

We know little of this visit, for our sources virtually ignore it or else confuse it with his later visit there. Presumably Manuel did his best to provide for the administration of the Despotate during the minority of his son.[133] He also made some effort to quell the constant fighting among the unruly *archons* of the Morea, whose proclivities to violence are clearly reflected in an

commentary to it on p. 428, has reckoned Manuel's journey to the Morea as in November–December of 1407. To support this, he argues only from such nebulous and imprecise evidence (the Venetian documents and the Chrysoloras request) as has just been discussed. Since the Byzantine year 6916 would have run from September 1, 1407, to August 31, 1408, such a conjecture is perfectly feasible, and the absence of any request for Venetian escort *to* the Morea and only *from* it by Chrysoloras can perhaps be taken to suggest that Manuel was *already* there. Nevertheless, it seems equally arguable that Manuel was still in Constantinople into the summer of 1408; and since his visit to the Morea does, as I have just said, seem to have been a brief one, it appears much more likely to me that the departure for the Morea came in the summer of 1408, which would still fit into the chronicle's dating of the year 6916.

133. It was suggested by Hopf, 70, that Manuel assigned as a guardian and regent for Theodore II an important official named Manuel Phrangopoulos. Thus also Mompherratos, Οἱ Παλ. ἐν Πελ., 30. But, as Zakythinos, *Le Despotat grec*, I, 166, points out, as credible a suggestion as this may well be, there is no evidence either to confirm or to refute it. We do have, however, an interesting passage in a letter by Manuel which was undoubtedly written during or after this visit to the Morea. Addressed to Manuel Chrysoloras, then in Western Europe, the letter opens with a rhetorical introduction on their correspondence and then proceeds: "And while Skaranos is worthy in wisdom, at the same time he is worthy in experience of what tasks he has now been assigned to do; all that remains is for him to be willing. Thus, if this factor be added, your kinsman and friend would be the best among the servants both to his homeland and to the Despot. At any rate, you know that such men prosper in my sight—and justly. And, as to what you ask that I do for him, there are two things, neither easy. He knows this better than everyone, since he is both my overseer and is also well aware of what is needed. But for your sake one of your demands, and the better one, will be granted to him now by me; and the other perhaps hereafter. And the interval of time should cause no injury, since he has my favor." (Letter μθ´, ed. Legrand, 74–75: translated here are ll. 10–21.) While this passage is unusually direct in saying what it says, it is obviously well-nigh impossible to fathom what specifically it is talking about. But the reference to the Despot is a healthy clue. I have found no information at this writing to identify Skaranos. But, from the context, there seems little reason to doubt that he was someone appointed by Manuel to an important post at the side of the young Despot. Could the word "overseer" (λογιστής) imply that this man actually had been made young Theodore's guardian and regent himself, instead of Phrangopoulos as Hopf concluded? We have no way of knowing, although one might be inclined to doubt this conclusion from the trace of skepticism in Manuel's reference to him.

interesting passage from a letter that Manuel wrote to Euthymios during or after this visit:

. . . For, as it seems, it was destined of old for the land of Pelops to esteem the state of fighting one with another as better than peace. And if someone should not provide a pretext to someone else, no one is so stupid as not to be able to fabricate and to invent one by himself. For each one wishes to exercise himself in arms, as an exercise in accordance with his very nature. Would that their needs lay that way, for their circumstances would then be better! And, since I understand these circumstances precisely, I consider nothing else more important than their peace one with another. This problem often distracted me from my meals and even from my proper sleep, and I have at times been generally negligent of necessities. So this has been the reason for your having been deprived of the customary letters.[134]

Any other activities that we may attribute to Manuel during this visit are essentially conjectural. Visiting the residence and tomb of his late brother, he may have conceived the idea of writing his important *Funeral Oration for His Brother Theodore* for a ceremony commemorating the Despot's death.[135] Apparently Manuel also at least contemplated the idea of building the wall across the Isthmus, the Hexamilion, a project he was not able to carry out until seven years later.[136] But such plans seem to have

134. Letter να', ed. Legrand, 77–78; translated here are ll. 13–23. Zakythinos, *Les Despotat grec*, I, 174, has translated virtually all of this passage into French. In Manuel's text the passage is embedded in an otherwise routine jumble about friendship and the joys of correspondence, with regrets over the distractions which, he says, have hindered his writing. Zakythinos, *ibid.*, has employed this passage in connection with Manuel's 1415 visit to the Morea, but it refers without doubt to the period of 1408 instead. The position of this letter in the manuscript (i.e. *Parisinus gr. 3041*) is a possible indication of this fact, and so also, perhaps, is the letter's address. Following the superscription "To the priest, lord Euthymios" is the continuation in a different hand, "but later Patriarch of Constantinople." This addition raises problems for the dating of this letter: see below, pp. 519–520. But if it can be accepted with any degree of assurance, its reflection of chronology is obvious, since Euthymios became Patriarch in October of 1410.

135. See Appendix XXII below.

136. See above, n. 130. Note, however, that the plan to rebuild the Hexamilion was not original with Manuel, even as early as 1408. His late brother had broached the project to Venice years before (deliberations of Aug. 25, 1394, and Feb. 22, 1396: Thiriet, *Régestes*, I, no. 864, p. 204, and no. 897, p. 211), reviving it later in concert with his then allies, the Hospitalers, at which time (Apr. 22, 1401: ed. Sathas, II, no. 239, p. 27, lacking in Thiriet; and May 6, 1401: Sathas, II, no. 241, p. 30, Thiriet, II, no. 1017, p. 18) the Senate gave cautious approval. Theodore's distractions and death left Manuel heir to the scheme.

been cut short by the arrival of the news of the second death in the Imperial family at this time.

In September of 1408, John VII donned the monastic garb as the monk Ioasaph—the same name his great-grandfather, John Cantacuzenus, had chosen—and passed on to whatever reward awaited him after his turbulent and warped life.[137] It was a tragic life in a way. For all the shabbiness and double-dealing of much of his career, and for all of his apparent mediocrity of talent, he had served with reasonable faithfulness in 1399–1403, and he is perhaps entitled to some small degree of our sympathy if only as a victim of hard circumstances.[138] But Manuel may well have heaved a sigh of relief at the news, and he could hardly have

137. The date usually accepted for the death of John VII is September 22, 1408, as given in the marginalia of a chrysobull of John (=Dölger, *Regesten*, no. 3209, p. 77), cited by Dölger, "Johannes VII.," p. 36, n. 1; and given also in a note written by Demetrius Lascaris Leontaris, which is quoted by Mercati, "Sarebbe Stafidace l'epistolegrafo del codice laurenziano di S. Marco 356?," *Studi bizantini (e neoellenici)*, 2 (1927), p. 242, n. 1. Another date, however, September 10, 1408, is given by the Βρ. χρ. No. 47, p. 82, ll. 77–78; and this date seems to have attracted neither acceptance nor attention. All these sources give the monastic name that John adopted. In addition to them, the *Bulg. chron.*, 543, places the death of John VII in the year 6917, which would of course include September of 1408. Unfortunately, Jireček, in his commentary on this text ("Zur Würdigung der neuentdeckten bulgarische Chronik," *Archiv für slavische Philologie*, 14 [1892], 276), has mistakenly contradicted this statement with the incorrect assertion that John died on November 20, 1410, authority unstated; but he possibly followed Muralt, p. 792, no. 2, giving that incorrect date. Though it does not speak of his death, the Ἐκ. χρον. makes an unusually favorable comment on his memory. Concluding the passage translated above in n. 77, this text observes: "For he was outstanding in his virtue, so that even his tomb now cures diseases of all sorts" (p. 2, ll. 1–3).

138. Cf. Dölger, "Johannes VII.," 36: "The figure of John is certainly not pleasant. He presents us with the image of an unlucky prince who, in earliest youth, was violently and innocently made a cripple; who, in manhood, wavered back and forth without firmness between loyalty and treachery in order to attain those goals of his life which, from his point of view, had been his from the cradle. He therefore became a puppet of foreign powers which abused the fact of his miserable existence for their self-seeking aims. Always passive in pretended activity, John was, in the midst of the general corruption of the declining state, the victim of a dynasticism pushed to extremes, which, in this form, was originally foreign to Greek constitutional thought, and which entered as an unhealthy import from the West, dissolving into the Eastern understanding of government only after the beginning of the 14th century. Seen from these two points of view, the figure of John is not lacking in tragedy: in some respects his adventurous life might be reminiscent of the fate of the Turkish Prince Djem who, a century later, was treated as a hostage in the courts of Europe against Sultan Bayazid II and met a violent end in Rome."

been expected to mourn his nephew's passing in quite the way he did his brother's. To be sure, it undoubtedly spared Byzantium many complications that John should have died before Manuel, and childless as well. Only in this sad fashion, with the extinction of John V's accursed eldest line of descent, could the rift of thirty-five years' standing be finally and utterly ended.

But this event, the news of which may well have been unexpected to Manuel, presented the Emperor with a new task. With John gone from the scene, the government of Thessalonica had to be provided for in terms of the current appanage system. Cutting short his stay in the Morea, Manuel proceeded to the Macedonian city,[139] once the scene of his own former triumphs and tragedies. There he installed as Despot his third son, at the time probably no more than eight years old. The loyal Demetrius Leontaris, who had served all this time as the administrator and advisor of John VII, apparently remained for a while to guide the government in the minority of Andronicus.[140] While Manuel was still in this city, moreover, he issued an important *prostagma,*

139. The so-called *Anonymous Panegyric to Manuel and John VIII Palaeologus,* ed. Lampros, Παλ. καὶ Πελ., III, 164–165; actually, this text is by Cardinal Isidore of Kiev: see below, Appendix XXII. Dölger, "Johannes VII.," 36, suggests archly that Manuel "hastened to the bier of the deceased perhaps more to urge immediately, on the spot, his claims as heir than out of deep sympathy over the death of the hardly 40-year-old departed nephew." Sphrantzes, 1025C (Pseudo-Phrantzes, ed. Papadopoulos, 70; ed. Bonn, 65), speaks of the death of John, the journey of Manuel thereupon to Thessalonica, and his installation of the young Andronicus as Despot, all as having preceded the death of Theodore and Manuel's trip to the Morea. Certainly our other evidence justifies our regarding this statement of the order of the two sequences of events as a confused reversal on the part of the historian.

140. Ducas, ed. Grecu, 173–175, ed. Bonn, 133–134, tells of the honors bestowed upon Lascaris, and then has Manuel bring him home. But this alleged return of Leontaris to Constantinople must be a confusion or a mistake of some sort. For we have evidence that Leontaris was still in Thessalonica in February of 1415, the date of a document issued by him concerning the Athonite monastery of Vatopedi: text published by Arkadios Vatopedinos, no. 34, p. 335, of his "᾽Αγιορειτικὰ ἀνάλεκτα ἐκ τοῦ ἀρχείου τῆς μονῆς Βατοπεδίου," Γρηγόριος ὁ Παλαμᾶς, 3 (1919); cf. M. Th. Laskaris, "᾽Ιωάννης Η᾽ ὁ Παλαιολόγος ἐν Θεσσαλονίκῃ κατὰ τὴν πολιορκίαν τοῦ 1416," Τόμος Κ. ᾽Αρμενοπούλου (=Πανεπιστημίου Θεσσαλονίκης, ᾽Επιστημονικὴ ἐπετηρίς, 6, 1952), 341; also, Dölger, *Regesten,* no. 3204, p. 76. We know from Ducas, moreover, that Leontaris was in Thessalonica during the Mustafa affair in 1416: see below, pp. 342–343. The first evidence we have of Leontaris' activity in the government of Constantinople is his appearance as a witness to the renewal of the Veneto-Byzantine treaty on October 30, 1418: see p. 332, n. 61 below.

dated December 1, 1408, in which he took note of the harsh economic conditions in Macedonia since the Battle of the Marica in 1371 and ordered an easing of the tax burdens and property restrictions of the monasteries of Mount Athos.[141] Some time thereafter, Manuel left Thessalonica. Presumably, he returned directly to Constantinople.[142]

When Manuel did reach his capital, probably in early 1409, he

141. The text of this document is published by V. Mošin on pp. 165–167 of his "Akti iz svetogorskih arhiva," *Srpska Kraljevska Akademija, Spomenik,* 91 (1939); cf. Dölger, *Regesten,* no. 3321, p. 96; also, *ibid.,* nos. 3301 and 3322, pp. 90–91 and 96–97, respectively, for other important documents of the same type. For a discussion of it, see Ostrogorsky, *Pour l'histoire de la féodalité byzantine,* 161–163; *id.,* "Byzance, état tributaire de l'empire turc," especially pp. 51 and 57; Charanis, "Monastic Properties and the State in the Byzantine Empire," *Dumbarton Oaks Papers, No. 4* (1948), 117. (The latter scholar suggests that "The issuance of this order was doubtless prompted by the erroneous belief that the Ottoman danger had disappeared as a result of the battle of Ancyra in 1402 and the civil wars among the sons of Bayazid that followed." Rather, as has been stressed previously, Manuel was by no means under any such illusions at all, and this *prostagma* was actually the result of certain economic conditions, if not pious aspirations.) Needless to say, this document is also of great value, beyond its intrinsic importance and context, simply for the specific chronological data it gives on Manuel's remarkably ill-documented visit. One phrase in the text leaves no doubt that Manuel was actually in this city when he issued it: "Νῦν οὖν ἐλθούσης τῆς Βασιλείας μου εἰς τὴν θεόσωστον πόλιν Θεσσαλονίκην."

142. These statements, as with so much else about this visit, must remain essentially a conjecture, if perhaps a not unreasonable one. In view of the great attention given by Greek sources to Manuel's European journey and especially to his visit to the Morea in 1415, it is surprising that little or nothing of this 1408 visit in between is reflected in the sources. Perhaps the only explanation for this fact might be that the visit was very short and perhaps not very eventful. Also contributing to this silence may have been the confusion of this visit with the later one, inducing the historians either to amalgamate the events of each into a single one or to leave out the earlier one almost entirely. Among the other mysteries surrounding this 1408 journey is the question of transportation. We have no knowledge of whose ships were used to convey the Emperor to the Morea from Constantinople, from the Morea to Thessalonica, and then back to Constantinople. Since we have no mention of specific Venetian arrangements for this purpose in the available documents, we may perhaps assume that whatever ships were used did not belong to the *Serenissima.* Nor did Manuel call upon Venice after all for the promised escort home from the Morea, from all indications, perhaps because he had been obliged unexpectedly to go to Thessalonica first. If we assume that it really was the illegitimate daughter of Theodore I who was married to Suleyman in the latter's ultimate close alliance with Manuel about 1410 (see above, n. 88), she may well have been brought by Manuel to Constantinople from the Morea at the end of this particular visit.

found himself and his state in an increasingly ominous situation. While Chrysoloras was roving through Western Europe, and while Manuel's diplomatic probings there were being rejected or ignored, the struggle between the sons of Bayazid was moving toward its final climax. The remaining three brothers would not tolerate each other's existence much longer. Already by this time Suleyman had launched his offensive in Anatolia. By the end of 1409 Musa had been incited by Mechmed to distract Suleyman on his northern flank by attacking Rumelia from beyond the Danube. As a result, Suleyman was driven into a doubtless humiliating dependency upon the support and alliance of Manuel.[143] Even before the storm broke, Manuel could foresee

143. On these events, see also above, p. 252 ff. The sources seem to make clear that this final alliance between Suleyman and Manuel was not made until after Musa's first assault on his brother in 1410. Chalcocondyles, ed. Darkó, I, 160–161, ed. Bonn, 171–172, the *Chron. Barb. 111*, 43, and the Pseudo-Phrantzes, ed. Papadopoulos, 90–91, ed. Bonn, 86–87, portray Suleyman as crossing from Asia, or at least coming to Constantinople, only then making his alliance with Manuel. A visit by Suleyman to Manuel (at Chalcedon, which seems unlikely) to cement their alliance is described also by Konstantin the Philosopher, ed. Jagić, 294, ed. and trans. Braun, 33; cf. Stanojević, 440–441. Apparently unused, however, is a very valuable report of this period in a letter of the government of Ragusa to King Sigismund of Hungary, ed. Gelcich and Thallóczy, *Diplomatarium*, no. 133, p. 195. The letter is dated May 30, 1410, and this passage from it deserves to be quoted in full to make it better known: ". . . Hodie vero ad hec littora navigans quidam brigantinus, quie die XXVIII. presentis de Avalona recesserat, nobis retulit ambassiatorem domini Mirchxe a partibus Constantinopolis in diebus XV. descendisse ad Valonam, narrantem Constantinopolitanum imperatorem Gallipoli cum fortiliciis, dempta magistra turri, cepisse, eandemque circuisse per terram et galeis octo per mare, datisque induciis creditur nunc adepta; Celopiam vero cum magno gencium apparatu ad littora declinasse, petentem ab imperatore et Januensibus paregium, cui honesto modo denegatum fuit, et propter Crespie fratris molestias retrocessit. Avarnas et sex baronos Celopie, qui ad partes Galipolis susurantes venerant, a Musicelopia detinentur captivos." This text involves a number of problems, but certain things are plain. In the first place, "Celopia" refers now to Suleyman, in contrast to "Crespia," one of several Ragusan corruptions of the nickname for Mechmed I (cf. above, n. 82), and to "Musicelopia," who is of course Musa Çelebi. Secondly, if the Ragusans' information was correct, this report suggests that into the spring of 1410 Manuel hoped to take advantage of the civil strife among the Turks, even to the point of moving on the much-desired Gallipoli; and that Manuel may have deferred giving Suleyman his support until late spring or thereafter. An inscription of 1407–08 published by H. Gelzer ("Der wiederaufgefundene Kodex des hl. Klemens und andere auf den Patriarchat Achrida bezüglich Urkundensammlungen," *Berichte über der Verhandlungen der Königlich Sächsischen Gesellschaft der Wissenschaften zu Leipzig, Phil.-histor. Klasse*, 55, 1903, pp. 54–55) contains a reference to a τζαλαπί

that the coming conflict had possibilities both of advantage and of danger for Byzantium.[144]

Musa did not waste any time. Bringing his allies, the Voievode Mircea of Wallachia and the Despot Stefan Lazarević of Serbia, Musa invaded Turkish territory in early 1410, and at Jamboli, on February 13, he defeated Suleyman's Beylerbey of Rumelia.[145] Making a formal claim to Rumelia, Musa swept on and finally encountered his brother, who had by this time returned from Anatolia, before the walls of Constantinople. Attempts were made by the Byzantines to detach Stefan Lazarević from Musa's side.[146] On June 15, 1410, at the suburb of Kosmidion, the two

which Iorga, "Une Inscription grecque sous le Sultan Mousa, 1407–1408, dans le région d'Ochrida," *Revue du sud-est européen*, 10 (1933), 11–12, has thus construed as referring to Musa Çelebi. This interpretation seems very questionable, since Musa was apparently not yet in Rumelia in the year of the inscription (6916 = 1407–08), and the equivalent of the Turkish title *çelebi* may allude rather to Suleyman.

144. It was at this time that Manuel sent the embassy to Venice to make the proposals considered by the Senate on January 10, 1410 (see above, pp. 268–269, and n. 121), which included Manuel's suggestion for a league to take advantage of the Turkish civil war to destroy their power. Among those same proposals was included also a request for the transportation of the Emperor and his family wherever they might wish: to which the Venetians agreed, on condition of payment for this transportation, and that the route chosen be one customary to Venetian shipping. In view of its late date, this request seems to have nothing to do with Manuel's visit to the Morea after Theodore I's death. It seems explicable only as a provision on the Emperor's part for the possibility that flight from Constantinople might be necessary in the near future.

145. These events and dates are preserved in a pricelessly valuable short chronicle entry published by Lampros in his collection, "᾿Ενθυμήσεων ἤτοι χρονικῶν σημειωμάτων συλλογὴ πρώτη," Νέος ἑλλη-νομνήμων, 7 (1910; cited hereafter as "Lampros chron."), p. 151, no. 97, but curiously omitted from his Βραχέα χρονικά collection. Cf. Iorga, *Geschichte*, 349; Jireček, *Geschichte der Serben*, II, 146; Wittek, "De La Défaite," 21. Jamboli (or Djamboli) is a town, now in modern Bulgaria, some 90 kilometers due north of Adrianople.

146. Both Chalcocondyles, ed. Darkó, I, 161–162, ed. Bonn, 172–173, and the *Chron. Barb. 111*, 44, report this; but, while the former says that Stefan acceded and defected to Byzantium, the latter maintains that he ignored the effort and was alien ted from Musa only after the latter's triumph in 1411. Jireček, *Geschichte der Serben*, II, 146, simply has him giving up the fight after Musa's defeat, following Konstantin the Philosopher, ed. Jagić, 295–296, ed. and trans. Braun, 34–35, according to whom Stefan was actually welcomed by Manuel in Constantinople. It is likely that at least the attempt was made to influence Stefan. He was, after all, an important Christian prince with important ties to Byzantium. Manuel's Empress was of course a Serbian herself. Stefan's very title of Despot was itself a gift from

brothers clashed at last, and Musa was defeated. As the younger brother fell back, Suleyman pursued and extended his advantage by scoring another victory over Musa at Adrianople on July 11, 1410.[147]

Musa had thus lost the first round of his bid for power. But the long-range advantage was his. During the ensuing winter he built up his strength anew, while Suleyman allowed his advantages to deteriorate. Depicted by contemporary sources as given over to debauchery and moral corruption, Suleyman had apparently inherited and magnified his father's tendencies toward lapses into lethargy and degeneracy.[148] Moreover, his policies, as much as his personality, had cost him the loyalty of his subjects.[149] When, at the beginning of the next year, Musa again appeared with a formidable force and advanced to Adrianople,

the Byzantines. After having served with distinction as a loyal ally of Bayazid at Ancyra, Stefan had stopped in Constantinople on his way home. There John VII had bestowed this resounding title on him: Konstantin, ed. Jagić, 278; cf. Stanojević, 428–429; Jireček, *Geschichte*, 138; Alexandrescu-Dersca, p. 133, n. 3. Stefan's bond to John VII was quickly to be strengthened, for on a subsequent stop at Mitylene on Lesbos Stefan met Helena, a daughter of Francesco II Gattilusio (hence, John's sister-in-law), and married her: Konstantin, ed. Jagić, 278–279; cf. Stanojević, 429–430; Jireček, *Geschichte*, 139; Miller, "The Gattilusij," 415 (322). Stefan is apparently the "dominus despota" whose return home through Constantinople after the Battle of Ancyra is described by the Ragusan government in a letter of August 11, 1403, to Sigismund of Hungary, ed. Gelcich and Thallóczy, *Diplomatarium*, no. 92a, p. 123; his safe arrival home is likewise reported in a missive of August 23, 1403, *ibid.*, no. 92b, p. 124. For interesting reflections of Stefan's visit in the records of Pera, see Iorga, *Notes et extraits*, I, 69–70. In all, then, Manuel would rightly want Stefan on the Byzantine side in any concerted Christian action. Cf. Stanojević, 440–441.

147. Lampros chron., 151; cf. Βǫ. χǫ. No. 47, p. 82, ll. 65–67; Iorga, *Geschichte*, 351–352; Jireček, *Geschichte der Serben*, II, 146–147; Wittek, "De La Défaite," 21. Kosmidion is a suburb about 1 kilometer or so from the walls, along the Golden Horn.

148. According to Chalcocondyles, ed. Darkó, I, 163–164, ed. Bonn, 174, Suleyman made more territorial concessions to the Byzantines to hold their support, while they at the same time warned him against losing himself in his excesses. Cf. Muralt, p. 790, no. 5, and Hammer, I, 348–349, trans. Hellert, II, 142–143. Konstantin the Philosopher also reports (ed. Jagić, 279, 300, ed. and trans. Braun, 21–22, 41–42) Suleyman's love for wine as his downfall.

149. Cf. Wittek, "De La Défaite," 18–19, 20–22, according to whom Suleyman's friendly attitude toward the Christians had alienated the powerful Ghāzī elements in Rumelia, who sought only continuance of the Ghāzā, or holy war against the unbelievers. Musa was thus able to appeal to this disaffected and strong group and to dissolve the weak position of his brother.

Suleyman's position crumbled. His subjects went over to the energetic Musa. The deserted Suleyman fell into the hands of his brother, who had him strangled on February 17, 1411.[150]

If Suleyman had inherited his father's moral failings, Musa had fallen heir to Bayazid's ruthlessness, coupled with a determined energy and efficiency. Taking advantage of the warlike elements in Rumelia, Musa revived the Turkish aggressive posture and moved promptly to strike at those who had opposed his rise. The only Christian power that had any hope of gain was Venice, which had played a chary waiting game.[151] For the rest of the Christians Musa revived the atmosphere his father had fostered. In reprisal for his desertion, Musa attacked Stefan Lazarević of Serbia. More pertinent to our consideration, he attacked Byzantium. Constantinople was assailed, and other cities, such as Thessalonica and Selymbria, were also besieged. Manuel attempted to use Orchan, the son of Suleyman, against Musa. But, through the treachery of a powerful Turkish noble, the prince was betrayed to his uncle.[152] But Musa was less successful

150. Lampros chron., 151–152, alone of the Greek sources gives the date. in general, see Konstantin the Philosopher, ed. Jagić, 297–300, abridged ed. and trans. Braun, 35–42; cf. Stanojević, 442–445. Cf. also Wittek, "De La Défaite," pp. 21–22 and n. 2; Hammer, I, 349, trans. Hellert, II, 143–144; and Iorga, *Geschichte*, 353; Jireček, *Geschichte der Serben*, II, 148.

151. Venice for some time had been disenchanted with Suleyman. In his wars with Musa Venice studiously avoided taking any sides. After the actual hostilities had begun, the Senate, on July 24, 1410, instructed its *bailo* in Constantinople to await, at his own discretion, the final outcome of the struggle before sending the usual tribute money to Suleyman: text, ed. Iorga, *Notes et extraits*, I, 185; cf. Thiriet, *Régestes*, II, no. 1385, p. 93. On August 5, 1410, meanwhile, the Senate took the precaution of augmenting its naval force in Romania in view of the civil war: Thiriet, no. 1387, p. 93. On April 13, 1411, three months after Suleyman's death, the Senate made provisions for the return of the unpaid tribute money: Thiriet, no. 1414, p. 98. Then, on April 17, 1411, the Senate tried to chart some new course in view of Musa's victory. At first the *Sapientes* discussed investigating the possibility that Manuel might try to seize Gallipoli, and that, if he did not, Venice should do so itself. But Manuel was hardly in a position to seize anything, nor would Venice be, in view of the man with whom they would now have to deal. Wisely, the Senate voted down this proposal. Instead, it voted congratulations to its *bailo* in Constantinople for its handling of the tribute delay; and it instructed him to open negotiations with Musa about a maintenance of former treaty agreements between Venice and the Turks: Iorga, 194–195; Thiriet, no. 1415, pp. 98–99. Finally, on May 4, 1411, the Senate voted to send an ambassador to Musa to arrange terms: Iorga, 195; Thiriet, no. 1419, pp. 99–100.

152. Chalcocondyles, ed. Darkó, I, 166–167, ed. Bonn, 177–178, followed

at Constantinople, which he invested by land and sea. Fortunately, Manuel was able to assemble some ships and drive off at least the Turkish naval attack. This maritime action was commanded, we are told, by an illegitimate brother of the Emperor, also named Manuel.[153] The incident is interesting if only to suggest that Byzantium still had something it could call a fleet at this time.

In spite of this success, however, the Byzantines continued to be under siege on land by Musa. Once again, as in the nightmarish days of Bayazid, Constantinople had to contend with a

by the *Chron. Barb. 111,* 47–48, and the Pseudo-Phrantzes, ed. Papadopoulos, 91, ed. Bonn, 87. Also, Konstantin the Philosopher, ed. Jagić, 301–302, 305–306, ed. and trans. Braun, 43–44, 50; cf. Stanojević, 445 ff.; and Dölger, *Regesten,* no. 3330, p. 98. See also Hammer, I, 351–352, trans. Hellert, II, 146–148; Iorga, *Geschichte,* I, 353–355. Runciman, *The Fall of Constantinople,* 43, misconstrues his information to mean that Musa actually "recaptured" Thessalonica, which does not seem at all to have happened.

153. Chalcocondyles, ed. Darkó, I, 165–166, ed. Bonn, 176, followed by the *Chron. Barb. 111,* 47, and the Pseudo-Phrantzes, ed. Papadopoulos, 91, ed. Bonn, 87. The first of these sources adds the statement that the Emperor, jealous of this brother's success and esteem, had him seized and imprisoned with his children for seventeen years. (N.B.: Manuel only lived for some fourteen more years himself.) Such an accusation seems quite irreconcilable with Manuel's character, and either it is untrue—suggested perhaps, by its omission from the other sources—or it is a confused and incomplete representation of more facts not fully revealed. Cf. Berger de Xivrey, 155–156; Muralt, p. 794, nos. 7 and 8. It is interesting to note that the short chronicle published at the end of the Bonn edition of Ducas, p. 517, ll. 9–10, and republished as Βǫ. χǫ. No. 27, p. 47, ll. 40–41 (cf. Loenertz' *Chron. br. mor.,* No. 24, p. 407, with his translation and commentary, p. 429), after reporting a plague for the year 6918 (1409–10), mentions the death of ὁ μέγας δούκας Manuel. This title of Grand Duke was borne in late Byzantine times by the commander, nominal or otherwise, of the Byzantine fleet. (See Guilland, "Etudes de titulature et de prosopographie byzantines. Les chefs de la marine byzantine: Drongaire de la flotte, Grand Drongaire de la flotte, Duc de la flotte, Mégaduc," *Byz. Zeitschr.,* 44 [1951], 212–240, especially 233.) In view of the date involved, it seems unlikely that this chronicle passage has anything to do with the illegitimate Manuel. (Loenertz, "Pour l'histoire," 156, notes the possibility of this deceased Grand Duke being a Mamonas of Monemvasia.) Still, it is interesting to note that Chalcocondyles' warm description of the bastard Manuel portrays him as one skilled in warfare, a professional service man, as it were. Note also that the sophisticated Pseudo-Phrantzes calls him δǫουγγάǫιος, which was a title borne in earlier times also by commanders of the Byzantine navy. The *Chron. Barb. 111,* on the other hand, betrays its Italian sources by calling him a καπετάνιο, obviously an adaptation of the Italian word. Other than these references to him, we know nothing more of this illegitimate son of John V. Cf. A. T. Papadopulos, *Versuch,* 58.

Turkish investment. While this new siege could hardly have been as severe as the former one, it still posed a threat to the city. We have no way of knowing exactly how long it lasted.[154] But, with the help of their fortifications, the Byzantines were able to fight off the Turkish assaults.[155] For a time the situation seems to have reached something of a stalemate. But its outlook could hold much danger, and at this juncture it was diplomacy that had to be brought to bear. The Venetians, of course, ever anxious to have the Levantine cauldron simmer down, had their own brand of trimming diplomacy.[156] Manuel's diplomacy, however, was of sturdier quality.

154. Chalcocondyles, ed. Darkó, I, 167, ed. Bonn, 178, and the *Chron. Barb. 111*, 48, maintain that Musa arranged a truce with the Byzantines, and gave them as a hostage one of the younger sons of Bayazid, named Isa ('Ιησοῦς or 'Εσαί). But other evidence seems to rule out any possibility of such a truce, and the reference to a hostage is perhaps a confusion with Suleyman's presentation of them: see above, n. 88. On questions of terrritory seized by Musa, see Vakalopoulos, "Les Limites de l'empire byzantin," 61–62.

155. Ducas, ed. Grecu, 127–128, ed. Bonn, 92–93, describes heavy and valiant fighting. Once these early and violent states of the siege were ended, however, the Byzantine situation seems to have been relaxed enough to allow for ready access to the city. We have reports of the ceremonious reception by Manuel and the ecclesiastical authorities of Matthios, the Bulgarian Patriarch, "during the war of Sultan Mohammed I with his brother Μωσὴ τζαλαπή" which was actually to develop in earnest shortly: Gelzer, "Der wiederauf-gefundene Kodex," 100–102; Iorga, "Une Inscription grecque," 12. In addition, Manuel was free enough from pressing concerns at this time to write a gracious and trivial letter to the Mamluke Sultan of Egypt, accompanying a gift of five hunting falcons: Dölger, *Regesten,* no. 3328, pp. 97–98. This letter is reported to have reached its destination on June 25, 1411 (the 27th of the month of Ṣafar in the year of the Hejira 814). A description and a French translation of this letter are given by H. Lammens, "Correspondances diplomatique entre les Sultan Mamlouks d'Egypte et les puissances chré-tiennes," *Révue de l'Orient chrétien,* 9 (1904), 359–362.

156. On June 4, 1411, after they had voted to strengthen some of their naval forces in the Levant, the *Sapientes* discussed instructions to their agent to contract a treaty with Musa on lines similar to those of the previous one with Suleyman. It was decided that, if no such compact could be settled, the Venetians might then discuss the possibility of joint action with Manuel against the Turks. Aware even this early of the possible fluctuations of events, the Senate made provisions for the eventuality that Mechmed might already be the "Lord of Grecia"; and, perhaps not without a sense of humor, the Senate ordered additional letters to be drawn up with the name of the Turkish ruler left blank, to cover any eventuality: Iorga, *Notes et extraits,* I, 196–199; cf. Thiriet, *Régestes,* II, nos. 1423 and 1422, p. 100. On June 7, 1411, the Senate took note of progress in negotiations with Musa: Thiriet, no. 1424, p. 101. And, indeed, a pact was concluded with Musa on August

The elimination of Suleyman had left only two survivors in the power struggle. It was inevitable that they should clash sooner or later. Manuel could not fail to grasp the fact that an alliance with the natural interests of Mechmed was his own trump card at this point. Messages were sent to the Anatolian Sultan offering Byzantine alliance and support against Musa.[157] Mechmed saw his own advantage as clearly as Manuel saw his, and agreed. Thus, the third of Bayazid's four contending sons came to Constantinople to draw upon Byzantine assistance. Anatolian forces were brought across the Straits in Greek ships. But Mechmed had underestimated his task. In the first encounter with his brother, in July of 1412, he was defeated.[158] Mechmed returned

12/September 3, confirming the treaty of 1406 with Suleyman: Italian text, Thomas, *Diplomatarium*, 302–304, and Iorga, 200–202; Italian summary, (Predelli) *Commemoriali*, III, p. 354, no. 137 (cf. also *ibid.*, pp. 354–355, nos. 138 and 140). As a result, Venice was embarrassed when Manuel used a Venetian ship to transport to Thessalonica the Serbian prince Giorgio Branković, who had deserted Musa (cf. Iorga, *Geschichte*, 355; Jireček, *Geschichte der Serben*, II, 149). Hence, on March 7, 1412, the Senate felt obliged to report the matter to Musa, though it was agreed to leave Manuel's name out of the report: Iorga, *Notes et extraits*, I, 205; Thiriet, no. 1444, pp. 104–105. Indeed, Venice's diplomatic attention now had to be shifted to dealings with the Emperor. On May 5, 1412, the Senate heard complaints from a Byzantine envoy. Among these complaints (including one on the perennial dispute over the Kalopheros inheritance), the Emperor protested that the Venetians should be seeking to make peace with Musa while that prince was before the walls of the besieged Byzantine town of Selymbria— a reference to the signing there of the treaty of 1411 or to new negotiations? The Senate drily replied that the Turkish ruler must be sought where he was to be found and added the mealy-mouthed claim that these negotiations with Musa were designated to help bring about peace between him and Manuel: Thiriet, no. 1453, p. 106; cf. Dölger, *Regesten*, no. 3332a, p. 98. By this time also the Senate was aware that the treaty with the Emperor needed to be renewed. On May 15, 1412, an ambassador was chosen to conduct the negotiations: Iorga, 206; Thiriet, no. 1454, p. 107. Only on May 22 were provisions arranged for the ambassador's departure: Thiriet, no. 1461, p. 108; Iorga, 209. And, on July 22, 1412, the ambassador received his instructions for negotiating the treaty renewal: Iorga, 209–210; Thiriet, no. 1463, pp. 108–109. As it happened, the renewal was accomplished with remarkably little delay or haggling, on October 31, 1412: instrument text, Thomas, 304; cf. (Predelli) *Commemoriali*, III, p. 361, no. 161; also, Dölger, *Regesten*, no. 3333, p. 98. The dispute over Tenedos was apparently left dormant by this time.

157. Dölger, *Regesten*, nos. 3330–3331, p. 98. Ducas, ed. Grecu, 129, ed. Bonn, 93, portrays Manuel's decision to call upon Mechmed as a result of the revulsion and anger over an atrocity committed by Musa's Turks against a son of the diplomat Nicholas Notaras.

158. Contrary to other sources, Ducas, ed. Grecu, 131, ed. Bonn, 94–95,

to Anatolia, readying to cross back once more and assembling meanwhile a great coalition against Musa, including Stefan Lazarević as well as the Byzantine Emperor. By this time, as well, he could take advantage of his rival's internal difficulties. The savage Musa had begun to lose support in ways almost opposite to those of his unfortunate brother, Suleyman. His suspicions, his brutality, and his radical policies had alienated many important elements, especially among the aristocracy and the leadership.[159] As the final clash approached, it was obvious that it was to be the decisive one. Venice bided its time for its own interests.[160] Manuel and his allies waited and prayed and did what they could. On June 15, 1413, the Byzantines transported a new Anatolian army across the Straits. On July 5, 1413, the final battle was forced. Musa, deserted and fighting to the end, was captured and strangled in his own turn.[161]

The struggle was ended. Mechmed had finally emerged victorious. Sultan and Emperor quickly moved to make formal the amity that the conflict had bred between them. Mechmed, from all indications, was a man of honor and recognized his debt to Manuel by restoring to the Byzantines the territory they had held after the 1403 treaty—an arrangement which was probably Manuel's condition for Byzantine support—and by professing a devoted filial affection for Manuel.[162] But Mechmed was being sensible as well as honorable, for he knew full well that, after

has Mechmed defeated not once but twice, and has him flee to Constantinople, where he professes his deep indebtedness to Manuel. Cf. the *Chron. Barb. 111*, 49.

159. Cf. Wittek, "De La Défaite," 22–23.

160. Duplicating their caution of the last civil war cycle, the Senate, on July 24, 1413, while making arrangements for the payment of its tribute to Musa, provided for the possibility that Mechmed, already on the march, might have emerged as the victor: Iorga, *Notes et extraits*, I, 214–215; Thiriet, *Régestes*, II, no. 1496, pp. 115–116. The provision was a wise one, for by that date the conflict had indeed ended, in Mechmed's favor.

161. Wittek, "De La Défaite," 23; cf. Hammer, I, 354–358, trans. Hellert, II, 148–156; Iorga, *Geschichte*, 356–359; Jireček, *Geschichte der Serben*, II, 150; Stanojević, 445–451. Reports of this outcome are contained in Ragusan letters to King Sigismund, of July 13 and July 30, 1413: Gelcich and Thallóczy, nos. 148–149, pp. 224–226.

162. Ducas, ed. Grecu, 133, ed. Bonn, 97. Less detailed are Chalcocondyles, ed. Darkó, I, 172, ed. Bonn, 183, followed by the *Chron. Barb. 111*, 51, and the Pseudo-Phrantzes, ed. Papadopoulos, 93–94, ed. Bonn, 89–90. Cf. Pears, 113; Muralt, p. 795, no. 1; Dölger, *Regesten*, no. 3334, p. 98, as well as *ibid.*, no. 3332.

the setback of Ancyra, followed by ten years of disruptive civil war, the Osmanli state could not afford a resumption of immediate and full aggressiveness against Byzantium. Rather, it was peace that was needed for the moment to allow an internal restoration and realignment of the Turkish state, not yet fully a well-organized empire. To this task Mechmed meticulously set himself.[163]

If peace between Turk and Greek was now essential for Mechmed, it was certainly something of a blessing for Manuel. After the long agonies of resistance to Bayazid and then the disappointment of the Western journey, Manuel had been plunged into a period that, if at least more advantageous for Byzantium than the former one, must have seemed as nerve-wracking and perilous as it was challenging. The quest for aid from the West, modified as it might have been in terms of Manuel's personal attitudes, had continued, still with no real success. Rather, Manuel had been obliged to make the most out of the Turkish "Time of Troubles" on his own. Now, at last, that period was ended. In spite of perils, Byzantium had emerged from it with some profit. The Empire was again at peace with the Turks, and this time— the first and, indeed, the only such time in Byzantine history— with a personal bond established between the rulers of the Greeks and the Turks, a bond which promised an immediate outlook of repose and reasonable security for the Empire. Out of the "Time of Troubles" there had finally come, it seemed, a time of relief.

163. Cf. Wittek, "De La Défaite," 28, and *id., The Rise of the Ottoman Empire,* 48–51, who interprets Mechmed's task as the reconciliation of the two sundered halves of the Turkish realms: Anatolia, dominated by the traditional and conservative element of the 'Ulemā; and Rumelia, motivated by the militant zeal of the Ghāzīs. This reconciliation was effected only by the definite recognition of the Ghāzī point of view as the driving force of the Osmanli state, as symbolized by the transfer of the capital "from Brusa, the 'city of the theologians' to Adrianopolis, the 'city of the Ghāzīs,'" while, at the same time, the older Islamic point of view was accepted only as a broader background.

5. The Final Struggles, 1413–1425

The end of the Turkish civil wars, with the final triumph of Mechmed I in 1413, at last brought a seemingly stable peace to Byzantium. Manuel was now sixty-three years of age, an old man by most standards, yet still active and vigorous withal. He had been Emperor in his own right since his father's death for twenty-two years. It had taken all of these twenty-two years of humiliation and toil and struggle and trial for Manuel to bring his realm into an era of honorable peace and relative prosperity, in spite of the continued existence of Turkish power. With the advent of peace at last, the Emperor might well turn to the internal needs of Byzantium, now that this peace had given him sufficient freedom.

Manuel and Byzantium had much need of this interval of repose, to lick wounds and to go about restoring strength as much as was possible. Though its territories had been slightly enlarged as a reward of Manuel's diplomacy, the Empire was still but a wretched shadow of the past, and a travesty of the very pretension of Empire. The capital itself, the battered head of a shriveled and almost nonexistent body, had been ravaged further by the hardships of sieges and warfare. It has been estimated that the population of Constantinople during the fifteenth century was as low as between 40,000 and 60,000 people,[1] though

1. A. M. Schneider, "Die Bevölkerung Konstantinopels in XV. Jahr-

the figure must have been even smaller in the early years of the century during and after the Turkish attacks.

The effects of such ruin and depopulation were easily visible and readily commented upon. In a document we have elsewhere had occasion to examine,[2] the Patriarch Matthaios remarked upon the dreadful condition of the capital about the year 1401, during Bayazid's siege. He reflected upon the evils that had "brought on the disfigurement and desolation of all this great city," and he noted further that "the former beauties of this great city—once a paradise of luxury—have now become as a plain of destruction." The Patriarch's explanation for such woes was the sinfulness of his people and the wrath which they had drawn upon themselves from God. For his purposes, economic and political realities were not pertinent.

On a broader perspective, however, at least some contemporaries (and Westerners, at that) had a sharper eye for details. To document more accurately the ravaged state of Manuel's city, we are fortunate that, among the various descriptions by travelers of this period, there are at least two which characterize its condition vividly. The earlier one is that of the Castilian ambassador to Timur, Ruy González de Clavijo, who visited Constantinople in the autumn of 1403. His account of his stay there is long and rich in details, for he was obviously much impressed by this still remarkable city. But, in spite of his expressions of admiration and awe, an awareness of its evil times is made clear:

. . . But, however large the city and the great circuit [of walls], it is not very well populated, for in the midst of it there are many hills and valleys on which there are fields of corn and vineyards and many orchards; and in what areas there are these said cultivated places there are houses, like as villages; and this is in the midst of the city. The most populated area is in the lower section, at the base of the circuit which runs close by the sea . . .

hundert," *Nachrichten der Akademie der Wissenschaften in Göttingen, Philologisch-historische Klasse,* 1949, No. 9, pp. 233–244, especially pp. 236–237. But note also the article by F. Dirimtekin, "1453 muhasasrası esnasın da Bısans' in nüfusu" ("La Population de Byzance lors du siège 1453") in the *Türkiye Turıng ve otomobil kuruku Belletin Hazıran* (1954), no. 149, which is unavailable to me but which, according to a citation in *Byz. Zeitschr.,* 47 (1954), 481, estimates the population in 1453 as not less than about 80,000.

2. See pp. 208 ff. above for a complete translation.

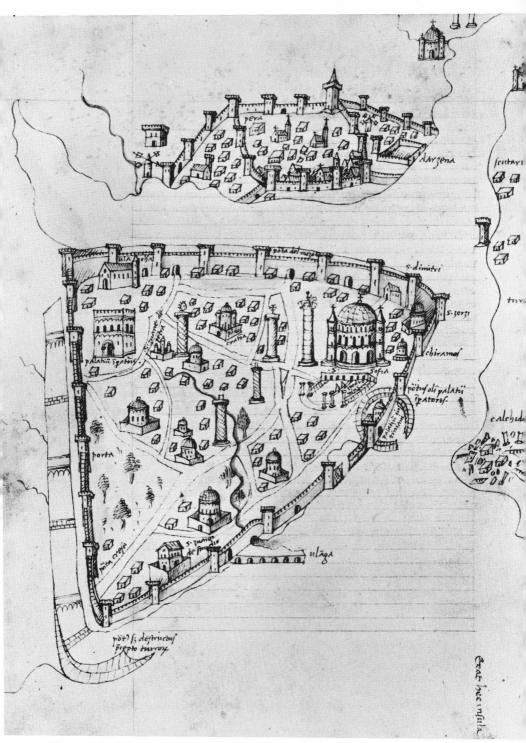

Figure 24: *View of Constantinople about 1420, after Buondelmonti.* Pen Drawing, Biblioteca Apostolica Vaticana, Rome, *Cod. Rossianus 702*, f. 32ᵛ (photo courtesy Biblioteca Apostolica Vaticana, Rome; see Appendix XXIV, C, 6, a).

Figure 25: *View of Constantinople about 1420, after Buondelmonti.* Pen and Wash Drawing, Biblioteca Nazionale di S. Marco, Venice, Cod. *Marciana Lat.* X, 123 (=3784), f. 22ʳ (photo courtesy Biblioteca Nazionale di S. Marco, Venice; see Appendix XXIV, C, 6, b).

. . . Moreover, throughout the city of Costantinopla there are many large buildings—homes, churches, and monasteries—the most of which are entirely in ruin. So it appears likely that in another time, when the city was in its prime, it was one of the noble cities of the world. And they say that in the present day there are in the city probably about a thousand churches, ranging from great to small. . . .[3]

Exactly a quarter of a century later, another Castilian visited the city and recorded similar conditions. Although Pero Tafur describes the city as it was in the autumn of 1437 and then early in the following year, its circumstances must not have been much different from those of Clavijo's time—certainly not any better. Tafur's comments in this vein at three different points are brief but telling:

. . . The Emperor [Manuel's successor, John VIII] treated me with great affection and as a kinsman, and he desired greatly that I should remain in his country and marry there and settle down, and I had some thoughts of doing so in view of what I have related, for the city is badly populated and there is need of good soldiers, which is no wonder since the Greeks have such powerful nations to contend with. . . .

. . . The Emperor's Palace must have been very magnificent, but now it is in such state that both it and the city show well the evils which the people have suffered and still endure. . . . Inside, the house is badly kept, except certain parts where the Emperor, the Empress, and attendants can live, although cramped for space. The Emperor's state is as splendid as ever, for nothing is omitted from the ancient ceremonies, but, properly regarded, he is like a Bishop without a See. . . .

. . . The city is sparsely populated. It is divided into districts, that by the sea-shore having the largest population. The inhabitants are not well clad, but sad and poor, showing the hardship of their lot, which is, however, not so bad as they deserve, for they are a vicious people, steeped in sin. . . . On one side of the city is the dockyard.

3. Ed. F. López Estrada, p. 57, ll. 3–9, 14–20, in my own translation; cf. ed. Sreznevski, 87–88, and trans. Le Strange, 87–88. Shortly thereafter, Clavijo's description of Pera presents a healthy picture, intentional or otherwise, of a contrast in bustle and prosperity. A portion of Clavijo's description of Constantinople is quoted, in Le Strange's translation, by J. Gill, "John VIII Palaeologus: A Character Study," *Studi bizantini e neoellenici*, 9 (1959), 152, or as reprinted in the author's collection, *Personalities of the Council of Florence, and Other Essays* (New York, 1964), 104–105.

It is close to the sea, and must have been very magnificent; even now it is sufficient to house the ships. . . .[4]

From these two similar descriptions,[5] we can readily see to what depths the economy of the truncated Byzantine state had sunk, even if little survives in the way of precise figures and documents. The once-great commerce of the capital had flown elsewhere. The Latin interlopers, especially the Genoese and Venetians, had won such commercial advantages in the past that they had taken over almost entirely the trade that had once made Constantinople such a fabulously wealthy mercantile center. Its customs income was reduced to a mere trickle while the outsiders enjoyed all the profit. Meanwhile, the debased coinage sank lower and lower in value, beyond all redemption by the Byzantine state's depleted metal reserves. Increasing political instability and wars restricted and ruined much vital trade. Even the very food supply system of the capital was on a precarious basis and frequently broke down. The economic exhaustion that had grown by the late fourteenth century thus went hand in glove with the further ravages of the Turkish advance, with its reduction of revenue-producing territories and with the great devastations from sieges of the capital, all to complete the abasement of Constantinople's economic situation.[6]

4. Quoted from the English translation revised and thoroughly discussed by Vasiliev, "Pero Tafur, A Spanish Traveller of the Fifteenth Century and His Visit to Constantinople, Trebizond, and Italy," *Byzantion*, 7 (1932), 75–122: the three passages are respectively on pp. 95, 111–112, and 113.

5. Of the remaining principal travel descriptions of this time, neither Schiltberger nor Buondelmonti, nor even the later Bertrandon de la Brocquiere, gives any real comments relevant here to the question of the city's great decay. The second of these accounts, however, is interesting in that various manuscripts of it contain interesting and valuable miniature views of the city. (Two of them are included here as Figures 24 and 25; see also below, Appendix XXIV: C, 6, a and b.) A general survey of the various travel accounts of the city in Manuel's lifetime and beyond, though with slightly different emphases and unfortunately omitting Tafur, may be found in J. Ebersolt's *Constantinople byzantine et les voyageurs du Levant* (Paris, 1918), pp. 46–60. In the same vein, see Zakythinos, *Crise monétaire et crise économique à Byzance du XIIIᵉ au XVᵉ siècle* (Athens, 1948), 36–37.

6. Little specific detail can be given for our particular period out of the context of late Palaeologan economic decline as a whole. For broad general surveys of this economic situation, see Zakythinos, *Crise monétaire*, 37 f., 40–43, and especially pp. 97 ff.; Heyd, *Histoire du commerce du Levant au moyen âge*, II, 257 ff.; G. Brătianu, *Etudes byzantines d'histoire écono-

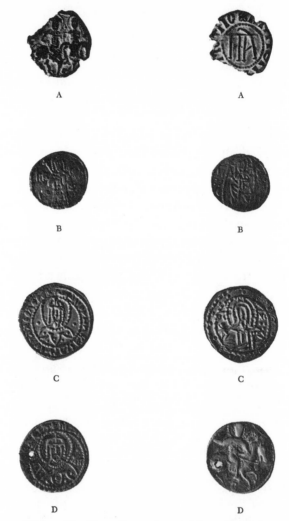

Figure 26: *Four Examples of Manuel's Coinage.* Dumbarton Oaks Collections, Washington, D.C. (photo courtesy W. Lane, Dumbarton Oaks, Washington, D.C.; see Appendix XXIV, A, III, 2, a-d).

In such dreary circumstances of decline, nothing which Manuel might have done could have made any major difference. A goodly number of Manuel's chrysobulls, *prostagmata,* and sundry other enactments have come down to us. But they reflect, on the whole, specifically *ad hoc* intentions—grants and pious foundations to religious institutions, settlements of disputes and ecclesiastical regulations, and adjustments of tax and property difficulties. To be sure, one can see some broad continuity of policy with regard to landholding.[7] But such long-range strands are rare. It may be that when the documentary material of this sort is more thoroughly published and examined, it will yet reveal more definite underlying currents of broad policy.[8] It seems unlikely, however, that one can ever really speak of much actual economic policy on Manuel's part. As the documents in-

mique et sociale (Paris, 1938), 167–168. On the coinage of this time, the most important study is Bertelè's "L'iperpero bizantino dal 1261 al 1453," *Rivista italiana di numismatica e scienze affini,* V, 5, 59 (1957), especially pp. 75–89. See also pp. 89–90 of A. Blanchet's "Les derniers monnaies d'or des empereurs de Byzance," *Revue numismatique,* IV, 14 (1910), 78–90. For a discussion of the unstable and often famine-producing food situation of the capital, see Brătianu's "L'Approvisionnement de Constantinople à l'époque byzantine et ottomane," *Byzantion,* 5 (1929–30), 83–107, especially pp. 100–102; also *id.,* "Nouvelles Contributions à l'étude de l'approvisionnement de Constantinople sous les Paléologues et les empereurs ottomans," *Byzantion,* 6 (1931), 640–656.

7. For the best discussion of tax and land-holding policies in Manuel's period, see Ostrogorsky, *Pour l'histoire de la féodalité byzantin,* 161–176. Ostrogorsky stresses the late Palaeologan effort—all in vain—to build some kind of base for military strength by seizing monastic properties to revive the old system of *pronoia* grants. The document of greatest significance here is Manuel's important *prostagma* of December, 1408 (Dölger, *Regesten,* no. 3321, p. 96; see above, p. 280, and n. 141). In it, Manuel alleviated the tax load of the Athonite monastery of Vatopedi and restored some of its confiscated properties, but not all; the text also comments most interestingly on the stringency of the earlier situation, after the Battle of the Marica in 1371, which had called forth such drastic measures.

8. The limitations of length and scope make impossible any systematic discussion here of all of Manuel's surviving enactments. Among his monastic grants, however, there are several documents which cast important light on this Emperor's policies, and on the economic conditions of the period. The publications of, or literature on, these documents may be traced from the listings in Dölger's *Regesten,* as follows: no. 3239, pp. 80–81 (1393); no. 3242, p. 81 (1394); no. 3301, pp. 90–91 (1404); no. 3304, p. 91 (1405); no. 3321, p. 96 (1408); no. 3322, pp. 96–97 (1409); and no. 3340, p. 99 (1414). (It might be noted here that this final section of Dölger's great reference work had not appeared at the time this book was written, so that all citations of it have had to be incorporated subsequently.)

dicate, his efforts in his hopeless situation could only be stop-gap attempts to meet explicit minor problems.

More to the point here, the surviving documentary evidence likewise gives no indication of any extraordinary increase in Manuel's devotion to internal problems during the period of Mechmed I's reign. To be sure, there can be no doubt that Manuel did turn his attention to internal affairs at this time. But it has unfortunately been all too common to assume that he did little more, regarding this time as one of rest at last; merely sweeping up the house after the party had ended, as it were. In the usual view, it is as if the reign of Mechmed was a period of such great tranquility for Manuel that he had little to fear from external factors. As we shall see, however, only when a detailed examination of this final epoch is made is it clear how false this common interpretation really is.

The best initial demonstration of this fact may be found in an episode which is normally pointed out as an illustration of the traditional view. This is Manuel's visit to the Peloponnesus in 1415. Manuel's stay there in 1408 had not been long enough for him to accomplish what he had seen needed to be done. In view of the importance of the Despotate of the Morea to Byzantium, it was only natural that Manuel should have taken advantage of his new freedom to attend to affairs there.

The story of the episode is long and intricate, with many distracting preliminaries. Leaving his eldest son, the future John VIII, as his regent in Constantinople, Manuel sailed from there on July 25, 1414.[9] He did not proceed directly to the Pelopon-

---

9. Sphrantzes, 1026B (Pseudo-Phrantzes, ed. Papadopoulos, 99; ed. Bonn, 96), gives simply the month of July and states the year as 1413; this date was accepted blindly by Muralt, *Essai de chronographie byzantine,* p. 795, no. 7. In context the year is obviously incorrect. Fortunately, we have another source which enables us to correct the error, in the remarkable Satire of Mazaris. One part of this work is a fictitious letter, dated November 21, the ninth indiction (1415), supposedly written by the protagonist/author to his friend (Manuel Holobolos) in Hades. This letter gives a pricelessly valuable account of Manuel's journey and of affairs in the Morea. In this text (ed. Boissonade, 177, ed. Ellissen, 242), the date is given as July 25 of the seventh indiction (1414), which fits the facts. (Mazaris also states that Manuel sailed "with one great ship and five triremes.") This correction of Sphrantzes was pointed out by Loenertz, in his article "Epître de Manuel II Paléologue aux moines David et Damien, 1416," *Silloge bizantina in onore di S. G. Mercati* (=*Studi bizantini e neoellenici,* 9, 1957), 294–296. For proof of John's presence in Constantinople as regent, see n. 23, and n. 87 below.

nesus, however, for he had to make two important stops along the way. The first was the island of Thasos, where there had been unrest and sedition for some time.[10] When Manuel appeared upon the scene, the island was apparently being contested by Giorgio Gattilusio, a bastard son of Francesco II, the Genoese Lord of Lesbos. It took Manuel some three months and a siege involving "stone-throwing machines" to reduce all to his authority once more. What is both helpful and puzzling in considering this incident is that we have a letter written by Manuel apparently to no less than this very Giorgio Gattilusio while the latter was under siege by the Emperor:

That you, then, behave foolishly in your own action is clear. For you would not be hazarding ventures beyond your merit were you capable of being moderate and, if you will, of knowing yourself fully. And that for those who have incurred this evil it is so great as to make it unnecessary to give them any punishment beyond their very association with such suffering—the present troubles themselves demonstrate. For, the undertaking has become as Scylla and Charybdis for you, since you would be slain, I suppose, should you remain within. So you see that the citadel which you now occupy, after you seized it rebelliously, is utterly weak and not such as would resist both the machines without its gates and the continuity of the war. Yet, should you wish to come forth, under constraint of your troubles themselves, you would certainly be saved, indeed, but you would then live in unending shame. For which reasons you "set your mouth against heaven, and your tongue walketh through the earth" [cf. Psalm 73:9] and the expressions of a boaster have turned round to the opposite for you.[11]

10. So says Mazaris, ed. Boissonade, 177, ed. Ellissen, 242.
11. Letter ξ′, ed. Legrand, 89–90, fully translated here. This letter raises many problems. The address in the manuscripts is not entirely certain for this letter and for the next one. The latter, ξα′, also supposedly addressed to the same person, is in quite a different tone. It is a brief but obscure reflection on the difficulties which a ruler faces in making his decisions. Unless one regards it as a kind of message of consolation to the defeated and deposed "tyrant" Gattilusio, it seems difficult to believe that it was written to the same man as its predecessor. That Manuel should have written even one of these two, if not both, to Gattilusio implies perhaps a certain familiarity with the man, unless it is taken as some kind of rhetorical exercise, a hypothetical letter to fit the circumstances. It is placed among his letters as a true piece of correspondence, though it does follow another rhetorical discourse which is really not a letter (νθ′). Amid these questions, however, it

After September of 1414,[12] Manuel proceeded on to his second stop, Thessalonica. It was there on November 28, 1414, that the Emperor wrote to King Ferdinand I of Aragon, informing him of his "recovery" of Thasos and of his arrival in Thessalonica.[13] There also Manuel was able to see personally to the affairs of the city that he had assigned to his third son, Andronicus, by

is obvious that at least the first of these two letters supposedly to Gattilusio, the one translated above, is plausibly connected with the Thasos incident.

The only other fighting with which it might be connected is that subsequently in the Morea; and we do have evidence, in Mazaris, of intensive siege operations, which would have involved the use of "machines" (μηχανάς) before a citadel. It is therefore quite possible that this letter could have been written to one of the *archons* whom Manuel besieged and chastized in the Morea (see p. 317 below), and I submit that this possibility ought to be given serious consideration. For the time being, however, I am accepting this letter in its usual association with the Thasos events. Mazaris, ed. Boissonade, 177, ed. Ellissen, 242, also referring to the three-month duration of Manuel's stay on the island, specifically speaks of the use of πετροβόλων μηχανημάτων here. The key to the problem, for the moment, is therefore simply the reliability of the letter's address, "To Georgios Gatelioutzes, when he was ruling Thasos as a tyrant" (or "illegally," or "rebelliously": ἐτυράννει); lacking in the *Parisinus gr. 3041*.

Little clearer is the involvement of the Gattilusii with Thasos at this time. It is true that the island later came under their control: see Miller, "The Gattilusij of Lesbos," 432 (330). From what we might conclude from Manuel's letter, assuming the association is correct, this particular member of the family may have tried to take advantage of the confusion of the Turkish civil wars to seize Thasos and establish himself on it. For what little else can be assembled about this illegitimate Georgio, see Loenertz, "Epître," p. 296 and n. 3. Concerning Manuel on the island, see Berger de Xivrey, *Mémoire sur la vie et les ouvrages de l'empereur Manuel Paléologue*, pp. 159–160, who did not use this letter or discover its possible relation to the incident; see also G. Perrot, *Mémoire sur l'île de Thasos* (Paris, 1864), p. 59, who had only the vagueness of the Pseudo-Phrantzes on which to base his statements. Citing no more than the same source, Mompherratos, Οἱ Παλαιολόγοι ἐν Πελοποννήσῳ, 35, asserts that the dissidents on Thasos were led by "the *archons* Asanes Raoul and Vranas." I find no support or background for this utterly contrary identification, save in a footnote (a) to Table IX, 2, in Hopf's *Chroniques gréco-romanes* (Berlin, 1873), with no specification of source or authority.

12. Sphrantzes, 1026B (Pseudo-Phrantzes, ed. Papadopoulos, 99; ed. Bonn, 96), says that Manuel seized Thasos in that month and then sailed on. Either this date or the three months ascribed by Mazaris, ed. Boissonade, 177, ed. Ellissen, 242, for Manuel's stay on the island may therefore be interpreted perhaps a bit flexibly. Muralt, pp. 795–796, nos. 2–3, still misled by (the Pseudo-)Phrantzes' faulty chronology, accepts the date as September 1413 and places the trip to the Morea immediately after, in the same year.

13. Dölger, *Regesten*, no. 3343, p. 100. For this letter, see below, pp. 333–334. Cf. Loenertz, "Epître," 296.

now about fourteen years old. At the same time, he turned his attention to the needs and requests of the monasteries of Mount Athos.[14] Finally, by the end of the winter of 1415, he had finished his work in Thessalonica, and he set sail for the Morea.

We are remarkably fortunate in having survive to us a letter by Manuel himself, in which he discusses at great length his visit to the Morea at this time. It is of such importance that any modern discussion of the subject could but be a commentary upon it. In spite of its great length there is little choice but to present the entire letter, in view of its vital significance for understanding this episode, as well as for the fascination of having

14. Four monastic grants by Manuel survive from this period. In August of 1414, even before his departure from Thasos, Manuel awarded to the Monastery of Vatopedi on the Holy Mountain a grant of land on the island of Lemnos: Dölger, *Regesten*, no. 3340, p. 99; text published by Arkadios Vatopedinos, in his " 'Αγιορειτικὰ ἀνάλεκτα ἐκ τοῦ ἀρχείου τῆς μονῆς Βατοπεδίου," in Γρηγόριος ὁ Παλαμᾶς, 3 (1919), no. 43, pp. 433–434; cited by Muralt, p. 796, no. 9, in spite of his assumption that Manuel was by then in the Morea. It was apparently in November of 1414, after his arrival in Thessalonica, that Manuel issued a chrysobull confirming a previous *prostagma* of nearly six years before (January of 1409; Dölger, no. 3322, pp. 96–97), on behalf of the Monastery of Docheiariou; in the text Manuel specifically refers to a petition addressed to him by some monks when he was in Thessalonica: Dölger, no. 3342, pp. 99–100; text published by Ch. Ktenas, in his "Χρυσόβουλλοι λόγοι τῆς ἐν "Αθω ἱερᾶς βασιλικῆς πατριαρχικῆς καὶ σταυροπηγιακῆς μονῆς τοῦ Δοχειαρίου," 'Επ. 'Ετ. Βυζ. Σπουδ., 4 (1927), 307–308 (no. 10); cf. also the comments of A. Sigalas in 'Ελληνικά, 1 (1928), 431–432. A *prostagma* of the year 6923 (1414–15) for the Monastery of Lavra seems also to be of this period: cited by E. Sophronios, in his " 'Ιστορικὰ μνημεῖα τοῦ "Αθω," 'Ελληνικά, 2 (1929), p. 384, n. μ'; not noted by Dölger. On these, cf. also Loenertz, "Epître," 296–297. Finally, we have still another *prostagma*, of December 20, 1414, in which Manuel confirms a previous grant (Dölger, no. 3211, p. 78) by his late nephew, John VII, in 1408, to the Monastery of Dionysiou: Dölger, no. 3344, p. 100; text and commentary in Dölger, *Aus den Schatzkammern des heiligen Berges*, I (Munich, 1948), no. 23, pp. 68–69. Manuel also devoted himself to ecclesiastical affairs in Thessalonica itself. For two monasteries there he issued a *prostagma* in March of 1415 (probably just before his departure from the city): Dölger, *Regesten*, no. 3346, p. 101; see Lemerle, "Autour d'un prostagma inédit de Manuel II. L'aulé de Sire Gui à Thessalonique," *Silloge bizantina in onore di S. G. Mercati* (=*Studi bizantini e neoellenici*, 9, 1957), 271–286.

We have only one specific source allusion to any other kind of activity which Manuel was involved in during this stay in Thessalonica. According to Konstantin the Philosopher (ed. Jagić, 271, ed. and trans. Braun, pp. 15–16), one of Manuel's acts then was to have a tower built by the Turks dismantled, for the purpose, the source says, of nullifying any claim by them on the city.

the Emperor's own extensive reflections on it. It is addressed to two "hieromonachoi" ("priest-monks," or celibate priests) named David and Damianos, whom the Emperor had apparently met during his dealings with monastic affairs in Thessalonica. They had seen a literary work by the Emperor in progress at that time, and they had requested a copy of it upon its completion. But Manuel's great preoccupations had delayed his fulfillment of their request. And it was only later, presumably at the end of his sojourn in the Morea in late 1415 or early 1416, that Manuel was able to write this missive to the two "priest-monks" to apologize for his delay and to explain in detail the reasons for it:

I know that this fruit of my exertions is come to you much past your expectations. The reason is that it has ripened late, inasmuch as the season has not provided it an atmosphere of proper climate. Thus, accordingly, it has remained unripe for a long time. But, now that it has only just succeeded in escaping hindrance to its attainment of fruition, it would seem to fulfill its function; for no sooner has it matured than, in order that it may not become useless from over-ripening, it goes to you now as if on wings. And it is not necessary to marvel, I suppose, that the book was not completed more quickly; rather, that it was finished at all, even after a long time. For, as if by some signal, many troubles of all sorts have come upon me, and it is not possible to have any leisure. All of which factors it would take a long time to relate; but to pass over them all forthwith, on the other hand, does not seem proper, since I know that you are eager to learn the news about me. For all these reasons, then, it is necessary to make clear to you in moderate length some of the events befallen at this time.

Well then, when we were not yet near to setting sail, the preliminaries were so ominous as to make us foresee that our journey would go on in like fashion. Which has, indeed, fully come to pass, even if it ended otherwise, at length, for the benefit of us who fare well in God's scale of judgment. So, that rough outbound voyage was not only of great length, but it was also not free of storms, nor was it either devoid of thunderclaps echoing in our ears—an ill-omened sound!—and of continuous bolts of lightning constantly flashing in our eyes, together with furious rainstorms and snowstorms in some places. All of which things, coming together all at once then, penetrated to the depth of our souls and instilled a trembling in our hearts, and wholly alarmed and confounded us—indeed, just as those experienced of these conditions understand perfectly. At other times, also, other winds blew by turns from all directions. And these winds, setting

upon our ships with such a frenzy—if we may describe it so charitably
—and, upsetting us in an instant, were threatening us with a terrific
shipwreck in the midst of the sea. Thus, waves were stirred up, rising
in crests over the decks of the ships—a fearful thing to be seen, to be
sure, if one endured even to look at them; but a yet more fearful thing
to be heard, since they were producing a monstrous din to our ears by
their dashing one after another against the ships. Indeed, it threatened, almost as if it could speak with a voice, to sink the vessels with
all hands. To tell the whole story, the voyage was just the sort of
thing to tear out our best hopes by the roots. Accordingly, as no one
was free from these fears, it made me, as you can imagine, go ashore
in the harbor still atrembling.

These, then, were the initial aspects of our departure. But those
after the trip were of the same kind. Now, one fact alone suffices to
disturb and to disquiet exceedingly the reflections and the thought
of every ruler whatsoever: I mean the need at a given time for as
much money as possible—in the absence of which "nothing can be
done that is needed," as the Orator said [Demosthenes, *Olynthiac I*,
20 (15); cf. n. 15 below]—while there is at the same time little wealth
within our borders, and not so much as would strain the hand of him
who carries it off. What may one say of what came thereafter? For,
my troubles on behalf of the common good are like unto blizzards;
and before all of them is that very task which seems to most people
entirely endless: I mean the fortification of the Isthmus so that, with
the aid of God's grace, we may favor all those dwelling therein with
freedom from fear. In comparison with these concerns, what flood of
woe could one not demonstrate as but a fair tranquility?

These factors, then, and such like them, and also—as the capstone
of our ills—the stubbornness and ingratitude of some by no means
granted me any leisure. At that time, moreover, the general emergency occupied all my attention. So how would it be possible, when
one is enmeshed in so many and such great problems, to arouse one's
reflections readily to another matter? In truth, however, something
else was added, something most bitter and enough to cripple in pro-
duction of words, I think one might say, the intellect of even a
Demosthenes and a Plato. For, from those who ought to acknowledge
the greatest debt there came plottings and deceits. How may one
speak of the manifold variety of such machinations which were
fabricated against us by them? Thus were they making proper repay-
ments to me, both for their deliverance from their dangers—since they
were "on a razor's edge" as their perils hung over them, and their
cities were in danger of being devastated by the first onslaught of
their enemies—and also for those blessings which they were now able
to enjoy bounteously.

For, it was now possible to till without fear, and to cultivate woodlands, and to sow groves cleared of trees; and sweet it was to look upon the billowing crop fields, and yet sweeter to reap them, and to attend to crops that had been neglected and to replant vineyards that had been left barren, and to plant new things in them; and at once to feast one's eye and to feast one's pleasure on the fruits of all these labors, and to revel in them to the point of satiety; and yet more, to sell at a higher price what is surplus if desired. There was in addition something better than this, or by no means less: to fatten herds and flocks and such other four-legged animals as are tamed. Inasmuch as now there was no more of the frightening onslaught of the barbarians, there was no hindrance, as there was formerly, to frequenting alike the borders and the citadels and to living as one's own master, whether in the plains or in the inaccessible places. And, to speak comprehensively, I believe that they themselves, and they from whom come their revenue, would never have expected to accomplish this, even in a dream.

Thus, no longer did anything constrain them still to seek some cave or fortress, in order to shut themselves in at night, nor a precipitous place passable only to chamois, or some deep thicket which may hide those who take refuge in it, so that they should not be as prey to their enemies. It no longer seemed necessary for them to seek such things, nor was it fitting that they suffer like people whose hearts were reared in terrors and those whose souls were never calm. For, since the old walls have been raised up, it seemed clear madness to endure without reason a long period of distress again, and to live in trembling instead of fearlessly, to be frightened by the rustlings of leaves and by shadows, to quit at an untimely hour of the night the place in which they may have been, and to seek after some very deep hollows and hiding places of wild animals—these were what they had been accustomed to do then. Now, it was surely possible, very possible, indeed, for them to alter to the contrary all these things that they had been accustomed to do when their fears were blooming and to enjoy the fruit of their happiness as a counterpoise to their former grievous circumstances. Thus now, entirely for the better, had it suddenly been altered. And so great came to be their freedom from fear that now even those who surpass hares in their cowardice did not desist from kindling great fires and lying down to sleep asnoring beside springs, having welcomed sweet sleep, in their soft eyes, as some poet would say, whether in fields or on hillocks, anywhere.

Such, then, were the benefits conferred on those ungrateful people. Yet, verily, I will not suppress the truth, for not all are ungrateful, nor is it fitting that the evil of some should become a disaster for the guiltless. Therefore, I will speak in defense of those who are with reason discontented; yet, not simply on behalf of all, since not all were the same in both their characters and deeds, but were different from each other, very basically. Lest, as it is said, "all things be as chaos" [cf. Plato, *Phaedo,* 72C], all possible justification is due those I have mentioned. But, on behalf of the worse party, not a word of defense should be wasted, since none is to be found even if one should strenuously wish to do so. There is a need, I think, for some distinctions, to show the variation among them. Within the three groups into which they are all distributed, those in office, those of consecrated garb, and the local people and foreigners, those better in character and in wisdom among them—and these are very quickly counted—approved very readily of not leaving themselves always as spoil and food exposed to the hands and mouths of their enemies; rather, they eagerly approved of the desire to exchange their manifest and customary dangers for those which lay in uncertainty and were not lasting.

And with them the swarms of Illyrians [Albanians] also agreed and consented, inasmuch as they were being very much harmed by the enemy, being both a people without cities and also used to spending their lives in fields and in tents. Therefore, those of sound thinking who had forthwith accepted their labors—as, indeed, all ought to have done—once they had spoken their opinion freely, spared not their feet, nor their hands, nor the entire body, supplying both night and day, if one must speak concisely, whatever things were required for raising up the wall. So, on behalf of these particular men there is certainly no need to speak any defense. Why, for those whose exertions were appropriate? But there were others, belonging to a rank by no means inferior to that of the foremost, but inferior to them in judgment, who neither did nor intended anything at all befitting their station or their proper repute, and who, in the delusion of folly, left no stone unturned in attempting to destroy the undertaking. And, while they were small in number, yet, they had communicated their defilement to a larger number who were more guileless—not to say more stupid.

Accordingly, they were priding themselves greatly on their success; nevertheless, they seemed to me to be choking in their bile, and as if they were losing their wits in the midday sun. For, who does not know that they were preferring the least before the best and the greatest evil before the greatest good? So they saw nothing wrong in their own ability to steal and to commit outrages on the most precious things of those who are free. And would that these acts were the worst of it! But there are yet others who emulate them, since they see nothing wrong in the murder of a brother who had supplied no ground whatsoever, save that of having something after which "their worships" may eagerly be lusting. So it would appear that they thought it plain nonsense, as they had been partners in reckless sinning, now thus to become partners in remorse, and to be held in constant dread of the discovery of some previous murder contrived against a brother who had done no injustice. Wherefore were they so out of their minds? I proceed now to explain. In long-standing maliciousness and in not wishing to withdraw from their customary extravagances, quite forgetting themselves, indeed, they rush headlong to their folly. Naturally! For, it is common that the majority of physical manifestations in nature change for the worse, and especially whenever something reaches its highest peak of condition, as the Physician says, philosophizing about good health. Thus, there are perils in being at a high pitch of condition, since our systems are not able to be at rest, nor to remain in the same state, nor, indeed, to advance whenever they have reached the utmost limit itself [cf. Hippocrates, *Aphorisms* I, iii]. Well and very soundly was this said by that wise man. For, if in any of our affairs there comes a point where it is not possible to progress, and where yet at the same time it is not possible to stay still, it is obviously necessary to move backward, and, in some cases, to change to the opposite course.

Perhaps some will seek to learn yet more clearly the pretext for such folly and how they seemed to become blind, they who certainly seemed to be even more clever than Themistocles at understanding expediency. One thing was the cause of all: their desire that they not be within those walls—those on the Isthmus, I mean. This was a genuine trap for them, since it allowed them not at all either to practice any further their former knavish tricks or to display their loyalty to the Despot merely to the extent of paying him lip service instead of by deeds. Rather, it forced them to confirm in their actions what they professed. Now, to be sure, doing this tilted the scale in favor of the Despot. And naturally they were not fond of their chastener. For, he who does not wish to be good comes to hate someone who does not allow him to be evil. And he who forces toward goodness one who is not naturally so disposed would, of course, also gladden the latter were he to die. For these reasons, then, they did not recognize as their real enemies those who were, in the fashion of wolves, with their mouths agape after them; nor were they mindful of the evils which they had experienced at their hands, nor did they heed counsels which were of themselves fully persuasive, and which were of the best possible guidance under the existing circumstances— by which we could perceive the future. Wishing, then, to exchange not one of their former opinions for a better one, they all but invited their own destruction, as if they were despisers of their own prosperity. For anyone willingly to act in such fashion, in which it is impossible to escape evil consequences, is little less than the same as hating one's prosperity. On behalf of these men not even their begetters would intercede. As for these men, then, who were malicious from their folly—if it is better not to say it the other way round [a pun on κακοήθεις ἐξ εὐηθείας]—God was not disposed to approve of their judgment, but He humbled their empty presumption and their pride in their shameful deeds; and He both made them become more moderate and caused those who admired them to change their tune.

These things, to be sure, are as they ought to be. But one should now be gracious to them. And well do I know that this will be so, since I judged them with kindness when imposing this justice. What is left now is to speak also about the remaining group, for whom it seems right that there should be exoneration. After all, toward this group—hitherto greatly discontented, yet, with some reason—I believe it is fitting not to be bitter. For, we ourselves were not beyond uncertainty and were not very confident about the outcome of our activities. Therefore, on behalf of these men, who were stricken, not without reason, by the seeming endlessness of the construction and, for many reasons, by the uncertainty of its termination, and who followed us in spite of this and worked together with all their might, there should be some defense, as I have proposed. And if to some this seems perhaps to be a transgression, yet, accordingly, upon more precise examination it would probably be found the best way to deal with our object—I mean, of defending their slowness. What seems a transgression in this matter will not, I believe, prove to be so. It will do no harm to object if I speak in defense of others: indeed, their defense will also be my own exoneration, no less than if my speech has been made on behalf of them alone. For this is just as it is with those who burn incense, since they are themselves the first to enjoy the smell of the odiferous fumes. After all, in that time and situation, their fearfulness should not be beyond forgiving, since circumstances then were delicately poised in the divine scale, while there were such difficulties among them as to banish altogether any optimistic hope from every heart, and to lead to the conclusion that anyone who had a hand in this venture would immediately experience evil consequences. For, the steepness of the task was such that it required no less than the hand of the Creator of All. Perhaps one should say rather "the magnitude of the task," or probably even both, so terribly difficult and fearsome a thing was it to undertake. But there was a need for speed in this matter; and of how much I will reveal.

One particular sentiment was inherent in all, and this same resolution was extended throughout: that, "since at last, beyond expectation, a certain foundation of the structure has been laid, what remains is to proceed, vying with the ever-flowing streams, and never to cease from the task." So, they deemed voluntary slowness to equal wishing to breathe no more. For, now the hostile beast [ὁ πολέμιος θήρ], even if he seems to be agreeable, yet is not in his soul and in his acts. And neither he himself nor the satraps who are our neighbors, and those who are around him, proved able to endure what was clearly beyond their expectation. For, they believed we were likely to need a considerable span of time if we were going to complete any of the construction. And for this reason, expecting to trick us, by feigning indulgence they have tricked themselves. But when they beheld the walls self-produced, as it were, yet not slowly, in accordance with their expectations, and not limping along, so to speak, and not exposed to their easy capture whenever they merely wished to take it, they were unable—however strongly they wished—to conceal their wrath and, if you wish, their violent madness, or fury, or reactions even worse to describe than these. And certainly they were spewing forth the poison that was lurking in their souls, saying that they were cheated and were not able to endure a damage that was compounded with shame.

These points, I believe, should be a reasonable excuse on behalf of those who are, with reason, discontented with the affair, and on behalf of myself, for not having discharged my obligation to you swiftly in accordance with your hopes. For there was, indeed, want of leisure to complete what you wished. And, on account of my preoccupations, no place whatsoever has been left remaining in which I may be at leisure. So, if I seem to be freed from your reproaches, and then, if another person casts my slowness in my teeth, should you employ your tongue against the man, I know well that I will be straightway beyond reproof.[15]

15. The text of this priceless letter is not in the usual manuscripts of Manuel's works. Hence, it is not in the Legrand edition of his correspondence, and it is overlooked in the discussions of Berger de Xivrey and Petit. The text survives, however, in a manuscript preserved in the famous Greek Abbey of Santa Maria di Grottaferrata in Italy. Attention was first called to it by Loenertz in his "Ecrîts de Macaire Macrès et de Manuel Paléologue dans les mss. Vat. gr. 1107 et Crypten. 111," *Orientalia Christiana Periodica*, 15 (1949), p. 192, no. 7. And it is to his subsequent effort that we are indebted for an edition of the full text, in "Epître," pp. 299–304, preceded by a French summary, 297–299. I have translated the entire text, preserving his paragraph divisions, although omitting the numbering he gives to each. (The identification of the three Classical citations is also his.) Later, presumably after his return to Constantinople in March of 1416, Manuel sent another (still unpublished) letter to David and Damianos (cf. Loenertz, "Ecrits," p. 191, no. 1; "Epître," p. 297), which accompanied a literary work which had been requested, a religious reflection on his recovery from an illness (cf. Loenertz, "Ecrits," p. 192, no. 3).

Returning, however, to the text of the above letter, a word might be added

An examination of the details of Manuel's activity in the Morea will fill in what the Emperor omits in his letter, also explaining much of his imagery and many of his allusions. At the same time, by keeping in mind this letter—for all its exaggerations and

on one of the Classical quotations it adapts from Demosthenes in the third paragraph. Since Manuel was a well-read man, we assume, it might be reasonable to suppose that his vague ascription of its source, "as the Orator [or, Rhetorician] said" (ὁ ῥήτωρ ἔφη), does indeed refer to Demosthenes, in the *Olynthiac*, I, 20 (15). (The full expression is also used by Libanius, *Sententiae*, γ', ed. Foerster [Teubner], VIII, p. 117, ll. 4–5; but it is doubtful if Manuel was familiar with it from here.) But another appearance of this expression must give us pause: it is in the popular compendium and textbook by the fourth-century rhetorician Aphthonius, the *Progymnasmata*, iv, ed. Rabe (Teubner), p. 7, ll. 11–12. We might well call to mind, in this instance, the example of Constantine Porphyrogenitus who, in his life of his grandfather, Basil I (*Vita Basilii* = *Theophanes Continuatus*, V, ed. Bonn, 1838, p. 257, ll. 12–13), puts this same expression in Basil's mouth when the latter's contemplation of the empty treasury is described. Basil surely did not say this himself. Since he seems to have been illiterate, Basil probably never had the opportunity to encounter it in Aphthonius, much less in Demosthenes (or Libanius). In all likelihood the Imperial biographer himself only knew it from Aphthonius and lifted the elegant saying from this source, probably his own former textbook. (On this case, cf. R. J. H. Jenkins, "The Hellenistic Origins of Byzantine Literature," *Dumbarton Oaks Papers*, No. 17 (1963), 39–52; 43–44. We also have another, earlier use of this same passage adapted in like fashion by John Lydus in his sixth-century work called *De magistratibus*. Here (ed. R. Wünsch, Teubner edition [Leipzig, 1903], p. 143, ll. 3–4; ed. I. Bekker [Bonn], p. 246, ll. 17–18) this expression is used with the very slightest changes in connection with the great drain which the Persian Wars constituted for the Imperial treasury. (This passage is noted and translated by Vasiliev, *Justin the First* [Cambridge, Mass.], 1950, p. 257, with no apparent recognition or acknowledgment of its borrowed origins.) Closer to Manuel's time is still another example of such adaptation of this popular expression by Anna Comnena in her *Alexiad*, I, xvi, ed. A. Reifferscheid (Teubner, Leipzig, 1884), p. 56, ll. 5–6; ed., with French translation, by B. Leib, I (Paris, 1937), p. 59, ll. 12–14; English translation by E. Dawes (London, 1928), p. 42.

These examples illustrate the problem one faces in encountering Classical quotations in Byzantine writings. Could Manuel's ῥήτωρ have been Aphthonius rather than Demosthenes? It might be just to give Manuel the benefit of the doubt in this instance. Yet, note further the case of the paraphrase (significantly, not a direct quotation this time) that Manuel draws from Hippocrates. The very same passage is paraphrased (again, not quoted exactly), even more succinctly, by Psellos in his *Chronographia*, VI, cxc, ed. C. Sathas (Paris, 1874), p. 194, ll. 2–5; ed. and trans. E. Renauld II (2 vols, Paris, 1926–28), II, pp. 64–65, ll. 14–17; trans. E. R. A. Sewter (London, 1963), p. 191. Thus, one should always bear in mind the likelihood that many of these oft-used quotations or paraphrases by Byzantine writers came not from the original Classical sources, but from the many texts, compendia, and handbooks (if not even from other Byzantine writers), all of which they had abundantly at their disposal.

disorganized hyperbole—it is possible to study this episode in an entirely new light.

After the stormy beginning of his voyage, Manuel proceeded on his course, stopping at Negroponte, where the Venetian *bailo* received him ceremoniously.[16] The Emperor at length reached the Peloponnesus on Good Friday, March 29, 1415, at the port of Kengchreai on the Saronic Gulf, some four or five kilometers from Isthmia.[17] The particular port of debarkation is noteworthy. That Manuel should go there instead of to a port with closer ac-

16. On April 24, 1415, the Venetian Senate approved of the reception and ordered reimbursement for its expenses: text, Sathas, *Documents inédits relatifs à l'histoire de la Grèce au moyen âge*, III, no. 660, p. 110. Cf. Zakythinos, *Le Despotat grec de Morée*, I, 168; Miller, *The Latins in the Levant*, 377. But, for all the polite formalities, the Venetians were uneasy about the presence of the Greek Emperor in the Peloponnesus. On June 11, 1415, alarmed over the loyalty of its Greek troops in Coron and Modon as a result of Manuel's proximity, the Senate gave orders to reorganize its forces there, eliminating this doubtful element: text, Sathas, III, no. 664, p. 113; cf. Thiriet, *Régestes des délibérations du Sénat de Venise concernant la Romanie*, II, no. 1578, p. 135. Cf. also Miller, *The Latins in the Levant*, 377; Zakythinos, *Le Despotat grec de Morée*, I, 172.

17. Sphrantzes, 1026B (Pseudo-Phrantzes, ed. Papadopoulos, 111; ed. Bonn, 107), gives only the month. But the Βρ. χρ. No. 18, p. 35, ll. 4–5 (in significantly similar wording), adds the specific date. Both sources name the port. Cf. Muralt, p. 798, no. 6. From other short chronicles Loenertz, "Epître," p. 295, n. 2, derives an alternate arrival date of the following day, March 30. (Muralt, p. 798, no. 7, uses this March 30 date improperly: see below, n. 31.) See also Loenertz' *Chron. br. mor.*, no. 25, p. 407, and his translation and commentary, pp. 429–432. Iorga, *Notes et extraits*, I, p. 233, n. 1, cites a source (still in manuscript in Venice, according to him, p. 122, n. 3), which reports that Manuel came with four galleys and two other ships, bringing contingents of cavalry and infantry, with masons and machines of war. The last were presumably those used on Thasos, were to be used again in the Morea soon, and were perhaps finally mounted on the completed Hexamilion. Loenertz' establishment of the dating of Manuel's arrival, on the basis of the short chronicle texts, has been denied recently by G. Schirò in his article "Manuele II Paleologo incorona Carlo Tocco despota di Gianina," *Byzantion*, 29–30 (1959–60), 209–230. Specifically in pp. 217–223, Schirò develops a drastically new chronology on the basis of a misuse of Sphrantzes and the wholly untrustworthy Pseudo-Phrantzes and of an important (but here inconclusive) extract which he publishes (pp. 228–230) and translates (pp. 210–211) from a Cephalonian chronicle in Greek on the Toccos of Yannina. All the relevant sources, however, have been examined thoroughly, and Schirò's theses have been completely rejected, in my own subsequent article, "On the Chronology of the Activities of Manuel II Palaeologus in the Morea in 1415," *Byz. Zeitschr.*, 55 (1962), 39–55. More generally on Manuel in the Morea, see Khoury, "L'Empereur Manuel II," 142.

cess to the heart of the Despotate makes it clear that he chose to use his time fully, at least at the beginning of his visit, for his principal aim. This aim, and the first of his tasks, was the construction of the Hexamilion, the wall across the Isthmus of Corinth. We have already seen that he had recognized the importance of this project and had contemplated execution of it during his visit in 1408.[18] This time he would not be put off or distracted, as he had been then.

The fortification of the Isthmus was nothing new. The earliest barrier athwart it dated back to 480 b.c., during the Persian invasion of Xerxes. A subsequent palisade was erected in an unsuccessful attempt to block the invasion of Epamanondas in 369 b.c., and in 279 b.c. there was talk of resorting to such a structure in the face of a threatened Gallic invasion. In Roman times a wall was erected in the reign of the Emperor Valerian in a.d. 253. It was only in the sixth century, however, that the wall across the Isthmus received its ultimate location and definition under Justinian, whose architect, Victorinus, raised an impressive structure extending from the Saronic Gulf to the Gulf of Corinth, terminating in fortresses at either end, with elaborate fortifications along its course and a great fortress on the site of ancient Isthmia. Over the centuries this rampart had fallen into decay. Manuel's task was not so much to build a new wall as it was to restore this earlier one (as Manuel himself notes at one point in his letter); it is still essentially Justinian's wall that constitutes the bulk of its remains today.[19]

18. See pp. 277–278 and n. 130 above.

19. The fundamental study on the history of the Isthmian wall in Roman and Byzantine times is that by Lampros, "Τὰ τείχη τοῦ ἰσθμοῦ τῆς Κορίνθου κατὰ τοὺς μέσους αἰῶνας," Νέος ἑλληνομνήμων, 2 (1905), 435–489, with additions in the same periodical, 4 (1907), 20–26, 240–243, and 5 (1908), 115–116. In this work Lampros has collected and discussed all the relevant source material. Note also the recent article by J. R. Wiseman, "A Trans-Isthmian Fortification Wall," *Hesperia*, 32 (1963), 248–275, on a distinct structure which is dated to the attack by the Gauls in 279 b.c. The present remains of the wall lie southwest of the modern Corinth Canal on an irregularly parallel course varying from 500 meters to almost 2 kilometers in distance. Discussion of its present state and of some excavations done around it may be found in R. J. H. Jenkins and A. H. S. Megaw, "Researches at Isthmia," *Annual of the British School at Athens*, 32 (1931–32), 68–89, especially pp. 69–79. Valuable comments on its history and present condition may be found in O. Broneer's article, "The Corinthian Isthmus and the

Under the Emperor's active supervision, the work was begun in April and was carried on at an urgent pace, as Manuel's letter emphasizes, so that within twenty-five days the wall had been reconstructed to its former size and strength.[20] The result was an accomplishment that greatly impressed Manuel's contemporaries.[21] Not the least among these was the famous Platonist,

Isthmian Sanctuary," *Antiquity,* 32 (1958), 83–84 and 88; and, on the large fortress of Justinian near the ancient stadium, see *id.,* "Excavations at Isthmia, Third Campaign, 1955–56," *Hesperia,* 27 (1958), 20–22, and "Fourth Campaign, 1957–58," *Hesperia,* 28 (1959), 320–321. But extensive and thorough study of these remains is still needed; I have been told by Prof. Broneer that some work in this line is now in progress.

20. Mazaris, ed. Boissonade, 177–178, ed. Ellissen, 242, alone gives the duration of the project; he says nothing of the size or features of the wall, speaking only of the two garrisons (πολίχνια εἰς φρουράν) at either end. Βρ. χρ. No. 18, p. 35, ll. 5–11, gives the date April 8 for the beginning of the work, while No. 23, p. 42, ll. 5–12, gives April 18. The latter of these two texts is probably incorrect, perhaps as the result of a copyist's addition of the extra digit. Otherwise, these two sources give essentially identical information, which is paralleled by Sphrantzes, 1026B–C (cf. Pseudo-Phrantzes, ed. Papadopoulos, 111–112, ed. Bonn, 108–109, following a long digression, and including interpolations from other sources), who also gives April 8 as the starting time. These three sources describe the walls as 3,800 fathoms (οὐργίαι) in length, with 153 towers, the number of those in the earlier wall. Chalcocondyles, ed. Darkó, I, 172–173, ed. Bonn, 184, describes it as 42 *stadia* in length; while the *Chron. Barb. 111,* 51, reckons it as six miles (μίλια) long—hence its name. On the other hand, the report to the Venetian Senate on September 23, 1415 (see pp. 314–315 and n. 25 below) gave the length at 3,750 paces, with 130 small towers and 19 large ones, plus 3 castles, which latter would doubtless be the two forts at either end and the large one of Justinian near the old stadium of Isthmia. Iorga, *Notes et extraits,* I, p. 233, n. 1, cites a Venetian source, which, he says, announces the completion of the Hexamilion on March 28, 1415. But this impossible date must represent a mistake at one point or another. See Barker, "On the Chronology," 48–55, for a convenient grouping of the major Greek source texts on Manuel's rebuilding of the Hexamilion and also of the Justinianic inscription which was found at the time. Cf. also Muralt, p. 798, no. 9.

21. Ducas, ed. Grecu, 139, ed. Bonn, 102, is the only one of the major Greek historians to ignore the building of the Hexamilion; indeed, he rather confuses this visit with that of 1408, as intended by Manuel to establish his son in the Despotate. By contrast, Chalcocondyles, ed. Darkó, I, 172–173, ed. Bonn, 184 (followed by the *Chron. Barb. 111,* 51), is under the impression that Manuel's *brother,* Theodore I, was still ruling there, and only later, ed. Darkó, I, 202–203, ed. Bonn, 216, does he speak of Theodore I's death and Manuel's supposed oration on it, statements obviously referring to 1408. At least one scholar has been misled by this confusion: R. Rodd, *The Princes of Achaia and the Chronicle of Morea, A Study of Greece in the Middle Ages,* II (London, 1907), 257–258, in his account of Manuel's 1415 visit, places the funeral oration at this later time, among

Georgios Gemistos Plethon, who was to use the building of the Hexamilion as his point of inspiration and departure for his subsequent grand schemes to reform utterly the Greek Morea.[22]

The importance that Manuel attached to his building of the Hexamilion may be observed also in his diplomatic relations with Venice during this period. After the completion of his great

other anachronisms. The building of the Hexamilion itself, however, is referred to by a number of short chronicles, in addition to the two cited in the previous note: Βρ. χρ. No. 19, p. 36, l. 30; No. 27, p. 47, l. 423 (also published in the back of the Bonn edition of Ducas, p. 517, ll. 11–13; this greatly confused text is emended by Loenertz, "Epître," p. 295, n. 2); and in the *Chron. Vat. gr. 162*, no. 16, p. 209, ll. 69–70; also by the short chronicle, ed. Veēs, no. 5. The principal accounts of the building of the Hexamilion are all discussed and translated in my article, "On the Chronology," including two particularly important ones, that in the Satire of Mazaris and the other in a panegyric by Demetrius Chrysoloras, neither previously translated. On the building of the Hexamilion in general, see Miller, *The Latins in the Levant*, 377–378, and also his "The Princes of the Peloponnese," *Quarterly Review*, 404 (July 1905), 125; Zakythinos, *Le Despotat grec*, I, 168–169; and, badly out-of-date on much of the chronology, Mompherratos, Οἱ Παλ. ἐν Πελ., 35–36.

As a vivid reminder of another impression this project made, there is also an interesting set of oracles, apparently originating as inscriptions, concerning the various buildings and rebuildings of the Isthmian wall. The third of them concerns Manuel. They have all been admirably discussed by E. W. Bodnar in his article, "The Isthmian Fortifications in Oracular Prophecy," *The American Journal of Archaeology*, 64 (1960), 165–171, especially pp. 166–167, 170. And, as an indication of how the project must have impressed outsiders, one may note that even the Serbian Konstantin the Philosopher cannot resist referring to it in a completely irrelevant context: ed. Jagić, 271, ed. and trans. Braun, 15–16.

22. Plethon (or Pletho) propounded his radical proposals for a total reorganization of the Morea—military, fiscal, social, economic, and intellectual—in two addresses, one to the Emperor Manuel and the other to the Despot Theodore II. Texts of both were published by Ellissen in his *Analekten der mittel- und neugriechischen Literatur*, IV (the same volume with Mazaris), Pt. 2, pp. 41–84, with appended German translations. More recent editions have been made by Lampros in his Παλ. καὶ Πελ., the one to Manuel in Vol. III, pp. 246–265, and the one to Theodore in Vol. IV, pp. 113–135. English translations of extracts from both may be found in E. Barker, *Social and Political Thought in Byzantium*, pp. 196–212. It was common to suppose that the one to Manuel was presented to the Emperor during his 1415 visit, but it is now clear on the basis of internal evidence that both writings doubtless date from later years. This question of their dating has been taken up by Zakythinos in his good brief discussion of Plethon's ideas, *Le Despotat grec*, I, 175–180. In greater detail, see J. P. Malakis, Ὁ Γ. Γεμιστὸς ἐν Πελοποννήσῳ, *1414–1437* (Thessalonica, 1939), especially pp. 16 ff.; and *id.* Γεώργιος Γεμιστὸς Πλήθων (*Texte*

construction work, Manuel wrote a letter, dated June 26, to the Venetian Senate about it. Only on July 23 next did the Senate send an answer, with apologies for its delay. In it the *Sapientes* extend their congratulations to Manuel for his arrival in the Morea and especially for his construction of the Hexamilion, a work of great benefit to the area and to the Christians in general. They promise Venetian cooperation in Manuel's activities in the Morea and also pledge the use of their galleys for the voyage of the Emperor or any of his sons to or from Constantinople.[23] And on the same date (July 23, 1415), the Senate followed up at least one of these promises with an order to its commanders in the Morea. This order was that, if the Turks should attack and attempt to destroy the newly constructed Hexamilion, the Venetian forces were authorized to aid the Greeks, should the Emperor request this help.[24]

The Hexamilion figured in further dealings with the Venetians when the Senate gave its answers to a number of requests by Byzantine ambassadors on September 23, 1415. The Emperor had taken care to give a detailed description of his new wall. But, in the process of building it, he had been obliged to lay such heavy impositions on the population of the Morea—a point inherent if not stated outrightly in his letter to David and Damianos—that many of these subjects had endeavored to escape

und Forschungen zur byzantinische-neugriechische Philologie, 32, Athens, 1939), in general. A good extended discussion of Plethon's ideas on these matters may be found in H. F. Tozer's article, "A Byzantine Reformer," *Journal of Hellenic Studies*, 7 (1886), 353–380 (save that, on pp. 355–356, Tozer seems to make the impossible suggestion that Manuel actually built the Hexamilion on the basis of nothing more than Plethon's suggestion). See also F. Massai, *Pléthon et le Platonisme de Mistra* (Paris, 1956), especially pp. 83 ff.; and Miller, *The Latins in the Levant*, 378–383; and, most recently, Vakalopoulos, Ἱστορία τοῦ νέου ἑλληνισμοῦ, I, 172–180. Note also J. Dräseke's article, "Georgios Gemistos Plethon," *Zeitschrift für Kirchengeschichte*, 19 (1899), 265–292, especially pp. 272–278.

23. Dölger, *Regesten*, no. 3351, p. 102. Text in Lampros, "Τὰ τείχη," 461–462; cf. Iorga, *Notes et extraits*, I, 232–233; Thiriet, *Régestes*, II, no. 1583, p. 136. The deliberation also refers to messages being sent to Manuel's son (i.e. John VIII), who is in Constantinople: see n. 87 below. The text describes the latter as "illustrissimus *genitor* vester," which, as Iorga, p. 233, n. 1, points out, is probably a scribe's error; for *genitor* we should doubtless read *filius*.

24. Text, Sathas, III, no. 668, p. 116; and Lampros, "Τὰ τείχη," 466–467; cf. Thiriet, *Régestes*, II, no. 1583, p. 136; on the significance of this suspicion that the Turks might react with force to the building of the Hexamilion, see pp. 318 ff. below.

them by fleeing to Venetian territory. Manuel requested the return of at least some of these fugitives, and Venice granted this much of the request; at the same time it arranged for the return of Greek refugees to Venetian lands from the Turkish sieges (by Musa) of Constantinople and Thessalonica. And, among other matters, the Senate also reaffirmed its promise to Manuel of escort for himself or his son (John VIII) from the Morea to Constantinople or vice versa.[25]

But Venice reacted differently when Manuel pressed questions concerning the Hexamilion more closely. When the Imperial ambassador Nicholas Eudaimonoioannes, or Evdaimonoyannis ("Nicholao de Monoiani"), brought before the Senate a number of Byzantine proposals, one of them was a request that the Venetians, who had praised Manuel's labor so highly, contribute to the expenses of the construction of the Hexamilion. This, now, was hitting a bit too close to home! On February 8, 1416, the parsimonious Senate reacted strongly, with protestations that their all-too-heavy expenditures on their other Levantine holdings could not permit them to contribute thus.[26] But at least a

25. Dölger, *Regesten,* no. 3352, p. 102. Iorga, *Notes et extraits,* I, 239–240; Thiriet, *Régestes,* II, no. 1592, p. 138. For other matters in this deliberation, see p. 336 below. The impositions on the Moreotes for the maintenance of the Hexamilion continued to drive them to flight. Again, on June 11, 1418, the Senate heard Byzantine requests to return such fugitives: text, Sathas, III, p. 177 (of no. 731); cf. Thiriet, no. 1697 (6), p. 165. See also below, n. 26, and n. 91.

26. Dölger, *Regesten,* no. 3354, pp. 102–103; text, Lampros, "Τὰ τείχη," 465; cf. Iorga, *Notes et extraits,* I, 243; and Thiriet, *Régestes,* II, no. 1599, p. 140. For other matters in this deliberation, see below, pp. 324, 335, 336, and also n. 80. Again, on June 11, 1418, when the question of Venetian help in the defense of the Hexamilion was raised, the Senate once more begged off on the grounds of heavy expenses elsewhere: [lacking in Dölger;] text, Sathas, III, p. 179 (of no. 731); cf. Thiriet, no. 1697 (12), p. 165; see also n. 90 below. When Venice finally did consider positively any role of its own in the defense of the rampart, it was on terms that would be to its own greedy advantage. On July 22, 1422, the Senate discussed the question of bearing some of the defense burden in relation to a demand for the cession of territory by the Despot to Venice: [lacking in Dölger;] text, Sathas, I, no. 78, pp. 115–119; cf. Iorga, 322–323; Thiriet, no. 1849, p. 196. In the same vein again, on February 18, 1423, when asked to join in defending the wall, the Venetians agreed to entertain the idea if they would be given financial support by the Moreote barons and would also be given the possession of the stronghold and territory of Corinth: [lacking in Dölger;] text, Sathas, I, no. 83, pp. 126–217; cf. Thiriet, no. 1870, p. 200 (see also p. 371 below). On this subject in general, see also Miller, *The Latins in the Levant,* 170–171, 192–196.

year later, on January 12, 1417, the Senate gave its assurance to Manuel that it would assist the Greeks in defending the wall in case of Turkish attack.[27]

It should also be noted that one of Manuel's first contacts with Pope Martin V, after the latter's elevation in November of 1417, involved the guarantee of Papal indulgences to Westerners who would contribute to the defense of the Hexamilion.[28]

As the Emperor labored on his great building task, it must have been a bitter disappointment to him to meet with opposition from his subjects of the kind of which he speaks at length in the long letter translated above. He himself points out how much he had to rely on the Albanian elements, who had been settled in large part, to be sure, by his brother for the very purpose of helping in the defense of the area.[29] And from the Venetian documents we have seen how the heavy burdens placed on the Moreotes had induced many of them to flee from the territory of the Despotate.

But, if passive resistance was bad enough, it was an even more grievous blow to have to face actually violent opposition. Manuel's expressions of horror and disgust in his letter make his feelings quite plain. Regardless of the common good, however, any strengthening of the security and stability of the Peloponnesus was bitterly resented by the restless barons of the Morea. Manuel's visit and his forceful activity on behalf of the defense of the Peloponnesus filled them with anger and alarm. To the horror of Manuel and his loyal supporters, the Emperor soon found himself faced with open insurrection.[30] Matters quickly

27. Dölger, *Regesten*, no. 3367, p. 104; Iorga, *Notes et extraits*, I, 258–259; Thiriet, *Régestes*, II, no. 1635, p. 150. For other matters in this deliberation, see n. 71, p. 336 below.

28. See p. 325 below.

29. Manuel, *Funeral Oration*, ed. Migne, 212C ff., ed. Lampros, p. 40, ll. 1 ff.; cf. Zakythinos, *Le Despotat grec*, I, 131; Miller, *The Latins in the Levant*, p. 367; Mompherratos, Οἱ Παλ. ἐν Πελ., 10.

30. We have a valuable complement to the relevant sections in Manuel's own letter and, indeed, a remarkable echo of the Emperor's own attitude, which suggests perhaps a personal acquaintance with it, in a passage from Mazaris, ed. Boissonade, 178–180, ed. Ellissen, 242–245. This passage relates that, after the Emperor completed the Hexamilion, the reckless "toparchs" threatened to destroy it and broke out into open rebellion. The writer vehemently and bitterly denounces their ingratitude, faithlessness, and baseness, and even refers directly or indirectly to a few individuals among them. Cf. Loenertz, "Epître," 295. For a translation of the passage, see Barker, "On the Chronology," 51–52.

came to a head. With an energy that belied his age, the sixty-five-year-old Emperor turned decisively to the second task of his sojourn in the Despotate. Marching forth, he met the dissidents, force against force. On July 15, 1415, he crushed at least a part of their revolt in battle. Near Kalamata in the southern Peloponnesus, the fortress of one of the insurgents, Eliavourkos, at Mandinia, was stormed and taken.[31] Following hard upon his victory, Manuel moved firmly to subdue the rest of these unruly elements. Such operations dragged on through the summer of 1415 and beyond, involving sieges and extensive campaigning. But the general outcome seems to have been a decisive triumph by Manuel over the malcontents. Some he deported to Constantinople. As for others, he destroyed their fortresses and forced them to abandon some of their wild ways, some of which he points out in his letter. If his curbs could not be permanent, as he doubtless realized, they at least brought some rest to the strife-torn land.[32]

31. The date is given by the Βρ. χρ. No. 19, p. 36, l. 31; and there is an allusion without date in the corrupted entry in No. 27, p. 46, ll. 3–4 (or, in the edition at the end of the Bonn edition of Ducas, p. 517, ll. 14–15); as it was to be for Schirò, this text is also a source of confusion for Muralt, p. 798, no. 7. Mazaris, ed. Boissonade, 178–180, ed. Ellissen, 242–245, also speaks of a specific battle, and, though he gives no date, he says that Manuel "advanced with a very large army against them." The Cephalonian chronicle text which Schirò has published ("Manuele incorona," 229–230) speaks of a battle, or a siege, at Mandinia in the southern Peloponnesus and names Eliavourkos, to whom Mazaris also alludes. Schirò attempts to distinguish between these hostilities and the battle reported in the faulty Βρ. χρ. No. 27 as between two separate battles at different times. But this interpretation is surely wrong, and the two events are almost certainly more or less the same or, at least, of the same general time: see Barker, "On the Chronology," 43–48. In general, see Zakythinos, *Le Despotat grec*, I, 170; Loenertz, "Epître," 295, and "Pour l'histoire du Péloponnèse au XIVe siècle," 157; Lampros, "Τὰ τείχη," 456. Chalcocondyles, ed. Darkó, I, 173, ed. Bonn, 184, and the *Chron. Barb. 111*, 51, say nothing of open hostilities, but hint at them by observing that the *archons* refused to contribute to the construction and that Manuel seized them and disciplined them.

32. Mazaris, ed. Boissonade, 179–180, ed. Ellissen, 244–245 (trans. in Barker, "On the Chronology," 52), comments on Manuel's campaigns, in terms which largely agree with the picture presented by the Cephalonian chronicle (ed. Schirò, "Manuele incorona," 229–230). Chalcocondyles, ed. Darkó, I, 173, ed. Bonn, 184, is the only source to report deportations specifically; cf. Muralt, p. 798, no. 7 (anticipating Schirò by mistakenly using the date March 30, 1415). Among the abuses which Manuel strove to curb was a barbarous custom called μασχαλισμός, dating back to antiquity, among the Maniotes of southern Laconia, of cutting off the fingers and toes of defeated enemies and

Thus, when Manuel sailed from the Morea and returned to Constantinople in March of 1416,[33] he left behind him a Despotate more secure and stable and more settled internally than it had been for many decades previously. His description, in his letter, of the blessings of the new peace there almost reminds one of Burgundy's speech in Shakespeare's *Henry V.* To all appearances this might seem a good job of internal policy well done. At this juncture, however, we may return to the point raised at the outset of this chapter. Reflecting on the conclusion of Manuel's letter, we may well remind ourselves of what was, after all, the real purpose of Manuel's visit to the Morea in 1415. He could not avoid involvement in the purely internal affairs of the Despotate, of course, and certainly would not have wanted to do so. But the extent to which he bore down on the restless *archons* was forced upon him to a great degree by these barons themselves. The real purpose of the visit actually had little to do directly with purely internal affairs, but was rather centered on one thing: the attempt to protect this important Byzantine realm from the threat of external invasion. By whom? Why, by "the hostile beast" (ὁ πολέμιος θήρ), Sultan Mechmed himself, and his ravenous henchmen.

This may seem, to those who cherish the old impression, a rather strong epithet for the man with whom Manuel was supposed to have enjoyed such allegedly blissful amity and peace. But we are well aware that, for all the officially peaceful relations between the Sultan and the Emperor, the Turks continued a hostile policy in Greece proper, if on a minor scale. We have seen already that Manuel and Venice foresaw a very real possibility

dipping these trophies in the cups from which they drank their toasts. The panegyrists who claim that Manuel completely abolished these quaint mores are quoted and thoroughly discussed by Lampros in his article on the subject, "Τὸ ἔθος τοῦ μασχαλισμοῦ παρὰ τοὺς μανιάταις τῶν μέσων αἰώνων," Νέος ἑλληνομνήμων, 2 (1905), 180–186. Cf. Miller, *The Latins in the Levant,* 384, especially his comment: "In a land where stones were so plentiful and imperial officials so rare, the towers [i.e. of the *archons'* fortresses] soon rose again, but this grim practice (μασχαλισμός, as it was called by the ancients), is never mentioned again."

33. This date is given by Sphrantzes, 1026C (Pseudo-Phrantzes, ed. Papadopoulos, 112; ed. Bonn, 108). The Emperor reported his arrival in his letter to King Ferdinand I of Aragon (see p. 334 below), dated March 25, 1416, and presumably written very soon after the Emperor's arrival: cf. Loenertz, "Epître," p. 297.

that the Turks might attack and seek to destroy the completed Hexamilion. Manuel maintains in his letter that the Sultan was aware of the intended project but did not object to it because he never really expected the Emperor to be able to carry it out. Therefore, says Manuel, the Sultan was furious when it was completed, to the obvious detriment of Turkish interests, as a barrier to freedom of entry for his troops into the peninsula. And we have some possible evidence that Mechmed may very well have at least contemplated reprisals against Manuel for his accomplishment.[34] Plainly, Manuel recognized the danger when the job was fully undertaken, as he makes clear in his letter. But it is also plain that he thought this effort to secure the safety of the Morea was worth the risk of offending the Turks and even of jeopardizing his accord with Mechmed.

More important, we can see in Manuel's letter something of his real attitude toward that accord. We may discount perhaps a certain degree of the proper hyperbole of a pious Christian Emperor, in converse with two holy men consecrated to the Faith, in order to rationalize his accommodation with the infidel Turk. But there is no escaping the decisiveness of Manuel's position. He makes crystal clear that the Turkish professions of friendship were not taken very seriously. Their aims were still ultimately the same, in spite of a kind of "peaceful coexistence" for the moment. When it suited their convenience, their old hostility would come forth openly once more. Peace with Mechmed could not be expected to be permanent or reliable. Thus, the current peace was merely a convenience, and Manuel could embrace it purely as a means of gaining time and staving off disaster while seeking to do what he could to bolster and strengthen the Empire.

It is true that the façade of amity was retained by both rulers. Certainly Mechmed, whatever may have been the possible reprisals he may have contemplated, chose to preserve that façade. Thus, if our information is correct, the Sultan even went so far as to go out from Gallipoli to meet the Emperor on his return

34. Iorga, *Notes et extraits,* I, p. 233, n. 2, cites a Venetian source which speaks of elaborate maritime preparations by Mechmed, which were reported as being intended for use against Manuel in retaliation for his construction of the Hexamilion. How true this report may have been is difficult to ascertain, especially in view of the subsequent involvement of Turkish naval forces in a battle with the Venetians a few months later (see n. 72 below).

voyage from the Morea. In his turn, Manuel is said to have entertained the Sultan on board his vessel with all outward cordiality before he proceeded on his way to Constantinople.[35]

Manuel understood, however, that, as this amity with the Turks could have no lasting foundations, he must take advantage of it while he could. Certainly any cessation of open hostilities with the Turks was to the Emperor's advantage. To understand Manuel's intentions, therefore, we must recognize that this façade of friendship with Mechmed enabled Manuel to win time for no less a purpose than to continue his quest for Western aid.

Here, then, is the key to Manuel's policy in this period. The peace with the Turks during the reign of Mechmed was only an external phenomenon of no basic significance. At the core of things there was simply a continuity of the old course. The felicitous conclusion of the Turkish "Time of Troubles" had not really changed anything. The old struggle continued, if in an atmosphere of slightly different outward tinting. *The* real enemy was still the Turk, and the Turk was still a *real* enemy. Sooner or later he must be fought again. Somehow Byzantium must still build its strength. And the best source, the only source, of such strength and support was still the Latin West, for all the long record of frustration and disappointment.

To follow this continuation of the basically uninterrupted policy of Manuel's government, we must trace it now on two separate planes. On the first of these we may take a series of negotiations which presents nothing less than a serious reopening of the question of the union of the Eastern and Western Churches. And in turning to this subject we but return to Manuel Chrysoloras on his mission in the West.

35. Thus Ducas, ed. Grecu, 139, ed. Bonn, 102–103, the only source to report such an incident. The rest of his account of Manuel's visit to the Morea is a hopeless confusion with the 1408 trip. And this particular description could be a confusion in turn with the later shipboard meeting of Manuel and Mechmed in 1421: see pp. 351–352 below. For what it is worth, the *Chron. Barb. 111*, 51, relates Manuel's building of the Hexamilion and his disciplining of the *archons*, and then adds (1. 29): "Wherefore the Basileus had much affection with the Sultan Mechmetes." Mechmed's reaction to Manuel's activities in the Morea was, if anything, apparently the opposite; but this statement could conceivably reflect some element of a show of friendship for Manuel in 1416 as Ducas represents it. The incident is accepted as fact by Iorga, *Geschichte des osmanischen Reiches*, I, 373; Pears, *The Destruction of the Greek Empire*, 151; Muralt, p. 799, no. 4.

As we have seen previously,[36] the first phase of Chrysoloras' diplomatic operations in the West on Manuel's behalf had taken him through many courts of Latin Europe and had brought him back to Italy in 1410. His destination then was Bologna, at that time the seat of the curia of the third Papal line, established at the Council of Pisa with the election of Alexander V on June 26, 1409. Following the Papal tradition of eagerness to pursue the old question of Church union, Alexander seems to have been in some sort of contact with the Emperor. At any rate, he made a point of inviting Manuel's roving ambassador to visit him in Bologna. But when Chrysoloras reached there in the middle of 1410, Alexander was already dead, having ended his days and his brief Pontificate on May 4 of that year. In his place was his successor, the ill-fated John XXIII. Nevertheless, contact had already been made with Manuel, and the Emperor apparently approved of this renewed approach to the familiar problem. With this prelude, the second phase of Chrysoloras' mission began.[37]

Chrysoloras remained thereafter in the company of Pope John. When that Pontiff moved to Rome in April of 1411, Chrysoloras went also and resided there during John's sojourn in the city.[38] When, in the summer of 1413, Pope John was driven out of Rome by his erstwhile supporter, King Ladislas of Naples, the Byzantine ambassador accompanied the fleeing curia. During their sojourn then in Florence, Chrysoloras was able to spend some time in his old haunts in this scene of former triumphs.[39] But John was soon to move back to Bologna, and then, still under pressure from Ladislas, to throw himself on the support of the Emperor Sigismund. The latter was in North Italy at the time on one of his innumerable projects, and his price for helping John was the calling of the long-hoped-for council to settle the troubles of the Church—and to enhance the Emperor's prestige as well. At

36. See pp. 261–267 above.
37. Cammelli, *I dotti . . . I, Manuele Crisolora,* 147–150. There is also some question about the possibility of a very brief trip home and back by Chrysoloras during this period: *ibid.,* 150–151. See also Goeller, "Zur Geschichte Manuels II. von Byzanz," 190–191.
38. Cammelli, *Crisolora,* 153–158. For one of Chrysoloras' writings of this 1411 residence in Rome, addressed to his kinsman Demetrius, see M. Baxandall, "Guarino, Pisanello and Manuel Chrysoloras," *Journal of the Warburg and Courtauld Institutes,* 28 (1965), 197–198 (English translation) and 203–204 (Greek text).
39. *Ibid.,* 158–159.

this point Chrysoloras, together with his nephew John, became involved in the negotiations to settle the convening of the council. This contact with Sigismund apparently had nothing immediate to do with any direct questions of Sigismund's sending aid to Byzantium. But, in the person of Chrysoloras, Byzantium was thus actively involved in the council from the outset and was committed to at least a renewed consideration of the problem of union. When the council was convened in Constance in November of 1414, Chrysoloras was present.[40] Unfortunately, however, the wise ambassador contracted a fatal illness, and on April 15, 1415, the death of Manuel Chrysoloras abruptly ended both a noble, fruitful life, and, at the same time, the second phase of his long mission for his Emperor.[41]

40. *Ibid.*, 161–163; and Loenertz, "Les Dominicains byzantins Théodore et André Chrysobergès et les négotiations pour l'union des églises greque et latine de 1415 à 1430," *Archivium Fratrum Praedicatorum*, 9 (1939), 12–15; also, Gill, *The Council of Florence* (Cambridge, 1958), 20–21; and G. Beckmann, *Der Kampf Kaiser Sigmunds gegen die werdende Weltmacht der Osmanen, 1392–1437. Eine historische Grundlegung* (Gotha, 1902), 89 and 117. Note also the following general studies: A. Doren, "Zur Reformation Sigismundi," *Historische Vierteljahrschrift*, 21 (1922), 1–59; O. Schiff, *König Sigmunds italienische Politik bis zur Romfahrt (1410–1431)* (Frankfurt, 1909); E. Göller, *König Sigismunds Kirchenpolitik vom Tode Bonifaz' IX. bis zur Berufung des Konstanzer Konzils (1404–1413)* (*Studien aus dem Collegium sapientiae zu Freiburg i. B.*, 7: Freiburg, 1901); H. Blumenthal, *Die Vorgeschichte des constanzer Concils bis zur Berufung* (Halle, 1897); and J. Aschbach, *Geschichte Kaiser Sigismund's* (4 vols., Hamburg, 1838–45), especially Vol. I: *Sigismund's frühere Geschichte bis auf die Eröffnung des constanzer Conciliums*. Material on the calling and beginning of the Council, and on Chrysoloras' role, will also be found in the more general works cited in n. 48 below. See also Dölger, *Regesten*, no. 3329, p. 98, on the unreliability of which, however, see Appendix XXI below.

Manuel Chrysoloras' involvement in negotiations with Sigismund is referred to in a bull of Pope John XXIII of December 1414, quoted by the *Religieux de Saint-Denys*, XXXV, xl, Vol. V, p. 456: "de simul cum eis dilectum nobilem filium Manuelem Chrysoloram, militem Constantinopolitanum, ad presenciam ejusdem regis transisimus." Curiously, that is apparently the only reference by this source to Chrysoloras' great final journey to the West: cf. pp. 264–265, n. 112 above. On the activities of his nephew, John Chrysoloras, in this connection, see n. 66 below.

41. Cammelli, *Crisolora*, 163–169; Loenertz, "Les Dominicains byzantins," 15–17; Gill, *The Council of Florence*, 21 (who mistakenly speaks of the *burial* of Chrysoloras on *March* 15, 1415). On Chrysoloras' death, see Vakalopoulos, 'Ιστ. τ. ν. ἑλλ., I, 316–317; *ibid.*, 315–319, for comments on Chrysoloras' career in general. Thomson, "Manuel Chrysoloras and the Early Italian Renaissance," 81–82, argues that the scholar-ambassador's conversion might actually have been encouraged and urged by the Emperor Manuel; and that there might have been a possibility that, had Chrysoloras

But the untimely deprivation of Chrysoloras' services by no means ended Manuel's involvement with these activities. Indeed, this last epoch of Manuel's life and reign witnessed his greatest surge of attention to ecclesiastical matters. Internally, Manuel seized upon an opportunity in 1416 to confirm and to extend the Imperial prerogatives and control over the Byzantine Church.[42] Even more important, however, was Manuel's continued and seemingly serious involvement with the work of the Council of Constance and the projects for Church union.[43] Even with the

not died at this point, he would have been chosen as the new Pope in a gesture of inter-Church understanding. As with some of Thomson's other ideas in this article, these are matters of pure conjecture, and cannot be taken very seriously, it seems to me.

42. According to the account given by Sylvester Syropoulos, *Historia Concilii Florentini* (The Hague, 1660), II, i–iv, pp. 1–3, the Emperor fell into a difference of opinion with his old friend the Patriarch Euthymios and imposed his will while he was still absent in the Peloponnesus in 1415. In retaliation, the Patriarch threatened what appears to have been a kind of Orthodox imitation of the Papal interdict. Fortunately, a severe dispute was avoided with the death of the Patriarch in the very month in which Manuel returned home, March of 1416: Sphrantzes, 1026C; Pseudo-Phrantzes, ed. Papadopoulos, 112, ed. Bonn, 108. (V. Laurent, "Les Dates du Patriarcat d'Euthyme II de Constantinople," *Byz. Zeitschr.*, 54 [1961] 329–332, has settled the date of his death on March 29.) Taking advantage of the vacancy on the Patriarchal throne, Manuel convoked a synod and pressured the bishops present into signing a confirmation in writing of the Emperor's heretofore only vaguely traditional rights and privileges in ecclesiastical affairs, before he would allow the selection of the new Patriarch (Joseph II). This incident has been presented and discussed thoroughly by I. K. Stephanides, in his article " Ὁ ἀκραῖος σταθμὸς τῶν σχέσεων Ἐκκλησίας καὶ πολιτείας τοῦ Βυζαντίου καὶ τὰ ἄμεσα ἀποτελέσματα αὐτοῦ (1416–1439)," Ἐπ. Ἑτ. Βυζ. Σπουδ., 23 (1953), 27–30; cf. Dölger, *Regesten*, nos. 3358–60, pp. 103–104. For the parallel episode under Manuel's father, John V, which paved the way for the 1416 incident, see V. Laurent, "Les Droits de l'empereur en matière ecclésiastique. L'accord de 1380–1382," *Rev. des ét. byz.*, 13 (1955), 5–20.

43. The course of Manuel's negotiations on the question of union is a long and intricate story. The most recent review of it is an excellent sketch by H. G. Beck in pp. 141–146 of his essay, "Byzanz und der Westen im Zeitalter des Konziliarismus," in the collection *Die Welt zur Zeit des konstanzer Konzils* (*Konstanzer Arbeitskreis für mittelalterliche Geschichte, Vorträge und Forschungen*, 9: Stuttgart, 1965), 135–148. Prior to this, an outline of Manuel's dealings with the Papacy was given by a particular specialist in this period, Fr. Gill, in his article "Greeks and Latins in a Common Council: The Council of Florence (1438-9)," *Orientalia Christiana Periodica*, 25 (1959), 265–267, reprinted in his collection, *Personalities of the Council of Florence, and Other Essays* (New York, 1964), 233–235. Subsequently, he has given an extended and generally excellent account of this course of events in his book, *The Council of Florence*, especially pp. 20–39. I have not been able to obtain the work by A. N. Diamantopoulos,

departure of Chrysoloras from the scene, the Byzantines were still well represented at the council, in response to Sigismund's invitation to Manuel to send delegates.[44] From this time, in the activities at the Council of Constance, we can date the beginning of the important work of those intermediaries of union projects, the two Greek Dominicans Andreas and Theodore Chrysoberges.[45] But even more important was the dispatch by Manuel from the Peloponnesus, in the beginning of 1416, of an embassy led by the Moreote noble Nicholas Eudaimonoioannes, and including his son Andronicus and John Bladynteros.[46] When this mission passed through Venice on its way to the council, Nicholas took the opportunity to submit a number of Manuel's proposals on February 8, 1416, including one on his related efforts to mediate between Venice and Sigismund.[47] From there the embassy proceeded on to Constance, to take an active part in the council's sessions there.

The Council of Constance was obliged to concentrate on three primary problems: the Hussite heresy, Church reform, and the Great Schism. To these concerns the council flitted back and forth throughout the forty-five sessions of its three and one half years. At least the first and third of these problems were dealt with decisively: at the beginning of the council, by the burning

'Απόπειραι πρὸς ἕνωσιν τῶν 'Εκκλησιῶν κατὰ τὸν ιε' αἰῶνα (Athens, 1924); but I gather from comments on it (e.g. Gill, *The Council of Florence*, p. 25, n. 7) that it is not very reliable.

44. Gill, *The Council of Florence*, 20–21.

45. On the first of these two men (primarily on his work in years following the period of the present study), see M. H. Laurent, "L'Activité d'André Chrysobergès, O.P., sous le pontificat du Martin V (1418–1431)," *Echos d'Orient*, 34 (1935), 414–438. More recent is the excellent study by Loenertz, "Les Dominicains byzantins," who gives (pp. 5–11) their background, and follows their activity up to 1430. These two brothers were possibly related in some way or another to the Chrysoberges who had been Manuel's companion in the latter's exile to Lemnos after 1387: see p. 66 above.

46. Dölger, *Regesten*, no. 3345, p. 100; Loenertz, "Les Dominicains byzantins," 23–29; Gill, *The Council of Florence*, 21–22; Muralt, p. 802, no. 10, with no idea of the true chronology. For further comments, see also Mercati, *Notizie* (*Studi e Testi*, 56), 475 ff. A propos Manuel's investigation of union possibilities, Muralt, p. 800, no. 10, refers to a decree of King Ferdinand of Aragon of January 6, 1416, which I have been unable to trace. According to this decree, Muralt says, "the Greeks promise to unite with the Roman Church when it should be united itself."

47. Dölger, *Regesten*, nos. 3354 and 3355, pp. 102–103. On this, see below, p. 335; cf. also above, p. 315.

of John Hus on July 6, 1415, and, toward the end, by the election of the sole Pope, Martin V, on November 11, 1417. Even if the second problem was left largely unresolved, the work of the council was of great significance for Western Christendom.[48]

Amid these great tasks, the question of Church union had to take a minor position and was essentially deferred. But it was by no means ignored. The Greek ambassadors stressed that their Emperor, Patriarch, Church, and nation were all eager and ready for union. A set of proposals, by the Emperor and Patriarch, for projected union were then submitted. The resulting sentiment among the Latins was one of encouragement and zeal. Nicholas Eudaimonoioannes, who was present at the time of the election and coronation of Pope Martin, quickly secured an audience with the new Pontiff to press the matter of union on behalf of the Greeks. Among the subjects discussed then was a demonstration of cordial intentions on both sides through the projected marriage of Manuel's two oldest sons to Latin princesses. In addition—already the practical element was showing through—the Pope acceded to the Byzantine request to grant indulgences to all Westerners who would make contributions toward the defense of the new Hexamilion.[49]

48. Among general accounts and discussions of this Council, note the following: the collection of essays entitled *Die Welt zur Zeit des konstanzer Konzils* (*Konstanzer Arbeitskreis für mittelalterliche Geschichte, Vorträge und Forschungen,* 9: Stuttgart, 1965); P. Glorieux, *Le Concile de Constance au jour de jour* (Paris, 1965); A. Franzen and W. Müller (eds.), *Das Konzil von Konstanz. Beiträge zu seiner Geschichte und Theologie* (Freiburg, Basel, & Vienna, 1964); G. C. Powers, *Nationalism at the Council of Constance (1414–1418)* (Washington, D.C., 1927); the indispensable C. J. Hefele and H. Leclercq, *Histoire des Conciles,* Vol. VII, Pt. 1 (Paris, 1916); J. H. Wylie, *The Council of Constance to the Death of John Hus* (Ford Lectures: London, 1900); J. N. Figgis, "Politics at the Council of Constance," *Transactions of the Royal Historical Society,* N.S. 13 (1899), 103–115; H. Finke, *Forschungen und Quellen zur Geschichte des konstanzer Konzils* (Paderborn, 1889); and B. Hübler, *Die constanzer Reformation und die Conkordate von 1418* (Leipzig, 1867). Some valuable contemporary accounts are usefully translated into English, with annotations, by L. R. Loomis, with J. H. Mundy and K. M. Woody, as *The Council of Constance: The Unification of the Church* (*Records of Civilization, Sources and Studies,* 63: New York & London, 1961); for more source materials, see *Acta concilii Constanciensis,* ed. H. Finke (4 vols., Münster, 1896–1928). Since the foregoing citations were compiled, there has also appeared the concise account (pp. 11–115) in Father Gill's general book, *Constance et Bâle-Florence* (=*Histoire des conciles oecuméniques,* 9: Paris, 1965).

49. Martin's letter to Manuel and his sons of April 1418, Baronius-

Pursuing the promising prospects that had seemed evident at the Council of Constance, the Papacy was seriously intent upon exploring this opening. In the coming years three Papal legates were chosen to be sent to the East to investigate the Orthodox intentions and disposition. The first of them, Giovanni Dominici, the Cardinal of San Sisto, was delegated to this task early in 1418. But he died on June 10, 1419, en route by way of Bohemia, before he could really begin his mission.[50] Meanwhile, Eudaimonoioannes and his embassy began their return trip to Constantinople. They carried with them letters to Manuel, to his son John, and to the Patriarch, urging on them the pursuit of Church union.

In ready response to these overtures the Emperor and Patriarch sent cordial answers, proposing a synod in Constantinople to study and settle the differences between the Churches. These replies were entrusted to John Bladynteros, who was sent back to the Pope. Martin V is reported to have responded in his turn, agreeing to the synod and promising to send a legate.[51] Actually, a legate had already been chosen, the second of the proposed Papal agents; for, on March 27, 1420, Piero Fonseca, CardinalDeacon of Sant' Angelo, was appointed to the task. But the subsequent outbreak of hostilities between the Turks and the Byzantines blocked his dispatch, and so this second attempt also came to naught.[52]

Raynaldus, *Annales ecclesiastici*, 1418, no. 17 (Vol. 27, p. 475); Syropoulos, II, v–vi, pp. 4–5. Cf. Dölger, *Regesten*, no. 3369, pp. 104–105; Loenertz, "Les Dominicains byzantins," 30–31; Gill, *The Council of Florence*, pp. 22–24, 27–28; Muralt, p. 801, no. 5. On the Latin marriages of Manuel's sons, see below, pp. 348–349. On the Hexamilion defense, see above, p. 316.

50. Gill, *The Council of Florence*, 23.

51. Dölger, *Regesten*, nos. 3374 and 3386, pp. 106 and 107; Syropoulos, II, vii–ix, pp. 5–7; cf. Loenertz, "Les Dominicains byzantins," pp. 31–32, 42–43; also Gill, *The Council of Florence*, 28–30, and 32, who presumes that this second Papal letter to Manuel was carried by Eudaimonoioannes on his second return to the East, escorting the Latin princesses. A reference to Bladynteros' second mission, which conveyed Manuel's answer to the first Papal letter, is apparently to be found in an expense entry of June 10, 1421, by the government of Ragusa on behalf of "dominus Johannes Plantiderus": Iorga, *Notes et extraits*, II, 198–199. And on June 13, 1421, the Commune of Florence wrote a letter to Pope Martin V, commending Manuel's ambassador "Johannes Platinterius" to the Pontiff's favor: text, ed. Lampros, Παλ. καὶ Πελ., III (1926), 126.

52. Gill, *The Council of Florence*, 30–31, 32–33; Loenertz, "Les Dominicains byzantins," 43–44. See Baronius-Raynaldus, 1420, nos. 27–28 (Vol. 27, pp. 508–509), for the Papal bull of August 21, 1420, calling for funds to

Meanwhile, however, Manuel was fostering talk of union himself, although by this time the old Byzantine linking of the question of union with prior Latin commitments to military aid was beginning to emerge.[53] But the expectations of the Pope were fanned anew by Eudaimonoioannes, who had apparently been sent back to the West to bring home the two Latin princesses being sought as brides for Manuel's sons.[54] Latin enthusiasm was still high. When the Turkish threat to Constantinople developed in 1422, Martin did his best to stir up some Western aid for Manuel.[55] The Pope also made his third effort at sending a legate to Constantinople. This time he was successful. On June 15, 1422, Antonio da Massa, a Franciscan, was appointed as Apostolic Nuncio to Constantinople. He arrived on September 10 follow-

support the projected journey of Fonesca to the East; cf. Gill, *The Council of Florence*, 31–32; Muralt, p. 805, no. 14.

53. For this course of negotiations, see below, pp. 331 ff.

54. Dölger, *Regesten*, nos. 3378, 3380, pp. 106–107; Gill, *The Council of Florence*, 29 ff. Eudaimonoioannes is mentioned as apparently being in Venice on April 2, 1419, according to a trivial deliberation of the Senate of that date over allowing Manuel's ambassador to export some timber from Venetian Crete to the Morea: Iorga, *Notes et extraits*, I, 290; Thiriet, *Régestes*, II, no. 1734, p. 174. For this ambassador's return voyage home and his role in the transportation of the Latin brides-designate, see p. 348 and n. 95 below. Eudaimonoioannes appears again in Venetian references on February 26, 1422. He is then described as an ambassador of the Despot of the Morea (but in the Morea, and not in Venice) in the Senate's complaint that Theodore II has broken promises made by his envoy: Iorga, p. 317; Thiriet, no. 1833, p. 193. Gill, *The Council of Florence*, p. 29, n. 3, cites a reference to the death of Eudaimonoioannes on November 1, 1423; cf. Mercati, *Notizie*, 478–479. If it is indeed true that he was the addressee of a letter of Cardinal Isidore, previously interpreted by one scholar as having been written to Manuel (see above, p. 192, n. 127), then Eudaimonoioannes' knowledge of Western languages may have been very extensive and his itinerary even more extended than our other sources indicate. At least one artistic memento of Nicholas Eudaimonoioannes survives to us. This is a richly embroidered *epitaphios*, a ceremonial covering used in the Easter rites of the Orthodox Church, donated by the ambassador in 1407. It is preserved in the Victoria and Albert Museum in London: a photograph of it is reproduced in that institution's publication *Late Antique and Byzantine Art* (London, 1963).

55. Baronius-Raynaldus, 1422, nos. 1–2 (Vol. 27, pp. 522–523), reports Martin's messages to various Western rulers and quotes a message of encouragement which the Pope sent to Manuel. (At the same time, the Pope sent an embassy to Manuel to try to induce him to make peace between his son Theodore II and the Archbishop of Patras: *ibid.*, no. 3, pp. 523–524.) Cf. Muralt, p. 810, no. 10; and Gill, *The Council of Florence*, 37. See also below, p. 369, for the Pope's continued efforts in the following year.

ing, and he had his initial audience with Manuel on September 16. But, before he could present the Papal communications at a second audience, the old Emperor was incapacitated by a paralytic stroke. Manuel's son, heir, and co-Emperor, John VIII, had to take his father's place when the legate was finally given due attention in October. Given his opportunity at last, Antonio da Massa formally set forth the Pope's expectations, which were rooted in the assumption that the accomplishment of union would be a relatively simple matter of Orthodox submission to Rome. Only after various delays and preliminaries did John VIII and the Patriarch Joseph submit the formal Byzantine answer, on November 14. In some respects it was not drastically novel, since it spoke again of the necessity of a council, and one in Constantinople, to discuss Church differences. But it made clear to the Latins at last the degree to which the Orthodox Church expected reciprocal compromise from the Latin Church. It was at last made plain to the Papacy that the eager expectations of the readiness and willingness of the Greeks to acquiesce in a mere "reduction" (*reductio*) of the former to the latter was after all an illusion on their part—an illusion perhaps fostered deliberately to some degree by Manuel's diplomacy. The results of this Papal mission were therefore a severe blow to Roman hopes.[56] It by no means ended the question of Church union, to be sure, but it showed that such a question would be a great deal more complex than had been realized. Thus, when the freshly convened Council of Siena heard the report of Antonio da Massa

56. Dölger, *Regesten,* no. 3406, pp. 110–111; Syropoulos, II, x–xi, pp. 7–8. Even more important is the personal report of Antonio da Massa himself to the Council of Siena, in Baronius-Raynaldus, 1422, nos. 6–15 (Vol. 27, pp. 525–529). For an excellent summary of it, see Gill, *The Council of Florence,* 33–36. We also now have the texts not only of the Latin Union proposals but also of the Greek responses to them, worked out by the Patriarch and his Synod on October 19, 1422, all recently published by V. Laurent, "Les préliminaires du Concile de Florence: Les neuf articles du Pape Martin V et la réponse inédite du Patriarche de Constantinople Joseph II (Octobre 1422)," *Rev. des ét. byz.,* 20 (1962), 5–60: texts, 31–47, with French translations, 47–57, and with thorough discussion of the background, 5–30. Excepting this new material, a good summary of these dealings is given by Loenertz, "Pour la chronologie des oeuvres de Joseph Bryennios," *Rev. des ét. byz.,* 7 (1949–50), 30–32, adding further the involvement of Vryennios and the anti-Union party, which strove to hinder these negotiations with the Papacy. See also below, p. 367. Cf. Berger de Xivrey, 178; Muralt, pp. 811–812, nos. 2–3, 6–15, and also p. 815, no. 10.

on November 8, 1423, it was recognized that immediate progress on the problem was not likely at that time and that the matter therefore had to be deferred.

It is difficult to tell how much of John VIII's answer of November 14, 1422, reflected his own initiative, and how much the remnant of his father's policies. But, at any rate, the question of Church union at this point moves past the time of Manuel's reign and on into that of John VIII himself. This transition is, of course, the great problem in discussing these negotiations for union, for they came to fulfillment only later, in the reign of John and at the Council of Florence in 1438–39. Thus, in their entirety they extend far beyond the scope of the present study. Nevertheless, the fact should be sufficiently self-evident that the true foundations for whatever ultimately was accomplished by John VIII were not his own doing, but belong squarely to the activities of Manuel's government.

What is important for us, however, is to note the difference between what Manuel intended and what his son finally concluded. To make this point clear, we must reflect on the basic conception of Manuel's dealings with the Latin West on union. And the inevitable fount of such reflection is a celebrated passage that sets forth strikingly exactly what Manuel regarded as the heart of his policy in this matter.

In his last years the Emperor was greatly concerned about some of his son's attitudes, which alarmed him. Hence, he devoted much care to giving him his advice.[57] On one such occasion, in the presence of the courtier-historian Sphrantzes, the old and wise Manuel addressed John as follows:

My son, surely and truly do we know that from the depths of the unbelievers' hearts there is great fear lest we should come to an agreement and should unite with the Latins [Φράγκοι]. For they believed that, should this be so, some great evil will come to them from the Christians of the West. For our course, consequently, attend to and keep active the question of the council, and especially whenever you have need of something to frighten the unbelievers. But, at the same time as you may do this, by no means should you actually take it in hand, inasmuch as I do not see that our people are suited for finding any manner of union and peace and of mutual understanding short of returning them [the Latins] to the arrangement in which

57. On this subject, see also pp. 382–383 below.

we were originally. And since this is nearly impossible, I am afraid that there would be an even worse schism; and, lo! we would then have been left naked to the unbelievers.[58]

As events were to prove, John ignored his father's shrewd if short-range advice. But nothing could indicate more clearly than this statement and its context the differences between the union policies of Manuel and his son and the basic conception itself of Manuel's policy.

Manuel's involvement, in the last years of his life, in negotiations for Church union were little more than calculated dabbling, diplomatic fencings, as opposed to the earnest and determined efforts on the part of John, then and thereafter. Their basic aims, after all, were the same: help from the West through the inducement of union. The important difference is that of approach. Personally, Manuel was little inclined to sympathy for union. It is true that in his earlier years he had pursued it during his Thessalonian venture; but it is not known whether it was achieved in that attempt, and certainly the attempt was of no help to him,[59] in itself perhaps a lesson. Moreover, when we recall to what intensity and length Manuel was provoked by a small criticism of Orthodox tenets when he was in Paris,[60] it is obvious that in his personal views Manuel was zealously, if not fanatically, opposed to compromise with conflicting Latin doctrines. But there was far more than merely personal motivation here. As ever, Manuel

58. Sphrantzes, 1046D–1047A. The translation by Gill, *The Council of Florence*, p. 30, n. 6, differs from my own partly because he has used the more elegant text of the Pseudo-Phrantzes, ed. Papadopoulos, 177–178; ed. Bonn, 178–179 (cited incorrectly, however). Another English translation, extremely free, may be found in C. Mijatović's *Constantine, The Last Emperor of the Greeks* (London, 1892), 24–25. Cf. also Ostrogorsky, *History of the Byzantine State*, 499; Berger de Xivrey, 178; and Walter, *La Ruine de Byzance*, 311. W. Norden, *Papsttum und Byzanz* (Berlin, 1903), virtually ignores Manuel's long relations with the Papacy, and he dismisses the Emperor in one pitifully small paragraph (p. 712), with a strained reference to this famous statement. It is noteworthy that Sphrantzes quotes this famous comment completely out of the context of Manuel's last years, and only as a kind of support for the historian's own skepticism regarding John VIII's union policies later on. This fact may raise some question as to the quotation's reliability. Regardless of Sphrantzes' motives in giving it, however, there seems little specific reason to doubt his essential trustworthiness in reporting the details of the court life with which he was so intimately associated.

59. See pp. 55–56 and n. 152 above.

60. See above, pp. 192–193.

understood the real factors involved, at once the psychology of his own people and of those with whom they were dealing, and at the same time the true nature of the problem they faced. As John was to find out after the Council of Florence, his father had really been right.

It is true that, at the outset of his negotiations with the Papacy, Manuel seems not to have renewed the former policy of his government: to require military assistance from the West before union could be seriously undertaken. To some extent this silence may have been due to Byzantium's less urgent immediate need as a result of the outward relaxation of emergency after 1402, and especially after 1413. But even before the death of Mechmed and before the outbreak of open hostilities with the Turks again, as we shall see, Manuel had revived once more this premise that military aid was the necessary collateral, if not an essential down payment, for any real chance of Church union. Again, the continuity of Manuel's policy, that of this late period from that of his earlier years, is obvious, regardless of the façade of peace with Mechmed.

It is to the second plane of Manuel's diplomatic activity in this epoch that we must turn for even more conclusive demonstration of the fact that the supposed period of peace and amity with the Turks at that time changed nothing of Manuel's basic policies. This diplomacy is essentially secular, although its links with questions of union are often confusingly intricate. But, to whatever degree one may choose to separate these planes, they still run in the same direction, and they demonstrate our repeated point about Manuel's real policy.

Once again, the copious Venetian documents provide the bulk of our information. Many of them, of course, concern merely routine dealings between Venice and Byzantium.[61] But many

61. On December 6, 1416, the Senate considered the complaints of a Venetian merchant in Constantinople against Manuel: Thiriet, *Régestes*, II, no. 1632, p. 149. In the same vein, an even stronger complaint was made by the Senate on March 11, 1418, in a letter to Manuel protesting strongly some alleged mistreatment of Venetians in Constantinople and referring to specific incidents: Iorga, *Notes et extraits*, I, 276; Thiriet, no. 1688, p. 163. (For more on this deliberation, see below, n. 111.) On July 21, 1418, the Senate answered a letter from Manuel dated May 31, evading the Emperor's own complaints, on questions of Greeks captured by Venetians in the naval battle off Gallipoli (see below, n. 72), of alleged Venetian customs frauds, of disputed duties, and of alleged cases of rape of two Greek girls by Venetians

of them give us vital insights into the course of Manuel's diplomacy with the West. At the outset we can see the main lines taking shape. On January 8, 1414, less than a year after the triumph of Mechmed and the confirmation of supposed peace with the Turks, the Senate responded to Manuel's plea for financial aid amid "the oppression which the Turks are making in his [Manuel's] regions." The Venetians replied that they were much too distracted by their own expenditures to provide any such money—unless, that is, the rest of Christendom should send aid, in which case Venice would also contribute. Secondly, the Senate thanked Manuel for his offer to mediate disputes between

in Constantinople. On the same date, the Senate also instructed its new *bailo* to renew the usual treaty with Byzantium on the same terms as previously and also to pursue complaints about Byzantine debts on the part of some Thessalonians to some Venetian citizens: Dölger, *Regesten*, nos. 3370–3371, p. 105; Iorga, 280–281; Thiriet, no. 1705, pp. 167–168. The *bailo's* credentials for treaty renewal were dated July 22 (Thomas, *Diplomatarium Veneto-Levantinum*, II, no. 170, p. 316); and only on July 23, 1418, was he given his instructions for the renewal terms (Thiriet, no. 1707, p. 168.)

There seems to have been no great difficulty regarding the treaty by now, for its renewal followed soon, on October 30, 1418: Dölger, *Regesten*, no. 3373, p. 105; Greek text, Miklosich and Müller, *Acta et diplomata graeca*, III, no. 35, pp. 153–163; Latin instrument of renewal, Thomas, *Diplomatarium*, no. 171, p. 317. (Among the Greek witnesses to the treaty were "the very beloved son-in-law of Our Majesty, lord Hilario Doria, . . . and of the domestics of Our Majesty, lord Nicholas Notaras, interpreter and knight [διερμηνευτικῆς καὶ καβαλλάριος], and lord Demetrios Leontarios [*sic*]...") But apparently Manuel would not give satisfaction in all matters. On March 17, 1419, it was decided to send a special Venetian agent to join the *bailo* in a stiff protest to Manuel about the continuation of alleged injustices against Venetian citizens: Iorga, 289–290; Thiriet, no. 1733, p. 174.

We have little more of such minor disputing for the next few years. On June 8, 1423, the Senate took notice of the need to renew the treaty again: Thiriet, no. 1885, p. 204; Iorga, 338. On June 13 the appropriate agent was chosen (Iorga, 338), and his credentials were dated July 25 (Thomas, no. 177, p. 341). In short order, on September 30, 1423, the treaty was confirmed for another five years, though by this time it was signed by the co-Emperor John VIII, Manuel being incapacitated (see p. 381 below): Dölger, *Regesten*, no. 3408, p. 111; Greek text, Miklosich and Müller, III, no. 36, pp. 163–173 (again with Demetrius Leontaris as a witness); Latin instrument, Thomas, no. 178, p. 341. Aroused by injuries allegedly suffered by Venetians in Constantinople and the Morea, on April 17, 1424, the Senate charged one of its commanders with the task of presenting complaints to "the old Emperor" Manuel, or to his son, the Despot of Constantine, who was regent in Constantinople during John VIII's absence (see pp. 381 ff. below): Iorga, 365–366; Thiriet, no. 1930, p. 215. Likewise again, on July 16, 1424: Iorga, 370–371; Thiriet, no. 1948, p. 219. By this time, of course, Manuel's health had incapacitated him for rule: see pp. 367, 381 ff. below.

Venice and Emperor Sigismund, the King of Hungary; it pointed out that the matter had already been handed over to Papal mediation.[62] Then, again, on July 24, 1414, the Senate also repeated its assurance that Venice was always ready to send help to Byzantium, but only when other Christian rulers provided it also.[63]

The "oppressions" referred to probably concerned Turkish activities in Greece, where the Emperor's personal attention was soon to be turned more fully. Even discounting exaggeration, the reference indicates in itself the artificiality of the outward peace with Mechmed. Plainly, Manuel considered his Empire to be still endangered by the Turks, and he was, at the outset of Mechmed's reign, still seeking Western material aid. In these years, however, a new approach was beginning to take shape. As always, any hopes for military aid from the West must bear in mind the important necessity of Venetian cooperation. But, in surveying the potentialities of various Western princes, the only one who now seemed to offer good promise of giving aid was again Sigismund. It was therefore Manuel's logical aim to attempt to reconcile Venice and the King, who had of late fallen into dispute and hostility over conflicting interests in Dalmatia.

Not that Manuel had entirely discounted other Western rulers. But in reality there seemed few who could promise much. The monarchs of France and England were of course entirely out of any consideration. This severely reduced the field of those who might provide initiative. Some ray of hope seemed to come from the Iberian Peninsula. Ferdinand I of Aragon was apparently disposed at first to continue his predecessor's practice of encouraging Manuel's hopes. Specifically, Ferdinand had taken it into his head to communicate to the Despot Theodore II his intention of coming personally to the Morea with an army. Having heard this, Manuel took the time during his stay in Thessalonica, on his own way to the Morea, to reopen personally his old contact with the Aragonese court. In a letter dated November 28, 1414,

62. Dölger, *Regesten*, no. 3335, p. 99; Iorga, *Notes et extraits*, I, 217; Thiriet, *Régestes*, II, no. 1514, p. 120.

63. Dölger, *Regesten*, no. 3338, p. 99; Thiriet, *Régestes*, II, no. 1544, p. 127. Among other points were a further rejection of Imperial complaints on the question of the Kalopheros inheritance; questions of treaty obligations; and commercial regulations; also, a rejection of a Patriarchal claim of authority over Greek priests in Venetian Crete.

and sent by way of a homeward-bound Catalonian ship, Manuel expressed his delight over the news of Ferdinand's promise. In passing, he informed the King of his own seizure of Thasos and arrival at Thessalonica on his way to the Peloponnesus, where he would look forward to welcoming Ferdinand personally.[64] Needless to say, Ferdinand never came, and upon his return to Constantinople, on March 25, 1416, Manuel wrote another letter to the King. He informed him of his own safe return home and archly asked the King what news the latter had himself. But this seems to have ended any real contact between Aragon and Manuel. Ferdinand I died later in 1416, and his successor, Alfonso V, was too greatly interested in other projects to pay much attention to Byzantium.[65]

In this dearth of potential champions, therefore, Sigismund emerged once again as Manuel's leading candidate for military leadership against the Turks on behalf of the Empire. Sigismund himself had assured Manuel that he still had hopes of mounting a new military expedition against the Turks for the relief of the Balkan Christians.[66] Hence, Manuel continued his efforts at me-

64. Dölger, *Regesten*, no. 3343, p. 100; text, Marinesco, "Manuel II Paléologue et les rois d'Aragon," 200–201; cf. *ibid.*, 195–196; also, Cirac Estopañan, *La unión, Manuel II Paleólogo y sus recuerdos en España*, 69–70.

65. Dölger, *Regesten*, no. 3357, p. 103; text of Manuel's letter, ed. Marinesco, "Manuel et les rois," 201–202; cf. *ibid.*, 196–197; also Cirac Estopañan, *La unión, Manuel II Paleógo y sus recuerdos en España*, 69–70. Before Manuel's return, on March 3, 1416, a certain Constantine Raoul Palaeologus—apparently a kinsman of the young John VIII, then regent in Constantinople—wrote to King Ferdinand to assure him of John VIII's good will and to ask fulfillment of a previous promise, not of aid, but of a gift of some dogs: text, Marinesco, "Manuel et les rois," 202–203; cf. *ibid.*, 197. This would seem to have been the last direct contact between the ruling houses of Byzantium and Aragon. The only currently known dealings of Manuel with Alfonso V were limited to the protests of a Byzantine ambassador, at Alfonso's court in 1419, over alleged outrages of some Italian and Catalan pirates: Dölger, *Regesten*, no. 3377, p. 106; Marinesco, "Contribution à l'histoire des relations économiques entre l'Empire byzantin, la Sicile et le royaume de Naples de 1419 à 1453," *Atti del V Congresso internazionale di studi byzantini*, I (=*Studi bizantini e neoellenici*, 5, 1939), 210.

66. We have a set of three letters which Sigismund addressed to Manuel during the period 1411–14, which are edited by H. Finke in his collection, *Acta Concilii Constanciensis*, I: *Akten zur Vorgeschichte des Konstanzer Konzils (1410-1414)* (Münster, 1896). In the first of these (no. 111, pp. 391–394), dated by the editor to May or June of 1411, Sigismund affirms his determination to renew his wars against the Turks, and stresses the importance of and need for the union of the Churches. The second (no. 112, pp. 394–399), dated to early 1412, includes some denunciations of his enemies

diation, in spite of the initial Venetian rebuffs. Even while he was busily occupied with his visit to the Morea, Manuel bore in mind this diplomatic aim. When the Byzantine embassy to the Council of Constance stopped in Venice, its leader, Nicholas Eudaimonoioannes, submitted to the Senate on February 8, 1416, a number of proposals, among them a renewed offer of mediation with Sigismund. This time the Senate was willing to accept the offer of Byzantine good offices, as long as the Hungarian King's terms were reasonable.[67]

the Venetians, stresses again the question of Church union, mentions the possible involvement of the Polish King against the Turks, and makes some typically Western comments on the understanding of Manuel's title as "Graecorum imperator" against his own title of "Romanorum imperator." The third (no. 113, pp. 399–401), dated with some question to the summer of 1414 is in response to messages brought by Manuel's ambassador, John Chrysoloras (Dölger, *Regesten*, no. 3339, p. 99). In it, Sigismund expresses sympathy for the difficult situation of Constantinople, surrounded by Turkish hostility, and he reports the calling of the Council, soon to meet in Constance; after which, he hopes, he will be able to turn his attentions to aiding Constantinople.

Any further messages and assurances from Sigismund to Manuel are not extant, but we know that his determination to mount a new campaign against the Turks remained active. So he wrote in a letter to the Commune of Ragusa, one of a pair of communications dated respectively September 22 and 25, 1416: texts, ed. J. Gelcich and L. Thallóczy, *Diplomatarium relationum reipublicae ragusanae cum regno Hungariae*, no. 180, a & b, pp. 276–279; cf. Stanojević, "Die Biographie Stefan Lazarevićs von Konstantin dem Philosophen als Geschichtsquelle," 457. Likewise, Sigismund was still nourishing his scheme in July of 1420, when Pope Martin V issued a bull to aid him in raising a crusade against the Turks in the Balkans: Baronius-Raynaldus, 1420, no. 26 (Vol. 27, pp. 507–508). In general, see G. Beckmann, *Der Kampf Kaiser Sigmunds gegen die werdende Weltmacht der Osmanen, 1392–1437* (Gotha, 1902), which, despite the date in its title, concentrates almost entirely on the period 1410–1437: on John Chrysoloras' embassy, see its pp. 59–60 and 117. See also the work by Göller, cited above in n. 40.

67. Dölger, *Regesten,* no. 3354, pp. 102–103; text ed. Lampros, "Τὰ τείχη," 465, and in his Παλ. καὶ Πελ., IV, 129–131; cf. Iorga, *Notes et extraits,* I, 243 ff.; Thiriet, *Régestes*, II, no. 1599, p. 140. For other proposals in this deliberation, see p. 315 and p. 324 above; also n. 70 and n. 80 below. (It is apparently this deliberation to which garbled and inaccurate reference is made by Muralt, p. 797, no. 5, under the year 1415.) In their disputes with Sigismund, the Venetians became sensitive about accusations made against them, alleging that they were collaborators with the Turks. On August 30, 1415, the Senate agreed to address a circular letter to Christendom to deny these charges, pointing out also their aid to Sigismund after the Battle of Nicopolis and their constant willingness, they said, to aid the Byzantines against the Turks: Iorga, 235. Another such message of justification was planned on September 10 following: Iorga, 236.

While Manuel was following this course, he became involved in another project. In the face of Turkish piracy in the Aegean, Pietro Zeno, the Venetian Lord of Andros, together with the Hospitalers of Rhodes and the Genoese governments of Chios and Lesbos, contemplated the advisability of a defensive league against the Turks and invited Venice to join. On August 31, 1415, the Senate expressed willingness and suggested further that the Byzantine Emperor might be asked to contribute some galleys as well.[68] Manuel was more than interested and seems to have tried to broaden the idea. In the response of September 23, 1415, to Byzantine envoys the Venetian Senate advised Manuel to conduct negotiations on the matter of a league through Pietro Zeno, but it promised to send a special ambassador to the Emperor.[69] When Eudaimonoioannes' mission was heard by the Senate on February 8, 1416, the Senate welcomed Manuel's urging about the organization of the league through Zeno, but it complained that the Genoese of Chios were holding back.[70] Finally, on January 12, 1417, the Senate responded to Manuel's inquiries with fuller discussion of the features of the league, which would be valid for only two or three years and which would limit its activities to the Straits and the Aegean Sea; the Senate also disagreed with Manuel's wish that the league remain secret.[71] Whatever came of this plan for a league, its results were ephemeral, for Venice had its own standing with the Turks to worry about.[72]

68. Text, Sathas, III, no. 672, pp. 119–120; cf. Thiriet, *Régestes,* II, no. 1589, pp. 137–138.

69. Dölger, *Regesten,* no. 3352, p. 102; Iorga, *Notes et extraits,* I, 239; Thiriet, *Régestes,* II, no. 1592, p. 138; for other proposals in this deliberation, see above, pp. 314–315. Two Venetian ambassadors are reported being dispatched to Manuel in the Morea by Thiriet's summary of the Senate's deliberation of January 4, 1416 (no. 1595, p. 139). But it would seem from what little is known that these envoys may have been on a different mission, if not a readily obvious one.

70. Dölger, *Regesten,* no. 3354, pp. 102–103; text ed. Lampros, "Τὰ τείχη," 464–465; cf. Iorga, *Notes et extraits,* I, 243; Thiriet, *Régestes,* II, no. 1599, p. 140; see also above, p. 335.

71. Dölger, *Regesten,* no. 3367, p. 104; Thiriet, *Régestes,* II, no. 1635, p. 150; Iorga, *Notes et extraits,* I, 258–259. Another item in this deliberation concerned the return of refugees from Musa's siege of Thessalonica. For other matters in it, see p. 316 above. Manuel's wish for secrecy might, of course, reflect his fear of going too far in unfriendly gestures towards the Turks.

72. It was not until some time after Mechmed's elimination of Musa that the Senate took up, on May 3, 1414, the question of opening negotiations

Manuel still continued to cling to the hope of reconciling Venice and Sigismund. Nicholas Eudaimonoioannes, apparently during the course of his return trip westward to fetch the Imperial brides, submitted to the Senate on January 17, 1420, a number of matters for discussion, including another urging of Byzantine mediation. The Senate expressed its willingness.[73] On the same day, however, the Senate heard another Byzantine ambassador who had been sent more specifically for this purpose. Manuel Philanthropenos ("Hemanuel Filatropino") portrayed to the Senate the awkward situation of Byzantium, unable, he af-

with the new Sultan: Iorga, *Notes et extraits*, I, 218; Thiriet, *Régestes*, II, no. 1526, p. 122. On July 19, 1414, the Venetian *bailo* of Constantinople was given instructions for negotiating a treaty with Mechmed: Iorga, 219–220; Thiriet, no. 1538, pp. 125–126. But friction soon developed, and on July 23, 1415, the Senate took note of Mechmed's anger over the failure of the *bailo* to attend to the appointed negotiations: Iorga, 233–234; Thiriet, no. 1584, p. 136. Thereafter, the *bailo* went on his mission. He was apparently still on it on January 7, 1416, when the Senate pointed out that any peace concluded with Mechmed should not hinder the hunting of Turkish shipping in the Straits: Iorga, 221–222; Thiriet, no. 1596, p. 139. But the negotiations dragged on. On April 2, 1416, the Senate sent an additional agent with further instructions: Iorga, 245–247; Thiriet, no. 1609, pp. 142–143. On the same date the Senate also made provisions for an attack on the Turkish fleet at Gallipoli if the circumstances should prove opportune: Iorga, 247–248; Thiriet, no. 1610, p. 143 (see also below, n. 80). On June 5, 1416, there was still no news of any peace agreed upon: Iorga, 249; Thiriet, no. 1614, p. 144.

Some time before this, however, matters had already been brought to a head. Almost by chance, the Venetian fleet had been drawn into action against the Turks at Gallipoli on May 29, 1416, and in the ensuing battle the Venetians won a resounding victory. This happy news was reported to the Senate on July 5, 1416: Iorga, 251–252; Thiriet, no. 1622, p. 145. Such a success naturally helped weight the negotiations with the Turks in Venice's favor. But these negotiations still dragged on at great length: see Thiriet, nos. 1641, 1642, 1645, 1647 (including instructions to keep Manuel informed of the course of negotiations), 1649, 1706, 1707, 1746, and 1750. Not until November 6, 1419, was the treaty between Venice and Mechmed finally settled, on terms very favorable to the former: text, Thomas, *Diplomatarium*, no. 172, pp. 318–319, and Iorga, 295–299. On the important fight off Gallipoli and its aftermath, see Hammer, I, 368–371, trans. Hellert, II, 170–174; Iorga, *Geschichte*, 370–372; Hazlitt, *The Venetian Republic*, I, 788–790; Heyd, *Histoire du commerce du Levant*, II, 277–278; also, Thiriet, *La Romanie vénitienne*, 368; Wiel, *The Navy of Venice*, 214; Vaughan, *Europe and the Turk*, 44–45; and K. A. Alexandris, Ἡ θαλασσία δύναμις εἰς τὴν ἱστορίαν τῆς Βυζαντινῆς αὐτοκρατορίας (Athens, 1956), 456–457.

73. Dölger, *Regesten*, no. 3378, p. 106; Iorga, *Notes et extraits*, I, 300–301; Thiriet, *Régestes*, II, no. 1757, p. 178; the other matters discussed included various minor grievances.

firmed, to maintain its position before the Turks without the help that the quarrels of Venice and Sigismund blocked. The *Sapientes* replied with expressions of their eagerness to settle these disputes, blaming their continuation on the intransigence of the Hungarian King, in spite of the efforts of the Pope and others to soften him. The Senate therefore cordially approved of the Byzantine ambassador's assignment to go to Sigismund, and it appointed an agent of its own to accompany him.[74]

The important mission of Philanthropenos was not, however, limited solely to seeing Sigismund. For, among those who were deeply interested in reconciling Sigismund and Venice, and in the crusade which might then be launched, was Jagiello (Vladislav V), the King of Poland, who had never given up his concern over an expedition against the Turks as part of the question of the union of the Churches. From Hungary Philanthropenos proceeded further to Poland, where he met Jagiello in August of 1420. And after that he went beyond, to confer with the King's cousin, Grand Duke Vitold of Lithuania, also an interested party. Jagiello was much enthused, and even wrote a letter to Manuel during the summer, stressing the relationship of the hoped-for aid to the question of union.[75]

As for the main aspect of his mission, Philanthropenos' efforts as far as Sigismund was concerned also seem to have met with some outward success. For, on February 17, 1421, the Senate received the returning ambassador, who reported that the Hungarian King had agreed to Byzantine mediation. The Senate

74. Dölger, *Regesten,* no. 3379, p. 106; Thiriet, *Régestes,* II, no. 1758, p. 178; Iorga, *Notes et extraits,* I, 301. Cf. Halecki, "La Pologne et l'empire byzantin," 55 and 56. Philanthropenos had previously appeared in Venice as a Byzantine ambassador as long before as 1396: see pp. 131–132 above. At that time he was the negotiator of the alliance between Sigismund and Byzantium prior to the Crusade of Nicopolis, which experience was doubtless the reason for his employment in this later mission. Indeed, in modern parlance, he may even have "held down the Hungarian desk" in the Byzantine foreign office.

75. Dölger, *Regesten,* nos. 3381–82, p. 107; Halecki, "La Pologne et l'empire byzantin," 55–56; Loenertz, "Les Dominicains byzantins," pp. 44–45; also Gill, *The Council of Florence,* p. 29, n. 4. Interestingly, it would seem as if Manuel had been in contact with Jagiello even earlier in this period, for there are references to an embassy and messages from the Emperor and the Patriarch reaching the Polish court in or about May of 1415: Dölger, *Regesten,* no. 3347, p. 101; Halecki, 52–53; Loenertz, 18–19. Even more obscurely for 1415, Dölger, no. 3350, p. 102.

noted its satisfaction and pronounced itself ready to negotiate.[76] Unfortunately, we do not know the details of the Byzantine prosecution of this projected mediation. Perhaps the subsequent outbreak of troubles with the Turks hindered the matter. But some efforts must have been made, for as late as December 30, 1423, the Venetian Senate referred to the obstinacy of Sigismund, which had blocked the success of such efforts.[77]

The embassy of 1420–21 did, however, serve to stir up some further activity in the West directed toward the talked-of crusade. Still zealously sanguine at the time over prospects for union, Pope Martin V took seriously the hope that Sigismund would at last set this crusade in motion. On July 12, 1420, the Pope issued a bull exhorting all Christendom to support the expedition with either arms or alms and making the usual provisions for indulgences in recompense.[78] Also, during this year, an emissary by the name of Gilbert de Lannoy was dispatched from the English and French courts to go to the East by way of Poland and Lithuania to investigate these serious portents of a crusade.[79]

Needless to say, all these promising efforts were to be barren of any actual results. But, bulky and diffuse as they may be, they demonstrate incontestably that, far from sitting back and enjoying the blessings of peace with the Turks, Manuel was actually preparing for action against them, and had by no means ended his former policies in quest of military and material aid from the West. The enemy was still the Turk, without doubt, even though Byzantium remained for the while in a state of professed peace and amity with Mechmed.

76. Thiriet, *Régestes*, II, no. 1802, p. 187. By this time, however, Sigismund had already antagonized Jagiello and Vitold, and had removed the likelihood of their cooperation with him in any effort, for the time being: Halecki, "La Pologne et l'empire byzantin," 56; also, more broadly, J. Goll, "König Sigmund und Polen, 1420–1436," *Mitteilungen des Instituts für österreichische Geschichtsforschung*, 15 (Vienna, 1894), 441–478; 16 (1895), 222–275; and J. Aschbach, *Geschichte Kaiser Sigismund's*, II: *Die Zeit des Hussitenkrieges bis auf die Eröffnung des basler Conciliums* (Hamburg, 1841).

77. Dölger, *Regesten*, no. 3408a, p. 111; Iorga, *Notes et extraits*, I, 350–351; Thiriet, *Régestes*, II, no. 1915, pp. 211–212. For more on this deliberation see p. 376 below.

78. Text, Baronius-Raynaldus, 1420, no. 26 (Vol. 27, pp. 507–508); cf. Gill, *The Council of Florence*, p. 29, n. 4.

79. On his mission, see Halecki, "La Pologne et l'empire byzantin," 56–57; cf. Gill. *The Council of Florence*, p. 29, n. 4.

But the façade of peace and amity had to be maintained. Even if Manuel had wished otherwise—and subsequent events were to show that he certainly did not—his lack of strength and continued failure to draw any help from the West would not have allowed him to break it. But just how thin a façade it was could not but be noticed when a crisis arose. Such a crisis was the episode of the pretender Mustafa.

The actual origins and background of the man who came forward as Bayazid's eldest son, lost to view since the Battle of Ancyra, have never been clearly established, although there is little doubt of his falseness. Early in 1415 this pretender attempted to make overtures to Manuel and then to Venice for support.[80] He succeeded in crossing to Europe, and there he was

80. On January 15, 1415, the Venetian Senate heard a report that a Venetian ship had recently taken aboard a Turkish agent who had been able by a ruse to gain passage to Constantinople. When he had learned, however, that the Emperor Manuel, to whom he had been sent, was not in the city but was away on his journey to the Morea, he had then revealed that his mission was to seek aid for the pretender Mustafa, and he had requested at least that his representations be listened to by the Senate. Whereupon the *Sapientes* decided to give him a hearing: Iorga, *Notes et extraits*, I, 225; Thiriet, *Régestes*, II, no. 1563, pp. 131–132. On January 18 the emissary stated his case, requesting transportation to Europe for his master and a league of alliance and assistance. The Senate replied that Venice was on friendly terms with Mechmed and was at the moment attempting to negotiate a treaty with him, so that it was therefore impossible to give Mustafa any formal support; nevertheless, Venice could assure the pretender its friendship. And at the same time the wily Venetians agreed among themselves that it would be advantageous to communicate all of the pretender's proposals to Mechmed: Iorga, 226; Thiriet, no. 1564, p. 132. It is difficult to determine if, and to what extent, the pretender's agents may have been in contact with Manuel after this. Dölger interprets the evidence to mean that the Emperor actually entered into a pact with Mustafa, together with Stefan Lazarević and the Qaramanian Emir, against Mechmed, in the summer of 1415: *Regesten*, no. 3348, pp. 101–102 (and cf. Khoury, "L'Empereur Manuel II," 143); but I am inclined to doubt that Manuel would in fact have taken so rash a step to endanger the peace with the Sultan, while the source cited in n. 81 below would suggest the unlikeliness of Stefan's involvement either.

At any rate, the *Serenissima* did not lose sight of Mustafa. In its reply to the proposals of Eudaimonoioannes on February 8, 1416 (see p. 335 above; also, pp. 315 and 336), the Venetian Senate reminded Manuel of the pretender's possibilities as a source of help to the Emperor and as an irritant to the Sultan: Dölger, *Regesten*, no. 3354, pp. 102–103; text, ed. Lampros, "Τὰ τείχη," 465–466 (the citations by Iorga, 243, and Thiriet, p. 140, to another edition of the text, are meaningless to me; Muralt, p. 797, no. 5, refers confusedly to these deliberations, under the year 1415). And on

able to secure the support of the Voievode Mircea of Wallachia and the unruly adventurer and troublemaker Djunaïd. During 1416 he made an effort to win over Rumelia from Mechmed.[81]

April 2, 1416, in the consideration of possible measures against Mechmed while negotiations with him dragged on (see n. 72 above), the Senate wanted a check kept on the movements of Mustafa and his supporter, the Voievode of Wallachia: Iorga, 247–248; Thiriet, no. 1610, p. 143. Cf. also Iorga, *Geschichte*, 366–367.

Though the Pretender Mustafa is first mentioned by name in our sources only in 1415, he may have begun his activities earlier. In a letter of the Ragusan Senate to Sigismund of Hungary, dated November 28, 1413 (text ed. Gelcich and Thallóczy, *Diplomatarium relationum reipublicae ragusanae*, no. 154, pp. 234–235), in the observation: "Audivimus insuper quemdam fratrem domini Crispie in Turchie partibus nuper surrexisse, potencius illis ut fratris hostem ad libitum dominantem." Could this be the false Mustafa, as early as 1413? By then, at any rate, all of the known brothers of Mechmed ("Crispia") were eliminated.

81. Mustafa's movements can be followed in the reports of the Ragusans to King Sigismund of Hungary. In one, dated June 28, 1415 (text ed. Gelcich and Thallóczy, *Diplomatarium*, no. 167, p. 249), reference is made to the preoccupation of Mechmed ("Chrisius") at Brusa with an attack by the Emir of Qaraman. The Ragusans then observe: "et eciam est de novo, quod dominus Muscat frater dicti Chrisii Theucer in contratibus Trebusonde prosperat paulatim Chrisii predictum fratrem suum. Preterea die XV. presentis appulit quedam chocha Ianuensium hos ad portus nostros de Constantinopoli, que confirmavit nova predicat vera fore inter Theucros." This "Muscat" is almost surely Mustafa, so that by the spring of 1415 he was still in northeastern Asia Minor, around Trebizond. In a report soon after, however, dated August 18 of this year, the Ragusans have his name correctly, with new information: for they refer to "do barones imperatoris Turcorum" who "aufugerunt ab eo ad fratrem suum Mustafa, qui moratur in Vlachia . . ." (*ibid.*, no. 168, p. 251). So, then, Mustafa must have crossed to Europe by early summer. Still another Ragusan letter, of October 12, 1416 (*ibid.*, no. 173, p. 261), refers to Mustafa's first assault on Rumelia: "De novis Teucrorum . . . [Mechmed, or "Crixia," is still occupied with the Qaramanian Emir's attack] . . . At Mustafa, frater dicti Crixie, videns ipsum Crixiam defulcitum gentibus, venit cum aliquibus Teucris secum colligatis et aliquibus Vlachis voivode Mirce usque in regnum Bulgarie, quod regnum continue vastat et dextruit. Stephanus autme despoth Sclavonie stat in quiete, quia dictus Crixia Teucer undique est occupatus." On these events, see also Iorga, *Geschichte*, 369–370; Stanojević, 456–457; and Muralt, p. 802, no. 11, who mistakenly places the episode in 1418. Djunaïd, or J̌uneid, or Güneyt, was a petty princeling from Smyrna who had been attempting to take advantage of the confusion in the Turkish wars of succession for his own aggrandizement. Changing allegiances as it suited his convenience, he had twice tried unsuccessfully during that period to carve out a principality for himself in western Asia Minor, and twice had been deported to administer posts in Rumelia, to keep him out of mischief. For a good summary of his career, see the article by J. H. Mordtmann on "Djunaid" in the *Encyclopaedia of Islām*, I, 1063–1064; also Hammer, I, 364–366, trans. Hellert, II, 163–167, for his

But the attempt was a failure. With Djunaïd, Mustafa was forced to flee before the Sultan, taking refuge in Thessalonica.[82]

His presence in this Byzantine city was a potential source of great embarrassment and danger. The angry Sultan addressed himself to Demetrius Lascaris Leontaris, the governor of the city during the minority of the young Despot Andronicus, and demanded the surrender of the pretender in the name of the current friendship between the Turks and the Greeks. Leontaris is reported to have put off the Sultan with a declaration of his own lack of authority to make such a decision, which was the proper responsibility of the Emperor alone. It was therefore to the government of Constantinople, presumably to Manuel himself, that Mechmed was obliged to turn. Manuel responded soothingly, not conceding the surrender of the fugitives, but promising to imprison them securely. It was agreed that the Sultan should provide annually the sum of 300,000 aspers for the maintenance of the pretender in his assigned place of exile of Lemnos, while Djunaïd was confined in the Monastery of St. Mary the Pammakaristos in the capital. Meanwhile, Manuel's son and heir, John, had appeared on the scene in Thessalonica and saw to the settlement and to the dispatch of the pretender to exile.[83]

earlier career. Ducas calls him Τζινεήτ or Τζινεήτης and Chalcocondyles calls him Ζουναΐτης: see Moravcsik, *Byzantinoturcica*, II, 313, and Nimet, *Die türkische Prosopographie bei Laonikos Chalkokandyles*, 45–46.

82. There has occasionally been some confusion about dating this first revolt of Mustafa, and some writers have placed it as late as 1418 or 1419. But in addition to the testimony of Sphrantzes, which will be presented in the next note, we have the corroboration of a letter of the Ragusans to King Sigismund. (There are two publications of this Latin text: in Gelcich and Thallóczy, *Diplomatarium*, no. 175, pp. 264–266; and in *Acta et diplomata ragusina*, ed. J. Radonić, I [=*Srpska kraljevska Akademija, Zbornik za istoriju jezik i Knjiženost srpskog narodna*, III, 2, Belgrad, 1934], no. 130, pp. 262–263.) Dated December 25, 1416, this letter includes the following passage (p. 265 or p. 263 in the respective editions): "Concerning news of the Turks: at present there is no army in the realm of Bosnia or Rascia, since their emperor [Mechmed] is occupied at Salonica concerning the blockade of his brother, who was in Wallachia, to whom the Constantinopolitan emperor shows favor." ("De novis Teucrorum: ad presens nullus exercitus est in regno Bosne aut Rasie, quia eorum imperator est occupatus Salonichi circa obsidionem fratris ipsius, qui erat in Vlachia, cui imperator Constantinopolitanus favorem exhibet.") This text leaves no doubt about the dating of the episode. Note also the brief account by Konstantin the Philosopher, ed. Jagić, 314, ed. and trans. Braun, 57; cf. Stanojević, 456 (with incorrect citation), and p. 458.

83. Dölger, *Regesten*, nos. 3361–65 (dated to autumn of 1416), p. 104.

Mechmed professed to be content with this arrangement, and thus the appearance of peace and friendship was maintained. But the Byzantines now held, in the pretender, someone who could serve as a useful instrument, if wisely used—or a potential danger, if not handled carefully. Such a stroke was in the best traditions of Byzantine diplomacy. Thanks to Manuel's clever

Ducas, ed. Grecu, 155–161, ed. Bonn, 117–121, gives the fullest account of these events, with the details of the settlement, and specifically relating the roles of Leontaris and Manuel himself, but ignoring John. Chalcocondyles, ed. Darkó, I, 190–192, ed. Bonn, 202–204, gives basically the same account, but with fewer details and names: he simply relates that, after the fugitives sought refuge, the Sultan demanded their return by "the ruler of Therma [=Thessalonica]" (ὁ τῆς Θέρμης ἄρχων), who sent word of the matter to "the Basileus of Byzantium," who in his turn concluded the agreement with the Sultan to imprison the fugitives. The *Chron. Barb. 111*, 52–53, gives an obviously denatured and corrupted account of how Mustafa failed in his attempted seizure of power and was himself seized by the Byzantines, who, amid Mechmed's gratitude, imprisoned the pretender on Mitylene (*sic*) with Djunaïd until the pretender died (*sic!*).

By contrast, Sphrantzes, 1026D–1027A (Pseudo-Phrantzes, ed. Papadopoulos, 112–113; ed. Bonn, 109) says that in the autumn of 1416 (under the year 1417, but still beginning the year with the previous September 1), the young John departed for the Morea. And at that time the "false" (πλαστός) Mustafa took refuge in Thessalonica, and "he" (John?) sent him into exile on Lemnos. Then there is a passage (pp. 173–174) of the so-called Anonymous Panegyric (actually by Isidore of Kiev) published by Lampros (Παλ. καὶ Πελ., III), in which there is an elaborate account of the Mustafa affair which makes "the Basileus" John the sole hero of the occasion; nothing is said of Leontaris or Manuel. On the basis of the last two sources, the involvement of John, on his way then to the Morea (see p. 346 below), seems certain, and Laskaris, in his article " Ἰωάννης Η′ ὁ Παλαιολόγος ἐν Θεσσαλονίκῃ κατὰ τὴν πολιορκίαν τοῦ 1416," has done well in presenting and stressing this evidence on the matter.

But how do the accounts referring to John fit in with those of Ducas and Chalcocondyles? Using all these sources save for the Panegyric, Iorga, *Geschichte*, 374, suggests an ingenious reconciliation: he assumes here that John arrived after the entry of Mustafa into Thessalonica, and has the future Emperor take charge of the fugitives from Leontaris and see to their exile. This would fit everyone in neatly, although it would not explain whether John had been specifically ordered by Manuel to take the matter in hand in the course of the journey to the Morea, or whether John simply happened to arrive there when the crisis arose and then took over the job on the spot. Nor is the exact handling of the two prisoners completely clear. Sphrantzes says that the pretender was sent to Lemnos and "thereafter to Myzithra [Mistra]." If this statement is not a corruption which refers to John's continuation of his journey, rather than to his dispatch of the prisoner, it may fit in reverse with the statement of Chalcocondyles that the fugitives were first imprisoned in the citadel of "Epidauros" (Monemvasia) and were later sent to Lemnos and Imbros. Imbros is not mentioned as an island of imprison-

manipulation of this windfall opportunity, he now had a valuable advantage in the sugar-coated "cold war" with Mechmed. And surely it must have been a great satisfaction to be able to turn the tables on the Turks and, for a change, exact a barely disguised tribute from them.

The appearance of the young Prince John in this episode signifies his first active arrival on the scene of events on his own. As a conscientious father and dutiful Emperor, Manuel had done his best to provide for the proper unbringing of his son.[84] As

ment by the other sources, and certainly we know that Mustafa was on Lemnos when he was subsequently released (see p. 357, below). Needless to say, the *Chron. Barb. 111*'s reference to Mitylene is worthless: the author probably confused the Italian word for Lemnos ("Stalimene") with Lesbos (represented by the city of Mitylene).

Is it possible that John took one or both of the two captives with him when he continued on to the Morea, before the final place of exile was established? After all, there might have been some lapse of time necessary for the negotiations with the Turks to settle definitely the arrangements for their confinement. Such an action on John's part is therefore not impossible, although it would seem clumsy. Ducas, by contrast, since he says nothing of John's role, simply relates that Leontaris put both prisoners on a "trireme" and shipped them off to the Basileus in Constantinople, who then in his turn sent them to their respective places of exile. Could it have been only Djunaïd who was sent to the capital, while Mustafa was taken on to the Morea by John after all? Only one non-Greek source has anything to contribute. But Konstantin the Philosopher, ed. Jagić, 314, ed. and trans. Braun, 57, speaks only in vague terms of the Sultan's complaint to Manuel and the retention of Mustafa by the Greeks.

Obviously, then, all our sources leave too many loose ends for us to be entirely certain of all details. But such uncertainties are no excuse for the terrible hash made out of the episode by Pears, 152 (apparently based on Muralt, p. 802, nos. 11–15), who places it in 1418 and identifies Mustafa's fellow fugitive and prisoner not as Djunaïd, but as "the chief of the Wallachs." See also Berger de Xivrey, 162–164; and Hammer (who accepts the pretender as the true Mustafa), I, 381–384, trans. Hellert, II, 190–194. As does Hammer (I, 384, trans. Hellert, II, 195), Taeschner in his chapter in the new *Cambr. Med. Hist.*, Vol. IV (2nd ed.), Pt. 1, p. 768, places at least the arrangement between Mechmed and Manuel regarding Mustafa, if not the entire episode, in 1421, but on what authority is not clear.

84. Not the least among Manuel's efforts in this line are some interesting literary works. The Emperor composed a long and noteworthy compendium of maxims and advice for his son, the so-called *Praecepta educationis regiae* (Ὑποθῆκαι βασιλικῆς ἀγωγῆς), in a style in which Krumbacher (*Geschichte der byzantinischen Litteratur*, p. 491) traces the influence of Isocrates. With this work should also be mentioned a set of so-called *Orationes ethico-politicae*, addressed also to his son, on various subjects of moral behavior suitable for a proper prince. The texts of these works may be found in Migne, *Patr. gr.* 156, respectively in coll. 313–384, and 385–557. Cf. the

John grew out of adolescence, Manuel took pains to furnish his heir with a wife. In 1411 there was secured as John's bride a little daughter of the Grand Prince of Moscow, Vasilii I, named Anna.[85] But the Turkish wars of succession through 1413 perhaps delayed her coming, and it was probably not until 1414 that she finally came to Constantinople, at the age of about eleven. At any rate, it seems to have been in 1414, when John was twenty years old and his father's attention was free to turn to such things, that the couple was married.[86]

John was left behind in Constantinople as regent when Manuel left on his journey to the Morea in July of that year.[87] When

comments of Petit in the *Dictionnaire de théologie catholique*, IX, p. 1929 (3: 1–2). Appended to the latter of the two works (ed. Migne, 557–561)· is an epistolary epilogue to the young John, which is included among the Emperor's correspondence as Letter νγ′ (ed. Legrand, pp. 80–83). The fact that this letter is placed as a separate work in the manuscript of Manuel's correspondence *after* two others (μθ′ and να′) which plainly bear on the Emperor's 1408 visit to the Morea (see above, p. 276, n. 133; and pp. 276–277 and n. 134), may or may not be of significance in dating at least the set of *Orationes*. Berger de Xivrey, 194–197, dates the *Praecepta* (nos. 68–69 in his enumeration) and the *Orationes* (his nos. 70–76; the letter, no. 77) both to the year 1406. Certainly their composition must have covered several years of the prince's early adolescence.

85. The award of Anna's hand to "Ivan Manouelevitch" of "Tzargrad" by her father is reported by an entry under the year 6919 (1410–11) in the *Sofiiskaya pervaya lietopis*, p. 258; cf. Muralt, p. 793, no. 5, who somehow adds the specific date of March 1.

86. Ducas, ed. Grecu, 133–135, ed. Bonn, 98, who gives her age, but no date for their marriage. He relates it in a context after the settlement of peace with Mechmed in 1413, however, and he says that she died three years after her marriage. Since we are told that she died in 1417 (see p. 347 below), she was therefore presumably married in 1414. Thus, Dölger, *Regesten*, no. 3337, p. 99, who, however, overlooks the betrothal in 1411. See Gill, "John VIII Palaeologus," 153 and 155 (reprint, 106 and 108); Muralt, p. 800, no. 5; also, more generally, Diehl, *Figures byzantines*, II, 272. For some diplomatic implications of this matrimonial alliance, see Halecki, "La Pologne et l'empire byzantin," 52. Dölger, *Regesten*, no. 3350, p. 102, notes a subsequent diplomatic contact between Manuel and the Muscovite court in the summer of 1415, though by way of the Patriarch and in connection with ecclesiastical matters.

87. Among various allusions to John's regency during Manuel's absence, the most clear is that in a deliberation of the Venetian Senate of July 23, 1415. On that date, instructions were given to a Venetian commander to go to Constantinople and, in the course of his mission, to pay his respects "to the son of the Emperor": Iorga, *Notes et extraits*, I, 234; Thiriet, *Régestes*, II, no. 1584, pp. 136–137. Another Senate deliberation of the same date also makes another undoubted reference to John in Constantinople at this time: see n. 23 above.

Manuel returned in March of 1416, his eldest son was halfway through his twenty-second year. Manuel apparently decided that it was time to give his heir some practical experience; and at the same time he used this opportunity to further the efforts of his own recent activities by making the Morea the scene of this experience. In the autumn of 1416 John departed for the Peloponnesus,[88] and on his way there he became involved in Thessalonica in the Mustafa affair, just discussed. Moving on to the Peloponnesus, John joined forces with his younger brother, the Despot Theodore II, and together they renewed Palaeologan expansionist policies in the peninsula. The rival to Byzantine authority there was the Navarese remnant of the old Latin Principality of Achaia, ruled by its last Prince, Centurione Zaccaria. According to our information, Manuel had been content during his busy 1415 stay to accept a recognition of suzerainty from Zaccaria.[89] With John's visit to the Morea, hostilities broke out. The Byzantines were able to make some substantial progress territorially with the acquisition of a number of towns and strongholds.[90] This activity aroused the concern of the Venetians, whose frequent complaints to Constantinople illustrate how actively Manuel kept, or was kept, in regular contact with events in this important Byzantine area.[91]

88. Sphrantzes, 1026D (Pseudo-Phrantzes, ed. Papadopoulos, 112–113, ed. Bonn, 109). See Laskaris, " 'Ἰωάννης," 342, for the necessary chronological adjustment; cf. Muralt, p. 800, no. 1.

89. Ducas, ed. Grecu, 139, ed. Bonn, 102, had been the only source to shed any light on Manuel's bearing with regard to the Navarese Principality during his visit; cf. Zakythinos, *Le Despotat grec*, I, 172, and Muralt, p. 798, no. 7. But recently, with Schirò's publication of the Cephalonian chronicle extract, we have gained some new information. According to this text (ed. Schirò, "Manuele incorona," 229), Prince Centurione . Zaccaria (called ὁ πρίγκιπας) went in person to pay his respects to Manuel, along with other local lords, when the Emperor arrived in the Peloponnesus in 1415. This text therefore confirms and strengthens the value of Ducas' statement. It is also interesting to note in this same chronicle text Manuel's cultivation of the Toccos of Yannina as useful powers and allies in the area, especially through Manuel's granting of the title and insignia of Despot to Carlo Tocco: see Schirò, 223–228, for a good discussion of Manuel's relations with this house.

90. On John VIII's activities, see Zakythinos, *Le Despotat grec*, I, 180–184; and Mompherratos, Οἱ Παλ. ἐν Πελ., pp. 40–48. See also Rodd, 258–259; Gill, "John VIII Palaeologus," 153 (105); Miller, *The Latins in the Levant*, 385.

91. On July 19, 1417, the Venetian Senate noted uneasily the commencement of hostilities by the two brothers against Prince Centurione and ordered

John returned from the Morea to Constantinople in 1418, probably in the late summer.[92] On his return he found that his child bride, the Russian Princess Anna, had died in August of the preceding year, during a plague in the city that spring and

a strengthening of their land forces in Coron and Modon: Iorga, *Notes et extraits*, I, 267 (see also the valuable supplementary material in his n. 3); Thiriet, *Régestes*, II, no. 1661, p. 156. But before this month was out the Venetian uneasiness had given way to protests. On July 25, 1417, the Senate wrote a letter to its *bailo* in Constantinople instructing him to complain to Manuel about the activities of his two sons who, it said, were violating all agreements to respect the rights of Venetian citizens and territory: text, Sathas, I, no. 48, pp. 65–66; cf. Thiriet, no. 1666, p. 157. Again, on the same date, the Senate ordered strengthening of its naval forces in the Morea in view of the rapid progress of the two brothers: text, Sathas, I, no. 49, p. 67; cf. Thiriet, no. 1667, pp. 157–158. And, at the same time, the Senate assured the ambassadors of Zaccaria that Venice would redouble its efforts to induce Manuel to intervene and halt his sons' activities: text, Sathas, I, no. 50, p. 68; cf. Thiriet, no. 1667, pp. 157–158.

During the autumn and winter, there were various negotiations and contacts with John, including questions of the Venetian effort to secure Patras (see Thiriet, nos. 1677 and 1679). And, on November 29, 1417, the Senate noted the continuation of its mediation efforts: text, Sathas, I, no. 62, pp. 90–91. Negotiations dragged on further. Some months later, on June 11, 1418, the Senate presented to the envoys of John (the "Imperator Iuvens") a long bill of its complaints: text, Sathas, III, no. 731, pp. 174–180; cf. Thiriet, no. 1697, pp. 164–165 (for other matters in this response, see n. 25 and n. 26 above). A few days later, again resorting to Manuel, the Senate made reply on July 21, 1418, to a letter from Manuel dated May 1 (which was itself in response to the Senate's own letter to him of March 11 and 12). The *Sapientes* again appealed to the old Emperor for redress against his sons: Dölger, *Regesten*, no. 3370, p. 105; Iorga, 281–282; Thiriet, no. 1705, p. 167. Cf., in general, Muralt, p. 802, no. 8. On November 9, 1418, the Senate was still taking note of the ravages of the brothers' Greek and Albanian troops, allegedly committed on Venetian citizens and territory: text, Sathas, III, no. 737; pp. 185–186; cf. Thiriet, no. 1714, p. 169.

Long after John had departed from the Morea the Venetian complaints continued. We note such protests to both the Despot and the Emperor Manuel against the ravages of Theodore II's troops: text (of the protest to the former only), Sathas, III, no. 764, pp. 207–208; cf. Thiriet, no. 1766, p. 180. Again, on May 8, 1421, the new *bailo* of Constantinople was ordered to protest personally, both to the Despot and "to the lord Emperor his father," about Venetian losses: text, Sathas, I, no. 75, pp. 109–112; cf. Thiriet, no. 1808, p. 188. Another complaint was lodged against Theodore on February 26, 1422, and it was agreed to send an ambassador to him: Iorga, 317; Thiriet, no. 1833, p. 193. This ambassador received his commission on April 2, 1422: Iorga, 319; Thiriet, no. 1840, p. 194.

92. Sphrantzes, 1027C (Pseudo-Phrantzes, ed. Papadopoulos, 113–114; ed. Bonn, 110) simply gives the year. Before this statement the historian notes that Manuel sent his youngest son, Thomas, to the Morea at the same time, apparently to replace John in a dynastic policy reminiscent of

summer.[93] There is no indication of what this loss may have meant to John personally, but it was soon to affect him not personally but politically. Seeking a new wife for his heir, Manuel took the opportunity to join his quest with his current negotiations with Pope Martin V and the question of union. Nicholas Eudaimonoioannes, Manuel's ambassador to the Council of Constance and to the Pope, was instructed to negotiate the details of marrying his sons to Latin princesses. The Pope agreed to this fine gesture of good faith on both sides.[94] Apparently on a second embassy to the West, Eudaimonoioannes attended to the matter of securing specific brides. In the summer of 1420, he arranged with Venice for the transportation of the two that he was bringing back with him: Sophia of Montferrat for John and Cleopa Malatesta for Theodore.[95]

a kind of modern troop rotation. Cf. Mompherratos, Οἱ Παλ. ἐν Πελ., 48; Muralt, p. 801, no. 1. But it should be noted that Thomas was only about nine years of age (see below, Appendix XV, for the time of his birth), and his dispatch was probably for purposes of education and training rather than of continuing any of John's work. See also Berger de Xivrey, 166, Zakythinos, *Le Despotat grec,* I, 184, and Miller, *The Latins in the Levant,* 385.

93. Sphrantzes, 1027C (Pseudo-Phrantzes, ed. Papadopoulos, 114; ed. Bonn, 110). His dating is apparently corroborated by a reference by the Venetian Senate, in a deliberation of September 6, 1417, to a plague then rampant in Constantinople: Iorga, *Notes et extraits,* I, 269; Thiriet, *Régestes,* II, no. 1676, p. 160. Cf. Gill, "John VIII Palaeologus," 153 (106); Muralt, p. 800, no. 5. Zakythinos, *Le Despotat grec,* I, 184, assumes that it was the death of Anna which drew John home from the Morea; but there is no proof whatsoever for this assumption. The Βρ. χρ. No. 44, p. 77, l. 4, places the death of "ἡ δέσποινα ἡ Ῥῶσα" in the year 6924 (1415–16), plainly an error, as are most of this chronicle's other entries.

94. Dölger, *Regesten,* no. 3369, pp. 104–105. See above, p. 325; cf. also Gill, *The Council of Florence,* pp. 23–24 and 27; Zakythinos, *Le Despotat grec,* I, 188–189; Muralt, p. 801, no. 5.

95. Dölger, *Regesten,* no. 3372, p. 105. On July 16, 1420, the Senate authorized the passage on a Venetian galley of Eudaimonoioannes and Cleopa, destined for marriage to Theodore: Iorga, *Notes et extraits,* I, 306; Thiriet, *Régestes,* II, no. 1782, p. 183. On August 30, 1420, the Senate gave orders for taking on board the *two* ladies who were on their way to marry sons of Manuel: Iorga, 307; Thiriet, no. 1791, p. 185. By the latter date, plainly, Sophia had joined the party. The sailing must have been soon after the latter date, for Sphrantzes, 1027C–D (Pseudo-Phrantzes, ed. Papadopoulos, 115, ed. Bonn, 110–111), reports Sophia's arrival in November (giving the year as 1418, which, though accepted by Muralt, p. 803, no. 1, should be, in accordance with n. 97 below, emended to 1420). In general, cf. Mercati, *Notizie,* 477–478; Mompherratos, Οἱ Παλ. ἐν Πελ., 48–49. It

Neither was to be happy in her marriage. As far as Sophia was concerned, it was to bring her years of misery. Despite a pleasing form, she was an unattractive woman, and she soon won the cordial aversion of her husband.[96] Nevertheless, their marriage in "the Great Church" of Hagia Sophia on January 19, 1421, was an important step for John, for it was also the occasion of his

might be noted that Cleopa's betrothal (if not the wedding) to Theodore was celebrated in a motet "Vasilissa ergo gaude" by the great composer Guillaume Dufay, then barely twenty and a member of the Papal Choir: see *The New Oxford History of Music*, III (London, 1960), 214. A similar epithalamium was composed by Dufay's contemporary and colleague Hugo de Lantins: *ibid.*, 235. On the question of whether or not Cleopa was allowed to retain her Roman Catholic faith during her marriage, as had been agreed, see G. Hoffmann, "Kirchengeschichtliches zur Ehe des Herrschers Theodor II Palaiologos (1407–1443)," *Ostkirchliche Studien*, 4 (1955), 129–137.

96. Ducas, ed. Grecu, 137–139, ed. Bonn, 99–102, gives a long account of the marital transactions, with a detailed description of Sophia. And he also states that John was so repelled by her that he would have nothing to do with her, neglecting her and relegating her to a remote part of the palace. He would gladly have sent her back home, says the historian, were it not that filial respect for his father's wishes hindered him. (Cf. Gill, "John VIII Palaeologus," p. 155 [108], who confuses her family name with that of Theodore's bride.)

A basically similar story is told by Chalcocondyles, ed. Darkó, I, 192–193, ed. Bonn, p. 205, who says that John refused to consummate the marriage. But Ducas also goes on to tell an elaborate story of an escape which Sophia finally undertook, with the connivance of the Genoese of Pera; and how, when there was an attempt to bring her back, Manuel prevented this, to his son's delight. Whereupon, says Ducas, she sailed back to Italy, to her parents, and to a nunnery. But this latter part of the story is surely wrong, for we are told that she was still in Constantinople late in 1424 (see n. 150 below), and Sphrantzes, 1031D, gives the reliable testimony of her homeward flight only after Manuel's death, in August of 1426. (The Pseudo-Phrantzes, ed. Papadopoulos, 125; ed. Bonn, 122, adds a brief comment more on this unhappy marriage, following the chronicle of the Pseudo-Dorotheos of Monemvasia: see Loenertz, "Autour du Chronicon Maius," 304–305.) Cf. Gill, "John VIII Paleologus," p. 155 (108) where he incorrectly gives the year as 1427; and *id.*, *The Council of Florence*, 24.

According to an entry in *Byz. Zeitschr.*, 22 (1913), p. 598, there is an article by O. F. Tencajoli entitled "Sofia di Monferrato imperatrice di Constantinopoli (1396–1437)," in a periodical identified as *La Donna*, 9 (Turin, 1913), no. 195, pp. 18–19. At the present writing I have been unable to identify or locate this article. However, see Diehl, *Figures byzantines*, II, 273–275. For Cleopa's no more happy marriage, see Gill, *The Council of Florence*, 24–25, and Zakythinos, *Le Despotat grec*, I, 189–191. Only after his father's death and his wife's flight did John finally find the love of his life, Maria, daughter of the Emperor of Trebizond, who became his third bride.

coronation as co-Basileus.[97] Thus was John formally elevated as his father's partner in the rule of the Empire.

The emergence of John in the government at this time is of great importance and was soon to be felt. As it happened, this emergence coincided significantly with the apparent growth of serious factionalism among the Byzantine leadership. One of the factions, following at least the outward policy of Manuel, accepted "peaceful coexistence" with the Turks, even to the point of virtual subservience when it seemed necessary. The other faction chafed under such conservatism and sought a forceful and hostile stance against the Turks. As time drew on, these factions were later to assume even more grave colorings. The war faction was to become the proponent of union with the Latin Church as the hope of safety, while the peace faction would become the rabid opponent of the union, even to the point of preferring surrender to the Turks—as one may recall in the celebrated assertion ascribed to Lucas Notaras on the eve of the final

97. Sphrantzes, 1027D (Pseudo-Phrantzes, ed. Papadopoulos, 115; Bonn, 111), gives the year as 1419. Berger de Xivrey, 167, notes an attempt to revise this to 1420; but Dölger has analyzed this and related sources in his important note, "Die Krönung Johanns VIII. zum Mitkaiser," *Byz. Zeitschr.*, 36 (1936), 318–319, pointing out the necessary emendations. (Curiously enough, Muralt, p. 806, no. 5—cf. also his n. 15—also had previously established the date correctly himself.) Dölger cites the obviously defective Βρ. χρ. No. 29, p. 54, ll. 27–28, which gives the year as 6900 (1391–92). And there is also No. 47, p. 82, ll. 81–82, giving the proper year of 6929 (1420–21). A third short chronicle entry, not available to Dölger then, is the *Chron. Vat. gr. 162*, no. 20, p. 211, ll. 95–97, which gives the completely impossible date of May 21, 6924 (1415–16), indiction 10 (which was 1416–17); this jumble obviously deserves no credence. It is possible that John had been crowned previously, perhaps at his first wedding in 1414. But Ducas, ed. Grecu, 133–135, ed. Bonn, 98, says only that the crown was withheld from little Anna at that time because of her tender age. Does this negative statement necessarily imply thereby that the crown was not given to John? It is true that some documents, especially the Venetian texts such as those cited above in n. 91, do refer frequently to John as Emperor before 1421. But this does not mean much: after all, at a later date other Venetian documents do not always speak of him as Emperor: see p. 381 below. Rather, the heavy emphasis on coronation in the sources for this second marriage seems to imply that it was only in 1421 that John was officially given the title of *Basileus*. Cf. Christophilopoulou, Ἐκλογή, ἀναγόρευσις καὶ στέψις τοῦ βυζαντινοῦ αὐτοκράτορος, 203, who points out that John is given the title of *Basileus* in the famous family portrait in the Dionysius the Areopagite manuscript (see pp. 263–264 above). But this is perhaps a mere acknowledgment of the obvious fact that he was the heir apparent.

fall.[98] But even before such ecclesiastical partisanship came to dominate the factionalism, the growth of a war party by itself was a development of grave implications. Not yet free of youthful impetuosity and rashness even at age twenty-seven, John was soon to align himself with this latter faction.

The first clear demonstration of the feelings of the war faction was to come soon enough. In this same fateful year of 1421, probably not long after John's coronation, came the last and most celebrated display of the façade of Turko-Byzantine friendship. The two motifs, the factionalism and the friendship, intertwine grotesquely in the account which has come down to us from the pen of the Imperial domestic and later historian, Sphrantzes. It is too vivid not to be given in full:

And . . . there came the Emir ['Αμιρᾶς] the lord Itzes [ὁ Κὺρ 'Ιτζής, plainly a corruption of Κυρίτζης, the Greek form of Mechmed's surname], or Mechemetes, that he might cross by way of the City into the East. And learning in advance, as in secret, from his people that "he proceeds in order to regulate the affairs of the East, and when he should return, he has as an object and intention to attack the city," all the magnates of the holy Basileus to whom this secret had been confided and all those among the higher clergy [ἱερομονάχοι] urged on the Basileus and counseled him that he should seize him. But he was not at all persuaded, saying: "I would not disregard the oath which I swore to him, even though I were certain that, should he come, he would be going to take us captive. And if he in turn should disregard his own oaths, the matter would rest with God, Who is much more powerful than he." But for this reason he did not send any of his sons for the reception of the unbeliever, but only the most excellent man Demetrius Leontaris, and Isaac Asanes, and the Protostrator Manuel Cantacuzenus, with many youths of the nobility and soldiers and gifts. And they met him in the neighborhood of Koutoulos and came with

98. Ducas, ed. Grecu, 329, ed. Bonn, 264: "It is much better to see ruling in the midst of the city the turban [φακιόλιον] of the Turks than the Latin headdress [καλύπτραν]" is the literal translation of the familiar comment, which is often rendered more freely. On the growth of factions up to 1421, Walter, *La Ruine de Byzance*, 308, suggests that the war faction was the product of a new generation which had grown up in such peace that it did not appreciate the hard realities of dealing with the Turks. But, as facts should have shown by now, this would have been a rather unlikely possibility at this time. (Walter also mistakenly describes John VIII as less than twenty-five years old at this time.) He further suggests that elements among the Turks were unhappy with the peace and were anxious to renew the fight with Byzantium.

him as far as the Diplokionion, while he was conversing, that is to say, along the whole route with Leontaris. And there, at the Diplokionion, were found the holy Basileus and his sons with a galley to transport him. And he boarded it, and they saluted each other in the midst of the sea from their galleys. And, holding conversation, they departed as far as to the further side, of the East, which is now called Skoutarion, but formerly Chrysopolis. He on his part, going out of the galley, went on into the tents which they had prepared in advance for him. And on their part, the Basileis were on the galleys, eating and drinking and sending food to each other, when he, mounting on a horse about evening, departed along the route which goes towards Nikomeidia. And the Basileis went back homeward.[99]

99. Sphrantzes, 1027D–1028C; cf. Pseudo-Phrantzes, ed. Papadopoulos, 115–116; ed. Bonn, 111–112. The historian was an eyewitness, in all likelihood; or, if not, he had access to reports of other eyewitnesses. He places these events in the year 1420, according to his surviving text, and this date is accepted by Berger de Xivrey, 169–171, Muralt, p. 804, no. 5, Iorga, *Geschichte,* 376–377, and Pears, 152; while Hammer, I, 384–385, trans. Hellert, II, 195–196, places it in the same year as the pact on Mustafa. But Dölger, "Die Krönung," points out justly that the historian's chronology during this period up into 1422 is entirely faulty, as it stands now, and that this episode belongs also to 1421; cf. his *Regesten,* no. 3384, p. 107 (dated winter 1420–21); also Khoury, "L'Empereur Manuel II," 143, who opts for 1420. The episode probably occurred in the late winter, for Sphrantzes continues his narrative immediately with the observation that, "crossing back over in the spring of the same year to the West by the route of Kallipolis, he departed to Adrianopolis." (Out of a vague allusion in Baronius-Raynaldus, for the correct year [1421, no. 23, Vol. 27, p. 522], Berger de Xivrey, 171, concluded that Mechmed relied upon the Genoese for his return crossing; he suggests some possible significance in the fact that the Sultan did not call upon the Byzantines for that return trip.)

It is interesting to note the route by which the original crossing was made. Koutoulos was apparently the modern Kurtuluş, a suburb of the modern city across the Golden Horn, approximately two kilometers from both the Horn and Galata—in other words, not very far from the area of the capital. (Was this a frontier point of Byzantine territory at the time?) But from here Mechmed was not brought into Constantinople, but was, instead, accompanied a distance of about three kilometers to the Diplokionion. The latter was a harbor on the Bosporus, apparently at the point now called Beşiktaş on the shore of the Dolmabahçe area (see Van Millingen, *Byzantine Constantinople,* 242–243) and roughly opposite Scutari, or old Chrysopolis. (See also Appendix XXIV: C, 6, below.) Therefore, when Mechmed entered Byzantine territory, no attempt was made to receive him in the capital. He was simply conducted to a ready point for a swift crossing. The two rulers and their entourages did not even join each other on the same boat or at the same table.

Incidentally, Vasiliev, in his "Pero Tafur," 116, notes the description (pp. 115–116) by Tafur of an occasion when the Turkish Sultan passed near the city walls on a campaign, when there seemed danger of a Turkish siege,

Manuel's firmness doubtless reflects well on his honor. But there was more involved than mere honor. It is obvious that both sides regarded Turkish hostility as a very real danger behind the friendly façade. But Manuel recognized that preserving the façade was essential. Adopting the proposal of the war faction would have been pure folly of the most disastrous sort, as Manuel surely realized. As false and as irksome as it may have been, there was simply no safe alternative to maintaining the façade.

Unfortunately, this incident was to be Manuel's last display of firmness—and almost the last demonstration of his constructive statesmanship.

The final crisis was not long in coming, as the crucial year of 1421 passed on. In the wake of this friendly meeting, Manuel sent the trusty Demetrius Lascaris Leontaris as his ambassador to Mechmed, after the Sultan's return to Adrianople in the spring. There seems to have ·been considerable diplomatic activity between the two rulers at this time, and, while there is no specific evidence on the subject, this embassy may have had something to do with a projected arrangement in Mechmed's will and testament, whereby Manuel was made the guardian of

and when a gift was sent to the Sultan. Vasiliev logically avoids any identification of this occasion with the siege of 1422; but, for some strange reason, he refers it instead to this meeting between Manuel and Mechmed I. In reality, Tafur makes it clear that this incident took place during his own stay in the city (late 1437–early 1438), and so the Sultan must surely have been Murad II and the incident must have nothing to do with the 1421 interview.

Finally, I note that Iorga, *Geschichte*, I, 376, followed uncritically by Dölger, *Regesten*, no. 3383, p. 107, affirms that Manuel made a new pact with Mechmed in 1420. The bases for this assertion are: first, Manuel's allusions to oaths in the passage quoted above from Sphrantzes (ed. Migne, 1028A; cf. Pseudo-Phrantzes, ed. Papadopoulos, p. 115, ll. 17 and 20; ed. Bonn, p. 111, ll. 14 and 17; and, second, an even more nebulous allusion to Manuel's necessity to accommodate himself to Mechmed in the Venetian Senate documents on Philanthropenos' mission in January of 1420 (Iorga, *Notes et extraits*, I, 301). But such "evidence" is utterly inadequate for such a flat assertion. The allusions must be rather to the general state of amity between Manuel and Mechmed established by their treaty of 1413, which had to be amended only once by the *ad hoc* agreements concerning the pretender Mustafa in 1416. Despite any irritations between them, there seems to have been no occasion at all requiring any new formalities between Emperor and Sultan to supersede the original 1413 accommodation; therefore, in the absence of any substantial confirmation of the flimsy source "evidence" adduced, I categorically reject the idea that any new pact was entered into in 1420. Manuel's scruples in 1421 about honoring his obligations to his ally refer surely to nothing more than the 1413 treaty and the amity it had sealed.

the Sultan's two younger sons.[100] Whatever his assignment, however, Leontaris was received with cordiality and honor. But full consultations with the Sultan were deferred.

Within three days Mechmed was dead. The ruler's demise, on May 21, 1421, was kept secret for a while to smooth the transition to his successor—the first instance of what was to become a common practice in Osmanli history. During this time, Leontaris was kept in isolation and ignorance. When he finally did discover the news, he was able to send a message to his government only with the greatest difficulty. During the period of uncertainty, however, there was the greatest anxiety in Constantinople. Manuel, who had retired into the Monastery of the Peribleptos because of a plague then raging, was the subject of many reproaches and recriminations from the war faction, which somehow construed the situation as proof that Manuel should have seized and killed the Sultan when he had his chance. The final arrival of Leontaris' report at length removed all doubt as to the fact of Mechmed's end.[101]

100. Sphrantzes, who alone reports the mission of Lascaris, says (1028C; cf. Pseudo-Phrantzes, ed. Papadopoulos, 116–117, ed. Bonn, 112–113) simply that the ambassador was sent "that he might learn and might inform in advance about the matters previously resolved and might test him [Mechmed] as a result of the fine affection and honor which they had displayed to him, both of the passage, and of such an ambassador—his personality, I mean—and also of the gifts which he brought." So vague a statement makes the embassy sound as if it were little more than a good-will mission. Yet, it could possibly have had something to do with the will arrangement, of which Sphrantzes says nothing, but which is reported by all the other historians of the period in one form or another. Its principal proponent is Ducas, ed. Grecu, 167, ed. Bonn, 126–127, who describes it as a provision of Mechmed's last illness to prevent civil war and murder. Chalcocondyles, ed. Darkó, I, 203, ed. Bonn, 216–217, followed by the *Chron. Barb. 111,* 55, asserts that Mechmed had a plan to divide his empire between his two (*sic*) sons, Rumelia to one and Anatolia to the other. In view of Mechmed's just reputation as the reunifier and restorer of the Osmanli state, it seems rather strange that he could have contemplated such a contradictory division of that state. That there was such a plan, indeed, seems rather doubtful, in view of the complete absence of any mention of it or of any effort to put it into effect after Mechmed's death. Cf. Dölger, *Regesten,* no. 3385, p. 107; Hammer, I, 385–386, trans. Hellert, II, 196–197; Iorga, *Geschichte,* 377–378; Muralt, pp. 804–805, nos. 7–8, mistakenly under 1420.

101. Sphrantzes, 1028C–1029A (Pseudo-Phrantzes, ed. Papadopoulos, 116–117; ed. Bonn, 113), gives these details of Leontaris' mission and its aftermath with a fullness which bespeaks his intimate acquaintance with court and government affairs. None of the other historians tell of this mission,

Now the Byzantines were faced with a new dilemma. What position should they take with regard to the succession to the Turkish throne? Ordinarily, such a matter would be not only none of their business, but also beyond their influence. The Byzantine role in the Turkish "Time of Troubles," however, had perhaps created sufficient precedents or habits to encourage the war faction to pretentious expectations. Normally the Byzantines would—and could—only have been content to acknowledge the accession of Mechmed's eldest son and designated successor, Murad II, and would have attempted to continue good relations with the Turks as far as possible. But the war faction sought to use the change of rulers to gain some advantage for Byzantium.

There seems to have been an effort to win concessions from the Turkish government during the transfer of power. And, when such efforts failed, it was proposed (in the parlance of modern diplomacy) to "unleash" the imprisoned pretender, the false Mustafa, after winning his promise of important concessions. A statesman as experienced and astute as Manuel could see that such a course would be rash and dangerous in the extreme. Hold-

but Ducas, ed. Grecu, 167, ed. Bonn, 128, reports that Mechmed's death was concealed for all of forty days. The same author, ed. Grecu, p. 163, ed. Bonn, 123, attributes his death to a hunting accident. The time of Mechmed's death is firmly established as May 1421 by the inscription on the Sultan's tomb in Brusa, which is transcribed and translated by Taeschner, "Beiträge zur frühosmanischen Epigraphik und Archäologie," *Der Islam*, 30 (1932), 147–148. But confirmation and amplification of this date is given by a short chronicle entry in an interesting Thessalonian account book, edited by S. Kougeas, "Notizbuch eines Beamtem der Metropolis im Thessalonike aus dem Anfang des XV. Jahrhunderts," *Byz. Zeitschr.*, 23 (1914–19), pp. 151–152, no. 80. This entry is worth quoting, not only for its further details on this question, but also for the unusually hostile attitude it displays toward the supposedly philhellenic Sultan: "On the 21st of the month of May of the 14th indiction of the 6929th year [1421], through a miracle of the great [St.] Demetrius, from a dysenteric and epileptic disease died the godless and impious Soultan Kyritzes [Mechmed I] the leader of the Saracens ['Αγαρηνῶν] who oppressed and troubled exceedingly Thessalonica and all Roman affairs." It should be noted that Alderson, *The Structure of the Ottoman Dynasty*, Tables XV and XXV, puts Mechmed's death on May 26, 1421: presumably this date might be derived from Turkish sources, but no citation is given. Alderson does, however, note the report (possibly unreliable, I suspect) by Ibn Arabshah (trans. Sanders, 187) that Mechmed died of poison. Curiously, in his chapter in *Cambr. Med. Hist.*, IV (2nd ed.), Pt. 1, p. 769, Taeschner gives the date of May 4 for Mechmed's death, though without source citation. Citing only Ducas, Runciman, *The Fall of Constantinople*, 44, mistakenly puts Mechmed's death in *December* of 1421.

ing the pretender as a form of diplomatic blackmail was one thing; throwing full support behind him in a bid for power, in the face of Turkish military might, was quite a different matter. Manuel protested strongly, but the war faction would hear no more of the old Emperor's course of moderation. Nor did the pleas and warnings of the Turkish government have any effect. Led by John VIII himself, the faction had enough influence by now to force its will. Manuel's strength was running out as was his time. In what must have been a moment of great weariness and despair, the old Emperor abandoned all responsibility to his son with the reported words: "Do as you wish. For I, my son, am both old and near to death. But the realm, and all things pertaining to it, I have given to you, so do as you wish." [102]

102. The sources for this episode are extremely contradictory. The basic text is that of Sphrantzes, 1029A–B (Pseudo-Phrantzes, ed. Papadopoulos, 117–118; ed. Bonn, 114), who speaks simply of the debate over supporting Mustafa in Rumelia as against recognizing Murad outright; of the hope for concessions, specifically Gallipoli; and of Manuel's words of virtual abdication to his son. But this account leaves something to be desired. For one thing, it speaks of the pretender as being in "Myzithra" or Mistra, which is in sharp opposition to all our other historical accounts (see n. 83 above). Moreover, there are points in the accounts of other historians which, though not irreconcilable with Sphrantzes' account, are not mentioned in it. In some ways his knowledgeable silence might itself be significant. But these other accounts have too much to recommend them to make such silence decisive.

Ducas, ed. Grecu, 171–173, ed. Bonn, 131–133, ignores the role of John and the debate over policy and attributes the Byzantine actions solely to Manuel. (Only later, ed. Grecu, 229, ed. Bonn, 182, does Ducas concede that, at some time before the Turkish siege of 1422, Manuel had yielded authority to John, in order, he says, to devote himself to study.) Ducas relates that, after the funeral of Mechmed and the accession of Murad in Brusa, Manuel was invited to renew the previous peace terms. The Emperor, however, sent two emissaries to congratulate the new ruler and to demand the surrender of Mechmed's two young sons to Manuel's care, as the late Sultan had wished; if this was not done, Manuel's embassy is supposed to have threatened, Mustafa would be supported instead. The Beylerbey of Rumelia, Bayazid, replied with the insistence that it was not proper for Muslim youths to be raised by infidels and offered the Byzantines continued peace on the old terms, without further concessions. Rebuffed in this quest, Manuel therefore turned to Mustafa, says Ducas. (This account has been accepted blandly, if not blindly, by Hammer, I, 400–402, trans. Hellert, II, 217–220, and by Muralt, p. 806, nos. 9–11, under the year 1420; and by Pears, 113, 152; also, Dölger, *Regesten*, no. 3388, p. 108.)

In his turn, Chalcocondyles, ed. Darkó, II, 1–3, ed. Bonn, 220–223, confirms Sphrantzes' description of the conflict between Manuel and John. According to this historian, as soon as the Greeks learned of Mechmed's death and Murad's accession in Brusa, they released Mustafa from Lemnos

Thus, by the late summer of 1421, the crisis in Imperial policy had come, and, on the initiative of the young John VIII, Byzantine support was thrown to the pretender. Demetrius Lascaris Leontaris was sent to Lemnos, apparently with the released Djunaïd, and Mustafa was offered Byzantine backing in seizing what he could of Rumelia, in exchange for the promise to surrender the important and ardently sought Gallipoli. This agreed, the pretender was conveyed to Europe, and, with the personal assistance of John VIII, Gallipoli was beseiged.[103]

and allowed him to go to Europe on the condition of promising them Gallipoli. Murad's deputies in Rumelia protested to the Greeks, and the Beylerbey Bayazid went personally to Byzantium to urge the Greeks not to support Mustafa, but instead to maintain peace now with Murad, offering twelve noble Turkish youths as hostages, 200,000 gold pieces, and whatever territory the Greeks might ask, including Gallipoli. But the young Emperor was not satisfied with such a course and advocated supporting Mustafa as ruler in Rumelia. His father objected on the grounds of treaty obligations and good faith, but John would not listen and pursued his own policy. Such is Chalcocondyles' account, much of it obviously an exaggeration or jumbling of details. The *Chron. Barb. 111*, 57–58, gives virtually the same story, interpolating short speeches. In one of them Bayazid is made to offer the twelve hostages, but only 100,000 florins. Another of these speeches is an interesting and otherwise wholly credible address by Manuel to his son warning against a breach with Murad, lest it bring down destruction on them.

Out of this mélange of sources it is difficult to make a coherent picture. Sphrantzes is still the most reliable one in general, and certainly there are basic flaws in the accounts of both Ducas and Chalcocondyles. The former is incorrect in ignoring John and making Manuel responsible for the support of the pretender. And the latter is wrong in seeming to place the release of Mustafa before the policy debate in Constantinople. Some details in both accounts, however, may be worth salvaging. The references by Ducas to an embassy by the Emperor to the Turks to demand the princes and those by Chalcocondyles to the embassy of Bayazid to the Emperor to offer hostages and more besides may perhaps reflect some preliminary jockeying for concessions of one kind or another. There is nothing specific in Sphrantzes' account to rule out the possibility that the war faction had first explored such avenues before finally pinning its hopes on Mustafa. Of course, such speculation may well be unjustified, and there may be no real reason to attempt to reconcile these sources or to interpolate details from one into another, assuming that one is bold enough to reject outright the accounts of both Ducas and Chalcocondyles in their entireties. Iorga, *Geschichte*, 379, skirts around this entire question and simply states that Byzantium supported Mustafa.

103. Sphrantzes, 1029B–C (Pseudo-Phrantzes, ed. Papadopoulos, 118–119; ed. Bonn, 114–115), gives the month of September as the date and has John personally bring Mustafa from his confinement in the Morea, a seemingly unlikely statement. Ducas, ed. Grecu, 173–175, ed. Bonn, 133–134, alone of the others speaks of Leontaris, together with Djunaïd. Chalcocondyles, ed. Darkó, II, 5, ed. Bonn, 225, ignores Leontaris, but con-

With Byzantine help the pretender made good progress. He passed on to Andrianople and, with the defeat of the Beylerbey Bayazid, won over the whole of Rumelia. When pressed, however, to fulfill his promise to the Byzantines, the pretender refused to surrender Gallipoli, on the grounds of a Muslim tradition which prohibited the restoration of conquests to the unbelievers.[104] The Byzantines then began to realize that they had been duped. But, in spite of contacts between Murad and Constantinople, they had no success then in divorcing themselves from their unfortunate mistake.[105] And, as 1422 dawned, the tide began to turn.

firms Sphrantzes' reference to John's presence at Gallipoli with Mustafa and Djunaid. Cf. Muralt, p. 806, nos. 1–3, under the year 1420; and Pears, 152–153; Dölger, *Regesten,* has no entries on the transactions with Mustafa.

Another source, apparently unnoticed previously, is a partly undecipherable text which gives a different dating. A short chronicle entry in the Thessalonian account book edited by Kougeas, p. 152, no. 81, is given by him in a fragmentary state, but its relevance is obvious, and its contents might be rendered roughly thus: "On the 15th of the month of August and in the above year [i.e., indiction 14, 6929, or 1421] the august Basileus lord Manuel [or John?] Palaiologos, by his expense and care and in his ships, restored [Moustapha . . .] in Kallioupolis as sovereign of all the West." The establishment of the Emperor's name in the text is not crucial, as we know that John might be implied implicitly even if not stated explicitly. But, barring possible efforts to harmonize them, we might well prefer this entry's dating to Sphrantzes', associated as the latter is, moreover, with a questionable statement of fact.

104. Ducas, ed. Grecu, 175, 181–201, ed. Bonn, 134, 139–156, gives a very detailed account (interrupted by a bitter digression on the progress of the Turks in the Balkans). He also gives a full account of the refusal by Djunaïd and Mustafa to surrender Gallipoli when it was demanded of them by Leontaris, Sphrantzes, *ibid.,* has the demand made by John himself after the capture of Gallipoli, very early in the pretender's success, it would seem; and John's demand is rejected. In his account of Mustafa's progress, Chalcocondyles, ed. Darkó, II, 3–4, ed. Bonn, 223–224, followed by the *Chron. Barb. 111,* 58, has the pretender put off the matter. Cf. Hammer, I, 402–404, trans. Hellert, II, 220–224; and Muralt, p. 807, nos. 7–8.

105. Ducas, ed. Grecu, 201–205, ed. Bonn, 157, 158–160, reports that Manuel, jolted by Mustafa's perfidy, sent to Murad to win peace, on terms of observance of Mechmed's will. (Ducas is the only historian to speak of this will as such and to pursue it throughout.) But when the Sultan's ambassador came to Constantinople he told the Emperor emphatically that peace on such terms or on condition of the surrender of Gallipoli to the Empire was impossible. Sphrantzes, 1029C (Pseudo-Phrantzes, ed. Papadopoulos, 118–119; ed. Bonn, 115), Chalcocondyles, ed. Darkó, II, 5–6, ed. Bonn, 225–226, and the *Chron. Barb. 111,* 58–59, all speak only about ambassadors sent by Murad to win the Byzantines from Mustafa's side. The latter two texts give more details and say that the embassies brought back the report that the Greeks would aid Mustafa. Cf. Pears, 153; Muralt, p. 807, no. 9.

Mustafa was apparently as incompetent as he was untrustworthy. In midwinter he made a totally unsuccessful attempt to fight Murad on his own ground in Anatolia, after crossing the Straits in Genoese ships on January 20. Instead, he was chased back to Europe. Ready at last to strike back decisively, the energetic young Murad crossed from Anatolia to Rumelia, also with the aid of Genoese transportation. The familiar story repeated itself. Mustafa was deserted by his supporters, including the faithless Djunaid. He fled and was caught. Murad had him executed as he would a common criminal.[106]

The young Murad II was no man to trifle with, and he quickly displayed his mettle. His intentions were no less than an immediate siege of Constantinople. Moreover, this was not to be

106. Again, the most detailed account is the one by Ducas, ed. Grecu, 205–229, ed. Bonn, 160–181, who also stresses that the ignominious execution of the pretender was intended to emphasize his spurious origin. But, for all his details, Ducas ignores Mustafa's campaign in Anatolia, which all the other sources report, and he stresses rather Mustafa's moral failings and debauchery. Sphrantzes' account, 1029C–D (Pseudo-Phrantzes, ed. Papadopoulos, 119; ed. Bonn, 115–116), is very brief, and it mistakenly places Murad's crossing in the summer. The account by Chalcocondyles, ed. Darkó, II, 5–7, ed. Bonn, 226–227, includes the extraordinary statement that Murad was able to cross to Europe because the Byzantine Emperor (which?) was too preoccupied with a lady-love to hinder him. The *Chron. Barb. 111,* 58–59, is the only one of the sources to ignore the role of Murad's Genoese transportation. We have a very fundamental report of Mustafa's crossing to Anatolia, with its actual date and with some figures of his forces, in a letter dated February 2, 1422, written by the Venetian *bailo* of Constantinople: partial text, Iorga, *Notes et extraits,* I, 316–317. And further dating is given in a short chronicle entry in the interesting Thessalonian account book, edited by Kougeas, p. 151, no. 78: "In the month of January, of the 15th indiction, the year 6930 [1422], there crossed over from Anatolia to the West by way of Kallioupolis, in a galley and in vessels of the Genoese without the consent of the Basileus lord Manuel Palaiologos, Mourates, the son of the Soultan, with [more probably, "in pursuit of"] Moustapha his uncle, the son of Bayazid; and he detached him from his army by treachery; being seized by Amourates, he was strangled in Andrianoupolis." Though the grammar is a bit corrupt, the narrative is clear. And it is of interest to note the allusion to the crossing being made without Manuel's permission. As for Djunaïd, however, ever the selfish opportunist, he hied himself back to Asia Minor for another attempt at winning himself a principality. He was soon brought to heel by Murad and duly executed. (See Muralt, p. 813, no. 22.) According to Konstantin the Philosopher, ed. Jagić, 314–315, ed. and trans. Braun, 57–58, Stefan Lazarević would have no part of Mustafa and supported Murad II; cf. Stanojević, 469. On Mustafa's fall in general, see Hammer, I, 405–410, trans. Hellert, II, 226–234; Iorga, *Geschichte,* 379–380; Pears, 153–154; Muralt, p. 807, nos. 10–14, under 1421.

merely a punitive demonstration, but an earnest attempt to take the city by assault.[107] Realizing their danger after the fall of the pretender, the Byzantines had sent ambassadors to the Sultan to attempt to mollify him. Murad would hear none of their pleas and treated them roughly.[108] One Turkish force was sent to attack Thessalonica.[109] On or about Wednesday June 10 an advance army of the Turks under the new Beylerbey of Rumelia, Michaloglu, encamped before the walls of Constantinople, after ravaging the surrounding countryside. And, a week or so thereafter, about June 20, Murad himself arrived.[110] Once more the city was invested by a Turkish siege.

107. We are fortunate in having, besides the extensive reports of the usual sources, a very valuable extended account of the siege by one John Kananos, Διήγησις περὶ τοῦ ἐν Κωνσταντινουπόλει γεγονότος πολέμου κατὰ τὸ ͵ϛϡλ´ ἔτος (text ed. Bekker, 1838, pp. 457–479 of the Bonn edition of [the Pseudo-]Phrantzes). The basic emphasis of the account is religious, and the central theme is the miraculous rescue of the city by the Virgin. As a result of this absorption, the author curiously neglects incidents reported by less extensive sources. But he does give a number of interesting details, with valuable reports of some of the fighting and particularly important descriptions of the Turkish siege operations, complete with a bewildering array of fascinating military terms.

108. Only two sources speak of this embassy. Sphrantzes, 1029D–1030A (Pseudo-Phrantzes, ed. Papadopoulos, 119–120; ed. Bonn, 116), names three ambassadors (Demetrius Cantacuzenus, Matthew Lascaris, and Angelos Philommates), and says that Murad brought them with him in chains when he advanced to the siege. Ducas, ed. Grecu, 229–231, ed. Bonn, 182–183, on the other hand, speaks of two embassies, the first in April; and he names different envoys (first Theologos Korax, on whom see n. 111 below; and then Palaeologus Lachanas and Markos Iagaris), also speaking in more detail of these diplomatic moves. He maintains that the ambassadors attempted to put the blame for the breach with the Turks on the arrogance of the dead Beylerbey and Vizier Bayazid, who would not fulfill Mechmed's will. Murad, says Ducas, was unmoved and detained the ambassadors a few days, then dismissing them when he was ready to march on Constantinople. Dölger, *Regesten*, nos. 3390 and 3391, p. 108, follows Ducas in distinguishing two separate embassies (April and June 8, respectively), making the one Sphrantzes reports the first of them.

109. This force was commanded by the general Baraq, the son of Evrenos, and it launched its attack on Thessalonica and its area on Saturday, June 13, 1422: so reports a valuable note from the interesting Thessalonian account book edited by Kougeas, p. 148, no. 49. For other sources, see Muralt, p. 808, no. 2, who, however, mistakenly places this attack at the end of 1421.

110. Sphrantzes, 1029D (Pseudo-Phrantzes, ed. Papadopoulos, 120; ed. Bonn, 116), says that Michaloglu (whom he calls Μιχάλμπεϊ) arrived on June 8, 1422 (his ascriptions of year being at last correct), and that Murad arrived on June 15. Kananos says (p. 458) that Μιχάλπαΐς arrived on Tuesday June 10, 1422 (a defective date in one way or another, since

The miscalculations of John VIII and the war faction had thus borne bitter fruit. Some elements among the Byzantines looked for a scapegoat. They found one in the person of a diplomatic interpreter, a Greek from Philadelphia in Asia Minor named Theologos Korax, who had emigrated to Constantinople during Timur's invasions, and who had been a favored negotiator with the Turks as a result of his knowledge of their language. Long under suspicion, justly or otherwise, for his popularity at the Turkish Porte, Theologos was blamed for the failure of yet another embassy, in which he had participated, to mollify Murad at the beginning of the siege. He was therefore accused of having entered into traitorous dealings with the new Sultan to surrender the city. Since John was occupied with the defense of the city, the alleged culprit was dragged before Manuel, in his retirement in the Monastery of the Peribleptos. Manuel attempted to question him fairly, but the Cretan contingents of his palace guard were so violently aroused against Theologos that a fair trial was difficult. The poor wretch was put to torture, and among his possessions were found letters and rich gifts which purportedly proved his guilt. His property was confiscated while he himself was sentenced to suffer the judicial mutilation of blinding, which was executed upon him by the eager Cretans with

June 10 was a Wednesday in that year; on the next page he repeats the date, again the 10th, this time without the day of the week), and then (p. 459) that Murad came on June 20 (no day given). Corroboration of Kananos' dating seems to come from a short chronicle which is usually very close in wording to Sphrantzes' text and obviously related to it. The Βϱ. χϱ. No. 1, p. 3, ll. 1–3, gives Wednesday June 10 for the arrival of Μιχάλπεϊς, and Saturday June 20 for Murad's appearance, both of which dates are in full agreement with the calendar for that year. These two sources disagree as to the time of day for the respective arrivals: Kananos says Michaloglu arrived "at the second hour of the day," while the chronicle says he came "at the fourth hour after midday." Kananos gives no hour for Murad, while the more detailed chronicle puts his arrival "at the sixth hour after midday." Kananos reckons Michaloglu's force at "twice five thousand," but gives no figures for Murad's force. Chalcocondyles, ed. Darkó, II, 7, ed. Bonn, 227–228, followed by the *Chron. Barb. 111*, 59–60, also distinguishes between the arrivals of Μιχάλογλη and Murad. Ducas, ed. Grecu, 231, ed. Bonn, 183, speaks only of one arrival and reckons Murad's army at 200,000. The inconsistencies between Kananos and the other sources are noted also by E. Colonna in her "Sulla Διήγησις di Giovanni Cananos," *Università di Napoli, Annali della Facoltà di Lettere e filosofia*, 7 (1957), 151–153; this article also includes (pp. 154–164) an Italian translation of the text. Cf. Muralt, pp. 809–810, nos. 7–9. (On Michaloglu's name, see Moravcsik, *Byzantinoturcica*, II, 191.)

Figure 27: *Constantinople Besieged by the Turks* (*in 1453*). Illuminated Miniature, Bibliothèque Nationale, Paris, *Ms. fr.* 9087, f. 207ᵛ (photo courtesy Bibliothèque Nationale, Paris; see Appendix XXIV, C, 7).

such zestful barbarism that he survived it no more than three days in his subsequent imprisonment.[111]

In such an atmosphere of suspicion and hysteria, the Byzantines were obliged to face this latest siege. Manuel, who had weathered so many such ordeals previously, was no longer in a position to give active leadership; but John was able to lead a vigorous defense personally and with distinction.[112] Although

111. Theologos Korax is first introduced when Ducas, ed. Grecu, 161–163, ed. Bonn, 121–123, gives his background and describes his earlier dealings with the Beylerbey and Vizier Bayazid, as well as his other close relations with the Turks. These relations aroused the suspicions of the Byzantines,. as events were to show, though not in the case of Manuel. Theologos Korax may well have been one of those who were named in a complaint of the Venetian Senate of March 11, 1418: Iorga, *Notes et extraits*, I, 276; Thiriet, *Régestes*, II, no. 1688, p. 163; see n. 61 above. The *Sapientes* protested against insults and abuses allegedly suffered by Venetians in Constantinople at the hands of Greeks, particularly two men, father and son, named Theologos. At any rate, he was among the emissaries sent to Murad after the fall of the pretender Mustafa, according to Ducas, ed. Grecu, 229–231, ed. Bonn, 182–183 (Dölger, *Regesten*, no. 3390, p. 108; see n. 108 above). The subsequent story of his last mission (Dölger, *Regesten*, no. 3392, p. 109) and of his fall, as told by Ducas, ed. Grecu, 231–235, ed. Bonn, 183–186, though not mentioned by any other Greek source, finds apparent confirmation in a Venetian source quoted by Iorga, *Notes et extraits*, p. 324, n. 1, which speaks of "a certain Theologo," a powerful and wealthy man who was blinded and deprived of his wealth on a charge of treacherous dealings with the Sultan. If the continuation of the story as Ducas tells it (ed. Grecu, 235, ed. Bonn, 186–187) is to be believed, there is perhaps confirmation of his guilt in the report that Murad, angry over Theologos' disgrace and death, blamed another Byzantine interpreter, one Michael Pylles, and had him tortured until he abjured his faith and adopted Islam. This episode of Theologos has been given attention only by Hammer, I, 411–412, trans. Hellert, II, 235–237, Berger de Xivrey, 175–177, Finlay, III, 489, and Muralt, p. 809, nos. 6 and 8 (mistakenly placing the episode *before* the beginning of the siege).

112. We have two interesting accounts of the respective dispositions of Manuel and John during the siege. Ducas, ed. Grecu, p. 233, ll. 4–6, ed. Bonn, p. 184, ll. 21–23, describes them (during the Theologos affair) thus: "For the Basileus was dwelling then in the monastery of the Peribleptos, weak and aged, but the Basileus John was busy at the defenses of the city." Compare this with Kananos, p. 471, ll. 13–16, who states that the old Emperor "was worn down by illness and old age and was unable to arm himself or to mount upon a horse, but was found within the palace and did what was in his power." And Kananos goes on to tell that John, on the other hand, went forth in arms to lead the defense. The fact that one of these sources places Manuel in the monastery and the other places him in the palace may or may not be of significance. Certainly, as we shall see (below, pp. 365 ff), he was to return from his retirement by the autumn of 1422 to direct the government once more, presumably from the palace.

the Turkish siege operations were elaborate and varied, complete with the use of primitive bombards—an ominous if temporarily ineffectual foreshadowing of their use in 1453—their efforts were not successful. The fortifications of Constantinople were still strong and the reported bravery of the defenders was sufficient to hold off the enemy. Nor were the assurances and signals of an alleged descendant of the Prophet, who had joined Murad's army as a kind of prophet-in-attendance, of any real help to the Turks.[113] Circumstances favored the Byzantines. The Venetians had considered attempting an effort at mediation between the Sultan and Byzantium,[114] but before they could make it, the siege had ended. Murad seems to have concentrated his hopes on one general assault on Monday, August 24, which was beaten back by the defenders, with the aid, they were convinced, of the city's traditional defender and protectress, the Virgin herself.[115]

113. After a valuable digression on the organization of the Janissaries and the establishment of the beylerbeylik, the administrative division of the Osmanli state, Chalcocondyles, ed. Darkó, I, 10–12, ed. Bonn, 231–233, concentrates his account of the siege on a discussion of Murad's bombards (τηλεβόλοι) and other firearms. The *Chron. Barb. 111*, 60, merely refers to these λουμπάρδες in passing in its very sketchy account of the actual siege and fighting. Otherwise, our sole information on the specific operations and events of the siege may be found in the work of Kananos, who describes in emotional terms the active fighting and the reactions of the Greeks. Kananos is also the only Greek source to speak of the Turks' prophet, whom he calls Μηρσαΐτες (cf. Moravcsik, *Byzantinoturcica*, II, 189), and whom he describes with proper Christian scorn and contempt; cf. Muralt, p. 810, no. 11.

114. On August 26, 1422, the Venetian Senate issued instructions to its *bailo* at Constantinople, who was to assure the Emperor of Venetian friendship, but should tell him that the Venetians would be unable to send any help to the besieged city before the next spring. For such help the Emperor should inquire of the Genoese and the Hospitalers. Meanwhile, the *bailo* was to offer mediation between the Emperor and the Sultan, even if Murad had already left the vicinity of the city. Provisions were also made for the possibility that the Emperor might be at peace with the Turks by that time. For this deliberation, see Iorga, *Notes et extraits*, I, 323–324, and Thiriet, *Régestes*, II, no. 1855, p. 197. On the same date the Senate ordered one of its commanders to go to Constantinople in the course of his mission, with alternate instructions in case of either peace between Emperor and Sultan or of a Turkish siege by land and sea. At the same time, the Senate discussed the possibility of making a naval demonstration before the Turks at the city. Text, Sathas, I, no. 79, pp. 118–123; cf. Thiriet, no. 1854, p. 197.

115. Sphrantzes, 1030A (Pseudo-Phrantzes, ed. Papadopoulos, 120; ed. Bonn, 116–117), gives the date of the general assault as August 22, but this is almost surely wrong in view of the weight of opposing testimony. Βρ. χρ. No. 6, p. 9, l. 8, gives August 24, 6930 (1422); and No. 47, p. 82,

After a brief duration of some two and one-half months, Murad's siege was broken and the Sultan abandoned it.

The spectacular misfiring of the war faction's temporary ascendancy had discredited it or, at least, its policies. In later years it was to emerge again with renewed vigor, when reconstituted on the side of the project for Church union. But its influence was apparently in eclipse for the time being. As a result of John's singular miscalculation and lack of judgment, his father, whose semiretirement in 1421 was by no means a total abdication, once again asserted his wiser will in the running of the

ll. 83–84, gives the date as the feast of St. Eutyches (which is August 24), in the wrong year (6931) but in the correct indiction (15). (Of the other short chronicles, the *Chron. Vat. gr. 162*, no. 22, pp. 211–212, ll. 104–105, simply refers to the attack without date.) This date, August 24, 1422, is also precisely the one given by the eyewitness Kananos (pp. 478–479), who this time gives the day of the week (Monday) correctly. Again, the Sphrantzes-related Βρ. χρ. No. 1 supports Kananos on dating and even gives the duration of the attack—surprisingly short, one would think. Its text (p. 3, ll. 3–6) reads thus: "And on the 24th of August, on Monday, he [Murad] assaulted it, that is Constantinople, from an hour before the beginning of midday to the completion of the second [hour] after midday, that is two hours." Kananos (p. 479) provides positively Herodotean casualty lists: of the Turks, "beyond a thousand" wounded or dead; of the Byzantines, less than one hundred wounded and no more than thirty dead. The Βρ. χρ. No. 47, p. 82, l. 85, is content to observe that "the Romans were victorious and many thousand Turks were darkened [i.e., slain]."

The long description by Kananos (pp. 471–479) is obviously that of a participant, or at least a witness, and is very highly colored and emotional. He tells (pp. 477–478), in great detail and conviction, of the appearance of the Virgin and of the divine aid which the defenders were doubtless convinced had come to their assistance. Sphrantzes, 1030A, is content to ascribe the departure of Murad to the "aid of God," leaving it at that. The reference by Chalcocondyles, ed. Darkó, II, 11–12, ed. Bonn, 233, to the assault and scaling attempt and the vague comments of the *Chron. Barb. 111*, 60, avoid any pious editorializing. While the allusions by Ducas, ed. Grecu, 235, ed. Bonn, 187, to Murad's siege operations come in the midst of a narrative which, as we are about to see, ascribes Murad's departure to more practical causes. Konstantin the Philosopher, ed. Jagić, 316, ed. and trans. Braun, 59, makes only passing allusion to Murad's siege, in the light of his good relations with Stefan Lazarević; cf. Stanojević, pp. 469–470. A tradition, then already legendary, of the supernatural deliverance of the city from the Turks is noted by Vasiliev, "Pero Tafur," 110–111, in the travel account of 1437–38 by this Castilian; Vasiliev is almost surely correct in associating the legend with this siege. On the siege in general, see Hammer, I, 412–415, trans. Hellert, II, 237–242; Iorga, *Geschichte*, 381; Pears, 114 and 152; Muralt, p. 810, nos. 13–14. Perhaps through a misprint, Runciman, *The Fall of Constantinople*, 13, puts the siege in 1423.

government.[116] In spite of his weariness and declining health, Manuel chose to take the initiative himself, at the height of Murad's siege.

Thanks to his son's folly, the situation had deteriorated to such a point that the only course now open seemed to be a repetition of John's very act: the support of a rival to Murad. What had before been a reckless blunder now became a political necessity. Presumably after further attempts to win peace from Murad had failed, Manuel turned to Murad's surviving brother, a youth of about thirteen, also named Mustafa. Writing to the boy's guardian and tutor, one Ilyas, Manuel proposed to support the little prince's claim to the throne against Murad. The offer was accepted. Frustrated in his great assault against Constantinople, Murad now realized the danger that this new threat of civil war would mean to him. He tacitly acknowledged Manuel's diplomatic parry by ending his investment of the city, departing from under its walls on September 6, 1422.[117]

116. We have already noted his role, retired as he may have been, in the Theologos affair. And there is ample indication of Manuel's dominating position in the government in the autumn of 1422: see n. 119 below.

117. Dölger, *Regesten,* no. 3394, p. 109. The principal source for this diplomatic move is Ducas, ed. Grecu, 235–237, ed. Bonn, 187–188, who makes indisputably clear that it was Manuel's step, even though the Emperor is curiously described as "being bedridden, and having, so to speak, death before his eyes each day." He says that one of Murad's young brothers was murdered, but that Mustafa was spared, under the tutelage of one Ilyas ('Ελιέζ) ; and he makes clear that Murad departed from Constantinople only after this plot had begun to be put into effect. But this latter point is not conveyed by Chalcocondyles, ed. Darkó, 12, ed. Bonn, 233, and the *Chron. Barb. 111,* 60, who rather imply that Murad's ending of the siege preceded the resort to the young Mustafa, which was the result of the failure of two peace-seeking embassies to Murad, one before the breaking of the siege and one after it; cf. Dölger, *Regesten,* no. 3393, p. 109. According to these sources, apparently Murad's abandonment of his attempt on Constantinople was simply the result of failure and had nothing to do with Byzantine diplomatic moves. But there seems to be no reason why the two separate accounts should be incompatible, and if there is no concrete evidence one way or another it seems quite likely that the Byzantines would have tried conciliation with Murad once more before resorting to the young Mustafa.

These two latter sources are also the only ones to give at this point the age (thirteen years) of the young prince (whose guardian Chalcocondyles identifies as 'Αλιάζης; for his name, see Nimet, no. 6, p. 34, and Moravcsik, *Byzantinoturcica,* II, 123). All of these matters are avoided by Sphrantzes, 1030A (Pseudo-Phrantzes, ed. Papadopoulos, 120; ed. Bonn, 116–117), who simply says that Murad withdrew from the city on September 6. In view of the frequent unreliability of his chronology for this period, this state-

Unfortunately, just at the crucial point of Manuel's last desperate diplomatic activity, his health broke. The aged ruler was already involved with the Papal legate, who had arrived on September 10, had been received briefly on September 16, and was due to have a subsequent audience for the accomplishment of his mission.[118] Then, on Wednesday September 30, the young Mustafa, or "Moustaphopoulos," arrived in the city with his supporters and exploiters to accept the Byzantine alliance. But on the next day, Thursday, October 1, 1422, the seventy-three-year-old Emperor was stricken by a paralytic stroke. The government was paralyzed with him for some days thereafter, until it was obvious that John would have to assume full responsibility in dealing with both the young Mustafa and the Papal embassy.[119]

ment might well be regarded with caution. But it is perhaps confirmed with some reliability by the more precise entry of the Βϱ. χϱ. No. 1, p. 3, ll. 6–7: "And on the 6th of September of the 1st indiction of the 6931st year [1422], on Sunday, he [Murad] went out from here an hour before the beginning of day." Ducas simply observes that when Murad withdrew he had been besieging the city for three months. Cf. Pears, 114–115; Muralt, p. 811, no. 1.

118. On this Papal embassy, see pp. 327 ff. above.

119. Sphrantzes, 1030A–B (Pseudo-Phrantzes, ed. Papadopoulos, 120–121; ed. Bonn, 117), gives the dates (without days), and his dates have usually been accepted at face value: e.g. Muralt, p. 811, nos. 4–5. That this acceptance is justified is perhaps shown by the closely related Βϱ. χϱ. No. 1, p. 3, ll. 7–13, which gives the same dates, and adds the days of the week. The chronicle's only divergence is in time of day. It specifies that Μουσταφόπασας crossed from "the East" "at the 5th hour after midday" on Wednesday the 30th; that he arrived "at the 3rd hour" on the 1st of October and "did bow down to our sovereign the Basileus, the holy lord Manuel" (Sphrantzes only says that he arrived to do so); and that Manuel had his stroke "at the first hour after midday" on the same day (not "after breakfast," μετὰ τὸ ἄϱιστον, as Sphrantzes says).

Without including dates, Ducas, ed. Grecu, p. 237, ll. 7–11, ed. Bonn, p. 188, ll. 9–14, gives a somewhat exaggerated representation of the facts: "And the Basileus Manuel lay breathing his last, having suffered a stroke, and in three days he discharged his debt, being most wise and virtuous in both discretion and propriety, leaving the realm to his son John, the last [*sic*] Basileus of the Romans, who was also first among all in qualities of rule." (The historian was apparently so carried away by his rhetorical balancing of the expression ". . . ὑστάτῳ . . . πϱώτῳ . . ." that he characterizes John as "the last Basileus of the Romans," which is of course incorrect; curiously enough, Ducas again makes this erroneous characterization of John at another point, ed. Grecu, 129, ed. Bonn, 93–94). The phrase ἀπέδωκε τὸ χϱεών is, of course, a euphemism for dying: and Ducas soon after (ed. Grecu, 327, ed. Bonn, 189) says that Manuel died in this same year, that is, 1422. This statement is baldly incorrect, for Manuel did not die yet. (Surprisingly, however, some of this confusion seems to have crept into the

The exact nature of the terms agreed upon with Mustafa's supporters is not clear, although it may have included a marriage alliance of the young prince with the Imperial family.[120] But,

thinking of Mompherratos, Οἱ Παλ. ἐν πελ., 52.) But the seriousness of his stroke apparently misled many of his contemporaries. Iorga, *Notes et extraits*, I, pp. 335–336, n. 4, cites a Venetian source which mistakenly reports the death of Manuel in early 1423. Likewise reports Sanuto, ed. Muratori, 973D; and Baronius-Raynaldus, 1423, no. 26 (Vol. 27, p. 556); cf. also Muralt, pp. 313–314, no. 27. (Muralt refers later, p. 816, no. 4, to a Venetian report of Manuel's death, again false, on April 18, 1425, three months before the actual event.)

Chalcocondyles, ed. Darkó, II, 12, ed. Bonn, 233–234, and the *Chron. Barb. 111*, 60, ignore Manuel and his disability and simply have the Turkish prince come to Constantinople to arrange terms of the alliance and then depart. Sphrantzes, however, says that, when Manuel was stricken, the prince was kept waiting in the city "many days" to no avail, and he then moved out to Selymbria briefly; after which he returned to Constantinople and passed back to Anatolia. It was presumably on the second trip through the city (if Sphrantzes' statement is correct, as it probably is) that John, by that time having assumed full power, arranged terms of the Byzantine alliance. The date of such transactions is not known. We do know, however, that negotiations with the Papal embassy were resumed not very long after Manuel's stroke, for John received the legate privately on October 15, and on October 20 John and the Patriarch formally heard the embassy on its business: see p. 328 above. Manuel's personal involvement with the Papal mission, and especially with the reception of Mustafa, and then the temporary disruption of these negotiations which his disability plainly caused, are irrefutable evidence that, at least by the end of Murad's siege, the old Emperor was again the hub of the Byzantine government, in spite of his ill health and age.

120. The anonymous and not very reliable late sixteenth-century *Historia politica Constantinopoleos*, 4–5, together with the virtually identical Ἐκ. χρον., 2–3, and derived from the latter, the history of the Pseudo-Dorotheos of Monemvasia, p. 405, all state that Mustafa was given as a wife the daughter of Hilario Doria, husband of Manuel's illegitimate daughter Zampia. This assertion is accepted by A. T. Papadopulos, *Versuch einer Genealogie der Palaiologen*, 70, who names this Imperial granddaughter Isabella, on the basis of the seemingly undocumented imagination of Hopf, *Chroniques gréco-romanes*, Table XII, 2 (who mistakenly makes the illegitimate Zampia/Isabella Manuel's half-sister, instead of his daughter). But the related sources aforementioned are the only ones to speak of this betrothal. Since there is a report of a marriage of a daughter of Doria to another Turkish prince (Suleyman: see above, p. 253, n. 88), there may be some doubt about the statement as a confusion of facts, especially in view of the tender youth of the prince in comparison with the doubtless greater age of Doria's daughter. Moreover, Sphrantzes' silence on the point is probably of some significance as well. On the other hand, since these texts, which relate the supposed marriage, speak thereafter of Murad's wrath, his futile attacks on the capital, and his wars against the Byzantines for "near to three years," is it possible that they confused the two Mustafas and that the one involved in such a marriage might actually have been the false pretender of 1421–22? Dölger, *Regesten*, ignores these dealings.

whatever the arrangements were, they soon proved futile. After some immediate success had favored the young Mustafa's cause, his energetic brother crossed to Anatolia, perhaps as early as January, certainly by spring of 1423. The little prince was betrayed to his brother and was delivered to the inevitable bowstring.[121] The puppet revolution died aborning. Thus ended pitifully Byzantium's last attempt—and even possibility—to intervene in the Turkish succession.

Byzantium was therefore left in a very awkward position during 1423. Murad was still hostile, if temporarily distracted in the beginning of the year by the revolt on behalf of the young Mustafa. Yet, there was still danger, as was recognized by more than the Byzantines alone. In spite of the disappointment of the Papal mission of the previous autumn,[122] Pope Martin V had not given up his interest in the Eastern question. In late winter of 1423 he sent Antonio de Massa, who had been the Papal legate to Constantinople, to seek aid from Venice for still-threatened Byzantium. On March 31, the Senate heard the Papal message and consulted on what aid the West ought to send. It was concluded that ten galleys were needed to augment those of the Emperor as soon as possible. Venice offered to send three at its own expense, but with the familiar qualification that the other Christian states must provide their contributions at the same

121. A complete and clear account is given in an important but generally overlooked short chronicle entry in the Thessalonian notebook edited by Kougeas, p. 154, no. 88. This text gives the date January 24, 6931, first indiction (1423), for Murad's crossing. But then it gives January 20 of the same year as the date of Mustafa's execution. In his discussion of these entries, Iorga, "Sur les deux prétendants Moustafa du XVe siècle," *Revue historique du sud-est européen,* 10 (1933), 13, suggests that we should read *February* 20 for the second date. But this suggestion is not fully justified by the wording of the text; hence, its value for dating is perhaps open to some doubt. Sphrantzes, 1030B (Pseudo-Phrantzes, ed. Papadopoulos, 121; ed. Bonn, 117), gives the season of Murad's crossing in general; Ducas, ed. Grecu, 237, ed. Bonn, 188–189, claims that Mustafa was only six years of age at his death (in conflict with Chalcocondyles, who makes him about thirteen: see above, n. 117), and who alone of the sources makes no mention of the tutor Ilyas' betrayal of the prince. See also Chalcocondyles, ed. Darkó, II, 12–13, ed. Bonn, 234–235, and the *Chron. Barb. 111,* 60. Cf. Muralt, 812, no. 16; Pears, 154. See, further, Konstantin the Philosopher, ed. Jagić, 315, ed. and trans. Braun, 58–59, who mistakenly places the episode of the young Mustafa *before* Murad's siege of Constantinople; this error is overlooked by Stanojević, 469. Alderson, Table V (p. 30), places the execution of Mustafa in December of 1423, surely too late. See also Hammer, I, 415–417, trans. Hellert, II, 242–245; Iorga, *Geschichte,* 381–382.

122. See above, pp. 327–329.

time. A proposal to join in some sort of accord for this purpose with the Genoese, the Hospitalers of Rhodes, and others was rejected by the Senate.[123] And, needless to say, such discussions produced nothing practical.

Unfortunately, we have little specific information on Byzantine affairs during the early months of 1423, but further storms lay ahead when Murad was freed from his internal troubles over Mustafa by the spring. Thus free, the Sultan apparently still cherished aggressive intentions against Constantinople itself.[124] And, as if such danger to the capital alone were not enough, there seems to have been friction in the Imperial family during the summer, involving Manuel's next-to-youngest son Demetrius and the Emperor's son-in-law Hilario Doria.[125] But Murad presum-

123. Iorga, *Notes et extraits*, I, 332–333; Thiriet, *Régestes*, II, no. 1876, p. 201; cf. Gill, *The Council of Florence*, 37–38.

124. Such is the assumption made by the Venetian Senate in its deliberation of June 8, 1423: partial text, Iorga, *Notes et extraits*, I, 336–337; cf. Thiriet, *Régestes*, II, no. 1885, p. 204. Note the comment by Ducas, ed. Grecu, p. 239, ll. 5–8, ed. Bonn, p. 189, l. 21 to p. 190, l. 1: "But with the Basileus John he was not by any means reconciled, but he nourished an enmity admitting of no truce. As he was not able, indeed, to do anything against the City, he directed the wrath in his mind toward the regions of Thessaly and toward the invasions of the Peloponnesus." Whereupon the historian speaks of Murad's attacks on Greece and his blockade of Thessalonica.

125. Sphrantzes, 1030C (Pseudo-Phrantzes, ed. Papadopoulos, 121; ed. Bonn, 118), gives the bare report that, during this summer, Manuel's son Demetrius, Hilario Doria, and the latter's (son-)in-law Georgios Izaoul fled to Galata, from which they intended to go over to the Turks; but instead they went to Hungary. Cf. Gill, "John VIII Palaeologus," 156 (109); and Muralt, p. 813, no. 19. The related Βϱ. χϱ. No. 1, p. 3, ll. 13–15, is even more terse, stating that on July 4 Demetrius crossed to Galata with Hilario Doria (Izaoul is not mentioned), and that on the 6th of the same month Demetrius himself (and apparently without even Doria) sailed to Hungary on a galley. We have no information on the incident other than these simple statements.

Demetrius was still well under the age of twenty at this time, but, in view of his reckless and selfish conduct in later years, such an act this early is wholly credible. What its cause might have been is not known, but it could have been the first of many open personality clashes with his eldest brother. (Iorga, *Geschichte*, 382–383, suggests that he was attempting to follow in the path of Andronicus IV and John VII and win support from the Turks as a pretender—at least a sound possibility.) What is even more curious is the involvement of Doria. Why should this old henchman of Manuel cast in his lot with the irresponsible young prince? There is one possibility. Could this suggested disaffection have some relationship to the supposed marriage of one of Doria's daughters to the defeated young prince Mustafa, if it did take place? Such speculation is provocative, but without any concrete basis. In the absence of any other available evidence this episode remains a mystery.

ably had learned not to waste his strength on the well-fortified capital itself. Instead, he directed his wrath against other Byzantine holdings, specifically the Morea and Thessalonica.

The former was the first to feel his vengeance. Theodore II had foreseen the growing Turkish threat to the Peloponnesus and had made various moves to win the cooperation of Venice in the defense of the Isthmian fortifications, but with little success.[126] In late spring the dreaded blow fell. An Osmanli army under the General Turachan hurled itself upon the peninsula. The great Hexamilion, the object of such toil and concern on Manuel's part, was as nothing. No attempt was made to man or defend it, and on May 21–22 the Turks passed through it as a hot knife would through butter, leaving it ruined once again. Ravaging as they went, the Turks met with serious opposition only from the large Albanian element, who were crushingly defeated and massacred at Tavia (the modern Davia, and the ancient Mainalos, in Arcadia) on June 5, 1423. Turachan's army made no effort at permanent conquest, but it departed only after having dealt a serious blow to the Morea.[127]

126. See n. 26 above; cf. also Zakythinos, *Le Despotat grec,* I, 192–196.

127. Our most important source for the dating of the fall of the Hexamilion is an anonymous Venetian letter (partial text ed. Iorga, *Notes et extraits,* I, 334–335), which recounts the desertion of the wall by its defenders and its destruction by Turachan, all on May 21; it speaks also of the Turkish ravages in the Morea. General allusions to the entire episode are made by Chalcocondyles, ed. Darkó, II, pp. 16–17 and 58–59, ed. Bonn, pp. 238–239 and 283, with no date; and by Sphrantzes, 1030B (Pseudo-Phrantzes, ed. Papadopoulos, 121; ed. Bonn, 117–118), who dates at least the first of the two events in May of 1423. (The *Chron. Barb. 111,* 61, mistakenly places Turachan's campaign after the conclusion of peace with the Sultan, and makes the destruction of the Hexamilion a fulfillment of its terms; but it does speak correctly of the massacre of the Albanians.) Of the short chronicles, the Βρ. χρ. No. 19, p. 36, ll. 33–35, gives the date of the fall of the Hexamilion as May 22, 1423, cites the Turkish progress in the Morea, and refers to the slaughter of the Albanians without date. No. 27, p. 47, ll. 65–67 (originally published at the end of the Bonn edition of Ducas, p. 518, ll. 13–17), gives almost exactly the same entry, with the addition of the date for the massacre at Tavia. For a harmonization of these two texts, see Loenertz' *Chron. br. mor.,* no. 28, pp. 408–409, and his commentary, pp. 434–435. The terse entry in the short chronicle published by Veēs, no. 6, p. 61, simply refers to the destruction of the Hexamilion in 1423. See Zakythinos, *Le Despotat grec,* I, 196–198; Mompherratos, Οἱ Παλ. ἐν Πελ., 52–53; Miller, *The Latins in the Levant,* 387; Hammer, I, 417, trans. Hellert, II, 246; Iorga, *Geschichte,* 382; Lampros, "Τὰ τείχη," 470–471. On the dating, see also Loenertz, "Pour l'histoire," 158 (who does not use the

Thessalonica was a less easy target, but the outcome of the Turkish attack on it was more serious than that from the attack on the Morea. The siege of the city by the Turks was a problem enough for the Despot Andronicus. In addition, Manuel's third son, though barely twenty-three years of age, was already suffering from the ravages of disease and was physically handicapped in bearing this burden.[128] But this disability was by no means the sole reason for the ensuing step taken, since the Imperial house was well supplied with healthy sons who might have replaced him. It was rather the fact that a vigorous Turkish siege ultimately reduced Thessalonica to such hardship and dire extremity and so taxed Byzantium's limited resources that it was decided to offer the city to the Venetians, with the sole condition that they respect Thessalonian rights and institutions. This extraordinary offer was considered by the Venetian Senate on July 7, 1423. The *Sapientes* accepted it and instructed an agent to proceed to Constantinople and assure himself of the Imperial government's wishes in arranging the cession.[129]

At the end of the month, on July 27, the instructions were given for taking over the city, with renewed concern over the approval of the government in Constantinople.[130] By September 14,

Venetian letter). For a discussion of the town of Tavia, see Lampros, "Tavia, eine verkannte mittelgriechische Stadt," *Byz. Zeitschr.*, 7 (1898), 309–315.

128. Andronicus' malady is variously identified. Ducas, ed. Grecu, 247, ed. Bonn, 197, speaks of it as epilepsy (ἡ ἱερὰ νόσος), while Chalcocondyles, ed. Darkó, I, 193, ed. Bonn, 205, calls it elephantiasis. The *Chron. Vat. gr. 162*, no. 15, p. 209, l. 67, and also no. 21, p. 211, ll. 100–101, describes Andronicus as a leper (λωβός); and likewise the Pseudo-Dorotheos, 492; and this attribution of leprosy is also followed by Spandugnino, *De la origine deli imperatori ottomani* (ed. Sathas, *Documents inédits*, IX), p. 149, l. 6, who calls Andronicus a "lazaroso."

129. The text of this important deliberation may be found in Sathas, I, no. 86, pp. 133–139; and a facsimile of part of it in a plate facing p. 32 of K. D. Mertzios' Μνημεῖα μακεδονικῆς ἱστορίας (Thessalonica, 1947); cf. Thiriet, *Régestes*, II, no. 1892, pp. 205–206. For more on this deliberation and that cited in the next note, see below, p. 381 and n. 154. It is important to stress that the central government was well informed of the affairs of Thessalonica, and took an active interest in them. Note, for instance, Manuel's personal involvement in some internal affairs of the city just two years earlier, in a bull dated June 4, 1421, addressed by Manuel to his son the Despot Andronicus and concerning a dispute over some property in the city: Dölger, *Regesten*, no. 3389, p. 108. Its text was published by I. Iveriotes in Γρηγόριος ὁ Παλαμᾶς, 1 (1917), 541–542; cf. the same author in the same journal, 5 (1921), pp. 844 ff. For another such document, see Dölger, *Regesten*, no. 3387, pp. 108–109.

130. The text of this equally important deliberation may be found in

all was arranged, and a Venetian squadron had reached the city to assume its government.[131] Thus did Thessalonica, long the second city of the Empire, pass once and for all out of the hands of the Byzantines.[132] Not that the Venetians were to enjoy its pos-

Sathas, I, no. 89, pp. 141–150; and a complete facsimile on a series of eight plates facing p. 40 of Mertzios' study; cf. the summary of Thiriet, *Régestes*, II, no. 1896, pp. 207–208. For the arrangements of July 13–25 for sending the Venetian agents, see Thiriet, nos. 1894, 1896, and 1897. For other provisions for establishing Venetian authority in Thessalonica, see Thiriet, nos. 1902, 1914, 1933, 1935, 1942, 1944, 1947, 1962, 1988, and so on.

131. This is the date from which the Senate reckoned its control of the city in its deliberation of October 20, 1423: Iorga, *Notes et extraits*, I, 347; Thiriet, *Régestes*, II, no. 1908, p. 210. Cf. Lemerle, "La Domination vénetienne à Thessalonique," *Miscellanea G. Galbiati* (=*Fontes Ambrosiani*, 27, 1951), 222. The date September 13 is given for Andronicus' surrender of the city in a notice appended by Loenertz to his edition of the *Chron. Vat. gr. 162*, no. 21, p. 211.

132. This Byzantine cession of Thessalonica to Venice has been the subject of some confusion. According to Ducas, ed. Grecu, 247–249, ed. Bonn, 197–198, it was the citizens of Thessalonica themselves, oppressed by the hardships of the siege, who agreed to offer the city to Venetian control, regardless of the wishes of the ailing Andronicus. On the other hand, all the other Greek sources speak of it as purely the Despot's affair. Chalcocondyles, ed. Darkó, I, 192–193, ed. Bonn, 205–206, simply says that Andronicus, unable to guard the city himself, yielded (ἀπέδοτο) it to the Venetians. Subsequently, ed. Darkó, II, 13–14, ed. Bonn, 235, he says that the Greeks in general yielded it to the Venetians for the same reason. But the remaining sources speak of a sale.

In a spurious passage which might alone be enough to demonstrate its inauthenticity, the Pseudo-Phrantzes (ed. Papadopoulos, 124–125, ed. Bonn, 122) says that Andronicus sold it to Venice for 50,000 gold pieces. (This same text, 64, confusedly interpolates this statement also into an earlier context, leading Muralt, p. 783, no. 13, to place the event fantastically in the summer of 1403; on this error by the Pseudo-Phrantzes, see Loenertz, "Autour du Chronicon Maius," 307 f. Muralt, p. 803, no. 17, then reports the sale by Andronicus once again, also on the basis of this text, but inexplicably in 1418! Finally, claiming Venetian sources, Muralt gives a sketchy account of the sale of the city a third time to Venice—without mentioning Andronicus—for the same 50,000 *hyperpyra*, in the correct year of 1423: pp. 813–814, nos. 20, 27, and 29.) The *Chron. Barb. 111*, 60, also gives the sum of 50,000 gold pieces. The *Chron. Vat. gr. 162*, no. 21, p. 211, ll. 101–102, gives 20,000 Venetian florins as the price.

Accepting the false testimony of the Pseudo-Phrantzes, modern writers had been wont to popularize the idea that Andronicus simply sold the city as his private possession. Yet, even Miller, in his sketch "Frankish and Venetian Greece: Salonika," republished in *Essays in the Latin Orient*, 280, though using a combination of stories, still stresses the idea of Ducas' account. And, as a result of the attention which Mertzios has drawn to the documentary evidence in his important study (in general, pp. 34–99), the

session to any great degree, for the city was to be wrested from them by the Turks after seven perilous years, on March 29, 1430.[133]

As 1423 drew to its end, the Byzantine situation was no better. Murad remained hostile. It was obvious that some outside assistance was needed. John VIII recognized this. Whether this

old and oversimplified view of the Pseudo-Phrantzes can be completely discarded. Cf. Lemerle, "La Domination vénetienne," 219–222; Ostrogorsky, *History of the Byzantine State*, p. 497, and n. 3. See also Heyd, *Histoire du commerce du Levant au moyen âge*, II, p. 280.

Yet, it is easy to see how the fiction of a personal sale by Andronicus might have sprung up. Note that, in its instructions of July 27, 1423, the Venetian Senate did concede (ed. Sathas, I, p. 144, ll. 17–21) that the *Signoria* might promise the Despot the annual sum of 20,000 to 40,000 aspers to offset his expenses and loss of income in Thessalonica: from compensation to purchase is a small step for the historian's imagination. Moreover, there are also various reports of territories offered to Andronicus in recompense for his surrender of Thessalonica: cf. Vakalopoulos' article, "Συμβολὴ στὴν ἱστορία τῆς Θεσσαλονίκης ἐπὶ Βενετοκρατίας (1423–1430)," Τόμος Κ. 'Αρμενοπούλου, pp. 133–136. According to Chalcocondyles, ed. Darkó, I, 193, ed. Bonn, 206, Andronicus went from Thessalonica to Mantinea in the Peloponnesus. At any rate, he was in Constantinople when he died on March 4, 1428. According to our sole reference to his death, Sphrantzes, 1034D (Pseudo-Phrantzes, ed. Papadopoulos, 137, ed. Bonn, 134), he had retired to the Pantokrator Monastery where he had taken the monastic name of Akakios; and there he was buried: cf. A. T. Papadopoulos, *Versuch*, 62. He left a son, John, of whom little is known: cf. *ibid*. For a recent critique of the work of Thiriet, Vakalopoulos, Mertzios, and others, on Thessalonica and the Venetians, see G. E. Ferrari, "Recenti studi veneto-tessalonicensi," *Archivio veneto*, V, 52/53 (1953), 137–145. More recently, J. Tzaras, "La fin d'Andronic Paléologue, dernier despote de Thessalonique," *Revue des études sud-est européenes*, 3 (1965), 419–432, has argued for accepting Chalcocondyles' report of Andronicus' retirement to and death in Mantinea, also contesting some of Mertzios' conclusions.

133. For good summaries of the Venetian rule in Thessalonica, see Lemerle, "La Domination vénetienne," pp. 222–225; Heyd, II, 280–281; Thiriet, *La Romanie vénitienne*, 371–372; and Miller, "Frankish and Venetian Greece: Salonika," 280–281. In more detail, see Vakalopoulos, *A History of Thessaloniki*, 65–75, and *id.*, "Συμβολή," 136–149. During their rule of Thessalonica, and the hostilities with Murad over it, the Venetians used the city also as a base for aiding the pretensions of yet another false Mustafa, who apparently also claimed to be the son of Bayazid. He seems to have been received first by the Venetians in the summer of 1423 (deliberation of July 10: Iorga, *Notes et extraits*, I, 339; Thiriet, *Régestes*, II, no. 1893, p. 206). Thereafter he was exploited by the Venetians around Thessalonica: see Thiriet, nos. 1949, 1980, 2000, 2004, 2018, 2132, and 2134. (During this period another Turkish prince, identified as "Ismaël," is referred to in Sathas, I, no. 96, p. 158, and in Thiriet, no. 1931: is this the same individual as the new false Mustafa?) But little is really known about this latest pretender: cf. Lemerle, "La Domination vénetienne," 222–223. See also Iorga, "Sur les deux prétendants Moustafa," 12–13.

recognition was a result of his father's reasserted influence in the light of the 1421 miscalculation or whether it was simply an understanding on his own part, we do not know. But by the end of 1423 John had returned actively to his father's old efforts to win Western military aid and to achieve this specifically by renewing mediation between its expected commander, Sigismund, and Venice. Previous efforts in this direction, as we have seen,[134] had not been notably successful in the past. Probably as a result of this failure, John chose to adopt his father's technique of personal diplomacy. He apparently had no intentions of duplicating Manuel's itinerary in the latter's great journey of 1400–03—certainly the situation of France vis-à-vis England would have prohibited that course anyway. Rather, John's mission was specifically concentrated on the question of Sigismund and Venice.

John sailed from Constantinople on November 15, 1423, leaving as his regent his brother Constantine,[135] who was then not quite twenty years of age. John's immediate destination was Venice, where the Senate allocated money on December 11 for the young Emperor's reception and expenses.[136] John was brought on a Venetian vessel, and on December 15 he reached the Lagoon City, where he was received with full honors.[137] He remained in Venice for more than a month. We have ample evidence of some of his transactions with the *Serenissima*. At the outset John raised the principal points: a request for Venetian assistance to

134. See pp. 332–339 above.

135. Sphrantzes, 1030C (Pseudo-Phrantzes, ed. Papadopoulos, 121, ed. Bonn, 118); cf. Muralt, p. 814, no. 3. In a possibly corrupt and certainly less precise entry, the related Βϱ. χϱ. No. 1, p. 3, ll. 15–17, puts John's departure, in Venetian galleys, on November 14, and sets his destination vaguely as "Φϱαγκία," which might be taken simply to mean the West in general. On Constantine's regency, see p. 381 below.

136. Iorga, *Notes et extraits*, I, 349; Sanuto, 972C–D.

137. Sanuto, 971C, who reports that John wished to go to the Pope ("in Ponente"—?) to ask for aid against the Turks. But there is no other evidence for any such visit to the Pope, or, for that matter, for any such intention on John's part; although it would not have been impossible as a planned adjunct to what was plainly John's primary mission. John's arrival in Venice (with the same date, December 15), and his negotiations for help there, are also described by another Venetian source cited in Baronius-Raynaldus, 1423, no. 26 (Vol. 27, p. 556); cf. Muralt, p. 814, no. 4. Citing other modern authors, D. J. Geanakoplos, in his *Greek Scholars in Venice, Studies in the Dissemination of Greek Learning from Byzantium to Western Europe* (Cambridge, Mass., 1962), 30, speaks erroneously of Manuel II himself as the Emperor received in Venice in 1423, instead of the actual John VIII.

Constantinople, and a renewed offer of Byzantine mediation with Sigismund. On December 30, 1423, the Senate gave its response. On the question of Venetian aid, the Senate recalled its former efforts on behalf of Byzantium and pointed out that it intended to organize a powerful fleet for the Levant in the spring; if, therefore, John was successful in his mission and was able to convince other Christian powers to contribute specific aid to Byzantium, then—and, as ever, only then—Venice would add its share. As to mediation, the Venetians declared that Sigismund had always been the obstacle to a peaceful settlement; in view of his continued hostility, the Senate said, Venice had been obliged to enter into a league with the Duke of Milan, Filippo-Maria Visconti, who was now to be informed of new peace moves and whose approval was necessary.[138] On the same day the Senate also considered other details which had been raised by John and his embassy.[139]

John tarried on in Venice. To ease his financial difficulties the Senate ordered on January 9, 1424, a daily allotment of money to enable him to pay his expenses,[140] and on January 13 it voted John a loan of 1,500 ducats which he had requested.[141] The Emperor's delay in Venice was the result of his having to await the reaction of the Duke of Milan to the latest moves for peace

138. Dölger, *Regesten,* nos. 3408a, 3409, and 3410, pp. 111–112; Iorga, *Notes et extraits,* I, 350–351; less adequate is Thiriet, *Régestes,* II, no. 1915, pp. 211–212. On the same date, December 30, the Senate ordered the armament of 20 galleys for its projected fleet for the Levant: Thiriet, no. 1917, p. 212. According to Sanuto, 971D, however, it was on January 12, 1424, that steps were taken to organize this fleet, which was undoubtedly the one of which the *Sapientes* spoke to the Byzantines.

139. John apparently bore letters from his father, touching on some matters (see also below, p. 382 and n. 155): Dölger, *Regesten,* nos. 3396 and 3397, p. 109; no. 3408a, p. 111. Among them was a proposal to pawn two rubies, one of which had been evaluated at 40,000 ducats. The Senate declared that it was not possible to evaluate them. Other matters included continued complaints against Byzantine imposts on Venetians and disputes over Jews in Constantinople who had become Venetian citizens. Also added was a concession of free transportation for the Emperor's son (John). Text, Sathas, I, no. 97, pp. 158–159; cf. Thiriet, *Régestes,* II, no. 1916, p. 212.

140. Iorga, *Notes et extraits,* I, 351; Thiriet, *Régestes,* II, no. 1918, p. 212. According to the report, John had been the victim of tricksters who had passed themselves off as members of his entourage and had thus fleeced him of his limited funds.

141. Doing so, we are told, in spite of the protests of their heavy expenses over Thessalonica and other Eastern possessions: Iorga, *Notes et extraits,* I, 351–352; Thiriet, *Régestes,* II, no. 1919, p. 212.

with Sigismund. On January 15 John had addressed some requests to the Senate, and in its response of January 17 the Senate urged John to set forth for Hungary to pursue his mission. To soothe his renewed agitation for Venetian assistance to Constantinople the Senate assured John of the *Signoria's* willingness to help and reminded him that the Venetian fleet which he had requested for that purpose would stand ready to do what was necessary.[142] Meanwhile, on the same date, January 17, the Senate took notice of a letter (dated January 12) giving Visconti's response, which was pronunced ambiguous. A clarification was requested, but, in spite of the uncertainty, it was decided to encourage John to proceed on his mediation mission to Hungary. The Senate therefore went ahead and informed the young Emperor of the situation and urged John, impatient to leave, to set forth on his mission, which was so important for Christianity and for his Empire.[143] But John delayed still further for some reason and did not finally leave the city until, at the earliest, the very end of the month.[144]

Leaving Venice, John went to Milan, presumably to confer with Visconti personally. He left Milan on February 9, 1424.[145] We know nothing of his activities threafter until March 17, when the Emperor wrote from Lodi to the Venetian Senate, requesting its dispatch of its news from the East, and also of a Venetian ambassador who might accompany him before Sigismund, now that the Emperor was providing him with the safe-conduct for his journey to Hungary. On March 23 the Senate promised that news would be sent. But, as for the requested ambassador, the Senate replied that its obligation to its league required much more cooperative and elaborate provision and advised the Emperor to designate a convenient place for a common gathering of all parties concerned.[146] John did not yet leave Italy, however.

142. Dölger, *Regesten*, no. 3411, p. 112; Iorga, *Notes et extraits*, I, 352–353; Thiriet, *Régestes*, II, no. 1920 (pt. 2), p. 213. On this fleet, see n. 138 above.

143. Iorga, *Notes et extraits*, I, 352 (two entries); Thiriet, *Régestes*, II, no. 1920 (pt. 1), p. 213.

144. He was presumably in the city on January 27 when the Senate accepted the Emperor's signed acknowledgment of his debt of 1,500 ducats, incurred that month: text, Iorga, *Notes et extraits*, I, 354; lacking in Dölger's *Regesten*.

145. Gill, *The Council of Florence*, 39.

146. Dölger, *Regesten*, no. 3416, p. 112; Iorga, *Notes et extraits*, I, 360–

Among other places, presumably, he visited Manuta and had some dealings with Gianfrancesco Gonzaga, its ruler, and Sigismund's Vicar-General in North Italy. For, back in Milan once more, John wrote to Venice on May 3 to arrange for the transfer to Gonzaga's agent of some pledges (*pignora*) that the Emperor had originally left in Venice in security against loans there.[147]

During the summer of 1424 John at last reached Hungary and met with Sigismund. One of the subjects of discussion, inevitably, was once again the question of Church union. The Western Emperor exhorted the Eastern Emperor to strive toward this goal,[148] an urging to which John doubtless listened sympathetically, in view of his general disposition in the matter. As for the principal concern of the mission, the effort at mediation between Sigismund and Venice, little of immediate importance appears to have come of it; although, after another year, there seems to have been a warming of relations and talk at last of cooperation against the Turks.[149] On balance, then, this initial adoption by

361; less satisfactory, Thiriet, *Régestes*, II, no. 1927, p. 214. At the same time, the Senate instructed its agent in Milan, who was conveying this correspondence, to show John's letter and the Senate's response to it to Visconti, and not to send the response to John if the Duke disapproved of it. On John's request for news, see also n. 151 below. Dölger, *Regesten*, no. 3415, p. 112, places about this time a treaty renewal with Genoa.

147. Dölger, *Regesten*, no. 3417, p. 112; text of John's letter, ed. Lampros, Παλ. καὶ Πελ., III, 353.

148. Syropoulos, II, xii, pp. 8–9. Subsequently (II, xxxiv, pp. 35–36), this writer refers to a claim by John that Sigismund had offered, during this 1424 visit, to make the Greek Emperor his heir to the Holy Roman throne in reward for healing the schism, should he accomplish it. Knowing Sigismund's passion for extravagant schemes, it is not impossible for us to believe that he might have made such a proposal, impossible of fulfillment as it would have been. Cf. Gill, *The Council of Florence*, 39. Dölger, *Regesten*, has no entries at all on this mission—appropriate, perhaps, to its fruitlessness. See also Beckmann, *Der Kampf Kaiser Sigmunds gegen die werdende Weltmacht der Osmanen*, 97; more recently, there is Moravcsik's article, "Vizantiiskie imperatori ich posli v g. Buda" ("Les Empereurs de Byzance et leurs ambassadeurs à Buda"), 250–252.

149. On October 30, 1425, the Senate received a large number of proposals from Sigismund suggesting peace and cooperation between himself and the Veneto-Milanese league, with detailed suggestions for common action thereafter against the Turk. The Venetians expressed interest: Iorga, *Notes et extraits*, I, 409–410; Thiriet, *Régestes*, II, no. 2006, p. 232. Thus, even after Manuel's death—and therefore beyond the scope of this study—there was once again what the old Emperor had so long been seeking, talk of joint military action from the West to combat the Turks. But, as always, talk did not necessarily produce results or action.

John VIII of his father's technique of personal diplomacy had little success to show for itself when John returned home by way of the Danube, on November 1, 1424.[150]

Thus, once again a Byzantine effort to obtain Western aid had been of little avail. By the time this effort had ended, however, the immediate need for aid had eased. For, at the beginning of John's absence—whether as a result of his own efforts or on the initiative of Manuel or of the regent Constantine, we do not know—an accord was at last reached with Murad. An ambassador, one Manuel Melachrinos, had been sent to explore once again the possibilities for peace. By this time Murad had become more conciliatory. Pursuing this opportunity, two more emissaries were sent out, Lucas Notaras and the historian Sphrantzes himself. On February 20 (or 22), 1424, peace was finally agreed upon, by the terms of which the Byzantines surrendered their title to a portion of territory, comprising some of the Marmora and Black Sea coast, which had been restored to them by Suleyman and Mechmed; they were also obligated once more to pay a large annual tribute.[151]

150. Sphrantzes, 1030D–1031C (Pseudo-Phrantzes, ed. Papadopoulos, 122–124; ed. Bonn, 118–121), relates at length how, at the end of October, a message arrived from John, who had reached the mouth of the Danube and was awaiting the ships to transport him home. The regent Constantine was absent on a hunt at the time, and the court official and historian tells how he himself took the message from its bearer and conveyed to the delighted mother, wife (who, in view of unhappy marital life, could hardly have been as delighted as depicted), and father the news of John's imminent safe return. Whereupon Sphrantzes proudly relates that, for his role in these glad tidings, the old Emperor bestowed rich gifts and a family heirloom upon him, and "the young Despoina" gave him one of her fine gowns for the historian's bride when he should marry. Cf. Berger de Xivrey, 179; Muralt, p. 816, no. 1. Though it lacks such personal details, more precise dates of John's return are given by the Βρ. χρ. No. 1, p. 3, ll. 19–23, which tells that two galleys sailed for Asprokastron (on the Black Sea?) on September 13 to fetch the Emperor John, who reached home thus on November 1.

151. Dölger, *Regesten,* nos. 3412, 3413 (the embassies), and 3314 (the treaty), p. 112; cf. also his no. 3407, p. 111, for an earlier approach to Murad, "about summer" of 1423. The Βρ. χρ. No. 1, p. 3, ll. 17–19, notes the signing of the treaty, and gives the date as Sunday February 20, which is a coherent date. But it is perhaps better to accept the fuller Sphrantzes, 1030C–D (Pseudo-Phrantzes, ed. Papadopoulos, 121–122; ed. Bonn, 118), who names the ambassador and who gives the 22nd as the date of the accord. According to him, Notaras—later to become the historian's bitter rival and enemy—involved himself with the embassy purely for the purpose of placing himself in a good light at court. Sphrantzes says that he himself was sent by the Empress (Helena) in order that he might keep both Manuel and the

Such was the final outcome of the rashness of John VIII and the war faction in 1421. By that one stroke Byzantium had been needlessly plunged into nearly fatal war with the Turks. Now, when the smoke was allowed to clear, the Byzantines found not only that they had failed in their effort to exploit the death of Mechmed and to win more concessions, but that they had also

absent John informed of the negotiations through his letters; and also as a personal representative of the Empress, who was herself related to Murad through his mother, the historian says.

This latter allusion is not entirely clear, and it has not been illuminated further by confusions in other sources. In a spurious passage the Pseudo-Phrantzes (ed. Papadopoulos, 94; ed. Bonn, 90) speaks of Murad's wrath against the Greeks being cooled, and a peace being arranged with them, through the intervention of "the lady Maro, his [Murad's] stepmother"; and then the Βρ. χρ. No. 50, p. 87, l. 16, mentions an alleged daughter of Manuel named "Mara," who was the *wife* of Murad and a stepmother of Mechmed II. But these references are perhaps confusions with a daughter of the Serbian Despot George Branković and his wife Irene Cantacuzena, also named Mara, who married Murad II in 1435: on her see the articles by J. Papadrianos, "The Marriage-Arrangement between Constantine XI Palaeologus and the Serbian Mara (1451)," *Balkan Studies*, 6 (1965), 131–138; by Babinger, "Witwensitz und Sterbeplatz der Sultanin Mara," Ἐπ. Ἑτ. Βυζ. Σπουδ., 23 (1953), 240–244 (especially pp. 240–241); and by *id.*, "Ein Freibrief Mehmeds II., des Eroberes, für das Kloster Hagia Sophia zu Salonik, Eigentum der Sultanin Mara (1459)," *Byz. Zeitschr.*, 44 (1951 = *Festschrift F. Dölger*), 11–20.

Sphrantzes says nothing of the terms of the treaty. Nor does Chalcocondyles, ed. Darkó, II, 17, ed. Bonn, 239, who simply says that "the Hellenes" made peace with Murad, and who mentions Notaras as one of the ambassadors. The terms are given, however, by Ducas, ed. Grecu, 245, ed. Bonn, 196, who also mentions Notaras and who ascribes the treaty to the efforts of the Emperor John. (But, since Ducas, as all the other sources save Sphrantzes, ignores entirely John's journey to Italy and Hungary, this ascription should be regarded with caution.) Ducas also sets the tribute as 300,000 aspers. A sum of 100,000 *hyperpyra* is spoken of by Sanuto, 975B, who gives the terms of the treaty according to a Venetian report from Coron, itself dated February 22. The *Chron. Barb. 111*, 61, ascribes the treaty to the plea of "the Basileus Palaiologos" and makes the strange statement that one of its conditions (it stipulates no others specifically) was the destruction of the Hexamilion; this source then states that Murad sent Turachan to destroy the rampart in fulfillment of the treaty. This is obviously absurd, since the latter event preceded the treaty by nine months exactly. On this treaty in general, see Khoury, "L'Empereur Manuel II," 144; Mompherratos, Οἱ Παλ. ἐν Πελ., 54; Hammer, I, 419, trans. Hellert, II, 249; Iorga, *Geschichte*, 383; Pears, 155; and Muralt, pp. 814–815, no. 5, and p. 816, no. 3 (entries which are slightly jumbled). Reflection on the date of this treaty, February 20/22, 1424, might help give some possibly significant meaning to John's request for news from the East, while he was in Italy, in his letter of March 17 to the Venetian Senate: see pp. 377–378 and n. 146. For a Genoese reflection (February 28, 1424) on this treaty, see Belgrano, "Studi e documenti su la Colonia genovese di Pera," no. 58, pp. 186–187.

been shorn of the slight territorial and other gains—Byzantium's last gains—which Manuel had won since the Battle of Ancyra. This peace at once proved the wisdom of Manuel's old policies and at the same time deprived the Empire of their results. No less significant, however, is the fact that this accord of 1424 also gave Byzantium its last respite from the Turks, the long, ominous calm before the final storm of 1453.

With this peace, and with the return of John, we reach the end of the specific political events of Manuel's life and reign. Indeed, in many respects we are by now already in John VIII's reign. There remains only to consider the question of what role or influence Manuel had in the government during the last years of his life. Manuel's stroke of October 1, 1422, incapacitated him completely for some time and rendered his full participation in governmental affairs impossible. Thus, when the treaty with Venice was renewed on September 30, 1423, it was John who conducted the negotiations, or, at least, who signed it.[152] And, as we have seen, when John departed on his journey in November of that year he left his oldest available brother, the Despot Constantine, as his regent.[153] It is interesting to note elsewhere how the Venetians regarded Manuel's status after his stroke. In their deliberations of July 7 and July 27, 1423, in discussing the efforts to secure Byzantine approval and cooperation in the cession of Thessalonica, whenever reference is made to "the Emperor," it is plainly in reference to Manuel, while John is not given that title.[154] We do not know how much of John's mission to Italy and Hungary was inspired by Manuel's ideas or in-

152. Dölger, *Regesten*, no. 3408, p. 111; text, Miklosich and Müller, III, no. 36, pp. 163, 172; cf. above n. 61.

153. See p. 375 above. Sphrantzes, 1030C (Pseudo-Phrantzes, ed. Papadopoulos, 121; ed. Bonn, 118), leaves no doubt about Constantine's status, referring to John's "making a Despot his brother, the prince lord Constantine, and leaving him in the city in his place [ἀντ' αὐτοῦ]."

154. For these two deliberations, see p. 372 above. In that of July 7, the *bailo* of Constantinople is instructed that he should go before the presence of "the Most Serene Lord Emperor in the event that he should be in convalescence, and, if not, you ought to go before the presence of his son ..." (text, ed. Sathas, I, p. 134, ll. 27–29). Two other such statements are found further on (p. 138, ll. 27–28, and p. 139, ll. 16–17, respectively, the latter a duplication of the original one just quoted). And, twice (p. 138, ll. 25–26; and p. 139, l. 30), the text makes clear that by "Imperator" is meant only the *father* of the Despot Andronicus, and not his *brother* John. Likewise, in the text of the July 17 deliberation it is clear that there also "the Emperor" means Manuel, while John is simply "his son" (ed. Sathas, I, p. 146, l. 23).

fluence, but the aged Emperor was involved in at least some of John's initial dealings with Venice through letters.[155] And, even during John's absence and the regency of Constantine, when the Venetians wished to register complaints to the government in Constantinople, they addressed them to "the old Emperor" and only alternatively to "his representative" or to "the Despot." [156] Plainly, to the Venetians Manuel was still the Byzantine Emperor and, at least nominally, the sole head of the Byzantine government.

According to Sphrantzes,[157] Manuel could be described as "bedridden" (κατάκοιτος) in 1424. But it is clear that he was completely lucid and able to converse reasonably freely with people.[158] And converse he did with his son John, whom he sought to advise. He was still worried about some of John's overly ambitious ideas and, as we have seen already,[159] gave his son some penetrating and revealing warnings about the quest for Church union. The historian Sphrantzes, by then an intimate of the Imperial family, was present when this conversation took place, and he tells us what happened after Manuel had given that celebrated advice to his son:

. . . But the Basileus [John], not accepting, as it seemed, the argument of his father, rose up, saying nothing, and departed. After a little meditation, his late and still-remembered father looked at me and noted: "While the Basileus, my son, is a fitting Basileus, yet, not so for the present time. For he sees and thinks on a grand scale, such as occasions warranted in the prosperity of our forefathers. But today, when our troubles are crowding close upon us, our state wants not a Basileus but a steward [οἰκονόμον]. And I fear lest from his schemes

155. The text of the deliberation of December 30, 1423 (discussed above, p. 376, and n. 139), begins: "Cum serenissimus dominus Imperator Constantinopolis *senior* per suos ambaxatores sub ejus litteris credulitatis, etc. . . ." (text, ed. Sathas, I, p. 158, ll. 34–35, italics mine). The *senior* Emperor is obviously Manuel. It is interesting to note that in neither this deliberation nor in that of the same date (see p. 376 above) also involving John's mission is actual mention made of the younger Emperor at all, even though he was at least physically present in the city.

156. Deliberations of April 17, 1424 (Iorga, *Notes et extraits*, I, 365–366; Thiriet, *Régestes*, II, no. 1930, p. 215) and July 16, 1424 (Iorga, 370–371; Thiriet, no. 1948, p. 219), complaining about Theodore II's alleged outrages in the Morea (see n. 61 above).

157. 1031A.

158. See n. 150 above.

159. See pp. 329–330 above.

and endeavors there may come ruin for this house. For, I observed his schemes previously also, and the advantages which he thought to obtain with Moustapha; and I saw as well the results of his exploits, into what danger they carried us." [160]

Unfortunately, as events were to show, John never did take to heart his father's discreet and realistic advice.

But Manuel's time was running out. Worn by his long years of toil and struggle for his realm, he apparently never fully recovered from his stroke. As his strength began to fail, he followed tradition by becoming a monk, under the name of Matthaios. He managed to survive his seventy-fifth birthday. Twenty-five days later, on July 21, the end came.[161]

160. Sphrantzes, 1047A–B. Unfortunately, the author injects his account of this conversation as a later recollection to demonstrate how wise Manuel was in the light of John's subsequent mistakes over the union question. He gives it no date, and it is therefore impossible to determine exactly when it took place, save that the appropriate reference makes clear it was after the mistake of 1421. This passage has been translated by Gill, "John VIII Palaeologus," 153 (105), who uses, however, the text of the Pseudo-Phrantzes, ed. Papadopoulos, 178; ed. Bonn, 179. This latter text, for the phrase which I have translated as "schemes and endeavors," gives the words ποιημάτων καὶ ἐπιχειρημάτων. Gill translates this phrase as "poems and arguments" and uses it to demonstrate John's literary education and propensities. In the first place, this is a mistranslation, for the words are a rhetorical linking of "deeds and undertakings" and have nothing to do with literary pursuits, real or imagined, as the context of the passage makes clear. More important, however, is the fact that the spurious Pseudo-Phrantzes has here changed the words of the original Sphrantzes text, which gives the expression ἐνθυμημάτων καὶ ἐπιχειρημάτων. Here the contrast is a more vivid one, and the complete irrelevance of the text to Gill's intended point is quite plain. There is also an abridged French translation of this passage in Berger de Xivrey, 178–179; and Walter, 308–309.

161. Sphrantzes, 1031C–D (Pseudo-Phrantzes, ed. Papadopoulos, 124; ed. Bonn, 121), which is generally accepted as reliable. Thus, Khoury, "L'Empereur Manuel II," 144; Muralt, p. 816, no. 6. The almost identically worded and obviously related Βρ. χρ. No. 1, p. 3, ll. 23–27, gives the same date.

But there is considerable disagreement among other sources on the exact date. The event is noted by five more of the short chronicles, each with a different date. An entry published by Lampros, first in his "... συλλογὴ πρώτη," no. 88, p. 149, and then in Παλ. καὶ Πελ., III, 360, gives the date as July 11, 6934, indiction 4 (1426). The Βρ. χρ. No. 15, p. 33, ll. 58–62, states the date as July 20, 6933, indiction 3 (1425), which is the closest of these variants to Sphrantzes' figures. Both these chronicles give Manuel's monastic name, and the latter also gives the place of burial. No. 38, p. 66, ll. 26–27, simply gives the year 6933 and refers to his adoption of the monastic garb and name "on the seventh day," which perhaps reflects some corruption of the text. No. 44, p. 77, l. 6, makes an even more bare statement of Manuel's

Manuel's remains were at last laid to rest on the same day in the Monastery Church of Christ the Pantokrator, and a laudatory funeral oration was pronounced by the young Bessarion, the future uniate Cardinal.[162] When the last rites were held, says the eyewitness Sphrantzes, they were attended "with such mournings and such assemblages as there had never been for any of the other [Basileis]."[163] One is tempted to recall such similar popular outpourings at the burial of Manuel's old acquaintance and host, the unhappy King Charles VI of France, when the latter died not long before Manuel, on October 21, 1422. In that case, the display of grief was the reaction of newly stirring nationalism to the fear that the death of the pathetic monarch

death, giving the year as 6931 (1422–23) and the indiction as the twentieth. This is of course impossible, there being only fifteen years to each indiction cycle; obviously, as with the other entries in this text, the number is probably a date of a month, the word for the month perhaps having been omitted, together with the proper indiction number which followed it. If it may be reconstructed with the aid of the Chronicle No. 15, we would then have another reckoning of July 20.

Even more startling, however, is a pair of entries in the *Chron Vat. gr. 162*, p. 212, the first of which (no. 23, ll. 108–110) gives the generally correct information that, after a long siege (here reckoned at nine years, two years too many), the Sultan took Thessalonica on Wednesday, March 29, in the year 6938 (1430), though adding an incorrect indiction number (2; it was actually 8). But then (no. 24, ll. 112–113), the chronicle states, with no specific date, that Manuel, upon hearing the news of "the [events] of Thessalonica," swooned and died. Since Manuel's death preceded by five years the fall of Thessalonica, we might be excused for exercising a modicum of critical caution over this statement, which is perhaps a confusion with Manuel's paralytic stroke on October 1, 1422. The most curious of all the mistaken datings for the Emperor's death, however, is that which appears in a fresco in Mistra, portraying Manuel, as noted below in Appendix XXIV, end of Section A, I. The transcription of this inscription by G. Millet in his "Inscriptions byzantines de Mistra," *Bulletin de correspondance hellénique*, 23 (1899), 97–156: no. x, pp. 120–121, is reconstructed to give the date of October 6932, indiction 2 (1423) for Manuel's death. The date is consistent with itself, but is demonstrably wrong. (Could at least the month be another confusion with Manuel's stroke in 1422?) What is surprising is that such an error should have occurred in a quasi-official form in such a center of presumably accurate governmental information as the capital of the Morea. For some other premature reports of Manuel's death, by Latins, see n. 119 above.

162. The Greek text has been edited by Lampros in his Παλ. καὶ Πελ., III, pp. 284–290. A fifteenth-century Latin translation was published in Migne, *Patr. gr.* 161, coll. 615–620. For a long while this latter was the only published version of the oration and, as such, was the only one known to Berger de Xivrey, 180.

163. Sphrantzes, 1031D (Pseudo-Phrantzes, ed. Papadopoulos, 124; ed. Bonn, 121). The Church of St. Savior Pantokrator still stands, and is shown

Figure 28: *Constantinople, the Church of St. Savior Pantocrator: Exterior from the East* (photo courtesy Ljubica Popović, 1961; see Appendix XXIV, C, 8).

symbolized the end of France as a nation and its imminent absorption by the English crown. In the case of Manuel, his subjects faced a threat which was, if less immediate, certainly no less horrible. Well might the Greeks reflect somberly on the passing of the wise old sovereign who had guided them devotedly through thirty-four years of turmoil and peril. Manuel's struggles were ended, and he had found rest at last. The final agonies of his state and of his people were yet to come.

in Figure 28. For comments on it and on Manuel's burial within it, see below, Appendix XXIV (C, 8).

For some more extensive discussions and descriptions of this Comnenian Church, the chief funerary church for the imperial family during Manuel's era, the following may be consulted: R. Janin, *La Géographie ecclésiastique de l'Empire byzantin*, I: *Le Siège de Constantinople et le Patriarcat oecuménique*, 3: *Les Eglises et les monastères* (Paris, 1953), 529–538; J. Ebersolt and A. Thiers, *Les Eglises de Constantinople* (Paris, 1913), 185–207; A. Van Millingen, *Byzantine Churches in Constantinople* (London, 1912), 219–240; and A. Hergès, "Le Monastère du Pantocrator à Constantinople," *Echos d'Orient*, 2 (1898–99), 70–78.

6. Manuel as an Emperor: Some Conclusions

Many of the most important observations that might be made about Manuel II Palaeologus as an Emperor have already been made in the course of the foregoing narrative. Indeed, in many cases the very establishment of many details and of an integrated narrative itself represents conclusions of sorts. Nevertheless, it might not be entirely out of place to pause here and review some general points, rounding out or extending some ideas inherent in what has already been said.

The basic theme thus far, of course, has been the development of Manuel's policies and the circumstances and attitudes that shaped them. At the outset, then, we should take note of one interesting point. This is the fact that the real author of Manuel's fundamental policy—that is, of seeking aid from the West as the only hope for Byzantine survival—was not Manuel himself, but actually his father, John V. To be sure, the Latinophile Demetrius Cydones, a powerful influence on Manuel in other ways, may have played an important role in encouraging both John V and Manuel to adopt this policy. Nevertheless, it is still John V who deserves the credit for establishing it first as an official governmental policy. Poor old John has long been the subject of much scorn. But if some of it may be justified, yet, for all his personal mediocrity, John did recognize for a while the basic fact of Byzantium's position. In the first half of the fourteenth century

Figure 29: *Emperors of the Palaeologan House.* Pen and Wash Drawing, Biblioteca Estense, Modena, *Cod.* α.S.5.5 (=Gr. 122), f. 294ᵛ (photo courtesy U. Orlandini, Modena; see Appendix XXIV, A, I, 1).

the Empire still had a chance to remain at least a Balkan state of some significance. But, by the time of Cantacuzenus' abdication in 1354, the process of decline had been allowed to go too far. First the Serbian challenge and then the more substantial Turkish threat made it clear that Byzantium was entering into a struggle literally for its life: the stakes were no longer goals of power or a restoration of former glory, but bare survival. It was therefore to John V's credit that he saw the danger and himself initiated the policy of the quest for aid from the West.

But his initiation proved premature. If the Latin West was slow or unwilling to rouse itself to the necessary effort at the end of the fourteenth century, it was even less in the proper frame of mind to do what was needed in the middle of the century, especially since some of the anti-Byzantine sentiment of the thirteenth century still lingered on among the Latins. After all his personal efforts and humiliations, John V was also intelligent enough to recognize this reality, especially when the crucial Battle of the Marica in 1371 caused his failure of nerve. John changed to his course of appeasement and thereafter became an almost helpless victim of the interacting dynastic strife and the ambitions of the Turks.

It is perhaps possible to level against John V, and perhaps Manuel as well, the charge that they made little or no effort to unite the Orthodox peoples of the Balkans in a coordinated alliance against the common threat. Certainly in John's case the charge might have some validity. Yet, here too there were problems of old animosities and suspicions, often even stronger than those connected with the Latin West. In the latter half of the fourteenth century there was little farsighted or authoritative leadership among these peoples. Their quarrelsomeness and inability to cooperate with each other consistently were easily recognized by the Turks and brilliantly exploited by them. As tragic as it is to think that these fellow Orthodox peoples could not have united against the mutual foe, it seems likely that they would have made unreliable, if not useless, allies for one another, even if Greeks and Slavs could have buried their age-old differences. Moreover, the one great Orthodox Slavic power that was not threatened directly by the Turks, Muscovite Russia, was in no position (or disposition) to send any major help, even when

Manuel begged it. John had therefore probably been right in feeling that the West offered the best possibilities for aid.

But it remained for Manuel to establish the quest for aid securely as the ultimate and definite policy of the Byzantine government. This role is hardly surprising, for we have seen that, long before his final accession, Manuel's personal inclination had been to oppose the Turkish advance. His independent venture in Thessalonica in 1382–87 was ill-starred and disastrous: but, at least in its successful phase, it was probably one of the most agreeable and satisfying times of his life. His submission thereafter to the then-current policy of appeasement was never voluntary or cordial. Even if he did have the will power to continue this unpalatable policy after his father's death, it was only the lesser of two evils, as he himself pointed out; and we have seen what bitterness and humiliation his years of subservience to the Turks brought to him. Only the recklessness and arrogance of the terrible Bayazid himself forced Manuel to abandon appeasement. But by this time the magnitude of the Turkish threat had made a full-scale policy of seeking Western aid not only desirable but also unavoidable.

Occasional details aside, Manuel's policies and outlook up to 1402 are reasonably clear and generally understood. It is only when we reach the confused period after the Battle of Ancyra that we have to insist on a revision of modern interpretation. In the foregoing text we have had ample occasion to challenge two grave misconceptions regarding Manuel's policy in the last twenty-odd years of his life: first, that after 1402, supposedly disillusioned with the West, Manuel rushed home and devoted himself simply to playing off the sons of Bayazid one against another; and, second, that after 1413 Manuel settled down for a restful breathing spell while cordial relations and peace flourished between Turks and Greeks and while Manuel attended to essentially internal concerns. There should hardly be any great need to stress much more the actual fact that Manuel never ceased to seek aid from the West at any time after 1402, or, for that matter, at any time after 1394.

What may merit some further discussion, however, is the new relationship of the quest for aid in the context of changed conditions after 1402. In simplest terms, how do we relate the seemingly contradictory policies of seeking aid on one hand and yet of acting in concert or peaceful cooperation with the Turks on the other? Of course, such double standards are by no means foreign to the traditions of Byzantine diplomacy and history. But there is a real relationship between these two strands. After all, Manuel was by all means a realist when it came to matters of state. He was too intelligent and sensitive a person not to recognize the truth when confronted with it. He therefore never forgot that Byzantium's only real enemy now was the Turks, whose successes could only increase danger to the Empire, and whose natural goal could only be the final destruction of its precarious existence. The Battle of Ancyra did not change the Turkish position: it merely shook it and gave the Christians a new opportunity. The old quest for aid, therefore, could only be stepped up to take advantage of that opportunity; for the only hope for Byzantine survival was in securing genuine Western interest and assistance. In this understanding Manuel was certainly correct.

Unfortunately, the Latin West was too reluctant or too distracted to make use of the opportunity. With his acute understanding of the Latins—the result of bitter experience—he realized how difficult it was to secure their aid, and how long it might be before he could do so. His realism therefore forced him into an outward paradox. If our assumptions are correct, Manuel himself may only have become involved originally in the struggles of Bayazid's sons against his will and as a result of the unauthorized commitments made by his nephew. But, as the Turkish "Time of Troubles" progressed, it must have become plain that the long-range policy of seeking Latin aid was not enough. Since the needed help from the West could not be counted on readily or promptly, in immediate terms Manuel had to make the best of the situation through direct dealings, and even cooperation, with the Turks. Thus, Manuel became involved in the wars of succession. As it proved, what limited gains were achieved with his limited resources were the result of his careful manipulation. And the peace he made with the ultimate victor, Mechmed I, was only a means for buying time to support his still-continued quest for aid. The right hand complements the left, each on its own plane of activity.

In pursuing this double-headed policy in his later years, Manuel was enmeshed in a second paradox, an even more curious one. Just as he, in his earlier years, had acted in defiance of his father, preferring resistance to appeasement, so, in turn, he found his own policies of moderation and precarious balancing challenged by his restless son John VIII. One is strongly tempted to wonder if Manuel himself ever reflected on this ironic parallel.

The contrasts between the goals and methods of Manuel and of his successor have already been remarked upon. But it ought to be stressed again that the basis for much of at least the ecclesiastical policy of John VIII, culminating in the union of Florence in 1439, was laid by Manuel himself. In his early and mysterious flirtation with the Papacy in 1384–85, then in his linking and subordination of union efforts to projects of prior Western aid, and then in his final concentration on the problem of union from 1415 on, Manuel's sole interest in the question was as a lever in his quest for aid. Michael VIII before him had been able to exploit this issue as a political football with important diplomatic success, if with unpleasant domestic repercussions. As we have seen, Manuel understood how dangerous the matter was, and he handled it with prudent—if not cynical—caution. His son was to demonstrate the wisdom of Manuel's caution when he abandoned it.

Manuel ruled Byzantium during a period of agonizing crisis. Had it not been for Timur, the crisis would surely have been the last fatal one. Events beyond his control spared Manuel from witnessing the final collapse in his lifetime and even allowed him to win some very meager territorial gains. But his reign and lifetime inevitably saw a drastic shrinking of Byzantine territory. With the weakening of the state and its resources came a weakening of the central authority. As a result, the epoch of Manuel was marked by a steady growth of the appanage system in Byzantine government. There had been ample precedents earlier in the fourteenth century, but only later was the practice to become firmly established. Manuel had held Thessalonica in his youth. His brother was given the Morea as a despotate. And, as a result of the family disputes, a separate enclave was held in succession by his brother Andronicus and his nephew John VII, in effect detaching that territory virtually as a dependency of the Turks.

Under Manuel himself, however, the parceling out of appanages, though more extensive, was never allowed to run away with itself. Byzantium never spawned its own Burgundy. Indeed, the system rather became a reasonably successful instrument of binding together what the central authority could not control directly itself. Thus, if the appanage of Thessalonica was used as the sop to end the long family feud with John VII, Manuel effectively resecured the territory by promptly replacing his nephew with his son Andronicus in its possession. Some of the recovered territory in the Black Sea area was later held by another son, Constantine. And the succession in the Morea was maintained through still another son, Theodore II. The case of the Despotate was, of course, an ironic exception to the general decay of the Empire elsewhere. In his own use of the appanage system, Manuel's father had already reclaimed the Morea for the dynasty and the central authority by sending Theodore I there to replace the moribund line of the Cantacuzeni. Building on the foundations laid by the Cantacuzeni in the middle of the fourteenth century, Manuel's family managed to pave the way for the ultimate eleventh-hour triumph of Byzantine authority in the Peloponnesus, which was to come within a few years after the old Emperor's death.

As Byzantine decline brought territorial constriction, it brought also a grave diminution of the resources of Byzantine polity. No longer was the Byzantine *Basileus* the grand exponent of lofty Imperial power and of "dollar diplomacy." Rather, in Manuel's celebrated journey to the West, we reach the ultimate reversal of the Empire's old position. Yet, for all its reduced means, the arts of Byzantine diplomacy and statecraft had not been entirely lost, and with Manuel the old wine could still be poured into new bottles. If his striking venture in personal diplomacy indicated his readiness to strike out boldly in a direction that was, for all the precedents, still strangely new, yet he could still use successfully many a time-worn device. He knew how to play off rivals one against another, and did so skillfully when it was possible; and he understood the old trick of having a pretender to a foe's throne ready at hand. Moreover, he also appreciated the advantages he still had in the prestige and glory of his rank as the successor of Constantine and as the living embodiment of the old Romano-Byzantine traditions.

With his varied talents and background, Manuel conformed in every way to the ideal of a perfect Byzantine sovereign. Certainly out of the entire Palaeologan house he is the most striking and appealing figure. His son Constantine XI has won a certain fame. But the glory of the gallant death of the last Palaeologus in the final drama of 1453 has elevated him perhaps beyond the merit of his otherwise rather moderate abilities. To match Manuel fairly, one must go to the other extreme, to the founder of the dynasty. Certainly Michael VIII (1259–1282) was a brilliant politician, a cunning diplomat, and a forceful ruler, one of the few natural-born sovereigns of his house, for all the illegitimacy of his accession. But Michael had little of the culture and none of the personal character or attractiveness that Manuel displayed. And we may wonder if Michael was endowed with the inner resources of moral strength that enabled Manuel to endure his terrible tribulations. Of the whole Palaeologan period, the only genuine equal to Manuel in brilliance, as a personality as well as an Emperor, was John VI Cantacuzenus, whose reign was after all nothing more than an illegal usurpation, an intrusion by one outside the dynasty itself. Indeed, when one considers the world of Manuel's own lifetime, there are few, if any, rulers of the age who could compare with him in culture, personality, and statesmanship; surely, at least not in Christendom.

Certainly, then, Manuel had all the capacity for becoming one of the greatest of Byzantine Emperors in many respects. Under ordinary conditions his accession could have marked the dawn of a golden era for the Empire. But, by the end of the fourteenth century, conditions were hardly ordinary any longer. Nor is the destiny of a state shaped only by the quality of its rulers. By this period the Byzantine rulers were no longer the masters of their own fate, much less of that of their realm. It was Manuel's personal tragedy that his age did not give him a fairer opportunity to display his capacities. It was Byzantium's own advantage, however, that in its time of great trial it at least had a genuine statesman to guide its blighted fortunes.

Yet, need Manuel's appearance in such unhappy circumstance be considered merely an unfortunate accident? One of the striking and important features of Byzantine history is that so often in a time of crisis the Empire was able to produce just the leader it needed. Capable leadership, rather than massive strength, was usually the key to Byzantine success. To be sure, however, the Byzantine state in previous crises still possessed some capacity for recovery which provided the necessary backing for such leadership. By Manuel's time that capacity had long since vanished, and the Byzantine state was an irrevocably doomed and dying relic. But the elements which had made Byzantine civilization what it was were not entirely spent, even then. In our still-feeble appreciation of the complex and fascinating age of the Palaeologi, we are at least beginning to recognize Byzantium's undiminished and even extended creative strength, especially in the field of art, amid its overall decay. Perhaps not the least significance of the reign of Manuel II is its demonstration that Byzantium still had the vitality and continued ability to produce leadership of the old high caliber, even in its most appalling political decline.

7. Manuel as a Personality and a Literary Figure

While this study has been devoted in the main to Manuel II's essentially political activities, it would not be out of place to round it out with a consideration of some other aspects of this Emperor's life in order to seek some further understanding of him as a human being.

To begin with a fundamental matter, we are perhaps better informed as to Manuel's physical appearance than we are on that of almost any other Byzantine Emperor—his own son John VIII being the most likely exception. In the three major portraits of Manuel that survive [1] we are confronted by the image of a well-proportioned figure with noble, flowing features and a long beard. Some elements of these portrayals are perhaps idealized to a

1. The most famous of the three major portraits is that in the manuscript of the works of Dionysius the Areopagite (discussed above, pp. 263–264 and n. 112), now in the Louvre. This shows not only the Emperor, but his Empress, Helen Dragaš, and their three oldest sons: see Appendix XV below. The second portrait, the sole major one of the Emperor alone, is an impressive miniature in a manuscript of his *Funeral Oration for His Brother Theodore*, now in the Bibliothèque Nationale in Paris, *Suppl. gr. 309*. The third is a sketch of the head of Manuel, with those of his father, John V, and his son, John VIII, in another manuscript, *Cod. gr. 1783*, preserved in the same institution. There are also a number of other representations of Manuel, both deliberate and presumed. These have been included throughout this book as illustrations, and all the known portraits of Manuel, of one kind or another, are discussed in detail and as a unit in Appendix XXIV, section I, below.

degree, but their general characteristics seem in reasonable accord, both with each other and with our other evidence.

In addition to the graphic representations of the Emperor, however, we also have two important verbal descriptions. One curious text, which is apparently a reasonably contemporary reference to Manuel, describes him as "a fair[-haired?] mortal, a hook-nosed, hoary, short leader of the Hellenes." [2] But there are some details of this characterization which are subject to controversy.[3] Far more reliable, however, as well as more significant,

2. " . . . ξανθὸς μέροψ, γρυπὸς πολιὸς βραχὺς Ἑλλήνων ἀρχηγός . . ." the phrase being from the third of the supposed prophecies regarding the Hexamilion, identified with Manuel II and expounded by Bodnar, "The Isthmian Fortifications in Oracular Prophecy," 166–167. Cf. also above, p. 313, n. 21.

3. In the first place, this seems to be the only concrete reference to Manuel's nose being bent or crooked. Bodnar, 167, suggests that some support for this feature might be seen in the sketch in the *Suppl., gr. 309,* of Manuel with his father and eldest son (Figure 32), the third of the major portraits mentioned above in n. 1. The lines of this sketch, however, are not decisive enough to settle the matter. Nor is Bodnar's further argument, that the seemingly straight nose in the two other major portraits represents idealization, completely convincing. On the other hand, if the two medallions from the Duc de Berry's collection (see below, Appendix XXIV, I, B, 1) are indeed representations of Manuel, we have in at least that of the Heraclius medallion valuable additional evidence. Compared with other authentic—and only full-face—portraits of Manuel, the Heraclius image (see Figure 15) could very well represent Manuel himself. If so, this portrait is of great value, for it would be the only representation of the Emperor in profile. And this profile shows him with a long but almost completely straight nose. Again, the possibility of idealization arises: but how far is it to be carried? For what it is worth, however, it might be mentioned that many of the best portraits of John VIII show him with a somewhat hooked nose. But, of course, the features of the son are not necessarily reliable evidence for those of the father.

Much more difficult is the matter of the color of hair. Ordinarily the word ξανθός would be taken as referring to hair color, rather than to complexion, with little problem. But then why does the prophecy text also include the word πολιός, "hoary," or "gray-haired"? The usual basis for the assumption that Manuel was "golden-haired," and the one used by Bodnar, 167 (and also cited by Berger de Xivrey, *Mémoire sur la vie et les ouvrages de l'empereur Manuel Paléologue,* 65) is drawn from the funeral oration for Manuel by Bessarion (see above, p. 384). For a long time this text was available only in a fifteenth-century Latin translation published by Migne, *Patr. gr.,* 161, 615–620. There the passage reads: "Ubi nunc est tua illa aurea caesaries . . . ?" ("Where now is thy golden hair . . . ?" 620A). In the first place, logic alone would make one suspicious: by the time Bessarion would have known him (not long after the building of the Hexamilion), Manuel's hair had long turned to gray—πολιός indeed! But there is an even more telling objection to this statement: it is not justified by Bessarion's original text. The original Greek was not available to Berger de Xivrey, but (a point overlooked

is the celebrated description of Manuel on the occasion of his entry into Paris on June 3, 1400. It should be recalled that Manuel was then only twenty-four days short of his fiftieth birthday and had lived a life of terribly aging strain. Yet, his physical agility, as well as his striking appearance, greatly impressed a contemporary observer:

. . . Then the Emperor, dressed in his imperial garb of white silk, seated himself on the white horse presented to him by the king [Charles VI of France] during his journey, mounting it nimbly without even deigning to set a foot upon the ground [i.e., in transferring himself from his own horse to the white one]. And those who—while marking his moderate stature, distinguished by a manly chest and by yet firmer limbs, though under a long beard and showing white hair everywhere—yet took heed of the grace of his countenance, adjudged him indeed worthy of imperial rule.[4]

This impressiveness of Manuel's appearance is further attested in a different and curious fashion by a comment of the courtier-historian Sphrantzes. In referring to the arrival of the young brother of Murad II, Mustafa or "Moustaphopoulos," in Constantinople in 1422, Sphrantzes notes the reaction of his followers to Manuel's appearance; and then he recalls, in passing, a hand-

by Bodnar) it has been published by Lampros in his Παλαιολόγεια καὶ Πελοποννησιακά, III, pp. 284–290. A close comparison reveals that the corresponding line there reads thus: " ᾿Ω οἷόν σοι βόστρυχον ταῖς ἀρεταῖς πεπλεγμένου ὁ δεινὸς ἀπετίλατο θάνατος...." ("O such a lock as thine, plaited with thy virtues, hath dread death plucked out....." p. 289, ll. 13–14). It is not impossible, of course, that the old Latin translation might have been based upon a more authentic Greek text than the one which survives to us now. But for the time being we must take them respectively at their face values and assume that the Latin version's use of "aurea" represents an error or an interpolation. Thus, the question of Manuel's hair color is not so easily established.

4. "Tunc imperator, habitum imperialem ex albo serico gerens, equo albo sibi a rege in itinere oblato, et super quem tunc ascendens agiliter non dignatus fuerat pedem ad terram ponere, insidebat. Et nonnulli qui notantes ejus staturam mediocrem, thorace virili ac membris sollidioribus insignitam, subque barba prolixa, undique canis ornata, vultus ejus venustatem attendebant, ipsum dignum imperio judicabant." *Religieux de Saint-Denys*, XXI, i, ed. Bellaguet, II, p. 756. The editor's own French translation, p. 757, is a trifle free, but it is followed heavily by Mijatović, *Constantine, The Last Emperor of the Greeks*, 77; likewise Stacton, *The World on the Last Day*, 115 (="Dereksen," 121–122). See also Berger de Xivrey, 65 and 100; and Schlumberger, "Un Empereur de Byzance à Paris et Londres," 108–109; cf. also above, p. 174.

Figure 30: *The Meeting of the Magi* [*The Reception of Manuel by Charles VI at Charenton?*]. Illuminated Miniature, *Les Très Riches Heures du Duc de Berry*, Musée Condé, Chantilly, f. 51ᵛ (photo courtesy Giraudon, Paris; see Appendix XXIV, A, II, 2, a).

Figure 31: *The Adoration of the Magi [Including Manuel and Charles VI?]*. Illuminated Miniature, *Les Très Riches Heures du Duc de Berry*, Musée Condé, Chantilly, f. 52ʳ (photo courtesy Giraudon, Paris; see Appendix XXIV, A, II, 2, b).

some compliment made by—of all people—the late Emir Bayazid.
The passage speaks first of the stroke suffered at that point by
Manuel:

. . . seeing whom, those Turks from the East with Moustaphopoulos
marveled, and from the sight of him alone said with amazement that
he resembled the founder of their faith, Machoumet; just as also
Bayazid, his enemy, once had said, that even whoever might know
him not as the Basileus, from the very sight alone of him is prompted
to say: "This man must be a king." [5]

From this description there can be no doubt that, regardless of
some uncertain details of his appearance, it was certainly an impressive one, to friends and enemies alike. This was a particular
asset to him in the delicate circumstances of his own and his
realm's position. He must surely have been aware of its value in
his venture in personal diplomacy in the West. And allied to advantages of outward appearance were apparently the blessings
of a strong constitution and presumably good health. Hence,
Manuel was able to bear the continuous emotional and physical
strains for which his great moral and spiritual strength could
not have sufficed alone. Aside from occasional references in his
writings to sickness, we almost never hear of him being really
gravely ill until his very late years. He seems to have felt that his
infirmities were sufficient by 1421 to justify his going into semiretirement, but it was only his stroke in the following year that
really broke his health. He must have been one of those people
who enjoy, on into a very ripe old age, largely undiminished
vigor which then crumbles completely upon the onslaught of a
severe sickness and physical breakdown. Yet, until then, Manuel
went right on fathering children in his fifties, leading military
campaigns in his sixties, and still presiding actively over his government in his seventies.

Moving from consideration of his physical characteristics to
that of his personality, we come to an even more nebulous
prospect. It is easy enough to draw general conclusions from the
known record of his political activity. There he appears to us as
a man of great nobility and integrity, a sensitive, responsible, and

5. Sphrantzes, 1030A–B (cf. Pseudo-Phrantzes, ed. Papadopoulos, p. 120,
ll. 21–26, ed. Bonn, p. 117, ll. 11–15).

Figure 32: *Manuel, between His Father and His Eldest Son.* Pen Drawing, Bibliothèque Nationale, Paris, *Cod. gr. 1783*, f. 2 (photo courtesy Bibliothèque Nationale, Paris; see Appendix XXIV, A, I, 2).

compassionate ruler over his suffering people, completely realistic about his circumstances, yet at the same time possessing a deep sense of tradition and of the glory of his rank; patient, earnest, with deep resources of fortitude and spiritual strength, and—with the possible exception of some wavering toward the idea of flight early in Bayazid's siege [6]—ready to accept with dutiful perseverance the crushing and almost hopeless burden placed upon him. Such would seem to have been his outward aspect.

It is more difficult to trace his inner nature. There seems to be good reason to assume that he was an affectionate family man. If we can take at face value his voluminous expressions of emotion, he was apparently devoted to at least his youngest brother, Theodore, and there is every indication that there was a very warm bond of feeling between him and his mother. Even his father, the much-maligned John V, with whom he was on bad terms at times, seems generally to have been regarded cordially by Manuel. Thus, in the great *Funeral Oration for His Brother*

6. See above, pp. 124–125, 146.

401

Theodore, we find Manuel characterizing his father as "a most excellent Basileus, who displayed great affection to his sons." [7]

Manuel's relations with his own personal family, however, are even more difficult to judge. There is nothing to indicate that his marriage with Helena Dragaš of Serbia was anything but happy, or at least tranquil. She is portrayed to us as a woman of character, and we know that she bore him a goodly number of children in his later years. It is true that Manuel sowed his share of wild oats and fathered at least several illegitimate children.[8] But all those of whom we have any knowledge were born unquestionably before his marriage to Helena, and there is nothing to suggest that he was other than faithful to her in their long years together.

His six sons were a mixed brood. None of them was particularly gifted, and they varied in quality from the gallant Constantine to the worthless Demetrius. One, Andronicus, was prematurely wasted and destroyed by disease before he could prove himself, while another, Theodore, was quickly revealed as incapable of consistent and responsible leadership in the Morea. The two youngest, Demetrius and Thomas, displayed capacities for little other than selfish ambition in their disgraceful rivalry in the Morea during the Empire's closing hours, undoing much of their family's previous good work. Perhaps proper fatherhood was difficult for Manuel in view of his age—he was forty-two when the eldest (John) was born; fifty-nine when the youngest (Thomas) came [9]—of his absences, and of his demanding preoccupation with affairs of state. Of his relations with his sons, we can trace little except in the case of his eldest, his successor, the mediocre John. As a literary-minded Emperor, Manuel was proud to wield his pen for the benefit of his heir's education.[10] But we have seen how Manuel came into conflict with John over governmental policy in 1422, with regrettable results,[11] and how

7. *Funeral Oration,* ed. Migne, 197C, ed. Lampros, p. 26, ll. 7–8, in which Manuel, praising Theodore's filial devotion, characterizes him as παῖς ὢν ἀρίστῳ βασιλεῖ πολύ τι τοῖς υἱέσι δείκνυτι φίλτρον. . . . This remark is translated in passing by Berger de Xivrey, 64, without citation of location.

8. See Appendix IX below.

9. See Appendix XV below for the birth dates of Manuel's sons.

10. See above, pp. 344–345 and n. 84.

11. See above, pp. 355 ff.

disappointed and concerned Manuel was over John's attitudes.[12] Virtually the only indication we have of John's attitude toward Manuel is the fact that John refrained from dismissing his unloved second wife, the bride of a political marriage arranged by Manuel, out of deference to his father, a deference that ended with the latter's death.[13] Otherwise, we know nothing of Manuel's personal standing with his children, nor have they left us any scraps of information or comments on their father, as he did on his.

In view of the bulk of Manuel's own surviving literary output, it is disappointing that we find so little personal information about him in it. To be sure, such cultivated detachment is not unusual in the literary idiom of his time and is often even more prominent in the writings of his contemporaries. But, in his case, this lack seems at once particularly acute and also particularly disappointing. Even in his letters the stilted rhetoric only rarely gives way to reveal something of his genuine feelings. But when it does, the results can be most vivid and compelling. The most notable examples of such self-revelation are, of course, the letters already discussed, which contain the outpourings of his anguish as a military vassal with Bayazid.[14] But passages or texts offering any really personal insights are unfortunately rare and sparse in his writings.

There is, however, one noteworthy instance in which Manuel relaxed to some degree and spoke of personal things. If still not devoid of rhetoric, it is a text that is nonetheless genuinely human and appealing. This comes at the beginning of a long letter to Demetrius Chrysoloras. The Emperor is at great pains to call attention to his crushing schedule, partly for the usual purpose of explaining his failure to keep up with his correspondence:

> For me there is a multitude of distractions which, by driving me on to other things, impels almost to abstain from those things without which it is not possible to survive. I have neglected the meal table, and time, and I take little thought for my food, whatever it may be.

12. See above, pp. 382–383.
13. See above, p. 349 and n. 96. Gill, "John VIII Palaeologus: A Character Study," 155 (107), also emphasizes John's tenacious retention of the historian Sphrantzes in his service after his father's death, in accordance with the latter's deathbed request, as a further display of filial deference.
14. See above, pp. 88–98.

I have shaken sleep from my eyes, and often my bed receives me only at dawn, just when it is necessary for those who sweep out the whole house and, in short, the entire household staff, to be roused out of bed so that they may undertake tasks that require their attention. Buzzing about the doors, these people are most annoying; and then comes an outcry from judges and plaintiffs and defendants; and what other such things as would be superfluous to relate, for it would be telling one who already knows. But the shouting of the servant crew, ringing through the house in which I would like to sleep, would easily awaken even a Dardanos or someone more sleepy than he. And then our own Antiochos—the old man, mind you, who was such a lover of slumbers as to go to sleep while riding horseback, and who would have exchanged everything for sleep—when he is not able, as usual, to snore through the tumult outside the door, though he calls down curses on such unsilent people, puts on some kind of shepherd's cap, stuffs his ears with his fingers, and fits his head into the deepest corner [of his bedclothes], he still gets scarcely any rest, so much is everything filled with clamor. Yet, the unavoidability of their function prevents any hindering of the disturbance. So, I have been careless of a diet that was approved by physicians: it was doing to one who is ill things that would cause sickness in a body which is healthy. It is impossible, moreover, to evade those outside, those inside, those whosoever are burdened with his particular problem: nay, there stands Latin, Persian [Turk], citizen, foreigner—even monk, no less— each demanding something else, and each shouting that he would be done injustice if he should not forthwith receive what he wants. It is absurd, then, to talk of pleasure, absurd to talk of repose: the best thing that could happen is something, anything, that would deliver me from these troublesome creatures each day. Such are my obligations, filled with difficulty. But what enlarges their difficulties is, I suppose, common both to us here and to you there—I mean our deficiency of material things, which inflicts injury on each individual and on our public affairs. For I know that deficiency dominates you also. But God is able to release us quickly from this, and may He yet grant us the good times of our ancestors! Still, this should also make clear how immoderately busy I am. For I have shaken off my zeal for books and all writing, and also my delight in them, a delight which holds advantage—as well you may imagine—for men's souls. I know, indeed, that this is detrimental for me, and I am practically in tears about it. But at the same time I am simply not able to rectify the matter, wishing as I do to pay heed to outward appearance. The present time, after all, does not permit me any leisure, even when the desire for relief admits no delay. These circumstances forced me out of every attempt at writing, to such an extent that I have scarce been able to begin this scribbling now in progress, which—well do I know!—you long to receive. So, therefore, needs must it be involuntarily that you endure not receiving anything, just as I myself endure thus my not finishing anything; although it may perhaps seem extraordinary that, when I had managed to carry burdens of this kind in alien territory— where it was necessary to cleave oceans and to cross rivers, to fear attacks of pirates and to bear with evils of a continuous land journey, and to bear many other things—since then, sitting back home in our own native land, released from all those toils, and eager to make an end to a piece of writing, I should now be unable to come by the time.

But, since obstacles have arisen in every quarter against my desire to accomplish something worth while, all that remains for me is my decision to entrust my difficulties to God: may He grant me better fortune and leisure, and may He allow me at last to be my own master, something highly desirable to intelligent people—since I am at present the slave rather of my urgent problems than of my own wishes. All this is certainly distressing. Nevertheless, there is one consolation which is sufficient for me: it is in the reflection that in his toiling the ruler will perhaps bring some benefit to his nation. Sweet to me, there- fore, are become my daily struggles and my nightly cares, alike to stay awake and alike to perservere at what needs to be done, no less in gladsome than in distressing things. Thus would it seem that, for those who wish to mull their cup with bitterness, the bitterness itself is not unmixed, even as there is no finding a life without sorrow among those who seem to be the most blest. . . .

(Manuel continues by emphasizing the importance of corre- spondence to him amid his trials, and he urges his friend to write.) [15]

15. Letter μδ', ed. Legrand, pp. 58–62: translated here are lines 1–72. Berger de Xivrey, 69–70, translates into French a very brief bit of the opening, but unfortunately he stops rather soon, after a scant eight lines. The letter was obviously written when Manuel was back in Constantinople after his great journey to Western Europe, to which he makes interesting allusion. (See above, p. 191, n. 126.) In spite of the normal exaggeration and rhetoric which one must always discount, the letter gives us perhaps some indication of Manuel's frame of mind when he plunged into the troubled post-Ancyra situation after returning home. Indeed, the reference to Turks as among those who pester him constantly might even suggest something of his involvement diplomatically with the sons of Bayazid, or at least with Suleyman, upon his return.

The allusions here to Dardanos and Antiochos are obscure; the latter, however, was presumably some sort of companion (ὁ 'Αντίοχος ὁ παρ' ἡμῖν,

Such reasonably personal and individual passages, however, are exceedingly unusual in Manuel's own writings. And one finds little in other contemporary material to shed light on the personal side of the Emperor's character. It is therefore of no small interest to come upon some slight suggestions of personal reflection—and unfavorable ones, at that—on Manuel in one of the important sources of the period. We have already had occasion to make use of the satiric work called *Sojourn of Mazaris in Hades*. While this violently and scurrilously vituperative picture of the selfish, grasping, unscrupulous, and immoral courtiers of the early fifteenth century must certainly be used with caution, there is no doubt that it reflects an intimate knowledge of Manuel's court. To be sure, Manuel himself seems almost to be held above the poisonous slander of this curious Lucianic and Aristophanic dialogue, and on the whole the author regards him with great respect, even admiration. In spite of this, however, there are three passages in the text from which one might clearly infer that the old Emperor was a difficult man to work under, to say the least. At one point the narrator speaks of his troubles at court and refers to "the angry tempers of the sovereign." [16] Again, shortly thereafter, Mazaris speaks of the "terrors and wrath of the Basileus" [17] and then suggests that Manuel used Mazaris and some of his associates as whipping boys:

as the text characterizes him), perhaps a palace servant of Manuel, possibly even a παρακοιμώμενος, a chamberlain, who sleeps in or near the Emperor's bedchamber. The allusion to trouble which is "common both to us here and to you there [κοινὸν . . . κἀνταῦθα κἀκεῖ]" may suggest something of the chronology of this letter, as well as the whereabouts of its recipient, Demetrius Chrysoloras. The latter seems to have served as a minister (μεσάζων) at the court of Thessalonica during most of the reign there of John VII (1403–1408), save for a brief visit to Constantinople in 1407 as πρέσβυς (cf. Dölger, *Regesten*, no. 3207, p. 77) after which he returned definitely to Manuel's court in the capital: Cammelli, *I dotti*, I, *Manuele Crisolora*, 198; P. Gautier, "Action de grâces de Démétrius Chrysoloras," *Rev. d. ét. byz.*, 19 (1961), 343; cf. also M. Treu, "Demetrios Chrysoloras und seine hundert Briefe," *Byz. Zeitschr.*, 20 (1911), 108. This letter is the second of a series (μγ΄, μδ΄, μς΄, μη΄, ν΄), which presumably dates from Demetrius' residence in Thessalonica. Hence the implied parallel which Manuel seems to make in this letter between "here" (Constantinople) and "there" (Thessalonica).

16. "... αἱ τοῦ κρατοῦντος ὀργαί...," ed. Boissonade, 144, ed. Ellissen, 213.

17. "... φοβερισμοὺς καὶ βασιλέως ὀργήν...," ed. Boissonade, 147, ed. Ellissen, 215.

. . . but whomsoever the most noble Autokrator wishes to affright and to strike with panic, whenever he sends them out on state service, he compares him with the miserable me, and [a colleague] and most wretched [another colleague], representing and convicting each of us as a monument of evil and of terror and of bad example.[18]

And, at still another point, Mazaris speaks of himself as "having been exceedingly vexed by the sovereign."[19] In view of the great strains and pressures to which Manuel was subject, it is not surprising that the old Emperor might have a short temper and might have become a difficult master to serve, demanding of his subordinates, and irascible toward those with whom he was displeased. Again, this text must be used with caution. But it cannot be dismissed lightly, even if its unfavorable reflection on Manuel seems to be unique. For, aside from the highly questionable tale concerning his alleged injustice to an illegitimate brother,[20] we have otherwise no authentically recorded instance of an act of real malice or spite on Manuel's part.

Another question which arises in discussing Manuel as a human being is that of his personal piety. We have one curious story in Clavijo, to the effect that Manuel had appropriated part of a relic from a monastery in Pera.[21] One can never be sure

18. "...ἀλλ' οὕστινας βούλεται ὁ γενναιότατος αὐτοκράτωρ φοβῆσαί τε καὶ ἐκπλῆξαι, ὁπόταν εἰς λειτουργίας ἐκπέμπῃ, ἐμή τε τὸν δύστηνον καὶ τὸν Μελικνάσαρ, καὶ ταλάντατον Βουλωτὴν παραβάλλει, ποιῶν τε καὶ ἐξελέγχων κακίας καὶ φοβερισμοῦ καὶ παραδείγματος στήλην." *Ibid.*

19. "...πλεῖστα ἀνιαθεὶς ὑπὸ τοῦ κρατοῦντος," ed. Boissonade, 165, ed. Ellissen, 231. In using these passages in this satire, however, we should bear in mind that it was written with the expectation that Manuel would read it himself. Indeed, it would seem as if the work had been written at the Emperor's express command and for his specific amusement. We learn this from a little epistolary epilogue by the author, apparently addressed to the Emperor, which does not appear in the editions of Boissonade and Ellissen and which survives only in a manuscript of the work they did not use; it has been published by M. Treu in his article "Mazaris und Holobolos," *Byz. Zeitschr.*, 1 (1892), 86–97: 86–87. This fact may add authority to its comments and prosopography, but it perhaps softens the seriousness of its vituperation and violent tone. This fact may also suggest that Manuel had a considerable sense of humor and was quite capable of enjoying a good literary joke at his court's expense, if not also his own to some extent.

20. As told by Chalcocondyles (see above, p. 285 and n. 153), whose bias is suspect here.

21. Clavijo, ed. López Estrada, 60–61 (cf. ed. Sreznevskii, 93; trans. Le Strange, 92), in telling of his visit to Galata, describes the relics he was shown at the Franciscan monastery there and relates that "moreover, there was displayed the right arm, with its hand, of St. Agnes, and it was very

how trustworthy this sort of tale really is, although it is not impossible that it does to some degree suggest accurately that Manuel shared the respect for holy relics so common in his age.[22] But certainly Manuel was not overly superstitious or scrupulous about relics, for we have seen how ready he was to use them as practical instruments of policy, a kind of "reliquary diplomacy," in his appeals to Western rulers for aid.[23]

Unfortunately, we have little evidence bearing directly on the Emperor's personal faith. His extant writings, however, do include a number of hymns and religious poems which indicate a highly polished formal piety. We also know from several of his works that he was deeply interested in theology and was far from meanly versed in it. He gave ample demonstration of his intense eagerness to leap to the defense of his Church and faith. Of course, in Manuel's case it is sometimes difficult to judge just how much of his writing is simply literary formality. In addition, in his case there is also the question of how much of his religious posture was simply a response to his position as Most Orthodox Emperor of the Christians. But there is every reason to assume that, regardless of the demands of policy and position, Manuel was himself a devout Orthodox Christian.

Manuel's rank as Emperor naturally obliged him to turn his attention to many concerns and to develop talents in many fields. Of Manuel as an administrator we know little, perhaps because there is little to know. In view of the destitute and constricted condition of his state, any coherent economic policy was probably all but impossible, save as a corollary to his quest for aid. As a result, the bulk of his surviving enactments in this sphere, as essentially stopgap or *ad hoc* measures, give little picture of any grand economic understanding.

expensively adorned. And it lacked the little finger, and they say that the emperor of Constantinople cut it off in order to put it among his relics, and that they are pressing litigation over it." Of course, Clavijo does not specifically state which Emperor was the culprit, and there is no telling how garbled the story may have become by the time he recorded it.

22. Clavijo also (ed. López Estrada, 36; cf. Ed. Sreznevskii, 54; trans. Le Strange, 63), in discussing one of the capital's churches, St. John in Petra near Blachernae, describes the relics, "to the which the emperor holds the keys." But this close control by the Emperor may suggest simply his awareness of the important value of these treasures, for the tourist trade or otherwise, rather than any particular piety toward them on his part personally.

23. See above, pp. 176–177, 183, 265, 511–512, and also p. 131 and n. 15.

As for military activity, so vigorously engaged in by many a Byzantine Emperor of old, Manuel's circumstances made him no stranger to warfare, but usually under conditions that gave him little opportunity to develop or display the qualities of a great general. Nevertheless, his performance is certainly not to be denigrated, but rather suggests some considerable capacity for military leadership. We have seen that in his Thessalonian venture, before the overwhelming power of the Turks was finally hurled against him, he was able to win some substantial victories over these formidable opponents [24]—a virtually unique achievement in Byzantine history. Though Bayazid's insistent use of Manuel as a military vassal was an undeniably political gesture, there is every reason to believe that Manuel participated actively and effectively; and these experiences, however bitter, inevitably contributed to his veteran military seasoning. In addition to field operations, Manuel had ample experience in siegecraft, not only offensive,[25] but especially defensive, for he personally directed the defense of Thessalonica in 1383–87 and the defenses of Constantinople during all the previous sieges of it during his lifetime, save that of 1422. During Boucicaut's expedition of 1399, Manuel shared the active command with the Marshal in its busy if restricted operations.[26] And even in his sixties, Manuel could still take to the field and trounce an opposing force during his visit to the Peloponnesus in 1415.[27] Though the size and extent of that last conflict are not known, surely any victories by force of arms over the rebellious barons of the Morea, as toughened a band of professional fighters and cutthroats as one could hope to encounter, was no mean achievement. Clearly, Manuel was not devoid of some military talent which, given more favorable opportunities, could have stood Byzantium in better stead and made Manuel the East Roman Marcus Aurelius.[28]

24. See above, pp. 46–49.
25. He participated in the Turkish reduction of Philadelphia: see above, p. 79. In his later years he besieged and captured the citadel of rebellious Thasos (see above, p. 299) and then blockaded and seized fortresses of the Moreote barons (see above, pp. 316–317).
26. See above, p. 163.
27. See above, p. 317.
28. At least one modern scholar has a considerably lower esteem for Manuel's talents in this field. In his recent brief discourse, "Angora, Florence, Varna and the Fall of Constantinople," 217, O. Halecki suggests that one of the reasons for the Christian failure to take advantage of the Turkish disaster at Ancyra was that Manuel, "an inspiring ruler in times of peace and

The most striking aspect of Manuel's personality and activities, however, is by no means a function of his status as Emperor. We have had ample occasion throughout the foregoing pages to have recourse to Manuel's voluminous writings. In them he makes clear that his literary activity was the cornerstone of his being, at once a passion from which he could never free himself, and at the same time a constant refuge to which he could and did always flee amid the crushing burdens and responsibilities of his official life.

And in the case of Manuel's literary activity we are, for a change, dealing with an aspect of his life on which there is much material. His interests began fairly early and were cultivated throughout virtually all of his adult life. Fortunately, too, the Emperor himself has left us an interesting reflection on his love of letters and its development. This comes at the beginning of a long and still unpublished discourse on theological matters in the form of a letter to one Alexius Iagoup (or Jacob). Though its emphasis is on Manuel's interest in theology, it reflects his broader preoccupations and various attitudes toward them:

When you came to me a day or two ago, you said that one of your intimates, in conversation with you on the previous day, claimed to be extremely concerned about me. For he professed to be much aggrieved that, when the cares of ruling scarce allow me to breathe, I choose to become involved with theology. But this, says he, is full of danger. For his part, as a friend, he reckons most important that I live my life with caution. Wherefore, had he thought I would have heeded what he said, he would have advised me to abstain altogether from theological study. Indeed, since my rank impels me to other business in this age that affords me many diverse problems, he would have advised me to direct my zeal altogether toward *them,* and in no way whatsoever to let myself be involved in a science that does not at all concern me; nor, on the other hand, to seek out anyone for instruction in what is needed to deal with the subject. After all,

a refined diplomat, was after all no strong military leader." Assuming the word "strong" refers to personal characteristics, this verdict is by no means a just one, as the foregoing recapitulation of the Emperor's military activities should indicate. It should also be borne in mind that no military leader, however gifted a field commander or tactician, is of any value without an army of some kind behind him. Manuel's great difficulty was that his resources allowed him no such force, and it was for the precise purpose of obtaining it—in essence, of making himself "strong"—that all his diplomatic efforts were being strained.

he claimed, a teacher of theology at once needs to be taught what is Truth from God Himself, and at the same time needs to be the most advanced expert in pagan Greek learning, or at least to have become a master in one of these respects before he tries to teach others. So that is certainly not within my reach now. Therefore, with matters as they stand, said he, it would accordingly be better for everyone—especially for the Basileus himself—not to wish themselves caught up in the toils of theology. And so he also said that he desires him [the Basileus] to make a written promise never by any means to seek involvement with theological dogmas, for never would he come anywhere near coping with so complex a subject.

Well now, these statements certainly raise many and varied issues, to dispute which requires both labor and leisure. And for me to answer them would, as you can imagine, require something like a year. But this most violent era, with its unspeakable difficulties, some present and others threatened, neither grants nor allows this. Wherefore, at first I decided there was no need to undertake any defense at all. But then, when you finished conveying his objections to me, you did demand an answer forthwith—though I suppose you will remember, for you wanted to have it so that you could answer your inquiring friend; and I was not at leisure, for the evening hymn to God was being sung. So, when I did have some leisure, even if not complete, I thought I ought to come to grips with the question. In the first place, such points as indicate that the man spoke these objections with no regard for my safety but merely that he was able to say with license at last things hitherto said in private and with discretion, when now there was nothing to stop him—since there was no one who would answer back—such points will be left aside for the time being, since, as I said, time does not allow for them. But, by contrast, the points that would cast discredit on me if I should remain silent—that is, if I were to think everyone ought to discuss theology all the time indiscriminately with everyone else—these points, then, will be discussed for your benefit, as briefly as is possible. In this latter respect, it is desirable that one who is occupied with such important matters should exonerate himself completely if anyone should find fault with him. Whereas, with regard to the other question, not to find fault with the fault-finder in the event he has found fault unjustly is, I suppose, certainly worthy of commendations or, at least, not of being found fault with.

So, then, when I was a child, it was not possible for me to frequent only the haunts of the Muses and to make this my sole employment, so that I could overtake every man of wisdom, even those who pride themselves in their learning. But, once I was out of my earliest instruction, toils followed one upon another. And it was necessary each day to alternate among my many teachers, who taught many other things—how to handle both bow and spear, and how to ride horseback. And then, once I had passed the age of children, though before reaching manhood, a different fortune ensued with my advancing age, one filled with storm and tumults, allowing one to prophesy from many signs that such fortune, then impending, would reveal our preceding troubles as a dead calm by contrast. Well, of course, to people who already know all these things it is superfluous to recount them. Everyone knows, however, that there were prophets of no mean rank who predicted that terrible times were coming. And come they did. So if, therefore, I ever in my childhood reaped the fruits of my studies, I cast aside at least the bulk of this, having been transferred elsewhere from my literary pursuits. For, many woes, brought together all at once, as if at some signal, thereupon attacked me: difficulties, and struggle with various calamities, and dangers one upon another. Such circumstances, blowing upon me with violent force, allowed no repose.

Thereafter a prison confined me, together with my father, the Basileus, and also my brother. Then indeed, as for all men in such circumstances, it was necessary to resort to activities of all kinds, so as to dissipate at least a little, in our leisure for these things, our cloud of despondency, and so as not to surrender completely to the evils both actual and suspected, which course would not be worthy of a man. At this time, therefore, it seemed good to me to take as my continuous activity a preoccupaton with books, nightly and by day, after performing my duty [i.e., of regular prayer] to God. But then, why do I say "by day"? There it was eternally a gloomy night. Wherefore, anyone who turned to any such occupation was obliged to use a lantern. Our prison cut off the rays even of high noon as effectually as, elsewhere on earth, night cuts them off from those who are outside of prison. Being destitute of any instructor, I was not able to advance in most respects in proportion to my many labors. Nevertheless, though, in the very continuity of my activity an utterly tyrannical desire for my studies sank deeply into my soul. Thus has it altogether prevailed, so as to make me into not merely a devotee of this activity, but an extreme fanatic.

But then, when three years had passed by and all our restraints were removed by God's hand, we returned directly once again to our former rank, and always was it necessary thus to be occupied with arms, and sometimes to move from one place to another, and not without danger of death. For, not even a brief truce did my ill fortune

Figure 33: *Constantinople, the Tower of Anemas* (photo courtesy Cyril Mango; see Appendix XXIV, C, 1).

concede. Once I had been ensnared by my studies, however, I was not able to put aside my desire. But, while I viewed fortune as an opponent, I regarded the aid gained from my studies as a trainer. So, I endeavored, by advancing in studies, to endure my dreadful ordeal and, at the same time, as long as I endured, to advance in studies. Wherefore, when I had progressed, I was also obliged to seek out many as my helpers toward what I was seeking; and, of course, I did not fail in my object. For I found men who enjoyed divine assistance and favor, and who were properly educated in classical learning. Not that it would be noteworthy if someone chooses to say the opposite—if, that is, he is one who expects to increase and enhance his own merits by detracting from others. Yet, even admitting that I have benefited considerably from the men I mentioned, I must grant that I have not really benefited all that much. For I own that from their spark no torch has been enkindled in me. Rather, from their great torch scarcely a spark have I been able to catch, nor has one become a part of me. And I am at a loss to decide whether I must blame the difficulties of our era for this failure, or whether I must indict my own innate stupidity. . . .

413

(From here Manuel returns to his interest in theology for the rest of the text.) [29]

The question of the attitudes of others toward Manuel's studies will be dealt with shortly. It is interesting, however, to note here the emphasis that Manuel placed upon the interval of his imprisonment, obviously that interval during the usurpation of his brother Andronicus IV (1376–79), as a valuable opportunity for advancing his studies.[30] What is more curious, however, is the omission of any direct allusion to the man who, probably more than anyone else, shaped and guided Manuel's literary development.

No study of Manuel Palaeologus is possible without some study of Demetrius Cydones of Thessalonica. Nor was Manuel the only person to be influenced by this man whose life spanned almost the entire fourteenth century and whose career is inseparable from much of the political and cultural history of Byzantium in that period. Minister and confidant of two Emperors, convert to Latin Catholicism, and ardently pro-Western politically and intellectually, Cydones was also a theologian and, most important of all, one of the central figures of Byzantine letters of the day. Few could have been better suited to be a mentor to the star-crossed younger son of John V. To be sure, we have little in the way of documented proof that this distinguished man actually was Manuel's official and formal tutor. But there is strong circumstantial evidence to this effect, primarily in the

29. As stated, the text of this long letter-discourse to Alexius Iagoup (Berger de Xivrey's no. 56) has not been published yet. But it may be found in the principal manuscript of the Emperor's works, *Parisinus gr. 3041*, ff. 72^v–85^v. It is from a microfilm of this codex, kindly provided me by the Bibliothèque Nationale in Paris through Dumbarton Oaks, that I have edited approximately the first three pages as a basis for the foregoing translation. This text may be found below, as Appendix XXIII. Actually, however, two brief extracts from this passage—and, arbitrarily, no more—were transcribed and published by Berger de Xivrey. The first of the two (lines 44–62 in the Appendix text below; paragraph three in the translation above) may be found in Greek in n. 1 on his p. 26, with his French translation, pp. 25–26; cf. Khoury, "L'Empereur Manuel II," 130. This same passage has recently been translated into English by Dennis, *The Reign of Manuel II Palaeologus in Thessalonica*, 14; and previously one brief sentence was also given thus by Vasiliev, *History of the Byzantine Empire*, 629. The text of the second of the two extracts (lines 63–79 below; the fourth paragraph above) was printed by Berger de Xivrey in his n. 1 to p. 44, with translations neither by him nor anyone else thereafter.

30. Cf. above, p. 32 and n. 84.

long and close relationship that flourished between them in Manuel's mature years. Indeed, we have fairly definite testimony from the Emperor himself. Manuel frequently sent copies of his own new literary works to Cydones, itself a revealing practice. A letter enclosed with one of them, his *Discourse of Counsel to the Thessalonians When They Were Besieged* of 1383–84, deserves quotation, both as an example of its kind and also for its own particular contents:

The ability to write is clearly better than being wealthy, is sweeter also than all sweet things, and, indeed, brings the greater glory. One may find, however, that it is perhaps entirely the opposite case with those who, while attempting to write, have not been trained thoroughly from childhood in the ways of letters. For anyone who wishes to learn how to write faultlessly, it is necessary first of all to have words in which men may take pleasure and matter to render them honored and envied, and to have a nature equal to the exercise, and an intelligence equal to the endeavor, and, in addition, to have the benefit of time. So, therefore, lacking all of the requirements I have enumerated, I thought it best to be content with silence and to hold fast to it with both hands: and I certainly have done this—for how long a time you know yourself, since you have not received my usual letters. But since the great affection and the equal good will which I nourish for your fellow citizens [i.e., the Thessalonians] have altogether overcome me, and since it appeared impossible for me to abide by my resolution—for there was need of my advice, and I said what seemed to me for the city's advantage—I do not conceal this defeat from you, and I reveal my composition. For, if it is just and safe not to share one's secrets with those who are not one's friends, it is far from just, and it is also dangerous, to keep anything a secret from such a friend as you happen to be to me. So, again I reveal my defeat to you, and thereby, as it were, I denounce myself to you. At the same time, however, I know well that you will be indulgent, since I imagine that you also, swayed by the influence of affection, have often trodden on rules and laws which you yourself set up. Nevertheless, as for this composition, should it seem to have been put together well, and not to be something to be concealed, you yourself will know in what ways you will reveal it. So, may you pluck yourself sweet fruit, as being the instigator of this; for you yourself supplied the seeds to me, and likewise by you was the watering bountifully poured forth. On the other hand, if it appears worth only casting into the fire, seek not to receive satisfaction from me: rather, it is you who owe it yourself, as the one who plants and waters and cultivates writing within me.[31]

The inference of this letter is obvious, and Cydones' role as Manuel's instructor has therefore been accepted as virtual fact.[32] Certainly such an assignment to Cydones would be completely understandable as a part of the general reconciliation which seems to have taken place in the late 1350's and early 1360's between the triumphant John V and the supporters of John VI Cantacuzenus, including Cydones.[33]

Cydones' influence on Manuel by no means ended with the young prince's attainment of manhood and his emergence on the active political scene, by the early 1370's. We have already had ample occasion to observe the flourishing and important correspondence between them for the next two decades. Manuel continued to value the wisdom and friendship of his old master and often sought his advice. Cydones on his part admired the genuine literary interests and talents of his brilliant pupil, now a friend, and he did his best to encourage them. There is more than mere flattery in his letter in which he praises Manuel as one who, in Homer's words, is able "to be both a speaker of words and a doer of deeds." [34] The strong bond between them provided by their common love of Classical literature is demonstrated by their exchange of letters over Manuel's dispatch of a manuscript of Plato which Cydones had asked him to procure for him from Mount Athos during the hectic Thessalonian period of 1382–87.[35]

31. Letter ια΄, ed. Legrand, 14–15, fully translated here; a very brief passage (ll. 31–35) was translated by Berger de Xivrey, 25; cf. also Dennis, 14. For the background of the *Discourse*, which this letter accompanied, and for Cydones' response, see above, pp. 52–53 and n. 145; and below, n. 34.

32. Cf. Berger de Xivrey, 24–25; Loenertz, *Les Recueils de Lettres de Démétrius Cydonès*, 110; Dennis, 14, and 20.

33. Cf. pp. 37 ff. For some good general comments on Cydones' career and intellectual role, see Setton, "The Byzantine Background to the Italian Renaissance," 52–57.

34. Cydones' Letter C. 204, L. 120; the Homeric phrase μύθων τε ῥητῆρ᾽ ἔμεναι πρηκτῆρά τε ἔργων is from *Iliad*, IX, l. 433, and is slightly abridged in Cydones' quotation of it, ed. Loenertz, I, p. 159, l. 24. Much the same sentiment may be found in Letter C. 187, L. 262, which was actually Cydones' reply to Manuel's Letter ια΄ (see above, n. 31). In it, Cydones specifically praises Manuel for his ability to follow his literary interests even amid the strains of defending Thessalonica; cf. Loenertz, *Echos d'Orient*, 37 (1938), 113; Dennis, 15.

35. Manuel acknowledged Cydones' request in his Letter γ΄, ed. Legrand,

Other letters written during the trying days of the siege of Thessalonica from 1383 to 1387 demonstrate Manuel's practice of falling back on intellectual distractions amid pressure and adversity. Indeed, at one point Cydones even felt obliged to warn Manuel against pursuing his studies to the extent of neglecting his military responsibilities in the beleaguered city.[36] In one case, however, Cydones expressed a different kind of disapproval when he heard that Manuel was making a compilation of Cydones' own letters. The latter—who himself copied many of his own letters systematically—protested to Manuel with ruffled modesty.[37]

As has already been demonstrated extensively, Manuel did not rely on Cydones for literary encouragement alone, but he profited also from his teacher's close contacts at court during the trying years up to his accession, often seeking advice from him.[38] Amid the humiliations of his military service with Bayazid, at least in 1391, Cydones was Manuel's chief confidant in the letters which provide us with so much priceless material on this episode.[39]

Their closeness continued in Cydones' final years, and Manuel still submitted his writings to his old master. The occasion of just such a gesture in one of Manuel's last letters to Cydones, with a closing tribute to the teacher's influence on the Emperor, was marked, however, by a note of real harshness. In late 1396 Manuel sent a copy of his *Ethical Dialogue, or Concerning Marriage* to Cydones, who was then on his final visit to the West. With it went a letter, which is worth quoting in full, not only as one of Manuel's last communications to his aged mentor, soon to die in Crete, but also for the curious sentiments it reflects:

3–5, at the same time appealing for his friend's presence in Thessalonica. Cydones responded in his own Letter C. 224, L. 276, and then commented further on the actual arrival of the manuscript subsequently in C. 219, L. 259. These letters are discussed and quoted by Dennis, 69–70.

36. Cydones, Letter C. 199, L. 304; cf. Loenertz, *Echos d'Orient*, 36 (1937), 474. By contrast, during Manuel's unpleasant exile on Lemnos after 1387, Cydones good-humoredly suggests in one letter (C. 234, L. 388) that Manuel is neglecting his studies in favor of hunting: cf. above, p. 66.

37. Cydones, Letter C. 205, L. 326. Manuel defended this venture in his own Letter ι', ed. Legrand, 14. Cydones commented further on the matter in his Letter C. 290, L. 263. Cf. Dennis, 96.

38. E.g., at the time of the fall of Thessalonica in 1387: see above, pp. 57 ff.

39. See above, pp. 88–98.

There comes to you the customary offering, writing sent to the father of writing. This is my own work, to which the troublesome impositions now upon me, become as a spur and as compulsions, led me. I know, at any rate, that this discourse will gladden you more than those which have come from me before this, since it reaches you while you are abroad and is a conversation between persons to whom you were once pleased to listen and whose sight you once said you regarded as a delicacy, being with whom, you also said, was not to be placed second to wealth [cf. Plato, *Phaedrus*, 227B]. But I myself, on the other hand, would wish this dialogue to gladden you not for this reason only, but also in its surpassing all my literary offspring which preceded it. At all events, if it should turn out in accordance with my intentions, it is thanks to you. For, he who furnishes the seed is himself the author of the begetting, as your comrade says.[40] But if, on the other hand, the results of my aspiration should work out to the contrary, and if, in addition, I should seem to you to have made no progress and even to be mentally incapable of producing writing, I will fall back on the argument of this troublesome time and other such factors, and perhaps I will reasonably excuse myself. But someone else, not unjustly, might put the blame on the gardener who has cut off the water: I mean you, who has put an alien country before your homeland, which latter has more claim on you than any other now, at a time when duty demands that you should endeavor by every means to help it; which is certainly clear proof that you do not bear your country the love which you ought. Do not imagine that, by lamenting its fate while you are sitting out of arrow shot, you are fulfilling your obligation to it! But in its evil state you ought to share its dangers and help it with deeds as far as is possible, if you have any intention of displaying yourself as a soldier worthy of more than a posting for desertion.[41]

40. "Ὁ γὰρ τὸ σπέρμα παρασχών, οὗτος τῶν φύτων αἴτιος ὁ σὸς ἑταῖρός φησιν" (ed. Legrand, p. 93, ll. 13–15). When Manuel speaks of "your comrade" (ὁ σὸς ἑταῖρος) in his letters to Cydones, he invariably means Plato. And Plato does, indeed, use this kind of imagery a number of times. But this does not seem to be a quotation (as the editor makes it), and the closest parallel in any of Plato's works seems to be a passage in a work Manuel thus had in mind at least twice in this letter, the *Phaedrus*, 277A: "ἀλλὰ ἔχοντες σπέρμα, ὅθεν ἄλλοι ἐν ἄλλοις ἤθεσι φυόμενοι τοῦτ' ἀεὶ ἀθάνατον ἱκανοί. . . ."

41. Letter ξδ´, ed. Legrand, 92–93, fully translated here; a brief passage is translated into French by V. Laurent in *Rev. d. ét. byz.*, 14 (1956), 201. The reference to "persons to whom you were once pleased to listen, etc.," apparently alludes to Manuel himself and his mother, who are the actual protagonists of the Dialogue sent with the letter. On the dating of this letter, see above, pp. 111–112, n. 32.

The reference to "putting an alien country before your homeland" and the extraordinary preachment which follows are quite startling. Let us recall that this letter was written just after the Battle of Nicopolis, at a time when Byzantium was facing a new peak of danger in the face of Bayazid's renewed onslaughts. And so we find Manuel actually rebuking Cydones for desertion of their country in a time of peril.[42] This letter raises interesting questions about a possible souring of relations between the old scholar and his exalted pupil at the very end of their relationship.

If Cydones played a fundamental role in fostering and encouraging Manuel's intellectual interests, he was by no means the only one. Manuel could feel well at home in the company of the large intellectual circle of the day. To be sure, outside of this circle there may have been some objection to the spectacle of the Emperor whiling away his time with scribblings while the state was suffering such wrenching agonies. We may recall an interesting and significant remark made by Manuel in the course of one of his letters, already quoted in full, written to Cydones during his trying military service with Bayazid. Commenting on the difficulties of finding time for his beloved correspondence while in the field, Manuel observes:

. . . As for those to whom it is not bearable that I should be engaged in literary pursuits when sitting at home, they would quickly make a

42. On Byzantium's post-Nicopolis situation in general, see above, pp. 137 ff. In regard to Manuel's cutting reprimand to Cydones for abandoning his country in its hour of need, two facts might be recalled. The first is that Manuel himself may well have contemplated doing exactly the same thing himself at two points during Bayazid's siege: see above, pp. 124–125 and 146. (In fairness to Manuel, it might be noted that our evidence for this contemplation is simply the speculation of the Venetian Senate in 1394 and 1397, which may have been based simply on their concern to keep in mind all possibilities of what might happen, rather than on any actual plan on Manuel's part.) The second fact is that Manuel himself, as we have already seen, wrote to Cydones just after the latter's departure in 1396, stressing how fortunate it was that his old friend had escaped the terrible post-Nicopolis situation: see the translation above, pp. 134–136. In the light of these two facts, Manuel's cruel sarcasm seems unduly harsh. Yet, this astonishing note of ill-feeling at the very end of their long and otherwise affectionate relationship can no longer be ignored in assessing that relationship. Moreover, this remarkable letter enables us quickly to discard the characterization by Zakythinos ("Démétrius Cydonès et l'entente balkanique au XIVe siècle," 47) of Cydones' final journey as a noble mission for nothing less than "afin de plaider, pour une dernière fois, la cause de son pays en danger." Cydones' voyage was a purely personal one and seems to have involved no official business whatsoever.

great outcry could they but see me doing these things here. For, with regard to all the evils which they are presently experiencing, and have experienced, they need only blame themselves. Yet, they would as easily blame my literary pursuits for making rivers flow backward, since they do not consider me guiltless of such charges, and you equally as well, for obvious reasons.[43]

But, whatever ill feeling Manuel's literary pursuits may have won him among some elements of his subjects, they elevated him to a particularly exalted position among the intellectuals of the day. The coterie which was proud to number Manuel a member included such outstanding figures as Demetrius Cydones himself, Nicholas Cabasilas, the great Manuel Chrysoloras, and Demetrius Chrysoloras, to all of whom Manuel wrote letters which have survived to us; it included further Manuel Kalekas, a fellow pupil of Cydones,[44] Georgios Gemistos Plethon, the great Platonist who admired the Emperor's reform measures,[45] and the celebrated Bessarion, the future cardinal, who delivered Manuel's funeral eulogy.[46] To such major cultural figures Manuel was a worthy intellectual peer as well as their sovereign. Not without meaning did Cydones repeatedly extol him as a true "philosopher-king" in the Platonic sense.[47]

And, indeed, among Byzantine Emperors Manuel's example is surely a rare one. Certainly an average Byzantine *Basileus* was likely to be highly educated and cultured. Many were ardent

43. Letter ιθ΄, ed. Legrand, 28–30; the passage translated here is ll. 25–31. For the full translation of the entire letter, see above, pp. 95–96.

44. On Kalekas, see H. G. Beck, *Kirche und theologische Litteratur im byzantinischen Reich* (*Handbuch der Altertumswissenschaft*, XI, 2, 1, Munich, 1959), 740 f.

45. Cf. above, pp. 312–314 and n. 22.

46. See above, p. 384 and n. 162.

47. See above, p. 84 and n. 1. On the subject of Manuel and his contemporaries in general, there is now an article by N. B. Tomadakes, "Μανουὴλ Β΄ ὁ Παλαιολόγος (†1425) καὶ οἱ λόγιοι τῶν χρόνων αὐτοῦ," Παρνασσός, II, 2 (1960), 561–575, which I have been unable to consult as of this writing. Also broadly on the intellectual climate and establishment of Manuel's day, see F. Fuchs, *Die höheren Schulen von Konstantinopel im Mittelalter* (=*Byzantinisches Archiv*, 8, Leipzig and Berlin, 1926), 65 ff., especially 68–69, and 73–74. L. Bréhier, *Le Monde byzantin*, III: *La Civilisation byzantine* (*L'Evolution de l'humanité*, XXXII, 3: Paris, 1950), 484–485, suggests that Manuel profited from his experience of Western scholarship and his observation of the Sorbonne when he reformed the University of Constantinople after returning from his journey; a point advanced even more emphatically by S. Vryonis, *Byzantium and Europe* (New York, 1967), 178. But I know of no evidence for this assertion.

admirers and patrons of culture. And some were also writers themselves. Casting back into "pre-Byzantine" times, one might cite Marcus Aurelius as the best parallel, the philosopher-emperor who is also a great doer of deeds as well as an intellectual and a writer. In the actual Byzantine line, the cases of Leo VI (886–912) and Constantine VII Porphyrogenitus (913–959) come to mind most naturally and immediately. The latter is perhaps the greatest rival to Manuel as a cultural figure among the Emperors of the East. But, for all his sincere passion for learning and for all his own active literary work, Constantine VII was probably of more importance as a patron and a stimulant than as an actually original contributor in many cases. Theodore II Lascaris (1254–1258), during the Empire's Nicaean period, was a zealous if unoriginal intellectual, whose highly artificial rhetoric and genuinely humanistic interests remind one rather strikingly of Manuel II. Manuel's own ancestor Michael VIII (1259–1282) also dabbled with a pen and even wrote a short autobiographical work. And Manuel's grandfather, John VI Cantacuzenus, who wrote actively after his encloisterment, is also high among the ranks of East Roman historians as "the only Byzantine Emperor to write detailed memoirs." [48] But none of the Emperors, with all their respective literary achievements, ever attained quite the same status as did Manuel as an equal of the cultural leaders of his day, as one of the principal active contributors to the intellectual life of his epoch. At once a great statesman and a major Byzantine literary figure, Manuel, among his fellow *Basileis,* is almost unique.

In view of the important role of literary activity in Manuel's life and of Manuel's important role in the literary activity of his age, one would be happy to find him a stirring and effective writer who made some valuable contribution to world literature. Alas, this is not the case. His subject matter is rarely of very broad interest. More damaging, his style is that of his day: elaborate, obscure, archaistic, artificial, highly rhetorical, and often devoid of any real substance. Almost equally applicable to Manuel's writings are the comments on Cydones by one of the most learned and experienced modern scholars of this period:

The letters of Demetrius Cydones, doubtless written with the ulterior motive of an eventual publication, are nevertheless true letters,

48. Vasiliev, *Hist. Byz. Emp.,* 688.

intended initially for a specific reader, usually well-informed about the matters which the author wished to discuss with him. How many allusions, intelligible to the recipient, must remain mysterious for us! This is, after all, the one difficulty common to all letter writing. But in the case of the Byzantines it is singularly aggravated. Written according to the precepts of a rhetoric hostile to proper names, to concrete details and to technical terms, their letters offer to us the image of their times in a distorting mirror of Classical antiquity. The reader sinks into the Cave of Plato, to draw awareness of the illuminated world from the outlines of a pageant of shadows. The nine *archons* preside over the destinies of the city, the *thesmothetai* are seated beneath the *Tholos,* the *Hellenodikai* pronounce judgment among the athletes of the Olympian gathering. The Triballians populate Serbia and the Moesians Bulgaria, and, ruling Asia Minor, the Persians threaten the freedom of the Hellenes. In that vast correspondence, only few strange words . . . would baffle a contemporary of Pericles. . . .[49]

As with so many Byzantine writers, Manuel could never escape the overwhelming consciousness of the traditions of the Classical past, which lay upon them almost as a kind of dead hand. Something of this outlook is reflected strikingly in one of Manuel's letters to a friend, Gabriel of Thessalonica. Even if much of its contents is stereotyped and stylized, it still reflects most interestingly something of the Emperor's attitude toward his own writing, and of the perspective of well-educated Byzantine intellectuals in general. As such it deserves to be better known:

It is said that once a peasant, upon beholding a palace, was so much astonished at its beauty that he came to loathe the hovel in which he was living and set it afire. If this is altogether absurd, then there is no need for any intelligent man to find fault with his own productions, should they be of some worth, merely because someone else's are a great deal better. Rather it is fitting to admire those things that are splendid but, at the same time, to bear with those that are not, just as one need not hate his own sons should those of his neighbors be more comely. I will not be distressed, therefore, and I will make it my rule not to discuss the point, inasmuch as I am well aware that my ability in the realm of writing is not on a level with those who are highly esteemed in this respect. On the contrary, I would

49. Loenertz, *Les Recueils,* p. vi; a portion of this passage is also quoted (in the original French) by Dennis, 20.

not want to rank myself at all with those possessing high reputation in the art of writing. For, I am not ignorant of the *Phaedrus* by Plato, son of Ariston. Nor, therefore, would I ever succumb to the desires of other people who encourage me to be overly proud. Nevertheless, it seems to me exceedingly stupid if, as regards the fruits of our effort that seem to be of some usefulness, we should obliterate them completely because they are not absolutely marvelous. Quite the contrary: if one will make this his law—I mean that the inferiors must keep silent out of deference to their betters— why then, I believe not one of our modern generation would dare to open his mouth, in view of the pre-eminence by far of the ancients. But this would be very unfortunate. After all, the best course for those of us who endeavor to write at all is to regard the works of the leaders in writing as our models, so far as is possible. At the same time, however, we must understand clearly that we do not approach them, and we are in no wise to be abashed by their superiority, nor to find it unbearable that our own compositions rank vastly below those of Demosthenes and Thucydides and their peers, inasmuch as the glories of the past have quite deserted the mortals of present times. Certainly if one should place the writings of the ancients beside those of the present age, he is "exchanging gold for bronze." [*Iliad* VI, 236.] For, such is the inferiority of our times that, reduced to the necessity either of writing as did those disciples of Hermes and the Muses once wrote, or else of not writing at all, no one nowadays would produce a single word, since it is not possible to talk on their level. And yet, should we abstain from the practice of writing, our education will be so undermined that it would become impossible for us to understand the dogmas from which is derived our True Faith.

With these points in mind, my worthy friend, I continue writing, not as much as I ought, but as much as my time allows, so that I will serve to those under my sway as an example in the love of letters, in order that they, as they mingle so much with barbarians, may not themselves become entirely barbarized. There comes to you, then, something from among the fruits of my own toils. And, if there be found in it anything worthwhile, you will point it out by what means you think best, nor will you keep it to yourself. If, on the other hand, it be judged absolutely worthless, a sponge will cure it [i.e., by erasing it], as Aristeides says. I mean to say, in the latter case, either deliver it over to the fire-god's hearth, or at least let it be seen by no one else: though I do not mean this to apply to the good Makarios, who is a true friend and who is distinguished in virtue.[50]

50. Letter νβ', ed. Legrand, 78–79, fully translated here; French translation of a very brief passage (ll. 20–23) by Berger de Xivrey, 146; virtually

Powerful as was their background in the content of Classical literature, even more formidable was the influence of its style on Byzantine writers. So anxious were these *literati* to preserve the glories of the ancient style that they shunned the crudities of the modern tongue which surrounded them and cultivated in their writings the idiom of the past with a zeal that resulted in a hot-house artificiality of extraordinary degree—imagine people today attempting to write English regularly in the manner of Chaucer or Beowulf or even Shakespeare, or French in the idiom of the *Chanson de Roland!* Inevitably, such effort produced a pedantic and crabbed abortion of style. Obscure and unusual tricks of Classical style are seized upon and used to absurd extremes. Logical syntax is distorted almost beyond recognition, and word order beyond all reason. Infinitives are used recklessly in place of participles; participles are exploited by the bushel as nouns. Key words are deliberately omitted, as if an architect had built his structure and then had gone about removing as much vital masonry as possible to see how much he could take away before it all collapsed in a meaningless heap. Conversely, vague and imprecise words are gleefully strewn about at every opportunity. Grammar and vocabulary become pawns in a learned game, in which each expert vies with the other to achieve a nirvana of esoteric enigma. Maintaining the Hellenistic tradition with remarkable fidelity on the one hand, and mirroring on the other the rhetoric typical of early Renaissance humanists, Manuel's principal concern is perfection of form, making of each work an exercise in empty and stylized patterns. In the process, content and substance are often lost or ignored and are almost always subordinate to demands of style and displays of elegance.[51]

It would be unjust, of course, to condemn Manuel alone for these distorting characteristics, some of which are inherent in the Greek language of itself. Moreover, Manuel was writing in an

the same passage is also translated (in English) by R. H. Jenkins in an article in *Dumbarton Oaks Papers, No. 17* (1963), p. 46. Precisely which of his writings Manuel sent with this letter is not clear, nor is the identity of the Makarios, to whom he alludes, fully plain. The reference at the end apparently draws upon Aelius Aristides, but I have been unable to locate or identify the citation.

51. For some of Manuel's Hellenistic models, see the Jenkins article just cited, *Dumbarton Oaks Papers, No. 17* (1963), 44–45.

idiom which was admired by the intellectuals of his time and culture, one which was taken for granted by them as the only true style worth attaining in learned and serious writing. But in some respects, it must be admitted, Manuel excels even his contemporaries in their exasperating idiosyncracies. It is small wonder, then, that his great legacy of extant writings attracts few modern readers, students, or admirers. For all his great importance as a literary figure, his works are of interest essentially to the scholar of Byzantine history and culture, a trial to be avoided by the layman, and a source of challenge and despair for the specialist.[52]

In spite of their difficulties and frustrations, however, Manuel's works remain sources of the most fundamental importance, of course, for the study of his life and reign in particular and for an understanding of late Byzantine culture in general. And, in truth, in comparison with the works of other Byzantine intellectuals, especially in the realm of correspondence, his writings often contain far more factual or descriptive substance than might have been expected. As a capstone to our consideration of this Emperor and his accomplishments, therefore, it behooves us to examine briefly the corpus of his surviving writings.[53]

52. Cf. Dennis, 95, on Manuel's letters, "which are not so much personal letters as brief literary essays on a variety of topics—classical literature, religion, philosophy and occasionally contemporary events and matters of a personal nature. In general, there is little spontaneity in these letters, overburdened as they are with classical allusions and written in conscious imitation of ancient models. Manuel must have spent much time in composing them, searching for the *mot juste* or the proper turn of a phrase, and in this he would seem to have been successful (although clarity is not his strongest point), for his letters occupy an important place in the history of Byzantine literature."

53. The most important discussion of Manuel's complete writings remains the bulk of L. Petit's excellent article on the Emperor in the *Dictionnaire de théologie catholique*, IX, 2, coll. 1926–1932, to which the present survey is but a supplement. Petit also lists various editions of Manuel's published texts, and only editions since his article are cited below. Before Petit's survey, Berger de Xivrey did draw up a detailed table in the final pages of his study (186–201), which he entitled "Essai d'une distribution chronologique des ouvrages de l'empereur Manuel Paléologue." In this table he assigned each work a number, from 1 to 109; these numbers are still worth noting, as is done here. But this list is, of course, badly out of date. Much of its chronology is totally wrong, many of Manuel's extant works were not known to him and were therefore not included, and, conversely, purely on the basis of references in other works, Berger de Xivrey assumed Manuel's completion of certain alleged writings which do not exist today. Of these last, the majority proba-

These come down to us in several manuscripts, most of them from the fifteenth century. The most important of these is undoubtedly that now in the Bibliothèque Nationale in Paris, the *Parisinus graecus 3041*. This deserves to be called the principal manuscript of his writings, not only because it contains a larger number of them than any other single manuscript—though by no means all or the most important of them—but also because it was apparently prepared under the direct supervision of the Emperor himself. The recognition of Manuel's personal involvement with this manuscript was first made by the great French scholar Boissonade almost a century and a quarter ago, in connection with the heavily marked-up and mutilated state of one of the works it contains, the Dialogue on Marriage (Περὶ γάμου). "Which dialogue," he observes, "after many erasures and attempts at correction, was at length completely crossed out from beginning to end, by the hand—who could doubt?—of the most august author himself." [54]

Amplification of this conclusion was made by Legrand, who, in his 1893 edition of Manuel's Letters, wrote thus:

This manuscript has undergone certain corrections . . . and some suppressions which, in our opinion, could only have been carried out by the august author of the Letters. This is the same hand which has amended the Περὶ γάμου, then has finished by crossing out this work. Boissonade was of the opinion that Manuel alone could have treated thus his work. [55]

bly never did exist, since most of the assumptions on which their existence is based are very questionable, to say the least.

To avoid the involvements and pitfalls of Petit's and Berger de Xivrey's respective methods, the following survey of Manuel's works is cast in terms solely of a review of surviving manuscripts. Of these manuscripts, the present writer has been able to examine only one directly, the *Parisinus gr. 3041*, and that only in a microfilm provided by the Bibliothèque Nationale, through Dumbarton Oaks. The other manuscripts are discussed on the basis of information published to date by other scholars and in the various manuscript catalogues.

54. "Qui dialogus, post multas lituras et correctionum tentamina, fuit demum a capite ad calcem totus cancellatus, manu, quis dubitet? ipsius auctoris augustissimi. . . .": *Anecdota nova* (Paris, 1844), p. 249, n. 1, the observation being made in connection with the text of Manuel's letter to Cydones which accompanied a copy of the Dialogue. For a photograph of two pages of that text, see Figure 34; see also Appendix XXIV (A, III, 4).

55. *Lettres de l'empereur Manuel Paléologue*, p. xii.

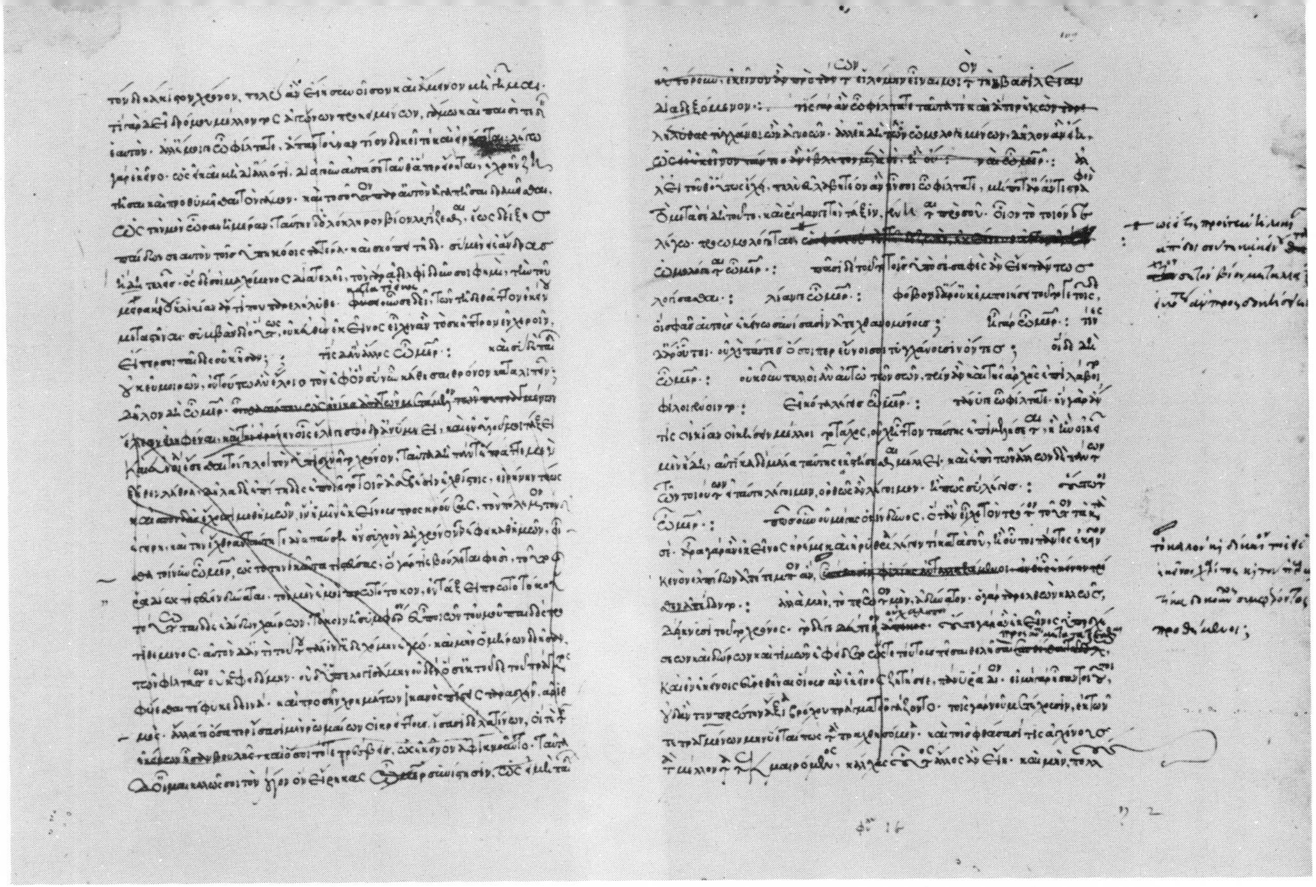

Figure 34: *Manuel's Proofreading: Two Pages of the Dialogue* Περὶ γάμου *Corrected and Then Crossed Out by His Own Hand*. Bibliothèque Nationale, Paris, Cod. gr. 3041, ff. 102ᵛ and 103ʳ (photo courtesy Bibliothèque Nationale, Paris; see Appendix XXIV, A, III, 4).

Between the work of these two scholars came that of Berger
de Xivrey, in 1853, whose description of this codex deserves full
quotation:

The Greek manuscript of which we speak, written on paper and
covered with a rich binding under the coat of arms of Henry II, is
characterized by a particularity of a kind which attracts notice. The
script, although featuring the invariable neatness and the regularity
which characterize the craft of calligraphy before typographic
competition, indicates as its date the first years of the century in which
printing was invented. The second part of the book, in a less elaborate
script, although it seems to be from the same hand, contains the
Annals of Nicephorus [*sic*] Choniates. The first part, which alone concerns us, is laden with corrections and excisions drawn by a practiced hand, which is nevertheless no longer that of a professional
copyist. This is evidently the author, who himself retouches his work
with a meticulous severity. His style is endlessly altered, by trans-
positions, or by equivalents substituted for the original expressions,
or by the introduction of some explanatory forms more conducive to
clarity; and, above all, in accordance with an eternal principle of
the art of writing, by frequent excisions. Not only phrases, not only
entire pages, but all of one work, are ruthlessly crossed out; finally, it
is as a well-corrected rough draft, a final copy carefully retouched by
the author, before the definitive form which a work ought to receive, at the moment of publication.[56]

That Manuel was himself the supervisor and reviser of this
Parisinus gr. 3041 has never since been questioned[57] and is,
needless to say, a factor of no small significance in examining this
manuscript. Here we have the closest possible link the modern
scholar could hope for with Manuel the writer, short of a complete holograph.

As the manuscript comes down to us, it begins with what might
have been taken to be a preface, in the usually florid and obscure
Byzantine style (f. 1^{r-v})—a passage which has been overlooked or

56. *Mémoire*, pp. 3–4. It might be noted here that the *Parisinus gr. 3041*
today is full of marginal markings which are almost surely those of Berger de
Xivrey himself, inserted for the most part to indicate passages that he wished
to quote and commendable at least for their restraint in those brave days of old
when manuscripts were held less inviolable than they supposedly are today.

57. Cf., for example, Loenertz, *Echos d'Orient*, 36 (1937), 271. More
recently, see also pp. 35–36 of G. T. Dennis, "Four Unknown Letters of
Manuel II Palaeologus," *Byzantion*, 36 (1966 [1967]), 35–40.

ignored by most descriptions of the manuscript.[58] The first body of actual material in it is a group of sixty-three letters, of varying length and content, numbered consecutively by the Emperor, or his copyist, in the margins. Of these sixty-three, two are not true letters: no. 59 (νθ′, ff. 35ᵛ–36ʳ; Berger de Xivrey no. 90) is a pretentious hypothetical address entitled: "As from a benevolent ruler to his well-disposed subjects in a critical time"; and no. 28 (κη′, f. 15ʳ⁻ᵛ; B. de X. 35) is a rhetorical exercise addressed "To a certain prattler" (τινὶ φλυάρῳ), whether an actual individual or not. Another letter, no. 53 (νγ′, ff. 33ʳ–34ᵛ; B. de X. 77) is actually a supplementary epistle appended to a larger work intended for his eldest son, John VIII, the full text of which, however, is not included in this manuscript. The remaining sixty texts are more or less true letters, addressed to a total of twenty-two individual friends, acquaintances, and contacts. Of these twenty-two people, the one to whom the greatest number by far were written (twenty letters) is his mentor Demetrius Cydones. Following in number are such important contemporaries as Demetrius Chrysoloras (8), Manuel Chrysoloras (5), the

---

58. This curious passage appears at the beginning of the manuscript as it now stands, and is plainly a fragment—that is, its beginning is missing, the text at the top of what is designated f. 1 commencing in the middle of a sentence. This means that *Parisinus gr. 3041* as we have it is incomplete, and lacks one or more of its opening folia.

Subsequent to my own cursory perusal of this curious fragment, Father Dennis has offered his own explanation of it in his recent article, "Four Unknown Letters of Manuel II Palaeologus," *Byzantion*, 36 (1966 [1967]), 35–40 (based on a paper delivered at the XIIIth International Congress of Byzantine Studies, Oxford, 1966). Father Dennis convincingly identifies this passage as a compression of the texts of two and a half letters from a series of four which, on the basis of a comparison with parallel texts preserved in the *Barberinus gr. 219* manuscript of Manuel's Letters, seem to have been addressed to Bishop Makarios of Ancyra during some awkward disciplinary action undertaken against this troublesome prelate during the years 1405–09. Since the full texts, with translations, of these "new" epistles are to be included in the forthcoming complete edition of Manuel's Letters, Father Dennis here provides English synopses, and sketches the background of these texts as he identifies them, ascribing them specifically to the year 1408–09. He also (p. 36) adds the calculation that the present f. 1 of the *Parisinus gr. 3041* was actually f. 27 of the manuscript as it was originally constituted. If this computation is correct, it raises some interesting questions as to what texts then preceded Manuel's Letters in this codex, and whether or not they were by Manuel himself—if so, then perhaps one or more of the texts lacking now in *Parisinus gr. 3041* but to be found in other manuscripts assembling his works.

Patriarch Euthymios (4), and Cabasilas (3). Of the remaining recipients only four received two letters, and the remaining thirteen were addressed only one letter each. These recipients include such individuals of note as the Emperor's mother, Helena Cantacuzena; his brother, the Despot Theodore I of the Morea; the Italian humanist Guarino; the Emperor of Trebizond (Manuel III?); and the Metropolitan Gabriel of Thessalonica. The others are individuals almost or entirely unknown to us. Manuel's selection—and these sixty-three are quite obviously only a gleaning from a much larger body of correspondence—was probably not, however, intended as representative of any meaningful ratio of recipients, but was doubtless based on criteria of style and content as met by these particular examples, which he chose to preserve above all others. His personal participation in the preparation of this collection assures us of the significance of this selection. There is also good reason to assume that the numerical order in which Manuel placed them is more or less chronological, a valuable asset in using these texts if the assumption is correct.[59]

The remainder of the manuscript is given over to a series of the Emperor's purely literary works, ranging in length and significance from the very trivial to the very substantial. In the order in which they appear—which is apparently without significance, chronological or otherwise, from this point—they are as follows: the discourse on the tapestry in the Louvre (f. 38^{r-v}; B. de X. 47); the hypothetical address by Timur to Bayazid (38^v;

---

59. That the manuscript order of the letters is chronological was asserted by Berger de Xivrey, p. 60, n. 3: "The more one examines attentively the collection of these letters, the better one recognizes that they have been placed carefully in chronological order. . . ." Though scrutinized critically by Loenertz, *Echos d'Orient*, 36 (1937), 271 ff., this assertion was cautiously acknowledged by him as a reasonable working hypothesis. As such, this hypothesis has been used in the present study as a qualified basis for certain chronological estimates. Legrand, in his edition of the Letters, scrupulously retained Manuel's sequence and numbering, save that he added as no. 64 (ξδ′)—a number never assigned by Manuel—another letter to Cydones which actually comes later in the *Parisinus gr. 3041*, at the head of the Περὶ γάμου, which accompanied it, a point to be noted presently. Legrand also included three other brief texts by Manuel, as may be seen in Petit's article, and Legrand also added two other texts not by Manuel. According to his preface, Legrand intended to append or to publish separately some notes and commentary on his edition. But he never did so: see Dennis, "Four Unknown Letters," p. 35, and n. 2.

B. de X. 54); the Psalm in celebration of Bayazid's death (38ᵛ–39ʳ; B. de X. 55); a religious poem of 812 lines of political verse (39ʳ–46ᵛ; B. de X. 83); a brief prose exercise on a Homeric subject (46ᵛ; B. de X. 2); the important *Discourse of Counsel to the Thessalonians When They Were Besieged* (47ʳ–51ʳ); [60] a frivolous discourse on drunkenness, adultery, and suicide (51ᵛ–60ʳ; B. de X. 1); [61] the long letter-discourse to Cabasilas (60ᵛ–65ᵛ; B. de X. 38); [62] an early panegyric celebrating the recovery of his father, John V, from an illness (66ʳ–72ʳ; B. de X. 15); the lengthy letter-discourse to Alexius Iagoup, discussing theological matters (72ᵛ–85ᵛ; B. de X. 56); a letter-discourse to Andreas Asanes on dreams (86ʳ–88ʳ; B. de X. 18); a letter to Cydones intended to accompany the work which follows it (88ᵛ; B. de X. 17); and the long *Ethical Dialogue, or Concerning Marriage*, the Περὶ γάμου (89ʳ–104ʳ; B. de X. 16). This last work is, of course, the one most heavily corrected by the self-critical Manuel, who finally seems to have reached such a point of dissatisfaction that he crossed out each and every page, often quite heavily. In this section of the manuscript we can see the author's own hand at work most fully, as the other scholars cited above have described. [63]

60. Berger de Xivrey, p. 8, n. 1, accepted the earlier and mistaken opinion of Hasse that this work was not by Manuel but by Cydones, and therefore he did not include it in his chronology of the Emperor's works. Since Petit's article, as noted previously, this text has been published in a critical edition by B. Laourdas in Μακεδονικά, 3 (1953–55), 295–302.

61. Since Petit's article, an extract from this text, which is entitled Μελέτη πρὸς μέθυσον, has been edited by G. Soyter, in his *Griechischer Humor von Homers Zeiten bis Heute* (Berlin, 1959), 102, with partial German translation and synopsis, p. 103.

62. Since Petit's article, of course, this text has been published in full in a critical edition by Loenertz, in Μακεδονικά, 4 (1955–60), 38–46.

63. Editions of this curious text have been undertaken but never carried out. Legrand, in the preface to his edition of the Letters (p. xi), claimed that he had transcribed this text, along with the *Discourse of Counsel to the Thessalonians* and the respective letter-discourses to Cabasilas and Iagoup, all of which he was prepared to publish. But this he never did. More recently, two successive modern scholars have considered an edition, but their schemes also have not been realized, at least at this writing. At the moment, the only part of this text currently in print is the extract published by Loenertz in the *Rev. d. ét. byz.*, 15 (1957), 183–184, and now translated above, p. 111. Editing this text would not be an easy task, in view of its mutilated nature after Manuel's markings. But it is worth making available, for it is a curious example of a Byzantine effort to expand upon a traditional subject, in the old dialogic form, with Classical models diligently kept in mind. Several ancient authors, including Theophrastus and Seneca, had written discourses on the

This last work is also a turning point in the manuscript. From here on the handwriting seems to change occasionally, perhaps as much as four different times—Berger de Xivrey's assumption to the contrary notwithstanding—and other, alien, elements intrude. Indeed, were it not for the fact that two of the ensuing works appear in other manuscripts of Manuel's writings, one might be inclined to question their authenticity, a temptation that is not easily allayed in perusing this manuscript. After a long Kanon, or liturgical poem, addressed to the Virgin (104^{r-v}; B. de X. 99),[64] which is apparently authentic and survives elsewhere, a definite change of script brings us to a Mitylenian Synaxarion, or Church calendar (105^r–127^r), a composition not by Manuel at all, but attributed to one Christopher of Mitylene;[65] then a brief prayer "for the storm-tossed" (127^v; B. de X. 98), which is found in another manuscript and is presumably by the Emperor. But next, in another change of script, comes a text by St. Athanasius (128^r–131^r); which is followed by two short texts, a brief discourse on the Seven Ecumenical Councils (131^r–132^v; B. de X. 100), and then a discourse on the condemnation of Paul of Samosata (132^v–133^v; B. de X. 101), both of which are attributed to Manuel; then a text that appears to be a translation of a passage from St. Augustine (133^v–134^v) provides another strange interruption, which is followed finally by a brief liturgy for Holy Saturday (134^v–136^v; B. de X. 102), also attributed to Manuel.

At this point the manuscript breaks off completely from anything possibly connected with Manuel: as it survives to us, the codex is concluded (137^r–283^v) with a compendium from the *History* of Nicetas Choniates, as noted above, containing additional passages interpolated from Acropolites. This final section is itself disjunct, since it also (with the change at 247^r) is in two different scripts. The relationship of this final section of the manuscript to the earlier part with which Manuel was involved

subject of matrimony, and the precedent that Manuel was most likely to have had in mind was Libanius' Θέσις (α'), Εἰ γαμητέον (ed. Foerster, Teubner, VIII, 550–561). Cf. Krumbacher, *Geschichte der byzantinischen Litteratur*, 491.

64. The text as given by Legrand, pp. 94–102, of his edition of the Letters, is lacking the final stanza. Discussion of this poem is included in T. Stratmann's article, "La Théotokos, prémices de justifiés," in *Irénikon*, 27 (1954), 122–141.

65. Berger de Xivrey, p. 8, n. 3.

is, of course, remote and obscure. Regardless of handwritings, considering the fact that Manuel's own corrections cease altogether after the end of the Περὶ γάμου, one may well wonder whether or not the manuscript beyond f. 104ʳ ever passed through his hands or had anything to do with him. This uncertainty raises problems which will have to be faced and resolved in any complete edition of his works.

Problematical as it may be in some respects, the *Parisinus gr. 3041* is still inevitably the fundamental manuscript of Manuel's writings. What is most curious about it is that it contains none of Manuel's really major and most bulky works. Interestingly enough, it is followed in this respect, with one exception, by another manuscript, which parallels extensively and perhaps significantly the *3041*. This is a codex, also of the fifteenth century, now in the Vatican Library, the *Barberinus graecus 219*. In addition to containing all but two of Manuel's numbered letters, in the same order as the *Parisinus gr. 3041*,[66] this codex repro-

---

66. The *Barberinus gr. 219*'s collection of Manuel's Letters (ff. 53ᵛ–88ᵛ) lacks what are to be found in *Parisinus gr. 3041* and in Legrand's edition as Nos. 53 (νγ', the supplementary epistle from the "Orations" to Manuel's son) and 59 (νθ', the address "from a benevolent ruler to his well-disposed subjects"); that is, two of the "non-letters" in the *Parisinus*-Legrand set. Following the sequence of the established Letters, however, the *Barberinus gr. 219* goes on to offer (89ʳ–90ᵛ) a grouping of four "Letters Raising Hypothetical Questions" numbered so as to continue the foregoing sequence of already familiar letters to which they are thereby added. It is these four texts which in fact constitute the full passage which survives in the fragment that begins the *Parisinus gr. 3041;* and it is, therefore, these four texts which have enabled Dennis to make his reconstruction of "Four Unknown Letters of Manuel II Palaeologus," as discussed above in n. 58. Thus, the *Barberinus gr. 219* constitutes an important source for the study of Manuel's Letters, in view of these divergences from the *Parisinus gr. 3041* collection. It is therefore ironic that the *Barberinus gr. 219* was the one major source not consulted for the published edition of the Letters that has so long commanded the field. This manuscript has been mentioned by Mountfaucon, but it had eluded the search of Legrand (*Lettres*, pp. vii-viii), who therefore did not use it in his edition: cf. Petit, 1926–1927. (For his part, Berger de Xivrey appears to have been either unaware of, or indifferent to, the existence of this manuscript; hence, the works by Manuel it alone contains are not in his table.) Legrand also used other manuscripts of Manuel's letters. The most important are a pair in the collection discovered by Theodore Avramiotis in Ragusa in 1890, one containing the complete sixty-three, all in order, the other the first forty-two of that sequence: see Legrand, *Lettres*, pp. viii-x; Petit, 1927. Eight letters (nos. 1–5, 7–9) also survive in another manuscript in the Bibliothèque Nationale, the *Coislin gr. 341*, folios 356–363. And one letter, νε', is also preserved in a manuscript in the Vatican Library, *Cod. gr. 1879:* cf. Appendix XXI below.

duces the following works: the 812-line poem (ff. 1ʳ–8ᵛ); the *Discourse of Counsel to the Thessalonians* (9ʳ–14ᵛ); the letter-discourse to Cabasilas (24ʳ–29ʳ); the panegyric on his father's recovery from illness (29ᵛ–36ʳ); the letter-discourses to Iagoup (36ᵛ–50ʳ) and to Andreas Asanes (50ᵛ–53ʳ); and, from the questionable group in the later part of the *Parisinus gr. 3041,* the short prayer "for the storm-tossed" (91). The manuscript also, however, contains several other works, certainly by Manuel, not included in the *Parisinus gr. 3041.* Some of these are minor, such as a short piece on "simplicity and peace in one's wishes" (90ᵛ), and a poem of 15 Anacreontic verses (92). But the next of these new works is a major one, the two parts comprising Manuel's lengthy discourse on the Procession of the Holy Spirit, refuting Latin views, written in Paris in 1401–02 (93ʳ–180ᵛ; B. de X. 49).

It is to still other manuscripts that we must turn to find Manuel's additional major works. There are three from the old Imperial Library in Vienna, which contain a mixture of large and small writings, including several to be found in the *Parisinus gr. 3041.* One, from the fifteenth century, was once the property of no less than the Cardinal Bessarion.[67] It begins with Manuel's compendium of advice to his eldest son, the so-called *Praecepta educationis regiae ad filium Joanem capita centum,* and its pref-

---

67. A new catalogue of the Vienna manuscripts is in preparation by H. Hunger; at this writing, however, only the first volume has appeared (Vienna, 1961). Until now, the frequent lack of adequate catalogues for various important European manuscript collections has been particularly acute in the case of Vienna. In his chronological table of Manuel's works, Berger de Xivrey consistently ascribed texts of works in one or all of these three Vienna manuscripts to "Biblioth. de Vienne, mss. 88 et 89." These numbers, lumped together without distinction of separate contents, represent the numbers assigned to our first two manuscripts by P. Lambeck, or Lambecius, in his catalogue of 1665–79: Vol. VII, pp. 154–160, and 160–161, respectively. Certainly they were the manuscripts used by Johann Loevenklau, or Leunclavius, for his edition of most of these writings as published in Basel in 1578, the editions which were then carried over into the Migne *Patr. gr.,* Vol. 156. Lambecius apparently omits mention of the third of our manuscripts. And Lambecius' numbers, amorphously used by Berger de Xivrey, must also be correlated with the confusingly distinct ones of Daniel de Nessel, whose own catalogue (often a reshuffled reprinting of parts of Lambecius') dates from 1690. Thus far, and for our purposes, Hunger has retained Nessel's numbering. This first Vienna manuscript under discussion, Lambecius' *Phil. gr. 88,* appears in Nessel's *Pars IV,* pp. 54–56, as *Phil. gr. 98,* which is also Hunger's number.

atory epistle (ff. 3ʳ–30ʳ; B. de X. 88–89); followed by the seven moral discourses, the ill-advisedly named *Orationes ethico-politicae*, also addressed to his eldest son (31ʳ–106ʳ; B. de X. 70–76) [?—with the appended Letter, number by Manuel was as νγ′, B. de X. 77?]; then a work found among the letters (as νϑ′) in the *Parisinus gr. 3041* and *Barberinus gr. 219*, the hypothetical disquisition to his subjects (106ʳ–107ʳ; B. de X. 90), followed itself by a morning prayer (107ʳ–111ᵛ; B. de X. 78 [and 79?]). These four initial works are followed then by another text found in the *Parisinus gr. 3041*, there so heavily marked-up: the Dialogue on Marriage (112ʳ–125ᵛ; B. de X. 16); and then, for the first time, one of Manuel's most important writings, the lengthy *Funeral Oration for His Brother Theodore*, introduced respectively by Gemistos Plethon's preface to it (126ʳ–127ʳ), an analysis by the *Hieromonachos* Ioasaph (127ᵛ), and Manuel's own Preface (or Προϑεωρία: 127ᵛ; B. de X. 109), the text of the work itself (128ʳ–175ᵛ; B. de X. 85) then being followed by a pair of brief elegaic poems by two contemporaries (175ᵛ).⁶⁸ Here the manuscript ends, as it survives today. But we know from its own table of contents that it originally continued with eight more works, six of them by Manuel, five of which appear also in our second Vienna manuscript.⁶⁹

68. This all-important Funeral Oration survives in no less than four other codices. From the fifteenth century there are two: one in the Bibliothèque Nationale, *Cod. gr. suppl. 309* (ff. 1ʳ–49ʳ), which also contains the superb portrait of Manuel alone as *Basileus* (see above, n. 1); and one in the Vatican, *Cod. gr. 1450* (ff. 3ʳ–42ʳ). A third, of the sixteenth century, is in the Escurial in Madrid, *Ms. Υ 1–4* (ff. 285ʳ–315ᵛ). And the fourth is a seventeenth-century copy by Combéfis, also in the Bibliothèque Nationale, *Coislin gr. 343*. Since Petit's article, a newer edition of the text was published by Lampros in his Παλαιολόγεια καὶ Πελοποννησιακά, III (Athens, 1926), pp. 11–19, with the other, supplementary, texts, pp. 2–10. These other four manuscripts contain most of the supplementary texts, the specific dispositions of them being noted systematically by Lampros in his notes. Manuel's Προϑεωρία may also be found by itself in still another manuscript at the Vatican, *Barberinus gr. 74* (f. 26ʳ), from the sixteenth century. Berger de Xivrey assigned Manuel's own Προϑεωρία a separate number under the erroneous impression that it was connected with an oration for a different individual: cf. Petit, 1928. I am lately informed, by the way, that Julian Chrysostomides is at present preparing a new critical edition of her own of the *Funeral Oration*, with extensive notes and commentary.

69. The eight missing works were, in this order: Manuel's Louvre tapestry description (B. de X. 47); his address of Timur to Bayazid (54); and his psalm on that Sultan's fall (55), all of which are shared with the *Parisinus gr. 3041*; next, a brief discourse by Demetrius Chrysoloras to Antonio

This second of the three [70] is from the sixteenth century and is closely related to the first, at least in its contents. It begins with precisely the same four texts found in the first: the *Praecepta,* initial letter and all (ff. 3ʳ–40ᵛ; B. de X. 68–69); the seven *Orationes,* with their concluding letter (41ʳ–138ᵛ; B. de X. 70–76, 77); the address to his subjects (139ʳ⁻ᵛ, Letter νθ′; B. de X. 90); and the morning prayer[s?] (140ʳ–146ᵛ; B. de X. 78 [and 79?]). It continues with five other small works, five of those missing from the first Vienna manuscript, though in a different order, beginning with a religious poem (146ᵛ–147ʳ; B. de X. 82).[71] And the remaining four of these five are all ones which are also found in the *Parisinus gr. 3041,* though not in the *Barberinus gr. 219:* the Kanon to the Virgin (147ᵛ–150ʳ; B. de X. 99); the description of the Louvre tapestry (150ᵛ–151ᵛ; B. de X. 47); the hypothetical address by Timur to Bayazid (152ʳ⁻ᵛ; B. de X. 54); and the psalm on the fall of Bayazid (152ᵛ–153ʳ; B. de X. 55). The manuscript is concluded (from f. 153ᵛ on) with legal texts from an earlier age, which have nothing to do with Manuel.

The third of the three Vienna manuscripts [72] is a hodgepodge of texts, mainly ecclesiastical or theological. But it repeats three of Manuel's works found in both the preceding codices, at one point or another: the *Praecepta* (ff. 49ʳ–59ᵛ; B. de X. 69), apparently without the prefatory letter (B. de X. 68); the religious poem (60ʳ; B. de X. 82); and the Kanon to the Virgin (60ᵛ–61ʳ; B. de X. 99).

d'Ascoli, followed by a response from d'Ascoli, followed then by Manuel's comments on both the foregoing; finally, Manuel's religious poem (B. de X. 82), and his Kanon to the Virgin (99), the latter of which is in the *Parisinus gr. 3041.* Of these eight works, five (1–3 and 7–8) are carried over into the second Vienna manuscript, while the other three works, including the one by Manuel of which Berger de Xivrey took no notice, survive in a manuscript at Grottaferrata, which will be described below presently.

70. Lambecius' *Phil. gr. 89,* pp. 160–161; Nessel's *Phil. gr. 42* in his *Pars IV,* pp. 29–30; and, likewise, Hunger's *Phil. gr. 42.*

71. Since Petit's article, this text has been published again, with extensive commentary, by S. Cirac Estopañan, in his "La Eucaristía y la paz del alma en una poesía del emperador Manuel II Paleólogo," *XXXV Congresso eucaristico internacional, Barcelona 1952, Sesiones internacionales del estudio,* II, 713–726: text, 721–722, followed by a Spanish translation.

72. Nessel's *Theol. gr. 252,* in his *Pars I,* p. 356, with no ascription of century. Hunger's catalogue as available to me did not yet extend to include this manuscript. I find no listing of this codex in the Lambecius catalogue, which omission presumably explains why Berger de Xivrey makes no allusion to it.

A few new and minor works definitely or presumably by Manuel, as well as other texts of two larger works, may be found in a pair of fifteenth-century manuscripts in the Vatican Library.[73] The first of them, *Vaticanus gr. 1107,* actually contains very little by Manuel, in fact only three works. The first two, the two parts of the Paris treatise on the Procession of the Holy Spirit (ff. 1^r–130^v, 130^v–134^v; B. de X. 49), and the *Praecepta* (137^r–167^r: B. de X. 68–69), are well known and appear elsewhere. The third is a letter by Manuel to the monks David and Damian (315^r–321^r), accompanying a literary work, the text of which is not included here; this letter was ignored by previous catalogues of the Emperor's works, and was not included in his own collection of them. The rest of this manuscript is devoted mainly to writings of Makarios Makres, many of which were formerly attributed to Manuel by mistake.[74]

The other of the two manuscripts, *Vaticanus gr. 1619,* includes four discourses attributed to Manuel, though they survive in no other currently known manuscript. These are: on the Dormition (ff. 1^r–14^v); on St. Mary of Egypt (15^r–29^v; B. de X. 106); on the Nativity (29^v–46^v; B. de X. 105); and in praise of John the Baptist (47^r–54^v). The next section of the manuscript (56^r–182^v) is devoted to some texts from Xenophon, but the codex returns to

73. Berger de Xivrey was aware of these manuscripts only from references by the seventeenth-century commentator Leo Allatius, and therefore his inclusion of their contents in his numbered table of Manuel's works is only scattered and partial.

74. These unauthentic works are discourses on the following subjects: on the seeming prosperity of evil-doers (168^r–199^v); on the death of a brother named John (200^v–219^v); on the Feast of the Fathers of the Seven Councils (219^v–236^v); on celibacy (236^v–253^v); in praise of the Archbishop Gabriel of Thessalonica (253^v–272^v; B. de X. 108); in praise of St. David of Thessalonica (272^v–288^r); and on the relics of St. Euphemia (288^r–297^v; B. de X. 107). These were all accepted as genuinely Manuel's by Petit, and a few of them had been assigned numbers by Berger de Xivrey on the basis of the mistaken references by Allatius. But Loenertz, in his article "Ecrits de Macaire Macrès et de Manuel Paléologue dans le mss. Vat. g. 1107 et Crypten. 161," *Orientalia Christiana Periodica,* 15 (1949), 185–191, has shown that most of these works are really by Makres, as can be seen in other manuscript copies of them under that author's own name. Moreover, except for the one new letter by Manuel, most of the rest of the manuscript is devoted to other works specifically identified as by Makres (299^r–303^v; 304^r–314^v; 323^r–342^v), with the final pages (343^r–358^v) given over to Manuel Kalekas. Petit's list must thus be reduced by the omission of these seven discourses.

Manuel with his prefatory letter and *Praecepta* (186ʳ–188ᵛ, 188ᵛ–210ᵛ; B. de X. 68, 69), which we have found consistently in the last four manuscripts enumerated. The remainder of this codex (211ʳ–228ᵛ) is devoted to material by Plutarch and is thus again irrelevant to Manuel.

Further, there is a codex of the fifteenth century given by Cardinal Bessarion to the Abbey of Grottaferrata, where it still exists, the *Cryptensis graecus 161*. Only recently brought to light, this manuscript contains, in addition to several works by Manuel, which are already known, a number of others not included in earlier listings of the Emperor's writings. The first of these (ff. 1ʳ–10ᵛ) is the letter to David and Damian which also appears elsewhere, in the *Vaticanus gr. 1107*, though generally unnoticed there; this letter accompanied a work by the Emperor which he sent to the two monks. Here there follow (11ᵛ) his Preface (Προθεωρία) to that work and then (12ʳ–65ᵛ) the work itself, a long address to his confessor after his recovery from a serious illness. Then the manuscript offers three works already known from various other codices, the pair of morning prayers (65ᵛ–70ᵛ, 71ʳ⁻ᵛ; B. de X. 78–79), and the Kanon to the Virgin (72ʳ–74ᵛ; B. de X. 99). Next comes the long and enormously important letter, also to David and Damian, on his activities in the Peloponnesus in the spring of 1415 (75ʳ–81ᵛ), also not included among Manuel's own numbered sequence of his letters. And, finally, there is the sequence of texts that are among those missing from the first Viennese manuscript: [75] the discourse by Demetrius Chrysoloras to Antonio d'Ascoli (82ʳ⁻ᵛ), d'Ascoli's answer to Chrysoloras (83ʳ–84ᵛ), and Manuel's own comments on both (85ʳ–88ᵛ).[76]

75. See above, n. 69.

76. The contents of this important manuscript were first publicized and catalogued concisely by Loenertz, "Ecrits," 191–193. Since then, he has published the text of the letter to David and Damian on the events of 1415 in the Peloponnesus, *Studi biz. e neoel.*, 9 (1957 = Mercati *Silloge*), pp. 299–304, with a French synopsis, pp. 297–299; this text is the one translated in its entirety above, pp. 302–308. The sequence of three works by Chrysoloras, d'Ascoli, and Manuel is also preserved in another manuscript, the *Cod. Vat. gr. 1879*, though all are given anonymously there, folios 322ʳ⁻ᵛ, 322ᵛ–324ʳ, and 324ʳ–328ʳ, respectively. Here this sequence is followed by the exchange of letters between Manuel (his νε′, f. 328ʳ⁻ᵛ) and Euthymios (ff. 328ᵛ–329ʳ), concerning a collaboration of theirs, presumably on Manuel's contribution to the sequence: cf. Loenertz, "Ecrits," p. 193 and n. 2; see also Appendix XXI below.

Not one of all the foregoing manuscript collections of Manuel's writings, however, includes still another work, a major one: his important and still largely unpublished *Dialogue with the Persian Mouterizes*, in twenty-six sections with an introductory letter to his brother Theodore, and a preface (B. de X. 22).[77] This work survives only separately and by itself, in two sixteenth-century manuscripts in the Bibliothèque Nationale, *Cod. gr. 1253*, and *Coislin gr. 130*, as well as in an eighteenth-century copy of the latter, *Cod. gr. suppl. 169*, in the same repository.

Such, then, are the surviving literary works by Manuel Palaeologus. In its emphasis upon the specific manuscripts, the foregoing survey perhaps appears a bit academic. But it may serve, it is hoped, both to document the scope and depth of this Emperor's literary work and also to list helpfully the specific manuscript resources available for the use of further research. And of the need for further research there can be no doubt. Even aside from questions of quality and content, though important by themselves, the mere fact that Manuel could have written such a great bulk of works, amid many distractions of a strenuous life—obstacles which he was the last to conceal!—must itself excite interest.

This cursory survey concludes our study of Manuel II Palaeologus. As with so much else in this supplementary chapter, the full scope of the material involved can only be hinted at. But even such a swift perusal of these writings indicates the extent of the task which lies ahead for scholars. A critical edition of Manuel's complete works, or at least of his major works, is greatly needed. And this should be an edition which would include, if not full translations, at least adequate synopses or analyses of the texts to guide the student. Only thus will this important corpus be made available for a thorough exploration by competent scholars. And only after this exploration has been soundly conducted will it be possible to understand and evaluate properly the total achievement of this unusually gifted man, who was not only the most remarkable of the Palaeologan rulers, but surely one of the outstanding figures of Byzantine history.

77. Since the citations above on p. 97, n. 17, there has appeared Trapp's article on its style, "Der Sprachgebrauch Manuels II. in dem Dialogen mit einem 'Perser,'" *Jahrbuch der Österreichischen Byzantinischen Gesellschaft*, 16 (1967), 189–197.

Appendices, Bibliography, and Indices

Appendices

I. The Pawning of the Byzantine Crown Jewels to Venice

(To Chapter I, note 30)

The identification of the "jewels" involved in John V's transactions with Venice in 1370–71 and thereafter has been a source of some confusion.

The issue derives from the original transaction, dated August 21, 1343 (indiction 11), by which the Venetian government loaned 30,000 gold ducats to Anna of Savoy, John V's mother, during her struggle with Cantacuzenus, the Byzantine crown jewels (presumably the bulk, if not all, of them) serving as security: Dölger, *Regesten*, no. 2891, pp. 9–10. These jewels (in the Greek, Κόσμια τῆς βασιλείας, loosely, "the insigniae of the Empire"; in the Latin, *jocalia imperii*, more specifically "the jewels of the Empire") were retained in pledge by the Venetians pending the expected repayment by the Byzantine government of the original loan plus interest. The redemption of these jewels, "quem habemus in pignore a domino Imperatore" in the Venetians' more-or-less repeated phrase of reminder, became a matter of prolonged concern to John V throughout his reign. They entered into his dealings with the Venetians repeatedly, but a mutually satisfactory arrangement for their return was never settled, though it seemed close at several points. As a result, the jewels remained in the treasury of St. Mark beyond the end of the Empire, for John V's successors were never in a position to make good on the debt. In virtually identical wording each time, a formal reminder of the debt was included in each renewal of the periodic treaties between Byzantium and Venice, for which we possess both the Greek texts (Miklosich and Müller, *Acta et diplomata graeca*, III: of John VII, 1390, p. 140; of Manuel II, 1406, p. 149, and 1418, p. 158; of John VIII, 1423, p. 168; 1431, p. 191; 1442, p. 212; and 1447/48, p. 220) and the Latin texts (Thomas, *Diplomatarium Veneto-*

Levantinum: 1390, p. 227; 1406 [p. 301]; 1418 [p. 317]; 1423 [p. 341]; 1431 [p. 346]; 1442 [p. 372]), as well as in that of 1450, for which we have only the Latin text (Thomas [p. 380]). Note also the formula in the earlier treaties under John V himself: of 1357 (Greek text, Miklosich and Müller, p. 125), of 1362, of 1363, and of 1370 (Latin texts only: Thomas, pp. 85, 90, and 154, respectively). Cf. Ostrogorsky, *History of the Byzantine State,* 469; and Zakythinos, *Crise monétaire,* 99; also Dölger, *ibid.* Most recently, a thorough study of the entire course of transactions between Byzantium and Venice in this matter, from 1343 to the end of the Empire, has been published by T. Bertlè, in his article, "I gioielli della corona bizantina dati in pegno alla Repubblica veneta nel sec. XIV e Mastino II della Scala," in *Studi in onore di Amintore Fanfani,* ed. A. Guiffrè, II: *Medioevo* (Milan, 1962), 90–177, including an extensive section (pp. 163–177) of the texts cf Venetian documents.

Scholars had come to speculate, meanwhile, that the "jewels" involved in John V's 1370–71 negotiations might not, in fact, be those of the 1343 transaction, but a second, quite different set. It is known, for example, that Byzantium acquired an alternate set of coronation regalia. For in his history, Cantacuzenus (III, 92, ed. Bonn, II, 564) describes the preparations made for his own coronation at Adrianople on May 21, 1346. Using his customary third-person narrative style, he writes: "And, entrusting to goldsmiths to prepare chaplets (στέμματα), and such other things necessary for the rite, when all were made ready, he was crowned...." Presumably, then, Cantacuzenus had made some sort of new coronation regalia. It may be that he did this simply because he was setting himself up as a usurper in an outlying city, away from the regalia in the capital. Or, possibly, new regalia might have had to be made anyway, in view of the pawning of the regular jewels earlier. Of course, we do not know the extent to which actual jewels—be they new ones, or remnants of the older set still in Byzantine hands—might have been used in Cantacuzenus' new regalia. But there might have been enough of value for this new regalia to furnish the added security which John now brought to his 1370–71 negotiations with Venice, according to the suppositions of Gibbons, 152, and Halecki, *Un Empereur,* 229. (Were that supposition correct, one might wonder what the retired Cantacuzenus himself would have thought at the time about such application of his regalia!) In addition, Loenertz, "Jean V Paléo-logue à Venise," 225–226, had further speculated that John him-self had not originally brought these extra "jewels" with him, but that Manuel had brought them—and not money, as the Greek sources have it—when he came from Thessalonica to his father's aid. It was therefore this second set of "jewels," and not the origi-nal 1343 set, of which the Senate authorized the dispatch back to the Byzantines in June of 1373: Thiriet, *Régestes,* I, no. 523, p. 131 (text published by Bertelè, "I gioielli della corona bizantina," no. 32, p. 176); cf. also Thiriet's "Venise et l'occupation de Ténédos," 225.

In his discussion (pp. 124–130) of this phase of the episode, however, Bertelè has asserted (specifically, p. 125) that this sec-ond set of jewels is a complete fiction. He argues that there is no reference in Venetian documents to a new set, as distinct from the original set of 1343, the redemption of which was rather itself one of the chief points of the 1370–71 negotiations. As for the "return" of Byzantine jewels in 1373, Bertelè states (pp. 129–130, with disappointingly little documentation on this point) that, however far the jewels actually were sent, they were not actually given back to the Emperor but remained in Venetian hands— one of several occasions during John's reign, in fact, when the Venetians were actually willing to ship the jewels all or part of the way back to Constantinople in expectation of a settlement of the Byzantine debt that was never achieved. And, expanding beyond Bertelè's arguments, J. Chrysostomides has since, in her article "John V Palaeologus in Venice (1370–1371) and the Chronicle of Caroldo: a Re-interpretation," *Orientalia Christiana Periodica,* 31 (1965), 76–84, attempted to sketch the actual nature and course of John's negotiations during this period.

The complementary arguments of Bertelè and Chrysostomides seem generally plausible and convincing. On their basis, it would now seem established that no second set of "crown jewels" was offered as additional security to Venice during the 1370–71 nego-tiations, and that what Manuel brought with him from Thessa-lonica was more probably cash, as the Greek sources have it, than new pawnables for security.

II. Turkish Attacks on Thessalonica in the Fourteenth Century and Their Source Problems, with a Supplement on Some Thessalonian Liturgical Acclamations

(To Chapter I, notes 40 and 161; to Chapter II, note 47)

A. *1372–1387*. Dennis, p. 33, and also p. 55, n. 13, asserts that the Turks attacked—though they did not take—Thessalonica on April 10, 1372, and that four days previously Manuel himself had fled the city by ship. These statements he bases on the *Chronicon breve thessalonicense*, ed. Loenertz, no. 6, p. 175. This text reads as follows: κατὰ τὴν ϛ′ τοῦ ἀπριλίου μηνὸς τῆς ι′ ἰνδ., ἡμέρᾳ τρίτῃ, ἐξῆλθεν ἀπὸ τὴν Θεσσαλονίκην ὁ δεσπότης ὁ Παλαιολόγος μετὰ κατέργου. τῇ ἑνδεκάτῃ τοῦ αὐτοῦ ἐν ἡμέρᾳ σαββάτου ἱππηλάτησαν οἱ Μουσουλμάνοι εἰς τὴν Θεσσαλονίκην. ("On the 6th of the month of April of the 10th indiction, on the third day [of the week, i.e. Tuesday], the Despot Palaeologus departed from Thessalonica on a galley. On the eleventh of the same [month] on Saturday, the Mussulmans [rushed?] into Thessalonica.") Thus, the text itself does not give any year, but only the indiction, the tenth. It can therefore apply not only to 1372, but—significantly—also to 1387.

Which year was it? A key to the matter is provided by the days of the week on which these dates fall. The original text says that Manuel fled on April 6, a Tuesday, and that the Turks did whatever the verb means they did on the 11th of the same month, a Saturday. Now, in 1372 April 6 *was* a Tuesday, but April 11 was a *Sunday*. Reading the latter date as April 10 instead of April 11, as Loenertz suggests in his notes to his publication of the text, makes it come out properly as a Saturday. Even if this seems a small adjustment to have to make, however, the fact that any chronological inconsistency exists in this text demands that its statements receive critical scrutiny. But more is involved here than the mere changing of one date.

Dennis, be it made clear, does not say that the Turks captured

446

the city in 1372—only that they attacked it. But if we are to use this source, we must be certain of what it says. The crucial verb must therefore be examined carefully. As it stands, this word is apparently corrupt in the text. Possibly it might be from ἱππηλατεῖν, "to ride," or "to drive a chariot." According to Loenertz (*Recueils,* pp. 117–118, n. 2), however, the word should be emended from ἱππηλάλησαν to ἠπιλάλησαν, reading the word as the Modern Greek verb πιλαλῶ (or πηλαλῶ). In this latter interpretation the verb itself would mean simply "they rushed." But one must bear in mind the preposition εἰς, with which the verb could take on a number of shadings. It could well be taken idiomatically to mean "they attacked." But the strength of the preposition is such that the meaning "they rushed into" or perhaps "they charged into" seems more plausible. (Indeed, could the very form of the verb, corrupted or not, as it appears in the manuscript with the root ἱππ-, actually be a reflection, conscious or otherwise, of the assumption that the Turks *rode into* the city? Such an implication would only make more remote the watered-down meaning of "attacked.") Certainly, then, there is at least a strong possibility that the verb means nothing other than actual entry into, or seizure of, the city of Thessalonica, rather than merely attack on it; perhaps even a great likelihood. This likelihood I chose to accept.

To apply the text to 1372, one must use it at its face value. If we make this application, we must reckon with the likelihood that the text would imply a capture of Thessalonica in 1372, since that is what the verb would be likely to mean. This is of course unfair to Dennis, who does not claim that Thessalonica was captured by the Turks in 1372. He would certainly recognize that to propose such an event would be a serious matter, as there is no evidence whatsoever otherwise for a capture in that year. Yet, the text seems to speak of capture, and this must be taken as a grave handicap to any use of this text for 1372. Another obstacle, if one which Dennis ignores, would be the impossibility of accounting for the whereabouts of Manuel himself, had he really been obliged to leave Thessalonica then. Of this, more in a moment.

I believe that the entire problem of this source can be resolved by accepting some previous suggestions by Loenertz himself (*Recueils,* pp. 117–118, n. 2) for interpreting this chronicle entry.

He originally corrected in a different fashion. First, he reversed
the days given for the two dates, and then he replaced the text's
eleventh (ἑνδεκάτη) of April with the ninth (ἐννάτη), instead of
with the tenth (δεκάτη)—perhaps a more tenable emendation
philologically. This change would solve the problem, for in 1387
April 6 *was* a Saturday and April 9 *was* a Tuesday. This was Loenertz' own original argument, and I believe he was correct then
when he did date this notice 1387.

In addition, we know from our other sources (see above, p. 59,
n. 161) that the 1387 capture of Thessalonica was in the month of
April; Dennis himself makes this clear, p. 155, n. 11. It seems to
be too much of a strain of coincidence to believe that, in exactly
the same month that an authenticated capture of the city takes
place in 1387, there would occur another capture, for which we
have the support of neither a reliable source nor context. Conversely, the mere fact that the chronicle entry fits 1387 so logically and so perfectly makes its acceptance for 1372 all the more
improbable as an alternative. And, plainly, the chronological
details of the text as it stands are too demonstrably untrustworthy
on their own to be taken as decisive proof of an improbable dating
without independent corroboration. (Ironically, however, Dennis
has neglected to note one point which might serve in his favor:
the text's characterization of "Palaeologus" as δεσπότης. In 1372
Manuel still bore only the title of Despot, whereas by 1387 he
was maintaining his claim to the rank of *Basileus*. This is a detail
which might give one just pause. But, in view of the unstable
legality of Manuel's rank and status in 1387, even this detail need
not be conclusive, and the less so in view of the obvious sloppi-
ness and unreliability of this text as it stands.)

The only independent corroboration which Dennis produces
for his use of this text and its statements in 1372 is Cydones'
Letter, C. 160, L. 77, to the Grand Primikerios Phakrases, apparently written in 1372. But this letter (trans. Dennis, 55–56) hardly
proves, as Dennis thinks, that Manuel was absent from Thessalonica, having already fled it. To be sure, the city is vividly
described in the letter as being under siege and suffering from its
pressures; and there is no doubt that the Turks were active in this
area at this time. To be sure, the recipient is certainly in a
position of importance in Thessalonica. But Cydones' phrase
"τοῦ βασιλέως δέ σε τοῖς πράγμασιν ἐπιστήσαντος" (ed. Loenertz, I,

pp. 109–110, ll. 25–26) does not necessarily prove that Manuel could not also have been in the city at that time. Moreover, even if this letter could be interpreted to indicate that Manuel had left, as Dennis concludes, could the bare interval of four days between the supposed departure of Manuel and the entry of the Turks—for entry is what the text means, in all likelihood—have been sufficient for Cydones to have written a letter to Phakrases under the circumstances which Dennis assumes? Such "corroboration" is all too fragile.

Finally, there is the question of Manuel's flight from the city, according to the text. Dennis' only fair justification for applying this entry to 1372 is the possibility that the difficult verb ἱππηλάλησαν really does only mean an attack, and not a capture (which would be untenable for 1372). But if the Turks merely attacked, why should Manuel have felt obliged to flee the city— and several days in advance? He certainly was brave and secure enough to endure sieges at other times. Conversely, we do know that in 1387 Manuel did have to abandon the city, being forced out of it by its citizens before they surrendered to the Turkish besiegers. And we know that Manuel left the city by ship. Obviously, the flight by Manuel which the text describes is that of 1387. To try to fit it to a different time is unnecessary and illogical. For, if Manuel did flee Thessalonica in 1372, as Dennis has it, how do we account for him thereafter, especially during the ensuing revolt of Andronicus. Of course, the silence of sources is not conclusive evidence of anything. But it is not unreasonable to expect that, had Manuel been out of Thessalonica, he would have played some traceable role in the events of 1373. But his very conspicuous absence from these events and from Constantinople until late 1373 make it likely that he was really still in Thessalonica.

In sum, then, I do not accept Dennis' use of this chronicle. The passage in this *Chron. brev. thess.* seems logically applicable only to 1387, and not to 1372, in the light of all the factors considered. Thessalonica may well have been under Turkish attack about 1372, but this text's allusion—be it to an attack or to a capture— does not belong to this year. The city was not abandoned by Manuel and was certainly not yielded to the Turks before 1387. Finally, it is plain that Manuel was in Thessalonica, and nowhere else, from his return there in the winter of 1371–72 until the late summer of 1373, after which he was in Constantinople to be proclaimed successor to the throne.

B. *1394?* There has long been disagreement on the question of whether Thessalonica was freed from the Turks after 1387 only to fall to them again in the early 1390's. This second capture has been asserted by such scholars as Lemerle, *Philippes*, 219–221; and Ostrogorsky, *Hist. Byz. Emp.*, p. 485, n. 4, and *Geschichte* (3rd ed.), p. 451, n. 1; while Loenertz, *Echos d'Orient*, 36 (1937), 482–483, had settled on the specific date for it of April 12, 1394, in which he has been followed by Ostrogorsky in the latter's chapter in the *Cambr. Med. Hist.*, Vol. IV, Pt. 1 (2nd ed.), 375 (and echoed later in the same volume in F. Taeschner's chapter, 764 and 766). A second capture had meanwhile been rejected by such scholars as Gibbons, 231; Charanis, "An Important Short Chronicle," 361; and (Loenertz' student) Dennis, 156. The question was raised again by Laskaris in his article "Θεσσαλονίκη καὶ Τάνα," in the Τόμος Κωνσταντίνου Ἀρμενοπούλου, 339–340, where he accepts the idea of a capture of the city in the early 1390's. Most recently, this capture has been asserted by Vakalopoulos, Ἱστ. τ. ν. ἑλλ., I, 123 but he gives the date as 1391, with no source citation and with no indication of the problem's complexity. Previously, however, in his "Οἱ δημοσιευμένες ὁμιλίες τοῦ ἀρχιεπισκόπου Θεσσαλονίκης Ἰσιδώρου ὡς ἱστορικὴ πηγὴ γιὰ τὴ γνώση τῆς πρώτης Τουρκοκρατίας στὴ Θεσσαλονίκη (1387-1403)," Μακεδονικά, 4 (1955–60), 20–34, Vakalopoulos had developed a more complex hypothesis: that, while the city was only captured and rendered tributary in 1387 by Murad I, in 1391 Bayazid aggressively imposed a tyrannical rule over it. At the same time, he had furthered this argument (on rather tenuous evidence, be it said: such as one of Cydones' letters, taking a misdating of it by Cammelli to 1391 as reliable) in his "Ὁ ἀρχιεπίσκοπος Γαβριὴλ καὶ ἡ πρώτη τουρκικὴ κατοχὴ τῆς Θεσσαλονίκης (1391-1403)," Μακεδονικά, 4 (1955–60), 371–373; and he has reasserted this position again, in passing, in his "Les Limites de l'empire byzantin," 57; curiously, in his most recent *History of Thessaloniki*, 63–64, he bypasses the issue completely.

This year of 1391 has been a popular one in the controversy. And indeed, when Ducas, ed. Grecu, 79, ed. Bonn, 49–50, speaks of a capture of the city by Bayazid, he seems to place it just after the accession of Manuel in 1391. Trying to balance all the confused source evidence and possibilities, and anticipating Vaka-lopoulos's speculations, the city's earlier historian Tafrali, in his study *Thessalonique au quatorzième siècle* (Paris, 1919), 285–287, had tried to avoid some of the difficulties inherent in the problem by developing an ingenious compromise theory. According to him, Turkish control of Thessalonica after 1387 was only formal, with a Turkish garrison in the town still yielding it certain inde-pendence under Greek authority; thus, all Bayazid had to do in 1391, upon the death of his vassal John V, was to impose more direct and complete Turkish control on the city. Such explana-tions, however, are hardly convincing. In the first place, what source references we do have on the question speak of a definite capture of the city. Secondly, on closer scrutiny, Ducas does speak of this capture in conjunction with a number of other events, between Bayazid's seizure of all the Byzantine territory up to the walls of Constantinople, presumably as he did at the beginning of his siege in 1394, on the one hand; and his dispatch of his general Evrenos to attack the Peloponnesus, that is in 1394–95, on the other hand. If we are therefore to reach an affirmative answer to this question, we must accept the fact that the city was actually taken captive by Bayazid, and was not simply subjected to more intensive control over an already subject city. And we must also discard the year 1391 as unlikely. After all, if the city somehow was back in Byzantine hands after 1387, Byzantium was still a loyal vassal to the Turks after 1391, and there seems little reason to expect that Bayazid would have made any serious territorial seizures from Manuel until after their falling out by 1394.

The Turkish sources, if not entirely conclusive, would seem to support this outlook. On the basis of such sources, Babinger, *Beiträge*, 16, places a Turkish capture of the city in April of 1394. And, indeed, one of the Turkish historians, Mehemmed Neshri (Serbian trans. Elezović), 77, does report the taking of Thessa-lonica by Bayazid, giving a date which is read as April 21, 1394. The fact of the event, if not the time, seems also to be confirmed by Konstantin the Philosopher, in a statement not often cited: ed. Jagić, 271; ed. and trans. Braun, 15–16 (Braun also quoting on p. 9 another text which speaks of the seizure of Thessalonica by Bayazid). Unfortunately, Konstantin places the capture of "Soloun," or Salonika, at some time after the Battle of Nicopolis; but his chronology is sometimes as confused as that of the Greek historians, and there can be little doubt that the event mentioned by him must have been that which the Turkish historians placed in April of 1394.

There is perhaps a further reflection of this dating in a comment by Nerio Acciajuoli in his letter of February 20, 1394, to his brother cited above, pp. 120-121, n. 47. Nerio says, "inpero che lo gran Turcho [Bayazid] *e venuto a Salonichi.*" What does he mean by saying that Bayazid "has arrived at Thessalonica"? Does the Emir arrive in a city he already possesses by that date? Does it mean that in arriving he has seized it? Or does he rather arrive to besiege it? In view of the April 1394 date in the Turkish sources, the last of these possibilities would seem most feasible.

What is seriously lacking is some Venetian documentation of the event. A Venetian text cited by Iorga, "Veneția in marea neagră," no. 28, pp. 1108–1109, dated April 26, 1392, speaks of some possible action being taken commercially against Turks of (or in? or occupying?) Thessalonica. But the reference is unclear. (It is not included in Thiriet's summary of this document, no. 813.) The Venetians did have some authenticated dealings with Thessalonica in 1393–94. On December 4, 1393, the Senate discussed a dispute with the Thessalonian authorities over their seizure of the persons and goods of some Venetian merchants, reprisals for which had been taken by the Venetian officials of Negroponte: partial text, Iorga, op. cit., p. 1110, no. 37; summary by Thiriet, *Régestes*, I, no. 838, p. 199. The affair was resolved by the following summer, as noted in another deliberation of the Senate, on July 16, 1394: Thiriet, no. 857, p. 203. Outwardly, these routine transactions tell us nothing regarding our problem. To be sure, the partial text of the former of these deliberations as given by Iorga concludes with the strange and vague line: "Liberetur lignum turcicum." This might perhaps have been construed to have some bearing on the problem. But Father Loenertz has kindly sent me transcriptions of both these Venetian deliberations, and in the authentic texts of this first one the problematical sentence does not appear. Thus, these deliberations are of very little use for us here. And the absence of any published Venetian documentation of this presumed capture of Thessalonica in 1394 is still a serious gap in our knowledge of the episode.

So, then, there are still many points of confusion and uncertainty, and there is still a need for more decisive source material.

For the time being I am inclined to accept the likelihood of such a Turkish reconquest, probably in the spring of 1394, after the rupture between Manuel and Bayazid. But how the Greeks recovered it after Murad's seizure in 1387 is still a mystery.

Most recently, and since the foregoing was written, Father Dennis has published an article on the problem, "The Second Turkish Capture of Thessalonica: 1391, 1394 or 1430?" in *Byz. Zeitschr.*, 57 (1964), 53–61. In this essay, Father Dennis examines in detail the various source reports and problems, and he comes to conclusions similar to those of Vakalopoulos: that in 1394 Thessalonica was not actually recaptured, but was possibly subjected to more direct and severe rule by Bayazid. But he is of the more general opinion that there was no actual break in Turkish control of the city from 1387 until 1402. His arguments bear weight, as far as the available sources allow them to go. For my part, I am not entirely convinced that Thessalonica might not after all have revolted and then, soon thereafter, been retaken, perhaps in the spring of 1394, after the rupture between Manuel and Bayazid. But such a hypothesis, if it were to be argued at all, would have to be based on more evidence than is presently at hand.

If there is anything to be gained from this problem—which I still consider open to discussion—it is the illustration it provides of the difficulties of our sources for this period. That so much uncertainty should surround the situation of the second city of the Byzantine world in this period indicates the serious limitations of the information we have available to us for it.

C. *Some Thessalonian Acclamations.* Though something of a premature anticipation chronologically, this is perhaps an appropriate place to note a different kind of association of Manuel with Thessalonica.

In the MS 2061 of the National Library in Athens there is a liturgical cycle which includes a set of ceremonial acclamations for the Emperor Manuel II Palaeologus and his wife, the Empress Helena. This material was identified by O. Strunk as belonging to the archiepiscopal church of Thessalonica in his study "The Byzantine Office in Hagia Sophia," *Dumbarton Oaks Papers, Nos. 9–10* (1956), 175–202: 180–181; this manuscript is further discussed by E. Wellesz in his *A History of Byzantine Music and Hymnog-*

raphy (2nd ed., Oxford, 1961), 117 ff. Strunk had therefore given the manuscript the general dating of between 1391 (which should, more properly, be 1392, the year in which he married Helena) and 1425, the years of Manuel's reign. Wellesz attempted to go further by associating the acclamations with a visit by the Imperial couple to Thessalonica, "shortly after 1403, when Sultan Bajezid had given back Thessalonica to the Byzantine Emperor" [sic].

Now, a precise dating in these terms is extremely difficult. The acclamations for the sovereigns are part of the office of the Feast of the Exaltation of the Cross. The regular date of this Feast in the Church calendar is September 14; and the acclamations would have been proper to the evening before, September 13. When one examines the historical record as we can reconstruct it, one finds that Manuel and Helena were probably never in Thessalonica together on this date. They may have passed near it, if not stopped at it, in the spring of 1403, shortly after it was restored to the Empire by the treaty of that year with Suleyman (not Bayazid). Helena was presumably with Manuel during the 1408 visit to the Morea, at the end of which the Emperor did go to Thessalonica to install his son Andronicus in the place of John VII; but they could not possibly have arrived there until after September 13/14, by at least several days, if not many weeks. Manuel was in Thessalonica in the autumn of 1415, on his way to the Morea again. We do not know when he arrived in the city, but it was probably after the Feast date; and, as far as can be known, Helena is not likely to have accompanied him on this trip. Manuel returned from the Morea in the winter of 1416, and was back in Constantinople by March 25 of that year; nothing is said of a stop in Thessalonica then. In all likelihood, then, these acclamations were never sung on this Feast in the presence of Manuel and Helena.

Prof. Strunk makes clear, however, that the chanting of acclamations for the sovereigns as an integral part of the liturgy for the Exaltation of the Cross *does not necessarily presuppose their actual presence*, but reflects rather the character of the Feast itself. Therefore, there is no point in attempting to date these acclamations and this manuscript by trying to find an occasion when Manuel and Helena were in Thessalonica themselves on September 13/14. But at least some narrower dating can be suggested in terms of current political conditions. The acclamation of Manuel and Helena as the reigning sovereigns is not likely to have been practiced before the city was restored to the Empire in 1403. But in the period beginning with that year the Imperial sovereignty was somewhat enlarged to include John VII, who actually ruled in Thessalonica in his own name as *Basileus* until his death in 1408. It is not likely that he would have sanctioned acclamations of only Manuel and Helena under his regime. Therefore, except for a few possible months of 1403, the period 1403 (autumn) to 1408 (autumn) would have to be eliminated. A *terminus ante quem* can be established by the fact that in 1421 Manuel's son John VIII was made co-Emperor, and would therefore have been included, with his new bride, in any liturgical acclamations chanted thereafter. We can therefore date these acclamations and this Thessalonian liturgical manuscript with some confidence to the period 1408–1421.

Pursuing the subject of surviving Imperial acclamations of this period, we may note also a set in honor of John V and his Empress Helena, together with his son and colleague Andronicus IV, with his consort Maria. This set of acclamations, also in a Thessalonian liturgical manuscript (Athens MS 2062), was noted both by Strunk, "The Byzantine Office," p. 199, and Wellesz, *A History of Byzantine Music*, p. 117 ff. Wellesz suggests dating these acclamations "to the period between 1379 and 1383, because these were the only years in which a kind of peace existed between the rebellious Andronicus and the old Emperor John who had made him Co-regent." If they do indeed date this late, the period should rather be between 1381 (the date of the actual peace settlement after Andronicus' 1376–79 coup) and a time by 1385 (when hostilities were renewed, and when Andronicus then died). It is not impossible, perhaps, to associate these acclamations with the joyous time of the settlement of 1381. In more likelihood, however, they belong rather to the years between 1355 (Andronicus' betrothal to Maria-Kyratza of Bulgaria) and 1373 (the year of Andronicus' first revolt against his father), during which time Andronicus was his father's acknowledged heir. The only argument which would support the later dating, to 1381 and after, would be the fact that Andronicus was probably not formally crowned with the full title of *Basileus* in the earlier period, whereas he was in the later one.

Textually and musically, the various sets of Imperial acclamations of the late Palaeologan period are all related, as Wellesz' discussion of them demonstrates. It is perhaps worth noting that a modern arrangement of the set for Manuel and Helena was performed in the course of the Byzantine Congress held in Ochrid in the autumn of 1961.

III. The Tower of Anemas

(To Chapter I, notes 58 and 67)

The Tower or Prison of Anemas apparently obtained its name from the days of Alexius I Comnenus (1081–1118) when a troublesome noble, Michael Anemas, was imprisoned there: see Anna Comnena, *Alexiad,* XII, vii. Clavijo twice (ed. López Estrada, 50 and 56; ed. Sreznevski, 76 and 86; trans. Le Strange, 79 and 86) states that the "castle" in which John V had been imprisoned by his son was later, after John's release, demolished by that Emperor's orders and was a ruin in the writer's day (1403). Clavijo's description of it fits what we know of the Tower of Anemas, save that he claims (probably through misunderstanding or misinformation) that it had formerly been used to house ambassadors. A ruin still survives in a section of the Comnenian Land Walls of Constantinople which has been identified with this infamous building: a view of it is given as Figure 33; see also Appendix XXIV (C, 1). One of the first to make this identification was A. G. Paspates, who discussed its history and described the discovery of the ruin in question in his Βυζαντιναὶ μελέται (Constantinople, 1877), 23–32. A somewhat journalistic and overly colored description of this ruin may be found in E. A. Grosvenor's *Constantinople,* I, 395–400. In Van Millingen, *Byzantine Constantinople,* one will find a more sober and scientific discussion of the matter, with a detailed description of the remains (pp. 131–142), an examination of the problems concerning their identification as the true Tower of Anemas (142–53), and an outline of the building's lurid history (154–163).

457

IV. The Visit of Andronicus IV to Murad I and the Cession of Gallipoli to the Turks

(To Chapter I, notes 76, 86, and 92)

The question of the dating of Andronicus' visit to Murad and of the Byzantine surrender of Gallipoli to the Turks involves a number of chronological problems.

Loenertz, *Recueils*, 114, stated that Andronicus' mission (and his cession of Gallipoli) took place on September 3, 1376, but gave no explanation of this dating. Dennis, 37–38, gave the same date for the trip, and cited as support two short chronicles. Of them Βϱ. χϱ. No. 47, p. 81, ll. 56–57, says that Andronicus went to Murad "on the 3rd [day] of the same month" of the Byzantine year 6885 (1376–77). But what month? The entry immediately preceding, and the first one for this year, notes the death of the Patriarch Philotheos, an event which is generally accepted as having occurred in the second half of 1376. No month is mentioned in this chronicle, and we have no indication of the month of the Patriarch's death in other sources I have studied. The entry immediately following, and the last one for this year, notes likewise "in the same month" the death of Maria Palaeologina, which is generally accepted as having occurred in 1377. The Byzantine year, of course, began with September 1, so that the year 6885 would include the last four months of our year 1376. Obviously, then, this short chronicle text is defective in one extent or another. The other short chronicle which Dennis cites, Βϱ. χϱ. No. 45, p. 77, l. 6, simply says that Murad took Gallipoli in 1377 (itself using the reckoning of the year in the Christian Era).

The only other reference given by Dennis in support of his dating is the colorful tale in the *Vita Caroli Zeni*, Jocapo Zeno's somewhat imaginative biography of his grandfather, Carlo. Specifically, this story concerns the supposed early attempt by Carlo Zeno to rescue John V from prison after Andronicus' 1376 coup: see above, pp. 32–33, n. 86. As this text tells it (ed. Muratori, *Rerum italicarum scriptores*, XIX, 215–216; re-ed. G. Zonta, *R.I.S.*, 19, 6, Bologna,

458

1940, 12–14), John, as an old friend of Zeno, sought the latter's help to obtain his release, sending a letter to him by means of the jailor's wife—conveniently, one of John's paramours. Zeno was able to approach John's prison by boat (which, from our knowledge of the Tower of Anemas, seems quite impossible), and to climb up to a window of his chamber. But John balked at immediate flight, claiming that this would not allow him to bring his sons, on whose release with him he also insisted. The chance was lost, and Zeno was obliged to leave alone. John then renewed negotiations, again through the jailor's wife, this time pledging to hand over to the Venetians the island of Tenedos. But the woman was caught by Andronicus—or, rather, by the wife of Andronicus, who was himself absent among the Turks at that time, says the account in passing—and under torture she revealed the plot. All that resulted was that Zeno escaped to Tenedos, and with the help of John's written pledge he secured the cession of the island.

So then, this text does casually mention the absence of Andronicus, who was at the Porte during the events described; events which certainly presuppose a date later than September of 1376, since John V was not imprisoned until October: see above, p. 28 and n. 67. Unable to understand the basis for Loenertz' and Dennis' assumption of the month of September for Andronicus' trip, I was fortunate enough to be able to explore this question in detail in a long personal correspondence with Father Loenertz. As kind as he is erudite, this scholar has both defined and amplified his position in the course of our letters.

The key to his argument is the passage in the *Vita Caroli Zeni.* While conceding its romantic and embroidered aspects, he regards this text as founded on reliable information, and he considers the tale in question as one which contains a strong element of truth. In his article "Notes d'histoire et chronologie byzantines," he had already used this source in connection with the seizure of Tenedos in 1376 by the Venetian commanders Marco Giustinian and Donato Tron, apparently at the instigation of Zeno. This seizure took place in October, as we know from other sources. Using the common link of the *Vita,* Father Loenertz has now come to the conclusion that the journey of Andronicus to Murad now must also be placed in *October,* and not in September. His arguments would therefore suggest the following sequence of events, all in the month of October: (1) John V surrendered and was impris-

oned with Manuel and Theodore by Andronicus in the first days
of the month; (2) immediately thereafter, on October 3, Andronicus left to see Murad (going with a returning Turkish army sent
to help him at the end of his coup?—see above, p. 28, n. 65);
(3) meanwhile, Carlo Zeno made two attempts to free John, at
least the latter, if not both attempts, during Andronicus' absence,
and he won from the imprisoned Emperor the promise to give
Tenedos to Venice; (4) after the plotting was discovered, Zeno
made his escape with some kind of a pledge by John of the cession
of Tenedos, and he fell in with the forces of Giustinian and Tron;
(5) on Zeno's initiative, the Venetian forces sped to Tenedos and
were able to assume control of the island.

This long and busy sequence of events may seem to strain the
limits of a single month, and there is doubtless still ample reason
for a margin of caution. Yet, on the whole, I now believe that
Father Loenertz' revised and extended argument offers the most
plausible explanation for the month of Andronicus' trip to Murad.
(It also enables us to suggest that Philotheos died at the beginning of October, and Maria Palaeologina later in that month, all
in 1376.)

It is even less easy to be certain about the date of the surrender of Gallipoli. Presumably, the official cession was made
by Andronicus at the time of his visit to Murad. But how much
time elapsed between then and the actual surrender and the
actual occupation by the Turks is impossible to determine precisely. Cydones' Letter C. 122 (No. 25), L. 167, which mentions
the cession of Gallipoli as a recent occurrence, has been dated to
the winter of 1376–77 by Loenertz (*Recueils,* 47, and in his edition), and certainly it was written before the summer of 1377.
Therefore, Gallipoli was in the hands of the Turks by the end of
the first half of the year. Then there is Cydones' *Oration on Not
Surrendering Kallipolis* (see above, p. 16, n. 38), which Charanis,
"Strife," 296–297, argues, I think rather correctly, belongs to this
period, placing it in early 1377 just before the actual surrender.
Charanis, p. 298 and n. 39, also gives as support the notice mentioned above from Βρ. χρ. No. 45. Ostrogorsky, *Hist. Byz. St.,*
483, has rejected this argument and has placed the cession of
Gallipoli in 1376, immediately after Andronicus seized power;
but his entire conception of Andronicus' relations with the Turks
is untenable (see above, p. 27, n. 63). Our only other source for

this cession of the important port is in the *Bulg. chron.*, 538; but this passage is so muddled and imprecise as to be virtually useless.

All points considered, it is perhaps safest to suggest that, while the formal cession was made in October of 1376, when Andronicus presumably visited Murad, the actual surrender of Gallipoli to the Turks followed at some time thereafter before the end of winter in 1377.

V. The Marriage of John VII

(To Chapter I, note 207; also Chapter III, note 73;
and Chapter IV, note 72)

The question of John VII's marriage is a thorny one. We know from our sources that he had married a daughter of Francesco II Gattilusio of Lesbos by the end of the fourteenth century, but we do not know when this marriage took place.

There is even some dispute about the girl's name. Sphrantzes, 1048A (Pseudo-Phrantzes, ed. Papadopoulos, 190, ed. Bonn, 191), records the death of "the Despoina, lady Eugeneia, the daughter of Gatelioutzes" on January 1, 1440, adding that she was buried in the Monastery of the Pantokrator. There seems little reason to doubt that the lady in question was the widow of the ill-fated and long-dead John VII; and it is interesting to note that she should spend her last days and receive her final rest in the bosom of her late husband's once-hostile family. On the basis of such a reference, Miller, "The Gattilusij of Lesbos," 414 (321), calls her Eugenia without question, and in this respect he is followed by most modern writers. On the basis of other vague source references, however, Dölger, "Johannes VII.," p. 29, n. 5, rejected this name and identified her as Irene. Few other scholars have taken up this name.

The major problem, of course, is that of the time of her marriage. Miller and others generally regarded it as having taken place about the late 1390's. This marriage must have taken place by the summer of 1397: for in the remarkable document that John had drawn up in that year (see above, p. 164 and n. 73), the Lord of Lesbos is significantly characterized as *reverendisimum et carissimum patrem imperii nostri*. But there are some source statements that might indicate an earlier date for this marriage. In the first place, Ignatii of Smolensk describes Gattilusio as a "kinsman," or perhaps an "in-law" (*"srodnik"*), of John VII. Of course, Francesco II was related to both John VII and Manuel II (as well as John V), since his mother, the wife of Francesco I, was the sister of John V, Maria Palaeologina. This reference, however,

462

obviously implies a closer relationship, that which Francesco II did attain sooner or later as the father-in-law of John VII. Does this mean, then, that the marriage took place about the time of the events of 1390? Or is this reference merely, as Kolias suggests (pp. 61–64), an anachronism on the part of Ignatii, reflecting a *later* marriage alliance? This latter explanation is perhaps plausible, given certain assumptions, but is hardly conclusive.

That Ignatii's description of Gattilusio really did signify something regarding the date of John VII's marriage had appeared possible in the light of some other sources. For some time there had been speculation regarding Venetian allusions to an "Empress of Constantinople" who passed through Venice in the summer of 1390, and some scholars adopted the theory that this mysterious unnamed Empress was the child bride or bride-to-be of John VII on the way to join her new husband, then in his precarious and—as it proved—brief occupation of the Byzantine throne. Thus Loenertz, *Recueils,* 120, and then, more fully, in his "Epître de Manuel II Paléologue aux moins David et Damien, 1416," p. 296, n. 2 (the latter being a concise summary of our knowledge of Eugenia up to that time).

A key to this line of thinking was the assumption that Francesco II Gattilusio was younger than John VII, since, as it was understood, Francesco was still in his minority when he succeeded his father as Lord of Lesbos in 1384; of this more in a moment. Hence, according to this line of reasoning, he was not likely to have had any children of very advanced age in 1390. Kolias, 63–64, did suggest that Francesco could have had a young daughter about five years of age by this time, though he rejects the idea of a marriage this early. Still, in the light of the Venetian references, it did not seem inconceivable to suppose that Francesco, already drawn to the pretender by ties both of blood and of Genoese national sentiment (which favored the disinherited Imperial line of Andronicus IV), could have concluded some sort of alliance with the successful usurper by 1390, sealing it with at least the betrothal of his little daughter to John VII. It was also not inconceivable that the girl, perhaps for purposes of raising and education, might have been in Italy at the time and was then brought by way of Venice (now no longer openly hostile to the line of John VII) to the East; hence the Venetian references. Why else, also, should Francesco have been in Constantinople in the late summer of 1390, except for the purpose of celebrating the nuptials, or at least of negotiating the betrothal, of John VII with his daughter, who would thus have come from Italy earlier in the summer? It would all seem to have fitted very neatly.

Alas, as interesting as such speculation was, the truth is that it is not justified on the basis of the Venetian documents involved. The four of them published with my article "John VII in Genoa," 237–238, provided through the generosity and efforts of Father Loenertz himself, make clear at last the true identity of "the Empress of Constantinople"—John VII's *mother*, and not any bride or betrothed of his. This clarification gives these texts great importance for other purposes as well (see "John VII in Genoa," 231–235), but it leaves us empty-handed once again as regards the present problem, since these texts have therefore nothing to do with John VII's marriage to Gattilusio's daughter.

In addition, the final pillar of the old theory can now be demolished as well. For it seems likely that the assumptions regarding Francesco II's age were incorrect. The conclusion that Gattilusio was only a boy on his succession to the rule of Lesbos in 1384, was drawn from the report in a Greek chronicle of the Gattilusii that his uncle, Niccolò Gattilusio, Lord of Ainos, was immediately associated with him in power. In publishing the chronicle, Lampros (in Νέος Ἑλληνομνήμων, 6, 1909, p. 39) therefore assumed that the uncle served as a regent during his nephew's minority. This interpretation was carried over into Miller, "The Gattilusij of Lesbos," 412 (319), and hence the assumption that Francesco II was too young to have a daughter of anything more than the most tender years in 1390. Thanks to suggestions and texts provided me by Father Loenertz, with the help of Dr. Enrica Follieri, however, I can now point out that the chronicle text itself by no means requires the conclusion that Niccolò was a regent or guardian for a boy; it indicates rather than Niccolò was made "co-ruler" (συνάρχων) with Francesco. (This prompts speculation as to another, quite different reason for such a step: could Francesco II have been an illegitimate son of Francesco I, requiring the bolstering of a full member of the family as an associate to legalize his succession?)

It is therefore quite possible that Francesco II was older in 1390 than previously imagined and was thus quite capable of having a daughter of reasonably marriageable age. Such a possibility therefore makes more meaningful the characterization, however vague, of Francesco II as a *srodnik* of John VII in 1390. This date, and allusion, may very well mark the marriage, or at least the betrothal, of John VII to Eugenia Gattilusio.

Since the above was written, Father Dennis has contributed some important new material to these subjects. He has, for one thing, made some further comments on John VII's Gattilusio marriage in his "The Short Chronicle of Lesbos," 16–17, in connection with his publication of a more reliable edition and exposition of the chronicle just mentioned.

Far more important, in his "An Unknown Byzantine Emperor, Andronicus V Palaeologus (1400–1407?)," *Jahrbuch der Österreichischen Byzantinischen Gesellschaft,* 16 (1967), 175–187, he added a new dimension to our understanding of John VII's life and marriage, and in the process he has suggested the existence of a previously undetected Byzantine sovereign—no mean feat by this time! Publishing for the first time a pair of texts (pp. 181–182, 183–187) which refer to the death, at age seven, of a young Emperor Andronicus, son of Emperor John and nephew of Emperor Manuel, Dennis argues that these texts could only refer to a son of John VII and Eugenia Gattilusio. The argument is quite plausible, and merits thorough study. The chief obstacle to accepting it immediately is that no previously known sources refer to this boy Emperor, who would have been the elder Palaeologan line's hope for survival. That none of the familiar Byzantine writers make mention of him seems strange, although the confused state of our sources for this period might explain that situation in part. There is, however, the very vague and flimsy allusion made by Clavijo to the idea of John VII's having a son and heir, as Dennis points out (pp. 178–179, quoting the text), in connection with the reported settlement of 1403 (discussed above in n. 76 to Chapter IV) whereby the succession in Constantinople would be accorded first to Manuel, then to John, then to Manuel's son, then to John's son. This Clavijo passage would appear, for the present, to be the only available corroboration of the existence of a son of John VII, if an indirect one.

Dennis suggests that, if John did have this son, he was probably born about 1400-1401, at least *after* Manuel's departure for the West. (Dennis observes: "it does seem somewhat unlikely that Manuel would have entrusted his capital to John for a period of several years if the latter had an heir.") The unexpected existence of this new heir at the time Manuel returned in 1403 would certainly have contributed a new concern to the older Emperor's relations with his nephew. In the texts Dennis publishes, the prematurely dead boy is clearly described as *Basileus.* "If," writes Dennis, "the young Andronicus was actually proclaimed co-emperor, and equivalently heir presumptive, during [the period of Manuel's absence], this could very conceivably have been one of the major factors in Manuel's anger in the summer and fall of 1403 which led him to banish John to Lemnos." Here we are on the most precarious ground of all. The fact that the boy would have borne the Imperial title at his death still gives us no indication of when it was bestowed upon him. Had John proclaimed him during his regime in Constantinople, the act would have been so bold, not to say illegal, that one can hardly imagine it would have attracted no attention at all in any other available sources. However *ex silentio* the argument, my present reaction is to think it more likely that John would have associated his son with him in his title only later, during his reign (as "Basileus of Thessaly") in Thessalonica, rather than flaunting his own dynastic claims so blatantly while still his uncle's regent in Constantinople. Nevertheless, John's very possession of an heir in 1403 could have contributed significantly to the tensions between him and Manuel on the latter's, and this new factor should therefore be reckoned now into the discussion above in Chapter IV (especially its n. 72) of Manuel's reasons for breaking his agreement with John.

It is clear that the Andronicus of Dennis' texts died before his father, and Dennis accordingly suggests about 1407–08 for the boy's death. Is any light thrown by this supposition on Manuel's haste to break off his Morean visit and get to Thessalonica immediately when John himself died soon after in September of 1408 (see above, pp. 278–279, and notes 137 and 139)? Manuel might or might not have known that his nephew's heir had pre-deceased him; but, even if he had, the fact that John VII had at one time possessed a son who might have succeeded him could have made Manuel particularly jittery about recovering the Thessalian appanage for his own family without any latitude left for further family schism.

At any rate, however far this new speculation may lead, it would now seem arguable that John VII's marriage to Eugenia Gattilusio was not entirely unfruitful, and that they may have had at least one child, with important political implications.

VI. John V's Destruction of Fortifications in 1391

(To Chapter I, note 213)

In his account of Bayazid's humiliating demands on John V, Ignatii of Smolensk simply reports the Emir as threatening that Manuel would "never leave my hands" unless John destroyed his "fortress" (Khitrovo translates the word as "chateaux"). Ducas, ed. Grecu, 75–77, ed. Bonn, 47–49, says that John constructed two new towers by the Golden Gate and built an additional fort— Ducas ignores the presence there of an existing fortress—and that in the following year, when the Emir was planning a campaign, Manuel was sent to serve in the Turkish army; as soon as Manuel reached him, says Ducas, Bayazid sent his demand to John. It is possible that new or renewed building activity by John served as the spark for the demand by Bayazid who simply, on the spur of the moment, used the presence of Manuel to halt activity of which he had become suspicious. Such seems to be the generally accepted view in all the general accounts: cf. Berger de Xivrey, 62–64; Muralt, p. 739, nos. 7 and 8; Pears, 96; Gibbons, 197–198; Charanis, "Strife," 306; Ostrogorsky, *Hist. Byz. Emp.*, 487; and also Van Millingen, *Byzantine Constantinople*, 70–71.

But when one ponders the statements of Ignatii, and even of Ducas, one is tempted to wonder if it was all as abrupt as that. We know that Ducas misunderstood, to some extent, the nature of John's building activity and that a fortress already existed there on the site of the present Yedi Koulé, the Turkish stronghold that incorporates elements of the old Byzantine structure (see Van Millingen, *ibid.*; and A. M. Schneider, "Yedikule und Umgebung," *Oriens*, 5 (1952), 197–208; see also Figure 5 and Appendix XXIV: C, 3). In fact, the bare statement in Βϱ. χϱ., No. 15, p. 32, ll. 39–43, of the Emir's command to John, says nothing of the new construction, but refers specifically to the destroyed fortifications as including those in which John had been besieged previously. And, knowing something of the usual Turkish shrewdness in exploiting the weaknesses of the Empire to their fullest advantage, we may assume, not unreasonably, that Bayazid may have deliberately intended, well in advance, to use the presence of Manuel in his army as a campaigning vassal as an instrument for his aims. The order to John to demolish fortifications, whether new or simply old, could then have been an example of such aims, perhaps only the first of a number.

That John's compliance was not absolute might have been concluded from an anonymous Russian description of the city, translated by Khitrovo (*Itinéraires russes*, 225–239), in which reference is made (pp. 231, 239) to "the castle of Kalojohn," which would be this fortress, judging from the description of it. Since Khitrovo dated this account 1424–53, it would seem as if John's fortifications were at least partly preserved. And this conclusion had been drawn by Van Millingen, *ibid.* But C. Mango, in his article "The Date of the Anonymous Russian Description of Constantinople," *Byz. Zeitschr.*, 45 (1952), 380–385, has contested Khitrovo's arbitrary and apparently groundless dating. He argues instead for a dating between late 1389 and early 1391, partly on the very grounds that the Russian pilgrim who wrote the account must have seen the *Kaluyanov Gorodok,* or "Little Town of Kalojohn," between the time John V built the fortifications, allegedly at the time of Bayazid's accession after Kossovo, and the time John V pulled them down on Bayazid's order. (It is interesting to note that Mango also discusses, pp. 384–385, a reference in this Russian text to prophecies attributed to Leo [VI] the Wise, according to which Manuel was to be "the last emperor of Tsargrad.")

As for the true extent of John V's compliance with Bayazid's order, however, there is apparently a legitimate reflection of this episode in a slightly garbled tale in another travel account, that of Bertrandon de la Brocquière, a Burgundian who visited Constantinople in 1432. He speaks of two strong "palais" at extremes in the fortifications, which had been destroyed as demanded and were in ruins when he saw them: *Le Voyage d'Outremer de Bertrandon de la Broquière,* ed. C. H. Schefer (*Recueil des voyages et des documents pour servir à l'histoire·de la géographie depuis le XIIIᵉ jusqu'à la fin du XVIᵉ siècle,* XII, Paris, 1892), 151–152; or ed. J. B. Legrand d'Aussy (appended to *Hakluyt's Collection of the Early Voyages, Travels, and Discoveries of the English Nation,* Vol. IV, London, 1811), 518; and trans. T. Wright, *Early Travels in Palestine* (London, 1848), 336.

VII. The Burial Places of John V and Andronicus IV

(To Chapter I, notes 142 and 214; also note 92)

Both of the short chronicles which tell of the death of John V (see above, pp. 80–81, n. 214) say that he was buried in the Monastery of the Hodegetria (ἐν τῇ μονῇ τῶν Ὁδηγῶν). This was not a normal place of burial and may well have been selected on the express wish of the Emperor himself.

If so, his reason is not readily clear. Possibly it might have had something to do with the fact that his father, Andronicus III, had died there in 1341 (Gregoras, XII, ii, ed. Bonn, p. 576, ll. 18–19). But a better explanation for this choice may perhaps be found in events of 1354. In that year, with the aid of Francesco Gattilusio —"le 'gangster' Gattilusio," as Walter (265) calls him—John V was able to gain entry into Constantinople by a ruse and bring about the final downfall of Cantacuzenus: Ducas, ed. Grecu, 67–69, ed. Bonn, 41–43. The gate by which this entry was made was the postern gate along the Marmora shore, "the small gate named after the [nearby Church of the] Hodegetria" ("ἐν τῇ μικρᾷ πύλῃ τῇ ἐπονομαζομένῃ τῆς Ὁδηγητρίας"). Cf. Miller, "Gattilusij," 407–408 (314–315); Van Millingen, *Byzantine Constantinople*, 258–259 (though this author mistakenly gives the year as 1355). It is therefore quite possible that John V may have desired that his mortal remains should rest in this venerable monastery-church adjacent to the portal that had been his gateway to final victory.

Clavijo says (ed. López Estrada, 54, ed. Sreznevski, 84, trans. Le Strange, 85) that in 1403 he saw the tomb of Andronicus IV in the Church of St. Mary of the Hodegetria, even though our other sources say that he was buried in the Monastery-Church of the Pantokrator. At a glance, this statement might lead one to the conclusion that Clavijo had misnamed the Pantokrator as the Hodegetria, since it is true that the celebrated Icon of the Theotokos Hodegetria, ascribed to St. Luke, was kept there, at least dur-

469

ing the Latin occupation (1204–1261): cf. Van Millingen, *Byzantine Churches in Constantinople*, 226–227. But this explanation is impossible for two reasons: (1) we know quite well that this icon was again kept at the Church of the Hodegetria during the Palaeologan period (see R. L. Wolff, "Footnote to an Incident of the Latin Occupation of Constantinople: The Church and Icon of the Hodegetria," *Traditio*, 6 [1948], 326); and (2) it is quite plain that the description which Clavijo gives of the church where he saw this tomb was the Hodegetria itself—indeed, his is one of our most important contemporary descriptions of the place.

There is therefore one obvious explanation for this misstatement: Clavijo mistook the tomb of John V for that of his son Andronicus IV, either through misunderstanding or misinformation.

VIII. A Reference by Manuel to the Dervishes

(To Chapter II, note 11)

. . . Καί, τὸ δὴ σχετλιώτερον, ὃς ἐν τοῖς τῶν Περσῶν ἱερεῦσαι [=ἱερεῦσι?] σεμνός, εἰρήσθω δὲ καὶ ἐπίτριπτος, μαυλωνᾶς ὀνομάζεται. Οἷς οὖν ἡ σεμνοτάτη αὕτη προσηγορία οὐδὲν πλέον παρὰ τῶν ὁμοφύλων ἐγένετο ἢ παρὰ τῶν Τριβαλῶν καὶ Ἰλλυριῶν, οἵ, δίκην ἀνθ᾽ ὧν πόρρωθεν ὑπὸ τοῦ ἔθνους πεπόνθασιν οἰόμενοι λαμβάνειν καὶ τὸν Χριστὸν βοῶντες ἐπεκδικεῖν, κτείνουσι μὲν τοὺς προστυχόντας πάντας ἑξῆς· δρῶσι δέ, ἀλλ᾽ οὐκ ἐμοὶ προσῆκε ταῦτ᾽ εἰπεῖν, παρ᾽ ἄλλων δ᾽ ἴσως ἀκούσῃ.

(Manuel, Letter ις΄, ed. Legrand, p. 22, ll. 20–26.)

Although not lacking some of the grammatical obscurity which characterizes almost any passage by Manuel, this one is also extremely difficult to interpret as to meaning. To my knowledge, there has been no previous notice taken of it nor any attempt to explain it; and it has been omitted or skirted over in what partial translations have been made of this letter. This is regrettable, for I believe that it contains an interesting and unusual meaning.

The key to the problem is the strange word μαυλωνᾶς. There seem to be three possible derivations of it. One is from the noun μαῦλις, "knife." What meaning would such an origin give our word? One might suggest the passive inference of "one marked by the knife," in terms of the Latin concept of the *homo sacer,* or else in the sense of a scapegoat, as might be concluded from the reference by Manuel in the next sentence to a seemingly parallel custom among the Balkan Christians. On the other hand, it might also be possible to take the word in the active sense, as perhaps something like "knife-wielders" or simply "knifers." One might then construe the relating of this Turkish custom to a custom among the Christian peoples not in the sense of a separate duplication of practice, but of familiarity with one and the same custom among the Turks by the Christians. That is, that the Turks were accustomed to give this name to certain of their religious leaders, and that the Christians in their turn were familiar with this custom, recognized the significance of the name, and sought to kill its bearers whenever they could.

Following this latter line of thinking, I was initially inclined to draw the tempting conclusion that this entire passage refers to the Ghāzīs. We know, of course, that the Ghāzīs were the fanatic Muslim warriors who believed in carrying on an unyielding Holy War against the unbelievers for the glory and advancement of an aggressive Islam. The possible meaning of the word μαυλωνᾶς would therefore fit them perfectly, rightly suggesting both the respect in which the Turks held them and at the same time the hatred and vengeance displayed by the Christians towards them, as Manuel seems to be saying. We might notice, moreover, that this passage follows a description of the massacres and desolation wrought by the Turks. And the sentence that immediately follows ("Ταυτὶ μὲν οὖν τὰ τοῦ φόνου.") makes quite clear that the passage is directly related to Turkish devastation and killing, the specialties of the Ghāzīs. We might, therefore, readily conclude that Manuel is speaking of how the Balkan peoples looked upon the μαυλωνάδες as particular enemies of their faith and authors of their woes and took special effort to kill them when they could.

As tempting as is this relation of our passage to the Ghāzīs, I have been turned from it by the generous advice of Prof. G. G. Arnakis, the distinguished scholar of Turkish institutions of this period. Prof. Arnakis has urged a shift of attention rather to two other possibilities for the derivation of the problematical word μαυλωνᾶς. One of these is a relationship to the Greek verb μαυλίζειν, "to pander" or "to seduce," with its noun form, μαῦλις, "procurer" or "pimp." If we take the first sentence independently, it is possible to make a reasonable meaning from some adaptation of this derivation alone. But in relation to the following sentences and in its entire context, such an explanation would not seem adequate; unless, that is, this derivation were supplemented by the third possibility. This possibility is that Manuel used his strange word as a transliteration or equivalent of a Turkish or at least a non-Greek word. Prof. Arnakis suggests that in such a case the original word well might have been the Arabic expression *mavlana,* or *mevlana,* which means "our lord."

Now this title was applied in particular to the early fourteenth-century mystic Djelaleddin, or Djalāl al-Dīn, al-Rumī, who was the founder of the *Mawlawīya,* or *Melevī* Order of Dervishes, known to the West as the "Whirling Dervishes." Prof. Arnakis further stresses the likelihood of irony, if not actually a pun, in Manuel's use of μαυλωνᾶς with all its salacious connotations as an equivalent for the name of the *Melevī* (or *Mavlavi*), suggesting disgraceful and indecent conduct. A possible objection to this explanation might be that this Order had an apparent reputation for tolerance and for an interest in reconciling Christianity with Islam. Of course, such a subversive aim might itself have earned the more scorn and hatred from the pious Manuel. But the specific identification of the *Melevī* (or *Mavlavi*) with Manuel's μαυλωνάδες might well be treated with caution for the moment.

Nevertheless, the relationship with the word *mavlana* is surely an important key to the problem. The adaptation of the Muslim salutation for (any kind of) a holy man might be construed more loosely as referring in general to dervishes and sundry other religious fanatics and devotees. Any respected Muslim religious leader, dervish or otherwise, would certainly be an enemy of the Faith in the eyes of Manuel and his fellow Christians. This seems the most plausible explanation, in the context of all the elements of the passage. It would also seem to confirm the assumption that Manuel's reference to familiarity with this epithet among the Balkan peoples does indeed, as already suggested, allude to a Christian hatred for these Turkish μαυλωνάδες and to a desire to kill as many of them as possible in retaliation for the ills suffered at the hands of the Turks.

These are only suggestions at this point. But it seems plain at the very least that our passage does indicate some degree of Christian awareness of Turkish institutions in the era of the Osmanli conquests. Such passages are not unknown, but they always deserve careful study when they are turned up. This one may well be worthy of further investigation by qualified scholars.

IX. The Marital Status of Manuel Palaeologus, and the Last Years of His Mother, Helena Cantacuzena

(To Chapter II, note 23; also notes 24 and 30; and Chapter III, note 36; Chapter I, note 214; Chapter VII, note 8)

Aside from the cryptic and probably meaningless Venetian reference of 1374 (see above, p. 23, n. 53), there is no evidence whatsoever of any actual marriage by Manuel prior to his union with Helena Dragaš.

We do know that he had at least one illegitimate daughter, named Zampia (Zabia) or Isabella, about whom we have some information. She may have been born in the 1370's, perhaps late in the decade, for by the 1390's she was of marriageable age and at that time she wed a Genoese named Hilario Doria. Although Manuel was to use other daughters of his family for political marriages, we do not know of any particular advantage that accrued from this alliance with a citizen of a state that was basically hostile to Manuel at the time; perhaps it was a love match. There is preserved (Miklosich and Müller, II, no. 430, p. 159) the profession of faith which signalized Doria's conversion to the Orthodox Church in April of 1392, presumably in connection with this marriage. We know that Manuel employed Doria on at least one important diplomatic mission: see above, pp. 158 ff. Apparently he continued to be close to Manuel. During Clavijo's visit to Constantinople in 1403 this Castilian ambassador was, by Manuel's express order, guided through the city's sites of interest by Doria (ed. López Estrada, 35, 49–50; ed. Sreznevski, 52, 74–76; trans. Le Strange, 62, 78–79), whom Clavijo specifically identifies as "his [Manuel's] son-in-law, whom they call Messer Ilario, a Genoese, who is husband of one of his daughters who is not legitimate." He appears later as a treaty witness in 1418 (see above, p. 332, n. 61); and in 1423, near the end of Manuel's life, he seems to have become disaffected (see above, p. 370 and n. 125); while at least one of his daughters by Zampia seems to have been used for a diplo-

474

matic marriage (see above, p. 253, n. 88; p. 368, n. 120). On Zampia in general, see also A. T. Papadopulos, *Versuch*, 70.

Manuel apparently had several other illegitimate children. In a chrysobull of September 1405 the Emperor confirms a foundation made in the church of Monemvasia by his brother Theodore to provide liturgies "on behalf of the souls of the children of My Majesty buried there": Dölger, *Regesten*, no. 3307, p. 92; text of this document, Miklosich and Müller, V, no. 5, pp. 168–170; also ed. Zachariae von Lingenthal, *Jus Graeco-Romanum*, III (Leipzig, 1857), pp. 713–715. But nothing else is known of these children, and the confused reference to them (supposedly a son and two daughters) made by Sphrantzes, 1026A (cf. Pseudo-Phrantzes, ed. Papadopoulos, 71, ed. Bonn, 66) is not much help. That reference has been discussed by Loenertz in connection with a supposed reference by Manuel himself to one of these children in one of his letters: first in *Echos d'Orient*, 37 (1938), pp. 112–113; then in much greater detail in his "La Date de la lettre ϑ' de Manuel Paléologue et l'inauthenticité du 'Chronicon Maius' de Georges Phrantzès"; but he subsequently altered his views in an afterthought appended to his article "Ecrits de Macaire Macrès et de Manuel Paléologue dans les mss. Vat. gr. 1107 et Crypten. 161," p. 103, n. 2.

Whatever our ignorance about these children, however, it is still plain that they must have been illegitimate, though by whom is not known, and that they were sired by Manuel before his assumption of the throne and his marriage to Helena Dragaš.

Chalcocondyles, ed. Darkó, I, 75–76, ed. Bonn, 81–82, followed by the *Chron. Barb. 111*, 35, tells the celebrated story of how the daughter of the Emperor of Trebizond had been sent to marry Manuel, but that his father, John V—a lascivious and lecherous old rogue, as the historian makes clear—was so captivated by her beauty that he took her as a bride for himself, in spite of his old age and infirmities. (Muralt, p. 739, no. 9, dramatically has him dying in her arms in 1391.) This story had generally been accepted by modern writers, including Berger de Xivrey, and especially by those who judge harshly the character of John V.

But this strange tale of Manuel's betrothal and deprivation has lately been subjected to critical scrutiny and finally exploded. Loenertz, first in "Pour l'Histoire du Péloponnèse," 180–181, and then in full detail in "Une Erreur singulière de Laonic Chalcocandyle," 176–181, has once and for all demonstrated the confusion and falsehood of this tale. One of the factors to be borne in mind is that Manuel's mother, the Empress Helena Cantacuzena, actually survived her husband by many years. (The death date of ca. 1385 in Papadopulos, 46 and 47, is completely unfounded.) This fact, of course, rules out the possibility of John's alleged second marriage, in spite of the assumption by Berger de Xivrey, 60, that she had died before her husband. To avoid any such complications, the assumption that Eudocia Comnena, the Princess of Trebizond, was simply kept as John's mistress is made by Gibbons, 198; and also, surprisingly, by V. Laurent, "La Date de la mort d'Hélène Cantacuzène, femme de Jean V Paléologue," *Rev. d. ét. byz.*, 13 (1955), 138, still needlessly crediting at least part of Chalcocondyles' story. Loenertz has argued, however, that this story represents a complete chronological confusion by Chalcocondyles.

His arguments have still not deterred Dölger from accepting something of this confusion in two entries in his *Regesten*. Citing as his source the Trapezuntine historian Michael Panaretos, Dölger reports (no. 3075, p. 50) for late 1360/early 1361 a Byzantine embassy sent to arrange a marriage between Manuel and Eudocia Comnena, daughter of Alexius III of Trebizond; and then (no. 3092, p. 52) he reports for 1363 the conclusion of an agreement to this effect. In point of fact, Pararetos merely states (ed. Lampros, in Νέος ἑλληνομνήμων, 4 (1907), p. 282, ll. 11–13) that in the year 6869 (= 1360–61) the embassy came from Constantinople to Trebizond to arrange a marriage alliance (συμπενθερείαν) between their houses, no specific names being mentioned; and then Panaretos says (ed. Lampros, p. 284, ll. 6–17) that in April of 6871 (1363) a Trapezuntine embassy including himself went to Constantinople to arrange with the Imperial family (which, by the way, is recorded as including former Emperor John-Ioasaph Cantacuzenus) the formal agreement for a marriage between "the son of the Basileus Palaiologos" and "the daughter of the Basileus of Trebizond Lord Alexios the Grand Komnenos." Again, no specific names are given, and Dölger's assumption that they were Manuel and Eudocia Comnena presumably reflects the influence of Chalcocondyles' story, even though that historian is not cited.

Above and beyond the fact that Chalcocondyles' highly suspect story would be the only reference to such a presumed marriage being pursued, a further study of Panaretos reveals the fallacies of these suggested identifications. Alexius III of Trebizond did have a daughter named Eudocia, but in 1380, Panaretos tells us (ed. Lampros, p. 290, ll. 11–15), she was married off by her father to a Turkish Emir: whether or not it was she who was involved in the earlier betrothal, it would seem unlikely that she was ever a partner to any Palaeologan marriage. Moreover, it was not Manuel but another of John V's sons who was to become involved in Trapezuntine affairs. Panaretos reports (ed. Lampros, p. 288, l. 22–p. 289, l. 3) the arrival in Trebizond on November 11, 1373, of the Despot Michael Palaeologus, John's youngest son, to become an "ally" (ὑπόσπονδος) of the Trapezuntine Emperor. Nothing is said at all here about a marriage, and it would therefore be mere supposition to suggest any connection between the earlier betrothal and Michael's appearance at this point. On the other hand, Panaretos says absolutely nothing anywhere to indicate that the earlier betrothal was realized in any actual marriage; had there been one, it seems reasonable to think that he would have mentioned it. Michael's contacts with Trebizond (see also above, n. 11 to Chapter I) are the closest thing to a realization of the alliance between it and Constantinople projected by the 1363 betrothal. They give us the only basis we have for speculating— and no more than that—about the identity of the son of John V intended in the 1363 agreement; bases, however, that are perhaps stronger than those used to identify the unspecified couple as Manuel and Eudocia.

When all the evidence is reviewed, it still seems best to agree with Loenertz that in all probability no Trapezuntine princess ever had anything to do directly with Manuel or John V, matrimonially or otherwise.

Nor can there be any doubt that John V left Helena Cantacuzena behind him in reasonably respectable fashion as his widow. We have ample testimony of her activities after his death. We know from the *Chron. Vat. gr. 162*, no. 15, p. 209, ll. 62–63, that at some time after his death (February 16, 1391) Helena Cantacuzena entered the Convent of τῆς Κυρᾶς Μάρθας under the name of Hypomene. (Curiously enough, this was the name chosen by her daughter-in-law, also another Helena, the widow of Manuel II, when she herself took the veil: see above, p. 100, n. 24. Could the statement in this source, which mentions the later Helena also only a little further on, have confused the two Empresses of identical name? Or did Helena Dragaš choose the same name indeed, perhaps to pay tribute thus to her mother-in-law?) This retirement from the world is also referred to by Cydones in his Letter C. 133 (No. 28), L. 222. (On this letter, see above, pp. 39 ff., and n. 105.)

But exactly when she took this step is not known. We have seen that she served as Manuel's regent in 1391: see above, p. 87 and n. 5. That she continued to be associated with her son in the affairs of government can be seen in an instruction by the Venetian Senate of July 20, 1392 (text on pp. 449–450 of Vol. II of Loenertz' edition of Cydones' Correspondence; cf. Thiriet, *Régestes*, I, no. 820, p. 196), in which specific reference is made to the Emperor and his mother together: see above, p. 105, n. 30. Loenertz, *Echos d'Orient*, 36 (1937), pp. 281–282 and n. 8, had concluded that Helena's retirement must be dated some time after July of 1392. But it is not easy to be certain of this, for we find her again referred to by Manuel in the important passage from one of his literary works a few years later: see above, pp. 111–112 and n. 32; and her continued association with him personally, if not governmentally as well, is suggested by Manuel in connection with the events of Serres in 1393/94: see above, p. 120, n. 47. These references do not prove categorically that Helena was not in a convent. Conceivably she could have taken the veil at any time after John V's death, but she might have enjoyed an encloisterment which did not cut her off entirely from the world and the government. But, in view of her plainly continuous association with her son up through much of 1394, it seems more likely that she did not take her monastic vows until perhaps that year, or at least at the end of her life, as was common for members of a Byzantine Imperial family.

At any rate, she was alive at least until before Manuel departed to the West, for he himself speaks of her in connection with the sale of Corinth to the Hospitalers (see above, p. 146 and n. 37). This is presumably our last reference to her. Laurent, *ibid.*, has come to the conclusion that this cession took place in or before 1396, and he demonstrates at least that Helena died between the end of August and the beginning of December in that year. In a subsequent note, "La Date de la mort d' Hélène Cantacuzène, femme de Jean V Paléologue, Un précision," *Rev. d. ét. byz.*, 14 (1956), 200–201, Laurent has convincingly reduced the margin to the month of November, 1396.

X. The Beginning and Duration of Bayazid's Siege of Constantinople

(To Chapter III, note 1; also note 26; and Chapter IV, note 15)

As mentioned above, p. 85 ff., n. 2, some modern writers have attributed the beginning of Bayazid's siege to a very early time. By now, however, we can place the date more accurately, not only from what we know of the context and aftermath of the Serres conference, but also from specific source material itself. Indeed, one of the authors most subject to this chronological confusion, Gibbons, himself cites (p. 232 and n. 4) a letter by Bayazid instructing preparations for the beginning of the siege of Constantinople. Gibbons also notes the date of this letter as 1394, and such a letter could well have been an actual order for the real commencement of the project.

We have other source material to authenticate this date. Βρ. χρ. No. 15, p. 32, ll. 45–47, states that Bayazid "provoked most grievous conflict against Manuel in June of the year 6903 [1395]," and that "he [Bayazid] prevailed strongly for very near to eight years." But then this chronicle places the terminal point of the siege, the Battle of Ancyra, in the correct year, 1402 (though in the month of August, which is incorrect). Hence, this chronicle errs in its statement either of the beginning date or of the duration of the siege. It is true that another short chronicle, the *Chron. Vat. gr. 162*, no. 17, p. 210, ll. 74–76, gives the duration of the siege as nine years; but the unreliability of its chronology is suggested by its totally inaccurate dating of the Battle of Ancyra, which it places in 1396 (perhaps a confusion with Nicopolis). Further support for a dating in 1396 might seem to appear in the entry in Baronius-Raynaldus, *Annales ecclesiastici,* 1393, no. 6 (Vol. 26, p. 540), which speaks of Bayazid turning on Constantinople after his defeat at Nicopolis Minor in 1393. But this entry, as has been noted above (pp. 86–87, n. 2), jumbles together events of several years, and its confused chronology is hardly very reliable. A duration of seven years is assigned to the siege by the

479

Bulg. chron., 542; but such a figure is incongruous—and hence suspect—in view of the fact that, while this text does give the correct years respectively for the Battles of Nicopolis and Ancyra, it ignores the role of the latter in ending it. One can hardly squeeze seven years out of the time between 1396 and some time before 1402. On the other hand, Chalcocondyles, ed. Darkó, I, 77, ed. Bonn, 83, while giving no date, states that the siege lasted ten years. Ducas, ed. Grecu, 79, ed. Bonn, 50, gives no dating in describing Bayazid's blockade; the unreliable Pseudo-Phrantzes, ed. Papadopoulos, 65, ed. Bonn, 60, on the other hand, blithely states that the siege began in the year 6900 (1391–92) and lasted "a long time." But here Chalcocondyles' usually faithful echo, the *Chron. Barb. 111*, diverges: this text states (p. 35) that the siege lasted *eight* years, thus confirming the first of the short chronicles just cited above.

More conclusively, we have a Patriarchal document (Miklosich and Müller, II, no. 626, pp. 463–467: see above, pp. 208–211 and n. 15) which was apparently written in 1400/01, and which speaks of the city as having been besieged continuously for six years by that time. Also, in his own letter of July 1, 1397, to the King of France (see above, pp. 155–156), Manuel speaks of the attacks of Bayazid which had been sustained "for about three years" up to that time. Finally, P. Gautier has recently offered two further texts to confirm this dating: in his article, "Action de grâces de Démétrius Chrysoloras," *Rev. des ét. byz.*, 19 (1961), 347, he calls attention to a reference by that contemporary writer which also clearly indicates 1394 as the year for the siege's beginning; while in "Un Récit inédit du siège de Constantinople par les Turcs (1394–1402)," *ibid.*, 23 (1965), p. 106, ll. 31–32, he offers another reference from after the siege that it had lasted eight years.

When all of the sources are sorted out, the conclusion that the siege did begin in 1394 is inescapable. This fact was pointed out early, for example, by Jireček, in a review of Iorga's *Geschichte* in *Byz. Zeitschr.*, 18 (1909), 584–585, refuting the latter's statement (p. 288) that the siege commenced in 1391. The 1394 dating has now been accepted with fair uniformity: cf. Khoury, 139 (though see above, n. 2 to Chapter II); and Ostrogorsky, *Hist. Byz. St.*, 488, and *Geschichte* (3rd German ed.), 454, as well as in his chapter in the *Cambr. Med. Hist.*, IV (2nd ed.), Pt. 1,

p. 375. Some writers persist in the old error, such as Taeschner in his chapter in *ibid.*, p. 766, where 1395 is given; the same year likewise in Thomson's rather casually documented "Manuel Chrysoloras and the Italian Renaissance," 77; also Runciman, *The Fall of Constantinople*, 39–40, giving 1396, before Nicopolis; and Stacton, 113 (= "Dereksen," 119), gives 1397, after Nicopolis.

Whatever the dissent, the fact is now clear: the siege began in 1394, as an aftermath of Manuel's post-Serres reversal of policy. Perhaps it began in the spring of that year; possibly even in June, as the first chronicle cited relates, marginally. But, as noted elsewhere (above, p. 123 ff.), it is possible that active hostilities did not envelop the city until after the end of July. At any rate, the siege commenced in either spring or summer of 1394 and lasted a total of eight years, give or take a month or so.

XI. King Sigismund's Letter from Constantinople after Nicopolis

(To Chapter III, note 22; also notes 17, 26, and 32)

Sigismundus dei gracia rex Hungarie, Dalmacie, Croacie etc. marchio Brandenburgensis etc. reverendissimo in Christo patri et religiosissimo militi domino Philiberto divina permissione sacre religionis hospitalis sancti Iohannis Iherosolimitani magistro dignissimo salutem et prosperos ad vota successus. Placuit Altissimo, ut ad urbem Constantinopolim licet alio quam sperabamus itinere veniremus. Quam circa obsessam invenimus et in statu positam valde gravi adeo, quod, si noster defuisset adventus, infra quam paucissimos dies Turchorum rapinis et spoliis patuisset. Sed nos attendentes, quod ipsius urbis perdicio toti christianitati dampnosa nimis esset, eo quod in mari vires infidelium nimis augerentur, pro consideracione ipsius, pro christianitatis bono ad eius defensionem atque custodiam galeas nostras cum illis imperatoris, Venetorum, Ianuensiumque dimisimus et alia multa tractavimus, sicut reverencie vestre admiratus vester seriosius explicabit. Hec quidem nos precipue christianitatis respectu fecimus. Vos autem preter christianitatem respectu lige, quam cum imperatore et Perensibus, sicuti ab eis didicimus, religio vestra habet, tenemini ad Romanie parcium conservacionem intendere et eis auxilium, quociens expedit, impertiri. Quapropter attente vestram ortamur reverenciam et rogamus, quatenus in dictarum parcium subsidium ex vestris aliquot transmittatis galeas, ut, donec per christianos fiet alia provisio, se valeant sustentare. Imperator siquidem et Perenses legatos suos ad Venetias et Ianuam transmittunt, a quibus interim sperant sustentacionem aliquam accipere. Nos autem eo potissimum animo in regnum nostrum revertimur, ut convocatis et congregatis undique christianorum auxiliis viribus omnibus hoc prosequamur negocium et pro christianitatis liberacione et corpus et animam et omnem coterie [= corone?] nostre sacre potenciam exponamus. Quocirca vobis [= nobis?] quippe bonum valde ac laudabile videretur, quod ad partes illas, ubi premissa tractabuntur, vos quoque religionis vestre destinaretis nuncios, ne religio ipsa milicie Christi precipue dicata in procurando christianitatis bonum cuipiam fortassis turpia [= tepida?] videatur. Dat. Constantinopoli, sub sigillo reverendissimi patris in Christo domini

482

archiepiscopi Strigonensis cancellarii regni nostri propter absenciam sigilli regii, Novembris die XI. MCCCLXXXXVI°.

Sigismund, by grace of God King of Hungary, Dalmatia, Croatia, etc., Margrave of Brandenburg, etc., to the most reverend father in Christ and most consecrated soldier, lord Philibert, by divine leave most worthy [Grand] Master of the Sacred Order of the Hospital of Saint John of Jerusalem, health and fortunate fulfillment to your wishes. It has pleased the Most High that we should come to the city of Constantinople, although in a fashion other than that in which we were hoping to go. Which city we found blockaded about and placed in a position so very grave that, if our arrival had not befallen, in less than the fewest days it would have been open to the plunderings and spoliations of the Turks. But since we are aware that the loss of this city would be an excessive damage to all Christendom, because on the sea the strength of the infidels would become excessively strong, in view of this, for the good of Christendom we have dispatched to its defense and guarding our galleys, with those of the Emperor, of the Venetians, and of the Genoese, and we have discussed many other things, as your admirable representative will explain to Your Reverence. This we did chiefly out of regard for Christendom. On your part, however, beyond consideration of Christendom, with respect for the league which your Order has with the Emperor and with the Peraiotes, as we have learned from them, do you hold fast to devote yourselves to preservation of the regions of Romania and to bestow aid on them, as often as it is advantageous. Wherefore carefully do we urge and beg Your Reverence, that for assistance of the said regions you send off some of your own galleys, so that they may be able to sustain themselves until there may be some other provision from the Christians. Of course the Emperor and Peraiotes are sending off their ambassadors to Venice and Genoa, from which meanwhile they hope to receive some support. We on our part, however, are returning to our realm with this particular intention, that by convoking and assembling succors from Christians everywhere we may pursue this business with all our powers, and for the liberation of Christendom we may expose both body and soul and all the might of our sacred crown. For which reason it would seem to us certainly very good and praiseworthy, that you also should appoint representatives of your Order to these places where the aforesaid steps will be discussed, lest this Order especially dedicated to the military service of Christ might seem to someone perhaps lukewarm in looking after the good of Christendom. Given in Constantinople, under the seal of our most reverend father in Christ, the lord Archbishop of Gran, Chancellor of our kingdom, because of the absence of the Royal Seal, on the eleventh day of November, 1396.

The text of this letter survives in a fourteenth-century *codex epistolaris* in the Biblioteca Barberina in Rome (*sign. xxx, 174*, fol. 28) and was published in an offering by H. V. Sauerland under the title "Ein Brief des Königs Sigismund von Ungarn an den Grossmeister des Johanniterordens Philibert von Naillac. Dat. Constantinopel, 1396 November 11.," in *Neues Archiv der Gesellschaft für ältere deutsche Geschichtskunde*, XXI, 2 (1896), 565–566. In spite of its obvious importance, this letter has generally passed unnoticed, and the only scholar I have found making use of it is Mercati in his *Notizie* (*Studi e Testi*, 56), p. 115, n. 2. Therefore, in view of both its interest and its neglect, this text is reproduced above (with my own translation appended) to make it more readily available. I have restored the three errors in the manuscript and have placed the editor's indubitably correct emendations of them immediately after, in brackets with question marks.

This letter is of interest for more than its mere proof that Sigismund did go to Constantinople. Of course, it also seems to bear out Chalcocondyles' statement about Sigismund's conferences with Manuel (*alia multa tractavimus*). But it also adds further points of importance. Sigismund speaks of a league among Manuel, the Genoese of Pera, and the Hospitalers. We know little about this league, but perhaps it was this to which the Venetian Senate referred on February 17, 1396 (see above, p. 131 and n. 15), in their allusion to a new understanding between Manuel and the Peraiotes. This letter also indicates that among the immediate and positive measures taken by the defeated King was his dispatch of the fleet organized for the Nicopolis campaign, including some furnished by Manuel (see above, p. 132), to the defense of Constantinople, at least temporarily, undoubtedly in expectation of just the renewed offensive against it which Bayazid did mount. We have ample evidence of the embassies which Sigismund says he sent to Venice. Indeed, on January 26, 1397, the Venetian Senate gave its response to just such an embassy: see above, pp. 142–143. We also know that Sigismund continued to talk of a new expedition, and we have noticed that at least on through 1397 Manuel himself took this talk seriously, continuing to regard Sigismund as the natural leader and focal point for the organization of any further military efforts. Indeed, the Patriarch so much as reports specifically the King's pledge to return the following spring: see above, p. 151.

The cleric whose seal the King was obliged to use was Nicholas Kanizsay, Archbishop of Gran (the Latin name, *Strigonii,* comes from the town's Hungarian name, Esztergom), an important and warlike prelate who had been one of the leaders of the successful raid on Nicopolis Minor in 1393 (see Atiya, *The Crusade of Nicopolis,* 7; Kupelwieser, *Die Kämpfe Ungarns mit den Osmanen,* 11; Muralt, p. 744, no. 13); he had participated in the great campaign and defeat of Nicopolis, and he had escaped therefrom with Sigismund. In the same band of refugees was Philibert de Naillac (cf. Delaville le Roulx, *Les Hospitaliers à Rhodes,* 236–237), the recipient of this letter. Naillac had been the Grand Master-designate of the Hospitalers since the summer of 1396, but only upon his return after Nicopolis did he assume the title formally (*ibid.,* 265). Modern writers (e.g. Atiya, *The Crusade,* 98) have been incorrect in stating that Naillac returned to Rhodes in the course of the same voyage which brought Sigismund home from Constantinople. This letter plainly indicates that by the time of its writing Naillac had already left the city, presumably for Rhodes, and had apparently arrived there. It might be added, incidentally, that among others who escaped with Sigismund from Nicopolis was the fascinating aristocratic adventurer and minnesinger Oswald von Wolkenstein: cf. Brauner, *Die Schlacht bei Nikopolis,* 49.

XII. A Venetian Grant to a Byzantine Ambassador

(To Chapter III, note 46)

1397.IV.8. indict. 5.

Anthonius Venerio, Dei gratia dux Venetiarum etc. uniuersis et singulis tam amicis quam fidelibus et tam presentibus quam futuris presens priuilegium inspecturis salutem et sincere dilectionis affectum.

Tanto benignius ducalis prouidentia consueuit personas discretas sibi deuotas et fideles honoribus preuenire ipsarumque fidem et deuotionem dignis retributionibus compensare ac ipsas dotalibus fauoribus conuallare et ipsarum petitiones liberalius exaudire quanto ducatui nostro deuotiores fide et operibus se ostendunt.

Attendentes igitur multiplicis fidei puritatem et deuotionis plenitudinem quam nobilis uir Nicola Notara Dermonophiti, natus uiri nobilis Georgii Notara Dermonophiti, habitatoris Constantinopolis, ad nostre magnitudinis excellentiam habere promptis affectibus se ostendit, qui in agendis nos, ducatum nostrum et singulas personas ducatus eiusdem tangentibus promptum et deuotum laudabiliter et incessanter se prebuit atque prebet, supplicationibus nobis sua parte porrectis gratiosius annuentes ipsum, nostrorum omnium consiliorum et ordinamentorum necessaria solemnitate seruata, perpetuo in nostrum ciuem et Venetum de intus tantum recepimus atque recipimus, et Venetum et ciuem nostrum de intus fecimus et facimus et pro Veneto et ciue nostro de intus in Venetiis tantum deinceps haberi et procurari omni effectu et plenitudine uolumus et tractari, ipsum sincere beneuolentie brachiis amplexantes et firmiter statuentes quod singulis libertatibus, benificiis, immunitatibus et honoribus quibuscumque quibus alii amici nostri et ciues Veneti gaudent de intus et perfrui dignoscuntur prefatus Nicola in Venetiis tantum perpetuo gaudeat et utatur, cum conditione quod in fontico Teutonicorum siue cum Teutonicis mercari non possit secundum formam consilii.

Nobis quoque idem Nicola prestari nobis fecit solemniter ad sancta Dei Euangelia fidelitatis debitum iuramentum.

In cuius rei fidem et euidentiam pleniorem presens priuilegium fieri iussimus et bulla nostra plumbea pendente muniri.

Datum in nostro ducali palatio, anno Dominicae incarnationis

millesimo trecentesimo nonagesimo septimo, mensis Aprilis die
octauo, indictione quinta.
(Venezia, Archivio di stato, *Privileggi* I, f. 125.)

I am indebted to Father Loenertz for the transcript of this
text. It is an example of common grant, an award by a city
to an individual of the rights and privileges of its citizenship,
though only when he is actually present in person within its confines (*de intus tantum*). It is interesting that such a grant should
be given to a Byzantine diplomat at this time and especially to
one engaged in so important an embassy as was this particular one
in 1397–98. But it is by no means unusual. Another instance of
this kind of grant, for example, may be seen in the case of no less
than Demetrius Cydones ("Chydhoni"), who was given the same
grant on January 20, 1391. The text of this document (published
by Loenertz in *Echos d'Orient*, 37, 1938, pp. 125–126) is almost
identical in most of its wording with our own here, and both
obviously represent a conventional form for such purposes.

Nicholas Notaras "Dermonophiti," son of Georgios Notaras
"Dermonophiti" (= Dermokaïtes?) and father of the celebrated
Lucas Notaras, appears from time to time during the reign of
Manuel as an important court functionary and envoy. For an
outline of his career as far as is known, see note 3 on pp. 229–331
of my article "John VII in Genoa, in *Orientalia Christiana Periodica*, 28 (1962).

XIII. Manuel's Letter of Appeal to King Charles VI of France

(To Chapter III, note 47)

(*Chronique du Religieux de Saint-Denys*, XVIII, viii, ed. Bellaguet, Vol. II, pp. 558–560:)

Circa medium octobris, Manuel Grecorum imperator, cum Turcorum incursus, quibus resistere non valebat, egre ferret, Francorum
adjutorium peciit et regi avunculum suum misit, qui imperatoris
apices presentaret statum imperii continentes. Epistole superscripcio
talis erat:

"Serenissimo excellentissimoque principi et domino, domino Karolo,
Dei gracia regi Francorum, fratri nostro precarissimo."

Et in eadem erant scripta que sequuntur:

"Serenissimo atque excellentissimo domino Karolo Francorum regi,
fratri nostro precarissimo, Manuelis in Christo Deo fidelis imperator et moderator Romeorum Palealogus salutem et prosperos ad
vota successus.

"Quia, frater, scimus potenciam maximam quam habet iste infi-
delis tyrannus turcus Basita, dominus Turcorum, inimicus Jhesu
Christi et tocius fidei catholice, et que potencia cotidie augmen-
tatur, nostramque et nostrorum miseriam atque penuriam, quam a
longo tempore citra passi sumus et patimur, et maxime ab annis
tribus vel circa, propter guerram, in qua adhuc sumus, contra nos
motam per dictum Basitam turchum, qui conatur totis viribus et
posse hanc nostram civitatem et christianos istarum parcium suo
dominio subjugare, et in totum nomen Christi de terre delere, non
parcendo die ac nocte in aliquo persone sue et subditorum suorum
laboribus et expensis; et cognito eciam quantum dampnum con-
tingeret toti christianitati, si dictus Basita turcus suam obtineret
intencionem de civitate predicta, quod absit; et cernentes eciam
procul dubio, quod civitas ista nullatenus durare potest usque ad
estatem venturam, qua expectamus et habere speramus auxilium
christianorum, mediante gracia Dei et vestre serenissime regie
majestatis, de qua multipliciter et effective speramus, ea propter
ordinamus ambassiatorem nostrum strenuum et desideratissimum

avunculum, imperii nostri nobilem et circumspectum virum atque
sapientem et expertum, dominum Theodorum Palealogum Canthacosino, latorem presencium, quem ad predictam vestram regiam
majestatem transmittimus; cui ipsa velit et sibi placeat in omnibus
eidem per ipsum exponendis oretenus nostra parte fidem plenarium
adhibere, ac si ea ab ore nostro proprio audiret viva voce. Insuper
firmiter credimus eamdem regiam majestatem invenire paratam
in omnibus de quibus ab ipsa indigemus, quia vidimus anno
proxime preterito, nulla ab ipsa facta requisicione, sed propria
voluntate, ipsam ob Dei reverenciam misisse magnam potenciam
suorum pro liberacione nostra et christianorum istarum parcium;
quod vere fuisset ad plenum, nisi casus inopinatus contingisset
propter demerita. Nos vero ad presens magis indigemus auxilio
quam tunc indigebamus propter debilitatem ad quam devinimus
occasione guerre supradicte, prout dicta vestra regia majestas
poterit informari a baronibus et nobilibus vestris, qui omnia
viderunt et de statu et condicionibus istarum parcium plenius sunt
informati.

"Datum in civitate Constantinopoli, anno Domini millesimo trecentesimo nonagesimo septimo, die prima mensis jullii."

Epistola vero ista in duabus columpnis pergameni contenta; que
scripta sunt in prima ydiomate greco habebantur, et in alia, ydiomate
latino. Nec tamen sigillo munita erat, sed de rubeo taliter signata in
fine . . . [lacuna].

XIV. The Reconciliation of John VII and Manuel in 1399

(To Chapter III, note 74; also note 80)

The various sources for this agreement must be weighed carefully. Roughly, they fall into two groups: those which tell the story and those which do not.

In the latter category are the Greek sources, which give a very faulty account of the episode. As observed elsewhere (above, p. 169, and n. 80), in his only references to this reconciliation Manuel himself states that he personally reached the conclusion that he must go to the West and appointed a government in his absence, over which he set his nephew, with whom he had made peace. A Patriarchal document, also as noted elsewhere (above, pp. 208–211), gives the same picture. Ducas, ed. Grecu, 83, ed. Bonn, 54–55, describes the reconciliation as Manuel's prudent plan to counter complaints within the city against John's exclusion from rule. Chalcocondyles (ed. Darkó, I, 78, ed. Bonn, 84), on the other hand, says that John fell out of favor with Bayazid, fled to Manuel, and reached an agreement with him under binding oaths. The Pseudo-Phrantzes, ed. Papadopoulos, 65–66, ed. Bonn, 61–62, gives essentially the same story with further elaborations, telling of the cordial reception of John by his uncle: see J. W. Barker, "John VII in Genoa," 217 and 220.

Nor do the remaining Greek sources help much. The *Chron. Barb. 111*, 36, simply says that the government was handed over to John VII while Bayazid was besieging the city; but the Emperor, who then leaves for the West, is identified as "John Palaeologus," in another of the frequent confusions of Imperial westward journeys. Of the short chronicles, the *Chron. Vat. gr. 162*, no. 17, p. 210, ll. 79–80, is differently confused, stating simply that the departing Manuel relinquished the rule to "his brother... the lord Andronicus." The Βϱ. χϱ. No. 15, pp. 32–33, ll. 53–54, simply states that Manuel made peace with his nephew John and left him in the government of Constantinople during

490

his absence in the West. No. 18, p. 35, ll. 12–14, helpfully includes the date, December 4, and states that John entered the city εἰρηνικῶς and that he came to an agreement with Manuel with an exchange of oaths; cf. Muralt, p. 766, no. 10. Virtually identical to this latter short chronicle text in wording are the last three of the four short chronicle entries published by Lampros in his Παλαιολόγεια καὶ Πελοποννησιακά, III, 360–361. One last Greek source, the anonymous late-sixteenth-century *Historia politica et patriarchica Constantinopoleos*, 3–4, merely says that Manuel left the government in the hands of his nephew, whose background is very briefly noted.

All the Greek sources, then, uniformly ignore the role of Boucicaut. This serious omission of fact is explained by Berger de Xivrey, 91–92, and by Delaville le Roulx, *La France en Orient*, p. 377, n. 1, as an indication of shame on the part of the Greeks over the necessity of foreign mediation in their internal quarrels. Whatever the reason, however, it is only in two Western sources that we find a full account of the episode. They are mutually independent, and their reliability in this instance is unquestionable.

The biography of Boucicaut, the *Livre des faits*, I, xxxiii, p. 606, tells how the Marshal realized the harm caused by the dynastic division and the need for an end to it. Hence, ". . . he himself went to fetch [*alla querir*] this nephew and his wife in a town called Salubrie, which lies on the frontiers of Greece, and conveyed [*mena*] him to Constantinople to his uncle who received him with great favor [*le receut à bonne chère*], for which all the Greeks were very joyous, giving thanks to God Who had conveyed [*mené*] the *Maréschal* to the land, Who had made this holy peace, and through Whom all their blessings would ensue." Whereupon it was agreed that John should hold and defend the city in Manuel's absence in the West.

Clavijo, ed. López Estrada, 27–28 (cf. ed. Sreznevski, 39–40; trans. Le Strange, 51–52), provocatively adds more details. In discussing the background of John and his claims to Thessalonica, Clavijo relates, ". . . this young emperor [John] had dwelt with Murate [undoubtedly a confusion of Bayazid with his father]; and as he was in a city of Turquia, which has the name of Selenbria, there arrived there Marshal Boucicaut [*Mosen Bochicarte*], governor of Genoa [i.e. later], with ten galleys, who seized [*tomara al*] the said emperor there by force [*por fuerça* or *fuerza*] and conveyed [*leuara* or *llevára*] him to Constantinople, and made him friendly with the emperor his uncle, on the condition that he [Manuel] give him this said city of Saloni in which he [John] might rule." Thereupon, the narrative continues, it was arranged that Manuel should return with Boucicaut to France to seek aid, while John should govern in Constantinople until Manuel returned home. Thus, not only does Clavijo give us the only reference to the prior agreement that John should ultimately receive Thessalonica, but he also makes the unequivocal statement that Boucicaut brought John from Selymbria *by force*.

Now, Clavijo derived his information on John VII from the best of sources during his visit to Lesbos, and his testimony in this respect is important, even if lone. It is of course possible that, looking back after the event and its unpleasant aftermath (still unresolved at Clavijo's time of contact), John had attempted to strengthen his position by claiming that he had been forced unwillingly into the agreement in the first place. But there is no real reason for us to doubt the plausibility of the statement. Certainly the wording in the *Livre des faits* by no means contradicts or rules out what Clavijo says on this point. Moreover, from what we can gather of Boucicaut's forthright and decisive personality, we can readily imagine his listening to an explanation of the situation, stalking out, sallying forth to Selymbria with a force, seizing the recalcitrant nephew by the scruff of the neck, as it were, and dropping him at the feet of his uncle to force the necessary reconciliation.

On the other hand, there is the patriarchal document of which mention has been made above. It states that John brought his mother with him, this source being the only one to mention Maria-Kyratza, who was hence still alive at this time; though this text ignores John's wife, Eugenia Gattilusio, whose return with John the *Livre des faits* mentions. The Patriarchal text also states that John brought with him a large number of followers as well. (One such follower, for example, was later involved in some litigation during John's regency: Miklosich and Müller, II, no. 652, pp. 502–505.) The accompaniment of such a retinue implies that John had more time to prepare his departure than an abrupt seizure would allow.

The truth is perhaps somewhere between the two extremes: John may have been given some leisure and freedom in returning to Constantinople, but he very well may have agreed to do so only under some pressure, if not physical constraint, from the forceful Boucicaut.

On this entire episode, see Dölger, "Johannes VII.," 30–31; Berger de Xivrey, 91–93; Delaville le Roulx, *La France en Orient,* 377; Gibbons, 237–238; Mompherratos, Διπλ. ἐν., 34–35; Silberschmidt, 196–197; and, lastly, Muralt, pp. 761–762, no. 8, and p. 762, nos. 3–4, where the Greek sources—the others are ignored! —have been terribly misunderstood and their details of the reconciliation absurdly dated to 1398.

Dölger, *ibid.,* 29–30, had suggested that, in this period of frustration and in the wake of his marriage to Eugenia Gattilusio, John VII had taken up residence with his father-in-law Francesco Gattilusio on Lesbos; cf. Wirth, "Zum Geschichtsbild Kaiser Johannes' VII. Palaiologos," 593–594, and 600. As Wirth points out, this is "rein hypothetisch," if not downright unlikely. Certainly the accounts of the 1399 reconciliation, especially those of the *Livre des faits* and Clavijo, make it incontestable that John was nowhere else than "Salubrie"/"Selenbria" at that time.

XV. Manuel's Family in the Morea, and His Subsequent Children

(To Chapter III, note 82; also Chapter VII, note 9)

In their accounts of Manuel's departure for the West in 1400, both Chalcocondyles and the Pseudo-Phrantzes mention only that Manuel left his wife in the Peloponnesus as he set sail for Italy. But Ducas observes (ed. Grecu, p. 85, ll. 16–17, ed. Bonn, p. 56, ll. 2–4) that Manuel "left there the Despoina with their children; for he had the recently born [βρέφος] John and the infant [νήπιον] Theodore."

Ducas' description of John must be taken rather loosely, since he was by then seven years old, having been born on December 17 or 18, 1392: see above, p. 104, n. 28. Manuel himself, prefacing his so-called *Praecepta educationis regiae* with an introductory letter to his eldest son, begins the work with an allusion to John's age at the time of his return from the West: "Having left you in Peloponnesus, when I returned from Italy—O how was I able to endure the separation?—you were still but a boy [παιδίον] ..." (ed. Migne, *Patr. gr.*, 156, 313A). Berger de Xivrey suggests (p. 142) that this work was written about 1406 when, at the age of fourteen, the future John VIII became, in Manuel's own expression, "an adolescent" (μειράκιον). When Clavijo saw John on October 28, 1403, he described the boy as being eight years old: ed. López Estrada, 34–35; ed. Sreznevski, 50–51; trans. Le Strange, 61. Actually, of course, the young John was almost eleven.

As for Theodore, A. T. Papadopulos, *Versuch*, 60, estimates that he was born after 1395. But there is no source evidence for this guess, and since his estimation is apparently based only on the false assumption that John VIII was born in 1394, it need not be taken too seriously. Ducas' term νήπιον could also suggest a wide range of age.

Of Manuel's four other sons, at least three would seem all to have been born after the Emperor's Western journey. The date of birth of his fourth son, the future Constantine XI, has been reckoned from Sphrantzes, 1061B (or rather more usually from the Pseudo-Phrantzes, ed. Bonn, 291) which gives Constantine's age at death as forty-nine years, three months, and twenty days: this would place his birthday on February 9, 1404. Thus Papadopulos, 62; cf. Lampros in Νέος Ἑλληνομνήμων, 4, (1907), p. 417, n. 1; also C. Mijatović, in his unreliable book, *Constantine, The Last Emperor of the Greeks* (London, 1892), 78, who also states that Constantine was "the eighth of the ten children of Manuel Palaiologos and Irene [sic] Dragasses," although his bases for such a computation are unknown to me. But usually overlooked is the more authoritative statement by Sphrantzes elsewhere, 1025B, that Constantine was born on February 8, 1405. It is undoubtedly on the basis of this statement that this date is correctly put forward by Loenertz, in "La Date de la Lettre θ′ de Manuel Paléologue," 98, and then later by him in "Une Erreur singulière de Laonic Chalcocandyle," 182. In this latter place Loenertz points out Sphrantzes' later error of a year in the reckoning, so long accepted, of Constantine's age at death.

For Manuel's third son, however, we know no precise date of birth. Since Andronicus is not mentioned among the children left behind in 1400, assuming Ducas did not overlook him, he was presumably not born at that time. As there is no evidence to warrant suspecting Helena of misconduct during her husband's absence, there would thus be two possibilities for his birth date: either Helena was pregnant with him when Manuel left and Andronicus was therefore born before the end of 1400; or, since Manuel rejoined his wife in April of 1403, Andronicus was born at the beginning of 1404. Fortunately, we have some incontestable circumstantial evidence. For one thing, in the famous portrait brought to Paris in 1408 by Chrysoloras (see Figure 6, and below, Appendix XXIV: A, I, 3; also pp. 263–264 above) Andronicus appears with his two older brothers, and he is represented as not much younger than Theodore. More decisive, since Clavijo saw Andronicus in his audience with the Imperial family on October 28, 1403, it is obvious that the first of the two possibilities is the only one really possible. Therefore, Manuel did not see his third son until perhaps some two years after his birth, when the Emperor returned from the West—again, accepting Ducas' failure to include him among the children left behind in 1400 as conclusive.

The birth date of Manuel's fifth son, Demetrius, is unknown.

But that of the sixth, Thomas, may be placed in the year 1409 (cf. Papadopulos, 65), since Sphrantzes, 1073D (Pseudo-Phrantzes, ed. Bonn, 415), reports that Thomas was a little past his fifty-sixth year when he died on May 12, 1465. There seems to have been still another son, named Michael, coming between Constantine and Demetrius, who died of the plague apparently in infancy; but he is mentioned only by Sphrantzes, 1026A (cf. Papadopulos, 55). If this Michael was an actual child of Manuel and Helena, his birth must have come in 1406 or 1407, moving Demetrius' birth in all likelihood to 1407 or 1408. Other than the obscure Michael, Chalcocondyles' survey of Manuel's children, ed. Darkó, I, 192 ff., ed. Bonn, 205 ff., gives them in correct order. But the list given by the Pseudo-Phrantzes, ed. Papadopoulos, 124–125, ed. Bonn, 121–122, is completely untrustworthy, as Loenertz has made clear in "La Date," 99.

The discussion here has spoken only of Manuel's sons. On the basis of the law of averages, we might assume that he and Helena may have had some daughters as well, but their number and names are not clearly recorded for us.

XVI. Manuel's Letter of Thanks to King Henry IV of England

(To Chapter III, note 106; also note 61)

Universis Christi fidelibus ad quos praesentes litterae pervenerint Manuelus, Deo devotus, Imperator et moderator Romeorum Paleologus et semper Augustus, salutem in omnium Salvatore.

Noverit Universitas vestra quod, cum tria millia marcarum, tempore clarae memoriae Domini Ricardi, nuper Regis Angliae post Conquaestum Secundi, a clero et populo regni sui Angliae pro defensione partium Romaeorum contra invasionem inimicorum Fidei Christianae collectae fuerint et levatae, et per Reginaldum Grille, mercatorem de Janua, de dicti Regis voluntate receptae; idemque Reginaldus, et alii, ad solvendum dicta tria millia marcarum nobis, Imperatori praedicto, infra certum terminum jamdiu effluxum, per suas litteras dicto Domino Ricardo Regi et heredibus suis fuerint obligati, ac hujusmodi solutio infra dictum terminum facta non fuerit; et quamquam eo pretextu vigore dictae obligationis, praedicta tria millia marcarum excellentissimo et illustrissimo Principi, Domino Henrico, Dei gratia nunc Regi Angliae, debeantur; idem tamen nunc Rex, attendens et considerans immensos labores ac onera expensarum per nos circa persecutionem praefati negotii penes quoscumque Catholicos Principes et alios Christi fideles hactenus supportata, summan trium millium marcarum auri de Thesauro ejusdem Regis, in recompensationem tantae summae, per praefatum Reginaldum modo quo supra receptae, nobis de gratia sua speciali donavit.

Quam quidem summam per manum honorabilis et religiosi viri, Fratris Petri de Holt, Prioris Hospitalis Sancti Johannis de Jerusalem in Hibernia, ex hujusmodi generoso dono recepimus, cum immensis actionibus gratiarum. Et ideo praefatum Reginaldum ac alios quoscumque quorum in hac parte interesse versatur inde quietos facimus per praesentes, quas nostri sigili appensione fecimus communiri.

Datum Londoniae in crastino Purificationis Beatae Mariae, Anno Domini (secundum cursum et computationem Ecclesiae Angli-

canae) millesimo quadrigentesimo, et regni dicti Regis Henrici
secundo.

To all the faithful of Christ whom the present letter reaches,
Manuel, faithful to God, Emperor and Ruler of the Romans,
Palaeologus, and ever Augustus, health in the Savior of all.

Your whole world knows well that, when three thousand marks
in the time of the Lord Richard of illustrious memory, recently
King of England, Second [of that name] after the Conquest, were
collected and raised by the clergy and people of his realm of
England for the defense of the regions of the Romans against the
invasion of the enemies to the Christian Faith, and were received
by Reginald Grillo, a merchant of Genoa, by the will of the said
King; and this same Reginald and others were committed by their
letters to the said King Richard and to his heirs to paying the said
three thousand marks to us, the said Emperor, within a certain
time limit long expired, and the payment of this sum within the
said time limit was not made; and although on this account, in
force of the said commitment, the said three thousand marks are
owed to the most excellent and most illustrious Prince, the Lord
Henry, by grace of God now King of England, nevertheless this
same man, now King, attending to and considering the enormous
labors and burden of expenses thus far borne by us concerning
prosecution of the aforesaid negotiations with various Catholic
Princes and other faithful of Christ, has given to us, of his special
grace, the sum of three thousand marks of gold from the Treasury
of this same King in recompense of such a sum received in the
above fashion by the aforesaid Reginald.

Which sum, indeed, from this generous gift we have received
through the hands of the honorable and pious man, Brother Peter
de Holt, Prior of the Hospital of Saint John of Jerusalem in Ireland,
with very great expressions of thanks. And for that reason, the
aforesaid Reginald and whomsoever others are involved in this
matter we thereafter set at peace through these presents, which
we confirm by the appending of our seal.

Given in London on the morrow of the Purification of the
Blessed Mary, in the Year of the Lord (after the sequence and
reckoning of the English Church) the one thousand four hundredth, and the second of the reign of the said King Henry
[i.e. February 3, 1401].

The text of this letter is preserved in a manuscript of the
Cottonian Collection (*Nero, B. xi.*, fol. 174); it is an original copy,
on vellum, and (according to the editor, p. 57, n. 1) "the mutilated

remains of the seal are still attached to the letter." This text has been published by Hingeston, *Royal and Historical Letters* (the first and only volume of a projected series never continued), no. 25, pp. 56–57. In view of its relative unavailability, it is reproduced here, with my own translation.

In his footnotes, Hingeston points out that during this period the English Church followed the late Roman tradition of beginning the year on March 25; therefore, the year 1400 as given by the text must be read as 1401. It is also interesting to note the attempt here to adapt into current Latin the standard formula of the Byzantine Imperial signature: [Μανουὴλ] ἐν Χριστῷ τῷ Θεῷ πιστὸς βασιλεὺς καὶ αὐτοκράτωρ Ῥωμαίων [ὁ Παλαιολόγος], with the added καὶ ἀεὶ αὔγουστος. For an even more literal Latin rendering of this formula in a subsequent letter (though not from Manuel), see the opening of the text in the following Appendix (XVII).

XVII. John VII's Letter to
King Henry IV of England

(To Chapter IV, note 17)

Serenissimo Principi et potentissimo Domino, Henrico, Dei gratia, Regi Angliae, consanguineo nostro praecarissimo, Johannes, in Christo Deo fidelis Imperator et Moderator Romeorum, Palaeologus, salutem in Eo per Quem reges regnant.

Magnis instantibus nobis periculis, necessariis indigemus auxilliis; ideoque inclitam regiam Majestatem vestram rogamus et requirimus quatinus ipsa dignetur, propter nomen Salvatoris Jhesu Christi, et ob famam quam ipsa Excellentia regia habet in toto orbe terrarum, conferre ad auxilium et subsidium huic civitati nostrae Constantinopolitanae, quae quidem ex longissima tempestate, et angustia guerrarum habitarum, quas praesentialiter habet cum Turchis infidelibus, persecutoribus nominis Christiani, tandem extenuata viribus et potentia ac facultatibus quibuscumque, jacet prostrata, non valens ulterius hostes offendere, immo nec ab ipsis se defendere; pereclitatur subire jugum ipsorum infidelium Saracenorum, nisi a vestra, et aliorum Regum et Principum Christianorum potentia, mediante Divina Gratia, sublevetur a periculo cladis.

Et si forte regia Celsitudo vestra in praesenti non valet tantum quantum gliscit subsidium et auxilium conferre, prout nobis scripsit serenissimus et excellentissimus Dominus et Pater meus, Dominus Imperator, saltem dignetur regia clementia vestra subsidium et succursum impendere ac conferre de gentibus-armorum et pecunia, in tanta parte quod dicta civitas valeat a praedictis periculis et hostium incursibus praeservari, usque ad majorem et magis ordinatam provisionem auxilii et succursus fiendam a vestra Majestate, una cum ceteris Regibus et Principibus Christianis, eo quod quia si (quod absit!) amitteretur dicta civitas de manibus Christianorum, quae civitas potest Domus Dei nuncupari, cederet ad damnum et dedecus omnium fidelium Christianorum, et timendum est quod deleretur et amitteretur nomen Jhesu Christi de istis partibus Orientis.

Ceterum, inclite Rex, quia rectos decet collaudatio, non debemus nec possumus sub scilencio [=silentio] praeterire illos qui virtutum operibus illustrantur, et actus laudabiles non desinunt quotidie exercere; sane cum nobiles nonnulli ex vestratibus in hujus urbis defensione commorantes, sint per eorum opera dignis laudibus merito excolendi. Ideo, intervenientibus eorum bonis operibus, adsurgimus vobis ad gratiarum actiones referendas valdo dignas, quoniam ipsi ad omnem defensionem hujus civitatis ab hostibus, et ad nostrum commodum et honorem, solertem et intrepidam curam contulerunt, velut optimi operantes, nihil de contingentibus omittendo quod respiceret bonum et securum statum nostrum et dictae nostrae Civitatis, et civium ejusdem. Nec enim clarissimae Angliae novum est producere tales fructus.

Valeat et augeat inclita regia Celsitudo vestra praelibata in optatis feliciter per tempora longiora!

Datum in urbe Constinopolitana [=Constantinopolitana], Anno a Nativitate Domini Millesimo CCCC^{mo} secundo, die prima Junii.

The original of this text is in the British Museum in the Harleian Ms. No. 431, fol. 10. It was published previously by Hingeston, *Royal and Historical Letters,* no. 42, pp. 101–103.

Aside from its obvious historical value, this letter has two interesting aspects. One is the presence of certain stylistic elements in the text. Its drafter seems to have been a competent Latinist, and the style here is generally a little smoother than that of Manuel's letter in the preceding Appendix. In comparison with the crude attempt there (cf. the end of the letter in Appendix XVI), the rendering into Latin here of the Imperial title is a far more literal and successful approximation of the original Greek formula: ['Ιωάννης] ἐν Χριστῷ τῷ Θεῷ πιστὸς βασιλεὺς καὶ αὐτοκράτωρ 'Ρωμαίων [ὁ Παλαιολόγος]. And at the end of the salutation, the phrase "in Eo per Quem reges regnant" reflects the Septuagint verse in Proverbs viii, 15, "δι' ἐμοῦ βασιλεῖς βασιλεύουσιν" ("Per me reges regnant" in the Vulgate). Adaptations of this phrase were common in Byzantine texts: note one, for example, in the last line of the *Prooimion* of Constantine Porphyrogenitus' *De administrando imperio.* Even more interesting, aside from occasional reflections of Greek phrases, is the obviously French origin of such a phrase as "*de* gentibus-armorum." Possibly it is some indication of the nationality of the scribe who drafted or translated John's letter. Could he have been one of the French members of Chateaumorand's garrison?

The second point of interest is the paragraph on Englishmen

serving in Constantinople. Obviously this passage was added to
curry extra favor with Henry and to emphasize supposed precedents for English help to the Byzantines. Therefore we cannot
expect much precise information from it. But the text seems to
make clear that the Englishmen helping in the defense of the city
against attacks, presumably during the Turkish siege, are there at
the time the letter is being written.

It is interesting to speculate just how much this allusion might
refer back to the presence of Anglo-Saxons in the old Varangian
Guard in the eleventh century and thereafter. Though it might
seem hardly flattering or tactful to us to remind the English King
of men who were in point of fact but refugees from the Norman
Conquest, such subtle distinctions might not have meant much
to the Byzantines of the early fifteenth century, whether or not
they even would have to the English themselves of that time.
Actually, though it might appear unlikely that a recollection of
the eleventh-century Varangians should linger in Constantinople
as late as Manuel's day, we must not forget that the Byzantine
memory was long. That such recollection did exist is suggested,
for example, by the English historian Adam of Usk, a contemporary of Manuel, who reports a comment he himself heard from
Byzantine ambassadors in Rome in 1404. This comment (pp.
96–97 in Thompson's edition, and p. 272 in his accompanying
translation), referring to axe-bearing warriors "of British race"
among the Greeks, has been taken to be an actual allusion to the
Britons (Anglo-Saxon or otherwise) of the old Varangian Guard:
see Vasiliev, "The Opening Stages of the Anglo-Saxon Immigra-
tion to Byzantium in the Eleventh Century," *Seminarium Konda-
kovianum,* 9 (1937), 39–70, specifically p. 69 (who, however,
does not make use of the further evidence of this letter itself).

On the other hand, whether or not his comment was intended
to reflect to so distant a past, John does seem to be speaking, at
least in part, of Englishmen of his own day: men of quality,
knights of good family who were a credit to their homeland in
"overseas service" fighting against the Infidel in Constantinople
in recent times. We may recall the case of the Knight in Chaucer's
Canterbury Tales, a work roughly of this epoch. The description
of the Knight in the Prologue identifies him with many actual
campaigns or events in the East, although nothing is said to indicate that he had anything directly to do with Byzantium. But

his background at least shows that it was a common practice in this period for restless English knights to hie themselves off to wherever a good fight might be found—all on behalf of Christendom, of course. It is therefore surely possible, if not probable, that some Englishmen of this stripe had lately been serving in Constantinople, at least as individuals. It might well be to such individuals, then, that John VII would be referring in his letter to Henry IV.

XVIII. Byzantine Relations with Timur

(To Chapter IV, note 23; also notes 16 and 18;
and to Chapter III, note 111)

We have ample evidence that Timur was in active diplomatic contact with various Christian rulers, and a number of communications between them survive.

As for contacts with Byzantium, there are several traditions. For example, the old history by Cantemir (*History of the Growth and Decay of the Othman Empire*, trans. Tindal, 53) claims that the Byzantine Emperor sent to Tamerlane, begging him to fight Bayazid and offering to submit to the Tartar's authority; and Cantemir makes the preposterous suggestion that Tamerlane's noble reaction to this plea was one of the principal reasons for his war against Bayazid. As early a work as the sixteenth-century Theodoro Spandugnino's *De la origine deli imperatori Ottomani* (ed. Sathas, 147) reports the obviously inaccurate story that *Emanuel Paleologo*, both before and after Timur's victory, offered Constantinople in submission to the Tartar. And even the contemporary French source, the *Religieux de Saint-Denys* (XXIII, x, ed. Bellaguet, III, 50), reports that "On the other hand he ['Tambellanus'] announced in letters to the governor of the Constantinopolitan empire [i.e. John VII] that he should recall his nephew [a mistaken reversal: read 'uncle'] from Francia, promising that whatsoever the impious Basita had taken away from him he would generously restore." We might also recall that the Turks subsequently made the claim that the Byzantine Emperor had stirred up Timur against them and was thus responsible for their disaster at Ancyra. This accusation was made as early as 1411 by Musa when he wished to excite the Turks against Manuel following the defeat of Suleyman: Ducas, ed. Grecu, 125, ed. Bonn, 91. It was used thereafter by Mechmed II in 1453, in a speech put into his mouth by Critobulus: ed. V. Grecu (Bucharest, 1963) 69–71; ed. K. Müller, *Fragmenta historicorum graecorum*, V (Paris, 1883), 64; trans. C. T. Riggs (Princeton, 1954), 28. In these instances, the charge was simply a matter of propaganda.

504

Still, Dölger, *Regesten,* no. 3278, p. 86, asserts that Manuel himself made an appeal to Timur to attack Bayazid before his departure for the West in 1399; on somewhat shaky testimony, it seems to me.

Nevertheless, there was perhaps some basis for part of these traditions. According to Clavijo, ed. López Estrada, 93, ed. Sreznevski, 145–146, trans. Le Strange, 135, the "emperador di constantinopla" (whom Le Strange wrongly identifies with Manuel) and the Genoese of Pera together had offered to send military aid to Timur or at least to use their ships to block Turkish passage of the Straits; and that the Greeks at least promised to send a subsidy of money to the Tartar. This writer, of course, had access to information and accounts which should have been reliable to one degree or another.

We have already noted Clavijo's evidence that John VII had come to an understanding with Bayazid as to surrendering Constantinople: see above, pp. 214–215 and n. 18. If such an understanding had indeed been made in good faith—assuming that one could use such an expression in this context!—any alleged dealings by John with Timur as well might seem paradoxical. But surely there need be nothing strange, especially to a Byzantine, in playing both sides against each other. Certainly the Byzantines would hardly have regretted the defeat of Bayazid. Thus, a report of dealings by John with the Tartars is entirely credible.

As it happens, we have independent confirmation of such dealings. Georgio Stella, *Annales Gennenses* (Muratori, *R.I.S.,* 17), 1194, reports that Timur was in contact with various Christian rulers, including the "Imperator Graecorum" and the Genoese; and he also reports that the latter flew Timur's banner over Pera ·as a token of respect; cf. Delaville le Roulx, *La France en Orient,* 390; Heyd, *Histoire du commerce du Levant,* II, 267.

Far more important, however, is another portion of the Venetian Senatorial deliberation, already cited (above, p. 212 and n. 16), of September 10, 1401. The report to the *Sapientes* at that time by their Genoese informant included the news that two messengers from Timur had arrived in Pera on August 19 of that year and had attempted to dissuade the Emperor and the Genoese from coming to any peace terms with Bayazid, whom Timur hoped to attack shortly; the report added that the Genoese informant was ignorant of the response which the two ambassadors carried with them upon their departure: Dölger, *Regesten,* no. 3197, p. 74; text, Iorga, *Notes et extraits,* I, 113.

Actually, at least one of these two ambassadors was none other than an emissary originally sent from the court of Charles VI of France, with the connivance (if not partly on the initiative) of Manuel himself, as part of a grand Christian effort to induce the Tartar to strike down the Turk. This was a Dominican whose name, some variations in spelling aside, seems to have been Francesco Sandron. Nor was he the only emissary to Timur from Western Europe, for at the same time another Dominican was in the company of Timur. He was one John Greenlaw, originally Bishop of Nakhšivan, from which he was translated on August 26, 1398, to the Archepiscopate of Sultaniya (the ancient Tigranocerta in Lesser Armenia), a post that bore with it the pompous title of *Archiepiscopus totius Orientis:* on him see Delaville le Roulx, *La France en Orient,* 391; Hingeston, *Royal and Historical Letters,* p. 419, n. 2. (P. B. Gams, *Series episcoporum ecclesiae catholicae,* Ratisbon, 1873, p. 454, puts the end of John [II]'s episcopate in Sultaniya in 1401: if this date is correct, was he therefore detached from his see specifically for this diplomatic project?) On the missions of the two in general, see Alexandrescu-Dersca, *La Campagne de Timur en Anatolie,* 38–40, 92–93; H. Hookham, *Tamburlaine the Conqueror* (London, 1962), 218, 219, 243, 256–259; Delaville le Roulx, *La France en Orient,* 389–391; Heyd, 266–267; Mompherratos, Διπλ. ἐν., 46 ff.; cf. also Gibbons, 249. I am dependent upon the reference in *Byz. Zeitschrift,* 60 (1967), 430, for reference to a discussion of John of Sultaniya's mission (and visit to Wallachia and Moldavia in the course of it) by Ş. Papacostea, "Un călător în ţările române în veacul al XV-lea," in *Studii* (Bucharest), 18 (1965), 171–174, which I have not seen.

Of these two men it is the Archbishop John who is of interest for us in connection with Manuel; for, presumably when these missions were being organized, Henry IV of England drew up as John's sovereign a series of letters of recommendation to various rulers to pave the Archbishop's way for his important negotiations in the East. The first three of these letters are addressed respectively to the Emperor of Abyssinia, the King of Cyprus and Armenia, and the Doge of Venice: published by Hingeston, *Royal and Historical Letters,* nos. 147, 148, and 149 respectively, pp. 421–425. But another letter, *ibid.,* no. 151, pp. 427–428, is addressed to none other than Manuel himself. This indicates without doubt that the Emperor was actively involved in the Christian negotiations with Timur. Thus, in addition to his pleas to Western rulers, Manuel took care to be alert to new possibilities in the East.

At any rate, the response received by these ambassadors in August of 1401 would seem to have been favorable and may even have been exactly the messages reported by Clavijo, if we can believe an important text found in Marino Sanuto, 797–798 (reproduced in Alexandrescu-Dersca, 123–124, and Mompherratos, Διπλ. ἐν., 60–62). This purports to be a letter, dated May 15 (1402), from Timur to "Il Procuratore Principe dell' Imperadore Chirmanoli," that is, Manuel's regent, John VII. It speaks of the message brought by one of these ambassadors, and it is plainly an answer thereto. Hence the seeming confirmation of Clavijo's statement, for the latter discusses payment of tribute to be made to the Tartars by the Byzantines and the matter of blockading the Straits against the Turks: cf. Alexandrescu-Dersca, 51; Mompherratos, Διπλ. ἐν., 47 ff.

There are also other reports and traditions regarding Timur and the Byzantines after the Battle of Ancyra. We are told by the Persian Sheref ed-Dīn (*Histoire de Timurbec,* trans. Petit de la Croix, Vol. IV [Paris, 1722], 37–39)—in terms construed by Heyd, p. 267, to suggest a previous offer—that Timur called upon John (and the Genoese) after his victory to make good on their promise of tribute: cf. Alexandrescu-Dersca, 86–87; see also Dölger, *Regesten,* no. 3199, p. 74, on an embassy of September 2, 1402, sent by John and the Genoese in such a connection. That John was at least ordered by Timur to recognize Tartar suzerainty, and that John did so, is recorded by one other European source, according to Grousset, *L'Empire des steppes,* 532. Moreover, Chalcocondyles, ed. Darkó, I, 148, ed. Bonn, 160, claims that after the battle Timur demanded that the Byzantine Emperor supply him with ships for a crossing to Europe. Apparent support for this statement might be found in a letter written by Giovanni Cornaro, a Venetian commander on Crete, dated September 4, 1402 (p. 127 of the text, reproduced from Sanuto, 795, by Alexandrescu-Dersca: cf. above, p. 219, n. 27), stating that Timur had demanded of the Byzantine Emperor some galleys and the cession of parts of "Grecia," including Gallipoli (which was not in his hands). Cf. Mompherratos, Διπλ. ἐν., 51, who uses a corrupted text. If this report is correct, even to the extent only of indicating that Timur did at least briefly contemplate carrying the war across into Europe, one can understand the confusion and terror on the part of the Christian powers which flourished for some time. On the other hand, a letter written by the Venetian Tommaso de Molino to Piero Cornaro at the end of September, 1402 (text in Sanuto, 799–800, reproduced by Alexandrescu-Dersca, 138–140), mentions that Timur had offered to the Greeks a force of 5,000 men to carry on the struggle against the Turks; cf. Heyd, 267.

Whatever the questionability of some of these various reports, the bulk of the evidence discussed here leaves no doubt that the Byzantines were in active contact with Timur. Apparently such contact was initiated by Manuel with the assistance of Charles VI of France and the other Christian rulers sponsoring the embassies to the Tartars. When brought into these negotiations, in spite of any existing understanding he might have reached with Bayazid, John VII himself was willing to cultivate Timur on his own part. Promises were made to the Lord of Samarkand, apparently the very ones mentioned by Clavijo; and, regardless of how hesitantly or deceptively John may have given them, Timur presumably expected that he could look to the Greeks for support and subservience.

It should be noted that there is a recent study on this subject by I. I. Umniakov in the *Trudy* of the Tashkent (Uzbekistan) University, N.S. 61 (1956), 179–200, which I have been unable to obtain in spite of diligent searching.

Finally, before leaving this theme, mention should be made of one further extension of it, even if it is somewhat out of place here chronologically. For the repercussions of the embassy of John Greenlaw, the Archbishop of Sultaniya, continued even after the period of 1401–1402. Some years later, in 1407, Konrad von Jungingen, the Grand Master of the Teutonic Order, upon hearing reports of Eastern affairs from this prelate, wrote a set of letters dated January 20 of that year, at Marienburg. One of these letters was addressed to Manuel II. It was simply an appeal to Manuel to end the schism of the Eastern Church. See K. Forstreuter, "Der Deutsche Orden und Südosteuropa," Kyrios, *Viertel-*

jahresschrift für Kirchen- und Geistes-Geschichte Osteuropas, 1 (1936), 266–267, with the Latin text of the Grand Master's letter appended on p. 271. There is apparently no record of Manuel's receiving it or reacting to it. It certainly left no impression on his course or policies in 1407 and thereafter.

XIX. Manuel's Supposed Visit to the Pope

(To Chapter IV, note 37, and note 31; also Chapter III, note 89)

In his constricted account of Manuel's journey, Ducas (ed. Grecu, 85, ed. Bonn, 56) mentions both Florence and Ferrara among other cities which Manuel visited, but in no order or relation to the Emperor's actual route as we know it. We can be reasonably certain that Manuel did not visit Florence on his first traversal of Italy. Therefore, if Ducas' information is at all correct, a stop in Florence would have occurred only on the return trip.

As for the supposed visit to the Pope, the *Livre des faits*, I, xxxv, p. 608, relates that Manuel "was before the Holy Father, who granted indulgences [*qui donna grand pardon*] to whomever would make contributions to him [*à quiconque luy feroit bien*]." This passage appears after the account of Manuel's actual visit to the French King, but on the other hand it precedes a reference to his visit to England; hence, the location of the statement in the text is probably of little value in itself, since Manuel could have made no visit to either Pope between his residences in Paris and London. Then, too, the reference to the grant of indulgences might perhaps relate the visit to the granting of the Papal bull of May 27, 1400, by Boniface IX (see above, p. 172).

At any rate, these source statements seem to indicate strongly that Manuel did visit a Pope personally. In view of Benedict XIII's indisposition in Avignon, the Pope whom Manuel saw was likely to have been Boniface IX. Certainly the consensus of scholarly opinion seems to be that Manuel did meet this Pope, and that in such case the interview probably took place in Florence, at this later stage of Manuel's journey. On the visit to the Pope, see Halecki, "Rome et Byzance au temps du grand Schisme d'Occident," 514. And on the entire question of Manuel's route and this visit in general, see Vasiliev, "Putešestvie Manuila," 292–294 (72–74); also Berger de Xivrey, 116–119; Schlumberger, "Un Empereur de Byzance à Paris et Londres," 137–139 (47–48).

In connection with this supposed meeting with the Pope, we

should note a tale which appears in the late sixteenth-century *Historia politica et patriarchica Constantinopoleos,* 4:

> ...And this Basileus [Manuel], taking ship and departing to Italy, and seeking many things, the Pope and the other rulers indeed promised to give him aid, but they did not give it, as the outcome revealed; giving as their excuse that the Basileus on one of the feasts would not accede to doing obeisance to the maniple on the right arm of the suffragan, adorned on the upper part with a woven image of Christ. Wherefore the Pope, taking this opportunity, wrote to all the Italians: "To the Basileus of the Romans, who has not acceded to do obeisance to the image of Christ, whoever will give aid will be excommunicated." And hearkening to such things, he who had been nourished in such great hopes withdrew from there and rushed to Venice, having accomplished nothing of the things for the sake of which this most Christian Basileus had gone and which he had sought.

(The related Ἐκ. χρον., 2, differing from this text only in some details of wording, gives a few further details, however, such as the Emperor's basic objection to kissing the hand of a *Latin* ecclesiastic; but the fundamental story is the same between these two texts. This same latter text is carried over also into the history of the Pseudo-Dorotheos of Monemvasia [ed. of Venice, 1750], 404–405.)

This curious tale is recounted and emphatically rejected as a fabrication by Berger de Xivrey, 117–119 (quoted by Schlumberger, "Un Empereur," 138–139 [47–48]), and is also discussed by Vasiliev, "Putešestvie Manuila," 294 (74), who both take note of the misinterpretation of this passage by Edward Gibbon. See also Halecki, "Rome et Byzance," 517–518. But, as spurious as the bulk of this story doubtless is, it nonetheless may add some small support to the assumption that Manuel did indeed visit the Pope —and at this phase of his journey, that is, on his way home.

As this book goes to press, the indefatigable Father Dennis has kindly supplied me with the typescript draft of a forthcoming article of his, entitled "Two Unknown Documents of Manuel II Palaeologus," scheduled to appear in the *Travaux et Mémoires,* 3 (1968). In this piece, Father Dennis offers the full Latin and Greek texts of two documents issued by Manuel during his stay in Paris, with extensive commentary. One of these two is particularly relevant here, since it is a letter to Pope Boniface IX, dated July 5, 1401, accompanying the gift of a relic to the Pontiff. Father

Dennis suggests that the letter and the relic were intended to be conveyed to the Pope by Demetrius Palaeologus in the course of the latter's mission to Florence in the summer of 1401. Father Dennis also suspects that, if Manuel ever did meet Boniface IX personally, such a meeting would have occurred during the Emperor's journey *to* France, in May of 1400, not on the trip *from* France in early 1403; that is, in connection with the Roman Pope's bull of May 27, 1400, as discussed above (p. 172). This 1401 contact would therefore represent, Dennis thinks, Manuel's efforts to remain in touch with the Roman Pontiff while at the same time trying to cultivate the Avignonese Benedict XIII.

The other document published by Father Dennis is a similar missive, likewise accompanying a relic, addressed to Queen Margaret of Denmark and the other two Scandinavian kingdoms, and dated November 20 (Latin text) and 23 (Greek text), 1402. This document is of interest on two counts. First, it reveals yet one more court with which Manuel was in contact during his journey; and, at that, at the very end of his Paris sojourn, stressing anew that, even after the Battle of Ancyra, he continued to put hope in such contacts in his continuing quest for aid. Second, it prompts Father Dennis to suggest some reflections on the date of Manuel's departure for Paris. From the statement of the *Religieux de Saint-Denys* it can be computed that Manuel left Paris on Tuesday, November 21, 1402: see above, p. 220 and n. 31. Does the later date of this document therefore suggest that this computation or statement is wrong, by at least two days? Might we re-compute the date as November 28, one week later?

At any rate, I am again indebted to Father Dennis for providing me with this material in advance of his publication of it.

XX. Manuel's Literary Revenge on Bayazid

(To Chapter IV, note 80)

Some remarks the leader of the Persians and the Scythians [i.e. Timur] might have made to the proud tyrant of the Turks [i.e. Bayazid] who talked grandly and insolently and who was insufferable in his boasts when he prospered, but who turned quite the opposite after his defeat.

As it seems, the mere desire, held long and from the beginning, to wage war is in its very essence a hostile act. And one who is impelled by such a nature is not able to restrain himself from endeavoring to cause trouble on all occasions. So then, you attempted, all the while your enterprises were proceeding according to your wishes, to oppose yourself to my interests with posturings and with insults—for in the actual realities your strength allowed no more—and now, when your pride, which was so fixed and so great, has collapsed, and when your vain arrogance has waned to nothing, even now you are no less hostilely disposed toward us, if in different fashion. So it is that, weeping after your defeat—for, since you failed to recognize that this life is filled with constant ebbing and flowing, you did not expect, as the events have shown, that your good fortune would decline, although this is an accustomed fact, neither unlikely nor inadmissible—you now belittle my brave exploit, and you sting no less now than formerly by forthwith casting aside your pride. Indeed, here I was, believing that I would obtain some brilliant and enduring renown for having prevailed over a man himself supposedly brilliant in the great achievements of his valor. Yet, you refute my glory as but a deception by covering yourself with shame and proclaiming yourself a man easily overcome in the gestures by which you fail to bear your misfortune manfully. Therefore is your past record of victory assigned to chance, not to valor. So do you strive against me even now and discredit my success, turning round to the contrary my glory on your account. For, since I have conquered someone who is devoid of bravery, how may I then appear brave in this victory? Away with gold, therefore, away with all booty and your great wealth collected from all sides, since the glory for which I longed is lacking! This it was that led me, who had already grown old,

513

from the ends of the earth against you. And now I find that my labors have been cheated!

This first work (ed. Migne, *Patr. gr.*, 156, 280C–281A; ed. Legrand, pp. 103–104 of his edition of Manuel's correspondence, fully translated here; partial French translation by Berger de Xivrey, 128, partially reproduced by Schlumberger, "Un Empereur de Byzance à Paris et Londres," 144 [52–53]) is one of the two in which Manuel marked the downfall of his old enemy Bayazid. As can be seen, it is cast in the form of an address to Bayazid spoken hypothetically by his conqueror, Timur, composed in a kind of exercise in style and character portrayal known as ἠθοποιΐα. One can well imagine that Manuel felt impelled to celebrate in some way the event that brought him such relief. We have little indication of much genuine spitefulness in Manuel's character, but a sudden appearance of it in this case hardly merits surprise or apologies. What is interesting is that this little monologue seems by implication to heap cultivated scorn not only on the vanquished but on the victor as well. Manuel's little essay is not the only one of its kind, however, for we have another, later (late sixteenth-century) specimen of exactly the same thing, by one Manuel Moros, a Cretan: this has been published by M. Treu, "Eine Ansprach Tamerlans," *Byz. Zeitschr.*, 19 (1910), 15–28, and is entitled Δημηγορία τοῦ Περσῶν βασιλέως Τεμίρη, text on pp. 15–20.

Having unburdened himself of this reaction, Manuel also penned another work on the subject of Bayazid's downfall, but in quite a different style. This is an even shorter little effort, which is the pious Emperor's hymn of thanksgiving to God.

> In the form of a Psalm about the Saracen Thunderbolt, when God looked upon His people and, through his enemies, slew him who was a beast in every way.

> Highest is the Lord in authority; our God forever and ever; and ere His powers were put forth upon all the earth He Himself was and will remain. Now did brutish men join together; for I saw His thunderbolt kindled against the native vanity of him who His wonders worked upon them, and their darts weakened, and mocked at the forebearance of God's goodness and at the generosity of His providence. God restrained His wrath, yet he despised Him. While he blasphemed, He was long-suffering; and the infidel

held his head high; he dreamed of the world, and would not allow the Lord of Heaven to rule it. But, in the boasting of his power, and in his trust in great numbers to abuse the flock of God, the confluence of evils came upon him, and he has paid at once for all his wrongdoings from the beginning. Know then, all the earth, and let not a son of earth be exalted in himself. For to God's spirit everything yields, and, after holding back for a long time, on a sudden He exacts a reckoning. But he that hopeth on Him, let him not fear evil: for those abiding patiently He saves, even if He may exact from them a sacrifice of contrition and requite them for it; because He is as a sea of worthiness. Let His people give Him glory, and let those who trust in Him be filled with good hopes.

As the title implies, this work (ed. Migne, *ibid.*, 281A–C; ed. Legrand, *ibid.*, 104; fully translated) is cast in the style of a Biblical Psalm. It is worth analyzing stylistically, for it shows how freely a Palaeologan writer such as Manuel could handle his models. This is especially interesting, since the practice of paraphrasing or parodying Psalms is a rather uncommon one in Byzantine literature.

In actual fact, the language of the Psalms is drawn upon only broadly here. It is true that there are cases in this text where Manuel uses expressions and turns of phrase in ways almost identical with obvious prototypes in the Psalms. Thus, compare Manuel's phrase "οἱ πεποιθότες εἰς αὐτόν" (line 24 in Legrand's edition) with "οἱ πεποιθότες ἐπὶ κύριον," (Psalm cxxiv [25], verse 1). Likewise, compare Manuel's "δότω δόξαν ὁ λαὸς αὐτοῦ" (l. 23) with the two Psalm expressions "δότε δόξαν τῷ θεῷ" (lxvii [68], 34), and "εἴδοσαν πάντες οἱ λαοὶ τὴν δόξαν αὐτοῦ" (xcvi [97], 6). There is also the obvious similarity between Manuel's line "ὁ θεὸς ἡμῶν εἰς αἰῶνα αἰῶνος" (ll. 4–5) and the Psalmist's "ὁ δὲ θεὸς βασιλεὺς ἡμῶν πρὸ αἰῶνος" (lxxiii [74], 12), especially in view of the use of the very common words "εἰς αἰῶνα αἰῶνος" (xxxvi [37], 29; etc.). And, working down to a simple usage of individual words, there is no small echo in the whole of Manuel's opening, through the words " ... ἦν ὁ αὐτὸς καὶ μενεῖ" (l. 6), of the Psalmist's line "ὁ κύριος εἰς τὸν αἰῶνα μένει" (ix [9], 7).

Indeed, Manuel is less likely to transpose into similar contexts entire phrases or expressions from the Psalms than he is simply to use words or turns of phrasing themselves employed in the Psalms, but in different ways. Thus, compare his "γνώτω δὴ πᾶσα ἡ γῆ"

(l. 17) with the two Psalm passages "γνῶτε ὅτε κύριος αὐτός ἐστιν ὁ θεός" (xlix [100], 3) and "φοβηθήτω τὸν κύριον, πᾶσα ἡ γῆ" (xxxii [33], 8). Compare further Manuel's "ὁ δὲ ἐλπίζων ἐπ' αὐτὸν μὴ φοβηθήτω κακά" (l. 20) with "μακάριος ἀνὴρ ὃς ἐλπίζει ἐπ' αὐτόν" (xxxiii [34], 8); his "ὑψοῦ τὴν κεφαλὴν ἦρεν" (l. 12) with "καὶ ὑψῶν τὴν κεφαλήν μου" (iii [3], 3); or even more far-fetched, Manuel's "καὶ μὴ ὑψούσθω ἐν ἑαυτῷ γηγενής" (l. 18), with "ὑψώθητι, κύριε, ἐν τῇ δυνάμει σου" (xx [21], 13), while the last phrase's exact words "ἐν τῇ δυνάμει" appear in an utterly different usage elsewhere in Manuel's text (ll. 14–15), and while Manuel's word "γηγενής" itself appears occasionally in the Psalms.

Manuel's independent usage of words which only rarely appear in the Psalms is illustrated by a reference to his "νῦν οἱ κτηνώδεις συνῆκαν" (ll. 6–7), of which the subject noun is a word that is found only once in the Psalms: "κτηνώδης ἐγενόμην παρὰ σοί" (lxxii [73], 22). But, while some of Manuel's vocabulary includes words that are used but rarely in the Septuagint Greek of the Psalms, it includes a far larger number that never appear there.

It can be seen that Manuel avoided a literally slavish imitation of the style of the Psalms, in general or in particular examples. For better or worse, he was content to use his prototypes as a broad kind of pattern and to preserve otherwise much of his own peculiarities of style in composing this pious reflection "about the Saracen Thunderbolt" ("περὶ κεραυνοῦ τοῦ ἀγαρηνοῦ"), exulting in the destruction at long last of him who had done so much evil, by Him Who does not forget His people when they wait and trust in Him. But the very failure of Manuel to capture or reproduce fully the style of his Scriptural models is in itself revealing. Byzantine intellectuals as a rule, and particularly in the late periods, felt much less at ease in the idiom of the Bible than they did in that of the Classical authors on whom they had been reared. For them, to write good Greek was to write in the idiom of the ancients, as far as they understood it and were capable of reproducing it. Thus, as dreary and pedantic as their imitations of Classical models may be, they still show a keen feeling for the niceties of ancient style; as imitations, these works are successful. But when confronted by a Scriptural antecedent, as in this case, the Byzantine stylist is not very effective in capturing either the flavor or the spirit of what is essentially a strange idiom for him. (For a similar free use of imprecise paralleling of Biblical material elsewhere in Byzantine literature, see G. Buckler's *Anna Comnena, A Study* [Oxford, 1929], 194–196.)

It is worth noting that, besides the one already cited, there are other specimens of Byzantine literary reactions to Timur's victory over Bayazid, in less constricted or artificial styles. One such reflection on these seemingly miraculous events is a discourse attributed to John Chortasmenos, at least a portion of which has been translated into German by H. Hunger in his *Byzantinische Geisteswelt* (Baden-Baden, 1958), 282–286. (On this author in general, see *id.*, "Johannes Chortasmenos, ein byzantinischer Intellektueller der späten Palaiologenzeit," *Wiener Studien*, 70 [1957], 153–163. Note, however, that P. Gautier has more recently, in publishing this text as "Un récit inédit du siège de Constantinople par les Turcs (1394–1402)," *Rev. des ét. byz.*, 23 [1965], 100–117, denied the attribution of its authorship to Chortasmenos.) But another, a more interesting, and, stylistically, a far more idiomatically Byzantine example than Manuel's has recently been published by Gautier, in his "Action des grâces de Démétrius Chrysoloras à la Théotocos pour l'anniversaire de la bataille d'Ankara (28 Juillet 1403)," *Rev. d. ét. byz.*, 19 (= *Mélanges R. Janin*, 1961), 340–357: Greek text and French translation, 348–357.

In conclusion, it is natural that these two little works by Manuel should be considered together as a related pair in view of their common subject matter. But there has been some speculation as to their date of composition. Berger de Xivrey suggests that they were actually written separately. He proposed (pp. 127 ff.) that Manuel wrote the first of them while on his way home from the West, perhaps while in the Morea awaiting Boucicaut. He points out (p. 129), however, that the second of the two was probably not composed until Manuel reached home or at least until he learned, presumably then, the news that Bayazid was really dead. Cf. Schlumberger, "Un Empereur," 143–144 (51–52).

There is nothing to disprove this thesis, and there is no absolute basis for assuming that the two works were of necessity composed at precisely the same time. The first certainly gives no indication that Manuel was aware of Bayazid's actual death when he wrote it—indeed, all to the contrary, since Bayazid is portrayed as a living captive—whereas the second one seems to make it clear that Bayazid was dead when it was written. Whatever interval of time may separate them, however, they cannot but be regarded as a pair, complementary demonstrations of Manuel's double reaction to Bayazid's fall and of his exacting the only kind of revenge he was in a position to enjoy—a literary one.

XXI. The Date of Manuel's Letter νϛ΄

(To Chapter IV, note 119; also to Chapter VII, notes 66 and 76)

This letter to Manuel Chrysoloras follows in the manuscript order a very brief note to the Patriarch Euthymios, Letter νε΄, concerning a literary work, in the writing of which Euthymios and Manuel had coilaborated. Presumably this writing was a commentary on an exchange between Demetrius Chrysoloras and Antonio d'Ascoli, the full sequence of which survives in two manuscripts today, the *Cryptensis gr. 161* and the *Vaticanus gr. 1879*: see above, p. 433, n. 66, and p. 438, n. 76. The latter of the two manuscripts also preserves this Letter νε΄ by Manuel and Euthymios' reply (ff. 328ᵛ–329ʳ): on the collaboration and this exchange of letters in general, see Mercati, *Notizie (Studi e Testi, 56)*, p. 517, n. 1.

Now there are interesting chronological problems regarding this Letter νε΄ itself. In the *Parisinus gr. 3041* the letter is headed "Τῷ πατριάρχη κυρῷ Εὐθυμίῳ." But recently, at the end of his article "Ecrits de Macaire Macrès et de Manuel Paléologue," p. 193 and n. 2, Loenertz has pointed out that, when this letter appears in the *Vaticanus gr. 1879*, it is addressed simply "Τῷ παπᾷ κυρῷ Εὐθυμίῳ." Loenertz contends that this latter address is the true one, and that the letter was therefore actually written *before* Euthymios became Patriarch in the autumn of 1410 (on October 26, 1410, according to the latest interpretation of the date, by V. Laurent, "Les Dates du Patriarcat d'Euthyme II de Constantinople," *Byz. Zeitschr.*, 54 [1962], 329–332).

To reject the testimony of the *Parisinus gr. 3041*, prepared under Manuel's personal supervision, in favor of that of another manuscript might seem rather drastic. But there is some reason for it if one considers the evidence. Loenertz points out, for instance, that the tone of Euthymios' reply is not what a Patriarch might write, but is rather that of a humble subject in relation to his Emperor. Further, if one examines the Emperor's four letters to Euthymios in the *Parisinus gr. 3041* as a group, some interesting possibilities arise. The first two of these letters, λθ΄ and μ΄,

519

written from Paris in 1401–02, are addressed simply "Τῷ παπᾷ κυρῷ Εὐθυμίῳ" ("To the Priest, lord Euthymios"). But for the third, written some time in the first decade of the fifteenth century, the address begins the same way, with the words " . . . μετὰ ταῦτα δὲ πατριάρχῃ Κωνσταντινουπόλεως" ("but later Patriarch of Constantinople") added in a different hand. And then Letter νε' bears the disputed address to Euthymios simply as Patriarch. Is it possible that the different hand adding to the address of να' was Manuel's own? More important, is it possible that the *Parisinus gr. 3041* was in preparation at this time, that the copy of Letter να' had already been completed when Euthymios became Patriarch, that Manuel then added, or had added, the additional phrase to the address of να' as a compliment to his newly exalted friend, and that, when Letter νε' was reached in the manuscript preparation Manuel then changed its original humble address to correspond to the new rank? If this is what happened, it would not only confirm Loenertz' thesis, but it might also tell us something about the possible date of preparation of at least part of this important manuscript. Only the absolutely certain establishment of the dates of the subsequent letters in this manuscript as much later than 1410 could destroy this explanation completely.

But, at any rate, we must recognize the importance of Loenertz' argument, certainly plausible in itself. If he is wrong, and if Letter νε' was written to Euthymios after the latter's elevation to the Patriarchate, its date would be no earlier than autumn of 1410; but if Loenertz is correct, then the date of νε' must be before that time. These speculations are of great importance in attempting to establish—on the basic assumption that the manuscript order of the letters is indeed chronological—a *terminus post quem* for Letter νς'.

It is impossible, however, to establish any useful *terminus ante quem* on the meager basis of the letters that follow this one in the manuscript. We can only say that its references to current Byzantine difficulties seem to indicate that the letter could not have been written after Mechmed's victory in 1413; by that time the Byzantine position was more favorable.

All we can do to determine the date of this problematical Letter νς' is to examine its contents in relation to the events of the nebulously general period in which we can place it. It was written to Chrysoloras while the latter was on his journey in the West, the first phase of which took him to Italy (1407–08), France (1408), England (1409), Spain (1410), and again Italy (1410): see above, pp. 263–266. At this same time the struggle between the sons of Bayazid was reaching a peak, Suleyman's campaign in Anatolia being succeeded by Musa's counteroffensive in Rumelia (1409–11), the defeat and death of Suleyman (February 1411), Musa's siege (1411), and the war between Musa and Mechmed (1412–13). Hence, Manuel's references in the letter to his difficult position, which are certainly more than empty exaggerations.

In consideration of these events, it is obvious that the letter could not have been written before Chrysoloras had made some kind of report on at least some part of his embassy, and it probably was not written before the struggle between Musa and Suleyman made the Byzantine position more serious—not before 1409, let us say. Another possible chronological clue is the Emperor's apparent urging at the end of his letter that Chrysoloras, unsuccessful in his efforts, should soon return home. This sounds as if the letter was therefore written to the ambassador at the end of an assignment. We know, however, that Chrysoloras did not return home. Rather, he died in the West, still in the midst of the second phase of his mission (see above, pp. 321–322). But this second phase was not really concerned with obtaining specific aid in the time of emergency. And, as this phase ended only with Chrysoloras' death, it seems unlikely that Manuel would be writing to him at any point during it with the thought that the mission was over and that Chrysoloras would soon be home. Rather, the letter gives the impression that it was written toward the end of the first phase of his mission, *before* Chrysoloras embarked on the second phase, which was undertaken either on his own initiative or on subsequent instructions from Manuel. In other words, in these terms the letter was probably not written after 1411.

This question of dating also involves another problem. In the letter Manuel is plainly speaking of one particular ruler with whom Chrysoloras had been dealing. There is no explicit identification of this ruler. But it is certainly interesting, as well as important, to speculate on his identity on the basis of a few clues provided by the text. The vital one, I believe, is the allusion to the ruler's situation as being, if not fully settled, at least much calmer than previously. No candidate for this identification is acceptable unless he fits this description.

Among the Western rulers from whom Manuel might be seeking important aid at this time, there seem to be only a few really likely possibilities. One of them may be ruled out immediately: Charles VI of France was by this time hopelessly insane, and his realm was torn by civil strife. Although the various Spanish rulers might seem relatively minor powers, a case could be made in the abstract for the King of Aragon. But Martin I died in 1410, and neither he nor his successor, Ferdinand I (with whom Manuel seems to have had no active relations for several years), would appear to fit Manuel's description.

There are only two real possibilities. One is Sigismund, by now the Holy Roman Emperor. He certainly would seem to fit best Manuel's reference to the ruler "whose duty requires him both to be concerned about and also to provide for all needs." If one were to translate τάξις as "rank" rather than as "duty," one might almost construe it as a reference to the title of Holy Roman Emperor. The prestige of his rank would also justify the importance and impact that aid from him would have in the eyes of the Turks. And, of course, Sigismund had long been, and was still to be, looked to by the Byzantines as a champion and potential leader of Western relief. Yet, one should never let the extravagance of Manuel's expressions be the sole basis for conclusions; in point of fact, there are obstacles to the acceptance of Sigismund as the ruler in question. Manuel says that the ruler does not even make promises, much less give those he will not keep: but Sigismund was always making promises, whether he could keep them or not, and he would not have let his own distractions curb his passion for great projects in the future. Moreover, Sigismund probably would not really fit Manuel's characterization of the ruler's situation, for his troubles never appeared calmer than they had been previously. Preoccupied by the problems of the Hussites and the Great Schism, as well as by various other affairs of his diverse realms and activities, Sigismund would not seem the most likely prospect for inspiring either Manuel's description or his immediate expectations. Further, though Chrysoloras did have dealings with this ruler during the second phase of his mission, we do not know that he was in any contact with Sigismund in the first, that is, by 1411. In terms of itinerary as we know it, Chrysoloras never visited Sigismund personally before 1414. (Be it noted here that Dölger, *Regesten*, no. 3329, p. 98, seems to be mistaken in implying that Chrysoloras was sent by Manuel to Sigismund by or before the spring of 1411. His evidence is the letter, dated May/June 1411, of Sigismund to Manuel, edited by Finke in *Acta Concilii Constanciensis*, I, no. 111, pp. 391–394, in which allusion is made to Chrysoloras. In point of fact, this allusion only seems to prove Chrysoloras' presence in Rome, not his appearance before Sigismund. For Sigismund speaks of some proposals of his concerning Church union that he has sent to Pope John XXIII, "with which articles, and the response thereupon of the Pope," adds Sigismund, "Your Majesty can become acquainted through your agent Manuel [Chrysoloras] *then in attendance there. . . .*" ["de quibus articulis et responsione papali superinde vestre magnitudini potuit innotescere per Manuelem nuncium vestrum *tunc ibi presentem. . . .*": ed. Finke, p. 393, ll. 6–8]. I therefore reject Dölger's entry as unwarranted and untenable, and I submit that there is no evidence for presuming that Chrysoloras visited Sigismund in or about 1411, or at any time before 1414; on the contrary, I continue to accept Camelli's account of Chrysoloras as being in Italy at this time, in the train of Pope John XXIII, as already indicated above, p. 321.)

The second possibility is Henry IV of England. Manuel's key description of the ruler's circumstances would fit him perfectly. By 1410 Henry's position internally in England had settled somewhat after the crushing of a number of grave revolts. And Henry seems to have been just the kind of crusty realist to refuse even to make promises if he felt his situation did not allow them. Moreover, if we accept the possibility of irony in Manuel's pompous reference to him as "the lofty ruler" ("τὸν ἄϰϱον ἄϱχοντα"), we might well take this letter almost as a foil to Manuel's earlier one, also to Manuel Chrysoloras (see above, pp. 178–180), containing such lavish and expectant praise of this very monarch. We have also seen previously (above, 213 ff., and pp. 189–190) that Manuel did register his recognition that this specific king would not fulfill his high-sounding promises, at least for the moment. What could be more natural, therefore, than that the Emperor should now warn his ambassador of this same ruler's shiftiness? Manuel's description of the ruler's status and prestige which might fit Sigismund more literally would also serve as deliberate hyperbole in an inverted parallel to his own former words of praise for this very man.

I therefore submit that, in spite of the very strong case that might be made for Sigismund, it is Henry IV of England who merits the dubious distinction of this identification with Manuel's ἄκρος ἄρχων, and that this letter really refers to Chrysoloras' dealings with this king in 1409. This identification, tenuous as it may be, perhaps gives us more basis for dating the letter. Since Henry died in 1413, any letter written concerning him obviously would have to antedate that year. Combining the possibility of the identification with Manuel's allusion to a plainly difficult situation at home and the prospect for Chrysoloras' return home, I think we are safe in assuming that this letter was written toward the end of the first phase of Chrysoloras' mission to the West, at the end of, or after, his trip to England. Its widest margin of date might thus be 1409–11; and regardless of the correctness of Loenertz' thesis regarding the dating of Letter νε′, I would suggest 1410 as the most likely time.

XXII. The Date of Manuel's *Funeral Oration for His Brother Theodore*

(To Chapter IV, note 135; also notes 120 and 139)

Chalcocondyles, ed. Darkó, I, 202–203, ed. Bonn, 216, possibly misled by an incorrect statement in Plethon's preface to this text, states that it was during the [1408] visit to the Morea that Manuel read his eulogy for his brother; and the so-called *Anonymous Panegyric to Manuel and John VIII Palaeologus*, actually by Cardinal Isidore, also gives this clear impression (ed. Lampros, p. 164). That this was the case was therefore accepted by Berger de Xivrey, 147–148, and for a long time it was the common assumption: for example, the clumsy catch-all entry (under 1407!) by Muralt, p. 789, no. 9, and also the biased and out-of-date comments of Miller, *The Latins in the Levant*, 370; even Khoury, 141 (using the date of 1407), maintains this tradition. (On the other hand, Mompherratos, Οἱ Παλ. ἐν Πελ., 37, succumbing to the confusion of some of the sources, actually has Manuel pronounce his oration toward the end of his 1415–16 visit.)

Lampros was the first, however, to suggest that the great Λόγος ἐπιτάφιος was not delivered personally by the Emperor. (His article on the subject, in the Σπαρτιατικὸν ἡμερολόγιον, 11 [1910], 33–42, is not available to me.) Since then, this point has also been developed fully by Zakythinos in his article "Μανουὴλ καὶ Ἰσιδώρος," 45–50 (1–6). One of the most important documents on this question is a letter to the Emperor by the very man who actually read the work in the Emperor's place, on the occasion of a commemorative ceremony presumably marking an anniversary of the Despot's death. This man was the "Hieromonachos" Isidore, later Metropolitan of Monemvasia. This Isidore has also been identified with the controversial Metropolitan of Kiev and later Cardinal. But this identification is a hotly disputed one, and Zakythinos' unhesitating acceptance of it has been most recently and most emphatically rejected by V. Laurent in his consideration of the question, "Isidore de Kiev et la Métropole de Monembasie," *Rev. d. ét. byz.*, 17 (1959), 150–157. Therefore Zakythinos' article should be used with caution on this point. (A further irony in this article is the fact that Zakythinos uses the Panegyric which Lampros had published as of anonymous authorship, apparently unaware that it is also by Isidore, that is, by Isidore of Kiev: cf. Mercati, *Scritti d'Isidoro* [*Studi e Testi*, 46], 6–7.)

Manuel had entrusted to this Isidore the task of reading the eulogy, and in Isidore's letter (text published by W. Regel, *Analecta Byzantino-Russica* [Petrograd, 1891], 65–69; an extract published by Zakythinos, 47–48 [3–4]), there is a description by the cleric for the Emperor's benefit of the effect which, he says, the long work produced on the select audience assembled to hear it, an audience which included the young Despot, Theodore II, Manuel's son and a nephew of the deceased.

Exactly when this assembly took place is not very clear. Zakythinos, 50 (6), suggests that it may have been in 1409, on the second anniversary of Theodore's death. And Mercati, in his discussion of the dating of the letter in his "Lettere di un Isidor Arcivescovo di Monembasia e non di Kiew," *Bessarione*, 20 (1916), 200–207, had reached essentially the same conclusion—although, obviously, he had strong opinions about the identification of the two Isidores which Zakythinos has taken for granted. From certain passages in the text of the eulogy itself, we might well conclude that Manuel intended to present his eulogy himself during his visit, for which purpose he would have had to prolong his stay in the Morea then on into 1409. But presumably he then had to entrust the reading of it to Isidore because this visit was cut short when the Emperor was required to leave the Morea before the appointed time, before the end of 1408, as a result of John VII's death and then the growing crisis in the Turkish wars of succession. (If these suppositions are correct, they may enable us to suggest that the date of Theodore I's death was at the beginning of the year in 1407; but on the problem of dating Theodore's death, see above, p. 272, n. 126.)

At any rate, even though unable to deliver his monster eulogy in person—if its original text was essentially the same as the one that comes down to us in "published" form, few would have been able to understand its highly artificial and obscure literary style, much less to keep awake through its inordinate length!—Manuel thought highly enough of the work to attempt to circulate it. He sent a copy of it to Manuel Chrysoloras, then in Western Europe, accompanying it with a letter (νζ′) in which he expressed further his great grief over the loss of his brother. Zakythinos reproduces a portion of this letter and arbitrarily dates it January 1410. I can see no basis for such a dating; on the contrary, especially in the light of dating the letter which precedes it in the manuscript (see Appendix XXI), this letter to Chrysoloras probably could not have been written much before 1411. Later, Manuel sent a copy of his Oration to Chrysoloras' pupil, the Italian humanist Guarino, together with his Letter ξβ′, in which he asked Guarino to translate the work into Latin. Mercati, "Lettere," 205, followed by Zakythinos, 47 (3), dates this letter to Guarino about October of 1417.

XXIII. Manuel's Letter-Discourse to Alexius Iagoup

(To Chapter VII, note 29)

Τῷ κὺρ Ἀλεξίῳ τῷ Ἰαγούπ.

Cod. Parisinus gr. 3041, ff. 72ᵛ–73ᵛ.

72ᵛ   Χθὲς ἢ πρότριτά μοι προσελθών, ἔφης, ὥς τις σοι τῶν ἐπιτηδείων
τῇ προτεραίᾳ συγγεγονώς, σφόδρα ἐμοῦ κηδόμενον ἑαυτὸν ἀπεδείκνυ.
ἔφασκε γάρ, ἀνιᾶσθαι δεινῶς, ὅτιπερ αἱ τοῦ ἄρχειν φροντίδες, μόλις
ἀναπνεῖν ἐῶσιν, ἔπειτ' ἐγὼ θέλω θεολογεῖν. κινδύνου δὲ εἶναι τοῦτο
5 μεστόν. αὐτὸν δέ, ἢ φιλοῦντα, τὸ σὺν ἀσφαλείᾳ με ζῆν περὶ πλείστου
ποιεῖσθαι. ὅθεν καὶ παρήνεσεν ἄν μοι, εἴ γε εἶχε θαρρεῖν ὡς οἷς ἂν
λέγῃ πεισθήσομαι, παντάπασιν ἀπέχεσθαι τοῦ θεολογεῖν· καὶ τοῦ σχή-
ματος ὠθοῦντος πρὸς ἕτερα, καὶ πράγματα παρέχοντος τουτουὶ τοῦ
καιροῦ παντοδαπὰ καὶ πολλά, πρὸς ταῦτα μὲν πᾶσαν ἐνδείκνυσθαι τὴν
10 σπουδήν· ἐπιστήμης δ' ἀντιποιεῖσθαι ἧς οὐδὲν ἐμοὶ προσῆκε μήδ' ὁπω-
στιοῦν ἐγχειρεῖν· ἀλλ' οὐδὲ τὸν ἄνδρα ἐπίστασθαι, ἐξ οὗ δυναίμην
μαθεῖν, ᾗ δεῖ χρήσθαι τῷ πράγματι. δεῖν γὰρ τὸν τῆς θεολογίας διδά-
σκαλον, παρὰ μὲν αὐτοῦ τοῦ Θεοῦ, ὅπη ἂν ἔχη τἀληθὲς διδαχθῆναι· εἰς
τοὔσχατον δὲ ἐληλακέναι τῆς τῶν Ἑλλήνων σοφίας. εἰ δὲ μή, τοῖν γοῦν
15 εἰρημένοιν κεκτημένον τὸ ἕτερον, τὸ τηνικαῦτα διδάσκειν ἑτέρους ἐπι-
χειρεῖν. ἐν ἡμῖν δ' οὐδένα [=οὐδὲν?] τοιοῦτον ἐστὶν εὑρεῖν νῦν. ὅ τε
τοίνυν ταῦθ' οὕτως ἔχει, ἄμεινον ἂν εἴη πάντας, μήτοιγε τὸν βασιλέα,
εἰς τοὺς τῆς θεολογίας ἀγῶνας μὴ ἐθέλειν ἑαυτοὺς ἐπισφαλῶς καθιέ-
ναι. ἔλεγε δὲ καὶ αὐτὸν ἐθέλειν ἐγγράφως ὁμολογεῖν, μηδαμῶς μηδέποτ'
20 ἐθέλειν θεολογικῶν δογμάτων ἐφάπτεσθαι. μὴ δὲ γὰρ ἂν ὅλως ἐφικνεῖ-
σθαι τοῦ μεγέθους τοῦ πράγματος.

   Πολλὰς μὲν οὖν πολλαχόθεν παρέχει τὰ ῥήματα ταῦτα λαβάς, οἷς
ἀντιλέγειν, ἔργον τε καὶ σχολή, καί με πρὸς ἔτος ἀποκρίνασθαι, πῶς
οἴει, παρακαλεῖ. ὁ δὲ βιαιότατος οὑτοσὶ καιρός, οὐ δίδωσιν οὐ δὲ συγ-
25 χωρεῖ, ἀμυθήτους δυσχερείας, τὰς μέν, ἤδη ἐπάγων, τὰς δ' ἀπειλῶν.
ὅθεν καὶ μὴ δ' ὁπωσοῦν τὴν πρώτην χωρῆσαι πρὸς ἀπολογίαν δεῖν
ἔγνων. ἐπειδὴ δ' ὡς διεπαύσω τἀκείνου διαπορθμεύων ὡς ἐμέ, ἀπό-
κρισιν ἀπήτεις εὐθύς, μέμνησαι δ' οἶμαι, ἠξίους γὰρ ἔχειν ὅτι ἂν ἀπο-
κρίναιο ἐρομένῳ τῷ φίλῳ· ἐγὼ δ' οὐκ ἐσχόλαζον, ὁ γὰρ ἑσπερινὸς
30 ὕμνος ἐτελεῖτο πρὸς τὸν Θεόν, σχολῆς ἤδη λαβόμενος εἰ καὶ μὴ καθα-
ρᾶς, δεῖν ᾠήθην μέσην χωρῆσαι. καὶ ὅσα μὲν εἰς τὸ ἐλέγξαι ἥκει, ὡς οὐ

528

προὔργου ποιούμενος τὴν ἐμὴν ἀσφάλειαν ταυτὶ τὰ ῥήματ' εἴρηκεν ὁ
ἀνήρ, ἀλλ' ὥστ' ἐξεῖναι λέγειν αὐτὸν μετὰ παρρησίας, μηδὲν ὂν ἔτι τὸ
73ʳ προσιστάμενον, ἅτε μηδενὸς ἀντιλέγοντος, ἃ / νῦν ἐν γωνίᾳ καὶ μεθ'
35 ὑποστολῆς, ἐν μέρει κείσεται τέως, τοῦ καιροῦ μὴ ἐπιτρέποντος ᾗπερ
ἔφην. ὅσα δέ, εἰ σιγήσαιμι ψόγον ἐμοὶ φέρει, εἰ δὴ θεολογεῖν ἡγοίμην
πάντας δεῖν πάντα καιρόν, καὶ πρὸς πάντας ὡς τύχοι, ταῦτα δέ [=δή?],
συντόμως ὡς οἷόν τ' ἐστίν, εἰρήσεται σὴν χάριν. ἀγαπητὸν γὰρ τὸν
περὶ τηλικάδε πραγματ' ἠσχοληκένον, ἀπολογησάμενον λῦσαι, εἴ τι τὶς
40 αὐτῷ μέμφοιτο, τὸ δὲ μὴ μέμψασθαι τὸν μεμφόμενον οἷς ἀδίκως ἐμέμ-
ψατο, ἤτοι ἐπαίνων ἄξιον οἶμαι, ἢ γοῦν, μὴ δὲ μέμψεως.
Ἐμοὶ τοίνυν παιδὶ μὲν ὄντι, οὐχ ὑπῆρξεν ἐς μουσεῖα μόνον φοιτᾶν,
καὶ τοῦτ' αὐτὸ μόνον ἔργον ποιεῖσθαι, ὅπως πάντα παρελάσαιμι σοφόν,
καὶ τοὺς ἐπὶ λόγοις σεμνυνομένους. ἀλλ' ἐκ τοῦ βουλευτηρίου ἐξερχό-
45 μενον, ἄλλοι ἐπ' ἄλλοις διεδέχοντο πόνοι. καὶ πολλοὺς ἦν ἀνάγκη καθ'
ἑκάστην ἡμέραν ἀμεῖψαι τοὺς διδασκάλους, οἳ πολλά τε ἄλλα, τόξά τε
μεταχειρίζειν καὶ δόρυ, καὶ ἱππεύειν ἐδίδασκον. τὴν δὲ τῶν παίδων παρε-
λάσαντα ἡλικίαν, πρὶν εἰς ἄνδρας ἐλθεῖν, ἑτέρα τύχη μετὰ τῆς ἡλικίας
ἐδέχετο, τρικυμίας οὖσα καὶ θορύβων ἀνάπλεως, καὶ πολλοῖς τεκμη-
50 ριοῖς διδοῦσα μαντεύεσθαι, ὡς καὶ ἡ μετ' ἐκείνην ἡμᾶς διαδέξεσθαι
μέλλουσα, ἄντικρυς γαλήνην λευκὴν ἀποδείξει τὰ φθάσαντα. καὶ εἰδόσι
μὲν καταλέγειν πάντα, περίεργον. πλὴν ἴσασι πάντες, ὡς οὐ φαῦλοι
τινὲς μάντεις γεγόνασιν, οἳ προΰλεγον ἐλεύσεσθαι τὰ δεινά. ἧκε ταῦτα.
καὶ ἡμεῖς ἐντεῦθεν εἴ τι τῶν λόγων παῖδες ὄντες ἐκαρπωσάμεθα, καὶ
55 τούτου τὸ πλεῖον ἀπεβαλλόμεθα, ἀπό γε τῶν λόγων μετενηνεγμένοι
ἄλλοτε. πολλὰ γὰρ ἄττα ἀθρόα ὥσπερ ἐκ συνθήματος τόθ' ἡμῖν ἐπέ-
θετο· δυσκολίαι τε καὶ διαφόρων πάλη συμφορῶν, καὶ ἀλλεπάλληλοι
κίνδυνοι. ἃ σφοδρᾷ τινι ῥύμῃ πνεύσαντα καθ' ἡμῶν, οὐδ' ἀναπνεῖν
συνεχώρουν.
60 Ἔπειτ' εἶχέ με φρουρά, ἅμα τῷ πατρί τε καὶ βασιλεῖ, καὶ δὴ καὶ
τῷ ἀδελφῷ. πᾶσι μὲν οὖν τοῖς οὕτως ἔχουσιν, ἀνάγκη πρὸς ἔργα τρέ-
πεσθαι παντοδαπά, ὥστε μικρὸν γοῦν τῇ περὶ ταῦτα σχολῇ, διασκεδά-
ζειν τὸ νέφος τῆς ἀθυμίας, καὶ μὴ τελέως ἀπειπεῖν πρὸς τὰ ὄντα τε καὶ
ὑφορώμενα κακά, ὅπερ οὐκ ἀνδρός. ἐδόκει τοίνυν τηνικαῦτα ἐμοί, τοῦτ'
65 ἔργον ἔχειν διηνεκές, τὸ βιβλίοις ἐνδιατρίβειν, νύκτωρ καὶ μεθημέραν,
73ᵛ μετὰ τὸ ἀφοσιοῦσθαι τὸ πρὸς τὸ θεῖον χρέος. καίτοι, τί λέγω / ἡμέραν;
νὺξ ἀφεγγὴς ἦν, ἀειδήποτ' αὐτοῦ. ὅθεν ἔδει λύχνῳ χρῆσθαι τὸν πρὸς
οἱανοῦν ἐργασίαν τρεπόμενον. τοσαῦτα δυναμένης ἡμῖν τῆς φρουρᾶς
καὶ μεσημβρίας σταθερᾶς εἰς τὸ τὰς ἀκτῖνας ἀποκρούεσθαι, ὅσαπερ
70 τῇ ἄλλῃ γῇ νυκτός, τοῖς ἔξω φρουρᾶς διατρίβουσιν. ὧν δὲ ἔρημος σοφι-
στοῦ, πλεῖστα μὲν ἐπιδοῦναι καὶ τῶν πολλῶν ἰσόρροπα πόνων, οὐκ ἐδυνήθην. τῇ δ' οὖν συνεχείᾳ τοῦ ἔργου, ἔρως μοι τῶν λόγων ἄκρως τυρ-
ραννικὸς ἐντέτηκε τῇ ψυχῇ. καὶ οὕτω γε τοῖς ὅλοις οὗτος κεκράτηκεν,
ὥστέ με τοῦτον οὐχ ἁπλῶς ἐραστήν, ἀλλὰ μανικώτατον ἀπεργάσασθαι.

75　'Ως δὲ δὴ τρία παρελήλυθεν ἔτη, καὶ φροῦδα πάντα γέγονε χειρὶ
Θεοῦ τὰ κατέχοντα, καὶ αὖθις ἐπανήκομεν εἰς τὸ πρότερον σχῆμα, αἰεὶ
μέν, καὶ οὕτως ὅπλοις χρῆσθαι ἐχρῆν, καὶ δὴ καὶ τόπους ἐκ τόπων
ἀμείβειν ἔστιν ὅτε ἠνάγκασμαι, οὐκ ἄν δε [=ἄνευ?] καὶ τοῦ περὶ τῇ
ψυχῇ δεδιέναι. οὐδὲ γὰρ ἐκεχειρίαν βραχεῖαν γοῦν ἐδίδου ἡ πονηρὰ
80　τύχη. πλὴν τῶν λόγων ἅπαξ ἁλούς, οὐκ ἐδυνάμην ἀποθέσθαι τὸν ἔρωτα.
ἀλλὰ τὴν μὲν τύχην, ἀνταγωνιστήν· ἀλείπτην δὲ τὴν ἀπὸ τῶν λόγων
ἐθέμην βοήθειαν. καὶ ἐπειρώμην, οἷς μέν ἐπιδοίην ἂν πρὸς λόγους,
ἀντέχειν πρὸς τὰ δεινά· οἷς δ' ἂν ἀντέχοιμι, ἐπιδώσειν πρὸς λόγους.
ὅθεν, καὶ πολλοὺς ἐδέησέ μοι παρελθόντι [=προελθόντι?] ζητῆσαι τοὺς
85　πρὸς τὸ ζητούμενον βοηθήσοντας· καὶ μέντοι γε, καὶ τοῦ σκοποῦ οὐκ
ἀπέτυχον. ἀνδράσι γὰρ ἐνέτυχον, θείας ἐπικουρίας τε καὶ ῥοπῆς, μετέ-
χουσιν ἀτεχνῶς, καὶ τὴν ἔξω σοφίαν, πεπαιδευμένοις ἐπιεικῶς. οὐ γὰρ
εἴ τῳ φίλον λέγειν τἀναντία θαυμάζειν χρή, εἴπερ ἀπὸ τοῦ τοὺς ἄλλους
ἐλαττοῦν, αὔξειν ἡγεῖται καὶ αἴρειν τὰ καθ' αὑτόν. ἀλλὰ καίτοι παρὰ
90　τῶν εἰρημένων ἀνδρῶν τὰ μέγιστα ὠφεληθῆναι δυνάμενος, οὐ τοσοῦ-
τον ὠφέλημαι. ὁμολογῶ γάρ, ὡς οὐκ ἀπὸ σπινθῆρος ἀνήφθη μοι πυρ-
σός. ἀλλ' ἀπὸ πυρσοῦ μεγίστου, μόλις τινὰ σπινθῆρα, ὅπερ οὐ γιγνόμε-
νον ἦν, λαβεῖν ἐδυνήθην. οὐκ οἶδ' οὖν, εἴτε τὰς ἀπὸ τοῦ καιροῦ δυσκο-
λίας αἰτιᾶσθαι πρὸς τοῦτο χρή, εἴτ' ἀβελτηρίαν τῆς φύσεως καταγνῶ-
95　ναι τῆς ἐμαυτοῦ. . . .

(In the foregoing transcription, all but one of the paragraph
divisions are my own. I have altered only occasionally the original
punctuation in the manuscript.)

Though the wording is distinctly different, it is perhaps not too
farfetched to suspect that when Manuel penned the two next-to-
the-last sentences (ll. 91–93) in the passage above he had in mind
at least the basic idea of a passage in Plato's *Epistle VII*, 341C–D:
"... ἀλλ' ἐκ πολλῆς συνουσίας γιγνομένης περὶ τὸ πρᾶγμα αὐτὸ καὶ τοῦ
συζῆν ἐξαίφνης, οἷον ἀπὸ πυρὸς πηδήσαντος ἐξαφθὲν φῶς, ἐν τῇ ψυχῇ
γενόμενον αὐτὸ ἑαυτὸ ἤδη τρέφει." More tangible, however, is the
apparent, or at least the plausible, derivation of a germinal
idea for Manuel's elaborate pun in ll. 40–41 from a passage in
the *Batrachomyomachia*, attributed to Homer, its ll. 149–150:
"... οἱ δὲ κάκιστοι/νῦν ἐμὲ μέμφονται τὸν ἀναίτιον...."

XXIV. Notes on the Illustrations

A. Portraits and Mementos of Manuel

I. *Authentic Portraits*

1. (Figure 29) *Emperors of the Palaeologan House* (Biblioteca Estense, Modena, *Cod. α.S.5.5* [= *Gr. 122*], f. 294ᵛ). This is one of a series of groups of Imperial portraits to be found in a fifteenth-century manuscript of the earlier historian Zonaras. Each ruler's name is indicated in key letters placed within his nimbus, and then fuller descriptions are placed over each head. These run as follows: Top row, from left to right: "Andronicus [III, 1328–1341] the son of Michael [IX, 1295–1320]"; "John [VI] Cantacuzenus [1347–1355]"; "John [V, 1341–1391], the son of Andronicus [III]." Middle row: "Andronicus [IV, 1376–1379], his [John V's] son"; "John [VII, 1390, 1399–1408], his [Andronicus IV's son"; "Manuel [II, 1391–1425], his [John VII's] uncle." Bottom row: "John [VIII, 1425–1448], the son of Manuel"; "Constantine [XI, 1448–1453], his brother"; and finally, as a symbolic filler of the pattern, a stylized portrait (note the different and earlier type of crown) of the first Byzantine Emperor, as it were: "St. Constantine [I, 'The Great,' 324–337]." At the bottom is an inscription that obviously belongs to this last inserted portrait, reading "Celebrated among the saints, and great Basileus, Constantine Chlorus." (The latter name is apparently taken over in confusion from Constantine The Great's father, Constantius Chlorus, 293–306.) These portraits are, of course, highly stereotyped and need not be taken too literally. But the artist has made some correct attempts at individual characterization: for example, John VIII's hooked nose. But for the almost unique forked beard (also suggested in the sketch noted next), this representation of Manuel is by no means incompatible with more reliable portraits of him. The portrayal here of John VII is the only one I know to exist; that of John V one of the only two. The left edge of this page had been trimmed off at an early time, leaving the page under it partially visible and prompting a later hand to

531

write in once again, at the bottom underneath it, the inscription's partially damaged opening words.

2. (Figure 32) *Manuel, between His Father and His Eldest Son* (Bibliothèque Nationale, Paris, *Cod. gr. 1783*, f. 2). This sketch, in a fifteenth-century manuscript containing texts by Codinus and other sources, has been reproduced several times, but is the victim of some confusion. It has been incorrectly cited by some scholars, and even the subjects have been conflictingly identified. Schlumberger, "Un Empereur," pl. VI (III) and pp. 145–146 (54) characterizes the two Emperors flanking Manuel simply as "deux de ses fils." But Lampros, in reproducing this sketch in his Λεύκωμα τῶν βυζαντινῶν αὐτοκρατόρων (Athens, 1930), pl. 86 (a), is surely more correct in identifying these two rulers as I have in the heading above. That the caption over the left-hand one indicates a John Palaeologus fits either case. But over the right-hand one may clearly be seen the letters Ιω, obviously indicating another John. And, if one compares this right-hand face with the portrait of John VIII in the preceding family group, noting also the plainly hooked nose common to other representations of this Emperor, there should be little doubt that Lampros was correct. In any case, the portrait here of John V and that in the preceding group are the only surviving likenesses of this ruler I have yet encountered. It might be mentioned that the crude additions to the sketch, which can be seen in our reproduction and which are clearly not by the original artist, appear in the reproductions of Schlumberger and of an earlier Lampros publication (Νέος ἑλληνομνήμων, 4 [1907], pl. Ζ'; but not in the Λεύκωμα), though they do not appear in other reproductions.

3. (Figure 5) *Manuel, with His Wife and Three Oldest Sons* (Musée du Louvre, Paris, *Ivoires A 53*, f. 1). By all means one of the greatest examples of Byzantine Imperial portraiture, as well as perhaps the best-known likeness of Manuel, this superb miniature serves as a frontispiece to the celebrated manuscript of the works of the (Pseudo-)Dionysius the Areopagite which Manuel Chrysoloras brought as his Emperor's gift to the Royal Abbey of Saint-Denys in 1408 (see above, pp. 263–264). It is reproduced very frequently, most notably in somewhat exaggerated color in Lampros' Λεύκωμα, pl. 84. The miniature shows the Virgin, with the Christ Child, conventionally identified with their initials,

blessing the Emperor and Empress. Manuel's caption is an enlarged version of the usual Imperial formula: "Manuel, in Christ Our God Faithful Basileus and Autokrator of the Romans, Palaeologus, and Ever Augustus." His wife's caption corresponds accordingly: "Helena, in Christ Our God Faithful Augusta and Autokratorisa of the Romans, Palaeologina." With them are their first three sons (the painting having been made either before or regardless of the births of the three other sons, Constantine, Demetrius, and Thomas: see Appendix XV above). The eldest, the future John VIII, is shown in miniature Imperial costume duplicating his father's, with the caption, "John, in Christ Our God Faithful Basileus, His Son." The second is identified as "Theodore Porphyrogenitus, [by God's Fortune?] Despot, His Son," and the third as "Andronicus, the Prince [αὐθεντόπουλος] Palaeologus, His Son."

4. (Frontispiece) *Manuel as Emperor* (Bibliothèque Nationale, Paris, *Cod. suppl. gr. 309*, f. VI). This superb portrait of Manuel alone is the sole illustration in a fifteenth-century manuscript of his *Funeral Oration for His Brother Theodore* and is also well known. The caption is the usual formula: ΜΑΝΟ[Υ]ΗΛ ΕΝ Χ[ΡΙϹΤ]Ω ΤΩ Θ[Ε]Ω ΠΙϹΤΟϹ ΒΑϹΙΛΕΥϹ ΚΑΙ ΑΥΤΟΚΡΑΤΩΡ ΡΩΜΑΙΩΝ Ο ΠΑΛΑΙΟΛΟΓΟ[Ϲ]. As in the foregoing family portrait, Manuel is represented in the full Byzantine Imperial regalia of the late period. Over (or embroidered onto) his purple gown he wears the gem-studded *loros,* by now highly stylized, the end of which is draped over his left arm. In his left hand he holds the traditional *mappa,* the red napkin or cloth used to signal the beginning of races and games in the Hippodrome; in his right hand is the sceptre surmounted by a cross, apparently tipped with pearls in at least the family portrait if not here. But this miniature adds a few details not evident in the family portrait: the Emperor's crown has jeweled pendants; and, with his feet in the traditional red (or purple) buskins, he stands on a red pillow embroidered with golden eagles. It is questionable if the Byzantine treasury, in its impoverished state in Manuel's day, really could have afforded to outfit Manuel in a genuine equivalent of this full regalia. Whatever the actual fact, however, at least on the basis of surviving art, Manuel was the last Byzantine Emperor to be depicted in the full Imperial garb in a formal portrait. (For a further discussion of this portrait of Manuel, and especially of

iconographic details, see Heisenberg, *Aus der Geschichte und Literatur der Palaiologenzeit,* pp. 26 ff.)

To the foregoing list of portraits two more should perhaps be added. The first is a small sketch supposedly showing Manuel, drawn by a Cretan artist of the late sixteenth century in a manuscript now in the Biblioteca Marciana in Venice, *Cod. Cl. VII, 22,* f. 78. This crude little sketch is so obviously stereotyped and fanciful that it can hardly be regarded as a real portrait of the Emperor's actual appearance. Those interested may find it reproduced in Lampros, Λεύκωμα, pl. 86 (b). The second portrait is, or rather was, in a fresco in the Church of the Saints Theodore in Mistra. It shows the Emperor kneeling in supplication before the Madonna and Child; unfortunately, however, the face is completely destroyed and the Emperor can be identified only from the inscription over his figure. A sketch of this damaged portrait is in G. Millet's *Monuments de Mistra* (Paris, 1910), pl. 91 (3); cf. A. Grabar, *L'Empereur dans l'art byzantin* (Paris, 1936), p. 101, n. 3.

II. Presumed Portraits
(Artistic Reflections of Manuel's Journey to the West)

1, a. (Figures 13 & 14) *Gold Medallion of Constantine the Great* [*Manuel?*] (Bibliothèque Nationale, Paris, Cabinet des Médailles).

1, b. (Figures 15 & 16) *Gold Medallion of Heraclius* [*Manuel?*] (Bibliothèque Nationale, Paris, Cabinet des Médailles).

The obverse of the first of these medallions purports to represent Constantine the Great proudly mounted on horseback. The obverse of the second bears a portrait supposedly of the Emperor Heraclius (610–641), while the reverse bears a representation of that Emperor's triumphant entry into Constantinople with the recovered True Cross after his victory over the Persians. Several specimens of these celebrated pieces—which seem to have existed in both gold and silver—survive: those shown here are the gold medallions which belonged to the Duc de Berry, who bought the Constantine piece in 1402 and owned the other by the time of his death in 1416, according to the descriptions of them in the inventory of his possessions. They have been studied and reproduced many times, most notably by J. Guiffrey, "Médailles de Constantin et d'Héraclius acquises par Jean, Duc de Berry en 1402," *Revue numismatique,* III, 8 (1890), 87–116, and plates IV–V. The most recent summary of the various debates and theories about them may be found in pp. 129–132 of R. Weiss' article, "The Medieval Medallions of Constantine and Heraclius," *Numismatic Chronicle,* VII, 3 (1963), 129–144 (with plates XI–XV); see also Marinesco, "Deux Empereurs byzantins en Occident," *Compts-rendus de l'Académie des Inscriptions et Belles-Lettres,* 1957, 24–26. Space forbids a full transcription of the respective inscriptions, which involve some difficulties of reading and of meaning or symbolism, especially in the case of the Heraclius medallion: see Guiffrey, 103–106; also G. F. Hill, "Notes on the Mediaeval Medals of Constantine and Heraclius," *Numismatic Chronicle,* IV, 10 (1910), 110–116; and Weiss, 138–140 (attempting to relate some of them to Byzantine formulae of Manuel's epoch). Disputes as to origin aside, our concern with these two pieces here is the result of provocative associations first suggested by Marinesco, *ibid.,* 26–27. He calls attention to the general period in which they must have been struck, about the turn of the fifteenth century; and he notes also certain similarities in them to the designs of the seals on Byzantine Imperial bulls, such as the one which Manuel sent out while he was residing in Paris at precisely the time these medallions were created. Thus, he suggests, "in drawing inspiration from the bulls, perhaps, an artist, unknown at the moment, had been able to produce, precisely during the residence of the Greek sovereign in Paris, the two 'gems' [*joyaux,* in the terminology of the Duc de Berry's inventory], the one representing Constantine, the founder of the Byzantine Empire, and the other Heraclius, the Emperor who recovered the Cross from Chosroës." Since the portrait of Heraclius in particular bears such a resemblance to the Byzantine portrayals of Manuel, at least this superb medal may well have been made by "an artist, very probably Flemish," who "had been able to see the Emperor." More recently, and apparently independently—since he seems unaware of Marinesco's article, or at least does not take note of it—Weiss has argued to much the same point. While acknowledging in his turn the possibilities of Manuel having been personally the model for these imperial images, Weiss, *ibid.,* 140–141, concentrates his attention on the parallelism of some of the medallion inscriptions to the Byzantine Imperial style in Manuel's time. He concludes that "the execution of both the medallions is actually connected with this very visit" by Manuel to Paris. Going even further, Weiss observes: "One can accordingly suggest that the person responsible for the inscriptions was actually one of the Byzantine officials who were in Paris together with the emperor Manuel II Palaeologus from 1400 to 1402." Whatever debatable points are involved here, there is good likelihood that these views, especially those of Marinesco, are correct. If so, these medallions, especially the Heraclius one, furnish us with an additional and particularly valuable idea of Manuel's general appearance. (Note that the Heraclius portrait, if it really does show Manuel, would be our only profile view of him; and that the picture of the Emperor on its reverse shows him with what seems to be a forked beard, which is attributed to Manuel in authentic portraits of him only in the two dynastic groups discussed in A, I, 1 [Figure 29] and A, I, 2 [Figure 32] above.)

2, a. (Figure 30) *The Meeting of the Magi* [*The Reception of Manuel by Charles VI at Charenton?*] (*Les Très Riches Heures du Duc de Berry*, Musée Condé, Chantilly, f. 51ᵛ).

2, b. (Figure 31) *The Adoration of the Magi* [*Including Manuel and Charles VI ?*] (*ibid.* f. 52ʳ).

These two splendid miniatures are from the earlier section of the great Book of Hours executed for the Duc de Berry by Pol de Limbourg and his brothers, the completion of which was interrupted by the Duc's death on June 15, 1416. They have been published previously by P. Durrieu, *Les Très Riches Heures de Jean de France, Duc de Berry* (Paris, 1904), pls. XXXVII and XXXVIII, with commentary respectively on pp. 205–206 and 207–208. The interesting bases of their inspiration have long been at least partially perceived. Durrieu, 97–99, took note of the undoubted Eastern and Byzantine influences on the details of these paintings as a result of such contacts as Manuel's visit; and he had pointed out further, pp. 39–40, the clear and literal use of the mounted figure of the Constantine medallion discussed above as the model for the King to the left in the miniature of the Meeting.

It was Marinesco, however, again the pioneer in this area, who suggested ("Deux Empereurs byzantins en Occident," 28–29; and in "Deux Empereurs byzantins, Manuel II et Jean VIII Paléologue, vus des artistes occidentaux," *Le Flambeau*, 40 [Nov.–Dec., 1957], pp. 759–761) that the rest of the scene is but an adaptation of the meeting between Charles VI and Manuel at Charenton on June 3, 1400 (see above, pp. 172–174). The lowest figure could well be the Emperor Manuel himself. Given the most obviously oriental aspect of the three Kings, and with features quite like Manuel's as we know them, this figure is dressed in a mauve or bluish-purple gown with a broad and ornamented white sash or corset (Manuel wore a white silk gown at the actual meeting: see above, p. 397); and on his head is a crown or hat which, with little stretch of the imagination, could be in the style of the celebrated one (or ones) worn by Manuel's son, John VIII, to the Council of Florence in 1438. More important, this figure is the only one to ride a white horse—the mounting of which was a great honor accorded Manuel on his arrival, even though it had been denied to the Emperor Charles IV of Luxemburg some years before (*Religieux de Saint-Denys*, XXI, i, ed. Bellaguet, II, p. 756). And the young-looking King at the upper right, suggests Marinesco, could be Charles VI himself, as he approached Manuel for their meeting. Marinesco stresses that the painters of this miniature were known to have been apprentices in Paris about the time of Manuel's arrival, or at least of his residence there. And this prototype would then make more meaningful the inclusion of such distinct Parisian landmarks in the background as Sainte-Chapelle, Notre Dame, the Abbey of Montmartre, and the fortress of Monthléry.

The second of the two miniatures carries over the figures of the previous one into the Adoration scene. The "Manuel" King again is the leading figure: looking even more like Manuel here, he is kissing the Child's feet. The "Constantine" King is to the right, prostrate in worship. Behind him the "Charles VI" King holds out his offering. All of the Kings are bareheaded, their crowns being held by their attendants, "Manuel's" the foremost. The background this time includes details from the city of Bourges, forming, as Durrieu suggests, a symbolic foil to the Parisian background of the other miniature on the opposite page and thereby juxtaposing the two cities associated with the Duc de Berry.

3, a. (Figure 7) *The Reception of Emperor Charles IV [Manuel ?] on the Road to Saint-Denys by Officials of Paris (Grandes*

Chroniques de France, Bibliothèque Nationale, Paris, *Ms. fr. 6465,* f. 444ᵛ);

3, b. (Figure 8) *The Meeting of Emperor Charles IV [Manuel P] by King Charles V before the Walls of Paris (ibid.,* f. 446ʳ);

3, c. (Figure 9) *The Arrival of Emperor Charles IV [Manuel P] at Saint-Denys (ibid.,* f. 444ʳ).

The third category of artistic reflections of Manuel's visit to France to which Marinesco has called attention is the group of representations purportedly of a visit made to France by Emperor Charles IV of Luxemburg in 1377, during the reign of King Charles V. The three miniatures reproduced here are from a sequence of eight bearing on this visit (in six of which the Emperor himself appears) in a manuscript of a chronicle of French Kings. These illuminations are ascribed without dispute to the great Jean (or Jehan) Foucquet (ca. 1415–ca. 1480), and all eight of them have been published by H. O[mont], *Grandes Chroniques de France enluminées par Jean Foucquet* (Paris, 1906), pls. 42–49 (those reproduced here being 45, 48, and 44, respectively); cf. also Durrieu, *Les Antiquités judaïques et le peintre Jean Foucquet* (Paris, 1908), pp. 97–98, and pl. XXIa (The Arrival at Saint-Denys). In all of these miniatures the Emperor Charles is accompanied by his son, the King of the Romans (Wenceslas), who either rides beside or behind his father, or, in the case of the Arrival at Saint-Denys, rides behind the horse-borne litter in which his father is conveyed.

Ignoring the inclusion of Wenceslas, however, Marinesco ("Deux Empereurs byzantins en Occident," 28–30) insists that the representation of Charles IV in these splendid miniatures by Foucquet, or at least in the one of the Arrival at Saint-Denys, "has nothing to do with the German Emperor." Marinesco suggests rather that these miniatures actually are, to one degree or another, portraits of Manuel II during the celebrated 1400–1402 visit. He concedes that this visit occurred years before Foucquet's birth. But, following the conclusions of Klaus Perls, Marinesco points out that Foucquet could very well have possessed sketches and models based on Manuel's appearance transmitted indirectly from the artist Jacques Coene, who was in the service of the Marshal Boucicaut.

Foucquet demonstrably had other links with prototypes of Manuel. Durrieu has wisely drawn attention (*Les Antiquités,* pp.

112–113 and pl. XXIII) to the incontestable influence of the reverse of the Heraclius medallion discussed above—for which Manuel was presumably the model—which shows the Emperor's triumphal restoration of the True Cross; this influence can be traced, through another Book of Hours of the Duc de Berry, to a representation of King "Salmanazar" in Foucquet's miniatures for the manuscript of *Joseph* (Bibl. Nat. *Ms. fr. 247*, f. 174). Moreover, one may compare Foucquet's miniatures in this Charles IV set to the corresponding sequence, often quite similar in themes, but vastly different in style and quality, in a similar French chronicle of the fourteenth century, quite close to King Charles V's reign: Bibl. Nat. *Ms. fr. 2813*, ff. 467–479, published by R. Delachenal, *Les Grandes Chroniques de France: Chronique des règnes de Jean II et de Charles IV*, Vol. IV (Paris, 1920), pp. 30–39, pls. 31–48. Such a comparison not only demonstrates Foucquet's vast artistic superiority and the great maturing of style over the crude and stereotyped paintings of a century before, but also shows the distinct differences between the appearances of the Emperor Charles IV in the respective portrayals. Foucquet's representations of the Emperor really look as if they could be of Manuel himself.

There are other features to be seen in the three specific miniatures reproduced here to add further credibility to Marinesco's hypothesis. We know that Manuel made at least one documented visit to Saint-Denys (and certainly many others), that this particular visit was very widely marked (see above, p. 181), and that Manuel cherished a certain affection for the Abbey (see above, pp. 263–264). Thus, there could have been some association of Manuel with the place in the popular and artistic recollection even in Foucquet's time. Note also that in the Reception by the Officials of Paris (a), the Emperor is mounted on a white horse (as is his son), as Manuel was in 1400. In accordance with the facts of Charles IV's visit (rather than of Manuel's), the Emperor's mount is no longer white for the actual Meeting by the King (b). But then, an artist as alert as Foucquet could be expected to observe details carefully. On the other hand, is it possible that the figure representing the King of the Romans in the Reception (a) might actually be an adaptation of the figure of King Charles VI, and that this Reception miniature might preserve some suggestions of the meeting of Manuel at Charenton?

III. Mementos

1. (Figures 11 & 12) *Seal on One of Manuel's Chrysobulls* (Cathedral of Palma, Majorca). This fine seal is one of several of Manuel's still extant. It is affixed to the bull of June 20, 1402, to the Anti-Pope Benedict XIII (see above, p. 198 and n. 133). The entire document, together with photographs of this seal, have been published by Marinesco, "Du Nouveau sur les rélations de Manuel II Paléologue avec l'Espagne," pp. 427–430 and figs. 3–4. As to the present location of this document, Marinesco remarks (p. 427): "We know neither at what time or in what manner the chrysobull, and the relics which accompanied it, reached the Cathedral of Palma on Majorca." The seal's artistic style is unusually fine for this period. On the obverse the Emperor is shown in stylized vestments, sceptre in his right hand and *mappa* in his left. The inscription is an abbreviation of the usual Imperial formula: Μανουὴλ ἐν Χ[ριστ]ῷ Αὐτοκράτωρ ὁ Παλαιολόγος. The reverse shows a full figure of Christ, His head flanked by the standard abbreviation of His name, $\overline{\text{IC}}$ $\overline{\text{XC}}$ ('Ι[ησοῦ]ς Χ[ριστό]ς). On the left is a strange symbol which, according to Marinesco (p. 430), is transcribed by V. Laurent as a superimposition of the initials Γ over Φ, with a rough breathing added, all interpreted as representing the name Γ[εώργιος] ὁ Φ[...?], presumably one of Manuel's secretaries or seal-keepers. This same symbol may be seen on the reverse of another (but slightly different) seal of the same period, also reproduced by Marinesco (his fig. 2).

2. (Figure 26) *Four Examples of Manuel's Coinage* (Dumbarton Oaks Collections, Washington, D.C.).

a. Bronze (W. Wroth, *Catalogue of the Imperial Byzantine Coins in the British Museum*, Vol. II, London [1908], p. 368, no. 14; H. Goodacre, *A Handbook of the Coinage of the Byzantine Empire*, London, 1957, p. 348, no. 6 [in silver]). *Obverse:* Manuel, nimbate, holding a sceptre in his right hand, on horseback, riding to the right beside a mounted and nimbate Saint, who holds a *labarum* or standard in his right hand. *Reverse:* the Palaeologan monogram ΠΑ surrounded by the inscription in the border, † ΜΑΝΟΥΗΛ ΔΕCΠΟΤΗC. In view of the use of the title "Despot," one might be inclined to identify the Saint as Demetrius and ascribe this coin to Manuel's early days as Despot of Thessalonica. But the use of Δεσπότης as a title on coins instead of the normal Βασιλεύς is common in this period and probably should not be taken to invite such an interpretation. Grabar, *L'Empereur dans l'art byzantin*, pp. 53–54 and n. 6, suggests that the Saint is Constantine the Great.

b. Bronze (Wroth, p. 638, no. 16; Goodacre, p. 348, no. 8 [in silver]). *Obverse:* Manuel in Imperial garb, holding a cross-topped sceptre in his right hand (?) (and a *mappa* in his left?), flanked by the monogram letters MA and N[OY]. *Reverse:* Christ, in nimbus within oval compartment, with His right hand raised in benediction.

c. Silver (Wroth, p. 637, no. 8; Goodacre, p. 348, no. 3). *Obverse:* bust of Manuel, crowned within nimbus, with scalloped "tippet" or neckpiece, surrounded by border inscription ΜΑΝΟΥΗΛ ΒΑCΙΛΕΥC Ο ΠΑΛΕΟΛΟΓΟC. *Reverse:* bust of Christ within cross nimbus, flanked by the standard initials I̅C̅ X̅C̅, surrounded by a dotted border.

d. Silver (Wroth, p. 638, no. 15 [in bronze]; Goodacre, [?] p. 348, no. 4). *Obverse:* bust of Manuel, crowned, and with nimbus, in a scalloped tippet (and holding a cross-tipped sceptre in his right hand?), surrounded by a border inscription which seems to read ✝ ΜΑΝΟΥΗΛ Ο ΠΑΛΕΟΛΟΓΟC ΒΑCΙ-Λ[ΕΥC]; to the left are what appears to be the letters ΔΜ. *Reverse:* a Saint on horseback, nimbate, riding to the right, with a sword in his right hand. Though the obverse pattern differs in details and inscription, the reverse design of this type is extremely similar to that of the single coin type which Goodacre (p. 350, no. 1) assigns to John VII, apparently with good reason. This similarity of patterns is both significant and understandable, especially if the letters on the obverse here, transcribed as ΔΜ, do indeed indicate that the Saint is Demetrius of Thessalonica, as the reverse of the John VII type clearly indicates with the same initials.

These specimens may give some idea of the general crudeness and ugliness of the Byzantine coins of this age. In addition to those illustrated here, there are two other types of Manuel's coinage which deserve mention. One is the only known type of gold coinage from his reign (Wroth, p. 635, no. 1; Goodacre, p. 347, no. 1), showing Manuel in full Imperial vestments, with his *loros* draped over his left arm and with an orb in his left hand, on the obverse; on the reverse is a stylized view of the walls of Constantinople, with six sets of towers, surrounding the city's Protectress, the Virgin Mary. The other is a bronze (Wroth, p. 639; Goodacre, p. 349, no. 10) which is interpreted as showing Manuel, in bust, on the obverse, and John VII with Manuel's Empress Helena, both crowned and nimbate, with a Cross between them (see above, pp. 238–239, n. 70). But be it noted that there is some likelihood that the figure with Helena actually represents their son, John VIII: cf. Grabar, *L'Empereur,* 56–57.

3. (Figure 18) *Manuel's Formal Signature: The Byzantine Treaty with Venice of May 22, 1406* (Archivio di Stato, Venezia, *Miscellanea, atti, diplomi e privilegi,* 928). Manuel's large and handsome signature on the final treaty (see above, pp. 260–261) is simply a writing out of the full Imperial formula: † Μανουὴλ ἐν Χ[ριστ]ῷ τῷ θ[ε]ῷ πιστὸς βασιλεὺς καὶ αὐτοκράτωρ 'Ρωμαίων ὁ Παλαιολόγος †A reproduction of this signature was also published by Dölger, *Facsimiles byzantinischer Kaiserurkunden* (Munich, 1931), no. 14, p. VII, with commentary, pp. 19–21.

4. (Figure 34) *Manuel's Proofreading: Two Pages of the Dialogue* Περὶ γάμου *Corrected and Then Crossed Out by His Own Hand* (Bibliothèque Nationale, Paris, *Cod. gr. 3041,* ff. 102ᵛ and 103ʳ). These two folios, open as one would see them in the manuscript, show the extensive insertions and emendations which Manuel first lavished on this particular text in the manuscript of his works. But then, dissatisfied with these changes, he struck out whole sections with rough strokes and at last ruthlessly crossed out the entire work in the codex by drawing at least one vertical line through each page (see above, pp. 426 ff.) The left-hand page (f. 102ᵛ), incidentally, includes (from the middle to the bottom of the page) the passage from this work which Loenertz published in the *Rev. d. ét. byz.,* 15 (1957), pp. 183–184, and which is translated above, p. 111.

B. People Associated with Manuel

1. (Figure 2) *John Cantacuzenus, Portrayed as the Emperor John VI and as the Monk Ioasaph* (Bibliothèque Nationale, Paris,

Cod. gr. 1242, f. 123). This celebrated miniature appears at the end of a manuscript of polemical writings of Cantacuzenus/ Ioasaph, a manuscript apparently in the hand of the Imperial monk himself, dating from the early 1370's, that is, about a decade before his death (1383). At the top is a stylized group of three angels, symbolizing the Trinity. At the left John appears in the full Imperial regalia: crown, cross-topped sceptre, *loros, mappa,* and bejeweled gown; and he stands on the pillow embroidered with golden double-headed eagles. The inscription on both sides of his head is the usual Imperial formula cited frequently here already, adding the Emperor's family names, pretentiously augmented as "Palaeologus, Angelus, Cantacuzenus." At the right, the former Emperor stands in his monastic garb as the monk Ioasaph. His right hand is raised in benediction, and in his left hand, as a symbolic substitute as well as a compositional parallel of the *mappa,* perhaps, is a partly unrolled scroll bearing the inscription Μέγας [ἐστιν] ὁ Θ[εὸ]ς τῶν Χριστιανῶν. A color reproduction of this miniature may be found in Lampros, Λεύκωμα, pl. 81.

2, a. (Figure 6) *Jean II le Meingre, Maréchal de Boucicaut, with His Wife, Antoinette de Turenne, Venerating the Madonna and Child (Heures du Maréchal de Boucicaut,* Musée Jacquemart-André, Paris, Dedication Page, f. 26ᵛ).

2, b. (Figure 17) *Jean II le Meingre, Maréchal de Boucicaut, Alone, Venerating St. Catherine (ibid.,* f. 38ᵛ).

In addition to his active life as a soldier, captive of Nicopolis, comrade in arms of Manuel II, energetic Governor of Genoa, Governor (after 1410) of Guyenne and Languedoc, and finally captive at Agincourt, the Marshal Boucicaut also had the good taste to commission the splendid Book of Hours which bears his name from an artist who in turn is known only as the anonymous painter of this manuscript. From it come these two portraits, one of them with his lovely wife. They have both been published previously by E. Panovsky, *Early Netherlandish Painting* (Cambridge, Mass., 1953), pl. 30, figs. 64 and 65. On this manuscript see also Panovsky's text, pp. 54–56, including the following description of it, which merits quotation:

... It seems ... that its execution extended over a number of years, which would not be surprising in view of the hectic life of the noble couple who had little time and presumably small inclination to press

the busy painter for delivery.... The inference is that the manuscript
was ordered and commenced about or shortly before 1400 (the com-
paratively quiet interval between the Marshal's glorious return from
Constantinople in 1399 and his departure for Genoa in 1401 being a
very plausible moment); that the work was continued, without too
much energy, during his absence; and that it was completed after his
final homecoming in 1409, say in 1410 or 1411.

External corroboration of this assumption may be found in a comparison of the dedication page (fol. 26ᵛ) with the St. Catherine page
(fol. 38ᵛ). Both miniatures ... contain a portrait of the Marshal. But
in the dedication page he appears as a man in his early thirties whereas
in the St. Catherine page he looks a good ten years older. And the
earlier likeness conforms to an ideal of youthful knighthood ... whereas
the later one is a notable example of individual characterization. Where
he pays homage to the Madonna, he is portrayed as a commander armed
and spurred; where he kneels before St. Catherine, he wears the long,
brocaded, fur-lined mantle, and the chain and pendant befitting the
Governor of Guyenne and Languedoc. The dedication page, a natural
point of departure for the illuminator, represents an initial invocation;
the St. Catherine page may be interpreted as the thanksgiving of the
warrior returned. These two leaves, then, may be taken to represent the
beginning and the end of an evolution within the "Boucicaut Hours"....

3. (Figure 19) *Manuel Chrysoloras* (Musée du Louvre, Paris,
Département des Dessins, no. 9849). This pen drawing is one of
two in the Louvre by the same anonymous early fifteenth-century
artist. (The other is of the contemporary King of Naples, Louis
II of Anjou.) The inscription identifies the person portrayed here
as "Maestro Manuello che insegno gramatica greca in Firençe,
1406" ("Master Manuel, who taught Greek grammar in Florence,
1406"). This sketch was published by H. Omont, "Note sur un
portrait de Manuel Chrysoloras conservé au Musée du Louvre,"
Revue des études grecques, 4 (1891), 176–177, who believes that
this is the only reliable portrait of the great Byzantine scholar
among all the supposed portraits which survive to us. Omont suggests that the portrait shows him in the role of a teacher, which
the inscription would seem to bear out; therefore he suggests that
the date of 1406 may only indicate the date when the drawing
was executed, and not the period of Chrysoloras' important teaching work in Florence, which fell in 1396–1400. But the inscription
may indeed refer to the actual presence of Chrysoloras in Florence in 1406. Between his return home with Manuel II in the

spring of 1403 and the final journeys of 1407–15, Chrysoloras seems to have made two other brief trips to Italy, in 1404 and 1405–06, about which we know very little: see above, p. 263 and n. 109. In all likelihood, this sketch was made, perhaps from life, during some visit which Chrysoloras may have made in 1406 to the scene of his former triumphs. The gown and book are drawn in such a crude style and are so inconsequential in relation to the head, which is obviously the focus of attention, that these trappings of pedagogy could well represent incidental interpolations of background with no immediate relevance to the year 1406.

4. (Figure 20) *Autograph Inscription by Manuel Chrysoloras in the Manuscript of the Works of Dionysius the Areopagite Brought as Manuel II's Gift to the Royal Abbey of Saint-Denys* (Musée du Louvre, Paris, *Ivoires* A 53, f. 237ᵛ). Here, in Chrysoloras' own handwriting, is the dedicatory inscription which he added at the end of the manuscript when he presented it to the Abbey. For this gift, and for a translation of the inscription, see above, p. 264. The text of this dedication reads thus:

Τὸ παρὸν βιβλίον ἀπεστάλη παρὰ τοῦ ὑψηλοτάτου βασιλέως καὶ/αὐτοκράτορος Ῥωμαίων κυροῦ Μανουὴλ τοῦ Παλαιολόγου εἰς τὸ μο/ναστήριον τοῦ ἁγίου Διονυσίου τοῦ ἐν Παρυσίῳ τῆς Φραγγίας ἢ Γαλατίας/ἀπὸ τῆς Κωνσταντινουπόλεως δι' ἐμοῦ Μανουὴλ τοῦ Χρυσολωρᾶ πεμ/φθέντος πρέσβεως παρὰ τοῦ εἰρημένου βασιλέως, ἔτει ἀπὸ κτίσεως/κόσμου, ἑξακισχιλιοστῷ ἐννεακοσιοστῷ ἑξκαιδεκάτῳ· ἀπὸ σαρκώσεως/δὲ τοῦ Κυρίου χιλιοστῷ τετρακοσιοστῷ ὀγδόῳ·/ὅστις εἰρημένος βασιλεὺς ἦλθε πρότερον εἰς τὸ Παρύσιον πρὸ ἐτῶν τεσσάρων.

C. Places Associated with Manuel

1. (Figure 33) *Constantinople, the Tower of Anemas.* These two towers project out from the Land Walls of Constantinople in the area of the Palace of Blachernae. The tower on the left has been identified as the Tower of Isaac Angelus, and that on the right, together with the network of chambers or cells within the main part of the wall which runs behind and to the left of the tower, has been identified with the Prison, or "Tower," of Anemas. This identification still leaves some inconsistencies with Byzantine descriptions of the dreaded prison, but it should be remembered that such inconsistencies could well be the result of later

Turkish alterations. For more on this structure, see Appendix III above.

2, a. (Figure 3) *A View of the Land Walls of Thessalonica, from the Outside.*

2, b. (Figure 1) *The Citadel of the Thessalonian Fortifications, from the East.*

These two views may give some suggestion of the ramparts behind which Manuel directed the defenses of Thessalonica, especially in the trying siege of 1383–87. The sea walls have all but disappeared, but the land walls still survive extensively. Particularly interesting is the Citadel, or Heptapyrgion ("Seven Towers," or "Yedi Koulé" in Turkish, a parallel to the fortress of the same names in Constantinople by the Golden Gate), the apex of the land fortifications, at the point where the eastern and western walls converge. On the fortifications of the city in general, see Tafrali, *Topographie de Thessalonique* (Paris, 1913), pp. 30 ff.; cf. p. 47 for a reference to a tower in the walls which seems to bear an inscription of Manuel himself; but cf. p. 45 for an identification of it to the earlier Manuel the Despot of Epirus.

3. (Figure 4) *Constantinople: The Golden Gate, from the Southwest* (1949). This is the present aspect of the great triumphal entry portal in the old Theodosian Walls, scene of many proud and dramatic moments in Byzantine history, now superstitiously bricked up and incorporated in the Turkish fortress of Yedi Koulé. In this view, the palisade of the moat may be seen in the foreground, and behind it the remains of the Propylaeum in the Outer Wall. Beyond is the Main Gate itself, a triple portal flanked by the two massive bastions that project from the Inner Wall. The bastions were fortresses themselves, but there were additional fortifications behind them, an earlier Byzantine Heptapyrgion ("Seven Towers"), which was the antecedent of the present Yedi Koulé ("Seven Towers"). It was in this additional Byzantine fortress that Manuel and his father, John V, were twice besieged in the dynastic civil wars, in 1376 and 1390. And it was this same fortress which John V was callously ordered to destroy by the arrogant Bayazid: see Appendix VI. The later Turkish fortress, a tower of which can be seen in the background to the left in the photograph, was apparently a reconstruction and extension of the earlier Byzantine structure.

4. (Figure 10) *The Royal Abbey of Saint-Denys, Paris, West Façade.* The magnificent and beautiful Abbey of Saint-Denys, or Saint Denis, dedicated to the national Saint of France and located in the Parisian suburb of the same name, was long the center of royal favor and artistic splendor before Manuel saw it in the early years of the fifteenth century. Its real origins may be credited to the powerful and enlightened Abbot Suger, whose grandiose building plans in the twelfth century were extended and climaxed in the thirteenth. Its construction thus extended from the crucial beginnings of Gothic architecture through the heyday of the style, making it one of the most important monuments of Gothic art. Unfortunately, it has undergone some transformation since Manuel visited it. The interior is now filled with the elaborate tombs of subsequent French Kings. The West Façade in particular has been heavily altered. The sequence of damage by lightning and misguided "restorations" in the nineteenth century brought about the loss of the North Tower. But some other disfigurements of the last century have been rectified, and the present condition of the building can still give us a good idea of what Manuel saw during his visit. On the building's history, see S. McK. Crosby, *L'abbaye royale de Saint-Denis* (Paris, 1953), especially pp. 66–72, observing also this book's splendid assemblage of illustrations. Also of particular importance is E. Panofsky's *Abbot Suger on the Abbey Church of St.-Denis and Its Art Treasures* (Princeton, 1946).

5, a. (Figure 21) *Mistra, the Palace of the Despots: General View from Above* (1961).

5, b. (Figure 22) *Mistra, the Palace of the Despots: The Façade and the Forecourt* (1961).

5, c. (Figure 23) *Mistra, the Palace of the Despots: The East Wall of the Throne Room* (1961).

These three photographs illustrate the residence of the Despots of the Morea in their remarkable hillside capital of Mistra. The main portion of the Palace (in the center of Figure 21 and in the background of Figure 22) is the original part. The other sections (to the right in Figures 21 and 22) were added later in the fourteenth and fifteenth centuries. In the courtyard before the Palace (the center foreground of Figure 22) the then Despot Constantine was acclaimed as the last Byzantine Emperor, the Eleventh of the Imperial founder's name, upon receiving the news of his brother John VIII's death at the end of 1448. Figure 23 shows part of the eastern wall of the large audience hall or throne room, visible in the main portion of the Palace in Figure 21. In this wall is the large recessed apse that curves out from the wall around it on the outside (as can be seen in the other two views, between the fourth and fifth of the wall's eight windows), which was the location of the throne of the Despots. Every occupant of that throne was a relative of Manuel: here sat his uncles, Manuel and Matthew Cantacuzenus, and the latter's sons, John and Demetrius; here sat Manuel's beloved brother, Theodore I, and Manuel's own sons, Theodore II, Constantine, and Demetrius; and, presumably, here sat Manuel himself, during his visits in 1408 and 1415.

6, a. (Figure 24) *View of Constantinople about 1420, after Buondelmonti* (Biblioteca Apostolica Vaticana, Rome, *Cod. Rossianus 702*, f. 32ᵛ).

6, b. (Figure 25) *View of Constantinople about 1420, after Buondelmonti* (Biblioteca Nazionale di S. Marco, Venice, *Cod. Marciana Lat. X, 123* [= *3784*], f. 22ʳ).

These stylized views are taken from two of the numerous surviving manuscripts of the fifteenth-century traveler Cristoforo Buondelmonti's *Liber insularum*, an enormously popular treatise in the fifteenth century and later. Of the many views of the city in each of the various manuscripts, eight (including the present two) have been brought together by G. Gerola in his study "Le vedute di Constantinopoli di Cristoforo Buondelmonti," *Studi bizantini e neoellenici*, 3 (1931), 249–279, in an attempt to trace their relationships. But a full study of all these views on a larger scale is still needed. They are, of course, untrustworthy for any precise information as to topography and monuments and are subject to wide variations, since they were copied one from another at various times with occasional instances of "updating" as well as inconsistencies that crept into them readily. But the same basic monuments are usually shown in all of them, crudely and not always accurately: Hagia Sophia and the Hippodrome, some of the monumental columns, some of the major churches (Holy Apostles, the Pantokrator, St. John in Petra, the Chora, St. John of Studion, and St. Mary of Blachernae), the so-called

Palaces of Justinian and of Constantine Porphyrogenitos. The Marciana view attempts to show the Land Walls (to the left) as the double walls they were. The Rossianus view makes the Land Walls only a single rampart, but makes some effort to suggest the vegetation that had taken over much desolate territory within the city's confines. In the upper portion of each view Pera is shown across the Golden Horn; and in the upper right-hand corner in virtually all of the views a pair of columns is shown, presumably representing the old harbor of the Diplokionion (see above, p. 352 and n. 99).

7. (Figure 27) *Constantinople Besieged by the Turks (in 1453)* (Bibliothèque Nationale, Paris, *Ms. fr. 9087*, f. 207ᵛ).

This fascinating miniature is one of three in a fifteenth-century manuscript, prepared for Philip the Good, Duke of Burgundy (d. 1467), of the travel account of the mid-fifteenth-century Burgundian traveler, Bertrandon de la Brocquière. It is, of course, involved with an event beyond the period of Manuel's lifetime, referring as it does to the final siege of the city by Mechmed II in 1453, and perhaps reflecting also the keen interest that the Burgundian court displayed toward the fall of the city then and to the entire Eastern Question. Here the various episodes and sights of the last siege are portrayed in quaint fashion: Sultan Mechmed II appears before his tent, at bottom center; the cannons and bombards and assault engines attack the walls while the sappers attempt to mine them; the Turkish fleet is hauled overland from the Bosphorus into the blocked Golden Horn behind Galata, at left; and the upper left, on the Asiatic shore, is seen a representation of the fortress of Anadolu Hisar, built by Bayazid some fifty-five years earlier. Constantinople itself is depicted most amusingly, with the double Land Walls manned by defenders; Blachernae is drawn to look like a French chateau, and Hagia Sophia becomes a Gothic cathedral. Even if the siege of 1453 is beyond the scope of this book on Manuel II, it is interesting to compare this representation of Constantinople with those in the Buondelmonti manuscripts. Moreover, the less fateful but still formidable siege of 1422, at the end of Manuel's life, foreshadowed remarkably the later one in view of Murad II's elaborate siege and assault engines and especially his use of cannons. Thus, some of the aspects of this 1453 view are not at all inappropriate to the 1422 attack.

8. (Figure 28) *Constantinople, the Church of St. Savior Panto-krator, Exterior from the East* (1961).

The old Comnenian triple church where Manuel was buried still stands, battered and neglected, and part of it is used as a mosque. The view here is from the rear of the building, showing the apses of the church's three sections. At least the dome of the North Church, at the upper right, is Turkish. The dome to the left of center in the photograph belongs to the Middle Church, where most of the tombs were placed and where Manuel was presumably laid to rest. But the exact site of his tomb within the church is not known. His bones were probably disturbed and scattered by his old enemies, the Turks, either when they finally entered his city in their triumph of 1453 or, more likely, when the church was "purified" to be converted into a mosque some time later. (Only recently, in 1961, some bones and stone fragments possibly from tombs were discovered, where they had been deposited in Turkish times, in some vaulting under the floor of the South Church, when work was done there by the Byzantine Institute.) The Middle Church has been completely cleared of all tombs and sarcophagi for some time, and, though the location of one unidentified tomb can be traced there presently, there is no way of knowing the actual number or placement of specific tombs within it. But the site must have been quite crowded with them, for it was a popular place of Imperial interment, not only in earlier times (here was buried, for instance, Manuel II's distant predecessor in name as well as time, Manuel I Comnenus), but also in the days of the Palaeologi. Many of Manuel's immediate family lay with him here: first his older brother, Andronicus IV (see Appendix VII); then, subsequently, the first three of his sons, joining him in reverse order of age, Andronicus, Theodore, and John; and, finally, his wife and Empress, Helena, on the very eve of the final disaster. Cf. Van Millingen, *Byzantine Churches in Constantinople,* especially pp. 229–230 (not without a few inaccuracies, however).

ACKNOWLEDGMENTS

All of the illustrations for this book have been selected and gathered by me, but not without much help from many sources. I am greatly indebted to the various libraries, institutions, and agencies, and their directors and staffs, for the respective material that they have made available to me as listed above. Though not mentioned among them, one individual I should like to thank is Sr. Juan Ainaud de Lasarte, Director-General of the Museos de Arte, Barcelona, for his courtesy and efficiency in providing me with the photographs of the seal from the Cathedral of Palma on Majorca. I wish also to thank Miss Ljubica Popović and Dr. Cyril Mango for allowing me the use of some of their personal photographs. In general, I should like to thank Professors André Grabar and Constantin Marinesco for their very valuable advice. Among the many staff members and colleagues at Dumbarton Oaks who have been generous with assistance, facilities, and suggestions, I should like to single out Mr. Wallace Lane, who prepared for me a number of the photographs used here; Mrs. Elizabeth Bland, the Assistant Curator of the Dumbarton Oaks Collection; Professor Paul Underwood, of the Dumbarton Oaks faculty; and Mr. Per Jonas Nordhagen, one of my fellow Fellows.

Bibliography

A. PRIMARY SOURCES

I. Greek Historical Sources

Cantacuzenus, John. *Historiarum libri IV* ('Ιστοριῶν βιβλία Δ), ed. L. Schopen, 3 vols., Bonn, 1828–32.

Chalcocondyles, Laonicus. *Historiarum demonstrationes* ('Αποδείξεις ἱστοριῶν),ed. E. Darkó, 2 vols., Budapest, 1922–27; ed. I. Bekker, Bonn, 1843.

Critobulus, Michael, of Imbros. 'Ιστορίαι, ed. V. Grecu, Bucharest, 1963; ed. C. Müller, in *Fragmenta historicorum graecorum*, V, 1, Paris (1883), pp. 52–164; tr. C. T. Riggs, *History of Mehmed the Conqueror by Kritovoulos*, Princeton, 1954.

Χρονικὸν περὶ τῶν τούρκων σουλτάνων (κατὰ τὸν Βαρβερινὸν Κώδικα 111), ed. G. Th. Zoras, Athens, 1958; cited as *"Chron. Barb. 111."*

Ducas. *Historia byzantina*, ed. V. Grecu, Bucharest, 1958; ed. I. Bekker, Bonn, 1834.

"Εκθεσις χρονική, ed. S. P. Lampros, London, 1902; cited as " "Εκ. χρον."

Kananos, John. Διήγησις περὶ τοῦ ἐν Κωνσταντινουπόλει γεγόντος πολέμου κατὰ τὸ ͵ϛϡλ' ἔτος, ed. I. Bekker, Bonn (1838), pp. 457–479 of the volume containing (the Pseudo-)Phrantzes; Ital. tr. by E. Colonna, pp. 154–164 of "Sulla Διήγησις di Giovanni Cananos," *Università di Napoli, Annali della Facoltà di lettere e filosofia*, 7 (1957), 151–166.

Panaretos, Michael. *Chronicle* (Περὶ τῶν τῆς Τραπεζοῦντος βασιλέων), ed. S. P. Lampros in pp. 266–294 of his "Τὸ τραπεζουντιακὸν χρονικὸν τοῦ πρωτοσεβάστου καὶ πρωτονοταρίου Μιχαὴλ Παναρέτου," Νέος ἑλληνομνήμων, 4 (1907), 257–295.

(Pseudo-)Dorotheos of Monemvasia. Βιβλίον ἱστορικόν, Venice, 1750.

(Pseudo-)Phrantzes. *Chronicon Maius*, ed. J. B. Papadopoulos (Bks. I and II only), Leipzig, 1935; ed. I. Bekker, Bonn, 1838; also, ed. and tr. V. Grecu, as a supplement to his edition of Sphrantzes (Academia Republ. Soc. Română, *Scriptores byzan-*

tini, 5), Bucharest, 1966 [not available as this book was written; therefore not cited]; see also Sphrantzes.

Short Chronicles. Βραχέα χρονικά, ed. S. P. Lampros and K. Amantos, 'Ακαδημία 'Αθηνῶν, Μνημεῖα τῆς ἑλληνικῆς ἱστορίας, Α', Athens, 1932–33, Τεῦχος α'; edition cited as "Βρ. χρ."

———. (Βρ. χρ. No. 27:) ed. I. Bekker, pp. 515–527 of his edition of Ducas, Bonn, 1834.

———. (Βρ. χρ. No. 52:) ed. J Müller, pp. 56–61 of his "Byzantinische Analekten," *Sitzungsberichte der philosophisch- historischen Classe der Kaiserliche Akademie der Wissenschaften, Vienna,* IX (1852), 334–419.

———. " 'Ενθυμήσεων ἤτοι χρονικῶν σημειωμάτων συλλογὴ πρώτη," ed. S. P. Lampros, Νέος ἑλληνομνήμων, 7 (1910), 113–313.

———. "Χρονικὰ σημειώματα περὶ Μανουὴλ καὶ 'Ιωάννου Η' Παλαιολόγου," ed. S. P. Lampros, Παλαιολόγεια καὶ Πελοποννησιακά, III (Athens, 1926), pp. 360–361.

———. "Chronicon breve de Graecorum imperatoribus, ab anno 1341 ad annum 1453 e codice Vaticano graeco 162," ed. R.-J. Loenertz, 'Επετηρὶς 'Εταιρείας Βυζαντινῶν Σπουδῶν, 28 (1958), 204–215; cited as *"Chron. Vat. gr. 162."*

———. "La Chronique brève moréote de 1423" [a collation of the Βρ. χρ. Nos. 19 and 27 with a previously unpublished text], edited, with translation and commentary, by R.-J. Loenertz, in *Mélanges Eugène Tisserant,* II (*Studi e Testi,* 232), Vatican City (1964), pp. 399–439; text, 403–409; cited as *"Chron. br. mor."*

———. *Chronicon breve thessalonicense,* ed. R.-J. Loenertz, pp. 174–175 of Vol. I of his edition of Cydones' correspondence (*Studi e Testi,* 186), Vatican City, 1956; cited as *"Chron. brev. thess."*

———. M. Gedeon, " 'Αναγνώσεις ἐκ τοῦ 'Ωρολογίου τῆς τῶν 'Ακοιμήτων μονῆς," 'Εκκλησιαστικὴ ἀλήθεια, 23 (1903), 380–382.

———. S. Kougeas, "Notizbuch eines Beamten des Anfang des XV. Jahrhunderts," *Byzantinische Zeitschrift,* 23 (1914–19), 143–163; text, 144–154.

———. B. T. Gorianov, "Neizdannyi Anonimyi vizantiskii Khronograf XIV veka," *Vizantiskii vremmenik,* N. S. 2 (1949), 276–293: text, pp. 281–287.

———. G. T. Dennis, "The Short Chronicle of Lesbos, 1355–1428," Λεσβιακά, 5 (1965), 3–24: text, pp. 5–7.

———. "Βραχὺ χρονικὸν τῶν ἐτῶν ἀπὸ κοσμογονίας 6903-6943," ed. N. Veēs, 'Ακρίτας, 1 (1904), 61.

Sphrantzes, Georgios. *Chronicon Minus,* ed. Migne, *Patrologia graeca,* 156, coll. 1025–1080; also ed. V. Grecu, together with Pseudo-Phrantzes (= Makarios Melissenos), Bucharest, 1966 [not available as this book was written; therefore not cited].

Syropoulos, Sylvester. *Historia Concilii Florentini,* The Hague, 1660.

II. *Greek Literary Sources*

A. MANUEL PALAEOLOGUS

Correspondence. Lettres de l'empereur Manuel Paléologue, ed. E. Legrand, Paris, 1893; reprinted, 1962.

———. *Discourse in Letter Form to Cabasilas* (Λόγος ἐπιστολιμαῖος πρὸς τὸν Καβάσιλαν), ed. R.-J. Loenertz, pp. 38–46 of his "Manuel Paléologue, épître à Cabasilas," Μακεδονικά, 4 (1956), 35–46.

———. R.-J. Loenertz, "Epître de Manuel II Paléologue aux moines David et Damien, 1416," *Studi bizantini e neoellenici,* 9 (1957 = *Silloge bizantina in onore di S. G. Mercati*), 294–304: text, pp. 299–304.

———. *Letter to the Sienese,* ed. S. P. Lampros, " Ἐπιστολὴ Μανουὴλ Παλαιολόγου πρὸς τοὺς Σιεναίους," Νέος ἑλληνομνήμων, 6 (1909), 102–104; and in Παλαιολόγεια καὶ Πελοποννησιακά, III (Athens, 1926), pp. 120–121.

Dialogue Which Was Held with a Certain Persian, the Worthy Mouterizes, in Angkyra of Galatia (Διάλογος ὃν ἐποιήσατο μετά τινος Πέρσου, τὴν ἀξίαν Μουτερίζη, ἐν Ἀγκύρᾳ τῆς Γαλατίας), ed. E. Trapp, *Manuel II. Palaiologos, Dialoge mit einem "Perser"* (*Wiener byzantinische Studien,* 2), Vienna, Graz, Cologne, 1966; excerpt, ed. and trans. T. Khoury, *Entretiens avec un musulman, 7e controverse* (*Sources chrétiennes,* 115), Paris, 1966; excerpts, ed. Migne, *Patrologia graeca,* 156, coll. 126–173.

Discourse of Counsel to the Thessalonians When They Were Besieged, ed. B. Laourdas, pp. 295–302 of " Ὁ «Συμβουλευτικὸς πρὸς τοὺς Θεσσαλονίκεις» τοῦ Μανουὴλ Παλαιολόγου," Μακεδονικά, 3 (1955), 290–307.

Funeral Oration for His Brother Theodore (Λόγος ἐπιτάφιος), ed. Migne, *Patrologia graeca,* 156, coll. 181–308; ed. S. P. Lampros, Παλαιολόγεια καὶ Πελοποννησιακά, III (Athens, 1926), pp. 11–119.

Moral Dialogue, or, Concerning Marriage (Διάλογος ἠθικὸς ἢ Περὶ γάμου), excerpt ed. Loenertz, *Revue des études byzantines,* 15 (1957), 183–184.

"*Orationes VII ethico-politicae,*" ed. Migne, *Patrologia graeca,* 156, coll. 385–557.

"*Praecepta educationis regiae*" ('Υποθῆκαι βασιλικῆς ἀγωγῆς), ed. Migne, *Patrologia graeca,* 156, coll. 313–384.

Psalm on the Fall of Bayazid, ed. Migne, *Patrologia graeca,* 156, coll. 281A–C; ed. Legrand, *Lettres de l'empereur Manuel Paléologue* (Paris, 1893), p. 104.

A Representation of Spring in a Woven, Dyed Drapery ("Εαρος εἰκὼν ἐν ὑφαντῷ παραπετάσματι ῥηγικῷ), ed. Migne, *Patrologia graeca,* 156, coll. 577–580.

Timur's Address to Bayazid, ed. Migne, *Patrologia graeca,* 156, coll. 280C–281A; ed. Legrand, *Lettres de l'empereur Manuel Paléologue* (Paris, 1893), pp. 103–104.

B. DEMETRIUS CYDONES

Correspondence (Complete). *Démétrius Cydonès Correspondance,* ed. R.-J. Loenertz, 2 vols. (*Studi e Testi,* 186, 208), Vatican City, 1956–60.

———. (Fifty Letters). *Démétrius Cydonès Correspondance,* ed., with French trans. by G. Cammelli, Paris, 1930.

———. (Six Letters). *Isocratis, Demetrii Cydone, et Michaelis Glycae aliquot epistolae, etc.,* ed. C. F. Matthaei (Moscow, 1776), pp. 33–46.

Oratio de non reddenda Callipoli, ed. Migne, *Patrologia graeca,* 154, coll. 1009–1036.

Oratio pro subsidio Latinorum, ed. Migne, *Patrologia graeca,* 154, coll. 961–1008.

C. MISCELLANEOUS

Anonymous (formerly attrib. to John Chortasmenos). Διήγησις περὶ τοῦ γεγονότος θαύματος παρὰ τῆς ὑπεραγίας Θεοτόκου ἐν ταῖς ἡμέραις τοῦ εὐσεβεστάτου βασιλέως κῦρ Μανουὴλ τοῦ Παλαιολόγου, κ.τ.λ., ed. P. Gautier, "Un Récit inédit du siège de Constantinople par les Turcs (1394–1402)," *Revue des études byzantines,* 23 (1965), 100–117: text, with French translation, 102–117.

Chrysoloras, Demetrius. *Canon to the Virgin,* ed. with commentary by P. Gautier, "Action de grâces de Démétrius Chrysoloras à le Théotocos pour l'anniversaire de la bataille d'Ankara (28 Juillet

1403)," *Revue des études byzantines*, 19 (= Mélanges R. Janin, 1961), 340–357: text, with French translation, 348–357.

Isidore of Kiev. *Panegyric to Manuel and John VIII Palaeologus*, ed. S. P. Lampros, Παλαιολόγεια καὶ Πελοποννησιακά, III (Athens, 1926), pp. 132–199.

Isidore of Monemvasia (and Kiev). *Letters*, ed. W. Regel, *Analecta Byzantino-Russica* (Petrograd, 1891), pp. 59–71.

The Life of St. Athanasius of the Meteora, ed. N. Veēs, "Συμβολὴ εἰς τὴν ἱστορίαν τῶν μονῶν τῶν Μετεώρων," Βυζαντίς, 1 (1909), 237–260.

Philotheos, Patriarch of Constantinople. *Antirrhetici libri XII contra Gregoram*, ed. Migne, *Patrologia graeca*, 151, coll. 733–1138.

Plethon, Georgios Gemistos. *Address to Manuel Palaeologus Concerning the Affairs in the Peloponnesus*, ed. A. Ellissen, *Analekten der mittel- und neugriechischen Litteratur*, IV, Pt. 2 (Leipzig), 1860, pp. 41–59 (German trans., pp. 85–105); ed. S. P. Lampros, Παλαιολόγεια καὶ Πελοποννησιακά, III (Athens, 1926), pp. 246–265.

––––––. *Address of Counsel to the Despot Theodore Concerning the Peloponnesus*, ed. A. Ellissen, *Analekten der mittel- und neugriechischen Litteratur*, IV, Pt. 2 (Leipzig, 1860), pp. 60–84 (German trans., pp. 105–130); ed. S. P. Lampros, Παλαιολόγεια καὶ Πελοποννησιακά, IV (Athens, 1930), pp. 113–135.

"The Satire of Mazaris" (Διάλογος νεκρικός, Ἐπιδημία Μάζαρι ἐν ʽᾼδου), ed. J. F. Boissonade, *Anecdota graeca*, III (Paris, 1831), pp. 112–186; ed. A. Ellissen, *Analekten der mittel- und neugriechischen Litteratur*, IV (Leipzig, 1860), pp. 187–250 (German trans., 251–314).

Social and Political Thought in Byzantium, passages selected and translated by E. Barker, Oxford, 1957.

III. Slavic and Oriental Sources

Anonymous Russian Description of Constantinople, French trans. by S. F. Khitrovo, *Itinéraires russes en Orient* (Geneva, 1899), pp. 225–239.

Ahmad ibn Muhammad, ibn Arabshah. *Timur the Great Amir*, trans. J. H. Sanders, London, 1936.

Bulgarische Chronik von 1296 bis 1413, ed. J. Bogdan, pp. 526–535 of "Ein Beitrag zur bulgarischen und serbischen Geschichtschreibung," *Archiv für slavische Philologie*, XIII, 4 (1891), 471–453 (Latin trans. by V. Jagić, pp. 536–543); cited as *"Bulg. chron."*

Ignatii of Smolensk. *Khoždenie Ignatiia Smolnianina*, ed. S. V. Arseniev, *Pravoslavnyi Palestinskii Sbornik*, 12, IV, 3 (1887); French trans. by S. F. Khitrovo, *Itinéraires russes en Orient*, Geneva, 1889, pp. 129–157; partial Modern Greek trans. by K. Meliaris, " 'Οδοιπορικὸν τοῦ 'Ρώσσου 'Ιγνατίου Σμολιάνιν (1389-1405)," Νέα Σιών, 32 (1937), 24–37, 97–98.

Konstantin the Philosopher. *Život Stefana Lazarevića Despota Srpskoga*, ed. V. Jagić in *Glasnik Srpskog ućenog društva*, 42 (1875), 223–328 (text, pp. 244–328); abridged text ed. with German trans. by M. Braun, *Lebensbeschreibung des Despoten Stefan Lazarevićs*, The Hague, 1956.

Lammens, H. "Correspondances diplomatiques entre les Sultans Mamlouks d'Egypte et les puissances chrétiennes (II)," *Revue de l'orient chrétien*, 9 (1904), 359–372.

Neshri, Mechmet. *Ogledalo sveta ili istorija Mehmeda Nešrije*, Serbian trans. by G. Elezović, *Srpska Akademija Nauka, Zbornik za istoistočnjacku istorisku i gradu književnu, Odeljenje društvenih nauka*, I, 3, Belgrade, 1957.

Sheref ed-Dīn. *Histoire de Timurbec*, trans. Petit de la Croix, 4 vols., Paris, 1722.

IV. Western Historical and Literary Sources

Adam of Usk. *Chronicon Adae de Usk, A.D. 1377–1421*, ed. and trans. by E. M. Thompson, 2nd ed., London, 1904.

Bertrandon de la Brocquière. *Le Voyage d'Outremer*, ed. C. H. A. Schefer (*Recueil des voyages et des documents pour servir à l'histoire de la géographie depuis le XIIIᵉ jusqu'à la fin du XVᵉ siècle*, XII), Paris, 1892; ed. J. P. Legrand d'Aussy (appended to *Hakluyt's Collection of the Early Voyages, Travels, and Discoveries of the English Nation*, IV), London, 1811; and trans. T. Wright in *Early Travels in Palestine* (London, 1848), pp. 283–382.

Clavijo, Ruy González de. *Embajada a Tamorlan*, ed. F. López Estrada, Madrid, 1943; ed., with Russian trans., by I. Sreznevski, *Dnevnik putešestviia ko dvoru Timura v Samarkand v 1403–1406gg.* (*Sbornik ruskago iazyka i slovesnosti Imperatorskoye Akademii Nauk*, XXVIII, 1), St. Petersburg, 1881; English trans. by G. Le Strange, London, 1928.

Froissart, Jean. *Chroniques,* ed. J. A. C. Buchon, 3 vols., Paris, 1836.

Livre des faits du bon messire Jean le Maingre, dit Bouciquaut, Maréschal de France et Gouverneur de Jennes, ed. J. A. C. Buchon, in Vol. III of his edition of Froissart (Paris, 1836), pp. 563–695.

The Life of St. Peter Thomas by Philippe de Mézières, ed., with commentary, by J. Smet, Rome, 1954.

Religieux de Saint-Denys—Chronica Karoli sexti (*Chronique du Religieux de Saint-Denys contenant le règne de Charles VI, de 1380 à 1422*), ed., with French trans., by M. G. Bellaguet (*Collection de Documents inédits sur l'histoire de France*), 6 vols., Paris, 1839–52; reprinted, 1965.

Resti, Giunio. *Chronica Ragusina,* ed. S. Nodilo (*Monumenta spectantia historiam Slavorum meridionalium,* 25), Zagreb, 1893.

Sanuto, Marino. *Vite di duchi di Venezia,* ed. Muratori, *Rerum Italicarum Scriptores,* 22, pp. 405–1252.

Schiltberger, Johann. *Reisebuch,* ed. V. Langmantel, Tübingen, 1885; trans. J. B. Telfer, Hakluyt Society, London, 1879.

Spandugnino, Theodoro. *De la origine deli imperatori Ottomani,* ed. K. Sathas, *Documents inédits relatifs à l'histoire de la Grèce au moyen âge* (Μνημεῖα τῆς ἑλληνικῆς ἱστορίας), IX (Paris, 1890), pp. 134–261.

Stella, Georgio. *Annales Gennenses,* ed. Muratori, *Rerum Italicarum Scriptores,* 17, pp. 951–1318.

Zeno, Giacomo. *Vita Caroli Zeni,* ed. Muratori, *Rerum Italicarum Scriptores,* 19, pp. 207–372; re-ed. G. Zonta, *R. I. S.,* 19, 6, Bologna, 1940.

V. *Documents and Diplomatic Sources*

A. CHRYSOBULL AND PROSTAGMA TEXTS

Arkadios Vatopedinos. " Ἁγιορειτικὰ ἀνάλεκτα ἐκ τοῦ ἀρχείου τῆς μονῆς Βατοπεδίου," Γρηγόριος ὁ Παλαμᾶς, 3 (1919), 326–339, 429–441.

Cirac Estopañan, S. "Ein Chrysobulles des Kaisers Manuel II Palaiologos (1391–1425) für den Gegenpapst Bennedikt XIII (1394–1417/23) vom 20 Juni 1402," *Byzantinische Zeitschrift,* 44 (1951), 89–93.

Dölger, F. *Aus den Schatzkammern des heiligen Berges,* I (*Textband*), Munich, 1948.

Ktenas, Ch. "Χρυσόβουλοι λόγοι τῆς ἐν Ἄθῳ ἱερᾶς βασιλικῆς, πατριαρχικῆς καὶ σταυροπηγιακῆς μονῆς τοῦ Δοχειαρίου," Ἐπετηρὶς Ἑταιρείας Βυζαντινῶν Σπουδῶν, 4 (1927), 285–311.

Mošin, V. "Akti iz svetogorskih arhiva," *Srpska Kraljevska Akademija, Spomenik,* 91 (*Drugi razred,* 70, 1939), 153–260.

Zachariae von Lingenthal, K. E. *Jus Graeco-Romanum,* Vol. III,
Leipzig, 1857.

——. "Prooemion zu Chrysobullen von Demetrius Kydones,"
*Sitzungsberichte der Königlich preussischen Academie der Wis-
senschaften zu Berlin,* 51 (December, 1888), pp. 1409–1422.

B. VENETIAN DOCUMENTS

Diplomatarium Veneto-Levantinum, ed. C. M. Thomas, Pt. II,
Venice, 1899; reprinted, 1964.

Documents inédits relatifs à l'histoire de la Grèce au moyen âge
(Μνημεῖα τῆς ἑλληνικῆς ἱστορίας), ed. K. Sathas, Vols. I and III,
Paris, 1880–82.

Iorga, N. "Veneţia in Marea neagră," *Analele Academiei Române,
Memoriile Secţiunii istorice,* II, 36 (1913–14), Pt. I, pp. 1043–
1070; Pt. II, pp. 1071–1118: documents, pp. 1058–1070, 1093–
1118, respectively.

Monumenta spectantia historiam Slavorum meridionalium, Vol. 4,
ed. S. Ljubić, Zagreb, 1874.

(Twenty-six Senate Deliberation texts), ed. R.-J. Loenertz, in Vol.
II of his edition of Cydones' Correspondence (*Studi e Testi,*
208) (Vatican City, 1960), pp. 434–454.

C. MISCELLANEOUS

Acta Concilii Constanciensis, ed. H. Finke, Vol. I: *Akten zur
Vorgeschichte des Konstanzer Konzils (1410–1414),* Münster,
1896.

Acta et diplomata graeca medii aevi sacra et profana, ed. E. Miklosich and J. Müller, Vols. I–III and V, Vienna, 1860–87.

Acta et diplomata ragusina, ed. J. Radonić, Vol. I (= *Srpska Kraljevska Akademija Zbornik za istoriju, jezik i književnost
srpskog narodna,* III, 2), Belgrade, 1934.

Annales ecclesiastici, ed., with commentary, by (C. Baronius and)
O. Raynaldus, Vols. 25–27, Bar-le-Duc, 1872–80.

Belgrano, L. T. "Studi e documenti su la Colonia genovese di Pera

(Prima serie)," *Atti della Società ligure di storia patria,* XIII, 2 (1877), 97–317.

"Ein Brief des Königs Sigismund von Ungarn an den Grossmeister des Johanniterordens Philibert von Naillac. Dat. Constantinopel, 1396 November 11.," ed. H. V. Sauerland, *Neues Archiv der Gesellschaft für älter deutsche Geschichtskunde,* XXI, 2 (1896), 565–566.

Diplomatari de l'Orient Català (1301–1409), ed. A. Rubió i Lluch, Barcelona, 1947.

Diplomatarium relationum reipublicae ragusanae cum regno Hungariae (= Raguza és magyarország összekötetéseinek oklevéltára), ed. J. Gelcich and L. Thallóczy, Budapest, 1887.

''Γράμμα τῆς κοινότητος Φλωρεντίας πρὸς τὸν αὐτοκράτορα Μανουὴλ Παλαιολόγον,'' ed. S. P. Lampros, Παλαιολόγεια καὶ Πελοποννησιακά, III (Athens, 1926), pp. 124–125.

''Γράμμα τῆς κοινότητος Φλωρεντίας πρὸς τὸν πάπαν Μαρτῖνον Ε' εἰς ὃν συνιστᾶται ὁ πρέσβυς τοῦ Μανουὴλ Παλαιολόγου Ἰωάννης Πλατυντέριος,'' ed. S. P. Lampros, Παλαιολόγεια καὶ Πελοποννησιακά, III (Athens, 1926), p. 126.

Iorga, N. *Notes et extraits pour servir à l'histoire des Croisades au XVᵉ siècle,* Vol. I, Paris, 1899 (Genoese and other documents), originally published in *Revue de l'Orient latin,* 4 (1896), et seq.

'' Ἰωάννου Η' Παλαιολόγου ἐπιστολὴ πρὸς τὸν δούκα Βενετίας Φραγκίσκον Φοσκάρην,'' ed. S. P. Lampros, Παλαιολόγεια καὶ Πελοποννησιακά, III (Athens, 1926), p. 353.

Monumenta spectantia ad unionem ecclesiarum Graecae et Romanae, ed. A. Theiner and F. Miklosich, Vienna, 1872.

Royal and Historical Letters During the Reign of Henry the Fourth, King of England, and of France, and Lord of Ireland, Vol. I: *A.D. 1399–1404,* ed. F. C. Hingeston (= *Rerum Britannicarum medii aevi scriptorum,* No. 18), London, 1860.

B. Modern Studies and Monographs

Alderson, A. D. *The Structure of the Ottoman Dynasty,* Oxford, 1956.

Alexandrescu-Dersca, M.-M. *La Campagne de Timur en Anatolie (1402),* Bucharest, 1942.

Alexandris, K. A. Ἡ θαλασσία δύναμις εἰς τὴν ἱστορίαν τῆς βυζαντινῆς αὐτοκρατορίας, Athens, 1956.

Anastasejević, D. "Jedina vizantijska carica Srpkinja," *Brastvo,* 30 (*Društvo sv. Save,* 50, Belgrade, 1939), 26–48.

Andreeva, M. A. "Zur Reise Manuels II. Palaiologos nach West-europa," *Byzantinische Zeitschrift,* 34 (1934), 37–47, 351.

Aschbach, J. *Geschichte Kaiser Sigismund's,* 4 vols., Hamburg, 1838–45.

Atiya, A. S. *The Crusade in the Later Middle Ages,* London, 1938.

———. *The Crusade of Nicopolis,* London, 1934.

Babinger, F. *Beiträge zur frühgeschichte der Türkenherrschaft in Rumelien (14.–15. Jahrhundert)* (*Südosteuropäische Arbeiten,* 34), Munich, 1944.

———. "Sawd̲j̲ī (3)," article in *The Encyclopedia of Islām,* IV (Leyden, 1934), 192.

———. "Witwensitz und Sterbeplatz der Sultanin Mara Ἐπετη-ρὶς Ἑταιρείας Βυζαντινῶν Σπουδῶν, 23 (1953), 240–244.

Barker, J. W. "John VII in Genoa: A Problem in Late Byzantine Source Confusion," *Orientalia Christiana Periodica,* 28 (1962), 213–238.

———. "On the Chronology of the Activities of Manuel II Palaeo-logus in the Morea in 1415," *Byzantinische Zeitschrift,* 55 (1962), 39–55.

Baştav, Ş. "Les Sources d'une histoire de l'empire ottomane rédi-gée par un auteur anonyme grec (1374–1421)," *Türk tarih kurumu, Belleten,* XXI, 81 (1957), 161–172.

Beck, H.-G. "Byzanz und der Westen im Zeitalter des Konziliaris-mus," in the co-operative collection, *Die Welt zur Zeit des konstanzer Konzils* (*Konstanzer Arbeitskreis für mittelalterliche Geschichte, Vorträge und Forschungen* 9) (Stuttgart, 1965), pp. 135–148.

———. *Kirch und theologische Litteratur im byzantinischen Reich* (*Handbuch der Altertumswissenschaft,* XI, 2, 1), Munich, 1959.

Beckmann, G. *Der Kampf Kaiser Sigmunds gegen die werdende Weltmacht der Osmanen, 1392–1437. Eine historische Grundle-gung,* Gotha, 1902.

Beldeceanu-Steinherr, I. "La Conquête d'Andrinople par les Turcs: La pénétration turque en Thrace et la valeur des chroniques ottomanes," *Centre de recherche d'histoire et civilisation byzan-tines* (Paris), *Travaux et Mémoires,* 1 (1965), 439–461.

———. "La Prise de Serres et le Firman de 1372 en faveur du

monastère de Saint-Jean-Prodrome," *Acta historica,* 4 (1965), 15–24.

Berger de Xivrey, J. *Mémoire sur la vie et les ouvrages de l'empereur Manuel Paléologue,* in *Mémoires de l'Institut de France, Académie des Inscriptions et Belles-Lettres,* XIX, 2 (Paris, 1853), pp. 1–201.

Bertelè, T. "I gioielli della corona bizantina dati in pegno alla Repubblica veneta nel sec. XIV e Mastino II della Scala," *Studi in onore di Amintore Fanfani,* II: *Medioevo* (Milan, 1962), 90–177.

———. "L'iperpero bizantino dal 1261 al 1453," *Rivista italiana di numismatica e scienze affini,* V, 5, 59 (1957), 70–89.

———. "Monete bizantini inedite o rare," *Zeitschrift für Numismatik,* 36 (1926), 1–36.

Blanchet, A. "Les Dernières monnaies d'or des empereurs de Byzance," *Revue numismatique,* IV, 14 (1910), 78–90.

Bodnar, E. W. "The Isthmian Fortifications in Oracular Prophecy," *The American Journal of Archaeology,* 64 (1960), 165–171.

Brătianu, G. I. "L'Approvisionnement de Constantinople à l'époque byzantine et ottomane," *Byzantion,* 5 (1929–30), 83–107.

———. *Etudes byzantines d'histoire économique et sociale,* Paris, 1938.

———. "Nouvelles Contributions à l'étude de l'approvisionnement de Constantinople sous les Paléologues et les empereurs ottomans," *Byzantion,* 6 (1931), 640–656.

Brauner, A. *Die Schlacht bei Nikopolis, 1396,* Inaugural Dissertation, Breslau, 1876.

Bréhier, L. *Le Monde byzantin,* I: *Vie et mort de Byzance* (*L'évolution de l'humanité,* XXXII, 1), Paris, 1947.

Broneer, O. "The Corinthian Isthmus and the Isthmian Sanctuary," *Antiquity,* 32 (1958), 80–88.

———. "Excavations at Isthmia, Third Campaign, 1955–56," *Hesperia,* 27 (1958), 1–37; "... Fourth Campaign, 1957–58," *Hesperia,* 28 (1959), 298–343.

Cammelli, G. *I dotti bizantini e le origin dell'umanismo,* I: *Manuele Crisolora,* Florence, 1941.

Cantemir, Demetrius. *History of the Growth and Decay of the Othman Empire,* trans. N. Tindal, London, 1734–35.

Cessi, R. "Amadeo di Acaia e la rivendicazione dei domini Sabaudi in oriente," *Nuovo Archivio Veneto,* N.S. 37 (1919), 5–64.

Charanis, P. "Coronation and Its Constitutional Significance in the Late Roman Empire," *Byzantion,* 15 (1940–41), 49–66.

———. "The Greek Historical Sources of the Second Half of the Fourteenth Century," *Bulletin of the Polish Institute of Arts and Sciences in America,* 2 (1944), 406–412.

———. "An Important Short Chronicle of the Fourteenth Century," *Byzantion,* 13 (1938), 335–362.

———. "The Monastic Properties and the State in the Byzantine Empire," *Dumbarton Oaks Papers, No. 4* (1948), 53–118.

———. "A Note on the Short Chronicle No. 45 of the Lampros-Amantos Collection," *Annuaire de l'Institut de Philologie et d'Histoire Orientales et Slaves,* 7 (1939–44), 447–450.

———. "The Strife Among the Palaeologi and the Ottoman Turks, 1370–1402," *Byzantion,* 16 (1942–43), 286–314.

Christophilopoulou, A. Ἐκλογή, ἀναγόρευσις καὶ στέψις τοῦ βυζαντινοῦ αὐτοκράτορος (Πραγματεῖαι τῆς Ἀκαδημίας Ἀθηνῶν, 22, 2), Athens, 1956.

Chrysostomides, J. "John V Palaeologus in Venice (1370–1371) and the Chronicle of Caroldo: a Reinterpretation," *Orientalia Christiana Periodica,* 31 (1965), 76–84.

Cirac Estopañan, S. *La unión, Manuel II Paleólogo y sus recuerdos en España,* Barcelona, 1952.

Cognesso, F. *Il conte verde (1334–1383)* Turin [1930].

Darrouzès, J. "Conférence sur la primauté du pape à Constantinople en 1357," *Revue des études byzantines,* 19 (1961 = Mélanges R. Janin), 76–109.

Delaville le Roulx, J. *La France en Orient au XIVe siècle,* 2 vols., Paris, 1886.

———. *Les Hospitaliers à Rhodes jusqu'à la mort de Philibert de Naillac, 1310–1421,* Paris, 1913.

Dennis, G. T. "The Byzantine-Turkish Treaty of 1403," *Orientalia Christiana Periodica,* 33 (1967), 72–88.

———. "Four Unknown Letters of Manuel II Palaeologus," *Byzantion,* 36 (1966), 35–40.

———. *The Reign of Manuel II Palaeologus in Thessalonica, 1382–1387 (Orientalia Christiana Analecta,* 159), Rome, 1960.

———. "The Second Turkish Capture of Thessalonica: 1391, 1394 or 1430?" *Byzantinische Zeitschrift,* 57 (1964), 53–61.

———. "An Unknown Byzantine Emperor, Andronicus V Palaeologus (1400–1407?)," *Jahrbuch der Österreichischen Byzanti- nischen Gesellschaft,* 16 (1967), 175–187.

Dereksen, David. *See* under Stacton, David Derek.

Diehl, C. *L'Empire oriental de 1081 à 1453* (*Histoire générale: Histoire du moyen âge,* IX, 1), Paris, 1945.

———. *Figures Byzantines,* Second Series, Paris, 1908.

Dölger, F. "Johannes VII., Kaiser der Rhomäer, 1390–1408," *Byzantinische Zeitschrift,* 31 (1931), 21–36.

———. "Die Krönung Johanns VIII. zum Mitkaiser," *Byzan- tinische Zeitschrift,* 36 (1936), 318–319.

———. *Regesten der Kaiserurkunden des oströmischen Reiches von 565–1453, 5: Regesten von 1341–1453* (*Corpus der griechi- schen Urkunden des Mittelalters und der neueren Zeit,* A: *Regesten,* I), Munich, 1965.

———. "Zum Aufstand des Andronikos IV. gegen seinen Vater Johannes V. im Mai 1373," *Revue des études byzantines,* 19 (1961 = *Mélanges R. Janin*), 328–332.

Dräseke, J. "Georgios Gemistos Plethon," *Zeitschrift für Kirchen- geschichte,* 19 (1899), 265–292.

Du Cange, C. *Familiae augustae byzantinae* (*Historia byzantina,* Pt. I), Paris, 1680.

Dujčev, I. "Le Patriarche Nil et les invasions turques vers la fin du XIVᵉ siècle," *Mélanges d'archéologie et d'histoire,* 78 (1966), 207–214.

Durrieu, P. *Les Antiquités judaïques et le peintre Jean Foucquet,* Paris, 1906.

———. *Les Très Riches Heures de Jean de France, Duc de Berry,* Paris, 1904.

Ebersolt, J. *Constantinople byzantine et les voyageurs du Levant,* Paris, 1918.

Falier-Papadopoulos, J. B. "Phrantzès, est-il réellement l'auteur de la grande chronique qui porte son nom?" *Actes du IVᵉ Congrès International des Etudes Byzantines* (= *Izvestija na bulgarskija archaeologicheski institut,* 9, 1935), 177–189.

Finlay, G. *A History of Greece from Its Conquest by the Romans to the Present Time, B.C. 146 to A.D. 1864,* Vol. III: *The Byzan- tine and Greek Empires,* Pt. 2, *A.D. 1057–1453,* Oxford, 1877.

Forstreuter, K. "Der Deutsche Orden und Südesteuropa," *Kyrios, Vierteljahresschrift für Kirchen- und Geistesgeschichte Ost- europas,* I (1936), 244–272.

Fuchs, F. *Die höheren Schulen von Konstantinopel im Mittelalter* (= *Byzantinisches Archiv*, 8) Leipzig & Berlin, 1926.

Gedeon, M. Πατριαρχικοὶ πίνακες, Constantinople, 1890.

Gelzer, H. "Der wiederaufgefundene Kodex des hl. Klemens und anderer auf den Patriarchat Achrida bezügliche Urkundensammlungen," *Berichte über die Verhandlungen der Königlich Sächsichen Gesellschaft der Wissenschaften zu Leipzig, Phil.-histor. Klasse*, 55 (1903), 41–110.

Gerasimov, T. "Edna medna moneta Joan VII Paleolog (1400–1403)" ("Monnaies de cuivre de Jean VII Paléologue"), *Izvestija Arkheologicheskaia Institut, Bulgarska Akademija na Naukite*, 20 (1955), 585–586.

———. "Les Monnaies de Jean VII Paléologue (1400–1408)," *Byzantinoslavica*, 17 (1956), 114–119.

Gerola, G. "L'Effige del despoto Giovanni Cantacuzeno," *Byzantion*, 6 (1931), 379–387.

Gibbon, E. *The History of the Decline and Fall of the Roman Empire*, ed. J. B. Bury, Vol. VII, London, 1902.

Gibbons, H. A. *The Foundation of the Ottoman Empire*, New York, 1916.

Gill, J. *The Council of Florence*, Cambridge, 1958.

———. *Constance et Bâle-Florence* (= *Histoire des conciles oecumeniques*, 9), Paris, 1965.

———. "Greeks and Latins in a Common Council: The Council of Florence (1438–9)," *Orientalia Christiana Periodica*, 25 (1959), 265–287; reprinted in the author's collection, *Personalities of the Council of Florence, and Other Essays* (New York, 1964), pp. 233–253.

———. "John VIII Palaeologus: A Character Study," *Studi bizantini e neoellenici*, 9 (1957 = *Silloge bizantina in onore di S. G. Mercati*), 152–170; reprinted in the author's collection, *Personalities of the Council of Florence, and Other Essays* (New York, 1964), pp. 104–124.

Goeller, E. "Zur Geschichte Manuels II von Byzanz," *Römische Quartalschrift für christliche Altertumskunde und für Kirchengeschichte*, 15 (1901), 188–191.

Goodacre, H. *A Handbook of the Coinage of the Byzantine Empire*, London, 1957.

———. "Notes on Some Rare Byzantine Coins," *Numismatic Chronicle*, V, 11 (1931), 151–159.

Grabar, A. *L'Empereur dans l'art byzantin,* Paris, 1936.

Grégoire, H. "L'Opinion byzantine et la bataille de Kossovo," *Byzantion,* 16 (1931), 247–251.

Grosvenor, E. A. *Constantinople,* 2 vols., Boston, 1895.

Grousset, R. *L'Empire des steppes: Attila, Gengis-Khan, Tamerlan,* Paris, 1939.

Guiffrey, J. "Médailles de Constantin et d'Héraclius acquise par Jean, Duc de Berry, en 1402," *Revue numismatique,* III, 8 (1890), 87–116.

Guilland, R. "Etudes de titulature et de prosopographie byzantines. Le chefs de la marine byzantine: Drongaire de la flotte, Grand Drongaire de la flotte, Duc de la flotte, Mégaduc," *Byzantinische Zeitschrift,* 44 (1951), 212–240.

————. "Etudes sur l'histoire administrative de l'empire byzantin: Le Despote, Δεσπότες," *Revue des études byzantines,* 17 (1959), 52–89.

Halecki, O. "Angora, Florence, Varna and the Fall of Constantinople," *Akten der XI. Internationaler Byzantinisten-Kongresses München 1958* (Munich, 1960), 216–220.

————. *Un Empereur de Byzance à Rome, Vingt ans de travail pour l'Union des églises et pour la defence de l'empire d'orient, 1355–1373,* Warsaw, 1930.

————. "The Last Century of the Crusades—From Smyrna to Varna (1344–1444)," *Bulletin of the Polish Institute of Arts and Sciences in America,* II, 2 (January 1945), 300–307.

————. "La Pologne et l'empire byzantin," *Byzantion,* 7 (1932), 41–67.

————. "Rome et Byzance au temps du grand Schisme d'Occident," *Collectanea theologica* (Lwów), 18 (1937), 477–532.

————. "Two Palaeologi in Venice, 1370–71," *Byzantion,* 17 (1944–45), 331–335.

Hammer-Purgstall, J. von. *Geschichte des osmanischen Reiches,* Vol. I, Pest, 1833.

Hazlitt, W. C. *The Venetian Republic, Its Rise, Growth, and Its Fall, 421–1797,* Vol. I: *421–1422,* London, 1900.

Heisenberg, A. *Aus der Geschichte und Literatur der Palaiologenzeit (Sitzungsberichte der Bayerischen Akademie der Wissenschaften, Philosophische-Philologische und Historische Klasse, Abhandl. 10),* Munich, 1920.

Heyd, W. *Histoire du commerce du Levant au moyen âge*, 2 vols., Leipzig, 1936.

Hill, G. F. "Notes on the Mediaeval Medals of Constantine and Heraclius," *Numismatic Chronicle*, IV, 10 (1910), 110–116.

Hodgeson, F. C. *Venice in the Thirteenth and Fourteenth Centuries*, London, 1910.

Hoffman, G. "Kirchengeschichtliches zur Ehe des Herrschers Theodor II Palaiologos (1407–1443)," *Ostkirchliche Studien*, 4 (1955), 129–137.

Hookham, H. *Tamburlaine the Conqueror*, London, 1962.

Hopf, K. *Chroniques gréco-romanes*, Berlin, 1873; reprinted, Brussels, 1966.

———. *Geschichte Griechenlands vom Beginn des Mittelalters bis auf unsern Zeit (1821)* (= Ersch and Gruber, *Allgemeine Encyklopädie der Wissenschaften und Künste*, Vol. 86), Leipzig, 1868.

Hunger, H. "Byzanz in der Weltpolitik vom Bildersturm bis 1453," in *Historia mundi*, Vol. VII (Bern, 1958), pp. 386–444.

———. "Das Testament des Patriarchen Matthaios I. (1397–1410)," *Byzantinische Zeitschrift*, 51 (1958), 288–309.

Inalcik, H. "Ottoman Methods of Conquest," *Studia Islamica*, 2 1954), 103–129.

Iorga, N. *Geschichte des osmanischen Reiches*, Vol. I, Gotha, 1900.

———. "Une Inscription grecque sous le Sultan Mousa, 1407–1408, dans le région d'Ochrida," *Revue historique du Sud-est européen*, 10 (1933), 11–12.

———. *Notes et extraits pour servir à l'histoire des croisades au XVᵉ siècle*, Vols. I and II, Paris, 1899.

———. *Philippe de Mézières, 1327–1405*, Paris, 1896.

———. "Privilegiu lui Mohamed al II-lea pentru Pera (1-iu Junie 1453)," *Analele Academiei Române*, II, 36 (1913–14), 69–92.

———. "Sur les deux prétendants Moustafa du XVᵉ siècle," *Revue historique du Sud-est européen*, 10 (1933), 12–13.

Jenkins, R. J. H. "The Hellenistic Origins of Byzantine Literature," *Dumbarton Oaks Papers, No. 17* (1963), 39–52.

Jenkins, R. J. H., and A. H. S. Megaw. "Researches at Isthmia," *Annual of the British School at Athens*, 32 (1931–32), 68–89.

Jireček, J. K. *Geschichte der Serben*, 2 vols., Gotha, 1911–18.

———. "Zur Wurdigung der neuentdekten bulgarische Chronik," *Archiv für slavische Philologie*, 14 (1892), 255–277.

Jugie, M. "Le Voyage de l'empereur Manuel Paléologue en Occident (1399–1403)," *Echos d'Orient,* 15 (1912), 322–332.

Khoury, T. "L'Empereur Manuel II Paléologue (1350–1425). Esquisse biographique," *Proche-Orient chrétien,* 15 (1965), 127–144.

Kling, G. *Die Schlacht bei Nikopolis im Jahre 1396,* Inaugural Dissertation, Berlin, 1906.

Kolias, G. " Ἡ ἀνταρσία Ἰωάννου Ζ´ Παλαιολόγου ἐναντίον Ἰωάννου Ε´ Παλαιολόγου (1390)," Ἑλληνικά, 12 (1952), 34–64.

Krammers, J. H. "Muhammed I," article in *The Encyclopedia of Islām,* III, Leyden (1936), 657–658.

————. "Mūsā Čelebi," article in *The Encyclopedia of Islām,* III, Leyden (1936), 740.

Krumbacher, K. *Geschichte der byzantinischen Litteratur von Justinian biz zum Ende des oströmischen Reiches (527–1453),* 2nd edition, Munich, 1897.

Kupelwieser, L. *Die Kämpfe Ungarns mit den Osmanen bis zur Schlacht bei Mohács, 1526,* Vienna, 1899.

Lampros, S. P. "Τὸ ἔθος τοῦ μασχαλισμοῦ παρὰ τοὺς μανιάταις τῶν μέσων αἰώνων," Νέος ἑλληνομνήμων, 2 (1905), 180–186.

————. Λεύκωμα τῶν βυζαντινῶν αὐτοκρατόρων, Athens, 1930.

————. "Τὰ τείχη τοῦ ἰσθμοῦ τῆς Κορίνθου κατὰ τοὺς μέσους αἰῶνας," Νέος ἑλληνομνήμων, 2 (1905), 435–489; 4 (1907), 20–26, 240–243; 5 (1908), 115–116.

Laskaris, M. Th. "Θεσσαλονίκη καὶ Τάνα," Τόμος Κωνσταντίνου Ἀρμενοπούλου (=Πανεπιστημίου Θεσσαλονίκης, Ἐπιστημονικὴ ἐπετηρίς, 6, 1952), 331–340.

————. " Ἰωάννης Η´ ὁ Παλαιολόγος ἐν Θεσσαλονίκῃ κατὰ τὴν πολιορκίαν τοῦ 1416," Τόμος Κωνσταντίνου Ἀρμενοπούλου (=Πανεπιστημίου Θεσσαλονίκης, Ἐπιστημονικὴ ἐπετηρίς, 6, 1952), 340–344.

Laurent, M. H. "L'Activité d'André Chrysobergès, O. P. sous le pontificat du Martin V (1418–1431)," *Echos d'Orient,* 34 (1935), 414–438.

Laurent, V. "La Correspondance de Démétrius Cydonès," *Echos d'Orient,* 30 (1931), 399–454.

————. "La Date de la mort d'Hélène Cantacuzène, femme de Jean V Paléologue," *Revue des études byzantines,* 13 (1955), 135–138.

————. "La Date de la mort d'Hélène Cantacuzène, femme de

Jean V Paléologue," *Revue des études byzantines*, 14 (1956), 200–201.

———. "Les Dates du patriarcat d'Euthyme II de Constantinople," *Byzantinische Zeitschrift*, 54 (1961), 329–332.

———. "Les Droits de l'empereur en matière ecciésiastique. L'accord de 1380–1382," *Revue des études byzantines*, 13 (1955), 5–20.

———. "Isidore de Kiev et la Métropole de Monembasie," *Revue des études byzantines*, 17 (1957), 150–157.

———. "Les Préliminaries de Concile de Florence: les neuf articles du Pape Martin V et la réponse inédite du Patriarche de Constantinople Joseph II (octobre 1422)," *Revue des études byzantines*, 20 (1962), 5–60.

———. "Σφϱαντζῆς et non Φϱαντζῆς," *Byzantinische Zeitschrift*, 44 (1951), 373–378.

Lemerle, P. "Autour d'un prostagma inédit de Manuel II. L'aulé de Sire Guy à Thessalonique," *Studi bizantini e neoellenici*, 9 (1957 = *Silloge bizantina in onore di S. G. Mercati*), 271–287.

———. "La Domination vénetienne à Thessalonique," *Miscellanea Giovanni Galbiati* (= *Fontes Ambrosiani*, 27, 1951), 219–225.

———. *Philippes et la Macédoine orientale à l'époque chrétienne et byzantine*, Paris, 1945.

Loenertz, R.-J. "Autour de Chronicon Maius attribué à Georges Phrantzès," *Miscellanea G. Mercati*, III: *Letteratura e storia bizantina* (= *Studi e Testi*, 123) (Vatican City, 1946), pp. 273–311.

———. "La Date de la lettre ϑ′ de Manuel Paléologue et l'authenticité du 'Chronicon Maius' de Georges Phrantzès," *Echos d'Orient*, 39 (1940–42), 91–99.

———. Démétrius Cydonès, citoyen de Venise," *Echos d'Orient*, 37 (1938), 125–126.

———. "Les Dominicains byzantins Théodore et André Chrysobergès et les négotiations pour l'union des églises greque et latine de 1415 à 1430," *Archivium Fratrum Praedicatorum*, 9 (1939), 5–61.

———. "Ecrits de Macaire Macrès et de Manuel Paléologue dans les mss. Vat. gr. 1107 et Crypten. 111," *Orientalia Christiana Periodica*, 15 (1949), 185–193.

———. "Une Erreur singulière de Laonic Chalcocandyle: Le prétendu second mariage de Jean V Paléologue," *Revue des études byzantines*, 15 (1957), 176–184.

Loenertz, R.-J. "Etudes sur le chroniques brèves byzantines," *Orientalia Christiana Periodica*, 24 (1958), 155–164.

——. "Fragment d'une lettre de Jean V Paléologue à la Commune de Gênes, 1387–1391," *Byzantinische Zeitschrift*, 51 (1958), 37–40.

——. "Jean V Paléologue à Venise (1370–1371)," *Revue des études byzantines*, 16 (1958), 216–232.

——. "Manuel Paléologue et Démétrius Cydonès, Remarques sur leur Correspondances: Première série," *Echos d'Orient*, 36 (1937), 271–287; ". . . Deuxième série," *Echos d'Orient*, 36 (1937), 474–487; ". . . Troisième série," *Echos d'Orient*, 37 (1938), 107–124.

——. "Notes d'histoire et de chronologie byzantines," *Revue des études byzantines*, 17 (1949), 158–167.

——. "Notes sur le règne de Manuel II à Thessalonique, 1381/82–1387," *Byzantinische Zeitschrift*, 50 (1957), 390–396.

——. "Pour la chronologie des oeuvres de Joseph Bryennios," *Revue des études byzantines*, 7 (1949–50), 12–32.

——. "Pour l'histoire du Péloponnèse au XIVe siècle (1382–1404)," *Revue des études byzantines*, 1 (1943), 152–196.

——. "La Première Insurrection d'Andronic IV Paléologue," *Echos d'Orient*, 38 (1939), 334–345.

——. "Un Prostagma perdu de Théodore Ier Paléologue regardant Thessalonique (1380/82?)," Ἐπετηρὶς Ἑταιρείας Βυζαντινῶν Σπουδῶν, 25 (1955), 170–172.

——. *Les Recueils des Lettres de Démétrius Cydonès* (*Studi e Testi*, 131), Vatican City, 1947.

Luke, H. C. "Visitors from the East to the Plantagenet and Lancastrian Kings," *Nineteenth Century*, 8 (1930), 760–769.

Maksimović, Lj. "Politička uloga Jovana Kantakuzina posle abdikazije (1354–1385)" ("The Political Role of John Cantacuzenus after his Abdication"), *Zbornik Radova, Vizantološkog instituta* (Srpska akademija nauka i umetnosti, Belgrade), 9 (1966), 119–193.

Malakis, J. P. Ὁ Γ. Γεμιστὸς ἐν Πελοποννήσῳ, 1414–1437, Thessalonica, 1939.

——. Γεώργιος Γεμιστὸς Πλήθων (*Texte und Forschungen zur byzantinische-neugriechische Philologie*, No. 32), Athens, 1939.

Mango, C. "The Date of the Anonymous Russian Description of Constantinople," *Byzantinische Zeitschrift*, 45 (1952), 380–385.

Marinesco, C. "Contribution à l'histoire des rélations économiques entre l'empire byzantin, la Sicilie et le royaume de Naples de 1419 à 1453," *Atti del V Congresso Internazionale di Studi Bizantini, Roma, 1936* I (= *Studi bizantini e neoellenici*, 5, 1931), 209–219.

––––––. "De Nouveau sur les rélations de Manuel Paléologue (1391–1425) avec l'Espagne," *Atti dello VIII Congresso Internazionale di Studi Bizantini*, I (= *Studi bizantini e neoellenici*, 7, 1953), 420–436.

––––––. "Deux Empereurs byzantins en Occident: Manuel II et Jean VIII Paléologue," *Compts-rendus de l'Académie des Inscriptions et Belles-Lettres*, January–March, 1957 (Paris, 1958), 23–24.

––––––. "Deux Empereurs byzantins, Manuel II et Jean VIII Paléologue, vus par des artistes occidentaux," *Le Flambeau*, 40 (November–December, 1957), 758–762.

––––––. "Manuel II Paléologue et les rois d'Aragon, Commentaire sur quatre lettres inédites en Latin, expédiées par la chancellerie byzantine," *Académie Roumaine, Bulletin de la Section Historique*, 11 (1924), 192–206.

Massai, F. *Pléthon et le Platonisme de Mistra*, Paris, 1956.

Mercati, G. "Lettere di un Isidor Arcivescovo di Monembasia e non di Kiew," *Bessarione*, 20 (1916), 200–207.

––––––. "Sarebbe Stafidace l'epistolegrafo del codice laurenziano di S. Marco 356?," *Studi bizantini [e neoellenici]*, 2 (1957), 239–242.

––––––. *Scritti d'Isidoro il Cardinale ruteno e codici a lui appartenuti che si conservano nella Biblioteca Apostolica Vaticana* (*Studi e Testi*, 46), Vatican City, 1926.

––––––. "Tre piccoli scritti di Caleca e la fine di Demetrio," in his *Notizie di Procoro e Demetrio Cidone, Manuele Caleca e Theodoro Meliteniota ed altri appunti per la storia della Teologia e della letteratura bizantina del secolo XIV* (*Studi e Testi*, 56), Vatican City, 1931.

Mertzios, K. D. Μνημεῖα μακεδονικῆς ἱστορίας, Thessalonica, 1947.

Meyendorff, J. "Jean-Joasaph Cantacuzène et le projet de Concile oecuménique en 1367," *Akten des XI. Internationalen Byzantinisten-Kongresses München 1958* (Munich, 1960), 363–369.

Meyendorff, J. "Projets de Concile oecumenique en 1367: Un dialogue inédit entre Jean Cantacuzène et le légat Paul," *Dumbarton Oaks Papers, No. 14* (1960), 149–177.

Mijatović, C. *Constantine, The Last Emperor of the Greeks, or The Conquest of Constantinople by the Turks (A.D. 1453)*, London, 1892.

Miller, W. "The Gattilusij of Lesbos (1355–1462)," *Byzantinische Zeitschrift*, 22 (1913), 406–447; reprinted in his *Essays on the Latin Orient* (Cambridge, 1921), 313–352.

———. *The Latins in the Levant, A History of Frankish Greece (1204–1566)*, London, 1908; reprinted, 1964.

———. "Monemvasia during the Frankish Period," *Journal of Hellenic Studies*, 27 (1907), 228–241; reprinted in his *Essays on the Latin Orient*, 231–245.

———. "The Princes of the Peloponnese," *Quarterly Review*, 404 (July, 1905), 109–135.

———. "Salonika," in *Essays on the Latin Orient*, 268–282.

Mompherratos, A. Διπλωματικαὶ ἐνέργειαι Μανουὴλ Β΄ τοῦ Παλαιολόγου ἐν Εὐρώπῃ καὶ ᾿Ασίᾳ, Athens, 1913.

———. Οἱ Παλαιολόγοι ἐν Πελοποννήσῳ, Athens, 1913.

Moravcsik, G. "Vizantiiskie imperatori ich posli v g. Buda" ("Les empereurs de Byzance et leurs ambassadeurs à Buda"), *Acta historica academiae scientarum hungaricae*, 8 (1961), 239–256.

———. *Byzantinoturcica*, 2nd ed., 2 vols., Berlin, 1958.

Mordtmann, J. H. "Djunaid," article in *The Encyclopedia of Islām*, I, Leyden (1913), coll. 1063–1064.

Muralt, E. von. *Essai de chronographie byzantine, 1057–1453*, 2 vols., St. Petersburg, 1871; reprinted, 1966.

Nimet, A. *Die türkische Prosopographie bei Laonikos Chalkokandyles*, Dissertation, Hamburg, 1933.

Norden, W. *Das Papsttum und Byzanz, Die Trennung der beiden Mächte und das Problem ihrer Wiedervereinigung bis zum Untergange des byzantinischen Reiches (1453)*, Berlin, 1903; reprinted, 1958.

Oeconomos, L. "L'Etat intellectuel et moral des Byzantins vers le milieu du XIVe siècle d'après une page de Joseph Bryennios," *Mélanges Charles Diehl*, I (Paris, 1930), 225–233.

Ostrogorsky, G. "Byzance, état tributaire de l'empire turc," *Zbornik Radova, Vizantološkog instituta* (Srpska akademija nauka i umetnosti, Belgrade), 5 (1958), 49–58.

————. *Geschichte des byzantinischen Staates* (*Handbuch der Altertumswissenschaft*, XII, I, 2), 3rd German ed., Munich, 1963.

————. *History of the Byzantine State*, American ed., tr. from 2nd German ed. by J. M. Hussey, New Brunswick, N.J., 1957.

————. "The Palaeologi," Chapter VIII in *The Cambridge Medieval History*, Vol. IV (2nd ed.): *The Byzantine Empire*, Pt. I: *Byzantium and Its Neighbours*, Cambridge (1966), pp. 331–387.

————. *Pour l'histoire de la feodalité byzantine*, tr. H. Grégoire (*Corpus Bruxellense Historiae Byzantinae, Subsidia*, 1), Brussels, 1954.

————. "La Prise de Serrès par les Turcs," *Byzantion*, 35 (1965), 302–319.

————. *Serska oblast posle Dušanove smrti* (*Posebna izdanja Vizantološkog instituta*, 9), Belgrade, 1965.

Pagano, D. C. *Imprese e dominio de Genovesi nello Grecia*, Genoa, 1852.

Panovsky, E. *Early Netherlandish Painting*, 2 vols., Cambridge, Mass., 1953.

Papadopoulos, J. " Ἰωάννης Ζ' ὁ Παλαιολόγος καὶ τὸ χρονικὸν τοῦ Φραντζῆ," *Byzantinische Zeitschrift*, 32 (1932), 257–262.

Papadopulos, A. T. *Versuch einer Genealogie der Palaiologen, 1259–1453*, Inaugural Dissertation, Munich, 1938; reprinted, 1962.

Papageorgiou, P. N. "Αἱ Σέρραι καὶ τὰ προάστεια τὰ περὶ τὰς Σέρρας καὶ ἡ μονὴ Ἰωάννου τοῦ Προδρόμου," *Byzantinische Zeitschrift*, 3 (1894), 225–329.

Parisot, J. *Cantacuzène, homme d'état et historien*, Paris, 1845.

Paspates, A. G. Βυζαντιναὶ μελέται, Constantinople, 1877.

Pears, E. *The Destruction of the Greek Empire and the Story of the Capture of Constantinople by the Turks*, London, 1903.

Perrot, G. *Mémoire sur l'île de Thasos*, Paris, 1864.

Petit, L. "Manuel II Paléologue," article in the *Dictionaire de Théologie catholique*, IV, 2, Paris, 1927, coll. 1925–1932.

(Predelli, R.) *I libri Commemoriali della Republica di Venezia, Regesti, III*, Venice, 1883.

Radojčić, N. "Die griechischen Quellen zur Schlacht am Kosovo Polje," *Byzantion*, 6 (1931), 241–246.

Radojičić, Dj. S. "La Chronologie de la bataille de Rovine," *Revue historique du Sud-est européen*, 5 (1928), 136–139.

Radojičić, Dj. S. "Listina manastira Petre od oktobra 1395 god. kao izvor za chronologiju bitke na Rovinama," *Bogoslovlje organ pravoslavnog bogoslovskog Fakulteta y Beogradu*), 2 (1927), 293–301.

Rados, K. Τὸ ναυτικὸν τοῦ Βυζαντίου, ὑλικόν, ὀργάνωσις, τακτική, ἱστορία, Athens, 1920.

Rodd, R. *The Princes of Achaia and the Chronicle of Morea: A Study of Greece in the Middle Ages*, Vol. II, London, 1907.

Roloff, G. "Die Schlacht bei Angora (1402)," *Historische Zeitschrift*, 161 (1940), 244–262.

Rosetti, R. "Note on the Battle of Nicopolis," *The Slavonic Review*, 15 (1936–37), 629–638.

Rossi, E. "Sulaimān Čelebi," article in *The Encyclopedia of Islām*, IV, Leyden (1934), p. 535.

Runciman, S. *The Fall of Constantinople, 1453*, Cambridge, 1965.

Salomon, R. "Zu Ignatij von Smolensk," *Beiträge zur russichen Geschichte Theodor Schiemann zum 60. Geburtstage von Freunden und Schülern dargebracht* (Berlin, 1907), pp. 241–270.

Samodurova, Z. G. "Malie vizantiiskie khroniki i ikh istorichniki," *Vizantiiski Vremenik*, N.S. 27 (1967), 153–161 [not available as this book was written; therefore not cited].

Sauli, L. *Della colonia dei Genovesi in Galata*, 2 vols., Turin, 1831.

Schlumberger, G. "Un Empereur de Byzance à Paris et Londres," in his *Byzance et Croisades: Pages médièvales* (Paris, 1927), 87–147; also separately, Paris, 1916, 58 pp.

———. "Jean de Chateaumorand, un des principaux héros français des arrière-croisades en Orient à la fin du XIVᵉ siècle et à l'aurore du XVᵉ," in *Byzance et Croisades: Pages médièvales* (Paris, 1927), 282–336.

Schneider, A. M. "Die Bevölkerung Konstantinopels im XV. Jahrhundert," *Nachrichten der Akademie der Wissenschaften in Göttingen, Philologisch-historische Klasse*, 9 (1949), 233–244.

Schreiner, P. "Hochzeit und Krönung Kaiser Manuels II. im Jahre 1392," *Byzantinische Zeitschrift*, 60 (1967), 70–85.

———. *Studien zu den* ΒΡΑΧΕΑ ΧΡΟΝΙΚΑ (*Miscellanea byzantina monacensia*, 6: Munich, 1967) [not available as this book was written; therefore not cited].

Setton, K. M. "The Byzantine Background to the Italian Renaissance," *Proceedings of the American Philosophical Society*, 100 (1956), 1–76.

Ševčenko, I. "Nicholas Cabasilas' 'Anti-Zealot' Discourse: A Reinterpretation," *Dumbarton Oaks Papers, No. 11* (1957), 79–171.

Silberschmidt, M. *Das orientalische Problem zur Zeit der Entstehung der Turkischen Reiches nach venezianischen Quellen,* Leipzig, 1923.

Sophronios, E. " Ἱστορικὰ μνημεῖα τοῦ "Αθω," Ἑλληνικά, 2 (1929), 333–384.

Stacton, D. D. *The World on the Last Day: The Sack of Constantinople by the Turks, May 29, 1453, Its Causes and Consequences,* London, 1965; previously published under the pseudonym "David Dereksen" as *The Crescent and the Cross: The Fall of Byzantium, May, 1453,* New York, 1964.

Stanojević, S. "Die Biographie Stefan Lazarevićs von Konstantin dem Philosophen als Geschichtsquelle," *Archiv für slavische Philologie,* 18 (1896), 409–472.

Stephanides, I. K. " Ὁ ἀκραῖος σταθμὸς τῶν σχέσεων Ἐκκλησίας καὶ πολιτείας τοῦ Βυζαντίου καὶ τὰ ἄμεσα ἀποτελέσματα αὐτοῦ (1416-1439)," Ἐπετηρὶς Ἑταιρείας Βυζαντινῶν Σπουδῶν, 23 (1953), 27–40.

Taeschner, F. "Beiträge zur frühosmanischen Epigraphik und Archäologie," *Der Islam,* 30 (1932), 109–186.

——. "The Ottoman Turks to 1453," Chapter XIX in *The Cambridge Medieval History,* Vol. IV (2nd ed.): *The Byzantine Empire,* Pt. 1: *Byzantium and Its Neighbours* (Cambridge, 1966), pp. 753–775.

Taeschner, F., and P. Wittek, "Die Vezirfamilie der Ğandarlyzāde (14./15. Jhdt.) und ihre Denkmäler," *Der Islam,* 18 (1929), 60–115.

Tafrali, O. *Thessalonique au 14ᵉ siècle,* Paris, 1913.

——. *Topographie de Thessalonique,* Paris, 1913.

Thiriet, F. "Una proposta di lega antiturca tra Venezia, Genova e Bisanzio nel 1363," *Archivio storico italiano,* 113 (1955), 321–334.

——. *Régestes des délibérations du Sénat de Venise concernant la Romanie,* 2 vols., Paris, 1958–59.

——. *La Romanie venitienne au moyen âge (Bibliothèque des Ecoles Françaises d'Athènes et de Rome,* 193), Paris, 1959.

——. "Venise et l'occupation de Ténédos au XIVᵉ siècle," *Mélanges d'archaeologie et d'histoire,* 65 (1953), 219–245.

Thomson, I. "Manuel Chrysoloras and the Early Italian Renaissance," *Greek, Roman and Byzantine Studies*, 7 (1966), 63–82.

Tozer, H. F. "A Byzantine Reformer," *Journal of Hellenic Studies*, 7 (1886), 353–380.

Trapp, E. "Der Sprachgebrauch Manuels II. in den Dialogen mit einem 'Perser'," *Jahrbuch der Österreichischen Byzantinischen Gesellschaft*, 16 (1967), 189–197.

Treu, D. "Demetrios Chrysoloras und seine hundert Briefe," *Byzantinische Zeitschrift*, 20 (1911), 106–128.

Turan, O. "The Ideal of World Domination Among the Medieval Turks," *Studia Islamica*, 4 (1955), 77–90.

Turner, C. J. G. "Pages from Late Byzantine Philosophy of History," *Byzantinische Zeitschrift*, 57 (1964), 346–373.

Tzaras, J. "La Fin d'Andronic Paléologue, dernier despote de Thessalonique," *Revue des études sud-est européens*, 3 (1965), 419–432.

Vakalopoulos, A. E. " Ὁ ἀρχιεπίσκοπος Γαβριὴλ καὶ ἡ πρώτη τουρκικὴ κατοχὴ τῆς Θεσσαλονίκης (1391-1403)," Μακεδονικά, 4 (1955–60), 371–373.

———. Οἱ δημοσιευμένες ὁμιλίες τοῦ ἀρχιεπισκόπου Θεσσαλονίκης Ἰσιδώρου ὡς ἱστορικὴ πηγὴ γιὰ τὴ γνώση τῆς πρώτης Τουρκοκρατίας στὴ Θεσσαλονίκη (1387-1403)," Μακεδονικά, 4 (1955–60), 20–34.

———. *A History of Thessaloniki*, tr. T. F. Carney, Thessalonica, 1963.

———. Ἱστορία τοῦ νέου ἑλληνισμοῦ, Α΄, Ἀρχὲς καὶ διαμορφὴ τοῦ, Thessalonica, 1961.

———. "Les Limites de l'empire byzantin depuis la fin du XIVᵉ siècle jusqu'a sa chute (1453)," *Byzantinische Zeitschrift*, 55 (1962), 56–65.

———. "Συμβολὴ στὴν ἱστορία τῆς Θεσσαλονίκης ἐπὶ Βενετοκρατίας (1423-1430)," Τόμος Κωνσταντίνου Ἀρμενοπούλου (=Πανεπιστημίου Θεσσαλονίκης, Ἐπιστημονικὴ ἐπετηρίς, 6, 1952), 128–149.

Van Millingen, A. *Byzantine Churches in Constantinople, Their History and Architecture*, London, 1912.

———. *Byzantine Constantinople, The Walls of the City and Adjoining Historical Sites*, London, 1899.

Vasiliev, A. A. *History of the Byzantine Empire, 324–1453*, Madison, Wisc., 1952.

————. "Pero Tafur, A Spanish Traveller of the Fifteenth Century and His Visit to Constantinople, and Trebizond, and Italy," *Byzantion,* 7 (1932), 75–122.

————. "Putešestvie vizantijskago imperatora Manuila Palaeologa po zapadnoi Evrope (1399–1403)," *Žurnal ministerstva naradnago prosveščeniia,* N.S. 39 (1912), 41–78, 260–304.

————. "Il viaggio di Giovanni V Palaeologo in Italia e l'unione di Roma," *Studi bizantini e neoellenici,* 3 (1931), 153–192.

————. "Was Old Russia a Vassal State of Byzantium?" *Speculum,* 7 (1932), 350–360.

Vaughan, D. M. *Europe and the Turk, A Pattern of Alliances, 1350–1700,* Liverpool, 1954; 2nd ed., 1965.

Voordeckers, E. "Les 'Entretiens avec un Perse' de l'empereur Manuel II Paléologue. (A propos de deux éditions récentes)," *Byzantion,* 36 (1966), 311–317.

Walter, G. *La Ruine de Byzance, 1204–1453,* Paris, 1958.

Weiss, R. "The Medieval Medallions of Constantine and Heraclius," *Numismatic Chronicle,* VII, 3 (1963), 129–144.

Werner, E. *Die Geburt einer Grossmacht—Die Osmanen (1300–1481). Ein Beitrag zur Genesis des türkischen Feudalismus (Forschungen zur mittelalterlichen Geschichte,* 13), Berlin, 1966.

Wiel, A. *The Navy of Venice,* London, 1910.

Wirth, P. "Wann wurde Kaiser Andronikos IV. Palaiologos geboren?" *Byzantinische Zeitschrift,* 55 (1962), 38.

————. "Zum Geschichtsbild Kaiser Johannes' VII Palaiologos," *Byzantion,* 35 (1965 [pub. 1967] = Mémorial Henri Grègoire), fas. 2, pp. 592–600.

Wittek, P. "De la Défaite d'Ankara à la prise de Constantinople," *Revue des études islamiques,* 12 (1938), 1–34.

————. *Das Fürstentum Mentesche, Studie zur Geschichte Westkleinasiens im 13.–15. Jhdt. (Istanbuler Mitteilungen,* 2), Istanbul, 1934.

————. *The Rise of the Ottoman Empire (Royal Asiatic Society Monographs,* 23), London, 1938.

Wolff, R. L. "Footnote to an Incident of the Latin Occupation of Constantinople: The Church and Icon of the Hodegetria," *Traditio,* 6 (1948), 319–328.

Wroth, W. *Catalogue of the Imperial Byzantine Coins in the British Museum,* Vol. II, London, 1908; reprinted, 1966.

Zachariades, E. A. Τὸ χρονικὸ τῶν Τούρκων σουλτάνων (τοῦ Βαρβερι-νιοῦ ˋΕλλην. Κώδικα 111) καὶ τὸ ἰταλικό του πρότυπο (ˋΕλληνικά, Πα-ράρτημα 14), Thessalonica, 1960.

Zakythinos, D. A. *Crise monétaire et crise économique à Byzance du XIIIᵉ au XVᵉ siècle,* Athens, 1948.

——. "Démétrius Cydonès et l'entente balkanique au XIVᵉ siècle," in his *La Grèce et les Balkans,* Athens, 1947, pp. 44–56.

——. *Le Despotat grec de Morée,* Vol. I, Paris, 1932.

——. "Μανουὴλ Β΄ ὁ Παλαιολόγος καὶ ὁ Καρδινάλιος ᾿Ισίδωρος ἐν Πελοποννήσῳ," *Mélanges offerts à Octave et Melpo Merlier,* III (Athens, 1957), 45–69.

ADDENDUM

Nicol, D. M. *The Byzantine Family of Kantakouzenos (Canta-cuzenus), ca. 1100–1460. A Genealogical and Prosopographical Study. (Dumbarton Oaks Studies, 11:* Washington, D.C., 1968) [not available as this book was written; therefore not cited].

Index to Literary Works by Manuel Cited, Discussed, or Translated

Note: This Index concerns only Manuel's literary works, in contradistinction to diplomatic ones bearing his name but doubtless not drafted directly by him; the latter are cited in appropriate places in the General Index. Dates establishable for these writings are given in parentheses where possible. All citations in standard type indicate references to or discussions of the works in question; citations printed in italics, preceded by the word *transl.*, indicate an English translation of a work, either complete or in part. Discussions of Manuel's style and intellectual interests are not indicated in this Index but in the General Index, under Palaeologus, Manuel II, Byzantine Emperor (1391–1425): GENERAL TOPICS.

General Index

Note: All individuals bearing legitimate family names (i.e. Palaeologus) are entered under these, rather than under their given names. This procedure does not apply to rulers of Western European dynasties. Citations printed in italics, preceded by the word *transl.*, indicate an English translation of a work, either complete or in part.

xxxi, 265; its relations with France, 177, 271, 375, 385; mentioned, 125, 339

Epamanondas, 311

Ephesus, 217 n. 24

Epidauros, 343 n. 83. *See also* Monemvasia

Epirus, Despotate of, xxxii, 46 n. 127

Epitaphios of Nicholas Eudaimonoioannes, 377 n. 54

"Escalime" (Lemnos), 240 n. 71

Esztergom, 485

Eudaimonoioannes, Andronicus, 324

Eudaimonoioannes, Nicholas: Byzantine ambassador (in 1416–18), xxxii, 315, 324, 325, 335, 336, 340 n. 80; (in 1419–20), xxxiv, 326 n. 51, 327 and n. 54, 337, 348; death of (1423), 327 n. 54; *Epitaphios* donated by, 327 n. 54; Cardinal Isidore's letter to, 192 n. 127, 327 n. 54

Eugenia Gattilusio. *See* Gattilusio, Eugenia

Eugenikos, *Protekdikos*, 211 n. 15

Euphemia, Saint, 437

Eurotas River, 231 n. 60

Euthymios II, Patriarch of Constantinople (1410–1416): installed, xxxi, 519; his dispute with Manuel, xxxiii, 323 n. 42; death of, xxxiii, 323 n. 42; Manuel's Letters to, 184, 185 and n. 116, 188 n. 119, 277 and n. 134, 430, 519–520

Evrenos-Bey, Turkish general, xxv, 127, 360 n. 109, 451

Fātima, 253 n. 88

Fāṭma-qatun, 253–254 n. 88

Ferdinand I, King of Aragon (1412–1416), Manuel's contacts with, 300, 318 n. 33, 324 n. 46, 333–334, 522

Ferrara, Manuel in (1403), xxix, 222, 510

Finlay, George, xxxviii, xl-xli

Fleet, Byzantine, 132, 268, 285 and n. 153

Florence: Manuel's appeal to, 188, 512; Manuel II in (?), xxviii, 222, 510; Manuel Chrysoloras in, xxii,

172, 321, 544–545; Council of (1438 ff.), 329, 331, 537; mentioned 326 n. 51

Fonseca, Cardinal Piero, Papal legate, 326

Foscarini, Francesco, Venetian *Bailo* of Constantinople, 212

Foucquet, Jean, 538–539

France: Manuel II's contacts with and appeals to, xxvi, 154–158, 255, 256 n. 96, 257, 480, 488–489; expedition from (1399), xxvi, 162 ff.; Manuel II in (1400, 1401–02), xxvii, xxviii, 168, 171, 172–178, 202, 203, 219–220, 397, 536–539; Manuel II leaves (1402), xxviii, 220, 512; Manuel Chrysoloras in (1408), xxx, 263–264, 545; its relations with England, 177, 271, 375, 384–385; mentioned, 125, 270–271, 379

Franciscans, 193 n. 129

Gabriel, Metropolitan of Thessalonica, 437 n. 74; Manuel's Letter to, 422, 430

Galata. *See* Pera

Galatia (Asia Minor), xxiv, 97

"Galatia" (France), 175, 264; "Galatians" (French), 136 n. 21, 268

Gallipoli (Kallioupolis): captured by the Turks (1354), xix, 4; recovered by Amadeo VI (1366), xx, 7; used by the Turks (1371), 16 n. 38; surrendered to the Turks by Andronicus IV (1376), xxi, 30, 31 n. 81, 458–461; sought by Venice, 217, 284 n. 151; Treaty of 1403 signed at, 227 n. 43; John VII meets Manuel II at (1403), 237, 238 n. 69, 242 n. 73; Venetian victory over the Turks at, xxxiii, 331 n. 61, 337 n. 72; taken by pretender Mustafa (1421), xxxiv, 357; sought by John VIII, xxxiv, 356–357 n. 102, 358; mentioned, 22 n. 51, 144 n. 32, 206, 230, 269 n. 121, 319, 352 n. 99, 359 n. 106, 508

Gattilusio, Eugenia, wife of John VII, 462–466, 492, 493

Gattilusio, Francesco I, Lord of Les-

Salisbury
London
Canterbury Dover
Calais

Paris
Charenton

Constance

SEE INSET
MAP

Rom

Naple

Venice
Chioggia
Po River
rrara Pola
avia
Genoa Moc
Bologna Rimini
Pisa Florence
Ancona
Siena